INTERNATIONAL POLITICS

Fourth Edition

INTERNATIONAL POLITICS

A Framework for Analysis

K. J. HOLSTI

University of British Columbia

PRENTICE-HALL, INC.   Englewood Cliffs, New Jersey 07632

Library of Congress Cataloging in Publication Data

HOLSTI, K. J. (KALEVI JAAKKO) (date)
  International politics.

  Includes bibliographies and index.
  1. International relations.   I. Title.
JX1305.H6 1983   327   82–3780
ISBN 0–13–473322–3   AACR2

Editorial/production supervision by Linda Benson
Cover design by Miriam Recio
Manufacturing buyers: Edmund W. Leone and Ron Chapman

Printed in the United States of America

10 9 8 7 6 5 4 3 2 1

ISBN 0-13-473322-3

Prentice-Hall International, Inc., *London*
Prentice-Hall of Australia Pty. Limited, *Sydney*
Prentice-Hall Canada Inc., *Toronto*
Prentice-Hall of India Private Limited, *New Delhi*
Prentice-Hall of Japan, Inc., *Tokyo*
Prentice-Hall of Southeast Asia Pte. Ltd., *Singapore*
Whitehall Books Limited, *Wellington, New Zealand*

Contents

6

Foreign-Policy Actions: Power, Capability, and Influence   144

7

The Instruments of Policy: Diplomatic Bargaining   161

8

The Instruments of Policy: Propaganda   192

9

Economic Instruments of Policy   214

10
Clandestine Actions and Military Intervention   241

11
Weapons, War, and Political Influence   268

PART IV
Explanations of Foreign-Policy Outputs

12
Explanations of Foreign-Policy Outputs   313

13
Law and World Opinion in Explanations of Foreign Policy   359

14
Ethics in Explanations of Foreign Policy   381

PART V
Major Forms of Interaction between States

15
The Interaction of States: Conflict and Conflict Resolution   399

16

The Interaction of States: Collaboration 438

Preface

Readers of books on international politics will be struck by the diverse approaches and methods of analysis. These range from works employing intricate descriptions of single events or crises, to broad, theoretical efforts that seek to explain broad patterns of behavior over a period of time. All approaches have their value, but perhaps ideally one general work should try to combine a reasonable amount of detail with a broader purpose of making generalizations and showing how they can be explained. If we are going to discuss the Soviet-American arms race, for example, we should be able to say something about arms races in general—why they start, what perpetuates the ever-escalating arms build ups, and how they end. The theorist who talks about arms races as one type of international phenomenon should also be able to illustrate generalizations with events or trends in the real world.

The reporters of current events have one important advantage over the theorists. Their stories, often filled with dramatic events and personalities, are entertaining. A work in theory cannot equally convey drama, but it can more adequately offer broad understanding of political life at the international level. My approach to international politics comes closer to that of the theorist. No single book can cover the field of international politics adequately at all levels of generality, from discussion of the most recent crisis to definition of analytic concepts. In formulating a framework for analysis, I have purposely excluded many aspects of contemporary international affairs because they have been handled more competently by others or because they are in the headlines every day. I make no reference to contemporary American foreign policy in the Far East, or to what the Chinese foreign minister said to the Russian ambassador in Peking last week about the frontier problems between the two countries. But the framework developed here leads the reader to ponder more general questions that will then facilitate an analysis of current events: What, in general, is the relationship of ideology to Soviet foreign-policy objectives? What types of roles do major powers see themselves as playing in various regions of the world? Given a conflict between two countries, how do diplomats typically bargain with each other? My overall purpose, then, is to present a framework that will help the reader understand what states seek through their governments and political leaders; how they operate in relation to others in periods of stability and war; what techniques they use to achieve or defend their objectives; how they are restrained—or unrestrained—by moral, ethical, or legal considerations; and how they resolve their conflicts. To the extent that current affairs and diplomatic history are discussed, I use them as means to an end—as illustrations of general propositions.

Since the appearance of the third edition, the agenda of international politics continues to grow. Optimism regarding East-West relations, rather prominent in the mid-1970s, has waned in the face of increased conflict, particularly between the Soviet Union and the United States. The second major cleavage in the international system, reflecting growing economic inequalities between rich and poor nations, has become a relatively permanent feature of the present system, generating a variety of contentious issues that were barely on the horizon a decade ago. The growing diplomatic influence of many developing countries can be applauded in terms of equity, but it has not made international life simpler. An increasing number of small states are following the examples set by the major powers in the use of propaganda, subversion, intervention, and economic pressures. And to complicate matters further, nonstate actors such as national liberation movements and large international business conglomerates have become increasingly involved in establishing items on the international agenda and operating as factors that help create both stability and crisis.

This edition discusses some of these changes and new issues. Its main focus, however, remains on the processes of international politics rather than on "problems." While the issues over which governments contend change from day to day, the means by which they are raised, promoted, and occasionally fought over have not changed in important ways since the first edition of this volume appeared in 1967. The main questions around which the framework is built therefore remain the same: *How* do states behave toward each other in different types of international systems, and *why* do they behave in certain ways? Because knowledge about how and why states act in international life is far from precise, some parts of the book are designed primarily to show how an analysis might be undertaken, in the hope that readers will attempt their own explanations. The pages that follow raise as many questions as they provide answers.

My thanks go to many students and academics who have over the years made numerous comments on strengths and weaknesses and occasionally offered useful suggestions for improvement. The revisions in this edition reflect the generosity of those who took the trouble to provide me with their thoughts: Michael A. Freney, United States Air Force Academy; Curtis H. Martin, Merrimack College; and J. Martin Rochester, University of Missouri. I am also grateful to Dory Urbano for cheerful and efficient typing.

K.J. Holsti
Vancouver, British Columbia

INTERNATIONAL POLITICS

PART *I*

Introduction

1

Approaches to the Study of International Politics

After the armies of Imperial Germany invaded Belgium in August 1914, launching one of the most destructive and futile conflicts in history, Prince von Bülow asked the German chancellor why all the diplomatic steps taken to avoid the war had failed. "At last I [Bülow] said to him: 'Well, tell me, at least, how it all happened.' He raised his long, thin arms to heaven and answered in a dull exhausted voice: 'Oh—If I only knew.' "[1] If the German chancellor did not understand all the reasons that had led to war, he and his policy-making colleagues knew quite well that many of their decisions were likely to end in catastrophe for both Germany and Europe. He also knew that Germany had only a slight chance of emerging victorious. Since a rational function of war is presumably to achieve a political goal at tolerable costs through the application of force, German policy makers in the summer of 1914 were not behaving rationally. Was such behavior unique? More than half a century later, Prime Minister Ian D. Smith of the self-governing colony of Rhodesia defied the British government, the United Nations, and most of the states of Africa by unilaterally declaring the independence of the colony. Smith and his advisers expected that the British government could not immediately prevent steps toward establishing full Rhodesian independence, yet they also knew that the declaration of independence would cause grave economic damage to the country, possible war with other

---

[1] Prince Bernhard von Bülow, *Memoirs of Prince von Bülow* (Boston: Little, Brown, 1932), Vol. 3, p. 166.

African states, or civil war between 6 million black Rhodesians and 200,000 white settlers. The British prime minister, Harold Wilson, had attempted to forestall the unilateral declaration by threats and promises conveyed through last-minute conferences and telephone calls with Smith. The last call was placed at six o'clock on a Thursday morning in a desperate bid to head off the illegal declaration. Reporting to the House of Commons on that conversation, Wilson recalled that he had "ended the conversation with a heavy heart, feeling that reason had fled the scene and that emotions, unreasoning . . . emotions at that, had taken command [of Prime Minister Smith] regardless of the consequences for Rhodesia, for Africa and for the world."[2]

Taking a longer-range perspective, other historical parallels that transcend time, place, and personalities can be noted. In the eighth century B.C., the princes of newly formed states in China successfully challenged the power and authority of the Chinese emperor, thereby putting an end to the Chinese feudal order. Similarly, in 1648, European diplomats and princes congregated in Westphalia to sign a peace treaty ending the Thirty Years' War. They also declared that henceforth the leader of the Holy Roman Empire could no longer extend its dominion into the territories of princes and sovereigns and that the latter were in no way obliged to respond to the directives of the emperor. This act symbolized the emergence of the modern European nation-state system, replacing the feudal political order that, as in China, had at least theoretically placed an emperor as head, with power radiating down through such lesser political entities as free cities, duchies, and developing dynastic territories.

Every historical occurrence is, of course, unique; the situations in which statesmen construct alliances, decide to go to war, declare independence, or make peace are all different. Yet, when historical phenomena are analyzed from a certain level of abstraction—not just as facts for their own sake—these situations have many common properties. The events the student of international politics attempts to understand may be unique, but, as the cases cited above suggest, they are also comparable. Smith and the German chancellor had to make many of the same kinds of calculations before acting, and both acted knowing that their decisions could easily lead to disaster. Both the Chinese princes and the European sovereigns 2,000 years later were determined to put an end to political orders in which emperors could intervene in subordinates' affairs and territories. Regardless of historical and geographical context, policy makers for different types of political units, whether tribes, city-states, empires, or modern nation-states, have attempted to achieve objectives or defend their interests by fundamentally similar techniques, of which the use of force and the construction of alliances are only the most obvious examples.

If Thucydides, Frederick the Great, or Louis XIV were to return to life in the latter part of the twentieth century, they would no doubt be astounded by the immense changes in technology, culture, and the lives of average citizens.

---

[2] *New York Times*, November 11, 1965, p. 1.

They would not be familiar with such international institutions as the United Nations, the International Court of Justice, or multinational corporations; nor would they understand immediately the rationale behind foreign aid programs or comprehend the destructive capacity of nuclear weapons. But they would recognize the types of threats and rewards modern governments make in attempting to achieve their objectives, the techniques of diplomatic bargaining, and the concern governments have for their international prestige. Certainly they would find little new in the attempts of states to conclude mutually satisfying military alliances or to remain uninvolved in the quarrels of the great powers.

The study of international politics, while it must account for the unique, new, and nonrecurring phenomenon, is also concerned with processes and patterns of behavior found typically in many historical contexts. All attempts to understand the disparate aspects of political life at the international level implicitly assume some regularities of behavior. The diplomatic historian tends to emphasize the uniqueness of the events he or she is describing and explaining, but when employing such concepts as the "balance of power" or "diplomacy," he or she is referring to classes or types of political behavior that transcend specific historical circumstances. Still, the historian concentrates mainly on single events and occurrences that are related to specific times, places, and personalities.

It is a bias of social scientists to assume the existence of regular patterns of behavior, to explain these in terms of specified variables,[3] and to use historical data primarily to elucidate or illustrate the generalizations they are attempting to make. Students of international politics try to understand and explain the causes and nature of war, imperialism, escalation, crisis, or alliance without having to describe every war, imperialist, escalation, crisis, or alliance in history. A valid generalization is one that can be used to describe all events of a given class. Any general statement about these phenomena must be based, of course, on accurate historical observation; but the social scientist is still concerned pri-

---

[3] A *variable* can be defined as any phenomenon or condition, a change in which produces a change in another phenomenon or condition. In the physical realm, for example, variations in temperature cause changes in the properties of water. We know from observation that when the temperature goes below a certain point, all other conditions being held constant, water freezes. There is an obvious functional relationship between the two variables, temperature and the state of the water. In the social sciences, relationships between variables may be much more difficult to identify and measure because (1) many variables inducing change may be involved simultaneously, and (2) it may be impossible to hold all other conditions constant while observation or experimentation is taking place. For example, we may wish to examine the conditions associated with outbreak of war. We could see if there is some type of relationship between the incidence of war and spending on armaments. If through a perusal of historical data we found a high correlation between variations in expenditures on armaments (independent variable) and incidence of war (dependent variable), we could say that the two variables are somehow associated. It would still remain for us to define the exact nature of the relationship and investigate other types of variables, such as perceptions of threat or degree of commitment to objectives, that may be involved in the outbreak of war. We can say with confidence that a lowering of temperature causes a change in the state of water, but we could not claim with certainty that rising armaments budgets cause wars, since so many other factors may be involved.

marily with classes or types of phenomena rather than with the particular details of each illustration. He or she is interested in the German chancellor in 1914 or Prime Minister Smith of Rhodesia as *examples* of the behavior of important policy makers facing situations of great stress, threat, and consequences; the historian is interested in them as individuals.

THE DEVELOPMENT
OF INTERNATIONAL RELATIONS
AS A FIELD OF STUDY

The line dividing a historian's approach to international relations from that of a social scientist is not as clear-cut as the comments above would indicate, for historians frequently attempt to uncover patterns of behavior and elements of recurrence in diplomatic relations, while many political scientists hold that the most valid approach to the subject is careful description of events that are assumed to be unique. In fact, a review of the history of this field of study reveals that most work has used a historical, descriptive, and developmental (analyzing the conditions that caused or helped bring about certain events or ideas) approach.

The earliest writings on international relations were largely concerned with proffering practical advice to policy makers. The Chinese philosopher Mencius in the fourth century B.C., Kautilya, a prime minister under the Indian emperor Chandragupta (326–298 B.C.), and Niccolo Machiavelli wrote works that are studied today for their insight into the kinds of problems that still confront statesmen. But the main purpose of these authors was not so much to provide general analyses of the relations between states as to offer advice on the most effective forms of statecraft. In eighteenth- and nineteenth-century Europe, diplomatic memoirs, studies on military thought and strategy, and works on international law proliferated. Few authors took the trouble to analyze the behavior of governments in their external relations from a systematic and detached vantage, although a number of observers did suggest that the "balance of power" was a more or less fundamental law of politics at the international level.[4] There were many philosophers, statesmen, lawyers, and military officials who claimed they knew what was wrong with the world and devised schemes for overcoming these deficiencies. It was not until the twentieth century that attempts at systematic analysis appeared.

Scholars in the United States first began to take serious interest in international problems following America's involvement in Asian and European politics at the turn of the century. Their studies, as well as those of many Europeans before World War I, were oriented largely to analysis of treaties and principles

---

[4] See Per Mauserth, "Balance of Power Thinking from the Renaissance to the French Revolution," *Journal of Peace Research*, No. 2 (1964), 120–36.

of international law. They were typically legalistic and moral in tone, based on the assumptions that most disputes were raised to be settled, that the "shrinking" world was making people more "internationalist," and that peace and stability could be constructed through the extension of democracy or the construction of international institutions, such as a world court, with power to enforce their decisions. International laws of neutrality and warfare and the problems of arbitration and disarmament were the main subjects considered in courses and texts in international relations.

Academic studies in the 1920s largely continued to expand on the prewar perspectives, although establishment of the League of Nations gave observers something new to write about. Institutes dedicated to the study of international law and organization were formed in Switzerland, Great Britain, and the United States. Articles in scholarly journals contained lengthy descriptions of international conferences and treaties, while popular and academic analysts presented innumerable commentaries on the proceedings of the League of Nations. Aside from these descriptive studies—from which one could deduce few generalizations—most work in the field during this decade had a normative orientation: Writers were less concerned with the variables or conditions affecting government behavior in external relations than with judging the policies of states according to their own values. The only new development in courses and texts, aside from the analyses of the League of Nations, was an emphasis on description of the "background" conditions of current international affairs.

Hitler's violent assault on the postwar order had important consequences on the ways in which scholars in the international-relations field approached their subject. Many observers became impatient with the descriptive, moralistic, and legalistic orientation of the 1920s and realized that, as important as treaties and international organizations were to international relations, objectives such as security and expansion, processes such as trade and diplomacy, and means such as propaganda and subversion had to be studied as well. Hence, while one group of scholars and commentators continued to emphasize the traditional concerns of law, institutions, and current affairs, another branched off to begin more systematic and comparative studies of objectives, processes, and means, as well as those "basic forces" (as they were then called) assumed to affect a state's foreign-policy behavior. These studies assessed the phenomenon of nationalism, the influence of geography on a country's foreign policy, and particularly the effect of "power" (or lack of it) on a nation's fate. Not infrequently, these same people were concerned with the strategies the democracies should adopt to ward off the threats posed by Hitler's Germany.

Most important, writers in this school attempted to become more analytical by defining concepts, exploring some ancient myths about international politics, and emphasizing the extent to which all states were equally interested in certain values and interests, such as security, power, territory, or peace. While these analysts remained occupied with current problems and described in detail the foreign policies of major powers, behind their teaching and research was the idea that detailed description should be used not only to acquaint the reader or student with facts, but also to illustrate some generalizations or theories about international politics. The emphasis in the classroom and in texts thus turned from efforts to inculcate in students certain attitudes about international politics ("We must strengthen the League of Nations") to creating understanding about reality, leaving the student to form his or her own judgments about the best ways to deal with contemporary problems.

Since the end of World War II, the study of international relations has seen important changes. With the development of basic animosities between the United States and the Soviet Union, the Middle East states, and China and its neighbors, the creation of weapons of mass destruction, and the rise of more than ninety new states, policy makers have had to cope with extremely difficult, dangerous, and, in some cases, unprecedented problems. Most academics, no matter how concerned with creating a scientific field of study, could not avoid becoming involved in the great policy and ethical issues of the day. Yet a definite trend away from descriptions, legal analysis, and policy advice has developed in the field. Its objective has not been to assess the main issues in the cold war or describe current international developments, but to create explanatory theories about international phenomena and, in some cases, even to propose the development of a general and predictive "science" of international relations. It is now possible to identify at least five different, if overlapping, "schools" of scholars who study international phenomena. The distinctions among these groups are not entirely clear, but the main differences arise over (1) the subjects to be studied, (2) the methods of analysis, and (3) the purposes of inquiry.

CURRENT "SCHOOLS" OF STUDY IN INTERNATIONAL POLITICS

Traditional Analysis

The first group includes those scholars who are continuing the traditional, predominantly descriptive, analysis of international politics and institutions: various states' foreign policies, certain international "problems," and international institutions. They analyze the historical and constitutional development of the United Nations or describe the results of international conferences dealing with such topics as the international law of the sea, control of narcotics smuggling, or nuclear strategy in NATO. Their purposes are essentially to report and analyze current international problems and to speculate on the sources and outcomes of various policy alternatives for specific states or for international organizations.

The Strategists

The second group, which has proliferated dramatically since 1945, might be called the "strategists." Their main concern has been to understand the logic of deterrence in the nuclear age, to analyze the impact of new weapons systems on deterrence, and to develop strategies to maximize national security while minimizing the possibility of nuclear war. The methods have ranged from logical analysis to the elucidation of policy alternatives inferred from the results of war games and game theory. Although much of this work has been essentially analytical, its policy implications have been great. In some cases, academic studies have become the basis of adopted military strategies; in others, they have provided rationalizations for decisions made by military leaders, or critiques of these decisions.

The Grand Theorists

Hans J. Morgenthau, in his classic treatise *Politics Among Nations* (1948), was the major developer of what might be called the "grand theory" of international politics. Unlike his predecessors, who saw their task mainly as reporting on current events or pushing for their favorite peace panacea, Morgenthau argued that the diverse data of international politics could be made coherent within the terms of a model of power politics. His major contribution was to show (1) that the field must seek to establish generalizations, not remain focused on unique events; (2) that interstate relations, in their essence, display patterns of behavior and recurrence; and (3) that the core of the subject is to explore the sources of state behavior (the search for power) and the resulting patterns of relations (the balance of power). A number of political scientists have subsequently developed their own "grand theories," which have made the field significantly more coherent than in the past. These theorists have emphasized such concepts as equilibrium, decision making, systems, and communications models as the central organizing devices for the field. Like Morgenthau, they have assumed that the most important aspects of foreign policy and international processes could be understood or explained by a single concept or set of interrelated concepts.

Middle-Range Theory

A fourth group of scholars has as its major purpose the empirical exploration of *selected aspects* of international politics and foreign policy. This group is problem-oriented, searching for precise description and explanation of specific phenomena. Theory, for these scholars, serves primarily as a source of hypotheses to be tested, rather than as a device for organizing the entire field. The subjects to be explored go far beyond the traditional concerns of international relations scholars, who focused on law, institutions, or current events. This new research delves into such questions as: How are foreign-policy decisions arrived at? How do "images," stereotypes, and ideologies affect policy makers' perceptions of reality and, consequently, their choices among alternative courses of action? How do policy makers react in periods of great stress, in crisis situations? Is a strategy of bargaining in which one side threatens to punish more effective than one in which it offers rewards? How do trust and suspicion affect the propensity of governments to enter into cooperative ventures? What conditions are most conducive to escalation in a crisis situation? What social, economic, and political conditions are most conducive to successful supranational integration? Is there a relationship between the amount of violence within a state and the amount of violence that that state employs in its external relations? Other scholars are involved in research that should tell us much more than we now know about the consequences of interdependence on national economic policy making, the origins and types of international conflicts, the conditions under which alliances are formed or disintegrate, and the relationship between the construction of alliances and the outbreak or incidence of war. As answers to these questions become available through systematic and comparative research, middle-range theories explaining specific phenomena are developing. If we do not yet have a "grand theory" of international politics, scholars have at least developed the components of, let us say, a theory of arms races or crisis decision making.

Some members of this group argue that the ultimate purpose of scientific analysis is not just explanation but prediction, and, they maintain, reliable predictions can be made only if the main variables affecting political behavior have been identified and relationships among the variables specified. These scholars might point out that economists can predict, once the relationship between variables is known, the general consequences of a lowering of bank interest rates, a rise in the supply of money, or an increase in public demand for a product. What would economists predict about a lowering of bank interest rates? Certainly not that John Smith or Jane White would apply for loans. But they could estimate that in the economy as a whole, there would be an increase of 5 percent in the volume of borrowing if interest rates were lowered by .25 percent. In other words, they can predict *classes* of events, not individual incidents of that class. Similarly, proponents of a predictive science of international politics claim that when enough basic propositions about the behavior of policy makers, states, and international systems have been tested and verified through rigorous research methods, predictive statements about classes of events and trends can be put forward with reasonable confidence. Although we all make casual predictions about specific events in foreign policy or international politics, a number of scholars have already made or tested propositions useful for understanding or predicting behavior in recurring situations. For example, the results of psychological experiments and historical research suggest that in times of crisis and high tension, policy makers tend to perceive and consider fewer alternative courses of action than when they are not under stress. On a broader scale, we can predict that alliances will tend to disintegrate if the members of the alliance cease to perceive a common potential enemy.

Notice that these statements are not laws; they do not state that in the next international crisis Prime Minister X will perceive only one course of action open to him or that NATO will be dissolved next year. They are, rather, *probability* or *tendency* statements about classes of events. Exceptions can and will occur, but experimentation or careful analysis of data has established that, in most instances, the dependent variable (perception of fewer alternatives or disintegration of alliances) can be predicted from knowledge of the state of the independent variable (level of tension or stress and degree of perception of a common enemy).

In order to conduct research into such questions, old methods of inquiry that relied primarily upon analysis of documents and treaties are no longer adequate. Investigators find it difficult to observe policy makers in action, and they are too impatient to wait forty to fifty years until all the documents are available. Moreover, many aspects of foreign policy making, diplomatic bargaining, or handling of international conflicts remain undocumented. Thus, scholars have recently fashioned a number of research tools that enable them to formulate and test propositions about their subject without having to go through meticulous documentary examination. The computer, which can analyze the contents and themes of thousands of documents in minutes once a key or dictionary has been formulated, is one important research aid. Surveys and interviews help to obtain information of public attitudes about international problems. Scholars have developed games or simulations of international politics that can be played by anyone. The researchers build into a game many features of reality, so that the pressures faced by lay "policy makers" (often undergraduate students) become to a certain extent similar to those faced by real policy makers. By observing the students' behavior (for example, when they decide to go to war; how they construct alliances, react to a major scientific breakthrough, handle conflicts, or solve the age-old problem of meeting domestic economic demands while providing arms for security) and by controlling certain aspects of "reality," the investigators are able to test propositions in a manner that would take years of research in government archives. As developed primarily by economists and psychologists, games can also be helpful in examining the conditions and variables, such as trust, suspicion, risk, rewards, or degree of communication, that affect bargaining behavior.

The systematic collection of data to test hypotheses has also been a feature of the work of this fourth group. Scholars in the past often arrived at generalizations on the basis of anecdotal evidence. For example, by citing the long history of French attempts to secure defensive frontiers against Germany and Italy, some scholars claimed that the (or a) basic source of foreign policy is a country's geographical location. This universal proposition was derived from examination of only one case. Or, more recently, citing the cases of Ghana or Indonesia, scholars have claimed that fluctuations in the prices of export commodities sold by developing nations have a great impact on the political stability of those countries. Researchers are now investigating propositions like these by employing data gathered from large samples of nations. The purpose is to see if there is any mathematical relationship between the quantified independent variables (in the two cases, geographic location and size of trade losses), and the dependent variables (various aspects of a country's foreign policy and the amount of political stability). Studies of this type, which presently predominate in academic circles, must be based on extensive data, including facts and figures about the countries' size, population, GNP, rate of economic development, literacy, defense spending, internal violence, foreign-policy actions, and the like.

"Peace Research"

The fifth type of scholarship combines the main characteristics of traditional analysis and empirical study—that is, it is deeply concerned with the problems of peace and war but argues that these can never be understood and ultimately controlled unless a vast amount of reliable knowledge about the subject is first created. The objective of the research is clearly normative—devising ways to control processes leading to violence—and the techniques are scientific and systematic. This type of scholarship has earned the unfortunate title of "peace research," a term that creates in the minds of the general public and government officials the notion of fuzzy-minded, naive intellectuals pontificating from their ivory towers about the ways to secure everlasting peace. Some of the work, however, has made important contributions to our understanding of such problems as the processes leading to war; escalation of violence; the relationship between individual personality characteristics and the phenomena of bigotry, prejudice, and national hostility; the economic consequences of disarmament and arms control programs; and the sources of public attitudes toward foreign countries and alien cultures. Whether the findings of these studies will ever be reflected in public policy remains to be seen. Much of the scholarly work on arms control and disarmament in the United States has been made available to the government, and a large amount is being undertaken by government officials themselves or by independent scholars under government contract. Other areas of "peace research" have not yet fared so well, for it is often a difficult political task to translate research findings into policy proposals acceptable to those who run governments.

INTERDISCIPLINARY EFFORTS

A unique feature of recent studies of international politics and foreign policy, aside from theoretical activity and attempts to create new research techniques, has been the extent to which they have become interdisciplinary, blending the data, concepts, and insights of all the social sciences. In the past, historians, political scientists, geographers, and legal scholars monopolized the field of international relations; today, anthropologists, economists, sociologists, and psychologists enrich our understanding of international relations by bringing their special skills to problems of common interest or opening previously neglected areas of inquiry. Sociologists and social psychologists help us to understand the nature and origins of public attitudes and opinions that affect foreign-policy issues; they have also provided a vast literature dealing with individual behavior in bargaining situations. Economists, aside from their interest in international trade and economic development, provide help in understanding political processes in developing countries. Anthropologists assist the development of the field by studying war and violence as cultural phenomena, characteristics of mediation and conciliation in primitive societies, and types of problems arising from cross-cultural contacts and economic progress in developing societies.

As much as the field of study has advanced as a result of new methods and interdisciplinary efforts, these contributions also have their limitations. For example, the literature of social psychology, which at first glance seems so relevant to foreign policy and international politics, is derived largely from experimental work employing small groups of people, usually students, in a laboratory setting. A certain amount of caution is necessary in transferring conclusions obtained in this fashion to diplomatic-political-military situations. No matter how carefully an experiment is constructed, it cannot replicate a real political situation. Results of experiments offered by the social sciences must thus serve primarily as *hypotheses,* which need to be tested against political experience and historical data before they can be verified. If small-group experiments suggest that willingness to communicate freely and cooperate vary directly with the amount of trust between people, we should not hastily conclude that the same propositions are necessarily valid in diplomatic relations. It remains the task of those who research in the field of international relations to see if the results of experimental situations can be verified in the diplomatic situation.

THE NEED
FOR ORGANIZING DEVICES

Some theorizing activity in the field is undertaken not for the purpose of constructing a predictive theory of international relations (assuming that it can be done), but for creating ordering devices or approaches that help the investigator and student make some sense out of the great diversity of data and events in international relations. Whatever the name of that device, whether a "quasi-theory," "model," "conceptual framework," or, more simply, a framework for analysis, its purpose is to help create understanding by ordering facts and concepts into some meaningful pattern. Gathering of facts or descriptions of events creates understanding of those facts and events but otherwise has little broader application. Only when these facts and events are fitted against some framework of concepts can they be seen essentially as illustrations of general and recurring processes in international politics. But an organizing device does more than just relate facts to general propositions.

Historians use the organizing devices of time, place, and subject matter (for instance, German foreign policy toward Poland from 1934 to 1939) as a means of helping them select relevant data, relate the data to each other, and determine the boundaries of their topic. Without such organizing devices there would be no place to begin, no limits to help research and description, and no way to determine what facts, conditions, or events are relevant to the subject.

Social scientists also use organizing devices; but because they are often interested in classes of social phenomena and processes rather than specific events bounded by time, place, and subject, their devices will be more abstract than those historians use. For instance, if we want to define the essence of international politics, we might say "power politics," in which case the boundaries of the subject would be determined largely by the definition we assign to those two words. But "power" and "politics" are very abstract concepts, more difficult to deal with than concepts relating to time and place. Yet, if we define international politics as "power politics" or "the quest for power," we have, however crude, some framework, approach, or quasi theory that provides the boundaries of the subject, establishes criteria of relevance, and helps fit some of the many facts of international life together. It designates key variables that help to explain the behavior of states in their external relations. In this case, power—how it is wielded and how much is available—is posited as the key explanatory variable to the understanding of a nation's foreign policies.

There are, of course, certain dangers in employing any approach, theory, model, or framework in social analysis. Although these devices help the investigator select data and relate concepts and variables, they may also act as blinders to other significant facets of the subject. One example of a popular model of international politics will illustrate this point. The "power politics" approach, very popular during the late 1930s and still enjoying considerable repute, assumes that no matter what the long-range objectives of states, their immediate objective is power over other states. International politics is conceived as a struggle for power among all states, either for expansion or defense and protection. Study focuses partly on the methods and techniques states use to maximize their power, but primarily on the "elements" of a state's power. Since it is assumed that states are successful to the extent that they have power, the approach demands lengthy consideration and assessment of each nation's "power position," which includes its geography, natural resources, population, technological level, available military resources, and national morale. In other words, because the approach emphasizes just one concept—power—it leads observers to try to discover what constitutes a state's power.

The power approach does explain some aspects of international politics, and it directs researchers to look for certain types of information that are useful to the student. But because of its undue emphasis on power and struggle, it conceals other important aspects of international politics. If some relations can be described as "struggle," surely Swedish-Norwegian relations are not, for the most part, adequately characterized by this term. As interesting as the *elements* of power may be, they do not determine how effective a state will be in its external relations. A state can be very well endowed with all the *elements* of power and still not achieve its objectives against even the weakest and smallest states. Thus, while the approach does explain a limited range of phenomena and helps to emphasize the importance of one variable—power—in international politics, it is burdened with oversimplicity, unexamined assumptions, and its Hobbesian view of international relationships.

LEVELS OF ANALYSIS

One final problem concerning organizing devices needs to be discussed before the framework of analysis in this book is presented. What should we use as the major unit of analysis in international politics?[5] Should we focus upon the actions and attitudes of *individual* policy makers? Or might we assume that all policy makers act essentially the same way once confronted with similar situations and therefore concentrate instead on the behavior of *states*? Or could we remove ourselves even further from individuals and examine international politics from the perspective of entire *systems* of states? Each level of analysis—individual, state, or systemic—will make us look at different things, so the student must be aware of the differences among them. For example, the classical theory of balance of power is an attempt to explain the behavior of many states over a period of time. It proposes that states will form coalitions and countercoalitions to fend off hegemonic drives and that a "balancer" will intervene on behalf of the weaker side in order to redress the balance or restore the old equilibrium. The behavior of *individual* political units is thus explained in terms of the state of the whole system (balanced or imbalanced) and the presence or absence of one aggressive state and a balancer. This type of analysis makes no reference to personalities, domestic pressures, or ideologies *within* states. Foreign-policy behavior is conceived as a reaction to the external environment, the state of balance or imbalance among *all* the units in the system.

If we look at international politics from the perspective of individual states, rather than from the state of the system in which they exist, quite different questions arise. We can attempt to explain the behavior of states by reference not just to the external environment (the system), but primarily to the domestic conditions that affect policy making. Wars, alliances, imperialism, diplomatic maneuvers, isolation, and the many goals of diplomatic action can be viewed as the results of domestic political pressures, national ideologies, public opinion, or economic and social needs. This level of analysis has much to commend it, for governments do not react just to the external environment or to some mythical balance or imbalance. Their actions also express the needs and values of their own populations and political leaders.

[5] J. David Singer, "The Level-of-Analysis Problem in International Relations," in *The International System: Theoretical Essays,* eds. Klaus Knorr and Sidney Verba (Princeton, N.J.: Princeton University Press, 1961), pp. 77–92; Kenneth W. Waltz, *Man, the State, and War* (New York: Columbia University Press, 1959).

Finally, we may study international politics and foreign policy by concentrating on the actions and behavior of individual statesmen. This is the usual approach of diplomatic historians, based on the sound point that when we say that "states" behave, we really mean that policy makers are defining purposes, choosing among courses of action, and utilizing national capabilities to achieve objectives in the name of the state. This level of analysis focuses upon the ideologies, motivations, ideals, perceptions, values, or idiosyncrasies of those who are empowered to make decisions for the state.

Which level of analysis gives us the most useful perspective from which to explain or understand politics among nations? Each makes a contribution, but each fails to account for certain aspects of reality that must be considered. We cannot understand Soviet foreign policy adequately by studying only the attitudes and values of its foreign minister, nor is it sufficient to analyze Soviet social and economic needs. We must have some knowledge, as well, of ideological considerations and of the general configuration of power, influence, domination, and subordination throughout the world. The main characteristics of the external environment are no less important than those of the state's internal environment. Therefore, all three levels of analysis will be employed at different times, depending upon the type of problem to be analyzed. The perspective of international systems is very broad, although not comprehensive, and provides the best approach for delineating the *main* features and characteristics of international political processes over a relatively long period of time. One can describe the essence of the types of relations among Greek city-states without examining the character of each city-state or the motives, ideals, and goals of each statesman in each city-state. Today, the structure of alliances, of power, domination, dependence, and interdependence in the world sets limits upon the actions of states and policy makers, no matter what their ideological persuasion or individual ideals are, and no matter what the state of domestic opinion is. The next two chapters will concentrate on the description of historic international systems, with a view to illustrating the general nature of relationships among their component political units. At the same time, the analysis will illustrate how the main characteristics of an international system affect the behavior of individual states. The system is thus only one variable used to explain how and why states act and interact. Subsequently, the focus will shift to an explanation of foreign-policy behavior primarily by reference to domestic national needs and values and to individual variables.

The organizing concepts for this study derive from the three questions that have traditionally made up the core of inquiry about foreign policy and international politics: (1) How do states act? (2) How do we explain the various aspects of their foreign policies? and (3) What are the main characteristics of the interaction between states? The last question is a modernized version of the ancient preoccupation with the question of war and peace.

We will begin by focusing upon the various aspects of behavior associated with the term *foreign policy.* Then, to provide historical depth and to illustrate how the environment influences state actions we will examine in Part II the types of international systems that have existed in the past as well as the main characteristics of the contemporary international system. The historical treatment also affords the opportunity to present a typology of international systems. (In Chapter 12, the typology is related to various *explanations* of foreign policy.)

Part III is primarily descriptive. We will be concerned with outlining the major *outputs* of states' foreign policies—what governments seek to achieve and how they go about it. These are defined, from the more general to the particular, as foreign-policy orientations (alliances, nonalignment, isolation), roles, objectives, and actions. Chapters 6 through 11 focus on the actions—the multifarious means of inducement governments use to achieve their objectives, fulfill national roles, and secure various orientations. We will start with simple techniques of diplomatic persuasion and end with a discussion of large-scale violence.

Part IV is the most difficult, because it attempts to explain how systemic, national, and personality variables can be linked to foreign-policy outputs. In addition, there is the question of law and ethics. To what extent can foreign-policy outputs be explained as meeting the demands of international law or of ethical principles?

To illustrate the framework used in Part IV, a problem for analysis might be posed. Suppose that after describing Soviet policies toward Afghanistan 1979–1980, we were asked to *explain* the goals and actions of Soviet diplomacy and military policy. We could, first, emphasize a type of explanation relying on *ideological* and *systemic* characteristics, such as the following: The Soviet government has traditionally been concerned with promoting and protecting the advance of socialism in a world formerly dominated by the "imperialists." Once the "revolution" in Afghanistan became threatened by counterrevolution the Soviet Union, for reasons of prestige, historical commitment, and internationalist solidarity, had an obligation to intervene militarily to "save" the revolution. In an essentially bipolar world, no great power can permit its main adversary (the United States) to make an important gain at its own expense. A successful counterrevolution in Afghanistan would represent a net increment to the power of the main adversary and would be a blow to the progressive forces of the world. An important feature of the contemporary international system—the growing might of the socialist camp—would be compromised by the defeat of the progressive forces in Afghanistan. Thus, the decision to intervene militarily can be understood primarily as a response to events which would have destabilizing consequences for the international system and historical development as perceived in Moscow.

Another line of explanation would emphasize Soviet *national needs.* No great power can afford to have near its borders a government hostile to it. The counterrevolution in Afghanistan was not only antisocialist, but anti-Russian as well. Not to intervene would have been to invite future troubles. A counter-revolutionary regime of a Muslim theocratic character might appeal for solidarity with the Soviet Union's Muslim population, thus raising the possibility of fomenting Soviet Muslim nationalism and possible secession. Such consequences would result in a direct threat to the national security and unity of the multiethnic Soviet federation. The intervention, then, was essentially a defensive move that any major power would have taken in similar circumstances. (What would be the reaction of the United States in the event of a socialist revolution in Mexico?)

A third type of explanation would concentrate on the personalities and perceptions of key Soviet decision makers and important groups in the Soviet policy hierarchy. Some commentators might point out that the Soviet military has assumed in recent years an important role in the formulation of Soviet foreign policy and that in the circumstances surrounding Afghanistan in the autumn of 1979, the military leaders saw an opportunity to test Soviet troops, weapons, and tactics in a combat situation. Afghanistan, in brief, provided an arena for displaying to civilian policy makers the effectiveness of Soviet military might. Others might point out that the intervention represented simply an escalation of commitments, an irreversible process in which the Soviets, like the Americans in Vietnam, became incrementally involved in Afghanistan. Soviet military advisors first went to the country in 1978, and their role eventually increased to participation in Afghan army combat missions, in which increasing numbers of Russians were killed. As the situation deteriorated, top military leaders began to argue for an active intervention to save a situation being bungled by the Afghans. The top Soviet civilian leaders' perceptions of the situation were parallel to those of the military; hence, they accepted the latter's advice. Finally, others might argue that Brezhnev had staked his personal reputation on committing Soviet support to the success of the Afghan socialist regime and that a failure to take effective action against counterrevolution could lead to his personal demise as the top Soviet leader.

All of these explanations probably have some validity or plausibility. The point to emphasize is that each focuses on different types of explanatory variables: systemic, national, or personal and decision-making. Chapter 12 attempts to show *under what conditions* each of the types of explanations is most satisfactory. After having read that chapter, the reader might wish to take several cases in recent diplomatic history to see if he or she can "explain" the case in terms of the relative importance of these variables.

Part V shifts focus to the *interactions* of states. The problem of peace and war is certainly the most important in international policies, so we will examine the behavior associated with conflictual relationships and collaborative interactions.

The key concepts, to summarize, are the *systems,* or environments, in which state action occurs; foreign-policy *outputs,* ranging from orientations to actions; the factors that *explain* those outputs; and, finally, *patterns of interaction* between states as revealed in conflict and cooperation.

INTERNATIONAL POLITICS,
FOREIGN POLICY,
AND INTERNATIONAL RELATIONS

If by now the reader is confused over the use of the terms *international relations, international politics,* and *foreign policy,* he or she joins the company of most experts in the field. There are many definitions of these terms but little agreement upon which are the most adequate or where the distinctions among them lie. This lack of consensus is no doubt related to the problem of organizing devices. How one defines these terms is largely influenced by what one wants to investigate, and what one investigates is largely a function of a particular approach, model, or theory.

Most studies in "world politics" or international politics have in fact been studies of foreign policy. They have concentrated on describing the interests, actions, and elements of power of the great powers. At what point, if any, does foreign policy become international politics? Distinction between the terms may be more academic than real, but it is roughly the difference between the *objectives* and *actions* (decisions and policies) of a state or states and the *interactions* between two or more states.[6] The student who analyzes the actions of a state toward external environment and the conditions—usually domestic— under which those actions are formulated is concerned essentially with foreign policy; the person who conceives of those actions as only one aspect of a pattern of actions by one state and reactions or responses by others is looking at international politics, or the processes of interaction between two or more states. The distinction is illustrated in the figure on p. 20.

This book will apply both perspectives, depending upon the problem under analysis. A discussion of state objectives, variables affecting their choice, and some techniques employed to achieve them is related closely to the study of foreign policy, while consideration of international systems, deterrence, and behavior in conflict situations comes closer to the idea of interactions between states.

As distinct from international politics and foreign policy, the term *international relations* may refer to *all* forms of interaction between the members of separate societies, whether government-sponsored or not. The study of international relations includes the analysis of foreign policies or political processes between nations; however, with its interest in *all* facets of relations between distinct societies, it would include as well studies of international trade unions, the International Red Cross, tourism, international trade, transportation, communication, and the development of international values and ethics. The student of international politics is not concerned with these types of relationships or phenomena, *except where they impinge upon official government objectives or where they*

---

[6] See Fred A. Sondermann, "The Linkage Between Foreign Policy and International Politics," in *International Politics and Foreign Policy: A Reader in Research and Theory,* ed. James N. Rosenau (New York: Free Press, 1961), pp. 8–17.

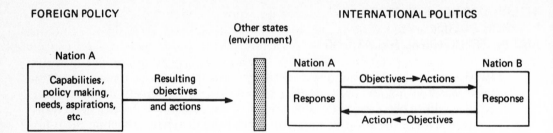

FOREIGN POLICY

INTERNATIONAL POLITICS

Other states
(environment)

Nation A

| Capabilities, policy making, needs, aspirations, etc. | Resulting objectives and actions |

Nation A

Response

Objectives→Actions

Action◄─Objectives

Nation B

Response

are employed by governments as instruments of inducement to achieve military or political objectives. An international ice-hockey tournament is an international or transnational relationship. So is a world congress of the International Political Science Association. But the student of international politics is interested in these events only if they have some reasonably immediate impact on intergovernmental relations. Where to draw the line is never entirely clear; "ping-pong diplomacy" interests us because it was a novel vehicle used by the Chinese government to establish more important diplomatic links with the United States, while a more ordinary table-tennis match between Australia and New Zealand would not be noteworthy. Similarly, the student of international relations is interested in all aspects of international trade. In international politics, we are concerned with international trade only to the extent that governments may employ economic threats, rewards, or punishments for political purposes, as when they promise to lower tariffs vis-à-vis another country in return for the right to establish a military base in that country.

DESCRIPTION, EXPLANATION, AND PRESCRIPTION

The purpose of this book is to help the reader understand the diverse phenomena of international politics and, in so doing, to think critically and analytically about the world. Now, of course, the term "understand" has different connotations. I will take it to mean that the reader will (1) obtain a few new facts; but more important, he or she will (2) see the similarity of processes in international politics and foreign policy, even when events are separated by decades; (3) be able to place facts in some sort of framework so that they connect better with each other; and (4) learn to appreciate the difficulties involved in explanations of foreign policies and international politics. This should result in a healthy skepticism toward those plans and ideas that will purportedly solve all the world's problems or those theories that, in a few pages, supposedly explain something as complicated as the motives of Chinese, American, Soviet, or Indonesian foreign policies.

Most of the book is descriptive; it seeks to show *how* states act and interact. In places, particularly Chapters 12 through 14, the analysis is more formally *explanatory;* it tries to identify those conditions within and between states that are likely to *cause* certain consequences we call foreign policy, international conflict, or cooperation. In scientific terms, the discussion is not elegant, since we cannot say that factors *a, c, g,* and *z* inevitably cause certain results in foreign policy or interaction between states. But we can demonstrate how and under what conditions public opinion, ethics, or international law, for example, are *likely* to be related (or unrelated) to certain foreign policies.

Unlike many of the treatises on international politics prior to World War II, this book contains very little prescription. It does not purport to solve the most pressing problems of the age; nor does it constitute a handbook for diplomats. From its pages the foreign minister of a country could not find recipes on how to solve his nation's foreign trade problems (although he might learn something about diplomatic bargaining tactics or how to maximize rational behavior in a crisis situation). The reasons that applied knowledge has been omitted are many, but perhaps the main one is the author's belief that before one can intelligently prescribe solutions to problems, it is best to begin by understanding the fundamental conditions and processes of international politics—how people and governments behave in their external relations.

SOME BIASES IN THE STUDY OF INTERNATIONAL POLITICS

No observer in a field so replete with complexities, ethical problems, and historical consequences could fail to reflect certain biases in his or her analysis. Even the most objective scholar is partly a prisoner of his or her experiences, the values predominant in his or her society, and the myths, traditions, and stereotypes that permeate his or her nation and environment. A general analysis of international politics presented by an Indian or Egyptian author, even if it employed a similar organizing device or frame of reference, would probably be very different from that in the succeeding chapters. One cannot avoid some distortion caused by different cultural perspectives. However, other sorts of biases are common in the field, and the student should remain aware of these.

First, many popular analyses of foreign policy and international politics reflect a preoccupation with essentially national problems. This is not so much a case of authors making value judgments that suggest that their country is right while others are wrong (this shortcoming is prominent in high school history texts, however) as it is a tendency to regard the most important problems and conflicts in the world as those in which their country is involved. No one can deny the importance of the postwar Soviet-American rivalry, but in many American texts there is a tendency to view almost all international political problems in terms of this rivalry. Hence, international politics becomes almost synonymous with the cold war, and solutions become identified with effective nuclear deterrents, the cohesion of NATO, and effective foreign-aid programs. Threats all seem to emanate from the Communist nations, and all Western actions appear only as responses to those threats. By using such concepts as objectives, capabilities, threats, punishments, and rewards—which all states have or employ—we are able to avoid much of the slanted phraseology of the cold war ("Communist imperialism," "free world," and "aggression"), which can only hinder understanding of the techniques of statecraft commonly used by all states, no matter what their ideological commitments. One can still have a strong attachment to radical, liberal, or conservative values and at the same time recognize that nuclear threats are no less threats just because they emanate from Washington or London instead of Peking or Moscow; nor are "information programs" any less propaganda just because Western countries have somewhat higher scruples than the Communists about presenting a reasonably balanced analysis of a foreign-policy situation.

A second prominent bias derives from the common interest in the unusual, the dramatic, and the violent. Anyone who reads newspapers regularly can see the tremendous distortion of reality in favor of violence and sensationalism. News media focus our attention on great international crises while they systematically neglect to mention peaceful relations between states. In fact, a majority of transactions between states are peaceful, unexciting, stable, predictable, and conducted with strict regard to treaty obligations.[7] These transactions do not make news. The average North American on the street has plenty of *opinions* on the Middle East crisis, Cuba, or Southeast Asia, even though his or her level of *knowledge* on these dramatic issues is often appallingly low. But how many know anything about the nature of relations among the Scandinavian states or the forms of cooperation among the Central American republics? An unceasing emphasis on violence and conflict naturally leads to perspectives that take "power politics" and cold warfare as the norms of interstate behavior, whereas they are really the exception.

SELECTED BIBLIOGRAPHY

Barber, Arthur, "The Citizen, the Scholar, and the Policymaker," *Background*, 8 (1964), 79–86.

Bobrow, Davis B., *International Relations: New Approaches.* New York: Free Press, 1972.

[7] In one study, Charles McClelland and Gary Hoggard counted and analyzed all the actions, verbal and otherwise, taken by states in the world in 1966, as reported in the *New York Times.* Thirty-three percent of the actions were classified as cooperation, 31.5 percent as conflict, and 33.5 percent as "participation" (government comments, explanations, consultations, and the like). We should not assume that almost one-third of all actions taken by governments in a given year are conflictful, however, because the newspaper bias toward reporting conflict-type events is not controlled in the study. See Charles McClelland and Gary Hoggard, "Conflict Patterns in the Interaction Among Nations," in *International Politics and Foreign Policy*, rev. ed., ed. James N. Rosenau (New York: Free Press, 1969), pp. 711–24.

BOYD, GAVIN, JAMES N. ROSENAU, and KENNETH W. THOMPSON, eds., *World Politics*. New York: Free Press, 1976.

BULL, HEDLEY, "International Theory: The Case for a Classical Approach," *World Politics*, 18 (1966), 361–77.

FOX, W.T.R., ed., *Theoretical Aspects of International Relations*. Notre Dame, Ind.: Notre Dame University Press, 1959.

FRANKEL, JOSEPH, *Contemporary International Theory and the Behavior of States*. New York: Oxford University Press, 1973.

GLASER, WILLIAM A., "The Types and Uses of Political Theory," *Social Research*, 22 (1955), 275–96.

HAAS, MICHAEL, "Bridge-Building in International Relations: A Neotraditional Plea," *International Studies Quarterly*, 11 (1967), 320–38.

———, ed., *International Systems: A Behavioral Approach*. San Francisco: Chandler, 1974.

HARRISON, HORACE V., ed., *The Role of Theory in International Relations*. Princeton, N.J.: D. Van Nostrand Company, Inc., 1964.

HOLSTI, K.J., "Retreat from Utopia: International Relations Theory, 1945–1970," *Canadian Journal of Political Science*, 4 (1971), 165–77.

HOLSTI, OLE R., "The Citizen, the Scholar and the Policy-Maker: Some Dissenting Views," *Background*, 8 (1964), 93–100.

KELMAN, HERBERT C., "Social-Psychological Approaches to the Study of International Relations: Definition of Scope," and "Social-Psychological Approaches to the Study of International Relations: The Question of Relevance," in *International Behavior: A Social-Psychological Analysis*, ed. Herbert C. Kelman. New York: Holt, Rinehart & Winston, 1965.

KNORR, KLAUS, and JAMES N. ROSENAU, eds., *Contending Approaches to International Politics*. Princeton, N.J.: Princeton University Press, 1969.

McCLELLAND, CHARLES A., "The Function of Theory in International Relations," *Journal of Conflict Resolution*, 4 (1960), 303–36.

———, *Theory and the International System*. New York: Macmillan, 1966.

MORGENTHAU, HANS J., "Common Sense and Theories of International Relations," *Journal of International Affairs*, 21 (1967), 207–14.

———, *Politics Among Nations*, 5th ed. New York: Knopf, 1973.

PALMER, NORMAN D., ed., *A Design for International Relations Research: Scope, Theory, Methods and Relevance*. Philadelphia: American Academy of Political and Social Science, Monograph No. 10, 1970.

———, "The Study of International Relations in the United States: Perspectives of Half a Century," *International Studies Quarterly*, 24 (September 1980), 343–63.

RAPOPORT, ANATOL, "Various Conceptions of Peace Research." Peace Research Society, Papers, 19 (1972), 91–106.

RIGGS, FRED, ed., *International Studies: Present Status and Future Prospects*. Philadelphia: American Academy of Political and Social Science, Monograph No. 12, 1971.

Rosenau, James N., "Games International Relations Scholars Play," *Journal of International Affairs,* 21 (1967), 293–303.

———, *International Politics and Foreign Policy: A Reader in Research and Theory,* rev. ed. New York: Free Press, 1969.

Russell, Frank M., *Theories of International Relations.* New York: Appleton-Century-Crofts, 1936.

Russett, Bruce M., "International Behavior Research: Case Studies and Cumulation," in *Approaches to the Study of Political Science,* eds. Michael Haas and Henry Kariel. San Francisco: Chandler, 1970.

Singer, J. David, "The Level-of-Analysis Problem in International Relations," in *The International System: Theoretical Essays,* eds. Klaus Knorr and Sidney Verba. Princeton, N.J.: Princeton University Press, 1961.

———, "The Relevance of the Behavioral Sciences to the Study of International Relations," *Behavioral Science,* 6 (1961), 324–35.

Starr, Harvey, "The Quantitative International Relations Scholar as Surfer: Riding the 'Fourth Wave,'" *Journal of Conflict Resolution,* 28 (June 1974), 336–68.

Sullivan, Michael P., *International Relations: Theories and Evidence.* Englewood Cliffs, N.J.: Prentice-Hall, 1976.

Tanter, Raymond, and Richard Ullman, eds., *Theory and Policy in International Relations.* Princeton, N.J.: Princeton University Press, 1972.

Thompson, Kenneth W., "Normative Theory in International Relations," *Journal of International Affairs,* 21 (1967), 278–92.

Waltz, Kenneth N., *Man, the State, and War.* New York: Columbia University Press, 1959.

Wright, Quincy, *The Study of International Relations.* New York: Appleton-Century-Crofts, Inc., 1955.

Yalem, Ronald, "Toward the Reconciliation of Traditional and Behavioral Approaches to International Theory," *Orbis,* 13 (1969), 578–99.

PART II

International Systems

2

Historic
International
Systems

An international system can be defined as any collection of independent political entities—tribes, city-states, nations, or empires—that interact with considerable frequency and according to regularized processes. The analyst is concerned with describing the typical or characteristic behavior of these political units toward each other and explaining major changes in these patterns of interaction.[1] While observers of international affairs have traditionally explained the behavior of states in terms of national attributes and needs, or individual characteristics of policy makers, the external environment and particularly the structure of power and influence in an international system may have profound effects on the general orientations or objectives of a state toward the rest of the world. Thus, the major characteristics of any international system can be used as one set of variables to help explain the typical orientations, objectives, and actions of that system's component political units. This chapter will focus on international structures and political processes of selected historical civilizations without, however, including lengthy descriptions of individual historical events or personalities, except where these had such a great impact on the system that

---

[1] The concept of "system" as it has been employed in "general systems analysis" is a formal method of analysis that can be used for studying social systems. We use the term in two ways: (1) as a description of regular or typical patterns of interaction among independent political units, and (2) as one variable that helps explain the behavior of the units comprising the system. For the difference between the usages of the concept, see Jay S. Goodman, "The Concept of System in International Relations Theory," *Background*, 8 (1965), 257–68.

they changed its major characteristics. Historical detail is sacrificed in order to emphasize typical or recurring patterns of behavior among interacting political units, permit greater understanding of comparative international politics, and assess the effects of structures and processes on the behavior of component political units.

Each historical system will be analyzed from five aspects. First, the *boundaries* of the system—the line between interaction and environment—will be designated. Any international system has identifiable boundaries—geographic, cultural, or issue lines beyond which actions and transactions between the component political units have no effect on environment, and where events or conditions in the environment have no effect on the political units. Although the Chinese states and the Greek city-states existed simultaneously in the fifth century B.C., there was no interaction between them; to the Chinese, the Greek political units were merely part of an unknown environment. Although the Greeks conducted exploration and trade that brought them into contact with many peoples in Eurasia, the political life of these peoples had little effect on Greek politics.

Second, what are the main *characteristics of the political units* whose interactions form an international system? We are concerned with the types of governments and administrations that political units developed, the role of the average citizen or subject in the political unit's external relations, and the methods by which resources of the unit were mobilized to achieve external objectives.

Third, any international system has a definable *structure,* a characteristic configuration of power and influence or persisting forms of dominant and subordinate relationships. Sometimes a system's structure is typified by concentration of power in one state, which then dominates others; in other eras, power may be diffused quite equally among a large number of states so that none is capable of dominating or leading the others for any period of time; or the structure may be polar or multipolar, where two or more antagonistic blocs of states, each led by states of superior strength, array against each other. We also want to identify the "great powers" of each era, analyze how they acquired their position, and describe the situation of the lesser political entities—satellites, neutrals, or reluctant alliance partners. This analysis also requires discussion of the *stratification* within each system and the criteria commonly employed to distinguish between "great powers" and lesser units. Descriptions of the structure of each system also include identification of the major subsystems, such as the most important rivalries, issues, alliances, blocs, or international organizations.

Fourth, each international system will be analyzed in terms of the most common forms of *interaction* among the component units—diplomatic contacts, trade, types of rivalries, and organized violence or warfare.

Finally, interactions and processes in most systems are regulated or governed by *explicit or implicit rules or customs,* the major assumptions or values upon which all relations are based. As regulators of each system, the techniques and institutions used to resolve major conflicts between the political units will also be considered. More detailed discussion of the major rules and institutions regulating contemporary foreign-policy behavior will be found in Chapter 13.

It would be impossible in two chapters to describe the main characteristics of these five categories for all international systems that have arisen and declined in history. This chapter will concentrate instead on three civilizations for which there is considerable historical evidence on interstate relations: the Chinese state system under the Chou dynasty, the Greek system of city-states, and the international politics of Renaissance Italy during the fifteenth century. The succeeding chapter will conclude with a discussion of the more familiar European state systems during the eighteenth and nineteenth centuries and the contemporary global system.

INTERNATIONAL POLITICS IN THE CHOU DYNASTY, 1122 B.C.–221 B.C.

Even though scholars on the Orient usually classify these nine centuries of Chinese history under the Chou title, there were at least two and possibly three fundamentally different structures in which international political processes took place. One was the feudal order, which lasted from 1122 B.C., with establishment of the dynasty, until approximately 771 B.C., when the central Chou monarchy was defeated by insurgent feudal lords and "barbarians" and forced to move its capital from Hao (near the present city of Sian) to Loyang, further east. This feudal epoch has been called the "Western Chou" period. The era from 771 to 483 B.C., known as the "Spring and Autumn" period, developed a system of independent states, sometimes arranged into two antagonistic blocs, replacing the small, hierarchical feudal order of the Western Chou period. The period of the "Warring States" (403 to 221 B.C.) was noted politically for conflict and competition among the larger states, decline of stable alliances and the polar power structure, and eventual destruction of the system itself.

Boundaries of the Chou System

During the Western Chou (feudal) period, the political influence of the Chou dynasts extended only to the territory of the lower Huang Ho basin, roughly the area between the Huang Ho and Yangtze rivers in central China. There were, of course, inhabitants throughout the territory that comprises modern China, and the Chou authorities had contacts with some of them, even though they were regarded as barbarians *(wu)*. Aside from these sporadic involvements with the *wu*, the Chou political units developed in isolation from the rest of the world. As the system of large independent states replaced the feudal structure, contacts were made with people on the Indian subcontinent, but there is no evidence that these interactions had any immediate political significance to the Chinese states. During the Warring States period, the larger political units extended their domain and sinicized many of the areas populated by the *wu,* so that by 221 B.C. parts of present-day Manchuria, the eastern tip of the Shantung Peninsula, and some territory south and east of the Yangtze River were organized politically and became components of the system.

Characteristics of the Political Units

In the feudal era, the main political unit was the Chou monarchy, which dispensed land, titles, and favors upon its vassals. The bureaucratic organization of the monarchy was already well-developed in this period and differentiated to serve a variety of government functions.

In addition to the central monarchy, which theoretically held title over all the known territory of China, a number of small feudal units, created and sustained by the central monarchy, also played an important political role. The Chou kings donated tracts of land, including towns and villages, to feudal lords and retiring civil servants in return for the payment of taxes. Vassals were also obligated to carry out certain other duties, such as following the king in wars and expeditions against the *wu,* guarding the frontiers of Chou lands, and supplying manpower to the king for his armies. The territorial extent of these feudal units varied considerably. Most consisted of walled cities and surrounding lands, extending over a radius of up to sixty miles;[2] but, in some instances, the monarch would reward a deserving noble with a tract of land the size of New York State. The noble could then subdivide the land into fiefs ranging in size from several fields to several hundred square miles, an area comparable to a large Texas ranch.[3] The literature of the period indicates that there were at least 130 large feudal states subservient to the central monarchy during the Western Chou period, although some authorities mention as many as 1,800.[4]

In theory, nobles and vassals were not allowed to expand their territory at the expense of neighboring feudatories without royal sanction. But even during the height of Chou power, feudal lords maintained some relations with each other (rather than directly through the monarchy) and in some cases fought wars over territorial spoils.

Within their own states, the nobles enjoyed considerable autonomy, appointing their own officials and levying taxes in accordance with their own needs. They maintained their own armies (partly for purposes of internal security) and, if they desired, could split up their land among relatives and subvassals,

[2] Owen and Eleanor Lattimore, *China: A Short History* (New York: Norton, 1944), p. 66.
[3] Dun J. Li, *The Ageless Chinese: A History* (New York: Scribner's, 1965), p. 47.
[4] There seems to be little agreement regarding the number of units in the feudal system. Richard L. Walker, in *The Multi-State System of Ancient China* (Hamden, Conn.: Shoe String Press, 1953), mentions that in 722 B.C., when the feudal order was declining rapidly, there were 170 states (p. 20); Edward T. Williams, in A *Short History of China* (New York: Harper & Row, 1928), mentions the existence of about 1,800 states during the height of the Chou dynasty (p. 56); and Friedrich Hirth, in *The Ancient History of China to the End of the Chou Dynasty* (New York: Columbia University Press, 1923), claims that about 130 states were noted in the Chou literature (p. 11).

creating even smaller political units (fiefs). During the early parts of the Spring and Autumn period (771 to 483 B.C.), the strength and independence of feudal lords grew rapidly at the expense of the central Chou authority. Emulating the administrative mechanisms within the Chou domains, the vassals themselves created regular government organizations as state functions expanded and became more pervasive in the lives of ordinary people. Large-scale irrigation and construction projects, collection and storage of grains, construction of walled cities, and organization and maintenance of armed forces required the establishment of coherent administrative structures and processes.[5] With the aid of administrative mechanisms that made them independent and self-sufficient, the feudal lords and royal princes were able not only to maintain control over their own expanding territories, but to resist the influence of the central monarchy as well.

Another development that strengthened the independence of the feudal states was the growth of rudimentary forms of nationalism. In the Western Chou period, popular patriotism had been directed toward village chiefs and the "Son of Heaven," the Chou monarch, and only occasionally to the feudal lord. But, after 771 B.C., ordinary people began to recognize and emphasize the differences in dialects, customs, religion, and cults among the states as their contacts with others began to proliferate, and the position of the Chou monarch—the symbol of unity—eroded. Pride in local distinctions and loyalty to the prince of the state became much more pronounced toward the end of the Spring and Autumn period. The significance of this development was that during the period of the Warring States, princes could more easily organize peasant militias and armies to fight their wars for them. In turn, peasants and townsmen believed that they were fighting not just as a duty to a feudal lord but for the independence and honor of their own state.[6]

In addition to the Chou monarchy, the feudal realms of the early Chou period, and the large independent states that developed in the Spring and Autumn period, a fourth type of political unit also existed in the Chinese system. This was the attached state *(fu-yung)*, independent only in relation to some purely local affairs. These attached states were mostly holdovers from the feudal era, small bits of territory that had not been conquered and absorbed by the larger feudal rulers as they developed their administrative mechanisms and armed forces. In external relations, the attached states were almost totally dependent upon their neighbors.[7]

The Structure of the Chou System

The center of influence during the Western Chou period resided with the political unit—the central monarchy—which could create or extinguish lesser political

---

[5] Walker, *The Multi-State System of Ancient China,* p. 37.
[6] *Ibid.,* p. 36.
[7] See Derk Bodde, "Feudalism in China," in *Feudalism in History,* ed. Rushton Coulborn (Princeton, N.J.: Princeton University Press, 1956), p. 56.

entities. The structure of the system in the feudal era was hierarchical. Most feudal lords were dependent upon the Chou monarchy for lands, subsidies, and protection against each other; but because of the difficulty of transportation and communication between units on the territorial fringes of the system, as well as the development of administrative mechanisms within the feudal units, there were different degrees of dependence and subservience between the small political units and the monarchy. The Chou kings ruled directly over extensive tracts of territory near the present city of Sian. Next to this they created a circle of small states, each ruled by a direct relative of the king's family. Because of close family and geographical relationships, these local rulers—usually princes—were in a weak position to increase their authority at the expense of the Chou monarch. Another circle of states farther from the capital was ruled by other nobles who had also received their territory from the king but who were distant members of the ruling house or relatives by marriage. Toward the fringes of the system (called the "region of tranquil tenure") the monarchs created a multitude of small states governed by former military or civil officials, who were awarded territory, villages, and towns in return for services to the Chou kings. The function of these states (termed *kuo*) was to watch over the activities of hostile tribes beyond the borders of the system. For this service, the vassals received special royal subsidies. At the farthest region of the system stood the area of "wild domain," land inhabited by barbarian tribes, Chou vassals whose loyalty was doubtful, and groups that retained sporadic connections with the Chou but were not wholly sinicized.

In part, this feudal structure was held together for several centuries by obligations that the vassals and members of the royal family had to fulfill toward the central monarchy or their immediate superiors. The relationships of dominance and subordination were also sustained by an official mythology, which held the king to be the "Son of Heaven," ruling by divine decree. A challenge to his power could thus be interpreted as a form of sacrilege.

But the Chou dynasts were incapable of preventing the eventual growth of power among the many vassals. The feudal lords through the centuries had consolidated political, military, and administrative power over ever-larger pieces of territory and had succeeded in creating self-sufficient states. By the beginning of the Spring and Autumn period, many of them had acquired or conquered enough territory to make it possible for them not to rely on the royal family for subsidies or grants of land. When ambitious nobles went to war and defeated a neighbor, they no longer turned the conquered rulers into subvassals but incorporated them and their land as integral parts of their own territory.[8] The smaller units were simply swallowed up by the larger.

Moreover, the rulers of these territories increasingly derived their authority from inheritance, rather than from the central monarchy. Regardless of lineage, they called themselves princes, and by the fifth century many were

[8] Li, *The Ageless Chinese*, p. 59.

known as kings.[9] By the beginning of the eighth century, successors of the original vassals and princes were already going to battle against each other and even against the Chou monarchy itself. In 707 B.C., a vassal actually defeated the Chou monarch's army;[10] and, fifty years later, a group of leaders from the more powerful states determined the succession of the Chou throne.[11] Increasingly, the central monarchy had to rely for its prestige and power on those theoretically subordinate to it. Between the eighth and seventh centuries, therefore, the patterns of dependency had become reversed. Although the monarch retained a certain ceremonial importance, leaders of independent states in no way felt compelled to observe the wishes of the king.

In four centuries, the structure of the Chou system changed from one in which the characteristic relationship was of a feudal type, with clearly established patterns of dominance and subordination, to a system in which a small number of independent states interacted with each other, with no permanent hierarchy of power and influence. The most important conditions that made this development possible were the relative isolation of many of the feudal units from the central authority,[12] their aggrandizement at each other's expense (thereby creating larger territorial units), growth of popular loyalties, and establishment of administrative mechanisms that made the political units more self-sufficient.[13] The number of units in the late Spring and Autumn and Warring States periods varied with each new conquest or absorption but fluctuated normally between ten and fifteen. By 230 B.C., there were only seven major states and three smaller entities remaining as independent units.

The processes by which smaller states were absorbed into larger ones normally involved the use of force. The state of Ch'i, for example, was particularly successful in expanding its territory at the expense of smaller neighbors. Chronicles of the period record that in 664 B.C., Ch'i "brought Chang to terms"; four years later, it "removed" Yang. In 567, Ch'i "extinguished" Lai and T'ang; and in 549, it "seized" Chieh-ken.[14] In other cases, the rulers of small states voluntarily sought the protection of larger units and ended up as protectorates, attached states, or quasi-independent provinces. In 645, the government of the state of Chin lost territory when it paid a ransom of eight cities in order to obtain the return of its ruler, who had been seized by the people of Ch'in. In some other cases, states either bartered or sold territory to others.

As unoccupied territory available for absorption declined, states warred increasingly between themselves. One result was a tendency toward the polarization of power between the states of the north, which (for ceremonial purposes

---

[9] Williams, *A Short History of China*, p. 62.

[10] Li, *The Ageless Chinese*, p. 50.

[11] Walker, *The Multi-State System of Ancient China*, p. 27.

[12] Cf. Wolfram Eberhard, *A History of China* (London: Routledge and Kegan Paul, Ltd., 1950), p. 34.

[13] The economic reasons for the decline of feudalism are discussed in Li, *The Ageless Chinese*, pp. 60–61.

[14] Walker, *The Multi-State System of Ancient China*, p. 29.

only) still identified themselves with the Chou monarchy but were under the effective leadership or domination of Ch'i, and the several states of the south under the domination of Ch'u. These two groupings constituted crude alliance subsystems and were also the instrumentalities of Ch'i and Ch'u, used partly for their own purposes. These two blocs were roughly analogous to the Western and Soviet blocs after World War II, except that they were never very stable. The period of the Warring States, for example, saw members of both blocs fight vigorously against their own allies.

In a system where territorial expansion became a prime objective of state policy and power was distributed among ten or fifteen large states, there was no role for neutrals. Those units that attempted to remain outside the quarrels of other states or alliances ultimately faced extinction, absorption by another state or bloc, or, in the case of the Chou (northern) alliance, a type of quasi independence that allowed for considerable cultural and political autonomy but not military neutrality.[15]

By the third century, whatever was left of Chinese unity dissipated as all states began to wage war against each other, regardless of alliance commitments or traditional friendships. Wars became great campaigns of massacre and annihilation, with serious consequences to the political and economic stability of both victors and defeated. Between 230 and 221 B.C., the westernmost state of Ch'in, a semibarbarian and partly isolated political unit, conquered Han, Chao, Wei, Ch'u, Yen, and finally Ch'i, bringing to an end the Chou dynasty and the system of independent states. The system was replaced by the Chin empire, ruled by the Han dynasty, which successfully destroyed all symbolic vestiges of feudalism and the political independence of separate territorial units.[16]

The forms and criteria of stratification during the Western Chou period were similar to those in the European medieval order: The status and prestige of each political unit was based upon the personal relationship between the central dynast and his vassals. Thus, each political unit was ranked at diplomatic and ceremonial functions according to the original title conferred on its leader by the monarch, corresponding approximately to the titles of prince, duke, marquis, earl, viscount, and baron. By the Spring and Autumn period, stratification became established upon the visible elements of a state's power and prestige; rulers who attended international conferences in the eighth century B.C. no longer ranked themselves according to the official titles of their feudal ancestors. Prestige and status in the system after 771 B.C. were based primarily upon a state's available military resources and secondarily upon the prestige, wealth, and family connections of its rulers. The number of four-horse military chariots was the most conspicuous indicator of a state's power.[17] Another indicator of

---

[15] *Ibid.*, p. 101.
[16] Li, *The Ageless Chinese*, p. 56.
[17] Cf. Cheng Te-k'un, *Shang China* (Cambridge, Eng.: W. Heffer and Sons, Ltd., 1960), p. 295. Richard Walker points out that even today, the translation of the term "great power" is commonly rendered in Chinese as a "country of ten thousand four-horse chariots."

a state's prestige and status was the number and quality of allies it could count upon for military assistance.

Since the Chinese were very conscious about their international ranking, they frequently attempted to impress neighbors, allies, and enemies by winning spectacular military victories or, if warfare was wanting, by conducting large military reviews before visiting dignitaries from other states. In 529 B.C., for example, the government of Ch'i organized a military performance in which it displayed more than 4,000 chariots.[18] Since the largest army mobilized for battle during the early Chou dynasty contained only 3,000 chariots,[19] it is clear that this state exhibited almost its entire military capability in an effort to impress others with its might.

Whether measured by available military forces, family connections, wealth, or allies, there was no persistent hierarchy of status or power after the strength of the Chou monarchy had declined to symbolic proportions. Military power and diplomatic status were diffused among a number of relatively large and equal states. These could be considered the great powers of the epoch, states that, although roughly equal with each other, determined the fate of lesser political units either by absorption or through leadership of alliances. During the early part of the Spring and Autumn period, no one state was predominant in the system, as alliance patterns shifted rapidly and leadership passed back and forth among Ch'i, Chin, and Ch'un in the north, and Ch'u, Wu, and Yueh in the south. During the latter portion of this period and throughout the Warring States period, however, power and status gravitated primarily to the leaders of the two main alliance systems, Ch'i and Ch'u, and ultimately to Chin, which conquered all the other states.

Below these great powers were smaller states, political units that maintained all the requisites of independence but, for lack of military capabilities, economic resources, family connections, or defense establishments (such as walled cities), had to rely for their survival upon the great powers and their alliances. A third tier of states included the *fu-yung*, or attached states, and smaller protectorates that owed their independence to the goodwill of their protectors. These units were seldom over eight square miles in size and, as the lowest units in the political order, did not have direct diplomatic access to the ceremonial center of the system, the Chou monarchy, but had to communicate indirectly through their protectors.[20]

Forms of Interaction

During the feudal period, levels of political and commercial interaction among the units were low, except when formal diplomatic and ceremonial exchanges were arranged between the dukes, princes, and other nobility and the central Chou monarchy. Interaction and communication followed closely the hierarchical

[18] Walker, *The Multi-State System of Ancient China*, p. 48.
[19] Cheng, *Shang China*, p. 295.
[20] Walker, *The Multi-State System of Ancient China*, p. 38.

pattern of authority in the system, although feudal units in close proximity naturally had many relations with each other.

In the Spring and Autumn and Warring States periods, each of the independent states conducted its external relations without reference to the official center of the empire. There was a proliferation of contacts between states, not only formal and diplomatic, but trade and commercial as well. The Chinese states never established permanent diplomatic organizations, but recurring occasions for arranging alliances, declaring war, making peace, or maintaining prestige in the system through ceremonial or military displays led to almost constant diplomatic exchanges between the units. Chinese sources of this period list such diplomatic exchanges as *ch'ao,* a court visit paid by one ruler to another; *hui,* meetings between permanent government officials of two or more states; *p'in,* friendly missions of information or inquiry; *shih,* exchange of emissaries; and *shou,* hunting parties where government representatives combined diplomatic affairs with recreation.[21] The ceremonies attending these types of exchanges were so lengthy that many states did have, in effect, permanent diplomatic communication with each other.

These exchanges often had a direct connection with a state's security or expansionist objectives, even when contacts ostensibly had ceremonial purposes. Almost all the major events in the life of a ruling family—assumption of a throne, burial of a former ruler, marriages between families or rulers, or even births of children into a ruler's family—required diplomatic representation from other friendly states, and these occasions were used for bargaining over state interests.[22] Marriages between ruling families were a means of creating and sustaining alliances, a practice familiar to students of early European diplomatic history.

A unique aspect of transactions within the Chinese system was the extent to which they occurred between states with different religious or cultural traditions. Though Ch'u and Ch'in were not fully sinified states, they were able to interact with the others essentially on a basis of equality. Apparently wars, alliances, and peace were made in the light of a state's immediate objectives and interests, whereas ideological or cultural distinctions remained largely irrelevant to a state's orientation toward others. Hence, if a state found it in its own interest to conclude an alliance with even the most uncultured barbarians at the fringes of the system, it would not hesitate to do so.[23]

Commercial exchange was another form of interaction. Normally this was a private affair of merchants, who were free to travel from state to state and conduct their transactions without administrative interference. However, insofar as grain and other commodities were necessary to feed armies, governments maintained an interest in having sufficient stores to support their forces in times of poor harvest. Since they could not always obtain adequate supplies

---

[21] *Ibid.,* p. 75.
[22] *Ibid.,* p. 78.
[23] *Ibid.,* p. 99.

from their own peasants, occasionally they had to send out economic missions to purchase agricultural products from other states.[24]

War was a frequent form of interaction between states during the Spring and Autumn and Warring States periods. It is recorded, for example, that Duke Huan of Ch'in went to war twenty-eight times in a reign lasting forty-three years.[25] In the feudal order, force (provided partly by the vassals) was used primarily by the Chou dynasts against the *wu* and occasionally against errant nobles whose actions were deemed damaging to the interests of the empire. In the system of independent states, all the units used organized violence as a method of achieving objectives—whether territory, slaves, "honor," or allies. During the feudal era, engagements were seldom fought as battles of annihilation, but more as trials of strength, finesse, and glory.[26] Fairly rigid rules of warfare prevailed (for example, a charioteer could not fight against anyone of lower or higher rank) and helped to moderate the destructiveness of battle. By the period of Warring States, however, wars had become great contests, fought brutally by huge armies numbering in the hundreds of thousands. Mass slaughter replaced duelling by charioteers, and the casualties of battle reached proportions enormous even by contemporary standards. In 274 B.C., a Ch'in general reportedly killed 150,000 enemy soldiers, and the massacre of prisoners of war was a common occurrence.[27]

The Chinese also used various forms of subversion and intervention in other states' internal affairs as methods of achieving their objectives. The number of dynastic quarrels and marriages arranged between families of different states led to situations in which one government could support certain claimants to the throne in a neighboring territory and, if it succeeded in creating disloyal factions or cliques, could then help foment revolutions or *coups d'état* and place a subservient, or at least friendly, ruler on the throne. According to one authority,[28] the Chinese states persistently employed the techniques of subversion to expand their influence into other areas. In the Spring and Autumn period, for example, there were at least thirty-six instances of successful subversion, frequently brought to a conclusion when the intervening state made a show of force at the last moment in order to ensure the victory of rebel elements.

The Rules of the System

In the latter periods of the Chou dynasty, there was considerable discrepancy between the official rules, traditions, and myths that were supposed to govern relations between political units and the actual behavior of independent states.

[24] *Ibid.*, p. 80.
[25] Li, *The Ageless Chinese*, p. 50.
[26] Kenneth S. Latourette, *The Chinese: Their History and Culture* (New York: Macmillan, 1959), p. 61; Marcel Granet, *Chinese Civilization* (New York: Meridian Books, 1951), p. 290.
[27] Cf. Eberhard, *A History of China*, p. 57; Li, *The Ageless Chinese*, p. 56.
[28] Walker, *The Multi-State System of Ancient China*, p. 86.

The official mythology and customary rules of behavior, buttressed by the writings of philosophers such as Confucius, emphasized unity, obedience to the "Son of Heaven," harmony among all parts of the political order, and the obligation of all lower entities—whether sons to fathers or vassals to lords—to higher authorities.

But practice during the Spring and Autumn and Warring States periods did not accord with the myths and customs appropriate to the feudal order. In a system of many powerful, ambitious, and independent states, such rules were anachronisms. Instead, the main units developed rules or customs that reflected the major political and military characteristics of the system. The official theories of hierarchy, imperial rule over all subjects, and attending patterns of superior-subordinate relationships were belied by the assumptions of later periods, which recognized that the great powers, at least, were more or less sovereign equals, free from all restraints imposed by the Chou monarchy. Treaties concluded after 771 B.C. were treaties between equals, even where the Chou authorities were involved. Obligations were entered into only by the consent of both parties to the treaty, and no authority had legal or customary rights in another independent state's territories, as they did in the Western Chou era. Even compacts between the Chinese states and various barbarian groups were concluded on a basis of equality. There was, however, no belief in the sanctity of independence; throughout the Spring and Autumn and Warring States periods, the larger units conquered and amalgamated lesser territories, with no intention of returning their independence after a short period of occupation. Conquered territories were simply annexed.

More explicit rules were formulated into treaties, which contained the specific obligations of states toward each other and provided means for enforcement. One guarantee of compliance with treaties was the practice of exchanging hostages. A state would concede several cities or members of the ruling family as hostages, to be kept—or destroyed—by the other treaty partner if the first broke its obligations. Among customary rules were those demanding that states send envoys to each other at frequent intervals, that members of the two main alliance systems send a minimum of one mission every three years to the court of the league president, and that "summit" meetings be held at least every five years.[29] Other rules prescribed in detail the types of conduct and behavior appropriate in warfare, although towards the end of the system the rules of warfare were systematically violated in great campaigns of annihilation.

Most conflicts during the feudal era were mediated directly by the Chou monarchy—except those on the periphery of the system, where central influence was at a minimum. With the decline of the Chou dynasty's effective position among the newly arising independent states, conflicts had to be resolved directly by those involved. During the early Spring and Autumn period, there were no institutions that could provide mediatory or conciliatory services; but, as the

[29] *Ibid.*, p. 81.

two alliance systems developed, they did establish techniques for resolving conflicts arising *within* the alliance. It was in the interest of the alliance—or at
least to the advantage of the predominant powers in each alliance—to maintain
peace and collaboration between alliance members. When disputes broke out
among them, therefore, other members often found it necessary to intervene,
either to secure a mediated resolution or, if that was impossible or improbable,
to threaten or force one or both parties to terminate their quarrel. In 546 B.C.,
moreover, some of the smaller states that had been increasingly victimized by
larger neighbors called a conference of states, which successfully drafted a multilateral treaty of nonaggression. This resulted in forty years of relative stability
and nonviolence in interstate relations. Whatever techniques were employed
by the Chinese states in the Spring and Autumn period were quickly cast aside,
however, in the period of Warring States, when conflicts were resolved almost
entirely by the use of force.[30]

We can now summarize two points that will be of particular concern
to us throughout this book: the sources of change from one system type to
another and the influence that the structure of the system has on the foreign-
policy outputs of the individual components. For the first, let us put in chart
form those social, political, and economic factors that brought stability or change
to the system. By stability, we do not mean the absence of war or conflict, but
rather that the *essential characteristics of the system* (boundaries, nature of the units,
structure, forms of interaction, and rules) remained essentially the same. Other
developments were occurring, however, that brought about fundamental changes
in any one or more of the system's characteristics.

How can these three fundamentally different types of Chinese international systems be related to the foreign policies of the typical states making
them up? How, in particular, can the structure of the system serve as one variable
explaining the foreign policy outputs of the political units?

In the feudal era, the units were weak in relation to the central monarchy
and had little freedom to maneuver in their external relations. Bound to the
center by traditional mythical and contractual obligations, the lesser units seldom
had a choice but to conduct their relations with each other in accordance with
the policies and rules set forth by the emperor. In parts of the Spring and
Autumn and Warring States periods, however, when military capabilities and
diplomatic influence were widely diffused among a number of relatively equal
political units and when the blocs were not operating, the structure placed fewer
limitations on external actions and objectives. To be sure, the smaller states
were virtual satellites or protectorates, but the medium and large states enjoyed
considerable freedom of action. They could forge or destroy alliances, seek
security through isolation, or attempt, although usually unsuccessfully, to defend
themselves by remaining neutral. Unlike the feudal system, wherein objectives
and policies were either set by the monarchy or agreed upon through bargaining

---

[30] Li, *The Ageless Chinese*, p. 53; Walker, *The Multi-State System of Ancient China*, p. 88.

Table 2–1 Sources of Stability and Change in Ancient Chinese International Systems

PERIOD	SOURCES OF STABILITY	SOURCES OF CHANGE
Western Chou (1122–771 B.C.)	"Son of Heaven" myth Emperor's control over all land	Poor communication between outer "states" and central monarchy
	Grants of titles Contribution of troops and taxes by units to emperor Emperor's superior military and administrative capacities	Developing administrative and military capabilities of states Beginnings of local nationalism Territorial aggrandizement by some states
Spring and Autumn (771–483 B.C.)	Continuing myth of emperor's unity Development of bilateral and customary rules to regulate interaction between states Development of conflict resolution mechanisms (mostly domination of small states by large) Easier communication Rough balance of power between major antagonists	Tendency toward polar power structure Development of increasingly large armies Decline of customary rules of warfare Growth of large states
Warring States (403–221 B.C.)	Weak operation of alliances	No more territory for external expansion Rise and predominance of Ch'in Destruction of blocs and balance between them Wars of annihilation

between the monarch and vassals, the diffuse system involved bargaining directly between competing independent states. The Chinese system during the Spring and Autumn period thus suggests that if power is diffused, the latitude for choice of foreign-policy orientations is substantial, but security from outside attack may be low. Strategy, alliance making, war, and rapid shifts in orientation toward neighbors and more distant states are characteristic features of the diffuse system. In the feudal system, on the contrary, most action is confined to court intrigues and secret bargaining, and major objectives are determined for the units by the emperor. Freedom of action is limited, but security from outside attack may be enhanced. In the bloc system of the Warring States period, the latitude of choice of lesser alliance partners was considerably restricted. The goals and diplomacy of all lesser states were made to conform to the interests of the bloc leaders. Generalizations such as these seem to be confirmed from other historical international systems as well.

THE EXTERNAL POLITICS
OF THE GREEK CITY-STATES,
800 B.C.–322 B.C.

The Greek world was geographically more extensive than its Chinese counterpart. While the Chinese remained isolated from most other cultural groups, Greek merchants and travellers found their way to India, the shores of the Baltic, Spain, and the north coast of Africa. Most of the famous city-states were located on the Greek peninsula and on islands of the Aegean Sea, but the Greeks also colonized locations throughout the shores of the Mediterranean, establishing their political organizations and culture in the areas on which the cities of Nice, Marseilles, and Naples are currently found. Since these people maintained commercial and diplomatic relations with the Phoenicians, Persians, Arabs, Indians, and various tribes in Europe and Southern Russia, the geographical boundaries of the system are difficult to establish. Persian expansion in the Aegean was a major threat to the interests of all Greek city-states on the peninsula; although the activities of the Phoenicians had little impact on relations between most Greek city-states, they determined the fate of several Greek colonies on the Italian peninsula. Non-Greek political units thus played an important, though sporadic, role in Greek life. Since the relations among city-states and colonies constituted the majority of interactions and transactions in the system, however, we will describe these rather than emphasize the Greeks' relations with the "barbarians," people of non-Hellenic culture on the fringes of the Greek world.

Nature of the Political Units

The city-state *(polis)* was the main form of political organization throughout the Greek world from the eighth century until Philip of Macedonia conquered the peninsula in the late fourth century B.C. Most of these units were comprised of a group of towns or a small city, usually walled, surrounded by relatively small areas of agricultural territory. Attica, for example, was the area occupied by the Athenian people. It included many small agricultural villages, but the city of Athens was the center of political life and administration, and the people throughout Attica were called Athenians. The population of the city-states varied from the largest, such as Syracuse, Acragas, and Athens, with about 25,000 male citizens, to the smallest, such as Siris and Thourioi in Sicily, which contained only several thousand inhabitants. In size, the city-states ranged from several hundred square miles, including outlying agricultural territory, to small towns built on the shores of the Mediterranean Sea comprising only several hundred acres. Most *poleis* were about 100 square miles.

The forms of government in the city-states varied from priest-kings ruling over tribal organizations, small oligarchies of the rich, and military tyrannies to freely elected governments, wherein citizens (omitting peasants, merchants, and slaves), whose tenure in office rotated frequently, formulated and administered policies directly.

The city-state cannot be understood adequately when described only in terms of its political institutions, for the Greeks considered the *polis* the *ideal* social organization for liberating an individual from a natural state and for providing justice, promoting fellowship and harmony, and training personal character. Despite the many economic, cultural, and language ties among Greek city-states, there was no struggle to create a common framework for uniting all the Hellenic people into a more viable empire. The Greeks emphasized the virtue of limited political organizations—small enough to allow for the assembly of all free citizens to help make political decisions and small enough for government and administration never to seem impersonal influences over the lives of citizens. The state and society were thus indistinguishable concepts among the Greeks.

Aside from the *poleis,* three other types of political units played roles in the Greek international system. One was the tributary state, a *polis* that came under the hegemony of another city-state but was allowed to maintain some degree of autonomy in internal affairs. During the fifth century, when Athens dominated the Delian League, a number of the smaller members of the alliance became tributary states. Most of these were obliged—ostensibly as alliance partners—to accept Athenian domination over their external relations, contribute to the Athenian treasury (officially, a contribution to the alliance), and make war and peace according to the interests of Athens. Failure to follow Athenian leadership resulted in serious punishment, including occupation of the recalcitrant city-state by Athenian troops and construction of permanent Athenian garrisons.

The third type of political unit was the military colony, *cleruchy,* which some city-states established to guard strategic territories, waterways, and trade routes. The *cleruchy* also served as an outlet for surplus population from the mother city-state, particularly after these cities grew to the point where their own agriculture could not provide adequate food supplies for the population.

Finally, many city-states also established nonmilitary colonies throughout the Aegean and Mediterranean seas. They erected these towns and cities primarily as new sources of food supply and areas for relieving population congestion at home. Many city-states also sent politically unreliable citizens and unwanted aspirants for public office to their colonies, sometimes in exile, sometimes to fill honorific positions. Although the original connection between the city-state and its colonies was one of dependence, after several decades most colonies became independent of their mother city-states and retained only formal religious ties. Otherwise, the colonies organized their own political administration and conducted their own external affairs.[31]

The Structure of the System

As each city developed during its formative years in relative isolation, the system originally displayed a highly diffuse structure of influence and power. Each unit was independent. Although frequent wars over territory, personal rivalries, and frontiers ended in the total destruction of some city-states, there were few permanent hierarchies of dominance-dependence. Some city-states had wider-ranging interests and activities than others, and consequently gained more prestige. By the fifth century, however, the structure of the system became more stratified and rigid, with city-states such as Athens, Sparta, Acragas, Corinth, Argus, and Thebes increasingly dominating the actions and transactions of the smaller units around them. The main sources of change from a diffuse to a "polar" international system, where power and influence coagulated around two blocs of states, were the rapid growth and extension of Athenian naval and commercial strength, and the threat of Persian penetration into the Ionian islands, Thrace, and Macedon.

As a response to this external danger, the Greeks established the Hellenic League into a military alliance and placed it under the leadership of Sparta and Athens. Despite the semblance of Greek unity during the Persian Wars (492–477 B.C.), there were serious conflicts between members of the League, mostly occasioned by the smaller city-states' fear of Athenian imperialism and expansion. Thus, after the Greek victories over the Persians, Athens' competitors, led by Sparta, formed a rival organization, the Peloponnesian League, an intricate alliance and collective security system designed to deter further Athenian expansion and in some cases to "liberate" areas already under Athenian domination. A bitter competition over trade and naval supremacy between Corinth and Athens led ultimately to the Peloponnesian Wars involving the two military alliances.

By the outbreak of these wars in 431 B.C., Athens had already become an empire, ruling directly or indirectly (ostensibly through a new multilateral alliance, the Delian League) over a number of independent and tributary city-states. But this hegemony was not created solely by Athens' commercial superiority or even by the imperialism of Cimon and Pericles. Many city-states voluntarily accepted Athenian laws, courts, and currency simply because these Athenian institutions were more admirable than their own arrangements.[32] Athens also provided many services for other city-states, such as leading the alliance against Persia, clearing the seas of pirates, and organizing trade connections with non-Hellenic peoples.

---

[31] For description of some of the city-states, see Kathleen Freeman, *Greek City States* (London: Methuen, 1948); for the colonies, Johannes Hasebrook, *Trade and Politics in Ancient Greece* (London: G. Bell, 1933), pp. 106–8.

[32] Adda B. Bozeman, *Politics and Culture in International History* (Princeton, N.J.: Princeton University Press, 1960), p. 86.

By 431 B.C., then, the Greek city-state system had become partly polarized into two large blocs. The Athenian empire led one bloc and was followed by its voluntary or tributary allies, including the prominent city-states of Rhodes, Miletus, Corcyra (a formidable naval power), as well as other units located in the eastern Aegean and northern and western Greece. Sparta led the Peloponnesian League, with Ellis, Arcadia, and Corinth as its most important allies. Unlike the Chinese system, wherein neutral status was not condoned, many city-states and colonies on the Greek peninsula and throughout the shores of the Mediterranean Sea remained free from direct involvement in the Peloponnesian Wars. The system was not, therefore, organized completely around the two blocs.

By the middle of the fifth century, an identifiable order of stratification had replaced the more diffuse, egalitarian distribution of power, status, and prestige found in the era when the city-states were relatively isolated from each other. The criteria according to which states were ranked during and after the fifth century were primarily military, commercial, and cultural. Sparta and Athens assumed leadership of the two blocs because of their military or commercial capabilities. Sparta gained respect and prestige from the fighting efficiency, bravery, and loyalty of its soldiers. Even those who abhorred Sparta's authoritarian political and social institutions admired the greatness of its armies.[33] Athens, on the other hand, wielded considerable influence over the other city-states by virtue of its citizens' aggressive commercial practices. When it had achieved a position of trading predominance, it could easily reduce smaller states to subservience by applying boycotts and embargoes on their trade. Other states moved voluntarily toward Athens, expecting profitable trade relations and protection of commercial routes by the Athenian fleet. Sparta, which possessed only one colony and few commercial connections, had to rely essentially on military force to achieve its objectives.

Also contributing to Athens' prestige and status were the cultural and political contributions of its citizens. Many city-states accepted direct Athenian rule or political leadership in external affairs in order to obtain the advantages of Athenian political institutions, laws, culture, and commercial practices. Above all, perhaps, cultural excellence was a criterion of greatness. Athens was to the Greeks what Paris was to Europe in the eighteenth century, the cultural center of the system—in Pericles' words, "the educator of Hellas."[34]

Forms of Interaction among the City-States

Prior to the fifth century, the city-states conducted little trade among themselves, as each unit was virtually self-sufficient in the few necessities of life and the commodities needed to sustain a fairly simple technology. Governments generally took no part in trading activities (except in some cases, to obtain revenues), and merchants faced numerous obstacles to successful transactions, including

[33] H.D.F. Kitto, *The Greeks* (Edinburgh: R. Clark Ltd., 1951), p. 94.
[34] *Ibid.*, p. 76.

land and sea pirates, nonconvertible monies, and nonenforcement of debts among citizens of different city-states.[35] By the fifth century, however, the growth of population and merchant classes and the need to obtain military supplies prompted rapid development in commercial activity among the units. Commercial transactions aided the city-states in their internal development but also led to important rivalries. By the time of the Peloponnesian Wars, private merchants no longer operated on their own, but relied extensively on governments to provide protection and open new sources of raw materials and markets. Simultaneously, many governments used trade to build up military resources and employed their merchants as agents through which they could place diplomatic pressure by threatening boycotts and embargoes on other city-states. The tradespeople of Athens, backed by the powerful Athenian fleet, were particularly aggressive in developing markets abroad, and the Athenian government occasionally helped them exclude the trade of rival city-states, such as Corinth, from sources of supply. By the time Athens dominated large parts of the Aegean Sea and the Gulf of Corinth, no city-state could conduct extensive overseas trade without the tacit approval of Athenian authorities.

One form of interaction that prevailed even in the early period of the city-states was the meetings of Greeks at religious festivals and councils. The Greeks observed one basic religious form and created a number of institutions (called *amphictyonies*) to maintain the purity of the religion and provide means for organizing common festivals and sacrifices. The shrines at Olympia and Delphi offered centers for interaction of all Greeks. Religion, then, was one of the unifying elements in the system (truces were always declared during the Olympic games) and helped the Greeks appreciate their common inheritance and distinguish themselves from the "barbarians" with whom they had developed many contacts. The religion did not, however, lead to any political unification among the many units; indeed, as each city-state had its own deities, religious symbols were often the basis for violence and conflict, not political cooperation. One of the major problems of the system was that despite the Greeks' propensity to fraternize with each other in social, religious, recreational, intellectual, and aesthetic matters, they were unable to carry these forms of cooperative behavior into political and military relationships.

If the political units could cooperate in some questions of common concern, generally their interests conflicted and their governments resorted to the use of force to resolve those conflicts. War was a recurrent phenomenon of the system, and most peace treaties were drafted to remain in effect for only a specified time. Part of the explanation for the frequency of violence lies in the coupling of religious and political symbolism within the city-states. In the early period of the Greek system, wars arising over territorial quarrels often developed into ideological crusades involving the honor and glory not only of the city-state, but also of its particular deities. For this reason, many

[35] Hasebrook, *Trade and Politics in Ancient Greece*, p. 85.

wars were fought with terrible brutality, resulting in destruction of the defeated city-state and sale of its inhabitants into slavery.

The sources of war varied. In the early period, wars over religious issues were numerous; one example was the conflict between Athens and Crissa, which erupted into armed violence after the Crissans destroyed Apollo's temple at Delphi. Border conflicts frequently led to warfare, and conflicts arising out of internal revolts and civil wars, in which outside city-states intervened, were not uncommon after the fifth century. War was also used to obtain control over strategic waterways and mountain passes. Athens used force several times to punish recalcitrant allies or city-states that had attempted to defect from the empire or Delian League to join the league of states led by Sparta. Finally, the search for booty and commercial advantage were important sources of military violence. Throughout the period, economic interaction became more prominent but did not always lead to cooperative forms of behavior. On the contrary, wars, conflicts, and rivalries tended to become more intense as the economic stakes involved in a quarrel increased. However, not every divisive issue could become a cause for a contest of arms, since wars were costly, destructive, and often indecisive. Other means of wielding influence had to be employed as well.

Among these was the practice of diplomacy, formal efforts by the government of one city-state to induce another city-state, through oral persuasion, to act in the interests of the first. Diplomacy was conducted through the medium of the ambassador, usually an honored citizen with oratorical skills, who was sent to persuade governing officials of another city-state to make formal decisions by concluding treaties of friendship, alliance, or commerce. In wartime, ambassadors—including those sent by the "barbarians"—normally enjoyed diplomatic immunities and were used primarily at the end of hostilities to negotiate the terms of peace, deliver prisoners, and make arrangements for burial of war victims.

Major Rules of the Greek System

The Greeks developed a number of rules, observed in treaties or custom, that regulated diplomatic relations and the conduct of warfare. These gave recognition to the independence and equality of the units and defined the limits of immunities for both diplomats and religious shrines in time of war; other rules pronounced standard procedures for declaring war, providing asylum, and conferring citizenship.[36] Since wars were often costly and indecisive, the Greeks also developed procedures for resolving conflicts short of force. Arbitration and conciliation, two procedures for interjecting third parties into diplomatic bargaining situations, were among the important contributions the Greeks made

---

[36] Arthur Nussbaum, *A Concise History of the Law of Nations* (New York: Macmillan, 1961); Coleman Phillipson, *The International Law and Custom of Ancient Greece and Rome* (London: Macmillan, 1911).

to subsequent diplomatic practices.[37] They occasionally employed these procedures for handling recurring boundary disputes, conflicts involving public debts, and quarrels arising from differing interpretations of treaties.[38] Normally, parties to a dispute honored the decisions of arbitrators, particularly since the arbitrators enjoyed great public prestige. Despite arbitral procedures, war and violence continued to be employed as means of settling conflicts, leading ultimately to the exhaustion of the most important city-states.

The fate of the Greek system was analogous to that of the Chinese: Both succumbed, after a long period of bitter strife between two major blocs, to a superior force that, although part of the system, was considered to be "barbarian" and alien. For the Chinese states, Ch'in was the danger lurking behind the Wei River; for the Greeks, Macedonia was the external threat.

It could be argued that the development outside Greece of much larger territorial and administrative units commanding extensive military power made the Greek city-states obsolete, just as developing dynastic states in sixteenth- and seventeenth-century Europe superseded the small independent walled cities of medieval Europe. By the third century B.C., no system based on such small units as the city-states could remain isolated from the new giants. Larger political units—first the Persians, succeeded by the Macedonians and ultimately the Romans—made the city-states appear weak and paltry in comparison. Either the Greeks would have had to unite into one large territorial empire, participating as just one of several larger entities in the politics of the Mediterranean area, or they would be engulfed, as they were, by new states that had previously been merely peripheral actors in Greek life. The small republics and city-states of Renaissance Italy were similarly engulfed by the larger dynastic states of Europe in the fifteenth and sixteenth centuries.

INTERNATIONAL POLITICS
IN RENAISSANCE ITALY

The unique character of politics in the Italian peninsula during the fifteenth century can be appreciated by comparing the system of Italian city-states and republics with the political structure in the rest of Europe. Although Europe at this time was not in its medieval period, its political organization maintained the major features of earlier centuries. Nation-states did not exist; there was no concept of ethnic nationhood that had any practical significance to the form of political organizations; and, even though kings reigned on thrones, few ruled

---

[37] The Greeks did not invent these procedures. Many primitive tribes and more extensive empires had developed procedures and institutions by which disinterested third parties attempted to reconcile two feuding families, tribes, or nations. The Europeans, however, developed the practice during the eighteenth and nineteenth centuries, using the Greek experience as a model.

[38] Marcus N. Tod, *International Arbitration amongst the Greeks* (Oxford: The Clarendon Press, 1913). For further discussion of arbitral procedures, see Chapter 15.

directly over a specified group of people inhabiting definable territories. Instead, there were many hierarchies of authority in the known areas of Europe. Some kings, to be sure, were sovereign and commanded the obedience of nobles on some questions of policy. There also existed hundreds of semisovereign walled cities and feudal lords, some of whom determined who would sit on the king's throne. The church hierarchy was an independent power on most ecclesiastical and moral issues of the day and wielded considerable influence in secular politics as well. Kings made treaties with their vassals, and vassals made contracts with each other—sometimes at the expense of the king; individual churches, monasteries, or convents had special privileges and immunities; peasants and independent cities formed protective leagues; in order to keep their thrones, kings often had to mortgage or sell their rights to territory. Europe was a patchwork of small, quasi sovereignties, states within states, and overlapping hierarchies, whose powers were defined in complicated contracts and oaths.[39]

   In contrast, a reasonably well-defined set of political entities had developed on the northern part of the Italian peninsula by the beginning of the fifteenth century. Venice had already existed for several centuries as an important trading state with the East. It had a regular system of administration, the rudiments of a diplomatic service, and historical interests upon which to base its diplomatic activities. The rest of northern Italy was rapidly developing into politically distinct pieces of territory.

The Boundaries of the System

According to historians,[40] the condition that most favored development of independent city-states and republics in Italy during the fourteenth and fifteenth centuries was the relative isolation of the peninsula from the rest of Europe. Not that there was any lack of contact between all areas of Europe, but the territories north of the Alps were still splintered into thousands of political authorities, and not even some of the more aggressive European kings could turn as far south as Italy in search of dynastic prestige or territory. They had too much to handle with their own vassals and pretenders to their thrones to intrigue among the Italian states. In addition, a number of crises like the Hundred Years' War, the fight between temporal and ecclesiastical authorities over control of the papacy, and recurrent chaos on the Iberian peninsula kept them either preoccupied or impotent. The periodic intrusion of non-Italian authorities into the system was, therefore, well within the bounds the system could tolerate without creating fundamental changes in its structure or patterns of interaction. It was when the Milanese prevailed upon the French to intervene on their behalf in 1494 that the system collapsed; after the fifteenth century, it became just another part of Europe, its politics integrally related to developments on the rest of the continent.

---

[39] Gerhard Ritter, *Die Neugestaltung Europas im 16. Jahrhundert* (Berlin: Verlag des Druckhauses Tempelhof, 1950), pp. 23–25.
[40] Garrett Mattingly, *Renaissance Diplomacy* (London: Jonathan Cape, 1955), pp. 59–61, 97.

What distinguishes the boundaries of the Italian system from those of China and Greece is that the inhabitants on the fringes of the system were not considered barbarians. If Europe was not unified politically during the fifteenth century, at least it was a cultural and religious unit, with only language and dynastic differences having any practical significance. Although the Italians did not interact extensively over political or commercial problems with other Europeans, the city-states or republics on the peninsula were not isolated. The boundaries of the system were defined by the predominant direction of political-diplomatic-military interaction, not by cultural or religious forms of interaction.[41]

Nature of the Political Units

An important political characteristic of the Italian states in the fifteenth century was lack of security and stability in their governments. Few governments, with the exception of the Venetian and papal authorities, could rule with safety of tenure, because few were established on secure foundations; most lacked any basis for legitimacy, whether historical, customary, or religious, being founded on force, fraud, and repression. The forms of government varied from outright tyrannies to rule by oligarchies. Venice was governed by a conservative aristocracy of patrician families, and the papal states were administered by a conglomeration of feudal lordships and petty tyrants, each more or less subordinate to the popes. A few of the units were genuine republics with various degrees of popular rule.[42]

The major units in the Italian system included the papal states, Venice, Milan, Genoa, Florence, and Naples. A number of smaller political organizations—often walled cities and areas in which political power had not yet attained any regular form—lay between the important states.[43] The concept of territoriality—that political power should be based on a specific piece of territory and sovereignty should extend only to certain natural frontiers corresponding with historical or ethnic divisions—had not yet developed, so the geographical bases of each unit were almost as ill-defined as the political bases for government and administration.[44]

The exceptional political unit of the era was Venice. Unlike its sister republics, it was not a new state, ruled by some faction or oligarchy of debatable lineage. Venice had been growing as a political and administrative unit for several centuries and had successfully expanded its commercial and military influence to the Adriatic area and the Middle East. The objectives its governors pursued were in many cases popularly supported; they were directly related to the welfare of the state's citizens rather than to dynastic or family interests. Consequently,

[41] If we were to consider cultural and religious forms of interaction as defining the boundaries, the Italian political units would become merely one subsystem of the general European system.

[42] Ritter, *Die Neugestaltung Europas*, pp. 24–26; Mattingly, *Renaissance Diplomacy*, pp. 94–95.

[43] Mattingly, *Renaissance Diplomacy*, pp. 78–79.

[44] Cf. Federico Chabod, "Was There a Renaissance State?" in *The Development of the Modern State*, ed. and trans. Heinz Lubasz (New York: Macmillan, 1964), p. 30.

Venice was one of the few states in this system that could count upon considerable support from its population in matters of war and peace.

The Structure of the System

The distribution of power—diffuse—and the patterns of domination-subordination within the Italian Renaissance system were similar to those in China during the early portion of the Spring and Autumn period, except that the number of units was considerably smaller in Italy. Why, then, didn't the Italian states form permanent coalitions around the central, powerful states, as had been the result of the diffuse power structure in both China and Greece?

The Italian states did conquer and annex smaller neighbors until the peninsula contained only six "major powers" and a few lesser entities. Once the number of units in China and Greece had been reduced, relations solidified around major antagonistic blocs or leagues of states. Each system had a polarized structure in its later years, except that in Greece, a number of city-states remained neutral in the major bloc conflicts. But in Italy, there was no polarization of power around two antagonistic centers. As the units quarreled and fought over territorial and dynastic interests, they concluded a number of alliances; but they shifted their allegiances almost annually, so that there was little time for connections between the states to assume more permanent characteristics.

The structure of the Italian system took on unique characteristics after the Peace of Lodi in 1454, when the three main antagonists in northern Italy—Venice, Milan, and Florence—created the Most Holy League, a collective security organization designed to make the status quo of relatively diffused power and equality among the major political units a permanent condition of the system. The Italians, unlike the Chinese and Greeks, apparently realized that continued strife and warfare among units of roughly equal capabilities and strength would ultimately endanger the independence of each; with this realization, they were able to reconcile their main antagonisms adequately to bring some stability to the system in the last forty years of its independent existence. Starting with a diffuse structure of power and influence roughly analogous to the Chinese and Greek systems in their early stages, only the Italians were able successfully to balance the many units and prevent any one from dominating the others. The Italian states thus avoided a polar structure of power, which might have led to a disastrous confrontation.

The major criterion for distinguishing the strength and prestige of the Italian states was money; for, without it, no government could field a professional army, establish a permanent diplomatic corps, or put on the feasts and celebrations used to impress both the local citizenry and visiting dignitaries. Lineage and historical or religious legitimacy were also noteworthy sources of a government's prestige, but since so few governments could claim these sanctions for their rule, other criteria must have been more important.

During the first half of the fifteenth century, there were no permanent subsystems on the Italian peninsula. Alliance patterns shifted frequently, and historical animosities between certain states did not always prevent the conclusion of alliances of convenience when it served the interests of both antagonists. In the period 1454 to 1494, however, the Most Holy League constituted a subsystem of considerable importance. Since the three original signatories—Milan, Venice, and Florence—invited all other states on the peninsula to adhere to it, the League was originally intended to be not merely a small alliance or bloc within a larger system, but a permanent organization or confederation of all the states of the system. It never achieved this aspiration, but in providing a legal basis for a particular distribution of power, it was a major source of the relative stability that ensued for forty years after it was drafted.

Major Forms of Interaction

Even though communications facilities within the peninsula were primitive, the small area encompassing the group of states allowed for considerable contact among them. Trade had existed for centuries and continued to be a major form of communication between the units, as well as with other areas of Europe. As in Greece, commerce led both to cooperative and conflictful types of relationships; some relationships increased the welfare of all parties on the basis of mutual advantage, but others led to acrimonious trade wars, sometimes ending in violence.

Renaissance Italy is most noted in the history of international politics for developing permanent diplomatic institutions for conducting foreign relations. Permanent embassies staffed by career diplomats were organized partly to enhance prestige, but also to enable governments to collect information about their allies or potential enemies on a systematic basis. Without envoys with direct access to the courts and councils of other states, how could governments, each in close proximity with the others, insecure, and vitally affected by their neighbor's diplomatic moves, obtain information about the latest intrigue, amount of money in a foreign treasury, size and morale of the army, or organization of plots and counterplots? Diplomatic reporting became one of the primary requisites for the formulation of successful external policies in fifteenth-century Italy. Aside from ceremonial and bargaining duties, the ambassador abroad served as his government's main source of information about new alliances, plans of aggression, secret agreements, and domestic strife.

After commerce and diplomatic communication, warfare was a common form of interaction. The Italian states employed violence recurrently to achieve objectives or settle conflicts. The objectives of war, aside from upholding a ruler's "honor" and prosecuting legal claims, were closely related to aspirations for increasing a state's capabilities by obtaining booty, new tax resources from an annexed province or city, or ransoms and indemnities. These were all legitimate objects of military campaigns. Kings, princes, ruling families, or elected councils often thought of foreign politics in terms of profits and losses, and since any increased source of revenue was an addition to a state's capabilities, war was well worth the small risks and costs of a military campaign.[45] Unlike the Greek wars, which were frequently fought by armed citizens and slaves and sometimes lasted for decades, the wars of the Italian peninsula during the first half of the fifteenth century were managed by professional officers *(condottieri)* and fought by mercenary troops. The forms of combat were mild by today's standards, as victory in the field normally resulted from a series of brilliant maneuvers rather than annihilation of the enemy's forces. After all, soldiers cost money and represented an investment not to be wasted. Machiavelli could report some battles in the fifteenth century in which casualties were limited to several horses and men.[46]

Another common technique for obtaining political and economic objectives was subversion of the political processes of a neighboring city or state. The prevalence of clandestine political operations can be accounted for by two characteristics of the Italian system. First, since the units were geographically and linguistically so close to each other, it was relatively easy for subversive agents to operate abroad as sources of information or links with plotting factions. Second, because the bases of political power and legitimacy in many of the units were so weak, the resulting domestic turmoil (with the exception of Venice and the papal states) presented opportunities for outside powers to intervene in an attempt to place their own men in power. Political instability and insecurity of regimes, a characteristic equally prevalent in many nations today, thus had numerous consequences for international affairs. As today, the Italians in each small political unit could not isolate internal problems from the external environment. It was this feature of the system that gave rise to so much diplomatic intrigue, conspiracy, and betrayal and set the standards of amorality often associated with the "Italian" diplomatic style, or "Machiavellianism."[47]

The Major Rules of the System

Since the works of Machiavelli are often cited as proof of the amorality or "power politics" of the fifteenth century, one would not expect the Italians to have developed explicit rules and principles that effectively restrained their behavior toward each other. Historians do not, in fact, assign credit to the republics and city-states for developing ethical or legal restraints to their actions. The medieval concept of "just war," which had established criteria under which force could be used legitimately, had no application in Renaissance Italy; no authority in the fifteenth century, either ecclesiastical or temporal, sought to judge the righteousness of a state's behavior. War was an accepted means of achieving objectives or resolving conflicts, and few questioned the right of governing authorities to engage in it. Since the turmoil of many republics' domestic affairs

---

[45] Mattingly, *Renaissance Diplomacy*, p. 134.
[46] Hans Morgenthau, *Politics among Nations* (New York: Knopf, 1950), p. 288.
[47] Bozeman, *Politics and Culture in International History*, p. 479.

created opportunities for subversion, there was no strict rule against intervention in other states' internal affairs. Assassination, bribery, and betrayal were common occurrences in diplomatic relations. Nor do we find evidence of the strong value placed on political independence that was so evident in Greece. Instead, the larger states annexed the smaller with impunity and were prevented from expanding indefinitely primarily by the countervailing power of other states or alliances. The concepts of sovereignty, equality, and territorial integrity had not yet developed as the bases upon which to conduct interstate relations.

In diplomatic bargaining situations, standards of honesty and good faith were rather low, although it did occur to some governments that a reputation for credibility might enhance their influence and prestige. Generally, however, the governments of the Italian units failed to recognize that diplomatic effectiveness might be related to moral and ethical principles. Gerhard Ritter, for example, has pointed out that all European ruling authorities in the fifteenth and sixteenth centuries regularly deceived each other in unscrupulous ways.[48] They had not yet developed a capacity to relate diplomatic means to ends and frequently undertook aggressive schemes and foreign conquests, which they could bring off successfully only by relying on intrigue, bluff, delaying tactics, and lucky breaks. Governments spent vast sums of money to bribe influential statesmen in foreign courts, arrange lavish "summit" meetings between princes, and despatch renowned orators and ambassadors to persuade other governments to act in the sending state's interests. These tactics seldom succeeded, because few governments, knowing their own standards of conduct, had any faith in the dependability of their rivals and pseudoallies.

There were, then, no fundamental rules of the system to help establish limits for action; yet, whether resulting from political conditions, lower-level technology, or financial considerations, a number of unwritten understandings or rulings were observed in the conduct of warfare. These helped keep organized violence between the units within tolerable bounds for the system. Unlike the Peloponnesian Wars, which drained the strength and vitality of so many city-states and made them vulnerable to outside invasion, the Italians were able to regulate their violence so that it would not cause total political collapse on the peninsula. Moreover, through the medium of the Most Holy League, the cities and republics made a most important decision implying that all states in the system should accept the distribution of power essentially as it had been arranged at the Peace of Lodi in 1454.

The Most Holy League never functioned as an effective instrument for the pacific settlement of conflicts. It had no institutional basis; and, during the last forty years of the fifteenth century, the Italian states did not radically alter their diplomatic style. Nevertheless, the diplomats and governments of these states apparently perceived that a treaty that sanctified the territorial status quo and provided a mechanism for enforcing that agreement was in their own interest.

[48] Ritter, *Die Neugestaltung Europas,* pp. 21–22.

Thus, they constructed through the Treaty of Venice (which established the Most Holy League) the ground rules for conducting interstate relations during the remainder of the century. In that document, the signatories promised to defend each other's territories against attack from any source, and each state undertook to provide military forces for joint action. In case of threat or outbreak of war, all members were to consult immediately and continue multilateral discussions until the danger subsided. Any member of the League that broke its obligations of nonrecourse to violence was to be expelled and, if necessary, disciplined by collective action.

In practice, the Most Holy League never fulfilled the expectations of its originators. Instead of existing in peace and stability, the Italian states continued to quarrel; and, in 1474, when the Pope and the King of Naples were implicated in a plot against the Medici rulers of Florence, they averted general war only by a narrow margin. The difference between the two halves of the century was more a diminution in the scope of violence than a growth of stability.[49] Whether the forty-year period of tension without large-scale violence was a result of the treaty or of a rough balancing of capabilities among the main units is difficult to judge. But, at least, after the Treaty of Venice, there were no wars that transposed the system into the hegemony of one state or into two antagonistic blocs, or that led to its collapse.

Nevertheless, the Italian system was engulfed by the general European political order in the last decade of the fifteenth century. Throughout the century, Italian tyrants, princes, and ruling families had called upon Europeans north of the Alps to intervene on their behalf in factional and interstate quarrels, and European rulers were eager to involve themselves in Italian affairs in search of crowns, lordships, and subsidies.[50]

These intrusions into peninsular affairs were not permanent and did not result in a major modification of the Italian system through coupling of European and Italian issues. Yet the habit of seeking extra-Italian involvement in alliances or domestic political quarrels eventually led to a more permanent European presence on the peninsula. In this way, the Italian city-states and republics became in effect just a group of smaller units in the wider European system of the sixteenth century. The French invasion of the peninsula in 1494, in response to a plea from Milan to counterbalance the House of Anjou's influence in Genoa and deter an attack of Milan's ally, Naples, was of such large scope that it amounted to a vast European intervention in Italian affairs. From that point, political isolation of the Italian peninsula was no longer possible, and, for the succeeding four centuries, the Italian states became merely the objects of French, Spanish, and Austrian rivalry, plunder, and expansion.

As in the Chinese system during parts of the Spring and Autumn and Warring States periods, the diffuse power structure on the Italian peninsula

---

[49] Mattingly, *Renaissance Diplomacy*, pp. 94–96.
[50] *Ibid.*, p. 61.

during the fifteenth century had an important effect on general foreign-policy orientations and the style of conducting relations between the units. The Italian city-states and republics were free agents, uninhibited by superior temporal powers or bloc leaders. They sought their objectives by forming and breaking alliances, seeking isolation, noninvolvement, or neutrality, or by intriguing in other states' internal affairs. Unlike the alliance partners of Athens and Sparta during the fifth century B.C. or the units in feudal China, whose actions were largely determined by a superior power, the Italian political units survived in a hostile environment by perfecting the art of diplomatic maneuvering. Latitude for choice among policy alternatives was wide, but security and certainty of success were scarce. If we examine international politics in Europe since the eighteenth century, we can observe how international structures, stratification systems, and interaction processes, as well as technological developments, can influence the behavior of each of the component units of an international system.

SELECTED BIBLIOGRAPHY

ADCOCK, FRANK, and J.D. MOSELEY, *Diplomacy in Ancient Greece.* London: Thames and Hudson, 1975.

BAYLEY, C.C., *War and Society in Renaissance Florence.* Toronto: University of Toronto Press, 1961.

BOZEMAN, ADDA B., *Politics and Culture in International History.* Princeton, N.J.: Princeton University Press, 1960.

EISENSTADT, S.N., *The Political Systems of Empires.* New York: Free Press, 1963.

FLIESS, PETER J., *Thucydides and the Politics of Bipolarity.* Baton Rouge: Louisiana State University Press, 1966.

GHOSHAL, U.N., "The System of Inter-State Relations and Foreign Policy in the Early Arthasastra State," in *India Antigua.* Leiden: E.J. Brill Ltd., Publishers, 1947.

GOODMAN, JAY S., "The Concept of System in International Relations Theory," *Background,* 8 (1965), 257–68.

GRAHAM, A.J., *Colony and Mother City in Ancient Greece.* Manchester, Eng.: Manchester University Press, 1964.

HANRIEDER, WOLFRAM, "Actor Objectives and International Systems," *Journal of Politics,* 27 (1965), 109–32.

HASEBROOK, JOHANNES, *Trade and Politics in Ancient Greece.* London: G. Bell, 1933.

KORFF, BARON S.A., "An Introduction to the History of International Law," *American Journal of International Law,* 18 (1924), 246–59.

LARUS, JOEL, ed., *Comparative World Politics: Readings in Western and Pre-Modern Non-Western International Relations.* Belmont, Calif.: Wadsworth, 1964.

LUBASZ, HEINZ, ed., *The Development of the Modern State.* New York: Macmillan, 1964.

MATTINGLY, GARRETT, *Renaissance Diplomacy.* London: Jonathan Cape, 1955.

MODELSKI, GEORGE, "Agraria and Industria: Two Models of the International System," *World Politics,* 14 (1961), 118–43.

———, "Comparative International Systems," *World Politics,* 14 (1962), 662–74.

———, "Kautilya: Foreign Policy and International System in the Ancient Hindu World," *American Political Science Review,* 58 (1964), 549–60.

NUSSBAUM, ARTHUR, *A Concise History of the Law of Nations.* New York: Macmillan, 1961.

PARKINSON, F., *The Philosophy of International Relations: A Study in the History of Thought.* Beverly Hills, Calif.: Sage Publications, 1977.

PHILLIPSON, COLEMAN, *The International Law and Custom of Ancient Greece and Rome.* London: Macmillan, 1911.

RUSSELL, FRANK M., *Theories of International Relations.* New York: Appleton-Century-Crofts, 1936.

WALKER, RICHARD L., *The Multi-State System of Ancient China.* Hamden, Conn.: Shoe String Press, 1953.

3

The European and Contemporary State Systems

What had occurred in Renaissance Italy continued throughout Europe between the fifteenth and nineteenth centuries, that is, the continent filled up with organized political power and administration. From feudal relations between the Holy Roman Empire, free cities, ecclesiastical authorities, duchies, aspiring monarchs, and small republics, there emerged an order of centralized political units led by dynastic families. These central monarchs eventually broke the power of lesser political authorities on their territories through bribery, coercion, or violence, and instituted nationwide administrative and judicial organizations.

This process did not occur simultaneously throughout the continent. As early as the latter part of the sixteenth century, Great Britain was a political unit with a defined territory in which a central monarchy ruled effectively over all subjects. Complex administrative mechanisms that extended to all areas and levels of society replaced the localized judicial and administrative organizations of the feudal period. Although nobles often resisted the monarchy, they did not have independent territorial bases or armies with which to challenge royal authority effectively.

Through marriages, alliances, and domestic and external armed conflict, the monarchs of France, Spain, Russia, and Austria were eventually able to create central dynastic orders as well; but the small states and principalities of Germany and Italy did not unite until the late nineteenth century. The nationalist impulses that helped them to unite were different from those conditions that had made possible the creation of central dynastic regimes in other parts of

Europe. Up to the nineteenth century, most of the important states in international politics were empires and dynastic orders whose boundaries were defined through innumerable royal marriages, alliances, ancient land titles, and wars. Nationalism was not a factor in dynastic politics. The European states that arose in the nineteenth and twentieth centuries, however, *resulted* from nationalism. They were organized around the remaining ethnic, religious, and language distinctions in Europe, not on dynastic interests. Prior to the nineteenth century, the state created the nation, whereas, in the last two centuries, nationalism has *preceded* and, in many cases, created the state.

THE INTERNATIONAL POLITICS OF EIGHTEENTH-CENTURY EUROPE

A significant feature of eighteenth-century European international politics was the relatively even distribution of diplomatic influence and military capabilities among the major states, a characteristic found also in China, Greece, and Renaissance Italy in certain periods of their history. England, France, Sweden, Spain, the Austrian Empire, Russia, Prussia, and Turkey (to the extent that the last was involved in European politics) were not significantly different in their domestic political institutions, armed might, or international prestige. This relatively equal distribution of power and influence made it possible for the dynastic states to shift alliance partners without radically upsetting the structure of the whole system. Alliances were based on the juxtaposition of constantly changing dynastic, economic, and colonial interests, not on ideological principles. Flexibility within the groupings of states was the result.

      The dynasts of the eighteenth century, as well as the aristocratic classes within each state, were united by strong cosmopolitan bonds and a common political culture. They commonly spoke French and identified themselves as the joint rulers of "Christendom" as well as the rulers of particular pieces of territory.[1] Royal families and many aristocrats were joined across state boundaries by marriage, while professional soldiers and diplomats, regardless of nationality, worked for the services that gave them the highest rank, salary, or prestige. There was no stigma attached to the German who commanded Russian forces or to the Italian who became one of the French court's most favored and trusted advisers. The Spanish diplomatic and military services in the eighteenth century were graced by such names as Konigsegg, Wall, O'Reilly, Fitzgerald, and Alberoni, while John Elphinstone, Sir Samuel Greig, and Peter Lacey made fine careers in the service of the Russian Tsarina. The continent was also unified through common support for the principles of royal legitimacy and dynastic

---

[1] The Holy Roman Empire, although of little practical consequence, still symbolized the cultural unity of the continent.

succession. Although radical political theories had already developed in England and France in the late seventeenth and eighteenth centuries, most literate upper-class subjects adhered faithfully to the royal mystique.

The stability of political life and the consensus in support of royal legitimacy helped preclude intervention and subversion as means of achieving political objectives. There were court intrigues of various types; but, if one dynast attempted to unseat another through military intervention or court subversion, he was undermining the principles of royal succession and the divine right of kings, principles upon which his own authority often rested.

Wars, too, displayed conservative characteristics. They were fought by professional and mercenary armies, usually for the purpose of outmaneuvering the enemy rather than annihilating him. Destruction of lives and property was often limited (although losses attributed to disease were high) because of the low level of military technology, high cost of maintaining a professional army, and high rate of desertion, as well as the limited objectives for which force was used—to obtain strategic territory, generate prestige for a dynast, or secure colonies. War was to be used, according to philosophers of violence such as Clausewitz, to impose the will of one sovereign upon another by defeating the latter's capacity to resist.[2] This purpose did not require annihilation, occupation, or the forcible imposition of alien social institutions onto other populations.

International politics of the eighteenth century have thus been characterized under various terms, each designed to illustrate the essence of the system. To some, it has been known as the period when the "balance of power" operated. Kings and their advisers could conduct foreign affairs as if they were playing a game of chess or strategy, easily calculating the power of their adversaries and adjusting their foreign-policy orientation through alliances or neutrality to achieve or defend their interests. If conflicts on the continent threatened to become too violent, the dynasts could play out their quarrels in the New World, where vast lands and commercial opportunities could be traded back and forth in wars and peace treaties. Others have called this era the "golden age of diplomacy," emphasizing the consensus of political values that prevailed in Europe; the cosmopolitanism of the upper classes; the regard for principles of royal authority and Christianity; and the propensity to resolve conflicts through skillful diplomatic bargaining, territorial exchanges, or alliance making, rather than through large-scale violence, propaganda, or subversion.[3]

But lying behind those conditions that helped to create stability and moderation in the politics of the eighteenth-century European state system were some characteristics that led to conflict. The religious wars of the preceding century were not easily forgotten, and their memory sustained international

---

[2] Karl von Clausewitz, *War, Politics, and Power,* ed. and trans. Edward M. Collins (Chicago: Henry Regnery, 1962), p. 63.

[3] For a characterization of eighteenth-century diplomatic relations that emphasizes the elements of stability in the system, see Richard Rosecrance, *Action and Reaction in World Politics* (Boston: Little, Brown, 1963), pp. 17–30.

hostilities and suspicions. Strongly held national sentiments did not exist at the grassroots level, but many peasants and townspeople were not entirely indifferent toward the policies of their rulers—particularly not toward those whom they regarded as alien in nationality or religion; insurrection against "foreign" rule was an occasional consequence of a system in which land and peoples were traded back and forth to satisfy the strategic requirements or to enhance the prestige of dynasts. Monarchs' sensitivity to the rules of etiquette as well as their status among foreign courts did not prevent them from occasionally employing deceit and fraud as diplomatic tactics. Wars, although less destructive by today's standards, were limited more by the crude military technology of the day than by any great concern over humanitarian principles. In other words, the elements of stability—cosmopolitanism, the principles of dynastic legitimacy, limited wars, shifting alliances, and a roughly equal distribution of power— did not prevent the occurrence of sharply contentious issues and frequent recourse to the use of force.[4] But various diplomatic procedures and mechanisms, operating within a common political culture, were adequate for the kinds of conflicts that arose. No one state conquered Europe; Europe did not collapse into chaos, inviting invasion from eastern adversaries; no technological developments fundamentally changed the main characteristics of political and economic life; and there were no important ideological incompatibilities that made divisions between states deep and rigid. If the eighteenth-century system was not entirely peaceful and stable, neither was it inflexible or unable to cope with the main issues of the day.

THE STATE SYSTEM OF THE NINETEENTH CENTURY

The periods from 1789 to 1939 and from 1945 to the present can be considered as containing distinct international systems. Although both have retained some of the features of the eighteenth century, several developments in the nineteenth and twentieth centuries have caused fundamental changes in the structure and processes of international politics.

Rise of Nationalism

The first was the rise of nationalism—development of strong emotional attachments to the central state (adding to the traditional loyalties to provinces or towns) and involvement of the average citizen or subject in his government's political life. This has had several important consequences. During the eighteenth century, statesmen and dynasts had been able to trade European and colonial territories with considerable ease, using ancient titles to lands and strategic

---

[4] See George Liska, "Continuity and Change in International Systems," *World Politics,* 16 (1963), 118–36.

and economic considerations as the predominant criteria for determining frontiers. In the succeeding century, nationalist leaders held that the only legitimate basis for political organization was a distinct ethnic or linguistic group; the state should be based, therefore, on nationality. The results of this doctrine were the rise of nationalist movements in the areas of Europe where the state did not correspond to ethnic distinctions, and the subsequent collapse of such multinational states as Russia, Austria–Hungary, and Sweden–Norway under the pressure of war and nationalist insurrection. A new type of European political phenomenon—movements for national independence—arose during the nineteenth century to supplement the more traditional concerns over which statesmen quarreled.

A second consequence of nationalism was that mass public involvement could be used by governments as a military and diplomatic bargaining capability. By invoking the theme of "sacred national honor," governments in the nineteenth century could mobilize their populations to support their diplomacy or wars, whereas, previously, dynasts had found it difficult to generate popular enthusiasm for objectives not rooted deeply in social and economic aspirations. Armies in the eighteenth century—taking personal oaths of loyalty to the king, queen, or prince—had numbered between 10,000 and 70,000; but, during the wars of the French Revolution, they were counted by the hundreds of thousands; and, during World War I, by the millions. The symbolic break from the eighteenth-century tradition of dynastic diplomacy came in 1791 when the French revolutionary regime instituted the *levée en masse,* a system of nationwide conscription designed to build a citizens' army to replace the older professional armed forces of the Bourbons. This army was sent abroad to "liberate" Europe from dynasticism and to conquer Belgian, German, and Italian territory for the greater glory of the French *nation,* not for the prestige of the French king.

Modern governments can create national fervor for their causes, but the greater involvement of the average citizen or subject also imposes restrictions on the policy makers' freedom of action. Foreign relations in the eighteenth century were never as simple as a game of checkers, even though dynasts and their advisers were relatively free to shift policies, objectives, and alliance partners without worrying about domestic reactions.[5] By the late nineteenth century, however, even the more autocratic regimes had to anticipate public reactions to their diplomatic maneuvers, while others had to accommodate pestering opposition parties in parliaments or worry about embarrassing newspaper editorials.

Technological Warfare

The second development of the nineteenth century with important consequences for international politics was the application of scientific and industrial technology to the conduct of warfare. Public enthusiasm over diplomatic and military

---

[5] In England, however, Parliament in the eighteenth century did impose important controls over the king's prerogatives in the conduct of foreign relations.

questions enabled governments to conscript large armies, and improvements in military technology enabled them to prosecute their military plans more quickly and violently. Starting with the wars of the French Revolution, armed conflicts tended to become increasingly wars of annihilation, in which violence could not be confined to military targets. Rising casualty figures, military and civilian, indicate the revolutionary developments in the art of warfare. In France, for instance, casualty rates in wars between 1630 and the outbreak of the revolution in 1789 fluctuated between one out of every 1,000 population and one out of every 200. During the wars of the French Revolution and the Napoleonic period, approximately one of every seventy-five French citizens was a victim of fighting.[6] In World War I, about one of every eighteen Frenchmen was either killed or wounded as a result of the conflict; and, in World War II, one out of every ten Russians suffered injury or loss of life. If international systems can be distinguished from each other, in part, by major changes in the processes of interaction and methods of resolving conflicts, then the nineteenth and twentieth centuries are markedly different from the eighteenth century in this one aspect alone: Major wars have become great social undertakings involving extensive civilian mobilization and destruction, fought for the purpose of annihilating the enemy and imposing political and social institutions upon the defeated nation.

The development of nuclear weapons has been the most revolutionary contribution of science and technology to war. In the past, some strategists argued that the invention of the machine gun, tank, or airplane made war "obsolete"; but the perfection of fission and fusion weapons has, indeed, made total war irrational, even if nuclear weapons could be used in a limited fashion for specific ends. No bank of heavy artillery or wing of airplanes can crush a nation's economy. Even the massive Allied incendiary strategic raids on Germany during World War II could not destroy Germany's capacity to produce war *matériel*. Strategic nuclear weapons, on the other hand, can quickly destroy the economic capacity of a nation (if it is reasonably concentrated in large urban centers) and most of its population, as well as endanger the lives and health of citizens in countries not directly involved in the nuclear salvo. Although there are means to reduce nuclear destruction, the only safety mechanism strategists have yet devised is the deterrent—the threat to retaliate instantly in case of a first strike. As Robert Oppenheimer has pointed out, the nuclear giants are analogous to two scorpions in a bottle; if one attacks the other, it can do so only at the price of its own destruction.[7] Nuclear weapons have thus added a new characteristic of vulnerability to international politics. Whatever protection could be afforded in the past by national frontiers or territorial fortresses, such contrivances

---

[6] Similar figures are cited in Hans Morgenthau, *Politics among Nations* (New York: Knopf, 1950), p. 293.

[7] "Atomic Weapons and American Policy," *Foreign Affairs*, 51 (1953), 529. Even optimistic military planners in NATO argue that a nuclear war in Europe would be over in 30 days at the most.

are of no significance today if war fought with nuclear weapons should break out in Europe or directly between the Soviet Union and the United States. As a unit of protection, the modern nation-state is as vulnerable to nuclear destruction as was the walled city or moated castle to the modern cannon.[8]

Ideological Conflicts

The third development in the nineteenth century with major consequences on the structure and processes of the European state system was the rise of ideological principles and political doctrines as a major motive or guide to foreign-policy behavior. Even though the wars of the French Revolution had territorial objectives, they were undertaken in the name of the universal principles of "Liberty, Equality, and Fraternity." Similarly, those who led the grand coalition against the French revolutionary and Napoleonic armies were partly motivated by a desire to safeguard the principles of royal legitimacy against radical French doctrines. Thus, many of the conflicts within Europe during the nineteenth century were fought in a context of the incompatible values represented by French revolutionary republicanism and royal legitimacy and conservatism. In this century, different and incompatible images of a world order have derived from the doctrines of Nazism, communism, and liberal democracy.

The international politics of the nineteenth century were thus uniquely affected by the growth of ideological issues, the increasing destructiveness of warfare, and the rise of nationalism and popular involvement in foreign relations. A development with equally great consequence on the structure and processes of international politics occurred in the latter part of the century, and all its implications are becoming clear only today. This was the extension of the European state system into the rest of the world and the subsequent rise of more than ninety new political units, mostly former colonial territories, as actors in the modern international system. The European continent was the primary arena for international politics during the nineteenth century; and, aside from the weak Latin American republics and several feudal leftovers, there were only about twenty important states that interacted regularly. Today there are more than 150 independent states, all conducting transactions through unprecedented levels of trade, diplomatic communication, travel, and occasional subversion and warfare. Contentious issues no longer arise predominantly in Europe, but appear most frequently in Asia, the Middle East, Africa, and Latin America. They no longer involve the major powers of the nineteenth century—Great Britain, France, Prussia, Germany, Austria-Hungary, and Turkey—but attract instead the involvement of extra-European powers, primarily the United States, the Soviet Union, and China. In short, the geographical boundaries of the nineteenth-century and contemporary systems have been extended from the Euro-

---

[8] This is the thesis argued by John Herz in his *International Politics in the Atomic Age* (New York: Columbia University Press, 1959), Intro. and Chap. 8. For further discussion of the effects of nuclear weapons on contemporary international politics, see Chapters 4 and 11, this volume.

pean continent to the whole world, and the number of political units in these systems has trebled in the last fifty years. Today we have a truly global state system.

THE CONTEMPORARY GLOBAL SYSTEM

The contemporary state system is in some ways similar to its nineteenth-century predecessor. Most main issues and characteristic forms of interaction are not significantly different from those in the European state system. Contemporary ideological issues trace their origins to nineteenth-century Europe; the question of nationhood and national independence still raises serious international problems; and the search for economic modernization that took place on the continent during the nineteenth century is only beginning in the developing countries. Diplomatic forms and procedures developed in Europe have extended to all areas of the world, even though they are almost unrecognizable when compared to eighteenth-century practices. The main rules governing international transactions are also an extension, development, and refinement of those that arose during the eighteenth and nineteenth centuries in Europe.

It is not difficult to understand why these characteristics of European international politics are still predominant in a global system. In 1875, less than one-tenth of Africa had been colonized by Europeans; twenty-five years later, only one-tenth of the area remained free of colonial administration. In the last three decades of the nineteenth century, Great Britain acquired over 4 million square miles of territory, France acquired 3½ million square miles, Belgium colonized almost 1 million square miles, and the Tsarist regime in Russia extended its control over territory amounting to a half-million square miles. The processes of establishing colonial administration and control differed in various areas; but, in each case, the administering powers unwittingly created aspirations among indigenous populations for many of the values they themselves cherished: independence in political life, industrialization of the economy, and international prestige. Despite the great variety of cultural contexts in which relations between states occur today, some important characteristics of the system represent an extension into new areas of the diplomatic, economic, ideological, and military traditions of the Europeans.

What sets off the contemporary international system from its European predecessor is (1) the rise in the number and types of states; (2) the great potential for destruction by those who possess nuclear weapons and modern delivery systems; (3) increased vulnerability of states to external intrusions, including subversion, economic pressures, and military conquest; (4) the rising importance of nonstate actors, such as national liberation movements, multinational corporations, international interest groups, and political parties transcending national frontiers; (5) the predominant position of influence that has been achieved by three essentially non-European states—the Soviet Union, China, and the United States; and (6) the great degree of dependence and interdependence between all types of actors. These differences will be discussed under the four categories of the preceding chapter—the nature of the political units, the types of stratification and structures of power and influence, the major forms of interactions, and the rules governing relations between actors.

The Nature of the Units

A major characteristic of the political units comprising the contemporary international system is their territorial basis. States today maintain systematic administrative control over people living in a well-defined territory. Some territorial divisions are artificial—particularly in Africa—in the sense that frontiers do not correspond to ethnic, language, or geographic distinctions; but in most cases the territorial boundaries of modern states are closely related to such distinctions. England can have no claim to continental French territory as long as language and culture serve as a basis for differentiating legitimate frontiers; but, when ethnic and linguistic differences did not matter in international politics, it was perfectly conceivable for the English to own territory in France, as they did until the seventeenth century. Although the units in many historical international systems derived their identity, strengths, and weaknesses from the territory they occupied, and although some even developed a concept of a frontier or boundary setting them off from other political units, not until modern times have the boundaries of states been so carefully defined and given such legal and ideological sanctity.

Despite the great value placed on independence, sovereignty, and territoriality, political, economic, and technological changes of recent decades have made the nation-state highly vulnerable to outside intrusions and, in some cases, to overwhelming external controls. Governments claiming sovereignty often rely on outside funds and arms to protect themselves from external and internal enemies. The Soviet Union, China, the United States, and other countries frequently siphon funds—and sometimes arms—to political parties, opposition groups, or military establishments in other countries; lobbyists representing other governments or multinational corporations abound in the capitals of most states; the Chilean junta hires a New York public relations firm to improve its "image" among the American people; most governments in the 1980s can do little to control high rates of inflation, because the forces producing price increases are mostly external. Thus, whatever our emotional commitment to the notion of independence, the interdependent and "penetrated state"[9] is the normal type of actor, not the exception. The domestic and foreign policies of countries are thoroughly intermixed as they were not in previous eras, and the possibilities of governments' undertaking major domestic policies without

---

[9] For some theoretical discussion of the penetrated state, see James N. Rosenau, ed., *Linkage Politics* (New York: Free Press, 1969).

considering the limitations imposed by external conditions are slight. Unemployment levels in Western Europe, for example, have as much to do with the price of Middle East oil or the interest-rate policies of the United States as with conditions on the continent.

The international systems of Greece or the Italian city-states were notable for their relative equality. There were great powers and lesser states, of course; but size, population, and military capability differentials were not extreme. In contrast, consider some of the differences today. If one compares actors according to size, they vary from the Soviet Union, which covers one-sixth of the world's land surface, to Singapore and Tonga, which cover only several hundred square miles, or the size of a metropolitan area. Population variations are equally extreme. Fewer than 100,000 people inhabit the Maldive Islands, a member of the United Nations. Many states in the global system have populations well under 1 million; but China has a population of over 900 million. The physical and population differences between the Soviet Union and Tonga are much greater than the differences between Athens and one of the smaller city-states in Greece, or between Prussia and Schleswig-Holstein in the eighteenth century.

Other differences may also be important for foreign-policy behavior and the structure of the international system. There are a number of states that are economically and technologically underdeveloped, whose populations suffer from high illiteracy, malnutrition, low productivity, land shortage, and very unequal distribution of wealth. Many of these states also have minority problems and have little hope for prolonged economic development because they lack natural and human resources. Even though they normally maintain administrative mechanisms providing a variety of government functions for citizens, their influence often barely reaches the grassroots level, where life is conducted according to tribal, village, or other traditional patterns. Political instability is rife; few of these states have resolved their major constitutional issues or developed political "rules of the game" that command widespread support. Political stability depends more on the influence or coercion of key personalities or groups—often the armed forces—than on widely accepted constitutional or legal principles. When these personalities change, or ruling groups become politically weak, corrupt, or demoralized, rebellion and civil war are often the result.

The important point about these characteristics, as far as the nature of the international system is concerned, is that they help create international dependencies. The lack of resources makes many developing states weak in all dimensions; to survive, they need outside sources of economic aid, frequent doses of humanitarian assistance to help cope with natural disasters such as droughts, military aid to build and maintain even rudimentary armed forces (which are often used more for maintaining the regime against its internal critics than against external attack), and markets for their exports.

A second important point, given the vast inequalities in the world, is that many weak microstates, such as Tonga, Lesotho, the Bahamas, Mauritius, and São Tomé—to name a few—have no foreign policies as we understand that term. They have little access to the decision-making points concerning global problems, and, for the most part, their actions have little impact on the global system as a whole. A few become involved in regional problems, but, in general, these actors are really *subjects* of international politics; they are highly vulnerable to events in their external environment, and, yet, their policies have little impact on that environment. They are acted *upon*, but, given their weak diplomatic, military, and economic capabilities, they act upon few others. Their major hope of influencing international problems is to join diplomatic or military coalitions (see Chapter 4).

Compared to these microstates, there are a number of nonstate actors that have a great deal more influence in the structure and processes of the international system. Although there are great varieties of nonstate actors functioning today, we will consider only those that have the most important impact on international politics. These would include (1) territorial nonstate actors, such as liberation movements, (2) nonterritorial transnational organizations, such as multinational corporations, and (3) intergovernmental organizations, such as NATO or the Food and Agricultural Organization.

Territorial nonstate actors include all political movements, parties, or cliques that, while focusing their activities within a state, establish linkages with other governments, political movements, or international organizations. The most common today are the various national liberation movements. They do not possess the attributes of sovereignty, yet their actions often have important consequences on the international system. The Palestine Liberation Organization, for example, maintains "diplomatic" relations with a large number of governments and militant groups abroad. It has its own "foreign policy," disseminates propaganda, maintains links with sympathizers throughout the world, and purchases arms from both governments and private concerns abroad. In the late 1960s, its actions virtually nullified the efforts of the Soviet Union, the United States, Egypt, Jordan, and Israel to begin peace negotiations; in 1970, the PLO, whose leaders and followers were concentrated primarily in Jordan, started military action against the Jordanian government. The war between this nonstate actor and the Jordanians almost caused the military intervention of Syria, Iraq, and the United States. Moreover, its activities have spread far beyond the confines of the Middle East. In attempts to obtain funds, notoriety, or retaliation against Israelis, some of its agents have participated in airplane hijackings, massacres of athletes and civilians, kidnappings, and plots to assassinate King Hussein of Jordan. By any measure, then, its activities have had an impact on the contemporary global system, including the foreign policies of the major powers. The same cannot be said for most of the microstates.

Nonterritorial transnational organizations are characterized by (1) organized activities occurring simultaneously in a number of countries, (2) objectives that do not relate to interests within any given territory, and (3) component parts that are essentially nonpolitical. The Catholic Church is perhaps the oldest organization with these characteristics. Although it has an administrative center in Rome, its activities occur in virtually every country in the world. Like all nonterritorial transnational organizations, its livelihood depends upon unfettered access to people living in all countries. Its activities are also transnational in the sense that if one component unit gets into difficulties, it can draw upon the financial, administrative, personnel, and spiritual capabilities of other units or of the entire organization. The Church, of course, has only a very indirect and intermittent impact on international politics, but occasionally its involvement becomes more apparent. The Pope has made pronouncements on a variety of international issues, including economic development, arms control, and the nature of political regimes. To the extent that these pronouncements influence public attitudes or the views of foreign-policy makers, the impact may be direct.

A newer type of nonterritorial transnational organization is the multinational corporation (MNC). Like the Church, its operations depend upon access to a number of societies. Also like the Church, its activities are primarily nonpolitical. The Church exists to save souls and to cultivate the spiritual life of people no matter where or how they live. The multinational corporation exists to make profits for shareholders and to expand markets. The component units of the multinational corporation are independent, yet tied together by financial and personnel bonds. If one unit gets into financial difficulties, it can be rescued from the headquarters or some other unit. If one of the units is no longer profitable, it can be closed down and reestablished somewhere else.

Most authorities on the multinational firm distinguish between nationally based firms that conduct some operations abroad and true multinationals. To be classified in the latter group, a firm must have some minimum number of foreign subsidiaries operating in various countries. A minimum of six countries is often used as the cutoff point. Others have listed as MNCs only those corporations whose assets, sales, earnings, production, and employment come significantly (perhaps 25 percent) from abroad.

Multinational corporations reflect the increasing globalization of the world economy. Just as in Europe and America, where most firms began with local markets and ultimately spread their activities to regions and then the entire nation, since World War II many industrial giants have continued expanding their productive and marketing activities to other regions of the world. Until the late 1960s, most MNCs were American- or European-based, but over the last decade Japanese firms have become prominent as economic actors in many regions of the world. Most recently, we have witnessed the appearance of MNCs whose home is a developing country (LDC). The Korean-based Hyundai firm operates a variety of enterprises throughout the world; Indian companies have projects in African countries such as Zambia, Somalia, and Tanzania; a number of Brazilian-based companies have built plants throughout Latin America and in several African countries. Many of these LDC-based MNCs specialize in technologies and products particularly appropriate for developing nations. Whatever the advantages and disadvantages of MNCs, they are becoming an increasingly visible form of economic organization, one which is no longer confined to the major industrial nations of the West. More than half the total production of manufactured goods in the world may soon—by the end of the century—be accounted for by the 200 or 300 largest MNCs, two-thirds of which are American.[10]

By their size in physical and financial assets, we would assume that multinational corporations have a great impact on the contemporary global system. The assets of some of the largest MNCs, such as Unilever, IBM, General Motors, British Petroleum, and Standard Oil of New Jersey, far outstrip the economic capabilities of small nations. How can we measure the *political* impact of such immense concentrations of wealth and centers of control over economic resources? By allocating factors of production and controlling investment flows, no doubt the activities of MNCs seriously influence the character of economic development. Payment of royalties and taxes; establishment of new plants or closing down of old ones; decisions on where to locate plants; and advertising— these and many other decisions can crucially affect a developing country's economic structure, tax revenues, level of employment, and consumption patterns. It can be argued, for example, that by fostering American-style consumerism through advertising, MNCs seriously distort development patterns in poor countries. Rather than promoting rural development, public transportation, or communal enterprise, MNCs try to create markets for middle-class needs and aspirations. By helping to destroy or alter indigenous cultural and economic patterns, moreover, the MNC may, at least indirectly, foster social strains and ultimately anti-American movements. Several important guerrilla groups in Latin America, for example, claim that MNCs lead not only to direct political imperialism, but to a more subtle form of cultural pollution. Whatever the indirect impact, it is hard to identify and measure. No doubt it is greater among small, weak countries than in the industrial countries, where a majority of the activities of MNCs are already located.

The direct *political* impact of the MNC is perhaps easier to deal with. While it is more intermittent, it is also more obvious. For example, MNCs have occasionally played an important role in the domestic policies of host states. The United Fruit Company's record of activities in the "banana republics" of Central America is well known: It primarily involved attempts to keep governments in power that would allow the company to operate unfettered by regulations and excessive taxes. When a government hostile to its interests came to power in Guatemala in 1952, the company apparently assisted in helping the American government, through exiles in Honduras and Nicaragua, to overthrow the Arbenz regime. In 1970, the International Telephone and Telegraph Company promoted a scheme for toppling the Allende government in Chile. Nothing came of the matter, as U.S. government officials had already undertaken their own program to oust Allende (see Chapter 10).

[10] See George Modelski, "Multinational Business: A Global Perspective." *International Studies Quarterly,* 16 (December 1972), 24.

Despite such examples of direct involvement in host-country politics, studies show that such episodes are exceptional. William Thompson studied 274 successful and unsuccessful military coups in the period 1946–1969 and found very little evidence of direct involvement by MNCs.[11] Likewise, there is little evidence that MNCs have been a significant factor either as causes of, or participants in, international wars. There are, however, a number of cases where the interests of an MNC and a home government coincided, so that the intervention of the home government against the host country served the interests of the MNC. Such was the case of the American government's involvement in the overthrow of the Mossadegh regime in Iran in 1953, after which American oil companies obtained new operating privileges in that country; the European oil companies' strong support of the French-British-Israeli invasion of the Suez canal in 1956; the direct role of the Union Minière Company in the Belgian government's support of the Katanga secession from the Congo in the early 1960s; and the pressure that American oil companies put on Washington to "do something" about Fidel Castro's nationalization of their assets in Cuba, so that the interests of the oil companies were probably one factor, among many, taken into consideration in planning the abortive Bay of Pigs invasion of 1961. Again, however, the evidence indicates that these are exceptional cases; although MNCs constantly seek, through persuasion of various sorts, to have the host governments treat their operations with a minimum of interference, or without high taxation, the occasions where such activity has included subversion are few. When a company prevails upon the home government to take up its case, if it feels it is being dealt with unfairly by the host government, there are regular and legitimate procedures provided under international law. It should be acknowledged, too, that often host governments have nationalized the assets of MNCs or instituted extremely high taxation rates and that these steps were taken without the threat or commission of retaliation either by the MNCs or the home government. An increasing trend for hosts to expropriate MNC assets without compensation suggests that impact does not flow in only one direction.

Intergovernmental organizations (IGOs) are also nonstate actors that often have important influences on international politics and the domestic orders of nation-states. Most IGOs reflect the interests of their members, but, occasionally, it makes sense to talk of the Common Market's "policy," the "action" of the United Nations, or the "reaction" of NATO. These organizations often develop a common "external" policy that has behind it all the forces of persuasion the organization can muster. And sometimes the policy may contravene the interests of any single member's state. Thus, the United Nations was instrumental in creating the Congo Republic and in reducing the possibilities of intervention into the Congo crisis by the United States and the Soviet Union. The

---

[11] Cited in Modelski, "Multinational Business," pp. 16–17.

Common Market has a single external tariff and, on many occasions, bargains as a single political actor in its relations with nonmembers. The Food and Agriculture Organization can be expected in the coming decades to play an important role in helping to set up food reserves; in some cases, its activities could spell the difference between mass starvation and life in some of the least-developed countries.

That intergovernmental organizations are fulfilling needs that cannot be met solely through the unilateral action of states is attested to by their dramatic growth over the past quarter century. The number has increased from thirty-eight in 1946 to more than 270 in 1982. Their variety and relative importance to international political questions vary greatly; but the important point is that many of them have a persistent and direct impact on the processes and issues of the contemporary global system, on the rules governing those processes, and on the foreign policies of virtually all the state actors in the system. In terms of their impact, they loom much more important than many of the smaller states in international politics.

International Stratification

Observers of contemporary international politics usually make distinctions between "super powers," "great powers," "middle powers," and "small powers." The basis for this type of classification is seldom explicit, but it is not difficult to place some states into each category. The United States and the Soviet Union are undoubedly "great powers," whereas Costa Rica would fit easily into the "small power" class. Others, however, defy instant categorization. Should India be termed a "great power" or a "middle power"? If we employ any single criterion, such as military capability, for differentiating the status of states, we may run into difficulties. The United States is militarily much more powerful than France, but this does not mean that on *all* international issues or in all relationships it enjoys greater status and influence than France does. We cannot assume that a "great power" is great solely by virtue of its military strength any more than we can assume that the nation that is most powerful militarily will also wield the most influence in the world. What is important is that today, policy makers "rank" states according to different criteria in different situations. Status and prestige are not objective facts; they result from subjective estimations of worth, and not everyone will agree as to what constitutes worth.

One study of differentiation among states[12] suggests that policy makers today judge other countries primarily on the basis of three criteria, each reflecting values that generally command esteem throughout the world. These include (1) a nation's level of technology, (2) its immediately available military capabilities, closely related to its technology, and (3) the reputation it can generate

---

[12] Gustavo Lagos, *International Stratification and Underdeveloped Countries* (Chapel Hill: University of North Carolina Press, 1963), Chap. 1. Lagos uses the concept of prestige as his third basis of stratification.

abroad through its day-to-day diplomatic conduct and political, economic, and social behavior at home.

During the eighteenth century, the royal family's connections and wealth and the size of the professional armed forces served as predominant indicators of international status. Today, the primary standard of judgment is technology and all the material things that derive from its application to economic activity. Economic growth and technological progress are among the main national objectives of developing countries, not only because they are necessary to sustain rapidly increasing population, but also because they are symbols of modernity and nationhood. We often hear of projects in both developed and developing countries that, from an economic point of view, are of questionable value— the steel mill that depends upon imported raw materials; the national jet airline that relies upon foreign personnel for its operation and maintenance; the modern highway that leads to no useful destination; and physically impressive but inefficient manufacturing concerns. These enterprises cannot be judged only for economic value, because they serve important social and psychological needs as well. They are tangible evidence of a country's modernity and search for status and prestige among other states. Similarly, am important value—quite apart from scientific knowledge—in space programs is the opportunities they provide for displays of technical and scientific prowess.

Military capacity, unlike technological level and economic activity, has always symbolized a political unit's status among others. No "great power" in the present or past has failed to maintain a large military establishment, and those states that aspire to great-power status allocate a large portion of their resources to developing an impressive military machine. Both the French and Chinese governments have claimed, for instance, that they could not hope to achieve great-power status unless they developed arsenals of nuclear weapons and modern delivery systems.[13] Nuclear weapons, delivery systems, and space technology are important components or symbols of great-power status. Like the displays of chariots in ancient China, these weapons and instruments are designed partly to impress others and thereby increase diplomatic bargaining influence.

In the past, it was not so difficult for states to impress neighbors, allies, and enemies by developing military forces. Dynasts were limited by the supply of funds, but if the money was available, any government could build a fleet of wooden ships or train a professional army of 20,000 men, armed with cannon and carts. All states were roughly equal, because all possessed basically an agricultural economy and a crude technology. Today, the costs of research and development, as well as the labor force and scientific and technological skills required

---

[13] In 1963, Communist China's foreign minister claimed that nuclear weapons, missiles, and supersonic aircraft were the most important indicators of the technical level of a nation's industry. Unless China possessed the most modern weapons, he suggested, it would "degenerate" into a second- or third-class nation. For the direct quotation, see Alice L. Hsieh, "The Sino-Soviet Nuclear Dialogue: 1963," *Journal of Conflict Resolution*, 8 (1963), 110.

to create and maintain a modern armed force, are beyond the capacity of all but a few societies. Some economically and technologically advanced nations have already learned that even with a highly skilled labor force and a heavy industrial base, it is difficult both to create modern armed forces and to maintain a reasonable level of economic growth. The governments of these nations have decided instead to obtain their most expensive equipment from the major powers' military arsenals and concentrate on developing less costly weapons. Certainly most developing countries cannot hope to achieve status by attempting to build military capabilities matching those of the industrialized states. In fact, as measured by military capabilities, the gap between developed and developing nations is growing wider, as is the gap between their economic levels. The cost of developing and producing the most sophisticated and destructive armaments has become prohibitive to all but a few nations. And yet, states such as Nigeria, Turkey, or Japan do not lack international status just because they do not possess the most modern nuclear weapons and delivery systems.

A state's status and reputation today may be based more on its diplomatic behavior and domestic socioeconomic and political institutions than on its technological level or military capacity. A government may enjoy a reputation for meeting its treaty commitments, being a loyal ally, or the quality of its trained diplomats. Or it may derive prestige from adhering to a particular foreign-policy orientation. Yugoslavia's active nonalignment, combined with the late President Tito's career and personality, has created for the country a prestige that is not warranted on the basis of military or technological capabilities alone. Today, many Afro-Asian countries underscore their independence by refusing to make alliances or special military arrangements with members of the NATO or Soviet blocs, while they scorn countries that do make such commitments. Governments and publics also tend to judge other nations by the character of their political leadership and economic and social institutions. Israel has a reputation in Western Europe and North America for being able to run democratic institutions successfully under adverse conditions, whereas Egypt's status may derive largely from the prestige of its political leaders. Sweden and Switzerland, while possessing some prestige in the developing world on account of their neutral foreign policies, are probably better known and admired in the Western world by virtue of their high standards of living and progressive social policies.

Because there are so many different standards for judging the status of nations, no single and permanent hierarchy of states—the great and the small, or the influential and the weak—exists. If governments generally rank each other by their armaments, technology, diplomatic behavior, and domestic institutions, this does not mean that these criteria are the most important in all issue areas or subsystems or that all the criteria are given equal weight by different policy makers. On the international trade issue, for example, one may find states ranked in one way, based on the general role they occupy in the international trade system, and another way on the issue of disarmament, depending upon which states possess the largest military capabilities, seriously tackle disarmament problems, and display a more reasonable diplomatic bargaining style. In the Communist subsystem, the ranking of states may be based on unique criteria, such as the state's (or party's) adherence to a particular doctrinal line, or even the revolutionary careers of its political leadership. Furthermore, even if the criteria of technological level, military capacity, socioeconomic institutions, and diplomatic behavior determine a country's status among most policy makers and publics, different governments may perceive the combination of these criteria in different ways.

The Structure of the System

Many observers have characterized the postwar world as "polarized." Since 1947, the United States and the Soviet Union have not only originated and defined most international issues, but have also taken the diplomatic and military leadership in dealing with them. Whether concerned with military policies, the fate of Germany, security for Europe, or arms control, the two major actors in each case have been the Soviet Union and the United States. But the structure of power and influence in the world is no longer polarized on all issues, for there are other problems in which quite different states are involved and where these two great powers have not assumed or appropriated leadership positions.

For example, in matters of foreign trade, still another configuration of power and influence exists. Here, the main actors are the nations that purchase the bulk of the world's raw-material exports, those that sell heavy machine goods, those that can control the flow of currency between nations by their fiscal policies, and the countries dependent upon foreign trade either to sustain a tolerable standard of living or help develop a modern economy. These would include the United States, Canada, most Western European countries, Japan, and the oil-producing nations. Even today, the Soviet bloc, including China, is not a major factor in international trade relationships and has little, if any, impact on the major diplomatic decisions affecting that trade. If the world is polarized on the trade issue, it is a north–south polarity, where producers of raw materials in many developing countries—oil producers excepted—receive low income from their export products but must pay high prices for heavy manufactured goods imported from industrialized nations.

In geographic, rather than issue, subsystems (the two are, of course, related), one may also find unique structures of power and influence. The United States may be a leader in Latin American affairs; its diplomatic and economic resources can be used in such a way that most Latin countries will adjust their behavior and interests to correspond with those of the United States. But the United States is certainly unable to provide such leadership in Africa, where it has few traditional interests, has relatively little economic influence, and receives slight sympathy for its position on many international issues. In brief, the structure of power and influence in the world is neither static nor universally definable. It appears under different configurations, depending upon the issue and geographic subsystems involved.

Nevertheless, relations between the Soviet Union and the United States still overshadow other issues areas to such an extent that for some purposes, the world may legitimately be characterized as polar. The fate of millions of people throughout Europe and in many developing countries depends upon decisions made in Moscow and Washington. But to the extent that China or the Arab states have begun playing an important part in defining and resolving international issues, there is, of course, a decline in polarity. On some questions, such as monetary policy or oil supplies, the Arab states have reached the rank of the great powers, for their actions similarly affect millions throughout the world. But on other issues, such as arms control, the use of the United Nations for resolving international conflicts, or security in Europe, the main actors remain the United States and the Soviet Union.

The argument so far is that there is no single system of stratification in the world, much less a single criterion according to which states are "ranked." The patterns of power and influence in the world change very much according to issue area and geographic location. And yet, as cold-war polarity declines, a fundamental cleavage in the international system, based on the level of economic development, is becoming more prominent as a potential source of international conflict. As a rule, influence on any particular global issue (as compared to a local or regional issue) tends to correlate highly with a country's general level of development. Decisions about armaments, international banking, monetary flows, trade patterns, and many other world problems are generally made by a fairly small group of industrialized countries. Thus, while it might be oversimplifying reality to argue that there are only two categories of states in the system today—the "haves" and the "have-nots"—various indices showing the patterns of trade, communications, influence, and dependency suggest that such a dichotomization is not too far off the mark and may become even more accurate as a characterization of the international system's structure in the future.

Some countries, like Taiwan, the two Koreas, Iran, Mexico, and Greece, were labeled "underdeveloped" only a few years ago. Although still far behind the economic and technological levels of the industrialized states, they have at least achieved a level where basic human needs are met reasonably, and, given favorable world economic conditions, they can expect growth to continue. The "haves," then, have been joined by an impressive number of former "have-not" states in a fairly short period of time. But prospects are not so bright for the most populous developing states. India, Bangladesh, Pakistan, Indonesia, and Egypt, whose combined populations are close to 1 billion, suffer from a combination of comparatively low growth rates, rapid population increases, lack of additional fertile land, and natural calamities.

Patterns of Interaction

Types of interaction between governments and peoples of the contemporary system's actors are unprecedented in comparison to historical systems. Transactions, whether in trade, tourism, diplomacy, private investment, or communication find no historical counterparts, and they are growing at exponential rates.

Take a few examples. The value of world exports (excluding the Communist countries) increased from $54 billion to $1,266 billion in constant (1963) prices between 1938 and 1977.[14] In 1948, only 14,000 people visited Greece as tourists; thirty years later, almost 3 million tourists visited that country. Mail-flow rates between nations have increased dramatically, as have the number of airline and shipping routes. And whereas a typical embassy of a major power located in Paris or London might have had a staff of a dozen or so at the turn of the century, today the figure is several hundred. The number of international civil servants approaches 1 million; a scant fifty years ago, they could be counted in the several thousands.

Of more political significance than aggregate growth rates, however, are the *patterns* of interaction, because they underline the types of cleavages, dependencies, and interdependencies that characterize the contemporary international system. Tourism is not distributed equally among countries. Neither are trade, foreign investment, diplomatic representation, and the various forms of communication.

Private foreign investment flows primarily from the United States to Canada, Europe, and Latin America. A secondary flow is from Europe to North America and, trailing far behind, to Africa, the Middle East, and Asia. Communist nations have recently begun to accept some private investment, usually in the form of joint ventures. Virtually all these funds come from North America and Western Europe. In brief, the flow of private investment is predominantly *between* industrialized countries, although most of the vast profits being made by Arab oil states are now being invested in the developed countries.

Tourism flows primarily between North America and Europe and secondarily between the Communist countries. There are insignificant amounts of tourism between Communist and non-Communist countries, whether developed or developing. Similarly, there is virtually no tourism originating from the developing countries.

Trade flows are primarily between non-Communist industrial countries, within the Communist bloc, and between the developing countries and the industrial countries. The composition of trade thus reflects patterns that were established at the height of colonialism. Most developing countries continue to export raw materials or partly processed goods and to import manufactured goods. There has been growth in manufactured exports by the developing countries, but it does not yet begin to compare with their imports of manufactured items.

These and other figures suggest a pattern of interaction that runs in most dimensions from Western industrial country to Western industrial country, from Western industrial countries to the developing countries, and from Communist country to Communist country. Virtually all the flows are unequal, again reflecting the cleavages mentioned in the previous section.

Dependence characterizes the relations between the developing coun-

---

[14] All statistics are taken from *United Nations Statistical Yearbook* (New York, 1963, 1968, 1972, and 1978).

tries and the industrial West, where dependence is defined as unequal degrees of reliance on markets and sources of supply and unequal ability of the members of a pair of states to influence, reward, or harm each other. Although there are some notable exceptions, such as the oil-producing countries, the actions or policies developing states undertake have little impact on the political or economic fortunes of industrialized states, even small ones. The policies of an industrialized state, on the other hand, often have significant consequences on a developing country; and any attempt to alter drastically or terminate the relationship is extremely costly to the latter, and less so to the former. Consider some of the dimensions or indicators of dependence.

The direction of airline flights remains predominately *from* New York, London, and Paris *to* the major cities of Asia, Africa, and Latin America. Air and ship communications *between* developing countries remain at rudimentary levels. Although some regional news agencies have been organized, and many developing countries beam programs abroad, the predominant pattern for the newer nations is to obtain their news from the major Western wire services. As Singer points out, for people in Nigeria to find out about an event in Ghana, less than 400 miles away, they must get news that has gone from Accra to London and then to Lagos. Naturally, the news they receive includes all the perceptual distortions of Western correspondents and editors.[15]

These patterns are repeated in many other types of interaction, whether foreign economic assistance, private investment funds, military aid and training, higher education, athletics, or even culture.

Most important from the day-to-day diplomatic perspective, the sources of information for developing nations' foreign-policy establishments are not only limited in scope, but also highly dependent upon the news media of the major industrial countries. A typical small developing country will have embassies in immediately adjacent states, in the capitals of some of the major powers, and perhaps in a few regional states. These countries have no special facilities for obtaining information about other areas of the world and must, therefore, rely on published accounts in the better Western newspapers. Few have the specialized skills and data-gathering capacities of even the smaller European countries. Again, the trend is toward diversification, but the unequal resources and flow of information remain characteristic.

If North-South relations are best described by the term *dependence,* the pattern of interaction between the Western industrial states is best characterized by the term *interdependence,* where flows, rewards, and costs are more nearly equal.[16] Although Western Europe and Japan remain largely dependent upon

---

[15] The analysis of various forms of dependence is presented comprehensively in Marshall R. Singer, *Weak States in a World of Powers: The Dynamics of International Relationships* (New York: Free Press, 1972).

[16] *Dependence* and *interdependence* are obviously relative concepts, or different ends of a continuum. State A can be dependent on B, but interdependent with C, and virtually irrelevant to D. Likewise, A can be economically dependent upon B, but militarily dependent upon C. Singer argues, however, that the various dimensions of dependence correlate highly with each other: If A is dependent in one dimension, it is likely to be dependent in all dimensions.

the United States in terms of nuclear deterrence, on other dimensions, including trade, private investment, education, and communication, interactions tend toward equality. Vulnerabilities, although hardly equal, are not as asymmetrical as they were in the early postwar years. Thus, economic trends in Europe can have a significant impact in the United States, as could a fundamental reordering of Great Britain's military relationship with North America.

A clear pattern of transactions between the socialist states and the Western industrial countries is only beginning to emerge. East-West trade configurations reveal a slight balance in favor of the West; but the makeup of trade suggests a complex pattern of vulnerabilities and dependencies. For example, by 1981, Poland was indebted to Western bankers by a sum of about $20 billion, a potential vulnerability that under extreme circumstances could be exploited by Western governments for political-military objectives. The socialist states are generally dependent upon the West for modern technology; while academics debate the consequences of this dependency, all agree that Western technology transfers do make a difference in the growth rates of socialist economies. But the dependence does not run only in one direction. Western European countries, such as Germany and Finland, are becoming increasingly dependent upon the Soviet Union for oil and natural gas supplies. To develop large export markets in the socialist countries involves some risk—in a crisis situation, those markets can be shut off, although only at a very high cost to those who are attempting to wield the economic weapon.

The Soviet Union, like its socialist allies, depends to a certain extent upon transfers of Western technology. Its unimpressive agricultural output creates another vulnerability: most years it must import large quantities of grain from the United States, Canada, and Australia. In 1980, the United States exploited this vulnerability by boycotting the sale of feed grains to Russia in retaliation for the Soviet Union's invasion of Afghanistan. Generally, then, dependence, interdependence, and vulnerability have dramatically increased in East-West economic relations—even to the extent that the socialist world has lost its immunity to inflationary pressures from the West. This is a significant difference in the pattern of interactions compared to the immediate postwar period. The implications of this fact are not entirely clear; we can conclude, nevertheless, that the economies of both types of systems are going to be influenced increasingly by trends and conditions in the other.

Major Cleavages in the Global System

The most pervasive and persistent conflict in the global system has been the competition, struggle, and occasional crisis between the socialist regimes of the East and the private enterprise, constitutional democracies of the West. The sources of the conflict go far back into history and involve fundamentally differing views about the nature of history, the relationship of person to labor, the normative value placed on investment capital, the role of individual rights, and many other problems. Basically, each type of regime perceives the other to be the exact negative of its own aspirations and values. While territorial issues and other similar problems exacerbate the conflict, the major sources of tension, hostility, and fear are philosophical and moral.

In terms of the characteristics of behavior in the cold-war system, the following are prominent:

1. A gain by one side represents a loss, and therefore a direct threat, to the other;

2. The stakes involved are the future of the world—whether it will be composed of independent states each pursuing its values and objectives unrestrained by ideological dogma and the brute military power of a hegemon; or whether there will develop a community of socialist states, all bound by an international division of labor, and each more or less arranging its domestic economies and foreign policies according to a Marxist-Leninist blueprint;

3. One's own behavior is always directed toward establishing stability and peace; the other side's initiatives, whether in diplomacy or arms deployment, are directed toward gaining unilateral advantages and, ultimately, some sort of victory. The Cold War is a constant struggle in many dimensions—propaganda, ideology, armaments, economic output, sports, and culture.

Other characteristics could be listed, but these are sufficient to point out that more than a conflict over some minor piece of territory is involved. The conflict, fundamentally, conditions the way policy makers (and publics) view the world, themselves, and their adversaries. Hence, to settle a single problem, such as Berlin, may help build a modicum of trust, but is insufficient to change well-established stereotypes and habits of diplomatic behavior.

Some progress in lessening East-West conflict levels has been made in recent years. Using the terms *détente* or *peaceful co-existence,* the adversaries have publicly claimed that their first obligation is to avoid nuclear war. Some steps to diminish the possibility of world holocaust have been taken, such as the Washington-Moscow hot line, limited arms control measures on strategic missiles, and agreements to consult in crisis situations. Levels of transactions between the two blocs have grown dramatically in the 1970s, thus increasing contacts in a variety of arenas. While these have helped to build up a common stake in ensuring mutual progress, they have not yet had an impact on the growing arms race between NATO and the Warsaw Treaty Organization. In its military and ideological dimensions, the Cold War runs unabated, with little hope that significant departures from customary ways of seeing each other will take place in the coming decade.

In addition to the well-known East-West cleavage in the international system, there is another source of system-wide conflict today: the fundamental disagreement between the industrialized West and many of the developing nations on how international inequality should be redressed in the future. The fact of inequality can hardly be disputed, whether it is defined in terms of the distribution of wealth in the world, the degree of dependence and vulnerability of states, or even, according to some, the vastly differing degrees of exploitation in the international economy. In the "radical" view, the poverty of most nations is the direct consequence of colonialism and its legacy, perpetuated through unequal trade; private investment, which extracts enormous profits from the developing countries; and the inherently unequal benefits accruing to trade partners, where one sells manufactured goods in exchange for raw materials.[17] The argument, which has become an accepted truth among leading figures in the developing countries, is that the terms of trade have steadily worsened over the past decades: today it takes more units of rubber, tin, hemp, or coffee beans to purchase one simple tractor than it did twenty years ago. In other words, the developing countries have to export more in order to buy the same amount. Adding to this problem is the propensity of the industrial countries to maintain high tariffs against manufactured imports from the Third World. While on the one hand most Western governments are committed to free trade and constantly exhort the developing countries to industrialize, on the other, according to the argument, they systematically restrict trade against the LDC's manufactured exports to protect domestic jobs. Foreign-aid programs, while ostensibly designed to assist in the development process, are in fact tied to the economic interests of the donors. Finally, there are numerous arguments against the activities of multinational corporations, as we have summarized earlier. There are, of course, other than economic dimensions of inequality, as the discussion of transaction flows indicates. But being easy to quantify, economic indicators are often particularly telling.

Arguments about the true state of inequality abound. To those who believe that any economic transactions within the capitalist system are inherently exploitative, the only answer to the problem is either total isolation and autarchy or socialist revolution and integration into the socialist international trade system. To those who argue that trade is inherently unequal only so long as the rules of the game are loaded in favor of the strong, the solution is drastic reform of the international trade system and regulation of foreign private investment. Measures such as preferential tariff treatment, cartels, and commodity agreements to stabilize prices and supplies are required. Most leading industrial countries have agreed to ad hoc measures such as food banks and some preferential tariff treatment; but, in the opinion of most LDCs, they have not gone nearly far enough.

Assuming that no drastic changes in international economic arrangements are on the horizon, what can we say about international economic inequality and its future? Table 3–1 allows us, however tentatively, to make some rough comments about the problem of the "gap" between nations. The table presents per capita income (pci) figures for a variety of countries, the percentage that each figure is of the American pci, and the average American income as a propor-

[17] A classical statement of this position is Johan Galtung, "A Structural Theory of Imperialism," *Journal of Peace Research,* 2 (1971), 81–117.

Table 3–1 Per Capita Incomes, Selected Countries, as Proportion of U.S. Per Capita Income

COUNTRY	1960	% U.S. PCI	U.S. ×	1978	% U.S. PCI	U.S. ×
U.S.A.	2502			9700		
Canada	1909	76	1.3	9170	95	1.1
Sweden	1678	67	1.5	10210	105	.9
England	1261	50	1.9	5030	52	1.9
Greece	410	16	6.1	3270	34	2.9
Japan	417	17	6.0	7330	76	1.3
Spain	317	13	7.9	3520	36	2.7
Mexico	307	12	8.1	1290	13	7.5
Brazil	233	9	10.7	1570	16	6.2
Nigeria	73	3	34.2	560	6	17.3
Indonesia	73	3	34.2	360	4	26.9
India	69	3	36.2	180	2	53

Sources: *United Nations Yearbook,* 1962, 1972; International Bank for Reconstruction and Development, *1979 World Bank Atlas* (Washington, D.C., 1979).

tion of the pcis of other nations. For example, the average Greek in 1960 earned only 16 percent of an average American's income. This means that the American's income was 6.1 times as great as the Greek's. Several conclusions appear from the figures. First, the United States is losing its income predominance, but mostly as measured against the increased gains of other industrial countries (Canada, Sweden, and Japan) and some new "have" nations such as Greece and Spain. Second, when measured in terms of proportions of incomes, the developing countries are "catching up" only very slowly, if at all. The average Mexican, compared to an American counterpart, is really only marginally better off in 1978 than in 1960. The Nigerians and Brazilians have made impressive strides in closing the gap, but Indians and Indonesians have made little progress. An Indian, in fact, is worse off today, comparatively speaking, than two decades ago. Of course, these figures may be skewed by the presence of two populous developing countries which face particularly intractable problems, India and Indonesia. Had we listed other countries, particularly those with oil resources, much more optimistic impressions might result. If we were to aggregate the statistics for all countries in the table, we would find that while the absolute "gap" between incomes continues to increase (e.g., the average Swede earned, in 1978, $10,020 more than the average Indian; in 1960, the difference was only $1609), the relative distances are beginning to close. But the process is so slow that it appears hopeless to talk about any form of economic equality between the industrial and developing countries during the next half century.

Trade figures support this conclusion. The proportion of the world's exports emanating from the developing countries—excluding OPEC oil exports—is not growing dramatically, even though in dollar terms it is. To the extent that exports constitute an important source of domestic economic growth,

Table 3–2 Value of Exports by Source and Destination, Billion Dollars

DIRECTION OF EXPORTS	BILLION $ 1970	% TOTAL WORLD EXPORTS	AGGRE-GATE	BILLION $ 1977	% TOTAL WORLD EXPORTS	AGGRE-GATE
From IND to IND	173	53		516	41	
From IND to LDC	42	13	68	173	14	58
From IND to SOC	9	2		34	2	
From LDC to IND	40	12		205	16	
From LDC to LDC	11	3	16	67	5	22
From LDC to SOC	3	1		12	1	
From SOC to IND	8	2		30	2	
From SOC to SOC	20	6	9	59	5	8
From SOC to LDC	5	1		18	1	
OPEC Exports	18	6	6	148	12	12
Total	329	99	99	1262	99	100

Key: IND = Industrial Countries
　　LDC = Developing Countries
　　SOC = Socialist Countries

Sources: *United Nations Yearbook*, 1956, 1977, 1979; International Monetary Fund, *Direction of Trade Yearbook*, 1972, 1980.

it is still the industrial countries which benefit most from it. Nevertheless, there is some perceptible movement toward a more egalitarian trade structure. In 1977, the exports of the industrial countries accounted for 58 percent of total world exports, whereas in 1953 they accounted for 72 percent. But the decline has not been taken up by most LDCs; the dramatically growing relative share of the OPEC countries—from $18 billion in 1970 to $148 billion in 1977— accounts for the declining share of the industrial countries.

Figures on asymmetry in dependence allow for somewhat more optimistic conclusions. Most developing countries have successfully begun to diversify their trade and investment relationships and to break down colonial-type patterns of product concentration in exports (e.g., Nicaragua exported mostly bananas). Several examples make the point. In 1965, 70 percent of Algeria's imports came from France; by 1976, the figure had declined to 27 percent. France purchased 73 percent of Algeria's exports in 1965, but only 14 percent a decade later. Most economic dependencies of the United States, England, and other former colonial countries show similar, if somewhat less dramatic, change. Yet, in a few instances, developing countries are becoming more dependent and vulnerable. El Salvador's trade ties to the United States were more pronounced in 1977 than in 1965; Gabon, a former French colony, received a higher proportion of its imports from France (68 percent) in 1976 than it did a decade earlier. Nevertheless, these and other countries are exceptions; the trend is clearly toward declining vulnerability and greater diversification. Yet, there is still a long way to go before one can begin to talk about equality of dependence (interdependence) or vulnerability. Indeed, in some senses, the situation has deteriorated; for the developing countries are not only buffetted by the economic fortunes of the industrial states (over whose policies they have virtually no influence), but also by constantly increasing oil prices. The latter phenomenon has burdened many LDCs with immense debt payments, thus retarding their economic growth.

The North-South cleavage, however measured, is likely to become a relatively permanent characteristic of the international system, with numerous consequences for the nature of contemporary international politics. Among these, for example, is the decreasing influence of the industrial countries in international fora, such as the United Nations (the United States can no longer command an automatic majority in either the Security Council or the General Assembly, as it could until the late 1960s); the agenda of international economic negotiations has to include the special problems of the developing countries; debates about international problems tend to focus increasingly around values such as equity and justice in addition to security and peace; and there are increasing strains within the Atlantic alliance, as some members, such as the Netherlands, adopt sympathetic policies toward the LDC demands, while others, like Germany and the United States, hold out for slow and piecemeal reform in only some issue areas.

The Major Rules of the Modern System

Territoriality, "impermeability," and political independence, the major characteristics of the nation-state as it developed in Europe during the sixteenth and seventeenth centuries, were also the bases upon which dynasts, diplomats, and lawyers of that period created the fundamental rules for conducting relations with each other. The three fundamental rules were, and continue to be, the sovereignty, territorial integrity, and legal equality of states.

By the conclusion of the seventeenth century, most of the dynastic states of Europe were politically sovereign—the central governments and their creations at lower levels of administration were the only rule-making and rule-applying bodies in defined territories. On the inside, political units such as duchies or walled cities were incapable of challenging the central authorities or making treaties with "outside" powers, and neither the Holy Roman Emperor nor the Church, as supranational institutions, could order kings and princes to undertake actions without their consent. The principle of sovereignty—that governments are the supreme lawmakers in their own territories—was little more than a legal doctrine expressing a situation that prevailed politically throughout large portions of Europe by the end of the seventeenth century. The principle was established firmly in the Peace of Westphalia (1648), which held that only sovereign (impermeable and independent) states could enter into treaty relations with each other, and that the Holy Roman Empire could no longer command the allegiance of its parts. This implied that a political unit that was not sovereign (such as a duchy *within* France) could not become a legal unit in the system; it could not make treaties, enter international organizations, or claim any other rights or duties under international law. This rule is still the basis of all interaction today; for, without legal sovereignty, as recognized by other states, a political unit, be it colony, protectorate, or liberation movement, has no legal standing among other states.[18] States are free, by virtue of their sovereignty, to govern as they wish within their own territory and to formulate their own external policies except where limited by self-approved treaty obligations.

The second major rule follows from the first. If a state is sovereign, it cannot allow, without its own consent, other political entities to make or apply their own rules on its territory; it has the corresponding obligation not to intervene in the internal affairs of other states or compromise their territorial integrity. In transactions between states, therefore, governments can attempt to influence each other's behavior only through established diplomatic channels. They cannot bypass relations with other governments and attempt to influence the domestic political processes of another country by establishing their physical presence (occupation) or laws on another's territory; nor can they attempt to persuade, cajole, or threaten its inhabitants by direct action against them on their own territory. In an age of subversion and extensive international propaganda, where states are "penetrated" and highly permeable to outside influences, this rule not only is violated systematically, but may be on the verge of obsolescence.

The third rule states simply that however they differ in size, population, location, or military capabilities, all states are equal with respect to legal rights and duties. All are, theoretically, sovereign and independent; all possess equally the rights of territorial integrity and self-defense; and all are equally obliged to avoid interfering in other states' internal affairs, to observe treaty obligations, and, since adoption of the United Nations Charter, to avoid the threat or use of force (except in self-defense) in relations with other states. From these three basic rules flow a number of more specific limitations on state action, as defined in treaties, international custom, and general principles of international law.

The three basic rules specify the accepted and expected forms of behavior in relations between states.[19] Through their regular observance they also constitute characteristic norms of behavior. This is not to deny occasional exceptions, particularly to the second rule of noninterference. But if these fundamental rules were not observed with reasonable consistency, the structure of the system and the nature of interstate relations would change radically. The Chinese states

---

[18] There are exceptions, however. For example, two constituent republics of the Soviet Union, Belorussia and the Ukraine, have separate representatives in the United Nations and maintain their own foreign ministries. The policies of these "states" do not, of course, diverge from those of the Soviet government. Although not a state, the PLO has achieved observer status within the United Nations.

[19] These rules are clearly outlined in the Inter-American Convention on the Rights and Duties of States, signed in Montevideo, Uruguay, in 1933.

did not place high value on sovereignty and independence, nor did they have a concept of permanent frontiers or territoriality. Since these rules did not constitute the assumptions behind all political action, there was a diminution in the number of politically independent states as the large and powerful engulfed the small and weak. In international history since the eighteenth century, however, the number of independent states has increased, not decreased. In particular, the number of very small and economically weak states has grown rapidly. It is significant that during the last two centuries, militarily aggressive states have seldom incorporated conquered states into their own territory; they have either temporarily occupied them, eventually restoring them to virtual independence, or have turned them into satellite states, political entities subservient in economic, defense, and foreign policies, but nevertheless maintaining some of the attributes of sovereignty. In several hundred wars or conflicts since the seventeenth century, states have not been commonly, as in the Chinese system, "removed" or "extinguished."[20]

FACTORS OF STABILITY, INSTABILITY, AND CHANGE IN THE CONTEMPORARY SYSTEM

Over a period of several centuries, the system of many small feudal states under control of the Chou monarchy became transformed into a structure in which power was diffused among several large states. Each state was independent of the others and constantly shifted alliance partners as new threats arose or subsided; these temporary alliances were the only form of political unity during the Spring and Autumn period. This structure eventually gave way to one in which power and influence were for the most part concentrated around two blocs or leagues of states. The Greek city-state system similarly changed its structure from one in which power and influence were diffused among a large number of relatively equal units to a configuration in which power accrued to two block leaders. These changes could be linked to economic, social, and cultural transformations within the political units, to the change of official myths, and to hostile intervention of outside powers. In feudal China, for instance, the small states on the periphery of the system were relatively independent of the center and able to seize surrounding territory, develop their military capacity, and establish administrative mechanisms adequate to cope with the problems of governing a larger territory and population. When size, military power, and economic welfare became values of importance, the small feudal political units incapable of change were either conquered by more powerful neighbors or lived on as insignificant anachronisms in a Chinese world of large states. We

---

[20] These statements do not refer, of course, to European imperialism, under which many tribes and petty states in the Western Hemisphere, Africa, and Asia lost their independence to the white man, or to the unification of Germany and Italy.

have similarly examined some recent social and technological developments that helped transform the eighteenth-century continental system of diffuse power and shifting alliances into a worldwide system of the twentieth century, in which, on most issues, the United States and the Soviet Union wield effective power and leadership.

Since any discussion of sources of stability and change in the contemporary system is likely to be conjectural and open to debate, great length would be required to support major assertions. Instead of receiving the author's views, readers may wish to speculate on their own—with the assistance of the accompanying statements—regarding some of the notable processes, conditions, events, or trends that seem to have important consequences on the global state system. The question is, Which processes, conditions, events, or trends tend to perpetuate the postwar patterns of interaction, stratification, or rules, and which ones tend to create a new type of international system? We can call the various factors *sources of stability and sources of change.* The following tables are certainly not comprehensive; they are designed to stimulate thought and discussion, not to answer questions. The reader can no doubt add other items to these lists.

The problem is that once the sources are identified, it is difficult to be certain about the consequences. In fact, many trends or conditions can have contradictory consequences as far as system change or stability is concerned.

Table 3–3 Sources of Stability in the Global System

PROCESS, CONDITION, TREND, OR EVENT	CONSEQUENCES FOR PATTERNS OF INTERACTION, STRATIFICATION, OR RULES
1. Costs of developing major nuclear or military strength	1. Helps sustain effective military polarity.
2. Continued incompatibility between communist and liberal philosophies	2. Helps sustain major East–West dimension of conflict. NATO and WTO remain major alliance systems in world.
3. Soviet-American collaboration to prevent nuclear proliferation	3. Helps sustain Soviet-American nuclear monopoly and, thus, military polarity.
4. Costs of research, development, and technological innovation	4. Sustains dependence of developing countries on industrial countries; the "gap" and asymmetrical interaction and dependency patterns persist.
5. Nationalism and desire for ethnic unity	5. Helps sustain ideology of sovereignty, and political independence as a major rule of system.
6. Development of direct satellite broadcasting	6. Indigenous cultures in Third World face continuous onslaught of Western culture and economic values; reinforces dependence.

Table 3–4 Sources of Change in the Global System

PROCESS, CONDITION, TREND, OR EVENT	CONSEQUENCES FOR PATTERNS OF INTERACTION, STRATIFICATION, OR RULES
1. Virulent growth of ethnic nationalism	1. Fragmentation of international system into ever-increasing number of small and conditionally viable states.[a]
2. Increase in number of small, weak states, liberation movements, etc.	2. Expanding possibilities for violence and international conflict; some conflicts could have major consequences in terms of power alignments (e.g., a national liberation war in South Africa—who would line up on which side; costs and consequences of such a war on African economies, etc.).
3. Development of China's economic and military strength	3. Breaks down postwar power structure; Chinese participation in global issues; possible Sino-Soviet war, with great consequences on distribution of power in international system.
4. Depletion of resources by industrialized countries	4. Increases power of scarce-resource-producing states; reversal of traditional dependence between rich and poor—or, at least, creation of interdependence.
5. Growth of important nonstate actors	5. Demands for new rules to regulate nonstate actors and to enhance sovereignty of state; decisions having great economic consequences on weaker states are made by nonstate actors.
6. Growth of Brazil as a major power	6. Decline of U.S. hegemony in Latin America; new leadership patterns appear in Western Hemisphere.
7. Revolutionary ideologies and technological developments	7. Increasing vulnerability of states to outside penetration; virtual demise of rule against interference in internal affairs.
8. Nuclear proliferation	8. Destroys effective U.S.-Soviet nuclear monopoly; possibility of local nuclear wars and escalation; effective "gap" between military haves and have-nots begins to narrow.
9. Growing collaboration of developing countries, demand for reform of international economic system	9. Declining economic hegemony of industrial countries; eventually, reduction of North-South cleavage in the system.

[a] The potentially disruptive influence of ethnic nationalism is revealed in the following statistics: Among 132 states, only twelve are ethnically homogeneous. In thirty-nine states (30 percent of total), the largest ethnic group does not constitute even a majority of the population. In fifty-three states (40 percent), the population contains more than five significant national groups. See Arnfinn Jorgensen-Dahl, "Forces of Fragmentation in the International System: The Case of Ethno-Nationalism," *Orbis,* 19 (Summer 1975), 653.

Direct satellite broadcasting will allow the industrial countries, which command the technology, to "reach" directly into the small communities of developing countries, communities that, in many cases, have up to now hardly been aware of an outside world. What will be the consequence? Some would argue that if television becomes an important conveyor of modernization ideas, then self-sustained development may take place and the dependence of the developing countries on the industrial countries will begin to decline. This would be an important change from the structure of interaction and dependence in the contemporary world. But others would argue that television could be a powerful vehicle for "Westernizing" people in developing countries; they would then want to model themselves on us, and, to the extent that this is not possible, frustration and conflict would ensue. The level of conflict between the "haves" and "have-nots" would thus significantly increase—another change in the characteristics of the contemporary system.

Another phenomenon with unknown consequences is nuclear proliferation. Most people assume that the likelihood of nuclear war increases with the number of states possessing nuclear military capabilities. But it can be argued equally fervently that the possession of awesome nuclear power instills in policy makers a sense of caution they do not have when playing with mere conventional armaments. A government might calculate that the use of conventional arms in a border war would be justified in terms of potential gains and losses. But would that government seriously contemplate the possibility of destroying an entire society for the sake of a few hundred square miles of disputed territory? One could also make the argument that nuclear weapons have become basically irrelevant to international politics except as symbols of status. They have not prevented the outbreak of crises; if they have deterred, they have deterred only the highly improbable—namely, a direct military strike by one major power against the other. The argument would then continue that as governments come to possess these weapons, they will learn that they are basically useless for the vast majority of problems that confront states. A counterargument might be that one should not predict the future on the basis of past Soviet and American behavior. The consequences of nuclear proliferation, therefore, remain problematical.

TYPES OF INTERNATIONAL SYSTEMS

By comparing historical descriptions of international systems, it is possible to construct typologies of political orders at the international level. But which criteria should be used to differentiate among the systems? The nature of the units that interact provides one basis of differentiation, but evidence is insufficient to suggest that the *forms* of political organization—whether feudal units, city-states, agricultural states, or nation-states—determine the unique characteristics of international politics in a given era. International systems could also be classified according to the types of issues that bring political units into conflict. Many of the Cold-War issues have been resolved, and today, resource depletion, economic inequality, and arms control are of paramount importance. But the most meaningful distinction may relate to the types of structures—the general patterns of power, dominance, and influence—that persist among units comprising the system. The significance of a system's structure lies in its influence on the general orientation of constituent units' external policies and on the restraints it can impose on the units' freedom of action.

If a system's structure is used as the differentiating criterion, we can outline models, based on the historical descriptions, above, of at least five different kinds of international systems: (1) the "hierarchial," (2) the "diffuse," (3) the "diffuse-bloc," (4) the "polar," and (5) the "multipolar." China in the Western Chou period (from 1122 until approximately 771 B.C.) is the only example of a hierarchical structure discussed in these chapters, but further historical examination would uncover other systems with similar features.[21] In this type of system, power and influence are concentrated in one unit, which has the authority to create lesser units and chastise errant units if they attempt to challenge the central authority's leadership and domination. The central authority maintains order and stability by offering rewards and subsidies such as grants of land or honorific titles, making threats of punishment, and vigorously inculcating official myths and ceremonies that emphasize the sanctity of superior–subordinate relationships. Interaction and communication within the system also follow the hierarchical principle. They are conducted primarily between the central authority and immediately subordinate units; units at the bottom of the hierarchy usually communicate with the central authority only through mediating states. Communication between the lesser units is, at best, sporadic and, in most cases, nonexistent. Alliances theoretically cannot exist, since all power flows from the top down. In the process of disintegration, however, ambitious subordinate units may secretly ally with each other to challenge the position of the central authority.

Power and influence in the diffuse system are distributed widely among the interacting units. There is an ill-defined hierarchy of status among states, established according to various criteria of stratification, but a comparatively large number of political units are of roughly equal size and military capability. None permanently dominates the others, although there may be some leaders of regional alliances. Diplomatic and military coalitions form frequently, are open-ended, and disintegrate rapidly once mutual objectives have been achieved. They do not form into stable blocs. These coalitions are unstable because the interests underlying them tend to shift quickly, members are not economically or ideologically dependent upon each other, and there are no fundamental ideo-

---

[21] Some features analogous to those of the Chinese system in the Western Chou period would be found in the Moslem empire and in the Holy Roman Empire before the seventeenth century.

logical issues dividing the alliances. Communication and interaction among the units is widespread, although geographic proximity and logistic factors undoubtedly make some units more involved than others in the major issue areas. China in the Spring and Autumn period and occasionally in the period of Warring States, Greece between the ninth and fifth centureis B.C., the Italian city-states in the first half of the fifteenth century, and Europe during the eighteenth, most of the nineteenth, and part of the twentieth century would fit the model of the diffuse system.

The diffuse-bloc system existed in the Greek period when the Athenian empire and the Peloponnesian League constituted powerful and relatively permanent blocs with surrounding allies or satellites, but many other city-states remained independent of bloc affiliations, pursuing their objectives with considerable freedom of action. The same general pattern was repeated in Europe in the last two decades of the nineteenth century and again in the four or five years preceding the outbreak of World War II; and it has reappeared, since 1955, when an increasing number of nonaligned states has successfully broken the military-diplomatic supremacy of the two bloc leaders. Patterns of communication and interaction in the diffuse-bloc system are similar to those in the diffuse system—they go in all directions, except that bloc members tend to become dependent upon, or subservient to, bloc leaders and to conduct relatively few relations with opposing bloc members or noninvolved states.

The polar model constitutes a generalization of the main features of power, influence, and patterns of communication and interaction found in China during portions of the period of Warring States (after the northern and southern leagues were formed), in Europe at the time of the French revolutionary and Napoleonic wars, immediately prior to World War I, and again in the period following World War II until approximately 1955. In this type of system, military power and diplomatic authority center around two bloc leaders, which dominate or lead lesser units by combining rewards—such as providing security and economic assistance—with implicit or explicit threats of punishment against recalcitrant allies. Interaction and communication seem to be primarily between the two antagonistic bloc leaders and between each of the bloc leaders and its respective client states. In the post–World War II period, however, interaction and communication among the *lesser* states of the Western bloc have been consistently high, while prior to 1956 it was largely absent within the Soviet bloc.

Conflicts and issues within the polar model seem to contain strong ideological overtones, although territorial issues and questions of spheres of influence may be mixed in with the competition over values. Strong value incompatibilities between blocs thus sustain cohesiveness within blocs. In ancient China, it was the "legitimate" league of Chou states against the partly "barbarian" southern bloc; in the years between 1789 and 1815, it was conflict not only between France and the rest of Europe, but also between the universal principles of republicanism and royal legitimacy; in our day, the principles of Marxism-Leninism conflict in many ways with democratic liberalism.

The multipolar system, examples of which could be seen occasionally during the Warring States period and, perhaps, in our own day, combines characteristics of other types. For example, with the rise of China over the past twenty years and the development of the Sino-Soviet conflict, the Soviet Union has adopted some policies aimed at reducing East–West hostilities. We would hypothesize that in the multipolar system, there is more flexibility between the blocs (that is, not all conflicts are seen as involving a life-death struggle between the blocs), more opportunity for short-term alliances and coalition shifts, and possibly somewhat less bloc cohesion than in the polar system. In the multipolar system, then, we would argue that the latitude of choice of bloc members, both leaders and followers, is greater than in the polar system; domestic needs, personality characteristics of key leaders, public opinion, and traditional policies can probably account for as much of the nations' foreign-policy outputs in the multipolar system as does system structure. In the polar system, on the other hand, foreign policy—at least for the smaller states—is determined essentially, if not exclusively, by the needs, ideologies, and aspirations of the bloc leaders.

These categories of international systems emphasize the recurrence of various power structures and interactions patterns in different historical contexts. Were there any other similarities between these systems? Each of the historical examples at some stage became transformed from the diffuse type to either the diffuse-bloc, multipolar, or polar type. Diverse conditions might be responsible for this phenomenon, but the trend is unmistakable. No system originally comprising a large number of roughly equal units, with power diffused among them, retained that structure for a very long period, and the usual direction of development was toward a polar structure.

Even polar structures were not very stable. Starting with the anti-French coalition between the eighteenth and nineteenth centuries, polar structures have developed into diffuse structures, only to turn into polar or multipolar structures again. In China and Greece, however, once power and influence were distributed between two bloc leaders, the wars that followed led ultimately to complete destruction of the systems. The descriptions of the systems thus suggest no patterns as to the types of system most conducive to stability among independent political units. The scope of violence in the hierarchical and diffuse systems, as well as during the last forty years of the unique Italian system, was limited. But this may be attributed as much to a crude military technology, small territorial basis of political organizations, and absence of overriding ideological issues as to the structure of the system. Also, in most of the historical diffuse systems, there was ample unorganized territory into which the states could expand. In China and Greece, eighteenth- and nineteenth-century Europe, and, to a lesser extent, in the first half of the fifteenth century in Italy, the political units could increase their territorial holdings without necessarily depriving other politically organized centers of their own territory. Africa, the Middle East, and Asia served more than once as convenient outlets for imperialist pressures in Europe. On the other hand, in polar or multipolar systems, the amount of space available for political expansion was usually limited, so improvement of one state's territorial position could be secured only at the expense of others.[22]

An examination of these systems also suggests that processes that lead to changes in their structures are occurring much more rapidly in the Western cultural context. Almost four centuries elapsed between the establishment of the hierarchical Chou system and its transformation into a diffuse structure during the Spring and Autumn period. The main characteristics of the Greek system when it had a diffuse structure remained essentially unchanged for almost three centuries. Today, technological innovation, economic development, and the effects of total war create rapid and radical changes in the world's power structure. England's decline as a major power in international politics occurred in less than two decades, and the rise of the Soviet Union and the United States took place virtually within the period of time that they were involved in World War II. Communist China's rise to prominence and diplomatic influence has occurred in little more than a decade. Nuclear war, major scientific discoveries, or depletion or discovery of natural resources could bring about even more radical shifts in the structure of power and influence in the near future.

SELECTED BIBLIOGRAPHY

ARON, RAYMOND, *The Century of Total War.* Garden City, N.Y.: Doubleday, 1954.

BHAGWATI, JAGDISH, ed., *Economics and World Order.* New York: Macmillan, 1972.

BLAKE, DAVID H., and ROBERT S. WALTERS, *The Politics of Global Economic Relations.* Englewood Cliffs, N.J.: Prentice-Hall, Inc., 1976.

CAPORASO, JAMES, ed., *Dependence and Dependency in the Global System,* special issue of *International Organization,* 32 (Winter 1978).

CARR, EDWARD H., *The Twenty Years' Crisis, 1919–1939.* London: Macmillan, 1946.

CLAUDE, INIS L., JR., *Power and International Relations.* New York: Random House, 1962.

COHEN, BENJAMIN J., *The Question of Imperialism: The Political Economy of Dominance and Dependence.* New York: Basic Books, 1973.

EMERSON, RUPERT, *From Empire to Nation.* Cambridge, Mass.: Harvard University Press, 1960.

FELD, WERNER J., *Nongovernmental Forces and World Politics: A Study of Business, Labor, and Political Groups.* New York: Praeger, 1972.

FRANK, ANDRÉ GUNDER, *Latin America: Underdevelopment or Revolution.* New York: Monthly Review Press, 1969.

GEERTZ, CLIFFORD, *Old Societies and New States: A Quest for Modernity in Asia and Africa.* New York: Free Press, 1963.

GROSS, LEO, "The Peace of Westphalia, 1648–1948," *American Journal of International Law,* 42 (1948), 20–41.

[22] See Rosecrance, *Action and Reaction in World Politics,* p. 239.

GULICK, EDWARD V., *Europe's Classical Balance of Power.* Ithaca, N.Y.: Cornell University Press, 1955.

HANSEN, ROGER D., *Beyond the North-South Stalemate.* New York: McGraw-Hill, 1979.

HERZ, JOHN H., *International Politics in the Atomic Age.* New York: Columbia University Press, 1959.

HOLSTI, OLE R., RANDOLPH SIVERSON, and ALEXANDER GEORGE, eds., *Change in the International System.* Boulder, Colo.: Westview Press, 1981.

HOROWITZ, IRVING L., *Three Worlds of Development: The Theory and Practice of International Stratification.* New York: Oxford University Press, 1966.

HUNTINGTON, SAMUEL P., "Transnational Organizations in World Politics," *World Politics,* 25 (April 1973), 333–68.

International Communication Agency, "Transnationals: New Dimension," *Economic Impact,* 33 (1981), 8–44.

JORGENSEN-DAHL, ARNFINN, "Forces of Fragmentation in the International System: The Case of Ethno-Nationalism," *Orbis,* 19 (Summer 1975), 652–74.

KAPLAN, MORTON A., *System and Process in International Politics.* New York: John Wiley, 1957.

KAUFMAN, EDY, *The Superpowers and Their Spheres of Influence.* London: Croom Helm, 1976.

KEOHANE, ROBERT O., and JOSEPH S. NYE, *Power and Interdependence: World Politics in Transition.* Boston: Little, Brown and Company, 1977.

———, eds., *Transnational Relations and World Politics.* Cambridge, Mass.: Harvard University Press, 1972.

LAGOS, GUSTAVO, *International Stratification and Underdeveloped Countries.* Chapel Hill: The University of North Carolina Press, 1963.

LALL, SANJAYA, and PAUL STREETEN, *Foreign Investment, Transnationals and Developing Countries.* London: Macmillan, 1977.

LEONARD, H. JEFFREY, Multinational Corporations and Politics in Developing Countries," *World Politics,* 33 (April 1980), 454–83.

LEVITT, KARI, *Silent Surrender: The Multinational Corporation in Canada.* New York: St. Martin's Press, 1970.

MODELSKI, GEORGE, ed., *Multinational Corporations and World Order.* Sage Contemporary Social Science Issues, No. 2. Beverly Hills, Calif.: Sage Publications, 1972.

MORSE, EDWARD L., "The Transformation of Foreign Policies: Modernization, Externalization, and Interdependence," *World Politics,* 22 (April 1970).

MOWAT, ROBERT B., *The European State System.* London: H. Milford, 1923.

NORTHROP, F.S.C., *The Taming of the Nations.* New York: Macmillan, 1952.

NYE, JOSEPH S., JR., "Multinational Corporations in World Politics," *Foreign Affairs,* 53 (October 1974), 153–75.

PENROSE, EDITH, "The State and Multinational Enterprises in Less-Developed Countries," in John H. Dunning, ed., *The Multinational Enterprise.* London: Allen & Unwin, 1971.

PLISCHKE, ELMER, *Microstates in World Affairs: Policy Problems and Options.* Washington, D.C.: American Enterprise Institute, 1978.

POUNDS, NORMAN, and SUE SIMONS BALL, "Core Areas and the Development of the European States System," *Annals of the Association of American Geographers,* 54 (1964), 24–40.

REJAI, MOSTAFA, and CYNTHIA H. ENLOE, "Nation-States and State-Nations," *International Studies Quarterly,* 13 (1969), 140–57.

ROSECRANCE, RICHARD N., *Action and Reaction in World Politics.* Boston: Little, Brown, 1963.

————, and ARTHUR STEIN, "Interdependence: Myth or Reality?" *World Politics,* 26 (October 1973), 1–27.

ROSENAU, JAMES N., ed., *Linkage Politics: Essays on the Convergence of National and International Systems.* New York: Free Press, 1969.

ROTHSTEIN, ROBERT L., *The Weak in the World of the Strong.* New York: Columbia University Press, 1977.

RUEBENS, EDWIN P., ed., *The Challenge of the New International Economic Order.* Boulder, Colo.: Westview Press, 1981.

SAID, ABDUL A., and LUIZ R. SIMMONS, eds., *The New Sovereigns: Multinational Corporations as World Powers.* Englewood Cliffs, N.J.: Prentice-Hall, 1975.

SINGER, MARSHALL R., *Weak States in a World of Powers: The Dynamics of International Relationships.* New York: Free Press, 1972.

SPIEGEL, STEVEN L., *Dominance and Diversity: The International Hierarchy.* Boston: Little, Brown, 1972.

TURNER, LOUIS, *Oil Companies in the International System,* 2nd ed. London: George Allen & Unwin, 1980.

TUCKER, ROBERT W., *The Inequality of Nations.* London: Martin Robertson, 1977.

————, *Storm over Multinationals: The Real Issues.* Cambridge: Harvard University Press, 1977.

United Nations, Department of Economic and Social Affairs, *The Impact of Multinational Corporations on Development and International Relations.* E/5500/ST/ESA/ 6, 1974.

VERNON, RAYMOND, *Sovereignty at Bay: The Multinational Spread of U.S. Enterprises.* New York: Basic Books, 1971.

VITAL, DAVID, *The Inequality of States.* New York: Oxford University Press, 1967.

WATERLOW, CHARLOTTE, *Superpowers and Victims: The Outlook for World Community.* Englewood Cliffs, N.J.: Prentice-Hall, 1974.

PART III

Foreign-Policy Outputs

4

Foreign-Policy Orientations and National Roles

The international system is the environment in which the units of international politics operate. Their goals, aspirations, needs, attitudes, latitude of choice, and actions are significantly influenced by the overall distribution of power in the system, by its scope, and by its prevailing rules. This section will shift the focus of analysis from systems to the units that constitute them. In order to explain what conditions make states behave as they do, we need first to describe what, typically, they do. Using the nation-as-actor approach for the time being, our concern will be to explore the components of foreign policy.

What is foreign policy? How do we make sense of all the phenomena that transcend national borders—sending a diplomatic note, enunciating a doctrine, making an alliance, or formulating a long-range, but vague, objective such as "making the world safe for democracy"? These are all foreign-policy outputs: actions or ideas designed by policy makers to solve a problem or promote some change in the environment—that is, in the policies, attitudes, or actions of another state or states. But there is a vast difference in scope between sending a single diplomatic note to a friendly state (a specific action) and defining what a nation will seek throughout the world in the long run. We will divide the notion of foreign policy into four components, ranging in scope from the general to the specific: (1) foreign-policy orientations, (2) national roles, (3) objectives, and (4) actions. This and the next chapter will describe the first three types of outputs and present some preliminary, anecdotal evidence explaining why certain governments adopt certain orientations, roles, or objectives.

Chapters 6 through 11 will describe various types of actions used to protect or achieve orientations, roles, and objectives. More formal attempts will be made in Chapters 12 through 14 to explain all these outputs.

Few states are at any given time concerned with direct threats to their security or "core" values. Some states are so weak in capabilities—the means by which they can influence the behavior of other states—that even if they were vitally interested in a problem, there would be little they could do directly to affect its outcome. The government of Malawi may have well-formulated views on Sino-Soviet relations; but, aside from occasional diplomatic statements, there is little its government can do by itself to influence the state of these relations. Moreover, some states are so geographically remote from the major scenes of international conflict or areas of collaboration that interest on the part of the government or the population as a whole may be difficult to generate. One would not expect the people of Iceland to be particularly interested in the problems of the Central African Republic, and their government would probably not be directly involved in African affairs. Many Europeans and Americans, whose governments maintain extensive commitments around the world and whose foreign-policy objectives and aspirations impinge upon the interests and values of many other societies, often forget that not all countries are equally interested in the great collaborative ventures and conflicts of our era. Many governments have few international concerns outside of advancing or protecting the private interests of their own citizens through routine trade and cultural contacts. Degrees of involvement in affairs of the system thus may vary from the maximum levels attained by major powers to the low number of official international transactions in which Iceland, Gabon, Tonga, or Mauritania are involved. Even the level of involvement of the great powers varies with different issue areas. The Soviet Union is a prime actor in many issue subsystems, from disarmament to colonialism, but it has not been vigorously engaged in the debates on trade and aid between the North and South.

A country's level of involvement in various international issue areas is at least one expression of its general orientation toward the rest of the world. By orientation we mean a state's general attitudes and commitments toward the external environment and its fundamental strategy for accomplishing its domestic and external objectives and for coping with persisting threats. A nation's general strategy or orientation is seldom revealed in any one decision, but results from a series of cumulative decisions made in an effort to adjust objectives, values, and interests to conditions and characteristics of the domestic and external environments.

By examining the structure of power and influence and the actions of political units in diverse international systems, it is possible to identify at least three fundamental orientations that have been adopted recurrently, regardless of historical context. These are (1) isolation, (2) nonalignment, and (3) coalition making and alliance construction. Ministers in the ancient Chinese system under the Chou dynasty recommended these strategies to their leaders, choice depending upon geographic location of the state and its position between other powers. Kautilya, the philosopher of interstate relations during the Chandragupta period in ancient India, also referred to these fundamental orientations as means of increasing power, gaining security, or conducting successful policies of imperialism. Even today, any state's general orientation and strategy toward the external environment can be described by one of these three terms.

In addition to describing the terms, we may ask: Under what circumstances have governments adopted these orientations? What domestic and external conditions help make these strategies or orientations successful, and when do they fail? At least four conditions or variables can help account for the selection of any particular strategy. First is the structure of the international system. The patterns of dominance, subordination, and leadership of an international system establish some limits on the freedom of action of the component units. By definition, it would be impossible for a state in a truly polar system to seek its objectives or defend its interests by isolating itself, nor would a political unit in a hierarchical system attempt to build coalitions against the center. Second, a state's general foreign-policy strategy can be linked to the nature of its domestic attitudes and social and economic needs. Third, the degree to which policy makers perceive a *persisting* external threat to their own values and interests will have great bearing on their orientation toward the external environment. Finally, a state's geographic location, topographical characteristics, and endowment in natural resources can often be linked to its choice of orientations.

ISOLATION

A strategy of political and military isolation is indicated by a low level of involvement in most issue areas of the system, a low number of diplomatic or commerical transactions with other political units and societies, and attempts to seal off the country against various forms of external penetration. Isolationist orientations are often based on the assumption that the state can best gain security and independence by reducing transactions with other units in the system, or by maintaining diplomatic and commercial contacts abroad while handling all perceived or potential threats by building administrative walls around the home base. How are the four variables of system structure, domestic attitudes and needs, threats, and geographic features related to isolationist strategies?

Logically, at least, an isolationist orientation would be adopted, or could succeed, only in a system with a reasonably diffuse structure of power, where military, economic, or ideological threats do not persist and where other states are regularly shifting alliances. A polar system is defined as an international structure in which all states, voluntarily or through compulsion, commit their military capabilities to the purposes of a bloc or bloc leader. In a hierarchical system, isolation might be possible only if the power of the central unit was so weak that it could not reach effectively to every vassal state. This was the case in China during the Western Chou period, when many of the smaller political units on the geographic periphery of the system were so physically isolated from the Chou capital that they were able to develop into powerful states with a minimum of interference from the emperor. They paid lip service to the "Son of Heaven"; but politically they remained independent while their strength grew to the point where they could effectively challenge not only other rising states, but the central monarchy itself. Throughout the Greek period, a number of city states and former colonies deliberately isolated themselves behind the barriers of the Mediterranean Sea as a way of escaping commitments to either side during the Peloponnesian Wars.

Political units that adopt an orientation of isolation are usually economically and socially self-sufficient. In order to maintain a "way of life," including social values, political structures, and economic patterns, the political unit does not have to change the external environment in its favor. Nor, in many cases, does it depend upon others to fulfill its social and economic needs. This does not mean that an isolated state necessarily fails to conduct commercial or diplomatic relations with other states. It may do so, but not to such an extent that conflicts in those relations could lead to unpleasant military consequences or military threats from abroad.

Isolation orientations can be linked directly to the presence of perceived threats, whether military, economic, or cultural. Some political units have remained isolated for centuries because geographic barriers prevented foreign incursions. But most have adopted isolation strategies as a means of coping with an actual or potential threat—not by meeting it in battle, but by withdrawing behind the frontiers and erecting defenses that would make the state impermeable to military attack or cultural infiltration.

Geographic and topographic characteristics are related in many ways to a strategy of isolation. Surrounding high mountains, wide seas, or uninhabitable plains or deserts will afford protection to political units, provided that other states in the system do not possess means for easily bypassing these features. Geographic remoteness reduces the number of potential threats; and protective topographical features provide natural shields behind which to hide, reducing further the number of potential threats. Until the nineteenth century, for instance, high mountain barriers and lack of access routes favored the sustained isolation of Nepal. Nepal was not far from the great centers of British military, economic, and political influence on the Indian subcontinent; but the natural barriers surrounding it were adequate to cope with most massive foreign intrusions. The British were diplomatically and commercially active in Nepal, but not to the extent that they were in other colonial or semicolonial areas. China invaded Tibet in 1950 and began building military roads in the Himalayan valleys, thus making Nepal's position much less secure. Because it is now much more accessible, it is more open to external influences, particularly to the effects of competition between Communist China and India. In other words, given the level of contemporary technology and military potential, Nepal's isolation strategy depends more on the state of Chinese-Indian relations than on geographic features.

The deliberate isolation of Japan for several centuries after the first Japanese contacts with Europeans is one illustration of a state's adopting this strategy in response to a perceived threat and taking advantage of its insularity. In this case, the Japanese emperors sealed off the islands (although they tolerated a minimum of trade with some Europeans) to prevent "barbarian" infiltration, meaning either territorial conquest or the more subtle pollution of Japanese culture and values by alien practices. By the middle of the nineteenth century, however, Western naval power in the Pacific had become so formidable that it could easily breach Japan's "impermeability." In 1854, Japan was isolated. Only five decades later it was making commercial and military coalitions with Great Britain, the United States, and several European countries; and it was acting as one of the important units in major conflicts of the Far East.

Examples of deliberate isolation as a foreign-policy orientation are not prominent in the second half of the twentieth century. For more than a decade, beginning in 1962, the Burmese government systematically reduced its contacts with the outside world and sealed itself off from foreign penetration. Foreign-aid missions (except some from international organizations) were expelled; tourism was proscribed by a rule limiting visitors to a stay of no more than forty-eight hours; the government refused to join regional alliances or even economic and cultural groupings; few Burmese students left to study abroad; foreign-owned private firms were nationalized; all incoming films and literature were censored; and new foreign capital investment was not invited. Burma remained a member of many international organizations, but even in those councils it remained silent and uninvolved. The reasons behind the isolationist orientation were many; but mostly they indicated a fear of becoming an object of great-power rivalry and of having Burmese economic activity dominated by foreigners or its society disrupted by alien cultural forces brought through foreign-aid officials, tourism, and Western-style advertising.

These examples indicate that there may be strong incentives for governments to choose strategies of isolation. Those who support these strategies are not, as many have argued, indifferent to the world around them; on the contrary, they may be realistically assessing international conditions and potential threats. Political units remote from scenes of conflict in the system, relatively independent economically and militarily, and suspicious that involvement would only jeopardize their social, economic, and political values often find that they can best maintain their values and achieve their aspirations through isolationism.

STRATEGIES OF NONALIGNMENT

Traditionally there has been confusion over the differences among such terms as *neutrality, neutralism,* and *nonalignment.* In one sense, they all signify the same type of foreign-policy orientation, where a state will not commit its military capabilities and, sometimes, its diplomatic support to the purposes of another state. Unwillingness to commit military capabilities to others' purposes is the hallmark of nonalignment as a foreign policy strategy, but there are some variations in the circumstances by which a state adopts a nonaligned policy; it is here that neutrality and neutralism have distinct meanings.

Neutrality refers to the *legal status* of a state during armed hostilities. Under the international laws of neutrality, a nonbelligerent in wartime has certain rights and obligations not extended to the belligerents.[1] These rules state, for example, that a neutral may not permit use of its territory as a base for military operations by one of the belligerents, may not furnish military assistance to the belligerents, and may enjoy free passage of its nonmilitary goods on the open seas and, under certain conditions, through belligerent blockades.

A neutralized state is one that must observe these rules during armed conflict but that, during peace, must also refrain from making military alliances with other states. The major differences between a neutralized state and a nonaligned state is that the former has achieved its position by virtue of the actions of others, whereas the latter chooses its orientation by itself and has no guarantees that its position will be honored by others. A state is often neutralized when the great powers agree to guarantee its nonaligned position through a multilateral treaty. The European powers neutralized Switzerland in 1815, Belgium in 1831, and Luxembourg in 1867. More recently, Austria (1955) and Laos (1962) were neutralized by agreement between the major Western governments and the Soviet Union. Under neutralization treaties, the state in question binds itself not to allow foreign troops on its soil or in any way to compromise its status by making military agreements or giving military privileges to other states on its own territory. In turn, the guaranteeing powers undertake not to violate the territorial integrity or rights of the neutral in both wartime and peace.

What motivates the great powers to establish and guarantee the neutrality of certain states? Sometimes, as in Laos, their own rivalry over the territory in question may lead to undesired results, or, more simply, the area under contention may not be worth a possible military confrontation. A solution to this situation is for both sides to withdraw and make an agreement that neither will again seek to gain military advantages in the territory. In other cases, a state may perform functions of value to the major powers, and it is understood that these functions can only be carried out if all nations observe neutrality. For instance, Swiss diplomatic establishments have frequently taken over minimal tasks of communication and representation for countries that have severed diplomatic relations. During both world wars, the Swiss performed many additional services for the belligerents: They cared for prisoners of war, arranged for transfer of stranded diplomatic personnel, and served as the main liaison agents for the small amount of secret diplomatic communication between governments

---

[1] Neutral status and alliance commitments are not necessarily incompatible. For example, if state A makes an agreement to assist state B only if state C attacks, it could still remain neutral if any state other than C attacked B.

at war with each other. Finally, the Swiss government, or the International Red Cross headquarters in Switzerland, has acted as a mediator or channel of communication in preliminary armistice or peace negotiations.

The most common form of nonalignment today is found among those states that, on their own initiative and without the guarantee of other states, refuse to commit themselves *militarily* to the goals and objectives of the major powers. Even though they lend diplomatic support to blocs or bloc leaders on particular issues, they refrain from siding diplomatically with any bloc on *all* issues. Their roles (see below) are *independent* in the system as a whole, although within regions they might well be aligned militarily, ideologically, and economically. The nonaligned states of Europe—Ireland, Sweden, Yugoslavia, and Finland—are usually sympathetic to Western values and interests but do not formally join military organizations such as NATO. They attempt to remain uninvolved in the major bloc conflicts, although on occasion they promote plans for nonviolent settlements. The nonaligned countries in the developing areas similarly avoid formal commitments to blocs, but they show a greater inclination to distrust the major Western powers, criticize publicly the actions of any state, and give vocal support to bloc actions when they are deemed in their own interests.

In the present international context, nonalignment strategies are mostly confined to military matters. On other issues, nations that consider themselves nonaligned do, in fact, create temporary diplomatic and economic coalitions. They have certain common interests, such as supporting anticolonial movements and organizing attempts to obtain better terms of trade from industrialized nations. In international trade conferences and on some issues in the United Nations, the nonaligned states combine to increase their influence vis-à-vis the industrialized nations and bloc leaders. The Group of 77, composed of approximately 115 developing countries, has acted as a reasonably unified diplomatic coalition at a number of international conferences, but most of its members claim to be nonaligned. Moreover, some nonaligned states have sought to create regional military alliances. Nonalignment thus appears more as an orientation toward East–West bloc conflicts than as a true strategy toward all issues in the system or in regions.

Successful strategies of nonalignment would seem possible in international systems with diffuse or diffuse-bloc structures. Theoretically, the military capabilities of member units in a hierarchical system are bound, by hereditary and contractual obligations, to the center unit. If the Chou monarchy was under attack from the "barbarians," or if it waged war to punish a recalcitrant vassal, the other units were obligated to come to its support by supplying foot soldiers and money. In the polar system, where all states belong to antagonistic blocs, there is similarly no room for, or tolerance of, states that attempt to remain neutral or noninvolved in bloc conflicts. In the Chinese system during parts of the Spring and Autumn and Warring States periods, units that attempted to maintain complete autonomy in foreign relations were either forced into alliances or annexed by more powerful neighbors.

Nonalignment orientations can be linked to a number of domestic considerations and pressures. Some political units have adopted this orientation as a means of obtaining maximum economic concessions from both blocs, recognizing that to make permanent military arrangements with one bloc would close off the other as a possible source of supply, markets, and foreign aid. Given the strong commitment of many governments in the Third World to achieve adequate economic growth rates as fast as possible, few can afford to restrict their international trade to any one area of the world. Much less can they afford to restrict their sources of economic aid. Some nonaligned governments feel that because of the political implications of aid agreements, the more sources of aid that are available, the more the nation can effectively counter threats to cut off aid by the donors. To be nonaligned is to maximize opportunities to meet domestic economic needs, while minimizing dependencies.

Nonalignment, it is often argued by its practitioners, also increases the diplomatic influence of those who adopt it as a foreign-policy strategy. They suggest that through alliances, nations give up freedom of action and lose the opportunity to formulate their policies in terms of their own needs. In too many instances, an alliance forces weak states to sacrifice their own interests for the needs of the great powers; and, when tensions turn into crises, the small alliance partners are usually unable to affect the outcomes, even though these may have serious consequences on their interests. As independent states, however, nonaligned nations have room to maneuver and may be able to influence the behavior and actions of *both* blocs.[2]

A strategy of nonalignment is particularly well suited to the domestic *political* conditions and needs of developing countries. By being expressed sometimes in anti-Western terms, it accords with the anticolonial attitudes of indigenous elites and mass political parties. By emphasizing dangers to the nation from the machinations of the great powers, it helps create national unity, a commodity sorely needed in societies torn apart by religious, tribal, or language conflicts. To many African and Asian nationalist leaders (most represent the first generation of native leaders), nonalignment foreign-policy strategies express and emphasize the independence of their countries. Understandably, they find that it pays political dividends at home and abroad not to give any impression of making military or ideological commitments to their former colonial overlords or to states that might compromise their independence in the future.

Nonalignment may be explained by perceptions of external threat as well as by domestic economic and political variables. Nations have traditionally sought to maintain their independence and territorial integrity by withdrawing or avoiding involvement in conflict areas. In the present international context, however, the fear is not so much of a *direct* threat to independence—except perhaps by way of "neocolonialism"—as it is concern that bloc conflicts will spill over into nonaligned areas or that regional conflicts in the developing

---

[2] This type of argument is ably presented by Alex Quaison-Sackey in his *Africa Unbound* (New York: Praeger, 1963), pp. 105–11.

world will attract great power intervention. The nonaligned states have had few concrete interests in the outcome of great coldwar crises such as Berlin, Hungary, or Vietnam. They have always expressed a fear, however, that such confrontations could escalate into nuclear warfare, which would eventually engulf them. Those nonaligned states that have perceived a *direct* threat emanating from one of the great powers have also considered abandoning the nonaligned strategy in favor of military alliances with those who could offer them protection.

Nonalignment as a strategy to defend independence and secure economic and social needs can usually be expected to succeed if the state in question is reasonably distant from the main areas of international conflict. States like Switzerland and Sweden managed to stay outside of both world conflicts in the twentieth century in part because of their geographic and strategic position. Even though neither was very distant from the main scenes of battle, both enjoyed favorable topographical and geographic features: The high mountains surrounding Switzerland constituted barriers that would have made Nazi invasion of the country extremely costly. The Germans could control both the Baltic Sea and parts of the North Atlantic by occupying Denmark and Norway, whereas control of Sweden was not crucial to either of these objectives. In other words, a strategy of nonalignment may be sustained successfully even in wartime if the area is of little strategic value to bloc leaders or various belligerents.

What other conditions can be linked to the success or failure of nonalignment strategies? Successful nonalignment is also basically a problem of credibility—convincing other states that the strategy is actually advantageous to their own interests. When a nonaligned or neutralized state compromises its independent position or is forced to compromise it by outside pressures, then the strategy will fail. Actions, not just words, have to conform to the expectations of other states.

To safeguard its position, particularly when a crisis or conflict develops around or near its frontiers, the nonaligned state must avoid any kind of military engagements with major powers. Usually this means that it must also have the capacity to resist incursions upon its territory or pressures by outside powers to use its land for military purposes. If the nonaligned or neutralized state cannot resist such pressures, it can no longer expect others to respect its special position.

The most difficult time to maintain a nonaligned orientation is during large-scale war. Throughout history, nonaligned and neutralized states have proclaimed their intention of remaining uninvolved in great-power conflicts, only to be invaded or forced into alliances by those who respected their position in peacetime. Leopold III declared Belgium neutral in 1936, but the Belgians hardly had the capacity to enforce this position against the Nazi war machine, whose most direct route to France lay through Belgian territory. Norway, too, declared its neutrality prior to the outbreak of World War II; but, as its geographic location was of importance to German military operations against Great Britain in the North Atlantic, it was invaded in 1940. Even where nonaligned or neutralized states are not invaded at the beginning of military operations, wars have a tendency to "spill over" into areas originally uninvolved. A neutral state such as Laos was unable to maintain its territorial integrity during the war in Vietnam, because its territory was useful to the North Vietnamese for infiltrating troops and matériel into South Vietnam.[3]

Successful strategies of nonalignment thus require the juxtaposition of many conditions, including favorable structure of power and influence in the system, national capacity to defend independence and territorial integrity against those who do not honor a neutral position, the benevolent attitude or indifference of the great powers, reasonable remoteness from the main centers of international conflict, and a reasonable amount of internal political stability. In times of great international conflict or widespread war, however, most nations gravitate either voluntarily or through coercion toward alliances.

DIPLOMATIC COALITIONS AND MILITARY ALLIANCES

Governments that seek to construct permanent diplomatic coalitions or military alliances assume that they cannot achieve their objectives, defend their interests, or deter perceived threats by mobilizing their own capabilities. Thus, they rely upon, and make commitments to, other states that face similar external problems or share similar objectives.

Of the five types of international systems, alliance strategies appear commonly in all but the hierarchical variety. In the Western Chou era, the feudal units were subservient to the central monarchy, and the only coalitions sanctioned by the leader of the system were those between itself and the subordinate units. Secret coalitions between the vassal states were deemed treasonable; but, as the superior–subordinate, contractual relations of the system decayed, owing to the growth of power among feudal units on the periphery, alliances became commonplace. In the diffuse system, alliances appear regularly but tend to be temporary in so far as state objectives derive from specific needs and interests rather than ideological aspirations. In the polar and diffuse-bloc systems, alliances tend to be closely knit structures in which the smaller alliance partners do not easily remove themselves from the bloc. Bloc alliances persist over a period of time, because they usually express deep ideological cleavages between bloc leaders, not just dynastic or commercial rivalries.

Alliance strategies are closely linked to domestic needs. States that share common economic problems are likely to form trading groups or diplomatic coalitions that maintain solidarity on trade issues. Thus, while on many problems today the developing countries do not constitute a bloc in the military-diplomatic

---

[3] The conditions that help sustain a policy of nonalignment are discussed by Risto Hyvärinen in "Neutrality in International Politics," an unpublished paper prepared for the Center for International Affairs, Harvard University (April 1964), p. 71.

sense, they have joined together on the question of obtaining more favorable commercial relations with the industrialized countries. The most effective economic coalition has been the Organization of Petroleum Exporting Countries (OPEC), which has successfully raised the price of oil in the face of strenuous consumer objections and attempts by the United States to pit the members against each other on non-oil issues. The member states obviously have a common interest in obtaining more revenue for their sole natural resource; but, acting singly, they could never achieve their objective, since consumers could just go to another supplier. By creating a cartel, or producers' monopoly, their bargaining power is enhanced far beyond the mere sum of their national strengths.

Nations that decide for various domestic or ideological reasons to undertake programs of territorial or revolutionary expansion may combine to form aggressive military alliances. Alliances have also bolstered weak regimes and served essentially domestic political purposes rather than defense against external threats. Throughout history, political units have offered their military capabilities to other states in order to help maintain friendly governments in power or perpetuate a particular dynasty against internal and externally supported rebellion or subversion. Although most alliances today are initially formulated for defense against a common external enemy, their effect may be to protect weak regimes against internal dissidence and revolution. Military aid given under alliance agreements may be used by the recipient to quell rebellions, while the military training assistance it receives often comes in the form of instruction in riot-control techniques and counterinsurgency warfare. In both Communist and Western alliance systems, some partners have joined basically out of the need to secure external protection against internal unrest.

Common perceptions of threat and widespread attitudes of insecurity are probably the most frequent sources of military alliances, whereas complementarity or common economic gains underlie economic coalitions. As Thucydides noted over 2,000 years ago and as modern experimental and historical studies have substantiated, mutual fear is the most solid basis upon which to organize an alliance.[4] Nevertheless, because in the face of common threats governments have also chosen neutrality (witness Belgium in 1936), we cannot say that this factor is a *sufficient* condition for the formation of an alliance; we cannot predict that if two states, A and B, commonly perceive C as an enemy, they will form an alliance. It is probably, however, a *necessary* condition: The chance that A and B would form a military alliance if they did *not* commonly perceive C as a threat would be low. Nor are other factors, such as internal stability in the partners, ideological affinity, and common economic values, while all significant in helping alliances cohere, sufficient in themselves to create or maintain the alliances. States, therefore, construct military alliances usually to act as deterrents

---

[4] Thucydides, *A History of the Peloponnesian War*, trans. Benjamin Jowett (Oxford: Ashendene Press, 1930), Book III, Par. 11.

against those that are making demands against their interests or posing immediate military threats. NATO was the primary Western response to the Berlin blockade, the Communist *coup d'état* in Czechoslovakia in 1948, and the expectation that similar actions, backed by the Red Army, would take place in France and Italy. The Warsaw alliance was formed in 1955 in response to the rapid recovery of West Germany during the early 1950s, its incorporation into NATO in the winter of 1954–1955, and the Communist expectation of a possible German "war of revenge" against East Europe.

Geographic characteristics are often relevant in the construction of alliances, although, as with other conditions, neither proximity nor topographical features are sufficient to cause alliances to be formed or to sustain them. Both Kautilya and Machiavelli advised their princes to form alliances with their enemies' neighbors, and certainly the possibility that the target of an alliance may have to fight a two-front war is one consideration underlying some modern alliances. The French interest in an alliance with Russia after 1871 was aroused in part by recognition that the best way to deter another Prussian attack would be to confront that country with a military response from both east and west. Hitler's nonaggression treaty with the Soviet Union in 1939 was designed specifically to prevent a Soviet-Western coalition, so that he could prosecute the war against France and England without having to worry about a Soviet attack in the east. In the 1950s, Secretary of State John Foster Dulles fixed the United States' defense perimeter on the very borders of the Soviet Union and China. Through NATO, SEATO, the Baghdad Pact, ANZUS, and mutual security treaties with Taiwan and Japan, Dulles hoped to create a military belt encircling the entire Communist world. Proximity to the Soviet bloc was an important factor in choosing alliance partners. Those that were farther away from China or the Soviet Union received less military and economic aid than did the "perimeter allies," unless they hosted air or naval bases for American strategic forces.

But for every case where proximity was a factor in alliance formation, we can probably cite cases where alliances were made by partners relatively distant from each other and from their common, perceived enemy. Indeed, one systematic study of 130 military alliances, nonaggression treaties, and ententes between 1815 and 1965 shows no relationship between the distances separating allies and the creation or duration of the alliance.[5] Thus, no generalization can be offered on the relationship between alliances and geography. In any case, common perception of threat would seem to be more important as a major source of an alliance orientation in foreign policy.

Types of Alliances

Military alliances can be classified and compared according to four main criteria: (1) the nature of the *casus foederis* (the situation in which mutual commitments

---

[5] See Ole R. Holsti, P. Terrence Hopmann, and John D. Sullivan, *Unity and Disintegration in International Alliances: Comparative Studies* (New York: John Wiley, 1973), Chap. 2.

are to become operational); (2) the type of commitments undertaken by the treaty signatories; (3) the degree of military integration of the military forces of the alliance partners; and (4) the geographic scope of the treaty.

THE CASUS FOEDERIS.   Although partners to an alliance have some similar or overlapping foreign-policy objectives, negotiators of the treaty are usually very cautious in defining the *casus foederis.* Some treaties, particularly those in recent years that have been used for offensive purposes, contain a very vague definition of the situation that will bring the alliance into operation. Because of universal condemnation of outright aggressive military alliances, offensive treaties seldom express their real purpose. The 1939 German-Italian "Pact of Steel," for example, provided: "If it should happen, against the wishes and hopes of the contrasting parties, that one of them should become involved in warlike complications . . . the other contracting party will come to its aid as an ally and will support it with all its military forces." The term "warlike complications" is so vague that it could (and did) commit Italy to assist Hitler in almost any situation. Soviet mutual-assistance treaties with Bulgaria and Romania (1948) also had such obscure definitions of the *casus foederis* ("drawn into military activities") that it was difficult to predict when and under what exact circumstances the Soviet, Romanian, and Bulgarian armies would begin military operations. In contrast to the vague *casus foederis* are those that contain a very precise definition of the situation in which the alliance is to be put into effect militarily. The NATO treaty, in Article 5, states that military measures can be taken only in response to an actual *armed attack* on one of the signatories.

COMMITMENTS UNDERTAKEN.   Alliance treaties also differ according to the type of responses and responsibilities required once the situation calling for action develops. The Soviet-Bulgarian treaty of 1948 unequivocally provided that if one of the parties is "drawn into military activities," the other will *"immediately* give . . . military and other help by all means at its disposal." This type of commitment is called a "hair-trigger" clause, because it automatically commits the signatories to military action if the *casus foederis* occurs. A similar clause is found in the Brussels pact among Great Britain, France, Belgium, the Netherlands, and Luxembourg. Since the clause establishes automatic commitments, it leaves little leeway for decision makers and diplomats to decide what to do once the *casus foederis* arises.

In contrast, some treaties only spell out vaguely the type of responses the treaty partners will make. The ANZUS treaty, which ties Australia, New Zealand, and the United States into a defensive alliance system, provides that each party will "act to meet the danger . . . in accordance with its constitutional processes." This treaty contains no precise military commitments, nor does it prescribe any course of action to which the parties commit themselves if one of them is attacked. Similarly, the renewed Japanese-American security treaty of 1960 provides only for "consultations" between the parties if Japan is attacked.

Alliance responsibilities may be mutual or one-sided. Mutual-defense treaties theoretically require all the signatories to assume equal commitments toward each other. According to the principles in the NATO and Warsaw treaties, an attack on any one of the signatories is to be considered an attack on all, requiring every signatory to come to the aid of the victim of aggression or armed attack. Other alliance treaties impose unequal burdens on the signatories. After "consultations," the United States may become obligated to defend Japan against external attack, but the Japanese are *not* obligated under the 1960 security treaty to assist in the defense of North America if war or invasion should occur there.

A variation of the unequal-burden treaty is the *guarantee* treaty, whereby one or more states receive guarantees for their security from a third party or parties, while the guaranteeing power or powers receive nothing in return except perhaps the possibility of enhancing stability and peace. Guarantee treaties of this variety were popular in the 1920s; one prominent example was the Locarno treaty of 1925, in which Great Britain and Italy undertook to come to the assistance of France, Belgium, or Germany, depending on which was attacked or was the target of a violation of the Franco-Belgian-German frontiers. For guaranteeing these frontiers, Italy and Great Britain received in return no tangible commitments from the beneficiaries.

INTEGRATION OF FORCES. Alliances may also be distinguished according to the degree of integration of military forces. Alliance treaties in historic international systems seldom provided for more than casual coordination of military planning, while national forces remained organizationally and administratively distinct. European alliances in the eighteenth century typically required signatories to provide a specified number of men and/or funds for the common effort, but otherwise set forth no plans for coordinated military operations or integrating forces or commands. Any coordination that did take place was the result of ad hoc decisions made after hostilities began. In one of the most enduring alliances of the nineteenth century, the Austro-German Dual Alliance of 1879, rudimentary military coordination was carried out only through the services of military attachés in Vienna and Berlin; and when the alliance was put to the test in 1914, German military and political leaders knew very little about Austria's mobilization plans.

Since World War II, the major leaders of both coalitions have sought to increase military integration to the extent that allied forces would operate, if war came, almost as one unified armed force. Integration may be accomplished by establishing a supreme commander of all allied forces (such as the Supreme Allied Commander, Europe, in NATO), standardizing weapons systems for all national forces (barely begun in NATO), integrating military personnel of different countries into one command structure (as proposed in the ill-fated European Defense Community), or permitting one of the major alliance partners to organize, draft, and direct all strategic and tactical war plans for the other partners.

Major alliances today also have permanent headquarters, continuous political and military consultations, innumerable meetings of technical experts, and a continuing avalanche of memoranda and staff studies.

Not only have some alliances become large organizations, but the manner in which they operate has changed since the eighteenth century. In that period, alliances were often concluded only *after* an armed attack had occurred, so that commitments were undertaken only for a very limited range of objectives. Today, however, alliances have a greater deterrence function. The purpose of the alliance is to prevent crises and increase diplomatic influence, not just to fight a war. Major contemporary alliances are built on the assumption of *bloc* politics and on the presence of almost permanently congruent foreign-policy objectives or permanent external threats. The lengthy sequence of threat perception–crisis– mobilization–declaration of war, a sequence that in the eighteenth century often lasted several months, can no longer be assumed with the new technology of warfare. The elements of speed and surprise, vital to military success, require that alliance commitments and war plans be agreed upon and drafted *before* any crisis occurs. In comparison to 200 years ago, alliance systems today are less flexible, more permanent, and more highly organized.

GEOGRAPHICAL SCOPE.   Finally, alliances differ with respect to the scope of their coverage. Soviet mutual-aid treaties are designed to cover only the territory of the state that is attacked or "drawn into military activities," but one of the major problems in drafting and interpreting the NATO treaty concerned whether the signatories could be committed to defend the overseas colonies or territories of France or Great Britain. The French and British governments insisted that NATO obligations extend to at least some of their overseas territories; so Article 5 of the treaty was drafted to read: ". . . an armed attack on one or more of the Parties is deemed to include an attack on the territory of any of the Parties . . . , on the Algerian department of France, on the occupation forces of any Party in Europe, on the islands under jurisdiction of any Party in the North Atlantic area north of the Tropic of Cancer, or on the vessels or aircraft in this area of any of the Parties." In 1965, coverage of the treaty was extended to Malta, which had received protection under Article 5 by virtue of being "an island under the jurisdiction of" Great Britain, but which received its independence in 1964.

Although these distinctions relating to the forms and types of alliances may seem quite technical, they are important because precise definitions of scope, *casus foederis,* and obligations lend predictability to the responses alliance partners will make in crisis situations. Predictability is an important element in international stability and may become crucial in crisis situations. One of the main objections against secret treaties and alliances is that decision makers cannot plan actions and predict responses of both friends and potential enemies if they are not familiar with treaty commitments and obligations. However, it must be acknowledged that treaties do not provide complete predictability, and that the circumstances of the moment will largely determine the responses alliance partners make in critical times. The NATO treaty, for example, stipulates that the parties will decide how to commit themselves only at the time an "armed attack" takes place against one of the signatories. Yet, if the Soviets launched a massive invasion of Western Europe, there is little doubt that previously drafted retaliatory plans of the NATO bureaucracy would come into effect almost instantaneously, with slight latitude for negotiations and discussions among the treaty partners. In such a situation, even when alliance commitments are common knowledge, do alliance strategies succeed?

No generalizations can be offered as to whether defensive alliances successfully deter aggression or provide stability for the international system. Presumably, a potential aggressor faced with an overwhelming coalition against it will not risk destruction of its society when it possesses foreknowledge of certain defeat. Yet decision makers do not always behave rationally in crisis situations, and there are enough examples (discussed in more detail in Chapter 11) of their going to war knowing that the probability of success was low to disprove this presumption. All we can say is that alliances probably inject a factor of caution among decision makers with aggressive designs; defensive alliances increase greatly the risks and costs to the aggressor, but do not necessarily prevent organized violence. We can only speculate on the wars that did not begin because alliances effectively performed the deterrence function; but both past and present reveal occasions when defensive alliances failed to deter, lower tensions, or promote stability in the system.

Strains in Alliances

Aside from poor military coordination or planning, one reason that alliances may fail to deter potential aggressors is that they lack political cohesiveness or are riven by quarrels and political disagreements. Presumably, any military coalition will be more effective to the extent that its members agree on the major objectives to be achieved, help each other diplomatically, and trust that once the *casus foederis* arises, the partners will in fact meet their commitments. In any international system comprised of independent and sovereign states, however, there is no automatic guarantee that even the most solemn undertakings will be fulfilled if those commitments are in conflict with the prevailing interests of different governments. Several situations can cause strains in alliances, impairing their effectiveness both as deterrents and as fighting organizations.

The first is when the objectives of two or more parties begin to diverge. If all partners of a defensive military coalition perceive a common enemy or threat, the alliance is likely to withstand strains caused by ideological incompatibilities or distrust arising from personality differences between political leaders. But if the objectives become incongruent, or the potential enemy of one alliance partner is not the enemy of the other, serious problems of cooperation and coordination arise and make the alliance more formal than real. The Franco–

Prussian alliance of 1741, for instance, lasted only several years before the diverging objectives of the signatories led to bitter quarrels over the prosecution of military campaigns. Frederick the Great was interested above all in destroying Austria and detaching Bohemia from Maria Theresa's realm; whereas French policy makers, less interested in dealing a blow to Austria, wanted to drive the English from the continent, in general, and from Flanders, in particular. The Prussians were hardly interested in these French objectives, with the result that there was no coordination of military operations, no trust in each other's diplomatic maneuvers, and, ultimately, no alliance.

More recently, the American-Pakistan alliance has been more a means through which Pakistan has received arms than a coalition leading to meaningful diplomatic cooperation. When the United States induced Pakistan to join SEATO in 1954, it regarded the Moslem country as a bulwark against communism. The purpose of the alliance, as seen from Washington, was to prevent Russia or Communist China from moving into South Asia. Pakistan, however, concluded the alliance primarily to obtain American arms and diplomatic support against India, its traditional enemy. Diplomatic relations between the United States and Pakistan reached a low point in the 1960s when Pakistan criticized the United States for failure to lend it support on the Kashmir issue and, as the Pakistan government saw it, for giving comfort to the Indians. Left virtually isolated on the Kashmir problem, Pakistan turned increasingly to Communist China, which was also embroiled in a border conflict with India. The American response to Pakistan's flirtation with China was manifested in reduction of economic and military aid. American diplomats desperately tried to induce the government of Pakistan to reiterate that the "common enemy" was China, a view the Pakistanis could not easily accept as long as their only diplomatic support against India came from Peking.[6]

Alliance cohesion is also apt to be strained if a threat arises against only one or a few of the alliance partners, so that other members do not perceive the same threat.[7] The Cyprus issue has long divided Greece and Turkey and created strains between each of them and other NATO members. Planning to fight an unlikely war against the Soviet Union seems less important to them than the emotion-laden ethnic issues surrounding the Cyprus conflict. Indeed, in this case, the alliance has functioned more as an arena for prosecuting an intraalliance conflict than as an organization for collective security.

A third factor that may lead to strains in military alliances is incompatibility of the major social and political values of allying states. By themselves, ideological incompatibilities seldom prevent formation of military coalitions as long as the parties face a common enemy. The study by Ole R. Holsti and his colleagues of 130 alliances, nonaggression pacts, and ententes reveals that ideology is not an important factor in creating alliances, although ideologically homoge-

---

[6] See Mohammed Ayub Khan, "The Pakistan-American Alliance: Stresses and Strains," *Foreign Affairs*, 42 (1964), 195–209.

[7] Holsti et al., *Unity and Disintegration in International Alliances*, p. 98.

neous partners are more likely to create alliances of high commitment (such as military undertakings rather than mere ententes).[8] We would hypothesize that in a condition of high threat, alliances of ideologically heterogeneous partners might cohere; but, given lack of a common enemy, or even a low level of threat perception, ideological factors would operate to reduce alliance cohesion. Certainly there are recent illustrations that would lend some support to the hypothesis. Ideologically mixed alliances may be confronted with misunderstandings and suspicion, usually expressed in unwillingness to share military secrets or coordinate military programs and campaigns, and a decided feeling that the other alliance partner is failing to live up to its commitments. During World War II, the Soviet Union, which for two decades had urged and worked for the overthrow of "decadent" bourgeois regimes in Western Europe, eagerly formed an alliance with these regimes once it was attacked by Germany. The threat posed by Nazi Germany to the rest of the world was so apparent that even Western liberal democrats and conservatives supported the alliance with the Communists. On the other hand, the wartime alliance operated with many irritations because of deep-seated attitudes of distrust and ideological differences. Stalin feared that the Western Allies would make a separate peace with Germany, leaving the Nazis free to crush his regime; alternately, he interpreted the failure of the Allies to invade France before 1944 as evidence of their intention to let the Nazis and Communists bleed each other to death so that the capitalists could come in later to pick up the pieces. Even at the administrative level, distrust was reflected in Stalin's refusal to allow British and American military officials to observe Russian operations in the field, let the Western Allies establish air bases on Russian territory, or permit Lend-Lease officers to investigate Russian military and matériel requirements. The allied wartime coalition was only a temporary marriage of convenience. On the other hand, the Anglo-American alliance is strong and withstands frequent disagreements between the two partners, not just because the overall interests of the two countries coincide, but also because the two countries represent similar cultural, political, and social traditions.

Development of nuclear weapons may, finally, have divisive effects on modern alliances.[9] In the post–World War II period, most states of Western Europe were eager to receive the protection of the American "nuclear umbrella." Militarily weak, they had no capacity to deter a possible Soviet invasion carried out by the massive Red Army in Eastern Europe and had to allocate their scarce resources for rebuilding their war-torn economies. By the 1960s, the situation had changed. Europe was recovered economically and entering a period of un-

---

[8] See *Ibid.*, pp. 66–68.

[9] For experimental evidence on the divisive effects of the spread of nuclear weapons technology, see Richard A. Brody, "Some Systemic Effects of the Spread of Nuclear Weapons Technology: A Study Through Simulation of a Multi-Nuclear Future," *Journal of Conflict Resolution,* 7 (1963), 663–753.

precedented prosperity. The Russians no longer possessed a military manpower advantage as compared to NATO. Most important, the nuclear monopoly held by the United States in the late 1940s and early 1950s had come to an end. Washington, New York, and Houston were as vulnerable to Russian nuclear attack as Leningrad, Moscow, and Baku were to an American nuclear salvo. In a system of Soviet-American *mutual* deterrence, some observers—particularly French military officials—questioned whether the United States would be willing to destroy itself in order to protect Western Europe from the Soviet Union.

These officials underlined their doubts by publicizing simple hypothetical situations. Suppose the Soviet government decided to take over West Berlin, an action the Russian army in East Germany could carry out with a minimum of immediate Western military resistance. Would the United States retaliate with nuclear weapons against the Russians, knowing that the Russians would respond immediately against American cities? In citing such situations, these observers have raised a fundamental question of military planning in the nuclear age. Is a deterrent really credible if the guaranteeing power—in this case the United States—knows beforehand that it must destroy itself to save others? During the 1960s, the French government argued that even though it found no fault with American *intentions* to defend Europe, it was not convinced that in all possible crisis situations, the Americans could be expected to live up to their commitments. This is not a uniquely American weakness, they emphasized. It is a fact of international life that no state is apt to invite its own destruction in order to defend others. In this kind of nuclear stalemate situation, the "others" must be armed with nuclear weapons so that if the "nuclear umbrella" fails to operate, smaller allies would still have independent means of deterring possible moves against their vital interests. It is to cover the 5 percent of hypothetical cases when the United States might not retaliate, the French argued, that Europeans must have their own nuclear weapons.

By itself, this type of reasoning would not create serious strains in an alliance—unless the holder of the "nuclear umbrella" does not want its allies to possess such weapons. This, indeed, has been the case in NATO, for, just as the French have been concerned that the United States deterrent may not be totally reliable, so American planners have expressed a fear that if the French develop an independent nuclear capacity—as they have—they might use the weapons in a manner contrary to American interests. It is assumed in Washington that if the French ever used their nuclear weapons, the situation would automatically drag the United States into the war. American strategists also point out that if the French have independent nuclear weapons, why shouldn't the Germans, Dutch, Belgians, and Italians have them as well? An alliance in which each nation is independently drafting plans to fight *its* kind of war for *its* political objectives is an alliance bound to lack coordination and common purpose. It is one of the paradoxes of nuclear weapons that although they are supposed to provide increased security for alliances, they may create political dissension instead. Because the consequences of nuclear war are potentially so terrible, a doubt must be raised about any alliance commitments in the atomic age: In the crisis, will any state risk its own destruction to save others?

NATIONAL ROLES AND ROLE CONCEPTIONS

All independent units in an international system (we have excluded colonies, satrapies, and highly penetrated states from the discussion) reveal one of the three traditional orientations. These orientations themselves reflect such factors as the structure of the system, perception of threats, levels of involvement, radical–conservative attitudes, and the like. However, national roles are foreign-policy outputs associated only with states that are involved in systemwide and regional affairs. Many of today's microstates, such as the Maldive Islands or Lesotho, although proclaiming or displaying some interests in other states, do not see themselves as playing any distinct role in the world. We can consider a national-role conception as the policy makers' definitions of the general kinds of decisions, commitments, rules, and actions suitable to their state and of the functions their state should perform in a variety of geographic and issue settings. Typical national roles are "regional defender," the role of protecting other states in a defined area, or "mediator," the role of assisting in international conflict resolution. Some people ascribed to the United States in the 1960s the role of "world policeman," even though there is little evidence that American policy makers thought in these terms. The Soviet Union's traditional role in relation to East Europe, as consistently enunciated in Soviet speeches, has been that of "regional defender" or "protector of the faith" (against the machinations of imperialism).

National role conceptions are closely related to orientations. Roles, too, reflect basic predispositions, fears, and attitudes toward the outside world as well as systemic, geographic, and economic variables. But they are more specific than orientations, because they suggest or lead to more discrete acts. For instance, we could predict with reasonable probability that a government that consistently portrays itself as a "mediator" would, when confronted with a regional or world conflict, offer to intervene in various conflict-resolving ways. If a state declares itself nonaligned, all we know is that, in relation to the two blocs, it will avoid military commitments. Other than that, we know or can predict little about its other foreign-policy activities or day-to-day decisions.

Types of Role

A study based on content analysis of speeches by high-level policy makers in seventy-one countries over the period 1965–1967 revealed that there are at least sixteen types of national roles that are components of the foreign policies of states.[10] The list below is arranged in order of the level of activity implied by the role conception. Those at the top reflect, generally, high involvement, usually of an active, radical, and strong character; those at the bottom refer to states whose orientations tend to reflect noninvolvement, few foreign-policy actions, conservatism, passiveness, and weakness.

1. **Bastion of the Revolution, Liberator.**   Some governments hold that they have a duty to organize or lead various types of revolutionary movements abroad. One task of their state, as they see it, is to liberate others or to act as the bastion of foreign revolutionary movements—that is, to provide an area that foreign revolutionary leaders can regard as a source of physical and moral support, as well as an ideological inspirer. Chinese foreign-policy pronouncements in the 1950s and 1960s were rich in allusions to the international role. Such allusions are also found in the statements of many leaders of newly independent nations.

2. **Regional Leader.**   The themes in this role conception refer to duties or special responsibilities that a government perceives for itself in relation to states in a region with which it identifies. These themes are prominent in Libyan statements on its position in the Middle East and occasionally in American conceptions of its international tasks.

3. **Regional Protector.**   This role conception, although it perhaps implies special leadership responsibilities on a regional or issue-area basis, places emphasis on providing protection for adjacent regions. Such role conceptions are routine in foreign-policy statements emanating from Australia, New Zealand, the Soviet Union, Great Britain, and the United States.

4. **Active Independent.**   Most government statements supporting the strategy of nonalignment are little more than affirmations of an "independent" role in foreign policy. Some states, however, say that independence should not imply isolation or noninvolvement. The themes in the role conception emphasize the necessity to increase involvement through establishing diplomatic relations with as many states as possible and, occasionally, to become involved as mediators in bloc conflicts. Active independent role conceptions are often found in the foreign-policy statements of high officials in Yugoslavia, India, Malaysia, and Rumania.

5. **Liberation Supporter.**   Unlike the bastion-of-the-revolution role conception, the role of liberation supporter does not indicate formal responsibilities for organizing, leading, or physically supporting liberation movements

---

[10] The full study is reported in K.J. Holsti, "National Role Conceptions in the Study of Foreign Policy," *International Studies Quarterly*, 14 (1970), 233–309.

abroad. Most developing nations see themselves as simple supporters of national liberation or anticolonial movements. They are, in brief, sympathizers of these movements. Therefore, we can predict, for example, that on colonial issues in the United Nations, these governments would always vote in an anticolonial manner.

6. ANTIIMPERIALIST AGENT. Where imperialism is perceived as a serious threat, many governments see themselves as agents of the "struggle" against this menace. The governments of the Soviet Union, Vietnam, and Libya, among others, are prominent antiimperialist agents.

7. DEFENDER OF THE FAITH. Some governments view their foreign-policy tasks in terms of defending values (rather than specified territories) from attack. President Kennedy, in his inaugural speech, for instance, claimed that the United States would "pay any price, bear any burden, meet any hardship, support any friend, or oppose any foe to assure the survival and success of liberty." In a similar vein, Walter Ulbricht, the former government leader of East Germany, saw his state as having a major responsibility for "defending the humanitarian traditions of the Europeans against Americanism and ruthless German militarism."[11]

8. MEDIATOR–INTEGRATOR. A number of contemporary governments perceive themselves as capable of, or responsible for, fulfilling or undertaking special mediation tasks to reconcile other states or groups of states. They see themselves as either regional or global "fixers." Such themes were frequent in foreign-policy statements coming from Canada, France, Rumania, the United States, and Yugoslavia for the period on which the study was based.

9. REGIONAL-SUBSYSTEM COLLABORATOR. The themes in this role conception differ from those in the mediator–integrator category in that they do not merely envisage occasional interposition into areas or issues of conflict; they indicate, rather, far-reaching commitments to cooperative efforts with other states to build wide communities, to coalesce, cooperate, and integrate with other political units. These themes are strong in some European nations regarding the Common Market, in most Communist states concerning cooperation among their ruling parties, and among some newer states like Malaysia.

10. DEVELOPER. The themes in this role conception indicate a special duty or obligation to assist developing countries. References to special skills or advantages for undertaking such continuing tasks also appear frequently. Most of the industrialized countries, both East and West, see this as one of their international or regional roles.

[11] German Democratic Republic, Ministry of Foreign Affairs, *Foreign Affairs Bulletin* (Oct. 30, 1967), p. 243.

11. BRIDGE.   This role conception usually appears in vague form, and it seems to stimulate no action. Whereas the mediator–integrator role implies various forms of diplomatic interposition into areas or issues of conflict, the bridge concept is much more ephemeral. Some states, such as Pakistan and Cyprus, merely mention that because of their unique geographic location or multiethnic culture, they are in a unique situation to create understanding among other states, or to act as a bridge in communications between other states.

12. FAITHFUL ALLY.   Policy makers see most alliances today as one-way propositions. Many governments receive alliance *guarantees* from other states, but in no way commit themselves to support the foreign-policy objectives of the guaranteeing state. A faithful-ally role conception is one in which the policy makers declare that they will support, with all means possible, their fraternal allies. They are not so much concerned with receiving aid as with giving the appearance of committing aid to others. East Germany and Great Britain, among others, often emphasize their alliance commitments in this way.

13. INDEPENDENT.   This role conception is enunciated by the leaders of a large proportion of the world's contemporary states. The statements simply claim that on any given matter, the government will pursue its own best interests; otherwise, they do not imply any particular task or function in the system. Many of the small states that have few foreign-policy objectives and are involved very little in world or regional affairs describe themselves as independents.

14. EXAMPLE.   This role conception emphasizes the importance of promoting prestige and gaining influence in the international system by pursuing certain domestic policies. For example, the former Prime Minister of Malaysia argued that his country could best contribute to the stability of Southeast Asia by undertaking internal development programs successfully and demonstrating to other states in the region that a multiethnic society can resolve its problems through democratic procedures.

15. INTERNAL DEVELOPMENT.   This concept refers not to a given task or function within the international system but to the notion that most efforts of the government should be directed towards problems of internal development. It also suggests a desire to remain noninvolved in international political matters. Such statements often come from Burma and Pakistan.

16. OTHER ROLE CONCEPTIONS.   Absent in this list is the notion of the *balancer,* a role that is traditional in diplomatic history. In the statements reviewed for this study, only the French government under former President de Gaulle alluded to a national task of balancing between great powers, or even lesser powers. Whatever the analytical utility of the concept of balance of power, it is clear that, today, most governments do not choose the balancer role. Finally, some governments have their own version of the *antiimperialist agent* role. China and Albania see themselves also as *antirevisionist agents.* A few nations, especially Nationalist China, see themselves as performing tasks amounting to an *anti-Communist agent role,* and many of the Middle Eastern states portray themselves as special agents in the struggle against Zionism.

The first conclusion about national-role conceptions and foreign policy is that most governments, and all of those that have a reasonably high level of involvement in international affairs, see themselves as performing several roles, in different sets of relationships, simultaneously. In the sample of seventy-one nations, the average number of national roles per state referred to in speeches, press conferences, and the like, for the two-year period, was 4.6. Some of the most active states, like Egypt, the United States, China, and the Soviet Union, saw themselves as playing seven or eight national roles in various international contexts. Smaller and less-involved states, such as Sri Lanka, Burma, Niger, or Portugal, had only one role conception. Most small states would have none. The study cited here generally displays that the more active a state is in international affairs, the more role conceptions it will develop. If this is true, then we would expect that national role conceptions accurately reflect different sets of relationships in which a state is involved.

In Chapters 6 through 11, we will discuss types of actions as components of foreign policy. Here, it might be useful to suggest the linkage between national-role conceptions and these actions. The hypothesis is that, in most circumstances, the specific foreign policy actions of a given state will be consistent with its national role conceptions. For example, if a government portrays itself as a bastion of the revolution, then we can predict that in any given revolutionary episode in the world, that state will take action, ranging from diplomatic and propaganda support to the provision of arms, and even active intervention, to promote that revolution. A faithful ally will support its protector's foreign-policy objectives and, in case of war, will probably meet its alliance commitments. And, in conflict situations, we would expect the self-styled mediators to make at least some diplomatic efforts or offers to resolve conflicts. There will be situations, of course, where knowledge of a nation's role conceptions will not enable us to predict actions or where actions will contradict the national-role conceptions. In certain situations (usually where there are rapid power shifts in the system, where aberrant personalities are concerned, or where a state is extremely weak), traditional national roles may be inconsistent with actions that are taken for short-run advantages. In the face of economic depression, for instance, we may expect that many governments will play down their developer roles in order to concentrate on saving their own resources. A faithful ally on the verge of civil war may be unable to meet its alliance obligations. Or, in the face of declining military strength, a government may drop a regional-protector role or may quietly dismantle military bases abroad without formally denying its traditional role.

SUMMARY

The relationship of national units to the international system—to other states—cannot be understood sufficiently in terms of actions, such as sending a note or declaring war. Governments often contemplate their relationships to the environment or to regional subsystems in terms that are broader than those very specific considerations underlying specific decisions. The first two components of foreign policy that reflect these broader concerns have been called orientations and national roles. These outline—sometimes vaguely, sometimes in considerable detail—how a nation and its government will generally relate themselves over a period of time to the outer world. They reflect basic national attitudes and needs, as well as external conditions.

Three major orientations have been observed repeatedly throughout history: isolation, nonalignment, and coalition formation. There are, of course, varieties of each, but basically they are all strategies that involve the making or avoidance of commitments to other states. They are adopted—often only gradually—in light of many considerations; but geographic location, perceptions of threat, national needs, and systemic characteristics may be the most important.

National roles outline the functions and tasks to which states see themselves committed within different international contexts. They thus provide guidelines for actions when specific situations arise in the environment. A government that defines itself as a bastion of the revolution, for example, will very probably provide diplomatic, military, and propaganda support (actions) to rebel groups operating in a neighboring country. National roles also reflect the general and specific objectives governments pursue within regions or in the world as a whole. We turn next to a third component of foreign policy, the goals governments seek to achieve abroad.

SELECTED BIBLIOGRAPHY

ANABTAWAI, SAMIR N., "Neutralists and Neutralism," *Journal of Politics*, 27 (1965), 351–61.

CRABB, CECIL V., JR., *The Elephants and the Grass: A Study of Nonalignment*. New York: Praeger, 1965.

DINERSTEIN, HERBERT S., "The Transformation of Alliance Systems," *American Political Science Review*, 59 (1965), 589–601.

FEDDER, EDWIN H., "The Concept of Alliance," *International Studies Quarterly*, 12 (1968), 65–86.

FRIEDMAN, JULIAN R., CHRISTOPHER BLADEN, and STEPHEN ROSEN, eds., *Alliance in International Politics*. Boston: Allyn & Bacon, 1970.

HAAS, ERNST B., "The Balance of Power as a Guide to Policy-Making," *Journal of Politics*, 15 (1953), 370–98.

———, "The Balance of Power: Prescription, Concept, or Propaganda?" *World Politics,* 5 (1953), 442–77.

HAMBLIN, ROBERT L., "Group Integration During a Crisis," pp. 220–30 in *Human Behavior and International Politics,* ed. J. David Singer. Skokie, Ill.: Rand McNally, 1965.

HOLSTI, K.J., "National Role Conceptions in the Study of Foreign Policy," *International Studies Quarterly,* 14 (1970), 233–309.

HOLSTI, OLE R., P. TERRENCE HOPMANN, and JOHN D. SULLIVAN, *Unity and Disintegration in International Alliances: Comparative Studies.* New York: John Wiley, 1973.

KEOHANE, ROBERT O., "The Big Influence of Small Allies," *Foreign Policy,* No. 2 (Spring 1971), 161–82.

LISKA, GEORGE, *Alliances and the Third World.* Baltimore, Md.: Johns Hopkins University Press, 1968.

———, *Nations in Alliance: The Limits of Interdependence.* Baltimore, Md.: Johns Hopkins University Press, 1962.

LYON, PETER, *Neutralism.* Leicester, Eng.: Leicester University Press, 1964.

NEUSTADT, RICHARD E., *Alliance Politics.* New York: Columbia University Press, 1970.

OSGOOD, ROBERT E., *Alliances and American Foreign Policy.* Baltimore, Md.: Johns Hopkins University Press, 1968.

ROTHSTEIN, ROBERT L., *Alliances and Small Powers.* New York: Columbia University Press, 1968.

RUSSETT, BRUCE M., "An Empirical Typology of International Military Alliances," *Midwest Journal of Political Science,* 15 (1971).

SINGER, J. DAVID, and MELVIN SMALL, "Formal Alliances, 1815–1939," *Journal of Peace Research,* No. 1 (1966), 1–32.

SIVERSON, RANDOLPH, and JOEL KING, "Alliances and the Expansion of War," pp. 37–49 in *To Augur Well,* eds. J. David Singer and Michael D. Wallace. Beverly Hills, Calif.: Sage Publications, 1979.

WALLACE, MICHAEL D., "Early Warning Indicators from the Correlates of War Project," pp. 17–36 in *To Augur Well,* eds. J. David Singer and Michael D. Wallace. Beverly Hills, Calif.: Sage Publications, 1979.

WILLETTS, PETER, *The Non-Aligned Movement.* New York: Nichols, 1979.

5

Foreign-Policy Objectives

Some aspects of international politics and foreign policy, such as general foreign-policy orientations and latitude of choice, can be accounted for by reference to systemic conditions. But political units do not just react or adjust to limitations imposed by the external environment. People grouped into nation-states and other types of political units have needs and *purposes,* many of which they can achieve or meet only by influencing the behavior of other states. A large portion of foreign-policy making is, to be sure, concerned with day-to-day problem solving as issues arise at home and abroad. Diplomats and foreign-office officials are normally concerned with immediate, mundane matters of narrow scope. However, most governments also have some objectives that they are attempting to achieve through the ordering of various actions and that reflect needs and purposes. The objectives may be very specific, relating to a particular problem (say, promoting a peace proposal for the Arab–Israeli conflict), or general (such as creating a common market in a given region).

Sometimes the term "national interest" has been used (or abused) as a device for analyzing nations' objectives. There has developed, in fact, a prolonged scholarly debate on the meaning of this concept, but little agreement has arisen. The vagueness of the concept is its main shortcoming. As Paul Seabury has noted:

> The idea of national interests may refer to some *ideal* set of purposes which a nation . . . *should* seek to realize in the conduct of its foreign relations. Wanting

a better word, we might call this a *normative,* civic concept of national interest. . . . A second meaning of equal importance might be called *descriptive.* In this sense the national interest may be regarded as those purposes which the nation, through its leadership, appears to pursue persistently through time. When we speak of the national interest in this descriptive sense, we move out of the metaphysical into the realms of facts. . . . It might similarly be said that the national interest is what foreign policy-makers say it is. A third definition might make the meaning of national interest somewhat clearer. The American national interest has often been an arena for conflict among individuals and groups whose conceptions of it . . . have differed widely. Disagreement about policy and action may arise even among men who are essentially in agreement about the general aims of their country in the world. But policy disagreements are usually due to differences among policy-makers about conceptions both of what the United States is and what its role in world politics, even its mission, should be.[1]

Even though there may be some immutable national interests such as self-preservation, to which everyone will agree, no one can claim with certainty that any other specific goal or set of goals is in the national interest.

Therefore, we will avoid the term and substitute the concept of *objective,* which is essentially an "image" of a future state of affairs and future set of conditions that governments through individual policy makers aspire to bring about by wielding influence abroad and by changing or sustaining the behavior of other states.[2] The future state of affairs may refer to concrete conditions, such as passing a resolution in the General Assembly or annexing territory; or to values, such as the promotion and achievement of popularity, prestige, or democracy abroad; or to a combination of the two. Some objectives remain constant over centuries and directly involve the lives and welfare of all members of a national society. Others change almost daily and concern only a handful of government personnel and citizens, for example, to protect a small industry from foreign competition. These are the interests of private individuals and groups, promoted by governments for the welfare of a few citizens—private interests translated into public policy.

Even if we use the term *objective* to describe a great variety of collective interests and values that operate in foreign policy, we should not assume that foreign ministers and diplomats spend all their time carefully formulating logical and coherent sets of collective or private goals to pursue systematically through the rational ordering of means to ends. Some statesmen or governments have, of course, spent time and resources to define the ultimate goals of their actions. Charles de Gaulle formulated a set of goals for France that, even if described in fairly mystical terms, was carefully thought out in accordance with his interpre-

---

[1] Paul Seabury, *Power, Freedom, and Diplomacy: The Foreign Policy of the United States of America* (New York: Random House, 1963), p. 86.

[2] Richard C. Snyder, H.W. Bruck, and Burton Sapin, "Decision-Making as an Approach to International Politics," in *Foreign Policy Decision-Making,* eds. Richard C. Snyder, H.W. Bruck, and Burton Sapin (New York: Free Press, 1962), p. 82; see also George Modelski, *A Theory of Foreign Policy* (New York: Praeger, 1962), pp. 8–11, 50.

tations of historical development and France's "destiny" in that development. Not all his actions were compatible with achievement of the goals, but generally he persisted in his plans despite widespread criticism from France's major allies.

If some governments operate to fulfill a series of logically consistent goals, many more do not seem to be working toward the achievement of any specific objective or, at best, seem to improvise policies to meet specific domestic or external crises or commitments. This is not surprising, for most transactions between governments are routine and unplanned, and serve primarily the interests and needs of a few private citizens. The work of a foreign office frequently appears to develop in a completely random fashion, with no discernible relationship between decisions arrived at and policies conducive to the achievement of collective goals. As one British diplomat has claimed, "most important decisions are often made, not as part of a concerted and far-sighted policy, but under the urgent pressure of some immediate crisis."[3] His comment is typical of criticisms aimed at the foreign policies of many countries—namely, that the governments have no real policies but only respond to the initiatives of others. They are concerned with solving problems as they arise, not with defining long-range objectives and formulating the means to achieve them. Some of the great foreign policies of the United States, such as the European Recovery Program, were products of planning, delineation of objectives, and assessment of costs. But, as Paul Seabury points out:

> All too often policy is the product of random, haphazard, or even irrational forces and events. Equally often it is the result of dead-locked judgements, an uneasy compromise formula. Often what appears on the surface as a nation's settled course of action may be due to indecision, unwillingness or inability to act. It may be no policy at all but simply a drift with events. Sometimes foreign policies are the product of statesmen's passive compliance with strong domestic political pressure—and thus products of contending political forces within the nation itself. Finally, policy may be due to statesmen's abdication of choice and rational judgement in the face of ruthless and strong external pressures.[4]

A second point we must remember when using the concept of objective is that governments often pursue incompatible objectives simultaneously. It is the task of policy makers to rank and choose among conflicting objectives and determine which are feasible within a specific set of circumstances. Disarmament, for example, has been conceived by many governments as both an end in itself and a means to achieve increased national security from foreign military threats. Yet, the implementation of any disarmament scheme would incur serious short-term risks to any nation's security. Many objectives of Soviet foreign policy seem to be similarly incompatible. Lenin often claimed that the interests of both the Russian nation and the Soviet state should be subordinated to the

---

[3] Quoted in Anthony Sampson, *Anatomy of Britain* (New York: Harper & Row, 1962), p. 311.

[4] Seabury, *Power, Freedom, and Diplomacy*, p. 5.

goals of proletarian internationalism—that is, to the victory of world revolution. But Stalin reversed Lenin's thesis and followed policies that promoted Soviet strength, often at the expense of foreign Communist parties. More recently, the Soviet government has distributed economic and military assistance to regimes—as in Iraq and Egypt—that persecute Communists. There is almost constant conflict among Soviet policy makers, who must attempt to reconcile short-run political and diplomatic goals with an ideological commitment to support the "international proletarian movement." Americans, too, have had their share of difficulties in reconciling policy objectives. For over four decades, the United States has publicly proclaimed its support for the principles of self-determination and national independence and its sympathy for anticolonial movements; but it has also supported allies that were attempting to retain their overseas territories by using American-supplied arms against native independence movements.

TYPES OF OBJECTIVES
IN HISTORICAL SYSTEMS

Among primitive tribes, distinction between collective interests of the political unit and private interests of its members is not always clear. Anthropological investigations of such groups as the Veddas, Australian aborigines, the Fuegians, and some North American Indians have revealed that, with the exception of common grazing rights, these people developed few *collective* interests that they had to achieve or protect in relations with other groups or tribes. At the same time, when one member of the collectivity was harmed in any way by outsiders, it became the collective duty of his own people to inflict revenge on the wrong-doer or his tribe. External objectives became more complex as tribal units achieved a higher level of civilization. Many groups became more sedentary and based their existence on a particular piece of territory that they had to defend or extend against others to survive. Other important collective objectives were access to, and rights over, water and communication routes. Independent political groups learned later the value of goods and slaves, which eventually become the objects of group conquest. Further economic and social development brought awareness of the needs or advantages of imperialism. In addition to plundering and robbing neighbors for goods and slaves, such groups as the Vikings, the early Anglo-Saxons, and the Danes systematically *occupied* and settled regions formerly held by militarily inferior peoples.

The promotion of value objectives through religious expansion or cultural imperialism is also typical of political units with concepts of collective interests. Drives for expansion in the Chou empire were often motivated by a desire to bring to the "barbarians" the benefits of Chinese culture. Forced conversion of the "heathen" to the Islamic religion was a major objective in the Saracen campaigns across North Africa and into Spain and France in the seventh and eighth centuries, and appeals to regain the Holy Land to destroy the Islamic "infidel" led to a series of crusades from Europe during the Middle Ages.

In the fifteenth and sixteenth centuries, Europe was composed of a complex of political units, including the largely symbolic Holy Roman Empire, dynastic states covering large and often noncontiguous areas, and hundreds of small dukedoms, religious states, and walled cities. The range of objectives among these units was equally wide. The Italian city-states were in almost constant warfare over issues of papal succession or objectives of territorial expansion and plunder. Conflicts also developed from the personal rivalries and ambitions of princes and were settled, like feuds, by private armies. International politics were typified by the conflicting private interests of dynasts and princes. And yet, higher purposes reflecting prevailing social and religious values were also present. The policies of Charles V, Holy Roman Emperor, King of Spain, ruler of the Austrian territories, the Netherlands, and various Italian holdings, were directed toward both extending his personal Hapsburg empire and creating a unified, Christian Europe. While he committed money and men to pursuit of his own glory and expansion of his personal wealth, he also led crusades against Islam in the Mediterranean area and Hungary.

The European state system in the eighteenth century is particularly interesting, because its members pursued in their external relations a combination of personal, dynastic, religious, commercial, and *national* objectives. Since monarchs (with the exception of Frederick the Great) believed that they ruled by divine right, and attributed their sovereignty and absolutism to the Lord of Creation, they considered their own family interests their most important concerns. The state served primarily as a vehicle for protecting the wealth, security, and patrimony of a particular dynastic line.[5] Among Louis XIV's main objectives, to which he committed the skills of his diplomats, were to place a Bourbon on the throne of Spain and to obtain his own election as Holy Roman Emperor. In the same period, the English kings were as much concerned with family interests in Hanover as with various threats to England posed by Spain or France. Some of the important diplomatic crises and wars between states in the eighteenth century arose from conflicting claims of private families.

Eighteenth-century states in Europe also pursued objectives that had little relationship to private dynastic interests—except that often they reflected on the prestige of monarchs. These included colonial ventures and expansion of trade and commerce. Statesmen such as Cardinal Fleury and Sir Robert Walpole exemplified those ministers who were increasingly organizing their policy objectives around other than religious or dynastic considerations. They had to respond to rising commercial interests and demands and thought in terms of national capabilities and national prestige. In addition to safeguarding dynastic objectives, these men quarreled over trade routes, rules governing navigation, strategic frontiers, colonies, and naval proficiency, all of which came to be regarded—not only in the courts, but also among the developing middle classes—as vital collective interests to be secured, extended, or defended. The major

---

[5] See Walter L. Dorn, *Competition for Empire, 1740–1763* (New York: Harper & Row, 1940), p. 10.

wars of the eighteenth century illustrate the rise of national objectives: The War of the Austrian Succession, as its name implies, concerned dynastic interests, but Frederick the Great's invasion of Silesia, trade rivalry, and the lure of colonial empire were important issues as well; and in the Seven Years' War (1757–1763), commercial and colonial objectives reflecting middle-class interests, as well as the British desire to obtain a monopoly of sea power, far outweighed dynastic concerns as factors in the conflict.

Even in our own era, political units seek to achieve a complete range of private and collective, concrete and value objectives. In some areas, state interests are still indistinguishable from dynastic interests. It is questionable, for example, whether the late Nicaraguan dictator Anastasio Somoza perceived that the interests of his country might be distinct from his private family interests. To him the primary objectives of foreign policy were to protect his ruling position and secure quantities of personal wealth and prestige. At the other extreme, we find governments that commit national resources to the expansion of messianic philosophies, regardless of what the effects will be on the personal lives, prestige, and fortunes of those who formulate these objectives. Between these extremes exist the vast majority of modern states, which seek to achieve collective objectives of national security; welfare of citizens; access to trade routes, markets, and vital resources; and sometimes the territory of their neighbors. Given the wide range of objectives that exist today, then, how can they be classified?

We will employ a combination of three criteria: (1) the *value* placed on the objective, or the extent to which policy makers commit themselves and their countries' resources to achieving a particular objective; (2) the *time element* placed on its achievement; and (3) the kinds of *demands* the objective imposes on other states in the system. From these we can construct categories of objectives such as the following: (1) "core" values and interests, to which governments and nations commit their very existence and that must be preserved or extended at all times (achievement of these values or interests may or may not impose demands on others); (2) middle-range goals, which normally impose demands on several other states (commitments to their achievement are serious, and some time limits are usually attached to them); and (3) universal long-range goals, which seldom have definite time limits.[6] In practice, statesmen rarely place the highest value on long-range goals and do not, consequently, commit many national capabilities or policies to their achievement—unless the goals are central to a political philosophy or ideology, in which case they may be considered "core" or middle-range interests. States that work actively toward

---

[6] Arnold Wolfers has outlined an alternative scheme for classifying goals. He distinguishes between *aspirations* and genuine *policy goals*, which correspond roughly to the distinction between long-range goals and others of more immediate importance. *Possession goals* refer to the achievement of national values and needs, while *milieu goals* are conditions outside the nation-state itself that a state seeks to change. Wolfers also distinguishes between *national goals* and *indirect goals*, which correspond roughly to my concepts of "collective interests" and "private interests." See Arnold Wolfers, "The Goals of Foreign Policy," in his *Discord and Collaboration: Essays on International Politics* (Baltimore, Md.: Johns Hopkins Press, 1962), Chap. 5.

achieving universal long-range goals usually make radical demands on *all* other units in the system and thus create great instability.

"CORE" INTERESTS AND VALUES

"Core" values and interests can be described as those kinds of goals for which most people are willing to make ultimate sacrifices. They are usually stated in the form of basic principles of foreign policy and become articles of faith that a society accepts uncritically.[7] Such terms as "command of the sea," a "frontier on the Rhine," and the "Monroe Doctrine" suggest basic foreign interests or goals that at one time were held sacrosanct by entire communities.

"Core" interests and values are most frequently related to the self-preservation of a political unit. These are short-range objectives, because other goals obviously cannot be achieved unless the political units pursuing them maintain their own existence. The exact definition of a "core" value or interest in any given country depends on the attitudes of those who make policy. There are, for example, many different interpretations of self-preservation. Some disagree over definitions of self—that is, what constitutes an integrated polity. Others will disagree equally on what policies contribute best to preservation. Some colonial regimes have been willing to grant independence to indigenous peoples voluntarily, whereas others have considered that overseas holdings constitute an integral part of the nation, which must be defended at all costs. Nevertheless, most policy makers in our era assume that the most essential objective of any foreign policy is to ensure the sovereignty and independence of the *home* territory and to perpetuate a particular political, social, and economic system based on that territory.

Some governments place equally great value on controlling or defending neighboring territories, because these areas contain ethnically related populations or assets such as a labor force and raw materials that can increase a state's capabilities, or because they believe that the major threat to their own territorial integrity might materialize through adjacent lands. Achievement of favorable strategic frontiers has been a traditional short-run policy objective to which states have been willing to commit great resources. Russians have traditionally attempted to dominate the areas between themselves and Western Europe, and the Soviets today are fully committed to the defense of Eastern Europe. They would probably react, as the Warsaw Treaty stipulates, to an attack on this territory as if it were an attack on the Soviet Union itself. The United States has similarly pledged through the NATO treaty to consider an attack on one of its European allies as an attack on itself. The objective of safeguarding American security by defending Western Europe has persisted since 1949, despite changes in administration in Washington. There is, then, almost unanimous

---

[7] Modelski, *A Theory of Foreign Policy,* p. 86.

agreement in the United States that the territorial integrity and independence of the Western European countries constitute a "core" interest of the United States.

Israel is an example of a small country that has committed great resources to the achievement of frontiers that would provide both security and lands traditionally considered to be part of the historical Jewish nation. To many Israelis, military control over the Golan Heights and occupation of the West Bank of the Jordan River constitute "core" interests that must be protected at all costs. The problem, of course, is that the West Bank lands are inhabited predominantly by Palestinians who consider that Israeli presence there is fundamentally inconsistent with their own "core" interest—which is to create an independent Palestinian state. Where the essential interests of two political units overlap in such a fashion, it becomes extremely difficult to develop some sort of political settlement that is satisfactory to both sides.

After self-preservation and defense of strategically vital areas, another prominent "core" value or interest is ethnic, religious, or linguistic unity. Today, no less than in the great era of nationalism in the nineteenth century, the most legitimate bases of frontiers correspond to ethnic, language, or religious divisions. Territories carved up according to historical or strategic criteria, where ethnic groups are arbitrarily divided between sovereignties, are likely to become areas of conflict as neighboring states attempt to "liberate" their own kin from foreign rule. Irredentist movements, subversion, and sometimes racial warfare are often the products of frontiers that divide ethnic, language, or religious groups. In almost all areas where such arbitrary divisions occur, governments make reunification a major objective of foreign policies, and sometimes place such a high value upon it that they are willing to employ large-scale force to achieve it. The Kashmir wars, intermittent crises over a divided Germany and Berlin, Austria and Italy over the Tyrol, tensions between Kenya and Somalia and Somalia and Ethiopia, and the wars in Korea, Vietnam, and Cyprus have arisen since World War II essentially because one government attempted through threats, subversion, or outright military attack to defend or incorporate into its own territory ethnically related people living in neighboring states.

The demands that pursuit of these "core" values or interests require of other actors in the system vary. States with well-established frontiers corresponding to ethnic divisions, which protect their territories and social orders through ordinary defense policies, are not likely to disturb even their immediate neighbors. Those that seek more favorable strategic frontiers or ethnic unity normally do so at the expense of the "core" values and interests of their neighbors, and thus create dangerous conflicts.

Such conflicts may not always lead to violence or war, because interpretations of "core" values or "vital interests" may change under different circumstances. The British were willing for decades to fight against any internal or external assaults on their empire as if they were fighting for the city of London. But in 1945, the economic and military strains of maintaining the empire were so great that many British leaders recognized they could no longer consider the colonies as "core" interests to be preserved at all costs. In the 1950s, reunification was considered by many Germans as a "core" value. By the 1970s, it was seldom mentioned as a foreign-policy objective.

A bizarre interpretation of "core" values and interests was the view propounded by Lenin that the development of world revolution was more important than saving either his Bolshevik regime or the independence of the Russian nation.[8] It was partly because of his exceptional commitment to world revolution that he was willing to concede to Germany in the Brest-Litovsk treaty almost one-quarter of Russia's traditional territory and one-half of its population. In this case, although the objective of world revolution was a middle-range goal if we are using the criterion of time, in terms of the value Lenin placed on its achievement it was a "core" interest. Lenin's successors have displayed quite different—and more traditional—attitudes, however, through their claims that the defense of Russian territory and the Soviet state, rather than promotion of revolution, is the first foreign-policy priority.[9] Lenin's priorities were exceptional; in most cases, policy makers explicitly state or reveal through their actions that the basic objective, for which any degree of sacrifice may be required, is defense of the home territory plus any other territory deemed necessary to self-preservation and perpetuation of a particular political, social, and economic order, or, as some call it, a "way of life."

MIDDLE-RANGE OBJECTIVES

Since there is such a variety of middle-range objectives, it would be useful to divide this category into three further types and illustrate each with contemporary examples. The first type would include the attempts of governments to meet economic-betterment demands and needs through international action. Social welfare and economic development—a primary goal of all governments in our era—cannot be achieved through self-help, as most states have only limited resources, administrative services, and technical skills. Interdependence means that to satisfy domestic needs and aspirations, states have to interact with others. Trade, foreign aid, access to communications facilities, sources of supply, and foreign markets are for most states necessary for increasing social welfare.

---

[8] Lenin's priority on the "world revolution" is illustrated by comments he made shortly after the Bolshevik revolution to a group of his friends: "We are creating a socialist state. From now on Russia will be the first state in which a socialist regime has been established. Ah, you are shrugging your shoulders. Well, you have still more surprises coming! It isn't a question of Russia. No, gentlemen, I spit on Russia! That's only one stage we have to pass through on our way to world revolution!" Quoted in Robert S. Payne, *The Life and Death of Lenin* (New York: Simon & Schuster, 1964), p. 418.

[9] As, for example, when former premier Khrushchev, in reply to Chinese claims to certain Soviet territory, announced, "Our borders are sacred and inviolable and any attempt to change them by force means war." UPI release from Moscow, September 13, 1964.

It can be argued, indeed, that with the very great demands people have placed on governments to provide them jobs, income, recreation, medical services, and general security, governments increasingly have to develop policies to satisfy expectations or face political defeat. In these circumstances, it may be difficult to gain much public support for other types of objectives, such as glory, territorial expansion, or power for its own sake.[10] Hence, the primary commitment of many modern governments must be to pursue those courses of action that have the highest impact on domestic economic and welfare needs and expectations. Canada provides one illustration. Official statements on Canada's external objectives indicate clearly that they are grounded in domestic needs rather than in designs to change the external environment. Many of Canada's present foreign-policy activities—expanding trade with the Pacific rim countries, strong pressure on other countries in the Law of the Sea conference to accept the 200-mile control limit, and expansion of cultural and scientific exchanges, for example—are described as necessary to promote economic growth, cultural development, social justice, and a better natural environment, all within Canada.[11] Directions to foreign-policy officials insist that all policy options should be measured against national gains in these dimensions. Similar uses of foreign policy to meet domestic welfare needs could be observed in countries such as Sweden, Belgium, Australia, Fiji, Ireland, and many others.

A variation of this type of objective occurs when governments commit themselves to promote private citizens' interests abroad, whether or not these relate to broad social needs. Instead of encouraging general expansion of trade or access to foreign markets, they might, under pressure from domestic groups or economic interests, undertake certain foreign-policy initiatives that have little connection with the interests of society in general. The American government in the early twentieth century, for instance, committed its power and resources to protect the foreign investments of private firms operating in Latin America. It intervened frequently, sometimes with force, in the internal affairs of Caribbean and Central American states essentially to guarantee the profits of these firms. It was thus translating private business interests into middle-range government objectives, even though the interests sometimes had little to do with the general level of social welfare in the United States.

A second type of middle-range objective is to increase a state's prestige in the system. In the past, as today, this was done primarily through diplomatic ceremonial and displays of military capabilities, but, increasingly in our era, prestige is measured by levels of industrial development and scientific and technological skills. In addition to responding to domestic pressures for higher living standards, political elites of developing states who are acutely sensitive to their material poverty may undertake massive development programs primarily to raise international prestige. Development has become one of the great national

---

[10] This thesis is developed in Edward L. Morse, *Foreign Policy and Interdependence in Gaullist France* (Princeton, N.J.: Princeton University Press, 1973), esp. Chap. 1.

[11] The official statement of the Trudeau government's foreign policy is *Foreign Policy for Canadians* (Ottawa: Queen's Printer, 1970).

goals of our times and is sought with almost as much commitment of resources as the securing of some "core" values and interests. This middle-range goal has no particular time element, but most of today's leaders in developing countries hope that they can begin to catch up with more economically advanced countries within their own lifetimes.

Industrialized countries and major powers can increase their international prestige through a number of policies and actions, including expansion of military capabilities, distribution of foreign aid, diplomatic ceremonies—including reciprocal visits by heads of state, and industrial and scientific exhibitions—and particularly through development of nuclear weapons and the capacity to explore outer space. An independent nuclear capability is probably the most important single indicator of a nation's military and diplomatic status today. The demands implied by the goal of increasing prestige are extensive, but they do not seem, at least in our age, to conflict with the "core" interests or values of other states.

A third category of middle-range objectives would include the many different forms of self-extension or imperialism. Some states make demands for neighboring territory even if that territory does not satisfy any important security requirements or ethnic unity. Territorial expansion becomes an end in itself, whether or not it fulfills any strategic, economic, or social needs. Others do not *occupy* foreign territory, but seek advantages, including access to raw materials, markets, and trade routes, that they cannot achieve through ordinary trade or diplomacy. Exclusive control and access may be obtained through establishment of colonies, protectorates, "satellites," or "spheres of influence." Ideological self-extension is also prevalent in many forms, where agents of a state undertake to promote its own socioeconomic-political values abroad or "convert" other peoples to a particular religious, cultural, or political faith.

European imperialism in Africa between 1870 and 1900 was a mixture of all these public and private, economic and ideological purposes. Often, private citizens journeyed to the "dark continent" to seek fortunes, put an end to the Arab slave trade, or convert "savages" to Christianity; later, they prevailed upon their governments to establish colonies and regular administrative services so that they could pursue their activities more easily and with greater security. Once a government had established such a colony to help its private citizens, it committed itself to maintain exclusive control over the area in question. In such cases, the interests of private citizens were converted to middle-range objectives of governments and, once the empires or colonies were established, developed into collective "core" interests to be defended at all costs.

More recently, Stalin's Russia, Mussolini's Italy, and Communist China have served as examples of states practicing regional self-extension for economic or strategic purposes, while simultaneously promoting an ideology or political value system abroad. Russian expansion into central Asia—a process started by the Tsars for religious, economic, and military purposes—was revived after 1917, as the drive to convert the indigenous peoples to socialism gave the objective new urgency. Italian expansion into Ethiopia and Albania between 1936 and 1941 was undertaken primarily for reasons of prestige—in the latter case, keeping up with Hitler's conquests elsewhere. The Chinese Communists expanded into Tibet in 1950–1951 for traditional, strategic, and ideological reasons.

LONG-RANGE GOALS

Long-range goals are those plans, dreams, and visions concerning the ultimate political or ideological organization of the international system, rules governing relations in that system, and the role of specific nations within it. The difference between middle-range and long-range goals relates not only to different time elements inherent in them; there is also a significant difference in scope. In pressing for middle-range goals, states make *particular* demands against *particular* states; in pursuing long-range goals, states normally make *universal* demands, for their purpose is no less than to reconstruct an entire international system according to a universally applicable plan or vision. As Lenin, one of the great modern visionaries, wrote in 1920:

> We have always known, and shall never forget, that our task is an international one, and that our victory [in Russia] is only half a victory, perhaps less, until an upheaval takes place in all states, including the wealthiest and most civilized.[12]

Since destruction and reconstitution of an established international order obviously conflict with the middle-range and "core" objectives of its members, any system that contains one or more actors committed to such plans will be unstable and typified by violent international conflict.

Some of these visions may be delineated explicitly, deriving from a coherent political or religious philosophy. Others, such as Hitler's concepts of the "Thousand-Year Reich" and the European "New Order," are merely vague images of a future state of affairs. But it is not the explicitness or rationality of a vision that creates international tensions and conflict; it is the degree to which a political unit is willing to commit capabilities and resources to its achievement. Whereas in recent years the Soviet government has been cautious in seeking to promote its long-range objectives, Hitler mobilized tremendous material and manpower resources in pursuit of his vision. Indeed, he was willing to destroy Germany and sacrifice all his middle-range objectives for the sake of creating the "New Order."

Contemporary Long-Range Objectives

Messianic plans for reorganization of continents or the entire world seldom succeed, because the threatened states coalesce, where otherwise their interests

[12] V.I. Lenin, *Collected Works,* Vol. 31 (Moscow: Foreign Languages Publishing House, 1961), p. 371.

might not coincide, to build a preponderance of military capacity and eventually destroy the revolutionary state in violent wars. Recent examples are the wars of the French Revolution, the Napoleonic Wars, Hitlers' defeat in Europe, and Japan's defeat in Asia after it had almost succeeded in building its "Greater East Asia Co-Prosperity Sphere." In the case of Soviet long-range goals, however, there is a new element in the vision. Although the Soviets conceive it their duty to promote and support revolution abroad, they are not required by their political doctrines to press too hard, for Marx claimed that the goal of world communism would be reached in any event through the inexorable laws of historical development. This element of determinism in Marxism allows Soviet policy makers a flexibility not found in other universalistic philosophies. They can either export revolution and support indigenous Communist movements through massive aid, or save their resources for economic development, secure in the knowledge that history will in any case develop according to the Marxist pattern. Napoleon, Hitler, and the Japanese imperialists did not believe that they had "history" on their side, and only through aggressive actions could they achieve their long-range objectives.

Even if Russian Communist leaders have perceived the possibility of choosing between giving historical processes a push or letting them take their course toward the predetermined end, they have attempted to draw pictures of the world as it would develop after the proletarian revolution had been completed. Since the Russian revolution inaugurated the first enduring Socialist order, it was natural that Bolshevik theoreticians would use the organization of their own society as a model for the entire world. Thus, the new world would be organized, at least initially, on the principles of federalism for the constituent units, a socialist economy, and government (or "dictatorship of the proletariat") by soviets (councils) of workers and peasants. But what was to be the position of nation-states in the new order—and particularly, what was to be the role of the first Socialist nation-state?

There is room for disagreement on the nature of the Soviet image of ultimate Communist world order. Some Western experts, citing Russia's relations with the satellites through the 1950s, the propensity of the Russian Communist party to define the goals, strategy, and tactics of the international Communist movement, and its domination of many revolutionary movements, argue that the vision is one of a communized world subservient to the interests of the Russian center—a Communist version of the Roman Empire.

Lenin's early pronouncements on the subject did not hint that the ultimate world federation of socialist states was to be dominated by Russians, but subsequent statements and actions by Communist leaders increasingly identified the Soviet Union as the nucleus of the new order. Progress toward the ultimate goals was thus closely linked to the aggrandizement and fortunes of the Russian state. Meanwhile, the original principle of voluntary accession of Socialist states into one great federation was increasingly belied by the Soviet interpretation of federalism within its own borders. Non-Russian parts of the Soviet Union were theoretically allowed autonomy in many political, social, and cultural affairs, but, in Stalin's era, the entire Union was ruled firmly from Moscow. Manifestations of "bourgeois nationalism" in constituent units of the Union were met with purges, mass executions, incarcerations, and forced migration of "unreliable elements." Soviet policy toward its Eastern European neighbors after World War II also contradicted the idea of voluntary federalism, which was to be one of the underlying principles of the new order under communism.

According to some Soviet theorists, even the principle of federalism was to be transitory. Federation was only a *method* designed to allow diverse peoples and cultures to unite politically. The Comintern Theses of 1920 declared that it would be necessary to strive for an ever-closer federal union, but that federation would be only a transition form toward complete unity. Federation, it was hoped, would foster the tendency toward creation of a single world economy regulated by the proletariat of all nations according to one common plan.[13] The expectation was that Soviet Russia would be joined (by force, if necessary, according to Stalin) by other Soviet republics in a federation that would eventually develop into a World Soviet Federation. This, in turn, would be transformed into a unitary, highly centralized world state.

Other observers of communism note a more egalitarian vision in Communist literature and philosophy.[14] Emphasizing the concept of a Communist "Commonwealth of Nations" based on fraternal relations among sovereign and equal parties and states, they argue that aside from organizing and supporting the overthrow of bourgeois regimes, Moscow would not necessarily be the center of an empire. As the oldest Socialist state, it would simply provide leadership and act as an example to other revolutionary states. Hence the vision is one of ever-expanding revolution to build a world order of sovereign states—not so different from the present system, except that all states would adhere to a common socioeconomic system and political philosophy.

Recent speeches containing evidence of Soviet long-range goals are ambiguous. At the 24th Party Congress in March 1971, for example, Party Secretary Leonid Brezhnev alluded to a world monolithic in ideology, but somewhat "free" in terms of sovereignty. He pictured the Socialist states in terms of a "well-knit family of nations, building and defending the new society together, and . . . enriching each other with experience and knowledge." This family would be "strong and united," and the "people of the world would regard it as the prototype of the future world community of free nations."[15]

How long will Soviet policy makers continue to regard the Communist

---

[13] See Elliott R. Goodman, *The Soviet Design for a World State* (New York: Columbia University Press, 1960), p. 233.

[14] See William Welch, "The Sources of Soviet Conduct: A Note on Method," *Background*, 6 (1963), 17–28.

[15] *Documents of the 24th Congress of the Communist Party of the Soviet Union* (Moscow: Novosti Press Agency, 1971), p. 19.

world state or commonwealth as the long-range objective of their policies? What time limits and how many national resources are they willing to commit to its achievement? Lenin anticipated the universal victory of socialism in his own lifetime, believing that the German proletariat would gain power either in 1918 or 1919 and the collapse of bourgeois regimes in the rest of Europe would follow shortly thereafter. To him, world revolution was a "core" value, or at least a middle-range goal, to be achieved even at the expense of Russian territorial integrity. In 1919, for example, he declared that it would not be long before communism had become victorious in the entire world, before he would see the founding of a worldwide Federal Republic of Soviets.[16] Later that year, he even predicted that by July 1920, all Communists would greet the victory of the "International Soviet Republic."[17] Since Lenin believed these developments would occur inevitably as a result of contradictions within capitalism and collapse of public order in many nations following World War I, the Soviet government could confine its activities to exploiting "revolutionary situations" abroad through agitation and propaganda. Unlike Stalin, Lenin did not believe, with the important exception of the Soviet campaign against Poland in 1920, that the Soviet state should use its military capabilities to impose Communist regimes abroad.

Stalin recognized that the new order could not be achieved unless the Soviet state used its national power, influence, and resources to this end. Construction of the new order became the objective not only of communism, but of Russian foreign policy as well. Stalin also did not hold to Lenin's optimistic predictions about imminent world revolution. Instead of anticipating the downfall of capitalism in the next year, or even during the next decade, Stalin's theoreticians spoke of long "historical stages" to which they could arbitrarily attach almost any period of time. As the tenets of Marxism–Leninism became irrelevant to the problems of modern society, the ultimate objective receded even further into the future. In 1935, for example, one Communist veteran told the Seventh World Comintern Congress that it would take communism a shorter time to achieve world victory than it did for the bourgeoisie to replace feudalism with capitalism. His estimate would place the world victory of communism somewhere around 1960. In 1952, however, a Soviet economist predicted that capitalism was undergoing its second stage of crisis (the first had occurred between the world wars) and that during this stage there would be a "lengthy" period of coexistence between capitalism and communism. Coexistence would no longer be necessary by the end of the present century, because by then communism would be victorious throughout the world.[18] To Lenin, the long-range goal was defined in terms of months; to Stalin, it was an objective that Soviet diplomats and the Red Army should pursue for two or more decades;

[16] Goodman, *The Soviet Design for a World State,* p. 32.
[17] *Ibid.*
[18] *Ibid.,* pp. 188–89.

to Khrushchev, the achievement of the mission was placed several generations ahead.[19] Today, the subject is seldom discussed. As the time limit passes into the remote future, middle-range goals such as construction of communism within Soviet Russia and development of Soviet diplomatic prestige around the world seem to occupy an increasing portion of Soviet policy makers' time and Russia's resources.

Former Secretary of State Henry Kissinger's long-range goals had not been stated as explicitly as those of Lenin. Nevertheless, Kissinger often indicated that his policies were oriented beyond the pragmatic resolution of day-to-day problems, as important as the latter may have seemed. The establishment of relations with China, the various moves toward the Soviet Union, termed *détente,* and the arms-control measures in SALT I and SALT II were basically just means of reaching the objective where "the solution of [our] difficulties by war becomes less and less conceivable and, over time, should have become inconceivable."[20] Underlying this objective was the assumption that extensive relationships and the creation of interdependence make war less likely.

The second major long-range objective, in Kissinger's view, was to get all governments—but particularly those in Western Europe, the United States, and Japan—to see that the facts of interdependence no longer allow countries to pursue national interests that are inimical to others. The world Kissinger attempted to promote is one where all governments recognize a "world interest," and shape their national programs and priorities to fit this greater interest. Kissinger saw that there are numerous forces creating a new "world structure." These forces, he implied, are beyond the power of any government to control. The function of foreign policy, then, is to adapt to these forces and to solve the problems they create without recourse to violence. Thus, while Kissinger had a vision of a different world order, he appeared less certain that foreign policy by itself can create such an order. But, in contrast to Lenin, there was no hint that the nation-state will cease to be the main actor in world politics.

Despite Kissinger's emphasis on the fact of interdependence, he did not believe that power can be distributed equally in the international system. The basic power structure for maintaining a semblance of international order depends upon a rough balance among five centers: the United States, Europe, the Soviet Union, Japan, and China. The essential thrust of his policies was to break down the cold-war barriers among these leading states and to build a network of economic, cultural, and diplomatic ties that might help reduce the likelihood of lethal conflict between them. Kissinger did not sanctify the idea of spheres of influence for each of these powers (for example, he was not overenthusiastic about the Conference on Security and Cooperation in Europe, which in a sense legitimized the territorial arrangements resulting from World War

[19] Khrushchev suggested that in North America, the present generation's *grandchildren* will live under socialism. This transformation, thus, could take place anytime between 1985 and 2020.

[20] Interview printed in the *New York Times,* October 13, 1974, p. 34.

II); but his actions in evacuating the United States from Southeast Asia and accepting covert interference in Chile suggest a recognition that each of the major powers has special interests in adjacent areas that must be respected. The pentagonal balance of power, then, would help provide stability not only in the mutual relations of the power centers, but in the developing world as well. Perhaps unfortunately, Kissinger's vision did not include a role for the greatly strengthened Arab states; he did not publicly recognize that interdependence in most instances exists only between the industrialized states and that the dependence of the Third World countries will eventually decline. Indeed, American resistance to the Group of 77's proposals for a new "world economic order" suggests that neither Kissinger nor his major advisors thought carefully about the roles of developing nations in the new diplomatic constellation. South Asia, Africa, and Latin America did not appear to have an important place in Kissinger's long-range views.

Even though leaders of a state may define long-range objectives such as those discussed above, the objectives do not necessarily determine the actions that will be used to achieve them. One of the frequent mistakes of armchair analysts is to assume that the only American objective abroad is to promote its liberal and free-enterprise values or that every Russian diplomatic maneuver is part of a carefully formulated plan to communize the world. Certainly in many of its actions, the United States actively seeks to promote abroad its own domestic values. This is one American middle-range goal. It rewards states with liberal political institutions; it has on occasion withheld recognition of governments—particularly in Latin America—that have not come into being through, or observed, constitutional processes; it has cut off foreign aid to governments that were constituted through violence; it has occasionally insisted that recipients of aid not use funds to build nationalized industries to compete against private entrepreneurs; and through its propaganda programs, it has emphasized the virtues of its own political and social values. On the other hand, where other interests and objectives have been more important, it has not attempted to promote its own "way of life" abroad. It has conducted transactions and formed alliances with all types of regimes; it has rewarded conservative groups, ignored the principle of self-determination, or remained officially indifferent to the values expressed in the economic and political life of other countries. It has intervened in the internal affairs of other states, sometimes to support conservative regimes against radical factions, sometimes to save liberal governments against plots on the right. The Soviet Union and China similarly pursue *all* ranges of foreign-policy objectives and commit varying resources to their realization. But these objectives, no matter how diverse, do not contain within them specific courses of action.

If a state wishes to secure more strategically advantageous frontiers at the expense of its neighbors, it can do so using almost any technique from persuasion to aggression. To persuade, it can offer a piece of its own territory as compensation, promise a friendship treaty, foreign aid, or a hundred other types of rewards. To coerce, it can build alliances or subvert the neighboring regimes and establish puppet governments that would then cede the desired territory. Certainly, the Soviet goal of a world Communist state, or a commonwealth of Socialist societies, does not prescribe any immutable strategic or tactical foreign-policy principles. With the exception of the Bolshevik war against Poland in 1920, Lenin did not believe that communism should be imposed abroad by the Red Army; but Stalin did appreciate the possibilities of using military power and succeeded in expanding communism by unleashing the Red Army. Each man held approximately the same long-range goal, but each sought to achieve it through different methods.

OBJECTIVES, NATIONAL ROLES, AND ORIENTATIONS

Most of the types of objectives discussed before derive from or are consistent with orientations and role conceptions. A government that sees itself as a bastion of the revolution will probably have at least some vague objective or plan to create a new revolutionary world or regional order. A government that sees itself as a regional collaborator will probably have an objective relating to the construction of a common market. Regional protector roles can be related to objectives of creating stable alliances.

States typically will have many more objectives than either orientations or national roles. This is because a number of objectives relate to private interests, peripheral problems, and issues that have only slight impact on the interests of other states. However, on major issues affecting security interests or access to markets and sources of supply, objectives may be deduced from national roles or orientations.

Contemporary Libyan foreign policy illustrates the relationships among the four types of foreign-policy outputs—orientations, roles, objectives, and actions. Toward the outside world in general, Libya has emphasized its independence, refusing to commit its foreign policy to the objectives of either of the super powers. While its sympathies have often been extended to the socialist countries, at least verbally, it has refrained from identifying itself as a member of the socialist bloc—despite its own domestic programs which are termed a form of "Arab socialism." The regime's self-conception is also one of an *active* independent, totally overturning the previous royal government's rather passive stance in regional and global affairs. The basic objective through this role has been to destroy Libya's dependence upon the West so that it can strike out in many different directions, promoting the cause against Israel and for Arab and Muslim unity. While blatantly anti-Western actions have been prominent in the range of Libyan foreign policy, they have been limited by the recognition that for reasons of internal development and to prosecute the war against Israel, Libya needs Western markets for its oil exports and Western technology and technicians.

Table 5–1 Orientations, Roles, Objectives, and Actions in Libyan Foreign Policy

ORIENTATIONS	NATIONAL ROLES	OBJECTIVES	ACTIONS
Global nonalignment	Active independent	1. Destroy neocolonial dependency ("core")	1. Nationalize foreign-owned oil industry 2. Establish diplomatic relations with socialist states 3. Maintain minimal relations with "imperialist" states for technology and markets
Regional alliances	"Anti-Zionist agent"	1. Destroy Israel ("core")	1. Provide funds and equipment to PLO and Syria 2. Boycott private firms dealing with Israel 3. Adopt vigorously anti-Israel resolutions in international fora 4. Denounce Egypt–Israel peace treaty; anti-Egyptian propaganda programs
	Leader of Arab states	1. Forge Arab unity (middle-range)	1. Diplomatic and military collaboration with radical Arab regimes 2. Political merger with Syria (1981) 3. Pan–Arabic propaganda programs
	Leader of the Muslim revolution	1. Create unity among all Muslim societies (long-range)	1. Foreign-aid programs for other Muslim states 2. Mediation between Philippine government and Muslim rebels in Philippines 3. Active participation in meetings of Muslim governments 4. Financial support for Pakistani nuclear program 5. Provide haven for Muslim leaders and revolutionaries (e.g., Idi Amin) 6. Intervene in Chad

In the regional context, the Libyans under Khaddafy have been willing to make all sorts of military and diplomatic commitments, pursuing basically an orientation of coalition-formation with any and all who share Libya's commitment as an anti-Zionist agent to the destruction of Israel and the creation of an Arab Palestine. Such large resources have been committed to fulfilling this role that we could term the resulting objectives as a "core" value. The activities to achieve the objectives have ranged from assassination attempts against Arabs with more moderate views about Israel, to the channeling of funds and equipment to the PLO and Syria. The promotion of Arab unity, a prominent middle-range goal, is also related, though not exclusively, to the role of the anti-Zionist agent. A role which carries with it less compelling commitments is that of the leader of the Muslim "revolution," a vague and rather amorphous self-conception that carries with it commitments to build increasing unity among all Muslim societies and a parallel sentiment to reduce the diplomatic and commercial influence of the Western countries in Muslim areas. As a leader of the Muslim renaissance, Libya has extended aid to a variety of countries, financed Pakistan's development of a nuclear capability, proposed solutions to the problem of the Muslim minority rebellion in some of the Philippine islands, and intervened on behalf of pro-Muslim faction in neighboring Chad's civil war. An illustration of the problems arising from incompatible objectives is also seen in Libya's case. While devoted strongly to the pan-Arab and Muslim causes, Libya was not willing to compromise its close relationship to the Soviet Union by condemning the lattter's invasion of Afghanistan in 1979. Here an important trade-off had to be made: reduced prestige among the Arab and Muslim countries in exchange for continued military supplies from the Soviet Union. In foreign policy, what a country does not do is often as important as what it does.

For a country as small as Libya (population = 2.6 million), it has taken an astonishing range of actions in fulfilling its orientations, roles, and objectives. These have ranged from quiet diplomacy, to assasination and subversion, to military intervention and extensive grants of foreign aid. Most countries of its size have much more limited aspirations and of course do not possess the where-withall to conduct a vigorous diplomacy. But Libya has the combination of a revolutionary regime dedicated to the reconstruction of the regional environment, including the elimination of Israel, and massive revenues obtained from the sale of oil. In the following chapters we will examine in detail how such actions are taken and the conditions under which they tend to succeed or fail. We are concerned, in general, with the various techniques governments employ to wield influence over other actors in the system and to achieve their objectives.

SELECTED BIBLIOGRAPHY

BEARD, CHARLES A., and G.H.E. SMITH, *The Idea of National Interest: An Analytical Study in American Foreign Policy.* New York: Macmillan, 1934.

FRANKEL, JOSEPH, *National Interest.* London: Pall Mall and Macmillan, 1970.

GOOD, ROBERT C., "National Interest and Moral Theory: The 'Debate' Among Contemporary Political Realists," in *Foreign Policy in the Sixties: The Issues and the Instruments,* eds. Roger Hilsman and Robert C. Good. Baltimore, Md.: Johns Hopkins Press, 1965.

HANRIEDER, WOLFRAM, "Actor Objectives and International Systems," *Journal of Politics,* 27 (February 1965), 109–32.

HERMANN, CHARLES F., "Policy Classification: A Key to the Comparative Study of Foreign Policy," in *The Analysis of International Politics,* eds. James N. Rosenau, Vincent Davis, and Maurice East. New York: Free Press, 1972.

"The Idea of National Interest," Symposium, *American Perspective,* 4 (1960), 335–401.

KAPLAN, MORTON A., *System and Process in International Politics,* Chap. 8. New York: John Wiley, 1957.

KNORR, KLAUS, "Theories of Imperalism," *World Politics,* 4 (1952), 402–31.

LICHTHEIM, GEORGE, *Imperialism.* New York: Praeger, 1971.

MODELSKI, GEORGE A., *A Theory of Foreign Policy.* New York: Praeger, 1962.

MOON, PARKER, T., *Imperialism and World Politics.* New York: Macmillan, 1926.

MORGENTHAU, HANS, J., "Another 'Great Debate': The National Interest of the United States," *The American Political Science Review,* 46 (1952), 961–88.

———, *In Defense of the National Interest.* New York: Knopf, 1951.

MORSE, EDWARD L., *Modernization and the Transformation of International Relations.* New York: The Free Press, 1976.

NUECHTERLEIN, DONALD, "The Concept of 'National Interest': A Time for New Approaches," *Orbis,* 23 (Spring, 1979), 73–92.

OSGOOD, ROBERT E., *Ideals and Self-Interest in American Foreign Relations.* Chicago: University of Chicago Press, 1953.

ROBINSON, THOMAS, "A National Interest Analysis of Sino-Soviet Relations," *International Studies Quarterly,* 11 (1967), 151–79.

SCHILLING, WARNER R., "The Classification of Ends, or, Which Interest is the National," *World Politics,* 8 (1956), 566–78.

SEABURY, PAUL, *Power, Freedom, and Diplomacy,* Chaps. 4, 11. New York: Random House, 1963.

WOLFE, BERTRAM D., "Communist Ideology and Soviet Foreign Policy," *Foreign Affairs,* 41 (1962), 152–70.

WOLFERS, ARNOLD, *Discord and Collaboration: Essays on International Politics,* Chaps. 2, 5, 6, 10. Baltimore, Md.: Johns Hopkins Press, 1962.

YALEM, RONALD J., "The 'Theory of Ends' of Arnold Wolfers," *Journal of Conflict Resolution,* 4 (1960), 421–25.

6

Foreign-Policy Actions: Power, Capability, and Influence

Orientations, roles, and objectives are composed of images in the minds of policy makers, attitudes toward the outside world, decisions, and aspirations. But policy also has a component of *actions,* the things governments *do* to others in order to effect certain orientations, fulfill roles, or achieve and defend objectives. An act is basically a form of communication intended to change or sustain the behavior of those upon whom the acting government is dependent for achieving its own goals. It can also be viewed as a "signal" sent by one actor to influence the receiver's image of the sender.[1] In international politics, acts and signals take many different forms. The promise of granting foreign aid is an act, as are propaganda appeals, displays of military strength, wielding a veto in the Security Council, walking out of a conference, organizing a conference, issuing a warning in a diplomatic note, sending arms and money to a liberation movement, instituting a boycott on the goods of another state, or declaring war. These types of acts and signals, and the circumstances in which they are likely to succeed, will be discussed in this and the following five chapters. Our organizing principle will be the amount of threat involved in the various techniques of influence. Diplomatic persuasion seemingly involves the least amount of threat; economic pressures, subversion, intervention, and various forms of

[1] A comprehensive treatment of how governments "signal" each other is in Robert Jervis, *The Logic of Images in International Relations* (Princeton, N.J.: Princeton University Press, 1970).

144

warfare involve increasingly great amounts of threat and punishment. To help understand what all these types of action or techniques of influence have in common, however, we will discuss in a more abstract manner the behavior governments show when they turn toward each other to establish orientations, fulfill roles, or achieve and defend objectives.

The international political process commences when any state—let us say state A—seeks through various acts or signals to change or sustain the behavior (for instance, the acts, images, and policies) of other states. Power can thus be defined as the general capacity of a state to control the behavior of others. This definition can be illustrated as follows, where the solid line represents various acts:

A seeks to influence B because it has established certain objectives that cannot be achieved (it is perceived) unless B (and perhaps many other states as well) does X. If this is the basis of all international political processes, the capacity to control behavior can be viewed in several different ways:

1. Influence (an aspect of power) is essentially a *means* to an end. Some governments or statesmen may seek influence for its own sake, but for most it is instrumental, just like money. They use it primarily for achieving or defending other goals, which may include prestige, territory, souls, raw materials, security, or alliances.

2. State A, in its acts toward state B, uses or mobilizes certain *resources*. A resource is any physical or mental object or quality available as an instrument of inducement to persuade, reward, threaten, or punish. The concept of resource may be illustrated in the following example. Suppose an unarmed robber walks into a bank and asks the clerk to give up money. The clerk observes clearly that the robber has no weapon and refuses to comply with the order. The robber has sought to influence the behavior of the clerk, but has failed. The next time, however, the robber walks in armed with a pistol and threatens to shoot if the clerk does not give up the money. This time, the clerk complies. In this instance, the robber has mobilized certain resources or capabilities (the gun) and succeeds in influencing the clerk to comply. But other less tangible resources may be involved as well. The appearance of the person, particularly facial expression, may convey determination, threat, or weakness, all of which may subtly influence the behavior of the clerk. In international politics, the diplomatic gestures and words accompanying actions may be as important as the acts themselves. A government that places troops on alert but insists that it is doing so for domestic reasons will have an impact abroad quite different

from the government that organizes a similar alert but accompanies it with threats to go to war. "Signals" or diplomatic "body language" may be as important as dramatic actions such as alerts and mobilizations.

3. The act of influencing B obviously involves a *relationship* between A and B, although, as will be seen later, the relationship may not even involve overt communication. If the relationship covers any period of time, we can also say that it is a *process*.

4. If A can get B to do something, but B cannot get A to do a similar thing, then we can say that A has more power than B regarding that particular issue. Power, therefore, can also be viewed as a *quantity*, but as a quantity it is only meaningful when compared to the power of others. Power is therefore relative.

To summarize, power may be viewed from several aspects: It is a means; it is based on resources; it is a relationship and a process; and it can be measured, at least crudely.

We can break down the concept of power into three distinct analytic elements: power comprises (1) the *acts* (process, relationship) of influencing other states; (2) the *resources* used to make the wielding of influence successful; and (3) the *responses* to the acts. The three elements must be kept distinct. Since this definition may seem too abstract, we can define the concept in the more operational terms of policy makers. In formulating policy and the strategy to achieve certain goals, they would explicitly or implicitly ask the five following questions:

1. Given our goals, what do we wish B to do or not to do? (X)
2. How shall we get B to do or not to do X? (implies a relationship and process)
3. What resources are at our disposal so that we can induce B to do or not to do X?
4. What is B's probable response to our attempts to influence its behavior?
5. What are the *costs* of taking actions 1, 2, or 3—as opposed to other alternatives?

Before discussing the problem of resources and responses, we have to fill out our model of the influence act to account for the many patterns of behavior that may be involved in an international relationship. First, the exercise of influence implies more than merely A's ability to *change* the behavior of B. Influence may also be seen when A attempts to get B to *continue* a course of action or policy that is useful to, or in the interests of, A.[2] The exercise of influence does not always cease, therefore, after B does X. It is often a continuing process of reinforcing B's behavior.

Second, it is almost impossible to find a situation where B does not

---

[2] J. David Singer, "Inter-Nation Influence: A Formal Model," *American Political Science Review*, 57 (1963), 420–30. State A might also wish state B to do W, Y, and Z, which may be incompatible with the achievement of X.

also have some influence over A. Our model has suggested that influence is exercised only in one direction, by A over B. In reality, influence is multilateral. State A, for example, would seldom seek a particular goal unless it has been influenced in a particular direction by the actions of other states in the system. At a minimum, there is the problem of feedback in any relationship: If B complies with A's wishes and does X, that behavior may subsequently prompt A to change its own behavior, perhaps in the interest of B. The phenomenon of feedback may be illustrated as follows:

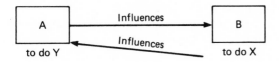

Third, there is the type of relationship that includes "anticipated reaction."[3] This is the situation where B, anticipating rewards or punishments from A, changes his behavior, perhaps even before A makes any "signals" about possible action. Deterrence theory clearly assumes that B—the potential aggressor against A—will not attack (where it might, were there no deterrent), knowing that an unacceptable level of punishment would surely result. A similar situation, but in reverse, is also common in international politics. This is where A might wish B to do X, but does not try to influence B for fear that B will do Y instead, which is an unfavorable response from A's point of view. In a hypothetical situation, the government of India might wish to obtain arms from the United States to build up its own defenses, but does not request such arms because it fears that the United States would insist on certain conditions for the sale of arms that might compromise India's nonalignment. This anticipated reaction may also be multilateral, where A wishes B to do X, but will not try to get B to do it because it fears that C, a third state, will do Y, which is unfavorable to A's interests. India wants to purchase American arms, but does not seek to influence the United States to sell them for fear that Pakistan (C) will then build up its own armaments and thus accelerate the arms race between the two countries. In this situation, Pakistan (C) has influence over the actions of the Indian government even though it has not deliberately sought to influence India on this particular matter or even communicated its position in any way. The Indian government has simply perceived that there is a relatively high probability that if it seeks to influence the United States, Pakistan will react in a manner contrary to India's interests.

Fourth, power and influence may be measured by scholars, but what is important in international politics is the *perceptions* of influence and capabilities held by policy makers and the way they interpret another government's signals.

[3] Herbert A. Simon, "Notes on the Observation and Measurement of Political Power," *Journal of Politics,* 15 (1953), 500–16. For further analysis, see David A. Baldwin, "Inter-Nation Influence Revisited," *Journal of Conflict Resolution,* 15 (December 1971), 478–79.

The reason that governments invest millions of dollars for gathering intelligence is to develop a reasonably accurate picture of other states' capabilities and intentions. Where there is a great discrepancy between perceptions and reality, the results to a country's foreign policy may be disastrous. To take our example of the bank robber again, suppose that the person held a harmless toy pistol and threatened the clerk. The clerk perceived the gun to be real and deduced the robber's intention to use it. As a result, the clerk complied with the demand. In this case, the robber's influence was far greater than the "objective" character of the robber's capabilities and intentions; and distorted perception by the clerk led to an act which was unfavorable to the bank.

Finally, as our original model suggests, A may try to influence B *not to do* X. Sometimes this is called negative power, or deterrence, where A acts in a manner to *prevent* a certain action it deems undesirable to its interests. This is a typical relationship in international politics. By signing the Munich treaty, the British and French governments hoped to prevent Germany from invading Czechoslovakia; Israeli attacks on PLO facilities in Lebanon are designed to demonstrate that PLO guerrilla operations against Israel will be met by vast punishments, the costs of which to the PLO would far outweigh the gains of the terrorist acts. Such a cost–benefit analysis, the Israelis hope, would deter the PLO from undertaking further operations. The reader should keep in mind the distinction between compellance and deterrence.

RESOURCES

The second element of the concept of power consists of those resources that are mobilized in support of the acts taken to influence state B's behavior. It is difficult to assess the general capacity of a state to control the actions and policies of others unless we also have some knowledge of the capabilities involved.[4] Nevertheless, it should be acknowledged that social scientists do not understand all the reasons why some actors—whether people, groups, governments, or states—wield influence successfully, while others do not.

It is clear that, in political relationships, not everyone possesses equal influence. In domestic politics, it is possible to construct a lengthy list of capabilities and attributes that seemingly permit some to wield influence over large numbers of people and important public decisions. Robert Dahl lists such tangibles as money, wealth, information, time, political allies, official position, and control over jobs, and such intangibles as personality and leadership qualities.[5] But not everyone who possesses these capabilities can command the obedience of other people. What is crucial in relating resources to influence, according to Dahl, is that one *mobilize them for one's political purposes* and possess the skill

---

[4] We might assess influence for historical situations solely on the basis of whether A got B to do X, without our having knowledge of either A's or B's capabilities.

[5] Robert A. Dahl, *Who Governs?* (New Haven, Conn.: Yale University Press, 1961).

to mobilize them. One who uses wealth, time, information, friends, and personality for political purposes will probably be able to influence others on public issues. A person, on the other hand, who possesses the same capabilities but uses them to invent a new mousetrap is not apt to be important in politics. The same propositions also hold true in international politics. The amount of influence a state wields over others can be related to the capabilities *mobilized* in support of *specific* foreign-policy objectives. To put this proposition in another way, we can argue that resources do not determine the uses to which they will be put. Nuclear power can be used to provide electricity or to deter and perhaps destroy other nations. The use of resources depends less on their quality and quantity than on the external objectives a government formulates for itself.

The *variety* of foreign-policy instruments available to a nation for influencing others is partly a function of the quantity and quality of capabilities. What a government seeks to do—the type of objectives it formulates—and how it attempts to do it will depend at least partially on the resources it finds available. A country such as Thailand, which possesses relatively few resources, cannot, even if it would desire, construct intercontinental ballistic missiles with which to intimidate others, establish a worldwide propaganda network, or dispense several billion dollars annually of foreign aid to try to influence other countries. We can conclude, therefore, that how states *use* their resources depends on their external objectives, but the choice of objectives and the instruments to achieve those objectives are limited or influenced by the quality and quantity of available resources.

THE MEASUREMENT OF RESOURCES

For many years, students of international politics have made meticulous comparisons of the potential capabilities of various nations, assuming that a nation was powerful, or capable of achieving its objectives, to the extent that it possessed certain "elements of power." Comparative data relating to production of iron ore, coal, and hydroelectricity, economic growth rates, educational levels, population growth rates, military resources, transportation systems, and sources of raw materials are presented as indicators of a nation's power. Few have acknowledged that these comparisons do not measure a state's power or influence but only its potential capacity to wage war. Other resources, such as diplomatic or propaganda skills, are seldom measured; but surely they are as important as war-making potential. Measurements and assessments are not particularly useful anyway unless they are related to specific foreign-policy issues. Capability is always the capability to do something; its assessment is most meaningful when carried on within a framework of certain foreign-policy objectives.

The deduction of actual influence from the quantity and quality of potential and mobilized capabilities may, in some cases, give an approximation of reality, but historically there have been too many discrepancies between the basis of power and the amount of influence to warrant adopting this practice as a useful approach to international relations. One could have assumed, for example, on the basis of a comparative study of technological and educational levels and general standards of living in the 1920s and 1930s that the United States would have been one of the most influential states in international politics. A careful comparison of certain resources, called the "great essentials,"[6] revealed the United States to be in an enviable position. In the period 1925 to 1930, it was the only major country in the world that produced from its own resources adequate supplies of food, power, iron, machinery, chemicals, coal, iron ore, and petroleum. If actual diplomatic influence had been deduced from the quantities of "great essentials" possessed by the major nations, the following ranking of states would have resulted: (1) United States, (2) Germany, (3) Great Britain, (4) France, (5) Russia, (6) Italy, (7) Japan. However, the diplomatic history of the world from 1925 to 1930 would suggest that there was little correlation between the resources of these countries and their *actual influence.* If we measure influence by the impact these states made on the system and by the responses they could invoke when they sought to change the behavior of other states, we would find for this period quite a different ranking, such as the following: (1) France, (2) Great Britain, (3) Italy, (4) Germany, (5) Russia, (6) Japan, (7) United States.

Indeed, many contemporary international relationships reveal how often the "strong" states do not achieve their objectives—or at least have to settle for poor substitutes—even when attempting to influence the behavior of "weak" states. How, for instance, did Marshal Tito's Yugoslavia effectively resist all sorts of pressures and threats by the powerful Soviet Union after it was expelled from the Communist bloc? Why, despite its overwhelming superiority in capabilities, was the United States unable in the 1960s to achieve its major objectives against a weak Cuba and North Vietnam? How have "small" states gained trading privileges and all sorts of diplomatic concessions from those nations with great economic wealth and military power? The ability of state A to change the behavior of state B is, we would assume, enhanced if it possesses physical resources to use in the influence act; but B is by no means defenseless or vulnerable to diplomatic, economic, or military pressures because it fails to own a large modern army, raw materials, and money for foreign aid. The successful exercise of influence is also dependent upon such factors as personality, perceptions, friendships, and traditions, and, not being easy to measure, these factors have a way of rendering power calculations and equations difficult. Aside from these situational factors, we may specify certain other conditions that help determine, regardless of military and economic capabilities, whether or not acts of influencing will succeed. These conditions, or variables, also help explain why states with very

[6] Frank H. Simonds and Brooks Emeny, *The Great Powers in World Politics* (New York: American Book, 1939).

weak capabilities are often able to resist the demands of the strong and sometimes achieve their own demands at the expense of the interests of major powers.

VARIABLES AFFECTING THE EXERCISE OF INFLUENCE

One reason that gross quantities of resources cannot be equated with effective influence relates to the distinction between a state's overall capabilities and the *relevance* of resources to a particular diplomatic situation. A nuclear force, for example, is often thought to increase the diplomatic influence of those who possess it. No doubt nuclear weaponry is an important element in a state's general prestige abroad and may be an effective deterrent against a strategic attack on its homeland or "core" interests. Yet the most important aspect of a nuclear capability—or any military capability—is not its possession, but its relevance and the ability to signal one's determination to use it. Other governments must know that the capability is not of mere symbolic significance. The government of North Vietnam possessed a particular advantage over the United States (hence, influence) because it knew that in almost no circumstances would the American government use strategic nuclear weapons against its country. It therefore effectively broke through the significance of the American nuclear capability as far as the Vietnam War was concerned. A resource is useless unless it is both mobilized in support of foreign-policy objectives and made credible. Likewise, nuclear weapons would be irrelevant in negotiations on cultural exchanges, just as the Arab countries' vast oil resources could not be effectively mobilized to influence the outcome of international negotiations on satellite communications. Influence is always specific to a particular issue, and resources must be relevant to that issue.

A second variable that determines the success or failure of acts of influence is the extent to which there are *needs* between the two countries in any influence relationship. In general, a country that needs something from another is vulnerable to its acts of influence. This is the primary reason that states that are "weak" in many capabilities can nevertheless obtain concessions from "strong" countries. Consider the case of France and Germany and some of the "weak" states in the Middle East. Both European countries are highly dependent upon Arab lands for oil supplies. They have an important need, which only the Arab countries can satisfy at a reasonable cost. On the other hand, the Middle Eastern countries that control these oil resources may not be so dependent upon Germany and France, particularly if they can sell their oil easily elsewhere. Because, in this situation, needs are not equal on both sides, the independent states (in terms of needs) can make demands (or resist demands made against them) on the dependent great powers and obtain important concessions. The German and French governments know that if they do not make these concessions or if they press their own demands too hard, the Arab states can threaten to cut off oil supplies. Their dependence thus makes them vulnerable to the demands and influence acts of what would otherwise be considered "weak" states. To the Arab states, oil is much more important as a capability than military forces—at least in their relations with major powers. In the form of a general hypothesis, we can suggest that, regardless of the quantity, quality, and credibility of a state's capabilities, the more state B needs, or is dependent upon, state A, the more likely that state A's acts—threats, promises, rewards, or punishments—will succeed in changing or sustaining B's behavior.

A third variable that has assumed increasing importance in the past several decades, and one that can be considered an important resource, is level of technical expertise. An increasing number of issues on the international and foreign-policy agendas are highly technical in nature: law of the sea, satellite broadcasting, international monetary matters, and the like. Many of these issues are discussed in international fora, where leadership often depends more on knowledge of the technical issues than on other types of resources. Those governments which come armed with technical studies, have a full command of the nature of the problem, and are prepared to put forth realistic solutions are more likely to wield influence than are governments which have only rudimentary knowledge of the problem and no scientific studies to back their national positions. A number of recent case studies have demonstrated conclusively that the outcomes of negotiations on technical questions cannot be predicted from the gross power of the participants and that knowledge, among other factors, accounts for more than raw capabilities.[7]

Understanding the dynamics of power relationships at the international level would be relatively easy if resource relevance, credibility, need, and knowledge were the only variables involved. Unfortunately, political actions do not always conform to simple hypotheses, because human characteristics of pride, stubbornness, prestige, and friendship enter into all acts of influence as well. A government may be highly dependent upon some other state and still resist its demands; it may be willing to suffer all sorts of privations, and even physical destruction and loss of independence, simply for the sake of pride. The government of North Vietnam was willing to accept a very high level of destruction of lives and productive facilities by American bombers rather than make diplomatic or military concessions to the United States.

Additional variables affecting the exercise of influence can be observed in the situation where two small states of approximately equal capabilities make similar demands upon a "major" power and neither of the small states is dependent upon the large—or vice versa. Which will achieve its objectives? Will both exercise influence equally? Hypothetically, suppose that the ambassadors of Norway and Albania go to the British Foreign Office on the same day and ask the

---

[7] See, for example, the case studies in Robert O. Keohane and Joseph S. Nye, *Power and Interdependence: World Politics in Transition* (Boston: Little, Brown and Company, 1977). See also David Baldwin's strong emphasis on the relevance of resources to particular situations in "Power Analysis and World Politics," *World Politics*, 31 (January 1979), 161–94.

British government to lower tariffs on bicycles, a product that the two countries would like to export to England. Assume that the quality and price of the bicycles are approximately the same and that the British government does not wish to allow too many imports for fear of damaging the domestic bicycle industry. Assume further that both the Norwegian and Albanian ambassadors offer roughly equal concessions if the British will lower their tariffs on bicycles. Both claim they will lower their own tariffs on English automobiles. Which ambassador is most likely to succeed—that is, to achieve his government's objectives? Chances are that the British government would favor the request of the Norwegian ambassador and turn down the representation by the diplomat from Tirana. The explanation of this decision can probably not be found in the resources of either of the small countries (both offered approximately equal rewards) or in need, since in this hypothetical situation Britain needs neither of the small countries' automobile markets. Norway would get the favorable decision because British policy makers are more *responsive* to Norwegian interests than to those of Albania. Albania represents a Communist state whose government normally displays through its diplomacy and propaganda strong hostility toward England.

After relevant resources, need, and knowledge, the fourth variable that determines the effectiveness of acts of influence is thus the ephemeral quality of responsiveness.[8] Responsiveness can be seen as a disposition to receive another's requests with sympathy, even to the point where a government is willing to sacrifice some of its own values and interests in order to fulfill those requests; responsiveness is the willingness to be influenced. In one study, it was shown that members of the State Department in the United States may take considerable pains to promote the requests and interests of other governments among their superiors and in other government agencies, provided that the requesting government feels that the issue is important or that the need must be fulfilled.[9] In our hypothetical case, if the quality of responsiveness is present in the case of the Norwegian request, members of the British Foreign Office would probably work for the Norwegians and try to persuade other government agencies concerned with trade and commerce to agree to a lowering of the tariff on bicycles. In the British reaction to the Albanian request, it is not likely that the government would display much responsiveness. Suspicion, traditional animosities, lack of trust, and years of unfavorable diplomatic experience would probably prevent the development of much British sympathy for Albania's needs or interests. Although Albania and Norway made similar requests and similar counteroffers, the lack of responsiveness on the part of the British officials toward Albania's government and its policies would probably account for their rejection of the

[8] The concept of responsiveness is introduced by Karl W. Deutsch et al., *Political Community and the North Atlantic Area* (Princeton, N.J.: Princeton University Press, 1957); developed by Dean G. Pruitt, "National Power and International Responsiveness," *Background,* 7 (1964), 165–78. See also Dean G. Pruitt, "Definition of the Situation as a Determinant of International Action," in *International Behavior: A Social-Psychological Analysis,* ed. Herbert C. Kelman (New York: Holt, Rinehart & Winston, 1965), pp. 393–432.

[9] Pruitt, "National Power," 175–76.

Albanian request. When the other variables, such as resources or need, are held constant or made equal, the degree of responsiveness will determine the success or failure of acts taken to influence other states' behavior.

If effective influence cannot be deduced solely from the quantity and quality of physical capabilities, how do we proceed to measure influence? If we want to assess a situation that has already occurred, the easiest way to measure influence is to study the *responses* of those in the influence relationship.[10] If A can get B to do X, but C cannot get B to do the same thing, then in that particular issue, A has more influence. If B does X despite the protestations of A, then we can assume that A, in this circumstance, did not enjoy much influence over B. It is meaningless to argue that the Soviet Union is more powerful than the United States unless we cite how, for what purposes, and in relation to whom the Soviet Union and the United States are exerting influence.

Predicting influence in a future situation, however, is more difficult. Since such factors as pride, traditional friendships and enmities, personality characteristics of policy makers, and unique circumstances cannot be measured, our task would be to assign values, however crudely, to only three of the variables discussed above: capability (composed of the relevance and degree of mobilization of resources); extent of needs or *dependence;* and extent of *responsiveness.* Below are some examples of how such an exercise might be conducted. Keep in mind, however, that the values on the scales are rough, subjective guesses, and that effective prediction of the probable outcome of any influence relationship would require precise indicators and measures of the variables. Let us outline, then, a situation where one government (A) is attempting to influence the actions, images, and decisions of another government (B). Each of the three variables is measured on a scale from 0 to 10. Our crude formula will be:

$$\text{A's resources} + \frac{\text{B's needs}}{\text{from A}} + \frac{\text{B's responsiveness}}{\text{to A}} = \frac{\text{Probability that A}}{\text{will succeed}}$$

One illustration might be the case where Canada attempts to arrange some preferential trade agreement with the Common Market. The resources mobilized by Ottawa are (1) a *guaranteed* supply of fuels—especially uranium—to the European countries, (2) offers of special considerations or tax write-offs for Europeans who wish to make direct investments in Canada, and (3) the skills, knowledge, and documentation of Canadian negotiators. We would assign a value of six to the first variable. On the question of need, the Europeans, having faced the Arab oil embargo of 1973–1974, are very sensitive to obtaining alternative and secure sources of supply. Thus, we would assign a value of seven to the second variable. Finally, although Canadian–European ties have not been extensive, responsiveness is reasonably high; we will assign a value of six to this variable. The sum of the three variables, then, is nineteen out of

[10] Robert A. Dahl, "The Concept of Power," *Behavioral Science,* 2 (1957), 201–15.

a possible thirty, indicating that there is about a 63 percent probability that Canada's objective will be achieved.

One final variable involving costs and commitments should be identified; it was omitted from the example because it is virtually impossible to measure. Success in the wielding of influence seems to be related also to the extent to which the objectives of the states are compatible or the degree of commitment each government has toward those objectives. If I am strongly committed to attending a poker game Friday night and you ask me to go to a football game, no matter what sorts of arguments you make, I will not go. The costs of breaking the commitment—displeasure of friends and possible dismissal from the poker group—would far outweigh the possible advantages of seeing a ball game. But where no significant costs are associated with not going to the poker game—perhaps there are already too many players—then I might well be persuaded to see some football instead. My interests are not well defined, I have no firm commitment to one course of action; hence, I will be more open to persuasion, provided that you have relevant resources (your offer to pay my way) and I recognize that you would rather not go to the game by yourself.

Thus, there is also an element of *probability* in predicting the outcome of influence acts and in measuring the degree of influence actors have over each other. It would be incorrect to infer that since A gets B to do X, A has *much* power, because it might not make much difference to B whether or not it does X. Or, in the case of nuclear deterrence, it doesn't make much sense to argue that the United States has much power over the Soviet Union because the Soviet Union has not attacked North America. The point is that such an attack has extremely low probability in any event; power could be inferred only if we knew the Soviet Union had strong intentions of launching an attack but was dissuaded by threats of American retaliation.

HOW INFLUENCE IS EXERCISED

Social scientists have noted several fundamental techniques that individuals and groups use to influence each other. In a political system that contains no one legitimate center of authority that can command the members of the group or society, bargaining has to be used among the sovereign entities to achieve or defend their objectives. Recalling that A seeks one of three courses of conduct from B (B to do X in the future, B not to do X in the future, or B to continue doing X), it may use six different tactics, involving acts of:

1. PERSUASION. By persuasion we mean simply initiating or discussing a proposal with another and eliciting a favorable response without explicitly holding out the possibility of rewards or punishments. We cannot assume that the exercise of influence is always *against* the wishes of others and that there are only two possible outcomes of the act, one favoring A, the other favoring

B. For example, state A asks B to support it at a coming international conference on the control of narcotics. State B might not originally have any particular interest in the conference or its outcome; but it decides, on the basis of A's initiative, that something positive might be gained, not only by supporting A's proposals, but also by attending the conference. In this case, B might also expect to gain some type of reward in the future, although not necessarily from A. Persuasion would also include protests and denials that do not involve obvious threats.

2. THE OFFER OF REWARDS.   This is the situation where A promises to do something favorable to B if B complies with the wishes of A. Rewards may be of almost any type in international relations. To gain the diplomatic support of B at the narcotics conference, A may offer to increase foreign-aid payments, lower tariffs on goods imported from B, support B at a later conference on communications facilities, or promise to remove a previous punishment. The last tactic is used often by negotiators. After having created an unfavorable situation, they promise to remove it in return for some concessions by their opponents.

3. THE GRANTING OF REWARDS.   In some instances, the credibility of a government is not very high, and state B, before complying with A's wishes, may insist that A actually give the reward in advance. Frequently, in armistice negotiations, neither side will unilaterally take steps to demilitarize an area or demobilize troops until the other shows evidence of complying with the agreements. One of the clichés of cold-war diplomacy holds that deeds, not words, are required for the granting of rewards and concessions.

4. THE THREAT OF PUNISHMENT.   Threats of punishment may be further subdivided into two types: (a) positive threats, where, for example, state A threatens to increase tariffs, institute a boycott or embargo against trade with B, or use force; and (b) threats of deprivation, where A threatens to withdraw foreign aid or in other ways withhold rewards or other advantages that it already grants to B.

5. THE INFLICTION OF NONVIOLENT PUNISHMENT.   In this situation, threats are carried out in the hope of altering B's behavior, which, in most cases, could not be altered by other means. The problem with this tactic is that it often results in reciprocal measures by the other side, thus inflicting damage on both, and not necessarily bringing about a desired state of affairs. If, for example, A threatens to increase its military capabilities if B does X and then proceeds to implement the threat, it is not often that B will comply with A's wishes, because it, too, can increase its military capabilities. In this type of situation, both sides indulge in the application of punishments that may escalate into more serious forms unless the conflict is resolved. Typical acts of nonviolent punishment include breaking diplomatic relations, raising tariffs, instituting boycotts and embargoes, holding hostages, organizing blockades, closing frontiers, or walking out of a diplomatic conference.

6. FORCE. In previous eras, when governments did not possess the variety of foreign-policy instruments available today, they frequently had to rely upon the use of force in the bargaining process. Force and violence were not only the most efficient tactics, but in many cases the only means possible for influencing. Today, the situation is different. As technological levels rise and dependencies develop, other means of inducement become available and can serve as substitutes for force.[11]

PATTERNS OF INFLUENCE IN THE INTERNATIONAL SYSTEM

Most governments at some time use all their techniques for influencing others, but probably over 90 percent of all relations between states are based on simple persuasion and deal with relatively unimportant technical matters. Since such interactions seldom make the headlines, we often assume that most relations between states involve the making or carrying out of threats. But whether a government is communicating with another over an unimportant technical matter or over a subject of great consequence, it is likely to use a particular type of tactic in its attempts to influence, depending on the past tradition of friendship or hostility between those two governments and the amount of compatability between their objectives and interests. Allies, for example, seldom threaten each other with force or even make blatant threats of punishment, but governments that disagree over a wide range of policy objectives and hold attitudes of suspicion and hostility toward each other are more likely to resort to threats and imposition of punishments. The methods of exerting influence between Great Britain and the United States are, typically, persuasion and rewards, whereas the methods of exerting influence between the Soviet Union and the United States in the early post–World War II era were typically threatening and inflicting punishments of various types. We can construct rough typologies of international relationships as identified by the typical techniques used in the act of influence.

[11] Francois de Callières, a renowned French diplomat of the eighteenth century, also suggested the utility of these techniques when he wrote, "Every Christian prince must take as his chief maxim not to employ arms to support or vindicate his rights until he has employed and exhausted the way of reason and persuasion. It is to his interest, also, to add to reason and persuasion the influence of benefits conferred, which indeed is one of the surest ways to make his own power secure, and to increase it." *On the Manner of Negotiating with Princes,* trans. A.F. Whyte (Boston: Houghton Mifflin, 1919), p. 7. In a treatise on foreign policy written approximately 300 B.C., Kautilya noted four fundamental techniques for obtaining the desired results from other Indian states: conciliation *(sama)*, gifts *(dana)*, dissension *(bheda)*, and punishment *(danda)*. See George Modelski, "Kautilya: Foreign Policy and International System in the Ancient Hindu World," *American Political Science Review,* 58 (1964), 553.

1. RELATIONS OF CONSENSUS. Relations of consensus would be typical between those states that have few disagreements over foreign-policy objectives, a high degree of mutual responsiveness, or a very low level of interaction and involvement in each other's affairs. An example of the first would be Anglo-American relations, and, of the last, the relations between Thailand and Finland. In the relations of consensus, influence is exercised primarily by the technique of persuasion and through the subtle offering of rewards. Since violence as a form of punishment is almost inconceivable between two countries, the military capabilities of neither actor are organized, mobilized, and "targeted" toward the other.

2. RELATIONS OF OVERT MANIPULATION. Here, there may be some disagreement or conflict over foreign-policy objectives, or state A might undertake some domestic policy that was disapproved by state B, such as a form of racial discrimination. Since there is some conflict, there will also be at least a modest degree of involvement between the two actors, or a perception that A and B are in some kind of a relationship of interdependence. The techniques used to influence will include, if normal persuasion fails, (a) offers of rewards, (b) granting of rewards, (c) threats to withhold rewards (such as not to give foreign aid in the future), or (d) threats of nonviolent punishment, including, for instance, the raising of tariffs against B's products. Militarily, in relations of overt manipulation, there is still no mobilization or targeting of military capabilities toward state B. Military capabilities are thus of little relevance to the power of each state toward the other. Examples of overt manipulation would include contemporary relations between Rumania and the Soviet Union and relations between France and the United States during de Gaulle's presidency.

3. RELATIONS OF COERCION. In relations of coercion, there are fundamental disagreements over foreign-policy objectives. Almost all actions that A takes externally are perceived by B to be a threat to its own interests. Involvement is therefore high, and the degree of mutual responsiveness is usually very low, if it exists at all. A seeks to influence B's behavior typically by (a) making warnings and threatening punishments; (b) inflicting nonviolent punishments; and, under extreme provocation, (c) the selective and limited use of force, as, for example, in a peacetime blockade. Military capabilities are likely to be targeted toward each other and become a relevant factor in power relationships, since they are often mobilized for threats and the policy makers labor under the assumption that they might have to be used. Examples would include relations between the Soviet Union and the Western coalition until détente, Cuba and the United States in the early 1960s, Syria and Israel since 1948, and Iran and Iraq in 1979.

4. RELATIONS OF FORCE. Here, there is almost total disagreement on foreign-policy objectives, and the areas of consensus are limited to a few necessities, such as communications. The degree of involvement is obviously extremely high. The typical form of exercising influence is through the infliction of violent punishment, although, in some instances rewards (say, peace offers) might be proffered. National resources are mobilized primarily with a view to conducting the policy of punishment. However, the quantity of military capabilities used will vary with the geographic and force-level boundaries that the disputants place on the conflict.

To summarize this analysis of power, we can suggest that power is an integral part of all political relationships; but in international politics we are interested primarily in one process: how one state influences the behavior of another in its own interests. The act of influencing becomes a central focus for the study of international politics, and it is from this act that we can best deduce a definition of power. If we observe the act of influencing, we can see that power is a process, a relationship, a means to an end, and even a quantity. Moreover, we can make an analytical distinction among the act of influencing, the basis, or resources, upon which the act relies, and the response to the act. Resources are an important determinant of how successful the wielding of influence will be, but they are by no means the only determinant. The nature of a country's foreign-policy objectives, the skill with which a state mobilizes its capabilities for foreign-policy purposes, its needs, responsiveness, costs, and commitments are equally important. Acts of influencing may take many forms, the most important of which are the offer and granting of rewards, the threat and imposition of punishments, and the application of force. The choice of means used to induce will depend, in turn, upon the general nature of relations between any two given governments, the degree of involvement between them, and the extent of their mutual responsiveness. Having analyzed the general techniques of wielding influence and the conditions under which power is likely to succeed, we may now turn to the specific instruments of inducement used to achieve objectives, ranging from simple diplomatic persuasion to the use of violence on a massive scale.

SELECTED BIBLIOGRAPHY

BACHRACH, PETER, and MORTON S. BARATZ, "The Two Faces of Power," *American Political Science Review*, 56 (1962), 947–52.

BALDWIN, DAVID A., "Inter-Nation Influence Revisited," *Journal of Conflict Resolution*, 15 (December 1971), 471–86.

———, "The Power of Positive Sanctions," *World Politics*, 24 (October 1971), 19–38.

———, "Power Analysis and World Politics: New Trends versus Old Tendencies," *World Politics*, 31 (January 1979), 161–94.

———, "Interdependence and Power: A Conceptual Analysis," *International Organization*, 34 (Autumn 1980), 471–506.

BELL, RODERICK, DAVID V. EDWARDS, and R. HARRISON WAGNER, eds., *Political Power: A Reader in Theory and Research.* New York: Free Press, 1969.

COX, ROBERT, and HAROLD K. JACOBSEN, *The Anatomy of Influence.* New Haven: Yale University Press, 1973.

DAHL, ROBERT, "The Concept of Power," *Behavioral Science,* 2 (1957), 201–15.

FERRIS, WAYNE H., *The Power Capabilities of Nation-States.* Lexington, Mass.: D.C. Heath, 1973.

FOX, ANNETTE B., *The Power of Small States: Diplomacy in World War II.* Chicago: University of Chicago Press, 1959.

GEORGE, ALEXANDER L., and RICHARD SMOKE, *Deterrence in American Foreign Policy,* Chap. 21. New York: Columbia University Press, 1974.

GROSS, ERNEST A., "Moral Power in International Relations," *Journal of International Affairs,* 12, (1958), 132–37.

HASKEL, BARBARA G., "Access to Society: A Neglected Dimension of Power," *International Organization,* 34 (Winter 1980), 89–120.

JONES, STEPHEN B., "The Power Inventory and National Strategy," *World Politics,* 6 (1954), 421–52.

KEOHANE, ROBERT O., and JOSEPH S. NYE, *Power and Interdependence: World Politics in Transition.* Boston: Little, Brown and Company, 1977.

KNORR, KLAUS, *Military Power and Potential.* Lexington, Mass.: Raytheon/Heath Co., 1970.

———, *The Power of Nations: The Political Economy of International Relations.* New York: Basic Books, 1975.

MACK, ANDREW J.R., "Why Big Nations Lose Small Wars: The Politics of Asymmetric Conflict," *World Politics,* 27 (January 1975), 175–200.

PRUITT, DEAN, "National Power and International Responsiveness," *Background,* 7 (1964), 165–78.

SIMON, HERBERT A., "Notes on the Observation and Measurement of Political Power," *Journal of Politics,* 15 (1953), 500–16.

SINGER, J. DAVID, "Inter-Nation Influence: A Formal Model," *American Political Science Review,* 57 (1963), 420–30.

7

The Instruments of Policy: Diplomatic Bargaining

In seeking to achieve objectives, realize values, or defend interests, govenments must communicate with those whose actions and behavior they wish to deter, alter, or reinforce. Today there are many occasions and media of communication that may be employed for conveying hopes, wishes, or threats to others. At the press conference, political rally, or banquet, government officials make statements directed not just to domestic audiences but to foreign governments and peoples as well. Nevertheless, most official attempts to wield influence abroad are carried out through formal diplomatic channels or by direct communication between foreign ministers and heads of state.

The subjects of interstate communication include definitions of a government's objectives, rationalizations for them, threats, promises, and the holding out of possibilities for concluding agreements on contentious issues. As will be seen, the function of diplomats is not so much to formulate their government's goals as to explain them abroad and attempt to persuade others to adjust their own policies to conform to those objectives. Diplomats are partially successful when they can get the government to which they are accredited to see a particular situation as their own government perceives it; they are totally successful when they are able to alter or maintain the actions of a foreign government in a manner favorable to the interests of their own government. Normally during the process of communication, those who formulate policy will reassess their objectives in the light of changing circumstances and varying foreign responses. Diplomats then convey the modified objectives to foreign governments; and the whole routine continues until consensus is reached through bargaining, until it is imposed by the use of force, or until one government abandons or withdraws from its objectives if they meet resistance abroad.

Objectives and diplomatic bargaining strategies are thus subject to constant reformulation on the basis of information and assessments provided by diplomats abroad and by various acts and signals governments make to each other. When mutual interest and consensus on a problem exist, the policy-formulating and policy-implementing processes may require only the length of time needed to fill in details on a piece of paper. When there is disagreement, misunderstanding, or incompatibility between two or more governments' values, objectives, and interests, the process may involve long periods of time. Both India and Pakistan, for instance, have maintained their basic objectives with regard to the states of Kashmir and Jammu for three decades although all of their diplomatic bargaining, threats, rewards, and use of force to resolve the issue have not succeeded in changing each other's position. The main purposes of this chapter are to illustrate some of the techniques of diplomatic bargaining and to discuss some of the contemporary problems attending diplomatic action. Before discussing these processes, however, it is necessary to examine some of the basic rules and traditions of diplomatic communication between independent states and analyze the position of the main medium for interstate communication, the ambassador.

THE INSTITUTIONS, RULES, AND PERSONNEL OF DIPLOMACY

The emissary is among the first of the distinct political roles established in human society. Between primitive tribes, whether friendly or antagonistic, communication was necessary; and special personnel, with certain religious, bargaining, or language skills, were appointed to conduct discussions on a variety of issues. Emissaries bargained over the allocation of hunting territory, settling of family or clan disputes, or planning of an intertribal marriage. Today, diplomats seek to extend national interests in foreign territories, protect the national society from a perceived threat, increase the volume of trade, resolve a conflict over contested territory, or regulate traffic in drugs.

It was not until the fifteenth century that the concept of a permanent mission, or legation, was instituted in Europe. Italian city-states during the late Renaissance period first developed a systematic diplomatic service and recognized the need for establishing a corps of professional diplomats. The functions of these early diplomats included obtaining information, safeguarding political and military interests, and expanding commerce. Indeed, organized diplomacy may have owed as much for its origins to the development of extensive trade networks in Europe and the Middle East as to political and military matters. The Venetian diplomatic service, for example, was originally a commercial organization. The new dynastic regimes emerging in Europe later emulated the diplomatic institutions established on the Italian peninsula; and by the eighteenth century, diplomacy was recognized as an important and honorable profession, even if its methods were not always so reputable.

Classical diplomacy operated among few political units: In 1648, for example, there were only twelve well-defined sovereign states in Europe, and the affairs of one did not frequently impinge on the interests of the other. In the present international system, not only are there more than 150 sovereign states, but their economic, political, and military interdependence means that almost any major domestic or foreign-policy decision in one will have repercussions on the interests of many others. In this setting, the problem of achieving mutually acceptable solutions to all issues is difficult and usually cannot be resolved through the relatively slow and cumbersome procedures of bilateral negotiations. Thus, a correlation between economic, scientific, and technological development and the growth of multilateral diplomacy can be observed. It is no accident that the most rapid growth of permanent multilateral diplomatic institutions occurred simultaneously with the fastest period of industrial and technological development in Europe. The bilateral patterns of diplomatic communication of the eighteenth century gave way first to ad hoc multilateral conferences and, more recently, to permanent multilateral diplomatic and technical organizations.

Until the latter part of the nineteenth century, most multilateral conferences dealt with the terms of peace following major European wars; but after the Franco-Prussian war of 1870–1871, governments began to send delegates to conferences dealing with the codification of international law (The Hague Conferences of 1899 and 1907) and the more technical economic problems that European governments commonly faced.[1] In 1875, a group of governments established the Universal Postal Union, the first permanent international machinery involving the membership of most of the states in the world. The idea of a permanent conference machinery was also put into practice in the League of Nations; and during the 1920s, other important ad hoc conferences were held in Genoa, Brussels, Geneva, and London to deal with economic reconstruction, German reparations, and disarmament. The machinery for Allied economic cooperation during World War I (The Inter-Allied Maritime Transport Council) was copied and expanded considerably during the war against Nazi Germany and Japan. There were also momentous meetings between the heads of state of the major powers at Ottawa, Cairo, Teheran, and Yalta; and the Allies created a series of interlocking conference systems to coordinate all aspects of the war effort and to plan for the postwar organization of the world.

Today, the concept of multilateral conference diplomacy is institutionalized in the United Nations and its specialized agencies. These organizations are widely known, but multilateral diplomacy also occurs constantly in thousands

---

[1] These conferences considered such disparate subjects as agriculture, regulation and production of sugar, international standards of sanitation, tariffs, international telegraphy, navigation on the Danube, the prime meridian, liquor traffic, statistics, maritime signalling, and weights and measures.

of ad hoc conferences and less formal meetings between diplomats or government officials. During the nineteenth century, for example, the American government sent diplomatic representatives to 100 conferences, or an average of one per year; in the period 1956–1958, American diplomats, specialists, and politicians attended 1,027 international conferences, an average of one per day.[2]

Not only has a large portion of diplomatic communication become channeled through multilateral institutions and organizations, but, even in bilateral relations, the institutional framework of communication has become increasingly complex as the range of issues common to any pair of states has expanded. During the eighteenth century, when foreign relations were concerned primarily with military, political, and dynastic problems, a country could be represented adequately in each major capital by an ambassador or minister and several secretaries. Envoys could perform their duties satisfactorily by keeping up on political developments in the country to which they were accredited and by applying tact, common sense, and intelligence to their contacts with foreign officials. Today, if diplomats at the ambassadorial rank are to achieve success in their efforts to influence the government to which they are accredited, they must command knowledge of a wide variety of affairs and subjects, including economics, propaganda techniques, labor relations, and all facets of political analysis. They frequently administer an embassy with a staff of several hundred specialists and secretaries. Office routine, expertise, and discipline within a bureaucratic organization have replaced the glamour and leisure of eighteenth-century salons and courts.

The last development of significance in diplomatic procedures has been the rapid increase in direct communication between heads of state. As modes of transportation have made travel a simple affair, high-ranking officials and policy makers can bypass the traditional diplomatic intermediary and maintain direct communication among themselves. These face-to-face confrontations may raise problems, since many presidents and prime ministers are not trained in diplomatic skills; but they have the compensating advantage of allowing constitutionally responsible officials to make decisions on the basis of their broad authority and to bypass the bureaucratic resistances or impediments to easy communication between governments. These officials often enjoy foreign travel because it raises their personal prestige at home and abroad and enables them to clarify their views personally to other heads of state. It is little wonder, then, that European leaders visit Washington or Moscow as often as twice each year, that most American presidents make at least several major trips abroad, and that leaders of nonaligned states are in almost constant personal communication with each other and with the major leaders of Western and Communist nations.

Whether conducted through trained diplomats or by heads of state, communication between governments representing widely diverse social, economic, and political systems is naturally liable to all sorts of distortion owing

[2] Elmer Plischke, *The Conduct of American Diplomacy,* 2nd ed. (New York: Van Nostrand Reinhold, 1961), p. 474.

to cultural differences, ideological cleavages, and plain misunderstandings. Since permanent diplomatic institutions were established in Italy during the fifteenth century, governments have commonly recognized that it is to their mutual advantage to observe certain rules of procedure that help make communication easier to conduct and less liable to distortion. Diplomatic bargaining processes become impaired if no one agrees as to who is entitled to represent a state or if diplomatic envoys are subject to harassment or intimidation by those to whom they are accredited. Three sets of rules concerning protocol, immunities, and noninterference have therefore been developed in Western international law and custom to facilitate communication between states.

Protocol

Diplomatic protocol is of considerable importance in assisting diplomats to pursue their tasks in an effective manner. Although the rituals of protocol may seem merely ceremonial leftovers of a previous era, they have a definite function even today. Rank, for example, constantly added irritants to international relations in the eighteenth century, and solution of the problem at the Congress of Vienna in 1815 has helped in many ways to reduce little frictions that may lead to poor relations and communication between governments. In the early years of modern diplomacy, the Pope claimed the right to decide the ceremonial order of the various dynasts' representatives; but, as the influence of the church in secular affairs declined, diplomats and their governments were left to their own devices—sometimes with disastrous results. Rank, protocol, and precedence had great symbolic significance; ambassadors and envoys frequently received orders not to permit other courts' envoys to precede them in ceremonial processions, for such acts could reflect adversely on the prestige and honor of their own dynast. In formal processions, for example, diplomats would plan strategies enabling them to gain favorable positions in the line. Several incidents have been recorded wherein coachmen were killed attempting to gain advantages over their rivals. It was not uncommon, moreover, for ambassadors to engage in duels to vindicate their honor and prestige when it was questioned by another envoy. In such circumstances, the candor and friendly personal relations necessary to successful diplomacy were not always easy to display.[3]

In 1815, four diplomatic ranks were established and universally adopted by European courts and foreign offices. The highest rank was assigned to ambassadors and papal nuncios, followed by envoys extraordinary and ministers plenipotentiary, ministers resident, and *chargés d'affaires.* These titles are still in use today and determine the ranking of diplomatic officials at ceremonial and political functions. The question of precedence was not, however, completely solved by agreement on the question of rank. Therefore, the delegates to the Congress of Aix-la-Chapelle in 1818 agreed that among members of the same rank, precedence should be established no longer on the prestige or power of the diplomat's

---

[3] See Hans Morgenthau, *Politics Among Nations,* 4th ed. (New York: Knopf, 1968).

government, but solely on the length of time the diplomat had served as ambassador in one country. Thus, if the ambassador of Luxembourg to the United States has served in Washington, D.C., longer than the Soviet ambassador, he or she always precedes the Soviet ambassador. Diplomats who have served the longest period in a foreign capital are normally referred to as the *doyens,* or deans, of the diplomatic corps and on ceremonial occasions always precede other ambassadors.

Another aspect of protocol that influences the efficiency of diplomatic processes is language, for precision in communication is one of the major requirements of effective diplomacy. To many outside government service, the style of written diplomatic communication seems at best specious and at worst hypocritical. Diplomatic correspondence today is largely devoid of the circuitous and formal phrases in use generations ago; it is still not unusual, however, to see notes stating, "I have the honor to acknowledge your excellency's note. . . ." or, "I feel constrained to advise you that my government cannot but acquiesce in the view that . . ." The use of such rhetoric is declining, and there is an increasing tendency in diplomatic communication to be frank and avoid any impression of being dilatory.

Formerly, by adhering to strict rules of etiquette, diplomats could phrase statements that gave precise meaning without creating the impression of impoliteness or belligerence. Gordon Craig cites the example of a meeting in 1859 between Napoleon III and the Austrian ambassador to France, when the Emperor in the politest terms expressed his regret that Franco-Austrian relations were not more cordial. If the Austrian ambassador was alert, he realized that Napoleon had really meant that unless the Austrians changed their foreign policy, a Franco-Austrian war was likely to ensue.[4] Although diplomats were aware of the meaning between the lines, the diplomatic environment at least *seemed* to be one of amity, courtesy, and common understanding. As will be seen below, much of the formality of diplomatic communication has been replaced by frankness and, in some cases, vulgarity, polemics, and intemperate namecalling.

Immunities

If governments are to seek to influence each others' policies and actions through effective communication, they must assume that their diplomatic agents abroad will not be abused or placed under conditions that would prevent them from engaging freely in bargaining and persuasion. Even among primitive people, envoys or messengers were usually regarded as sacrosanct and enjoyed special privileges and immunities when travelling abroad. Communication would have been impossible if emissaries had been treated as "heathen," burned, tortured, or eaten before delivering their messages. In ancient China, Greece, and India, as well as in the Muslim Empire, diplomatic immunities were regularly accorded

[4] Gordon A. Craig, "On the Diplomatic Revolution of Our Times" (The Haynes Foundation Lectures, University of California, Riverside, April 1961), p. 9.

to envoys and messengers from "barbarian" communities. On occasion, ambassadors were imprisoned or slain because they were suspected of trickery; but in most cases (as indicated in the ancient Indian *Mahabharata,* "The King who slays an envoy sinks into hell with all his ministers"), there were strong ethical sanctions and reasons of self-interest against violating diplomatic immunities.[5]

It is still the general rule of international law that diplomats and their embassies are to be treated as if they were on their native soil. They are immune from prosecution under the laws, customs, rules, or regulations of the government to which they are accredited. Those who enjoy diplomatic status (usually all the full-time foreign staff of the embassy) may not be molested by national police officials, nor may the premises of an embassy be visited by local law enforcement agents without the invitation of the embassy staff. If a French official enjoying diplomatic status parks his or her auto in a restricted zone in Stockholm, for instance, the official is not liable to fine, trial, or imprisonment by Swedish officials. However, if diplomatic officials commit serious crimes abroad, the host government may either demand that they be recalled or request that their immunities be lifted so that they can be indicted and tried in the receiving country's courts of law. A Central American diplomat was arrested upon his arrival in New York when police apprehended him attempting to smuggle a large amount of heroin into the United States. The State Department requested the foreign government to strip the man of his diplomatic status, which it consented to do; and he was eventually tried, convicted, and imprisoned according to American legal procedures.

If in this case the Central American government had refused to recall the ambassador or lift his diplomatic status, the United States could have declared him *persona non grata,* thus forcing the Central American government to recall him. In most cases, governments do recall their diplomats when requested to do so, and designating a diplomat *persona non grata* usually results from a diplomat's political actions, not from breaking a local law. Ambassadors and other diplomatic officials are usually declared *persona non grata* only when their efficiency has been impaired by indiscreet political statements, interference in internal affairs of the host country, or taking advantage of their status to indulge in espionage activities. During the cold war, there was rather rapid turnover of diplomatic personnel in the Western embassies in Moscow and the Soviet embassies in Western capitals, as numerous diplomats (many were intelligence agents posing as diplomats) were apprehended while conducting illegal intelligence activities. Retaliation also became an accepted practice; for example, if a British dipolmat was expelled from the Soviet Union, the British government normally

---

[5] See Frank M. Russell, *Theories of International Relations* (New York: Appleton-Century-Crofts, 1936), p. 42. In several recent instances, the Soviet government has promised immunity and safety to emissaries and delegations, only to imprison or execute them upon arrival. The cases in question involved a group representing the Polish underground in 1945 and the military and political leaders of the Hungarian revolution in 1956. The universal condemnation of the Iranian authorities' imprisoning fifty American diplomats for use as hostages in 1979–1981 derived from the recognition that a fundamental norm protecting interstate communication had been violated. If many governments acted similarly, international anarchy would result.

requested the immediate recall of a Soviet diplomat in London. Although the activities of diplomats during the cold war taxed the laws and customs of immunity, they were still recognized as essential to effective diplomacy, and there was surprisingly little discussion over the merits of either abandoning or proscribing them.[6]

Noninterference

If diplomatic officials ordinarily enjoy immunities from the laws of the country to which they are accredited, other customs have developed that limit the types of actions they can undertake in attempting to influence the policies of foreign governments. Chief among these is the stricture that they cannot in any way interfere in the internal political processes of another country. Normally, they are expected to confine official discussions to government personnel. Certainly they may defend their own government's policies to the foreign public by addressing private groups; but they must not make appeals to these people asking them to put pressures on their own government; nor can they provide funds to political parties, or provide leadership or other services to insurgents, political factions, or economic organizations.

These rules of noninterference are well established in law and customary practice, but as the domestic affairs of countries have increasingly important foreign-policy implications, the rules are in many cases circumvented. In 1919, President Wilson toured Italy exhorting the Italian people to press their government to make concessions at the Paris Peace Conference; foreign aid and technical personnel frequently "suggest" how foreign governments should reform their economy, organize a military force, or put down civil rebellion.[7] As will be discussed in Chapter 10, Nazi, Western, and Communist diplomats have amassed an impressive record of intervention in other countries' internal affairs by fomenting civil disorders, subsidizing subversive political factions, and disseminating covert propaganda.

THE FUNCTIONS OF DIPLOMATS

Aside from the main role of diplomats in bargaining and communicating information between governments, they perform several other duties that should be mentioned briefly. These can be classified under the headings of (1) protection of nationals and their property abroad, (2) symbolic representation, (3) obtaining information, and (4) providing advice and making overall policies.

---

[6] Most Communist governments and the United States still restrict the travel privileges of each others' diplomats. Certain areas of the United States, for instance, cannot be visited by Russian diplomats.

[7] For an analysis of the shoddiness of cold-war diplomatic practices in comparison to those of the nineteenth century, see Lord Vansittart, "The Decline of Diplomacy," *Foreign Affairs*, 28 (1950), 177–88.

Protection of Nationals

This function, which involves protecting the lives and promoting the interests of nationals residing or travelling abroad, is a routine task, although during catastrophes or civil disorders, the role of diplomats in this capacity may become very important. Nationals have to be protected or evacuated if necessary, they must be represented by legal counsel if jailed, and their property or other interests abroad must be protected if the local government does not provide such service. It is the general practice among major powers to assign consular agents rather than embassy personnel to perform these duties. Consulates, which may be established in many cities in a country, are diplomatic substations that serve travelers to and from the host country with regard to visas and other information, protect the interests of their own citizens when on foreign soil, and assist in commercial transactions. Consular agents occasionally perform the other three major functions of diplomats, but only when normal diplomatic communication has been disrupted.

Symbolic Representation

In their role as symbolic representatives, diplomats of other eras seldom did more than attend court ceremonies; today, however, ambassadors, in addition to attending ceremonial and social occasions, must address foreign groups and be present at all events with which their country is somehow connected, no matter how remotely. If a Soviet ballet group visits Paris, the Russian ambassador is expected to be on hand for the opening performance; if the United States has constructed a medical center for children in some developing country, the American ambassador must not only attend its opening but also display a continuing interest in its activities. Whether in agriculture, medicine, music, physics, or military policies, if their government has some stake in a project, diplomats must symbolize that stake by their physical presence and continuing concern. In their symbolic capacity, ambassadors are concerned with the totality of relations—whether political or not—between their own country and the one to which they have been sent.

Obtaining Information

Because information and data are the raw materials of foreign policy, the gathering of information—by official acts, at cocktail parties, or by covert means—is the most important task of the diplomat, aside from his bargaining activities. Precise information must be made available to those who formulate policy if there is to be a minimum discrepancy between the objective environment and the image of the environment held by policy makers. Data concerning military potential, personalities, and economic trends or problems may be supplied by intelligence units abroad; but intelligence experts work under limitations when it comes to assessment of trends, intentions, responses, attitudes, and motivations. Although diplomats may also provide a large quantity of raw data in their reports, their main role in providing information is to use their skill and familiarity with the foreign society to interpret the data and make reliable assessments and forecasts of responses of the receiving government toward their own government's policies. They might be asked to predict answers to some of the following questions: What are the implications for the host government's foreign policy if a new party is elected to power or a military junta gains control through a *coup d'état?* What is the influence of a certain columnist or radio commentator upon official policy and public opinion? What tactics are likely to be adopted by the foreign government in forthcoming negotiations over the allocation of foreign-aid grants? How would the foreign government react to a major diplomatic maneuver by the diplomat's government in another area of the world? What position might the foreign government take in a future international conference on tariffs, or on the regulation of narcotics, or on an issue before the General Assembly of the United Nations?

The success of diplomats in answering and assessing such questions will depend upon the scope and variety of sources of information they are able to cultivate among party leaders, government officials, trade unions, the press, and the military. Ambassadors or diplomats who rely too heavily upon one official source of information are likely to obtain only a distorted version of reality.

How do diplomatic officials obtain vital information? Most of it comes from reading and examining reports, debates, and newspaper articles published in the country where they are stationed. Since the volume of information in these sources is normally beyond the capacity of any one individual to assess, ambassadors rely on extensive staff assistance and full-time specialists concerned with a particular range of problems. Commercial attachés not only negotiate trade agreements and promote trade relations but also have the responsibility for knowing in detail the development, structure, problems, and leaders of the foreign country's economy. Cultural, agricultural, labor, scientific, and military attachés perform the same duties within their respective areas of competence, while intelligence officials attached to the embassy have the responsibility for obtaining more covert information.

Information is also obtained through informal means. "Entertainment," one diplomat claimed, "oils the hinges of man's office door." Although legislators and taxpayers frequently disparage diplomats for the time and money they spend on cocktail parties and dinners, there are definite advantages to these informal occasions. In a light setting it is often easier to persuade and obtain vital information. The strain of rigid protocol is removed and unofficial views can be exchanged, while the element of personal acquaintance—and sometimes plentiful quantities of liquor—may increase confidence and trust. Rumors can be assessed and verified, personal reactions elicited, and all types of interesting information obtained more easily at social functions than during official calls and in official communications.

The final important function of diplomats, aside from bargaining and negotiation, is to provide advice to those who formulate goals and plans of action and occasionally to make important policy decisions themselves. All diplomats serve in a sense as policy makers, because they provide a large portion of the information upon which policy is based. A principal contribution of diplomats in the policy-making process thus comes from their skill of interpretation and judgment about conditions in the country to which they are accredited. But even if diplomats are particularly useful in this capacity, it does not mean that their judgment will always be considered or that their advice or warnings will be heeded. Diplomats' influence in the formulation of a nation's goals will depend on a number of considerations. If they enjoy political prestige among the top policy experts at the home foreign office, if they have a reputation for reliability, initiative, and resourcefulness and refrain from attempting to sabotage official policy in its execution, they may be called upon frequently to make policy recommendations—their functions will include giving advice as well as providing information. They will probably not have any role in formulating the broad objectives of government policy abroad, but given those objectives, they may be asked to suggest the best ways to achieve them. On the other hand, if diplomats are new in their posts or careers, if they vigorously question official policy, and if their assessments are not reliable, it is unlikely that they will have much influence in policy formulation.

Beyond such general considerations, a number of conditions peculiar to modern diplomatic organizations diminish the influence of career diplomats in the policy-making process. One is the ease with which bureaucratic officials can combine policy making and diplomatic roles. Prior to World War I, the prevailing practice was for government officials to formulate external goals and strategies and then direct their diplomatic agents abroad to attempt to achieve them. With the modern means of travel at their disposal, foreign ministers can now visit foreign capitals and obtain their information firsthand; they can similarly become negotiators and perform the task of diplomatic bargaining as well as policy making. While they must still rely on ambassadors abroad for some information, there are few impediments, aside from the rush of business, that prevent foreign ministers from being policy makers, administrators, and negotiators simultaneously.

Another impediment to a significant role in policy making for diplomats is the limited environment within which they operate. Ambassadors generally develop considerable competence in handling bilateral relations between governments, but it is more difficult for them to perceive these relations in the broader context of overall foreign policy. Although political officials at the highest level of government lack detailed knowledge of conditions abroad, they act upon a broad understanding of situations, of which bilateral relations are only a part.

What to the ambassador may seem a logical and desirable policy to pursue in the bilateral system may be the wrong policy in view of the total substance of a country's foreign policy. Moreover, foreign ministers and high political officials also view policy in terms of the domestic political environment and requirements. The definition of the situation that operates in foreign-policy decision making includes an important domestic sector that is not always understood by the diplomatic agent who has lived abroad for a long period.

The bureaucratic structure and organization of foreign offices hinders many reports and recommendations from ambassadors abroad from reaching those who make policy at the highest level. In the eighteenth and nineteenth centuries, communications were slow, there were only approximately twenty states in the European system, and foreign contacts were limited to a few political or commercial affairs, so foreign ministers could keep abreast of all the activities of their diplomats. Today, most dispatches—including some potentially important ones—never get beyond the "desk officer" in the foreign ministry. High-level officials who formulate major policy decisions within the context of large organizations tend to become increasingly removed from the environment in which their diplomats operate. In a period of crisis between two countries, ambassadors may play a more significant role in recommending courses of action; but, even in this situation, they are merely experts whose advice may or may not be followed.

Finally, there are personal and social reasons that prevent diplomats in the field from initiating proposals on major policy decisions. Occasionally, diplomats are so afraid of being accused of lack of judgment by their superiors that they may prefer to avoid making any recommendations at all. Evading responsibility in this way may not be solely their fault, since most bureaucratic organizations have established policies, persisting by the sanction of time and tradition, that can only be changed by those with the greatest political strength. Diplomats who challenge these traditions are in many cases likely to become suspect. High-level officials in organizations that hold strong commitments to certain policies tend to overlook or downgrade information provided by ambassadors that contradicts or questions the validity of these policies.

One example is provided in a detailed study of the crisis preceding the outbreak of World War I. In the summer of 1914, Kaiser Wilhelm dismissed the accurate warnings of Prince Lichnowsky, his ambassador in London, as utter nonsense coming from "that old goat." Prince Lichnowsky's reports, the study reveals, did not conform to the Kaiser's view that England would remain neutral if war broke out between the major antagonists of the crisis. On the other hand, the highly inaccurate reports of the German ambassador in St. Petersburg supported the Kaiser's expectations that the Tsar's government was bluffing in its announced policy of supporting Serbia and were thus accepted uncritically.[8]

---

[8] Robert C. North, "Fact and Value in the 1914 Crisis" (Stanford, Calif.: Stanford Studies in International Conflict and Integration, 1961).

When diplomats are faced with circumstances wherein their advice is either rejected or ignored, it is little wonder that they judge their policy-making role to be insignificant. It is a fact, nevertheless, that most foreign offices suffer from rigid procedures and established policies that impel policy makers to downgrade "uncomfortable" information. As a former Secretary in the Australian Department of External Affairs has written:

> The only facts and opinions regarded [in foreign offices] as relevant will be those which fall within the framework of broad government policy, and which are compatible with the basic assumptions on which government policy is conceived. There will be "reliable" sources, those which support government policy, and "suspect" sources, which have the unfriendly habit of producing facts which do not support government policy. Very important human factors, of course, creep into activities of this nature. The desire for promotion, the need not to offend by producing embarrassing facts, the reluctance to report from overseas events which would suggest policy was wrongly based, are all most relevant influences in the final formulation of national policy.[9]

THE PURPOSES OF DIPLOMATIC COMMUNICATION

In most cases, the purpose of negotiation between two or more governments is to change or sustain each other's objectives and policies or to reach agreement over some contentious issue. However, such negotiations may have other purposes or side effects as well. Before analyzing the techniques diplomats employ in bargaining and securing agreements, these other objectives should be noted.

First, a large amount of diplomatic communication between governments is undertaken primarily for exchanging views, probing intentions, and attempting to convince other governments that certain actions, such as attending a conference, lowering tariffs, or proffering diplomatic support on a particular international issue, would be in their interest. Here there is no hard bargaining, and diplomats or government officials do not ordinarily employ threats or offer rewards. The majority of routine diplomatic contacts between governments are of this nature, and almost all visits by heads of states are undertaken not for bargaining, but simply for "exchanging views" and "consulting."

Second, bilateral diplomatic meetings or multilateral conferences may be arranged for the purpose of stalling or creating the illusion that a government is seriously interested in bargaining, even though it really desires no agreement. During the conduct of warfare, one state may agree to armistice negotiations to assuage public opinion, while it simultaneously steps up its military campaigns. By agreeing to negotiate, it may be able to draw attention away from its other activities.

[9] John W. Burton, *Peace Theory: Preconditions of Disarmament* (New York: Knopf, 1962), pp. 184–85.

Third, a government may enter into diplomatic negotiations primarily for the purpose of making propaganda; it uses a conference not so much to reach agreement over a limited range of issues as to make broad appeals to the outside public, partly to undermine the bargaining position of its opponents. In an age when "secret diplomacy" is viewed with suspicion and many diplomatic negotiations are open both to the press and public, a conference that is certain to receive extensive publicity around the world offers an excellent forum for influencing public attitudes. Soviet negotiators have earned a reputation for employing some international conferences for propaganda purposes, but any time two or more governments cannot agree—or do not wish to agree—upon the issues under consideration and yet desire to gain some advantages from their efforts, they are likely to use the proceedings primarily to embarrass their opponents and extol their own actions and attitudes. The open forum of the General Assembly offers one important arena for attempting to influence non-diplomatic opinion. Indeed, many observers of United Nations affairs note that most speeches made in that body are designed primarily for public domestic and international consumption, not for the information of other delegates. The many conferences on disarmament and arms control since World War II have similarly been exploited for propaganda purposes.

The trained observer can readily discern when a party to diplomatic negotiations is exploiting a conference or meeting *primarily* (since all "open" diplomacy involves some propaganda) for the purposes of influencing the attitudes of the general public rather than for changing the bargaining positions of its opponents. Persistent use of slogans, epithets, vague phrases (such as "general and complete disarmament") and repetition of totally unacceptable positions indicate that bargaining is not the real purpose of the discussions. Other techniques include repeated attempts to discredit the opposition, deliberate and frequent misrepresentation of the other party's positions, widespread discussion of subjects not on the agenda, or inconsistent statements. John Foster Dulles remembered how, when he was attending the Moscow Foreign Minister's Conference in 1947 as an observer, Soviet Foreign Minister Molotov would make lengthy speeches at the meetings, each inconsistent with its predecessor. In one instance he would proffer friendship to the defeated Germans and promise them help in reconstructing their economy; in the next he would please the anti-German sentiments of the Soviet population by demanding stiff reparations from the Germans; and to the Poles he promised generous portions of German territory.[10] An American delegate at one series of disarmament meetings in 1960 noted to the Soviet negotiators that they had employed the vague phrase "general and complete disarmament" 135 times in about two hours of speechmaking.[11] The plenary sessions of the Paris negotiations on the Vietnam war dragged on for four years, each side putting forth proposals that had been repeatedly rejected, and sometimes not even considered, by the other. The

[10] John Foster Dulles, *War or Peace* (New York: Macmillan, 1950), p. 67.
[11] Joseph L. Nogee, "Propaganda and Negotiation: The Case of the Ten-Nation Disarmament Committee," *Journal of Conflict Resolution*, 7 (1963), 515.

North Vietnamese in particular did not use these sessions for bargaining, for their government was committed to securing American withdrawal from the war and the collapse of the South Vietnamese regime by means other than diplomacy—primarily through military offensives. The Paris discussions were exploited for propaganda purposes; the Vietnamese envoys used postsession press conferences to castigate the other side and to prove the reasonableness of their proposals, when in fact they were demanding capitulation. This four-year charade thus had little to do with diplomacy. It was designed to give the appearance of negotiation when in fact the real bargaining was being conducted in the battlefields and in the North Vietnamese efforts to bouy the antiwar opposition in the United States.[12]

Diplomacy, however, is used primarily to reach agreements, compromises, and settlements where government objectives conflict. It involves, whether in private meetings or publicized conferences, the attempt to change the policies, actions, objectives, and attitudes of other governments and their diplomats by persuasion, offering rewards, exchanging concessions, or making threats.

THE NEGOTIATING PROCESS: PRELIMINARIES

Bargaining over contentious issues may begin through a series of signals by the parties to the effect that they wish to enter into formal discussions. As the long history of "peace feelers" during the Vietnam conflict reveals, it may take a great deal of time, and military successes or failures, before both sides are convinced that formal bargaining is a better (or supplementary) means of pursuing objectives. But even once the parties have agreed to enter into negotiations, a number of preliminary points have to be resolved before any substantive discussion can take place.

Table 7–1 lists some of the preliminary issues involved in the negotiating process. The location of the talks is usually dealt with first. If the negotiations are between adversaries, then the customary rule during the past two decades has been to select the city of a "neutral" state. Geneva has been the most popular location for multilateral conferences involving cold-war issues and disarmament, and Vienna and Helsinki have been used to discuss limitations on strategic armaments, troop reductions in Europe, and overall European security. If, on the other hand, the negotiations are between states that normally maintain friendly relations, they will usually take place in the capital of one of the parties.

The parties to be represented at the negotiations often raise problems. The usual criterion is, Who is involved in an issue area? Those who have some stake in the outcome are normally invited. But often there is the problem of parties with no formal diplomatic status. The early stages of the Paris negotiations

[12] There were, however, secret negotiations between the North Vietnamese and Henry Kissinger in 1970–1972, which, though often meaningless, eventually became crucial once the North Vietnamese, partly abandoned by the Russians and Chinese, decided they could not achieve their objectives on the battlefield.

Table 7-1 Formal Negotiating Process

SETTING	PROCESS	OUTCOMES
1. Open vs. closed meetings	1. Preparation of rules of the game (Talks about talks)	
2. Bilateral vs. multilateral meetings	a. Place (city)	
3. Stress or crisis situation, or more normal circumstances	b. Parties and size of delegations	
4. Time available (open or closed; e.g., ultimatum)	c. Languages, seating	
5. A mediator role? Or only direct participants?	d. Press coverage, etc.	
	2. Substantive bargaining	
	a. Presentation of positions ⟵	Original objectives of parties
	b. Presentation of demands or conditions	
	c. Symbolic acts or signals ⟶	New alternatives created or maximum and minimum conditions revised
	d. Persuasion ⟶	
	e. Promises	
	f. Threats	
	g. Commitments	
	h. Concessions ⟶	Possible outcomes:
		a. Treaty or "understanding"
		b. Postponement of negotiations
		c. Ending negotiations and leaving problem unresolved

over Vietnam, starting in 1968, involved lengthy discussions about whether or not the Viet Cong could have representation separate from the delegation of North Vietnam. This complicated question then brought up a related issue: What should be the shape of the table around which discussions would take place? Negotiations about this problem went on for several weeks, until eventually the United States accepted the Viet Cong as a distinct party to the negotiations. Finally, agreements have to be made on the problems of translation, publication of documents, the role of advisors, and, most important, whether or not the meetings will be open to the press.

All these matters may occupy a great deal of time. The average person may not be impressed with all the quibbling that goes on over matters that appear trivial. But many of these preliminaries are seen by the delegations or governments as reflecting upon questions of fundamental importance, including their bargaining strength and prestige. The implications of each minor procedural decision may be great. For example, the United States delegation initially opposed the seating of the Viet Cong as a separate party in the Paris discussions. It had to adopt this position because in previous public statements the American government had taken the position that the Viet Cong were organized and directed by Hanoi. To agree to the seating of the Viet Cong separately implied that the American view of the situation in Vietnam had been incorrect and that the Viet Cong did indeed represent a political movement indigenous to the Republic of Vietnam, quite separate from the government and Communist party of North Vietnam.

Before discussing the various ploys used in the substantive bargaining, we should point out that a number of conditions, or the "setting," surrounding the process may vitally affect the outcome. These are listed in Table 7–1. The first critical question to ask is, Are the meetings to be open or closed to the press? For reasons to be examined below, we could predict that if they are open, they will contain much propaganda, that the discussions will be prolonged, and that much of the rhetoric will be designed to impress the "folks at home," not the delegations sitting on the other side of the table. Are the meetings between two parties, or more? Is the situation perceived as critical by all the parties? If so, we could expect discussions to last only a short time. Closely related is the time that is perceived as available. If the parties see the situation as running out of hand, requiring *some* solution, then there will be great pressure to focus on immediate issues and reduce the amount of careful probing of intentions and evaluation of each of the opponent's statements. There may be a feeling that *any* solution is better than letting "events take their course" or permitting oneself the luxury of time to think matters over.[13]

---

[13] Hitler often tried to create an atmosphere of crisis when he confronted foreign diplomats. In discussions with Chamberlain, Daladier, and others on the Czech issue, he made it clear that if some solution were not devised quickly, the Reichswehr would march. The unfortunate diplomats always negotiated in an atmosphere of crisis and in a time setting that Hitler had manufactured. The outcomes of these negotiations might have differed if the foreign diplomats, not Hitler, had defined this important part of the setting.

Finally, the negotiations may be expected to take on particular characteristics if at least one of the parties plays the role of an official or unofficial mediator. Mediation will be discussed in Chapter 15; suffice it to say here that the bargaining process becomes more complicated, but favorable solutions are more likely if one party can propose sets of alternatives different from those put forth by the main protagonists or can make certain that communication between the adversaries does not break down.

THE NEGOTIATING PROCESS: INDUCING AGREEMENT

The choice of techniques and tactics to employ in diplomatic negotiation depends generally upon the degree of incompatibility between two or more nations' objectives and interests, the extent to which the nations are committed to those interests, and the degree to which the parties want to reach agreement. Diplomatic negotiations between friends and allies seldom display the same characteristics as those between hostile governments. Where there is already considerable agreement about the principles of an issue, negotiation may involve only working out the details or deducing the consequences from the principles.[14] When governments are responsive to each others' interests, moreover, they have a good basis for arranging compromises and exchanging concessions. In negotiations within the Common Market, for instance, the parties agree widely on the objectives of the organization and have intimate knowledge of each others' economic needs and interests. To a large extent, they can negotiate over essentially technical matters and do not have to worry about reconciling great principles. A common desire to reach agreement may also induce the bargaining agents to make concessions. The alternative is to adhere inflexibly to a position, prevent agreement, and accept the adverse publicity for adopting such a position.

Where objectives are fundamentally incompatible and both sides maintain strong commitments to their respective positions, the problem of influencing behavior, actions, and objectives through diplomatic bargaining becomes much more complex. Two stages toward reaching a settlement in such conditions are involved. First, one party must get the other to *want* an agreement of some sort; he must somehow make the other realize that any agreement or settlement is preferable to the status quo of incompatible positions or nonagreement or, conversely, that the consequences of nonagreement are more unfavorable to him than the consequences of agreement. Second, once the stage of "agreeing to an agreement" has been reached, the two parties must still bargain over the specific terms of the final agreement.

Of the two steps, the first is probably more difficult to achieve when commitments to incompatible objectives are strong; as long as one or both

---

[14] Fred C. Iklé, *How Nations Negotiate* (New York: Harper & Row, 1964), Chap. 11.

parties believe they can achieve their objectives through actions other than nego- tiations, diplomatic bargaining cannot lead to settlement. In the postwar negotia- tions over the status of Austria, negotiators from the Western allies and the Soviet Union met over 400 times before an agreement was worked out. It was clear that, with the exception of the last several meetings, the Soviet government did not wish to make an agreement or change its objectives toward Austria but was content to maintain the occupied status of the country. Negotiations were not used to bargain, but to mark time, discuss other issues, make propa- ganda, and give the impression that serious talks were proceeding. Only after other developments had occurred within the Soviet government and throughout Europe did the Russian government, over Foreign Minister Molotov's objections, decide that it wanted to conclude a permanent settlement of the Austrian issue. Once that decision was made, negotiations were completed in a matter of weeks.

If both sides have made the prior decision that agreement is more desir- able than nonagreement or maintenance of the status quo, it remains for them to bargain over the specific details of settlement. Diplomats can employ a great variety of bargaining techniques. Basically, they present their conditions, define their own objectives, and use persuasion by making arguments or presenting data to illustrate the correctness of their views or the degree of their needs. Occasionally they can use threats and offers of rewards to try to obtain acceptance of their proposals and, if this fails, reassess their original positions in terms of possible concessions that they hope will elicit agreement or a change in the objectives of the other side. All the time, they must simultaneously reveal their *commitment* to their bargaining positions, lest the other party assume that they do not feel very strongly about their conditions and would be willing to compro- mise them without significant compensations.

Promise of a reward is in a sense a bribe or inducement that offers some future advantage in return for agreement on a specific point under conten- tion. These may range from promises of "soft" peace terms, monetary loans, or diplomatic support at some future conference to such symbolic acts as unilater- ally releasing prisoners of war or suspending hostilities. One common ploy of governments that make extensive demands on the territorial status quo is to offer the reward of a permanent settlement of all other issues dividing two or more states if the other side will just give in on one specific territorial demand. Hitler promised that he would make no more territorial demands in Europe if only the Western powers would assist him in inducing the Czechs to cede the Sudetenland to him. He held out the possibility of a permanent settlement of all outstanding issues if this last problem could be resolved in his favor.

Threats can be conceived as the opposite of rewards, whereby state A announces that if state B does not do X, it will do Y, which will hurt or damage B's interests. In a general setting, if objectives between two or more states conflict, this can include a threat to start war, break diplomatic relations, impose economic embargoes or boycotts, institute a blockade, withdraw a foreign-aid program, or in other ways punish state B. In addition, threats more peculiar to a particular diplomatic negotiating situation can be employed. The negotiators of one side might threaten to break off discussions (implying that it would prefer nonagreement to continued stalemate or acceptance of B's conditions), reveal secret agreements, increase its terms of agreement, or "let the military take over."

The effectiveness of threatening actions depends above all on their *credibility*. State B has to believe that the threat will be carried out if it does not meet state A's demands. Credibility would seem to be established when B realizes that A can fulfill the threat and thereby damage B, without seriously harming its own interests. If, for instance, state A's diplomats threaten to walk out of a conference, and B knows that such action would seriously jeopardize the chances of obtaining an agreement it wants, it might very well be willing to make last-minute concessions to prevent a breakdown of negotiations.

The effectiveness and credibility of a threat would also seem to require that there be some symmetry between the *magnitude* of the threat and the issue under contention. If the Soviet Union threatens to start a nuclear war with Iran because the latter will not concede some relatively minor point in frontier negotiations, the threat will not seem credible; it is out of proportion to the issue at stake. Or, as Kenneth Boulding has summarized it, beyond a certain point, the higher the magnitude of a threat, the lower is the subjective probability that it will be believed.[15]

To be credible, threats must also appear to be one-sided. State A has to make it clear that if the threat is fulfilled, it will not damage its own interests—in other words, the costs to the target of the threat will be much greater than to the party that makes the threat.[16] If A threatens to walk out of a conference (usually after some signal, such as sending home the chief negotiator for "consultations"), but B knows that A would suffer serious public condemnation for "wrecking" the conference, the threat is not very credible. Indeed, B might be seriously tempted to call A's bluff, in which case A would be placed in a most difficult position.

In some instances, those who make threats may also have to take certain actions that demonstrate that they have the *capacity* to fulfill them. This might involve mobilizing troops, cutting off foreign aid or trade for a short period, ordering a reduction in embassy personnel, or staging a short walkout from a conference—all actions designed to indicate that the "real thing" can be done if necessary.

Finally, it may be advantageous to make deliberately vague threats or, as some might put it, ominous warnings. Although these may not be entirely

---

[15] Kenneth E. Boulding, *Conflict and Defense: A General Theory* (New York: Harper & Row, 1962), p. 255.

[16] In certain circumstances, a threat may be more credible if it would damage both sides. See Thomas C. Schelling, *The Strategy of Conflict* (Cambridge, Mass.: Harvard University Press, 1960), pp. 124–31.

credible, they have the advantage of giving the threatening side many alternative forms of punishing actions—or inaction—if the other side does not take heed. The common diplomatic phrases "we will not stand (or sit) idly by" while state B does something, or state B "must bear complete responsibility for the consequences of its actions" are threats of this kind. They do not commit the threatener to specific actions, but indicate that state B's actions are perceived as dangerous and *could* lead to counteraction or reprisal. The vague threat avoids placing A in a position where it cannot maneuver. As Jervis points out, there is an inherent conflict between the desire to make a credible threat and the desire to preserve freedom of action.[17]

The problem with making threats in diplomatic negotiations is that even if they are reasonably credible, the other side might test them. In this case, the threatener has to act and perhaps damage his own interests or back down and earn the reputation of being a bluffer. In other words, if the threat is actually challenged, it has failed its purpose. Between 1958 and 1962, the Soviet government threatened several times to sign a peace treaty with East Germany, in effect, giving the Communist regime there control over Allied access routes to West Berlin. In each instance, the Russians gave the three Western allies a time limit to join the negotiations or otherwise be left out altogether. The Allies refused to act and, instead, built up their military capabilities in West Germany and West Berlin to signify that if the Soviet Union fulfilled its threat, the Allies would fight, if necessary, to keep the access routes open. Each time the Soviet government failed, as threatened, to sign a treaty with the East German regime, the credibility of its threats declined further.

A problem partly related to that of making threats credible is establishing a *commitment* to a bargaining position. Diplomatic negotiations normally start with all sides presenting their "maximum" demands, usually the positions they would like ideally to achieve in the negotiations. Since diplomats realize that initial positions are maximum positions, they must probe to find out how far their opponents are willing to pull back from them. During the negotiating process itself, they bargain over various proposals until some point of compromise has been reached. But where that point is located depends on the effectiveness of persuasion, presentation of data and arguments, threats and rewards, and also on the extent to which diplomats can convince others that they and their government are committed to certain points, principles, and values. If the opponents know or suspect that a government is not deeply committed to one of its proposals or bargaining positions, they will be inclined to demand extensive concessions, hoping to attain a point of compromise much more advantageous to themselves. Compromise, after all, does not require that the parties place the point of agreement exactly halfway between the initial positions. An

---

[17] Robert Jervis, *The Logic of Images in International Relations* (Princeton, N.J.: Princeton University Press, 1970), p. 90.

important part of diplomatic negotiating strategy thus concerns the efforts of bargaining agents to show each other, as convincingly as possible, *why* a position cannot be compromised beyond a certain point.

One way is to argue that as much as the government or diplomatic delegation would like to make further concessions, it cannot do so for fear of alienating the public at home and jeopardizing the chances that any treaty or agreement would be approved by a legislative body. This is the ploy (often sincere, of course) that "public opinion" or parliamentary opinion is committed to certain positions, principles, or values, and that no agreement that compromises them could be concluded. In other words, diplomats try to create the impression that neither they nor their government has the authority to make concessions.[18] Another way is to transform a dispute over a relatively concrete issue such as a piece of territory into a matter of principle. This strategy, sometimes called "issue escalation," is also designed to illustrate commitment, for it is generally understood that concessions over principles are harder to make than concessions over trivia. Instead of treating the problem of access to West Berlin or defense of the offshore islands of Communist China and Formosa as narrow territorial issues, the United States chose to characterize them in terms of freedom versus communism. This has the effect of displaying commitment to the cause, and at the same time it enables the government to incite public enthusiasm for the principle, thus further displaying its commitment. Both citizens and allies can be rallied, whereas if the issue were characterized in legal or technical terminology, little public or international support could be generated. When one side has firmly displayed a commitment to a position, it is in a better position to resist demands for concessions.

The problem with establishing commitments is that governments and diplomats decrease their bargaining flexibility and in effect cut off the possibility of backing down in case one side seriously presses its demands.[19] If both sides remain committed—particularly, publicly committed—to fundamentally incompatible positions of principle, then little room remains for effective bargaining. By attempting to establish commitment or credibility to a position, negotiators and their governments may create such inflexibility that the possibilities of reaching agreement are closed out.

Persuasion through argument and presentation of information, offering rewards, making threats, and establishing commitments are thus the major techniques employed in the process of diplomatic bargaining between nations. Some of the problems common to these techniques are listed above, but each bargaining situation is unique, and no one can predict with certainty which methods of inducement will work. We can only suggest the conditions under which they would be more likely to succeed. In addition to the basic strategies involving

---

[18] Schelling, *The Strategy of Conflict,* p. 28.
[19] E. James Liebermann, "Threat and Assurance in the Conduct of Conflict," in *International Conflict and Behavioral Science,* ed. Roger Fisher (New York: Basic Books, 1964), p. 105.

threats, rewards, and commitments, a number of more specific techniques have been used recurrently by diplomats and need to be mentioned briefly.

One is to exploit the impatience of the opponents—particularly when they want an agreement quickly—and induce them to make concessions they might avoid were they content to engage in lengthy bargaining processes. The foremost ploys for exploiting impatience are haggling over minor details, introducing new and unexpected topics for the agenda, and evading crucial points. Conversely, overall settlements may be reached more quickly by starting with quick agreements on small and minor issues where considerable consensus already prevails, and subsequently exploiting this "momentum" to obtain concessions on important issues. A further technique is to offer large concessions at first, on the assumption that if you show your goodwill, the other side will feel compelled to reciprocate. This is a calculated gamble, for if the other side does not come through with important concessions, you are left with either having to maintain your initial concessions and continue making even more until some point of compromise is found, or retracting concessions, an action that, although frequently performed in disarmament negotiations, leaves you open to the charge of not negotiating "in good faith."

Finally, a government and its diplomats can threaten to increase its terms later on if the opponents do not take what is offered now. A familiar gambit by shopkeepers, this may be extremely effective if the opponent is, in terms of the specific issue under contention, much weaker. In the summer and fall of 1939, the Soviet government made territorial and other demands on Finland. When Finnish diplomats rejected most of the Soviet demands and proposals, Stalin and Molotov let it be known that once the Red Army had its say in the matter, the demands would increase. After the Soviet Union attacked Finland that winter and its armies made some headway against the Finns, Soviet demands did in fact grow stiffer, and the peace signed in March 1940 was considerably more disadvantageous to Finland than the original Soviet demands of 1939. The situation in wartime when one side is on the verge of defeat is also a propitious moment to employ this technique for inducing the opponent to agree to surrender or to armistice terms.

So far, the discussion might imply that all negotiations involve solely the statement of maximum positions which, after the employment of various tactics, are whittled down through compromises and concessions to some reasonably equitable distribution of advantages between the bargaining parties. This is indeed a common pattern, but there are other possibilities. In a situation of extreme power asymmetry, one party may be in a position to make a virtual *diktat.* It offers *its* terms on a take-it or leave-it basis. Some compromises may be made on matters of details, but the basic pattern is one where the weaker party is compelled to give legal sanction to a capitulation. This form of negotiation was common in Hitler's treatment of weak or defeated opponents and was attempted initially by the North Vietnamese in the Paris negotiations. Another type of negotiation involves the search for a general *formula* or set of principles acceptable to both sides. There is little bargaining involved in the sense of using threats or rewards; rather, one or both parties (often a mediator) searches for alternative solutions which are presented for consideration as a package. Once a formula is accepted, then bargaining begins in order to fill out the details. This type of negotiation has been prominent in the formulation of the Camp David agreements and the subsequent Israel–Egypt peace treaty of 1979.[20]

THE NEGOTIATING PROCESS: PROBLEM SOLVING

Most of the tactics just described are used primarily in situations where one government attempts to change the actions and policies of others—that is, to persuade them to do what they would not otherwise do. Problem solving, in contrast, is a process where two or more parties attempt to develop rules to handle some problem arising in the physical or diplomatic environment. Whereas in bargaining situations, a zero-sum condition prevails—the gain of one side is seen as a loss for the other—in problem solving, the parties generally see that common study of a problem, pooling of resources, and general cooperation may result in mutual advantage and that no major values will have to be sacrificed to obtain an agreement. Differences may arise over the exact specification of rights, duties, and costs, but these are primarily matters of detail that lie above an underlying consensus on objectives.

The thousands of scientific, cultural, technical, economic, and communications treaties and institutions are the result of parties' getting together to resolve some problem common to them, where they recognize that unilateral action would be fruitless. Examples include agreements and institutions to regulate fisheries (where, despite attempts to maximize catches, governments share a common interest in preventing the depletion of stock), mail, telephonic communications, the narcotics trade, international police work, and the like.

Negotiators in problem-solving situations usually begin by presenting data and technical studies of a problem. These form the basis of proposals put forth as draft treaties or constitutions for a new international organization. Often the technical research, analysis, and interpretation of the data are conducted by specialists from more than one government, working together. Although some of the more punitive diplomatic techniques discussed earlier are used occasionally, problem solving normally stresses the gains to be achieved through mutual concessions; and the diplomacy emphasizes that it is basically

[20] For the distinction between concession-type negotiations and searching for alternative formulas, see I. William Zartman, "Negotiation as a Joint Decision-making Process," in Zartman (ed.), *The Negotiation Process: Theories and Applications* (Beverly Hills, Calif.: Sage Publications, 1978), pp. 67–86.

in the national interest to make short-term sacrifices for greater long-term gains. The point to emphasize is that, of all diplomatic contacts between governments and between governments and international organizations, problem solving predominates. We are less aware of it because it is seldom newsworthy; it is certainly less dramatic than a great peace conference or summit meeting, and hence only infrequently makes the headlines. But beneath the issues of war and peace and the diplomatic interchanges that deal with these problems lies a vast network of contacts between governments, concerned primarily with coordinating and putting into treaty form those solutions achieved through quiet problem-solving procedures.

THE NEGOTIATING PROCESS: DIPLOMATIC STYLES

One of the interesting problems facing students of diplomacy is to describe and explain the different styles of diplomatic bargaining among governments.[21] In diplomatic negotiations, for example, do Russians evince certain bargaining styles that are unique or significantly different from those of, let us say, the English?

Many retired diplomats claim in their memoirs that certain countries or societies do have distinguishable diplomatic styles. Sir Harold Nicolson, a renowned British diplomat, argued on the basis of his long experience that the bargaining styles of a country's diplomats reflect major cultural values in their society.[22] He contrasted the "shopkeeper" style of British diplomats—one that is generally pragmatic and based on the assumption that compromise is the only possible reason for and outcome of bargaining—with the style of the totalitarian governments, particularly Soviet Russia in the 1920s and during the height of the cold war, and Nazi Germany in the 1930s. The diplomats of these regimes were known for rigidity in bargaining positions; extensive use of diplomatic forums for propaganda displays; coarseness of language; a strategy of trying to wear down opponents by harangues; interminable wrangling over minute procedural points; constant repetition of slogans and clichés; and, most important, the view that agreements were tactical maneuvers only, to be broken or violated whenever it was to one's advantage (to quote Lenin, "Agreements are like pie crusts: They are made to be broken."). Duplicity and deception were also common to diplomatic styles of the totalitarian regimes. Without the slightest qualm, the Nazi government could stage an incident that it then used to justify military action as a "reprisal" against a neighbor. Or the Soviet foreign

---

[21] Portions of this section are reproduced from K.J. Holsti, "The Study of Diplomacy," in *World Politics,* eds. Gavin Boyd, James N. Rosenau, and Kenneth Thompson (New York: Free Press, 1976). Copyright © 1976, The Free Press, a Division of Macmillan Publishing Co., Inc. Reprinted by permission of The Free Press.

[22] Harold Nicolson, *Diplomacy,* 3rd ed. (London: Oxford University Press, 1964).

minister could tell President Kennedy in 1962 that the Russian missiles being placed in Cuba were only "defensive," when in fact they were capable of reaching almost any target in the United States.

From these and many other examples, as well as Nicolson's analysis, we might be tempted to infer that the critical variable explaining differences in diplomatic styles is the degree to which a state is "open" or "closed." Undoubtedly, the ethical principles or cultural values expressed in "shopkeeper" diplomatic style are significantly different from those of the totalitarian style. British, French, and American diplomats were genuinely shocked at the standards of diplomatic conduct they faced among their opponents in the 1930s and during the height of the cold war. Yet, many western diplomats are biased in the direction of emphasizing the sins of revolutionary regimes (which are unorthodox largely because they do not accept the legitimacy of the international system or its norms or of their adversaries in negotiations), while forgetting their own lapses.

From what we know of bureaucratic and revolutionary politics in totalitarian regimes, and assuming that diplomatic styles reflect those politics as well as general cultural values, it is probably valid to argue that the *modal* behavior of Soviet and Nazi diplomats was indeed rigid, blustering, coarse, filled with invective, and, above all, untrustworthy. Any tactic to wear down opponents was considered legitimate—including, in some instances, threats against the lives of diplomats themselves. However, the long history of Communist–Western negotiations shows that when it was in their interest to do so, the Soviets, Chinese, and even the Nazis have bargained straightforwardly and have kept agreements.[23] That they were hard bargainers is less relevant.

On the other hand, Western diplomatic styles, reflecting "open" societies, have often lapsed from their own modal characteristics as listed by Nicolson and others. President Kennedy complained of Gromyko's duplicity on the missile issue in Cuba; yet, only one year earlier, the American ambassador to the United Nations had told the world that the Bay of Pigs invasion was organized by a few segments of the Cuban army defecting from the Castro regime. He did not indicate that the enterprise had been planned, organized, financed, and directed by the Central Intelligence Agency. The diplomacy of the United States during the Vietnam War was not noted for its candor; and, even in disarmament negotiations, Americans have been known to break one of the fundamental rules of bargaining: Once you have made a concession, you cannot retract it. The British, for their part, have no less frequently broken promises, violated legal principles, engaged in deceit, and blocked progress in negotiations. It would not be an exaggeration to claim, nevertheless, that whatever their bargaining tactics, British diplomats always maintain verbal decorum.

---

[23] See Lall, *How Communist China Negotiates.* One empirical study of Soviet bargaining behavior establishes that when the Russians want an agreement, their diplomatic style is largely devoid of propaganda, rigidity, and other "sins." See Christer Jönsson, *Soviet Bargaining Behavior: The Nuclear Test Ban Case* (New York: Columbia University Press, 1979).

Some important differences in diplomatic styles appear between "open" and totalitarian states, but the differences are most notable only when the "closed" states are undertaking highly expansionist policies or when they are largely isolated from contacts with the rest of the international system. As their goals become more pragmatic and inner-directed—toward meeting domestic welfare and economic needs, for example—their diplomatic styles tend toward the conventional. The "open" states, or at least the traditional Western major powers, generally adhere to a highly pragmatic style, where the major purpose of bargaining is to reach agreements rather than to emphasize side effects such as propaganda or intelligence work. But the style probably derives more from broad cultural and historical conditions than from the fact that they have demo-cratic political systems. It would be difficult to argue, for example, that Brazilian diplomatic style (representing a relatively "closed" state) is significantly different from that of Belgium. In brief, the "open"–"closed" dichotomy may help to explain *some* differences in diplomatic styles, but by no means all. The nature of a state's external objectives, its position in the international system, and bureaucratic traditions are probably of equal importance.

What of size? Although some foreign-policy problems of small states may differ from those of their larger neighbors, there is little reason to believe that the size factor alone can significantly influence the outlooks and styles dis-played by diplomats in bargaining or problem-solving situations. The differences between British and New Zealand, or French and Finnish diplomatic styles—if there are any—can probably be explained more convincingly in terms of cultural traits, historical traditions, or the general diplomatic situation they find them-selves in, than of size.

Does the level of development influence diplomatic styles? The answer would be yes—at least, indirectly. Many of the developing states are also *new* states, often in positions of great economic dependence and holding a not en-tirely unjustified opinion that, in most of their relationships, they can bargain only from a position of extreme weakness. Most of these states do not have long diplomatic traditions, and few have extensive foreign-affairs bureaucracies with years of experience. Henry Kissinger has argued that whereas the developed countries

> suffer from the inertia of overadministration, the developing areas often lack even the rudiments of effective bureaucracy. Where the advanced countries may drown in 'facts,' the emerging nations are frequently without the most elementary knowledge needed for forming a meaningful judgment or for implementing it once it has been taken.[24]

Although Kissinger may be exaggerating differences—certainly, his comments would not apply to countries such as India or Egypt—his subsequent discussion

[24] Henry Kissinger, "Domestic Structure and Foreign Policy," *Daedalus*, 95 (Spring 1966), 513.

of American diplomatic style does underline differences in foreign-policy behavior from the small developing states, particularly the more "revolutionary" ones. Whereas the developed states tend to be problem-oriented and react to situations as they arise, "charismatic-revolutionary" leaders want to create entirely new international environments and tend to develop fairly well thought-out sets of long-range objectives. Construction of "new orders" rather than piecemeal manipulation of problems is their main characteristic.[25]

We would expect in these circumstances that the diplomacy of the more radical developing states (Indonesia under Sukarno, Iran under Khomeiny, Guinea under Touré, and Libya under Qaddafi) would be distinct, particularly emphasizing moralistic rhetoric and the evils of the world (primarily imperialism) of which they are the main victims. Instead of problem solving based on laborious and unexciting accumulation of data, this form of diplomacy would be more comfortable in a setting where great debates and propaganda are appropriate. The reader may wish to consult some of the speeches before the United Nations General Assembly to see if there are discernible differences in rhetoric between the developed states and some of the emerging nations. Certainly the evidence about foreign-policy behavior in general, as will be discussed in Chapter 12, does not indicate that developing countries operate in a manner fundamentally different from many other states. With only a few exceptions, and, unlike the totalitarian states of the 1930s and the cold war, diplomacy as an instrument of revolutionary upheaval and systematic invasion of foreign lands is not to be seen among the developing countries. Because they are weak and often poorly informed, their bargaining strategies might differ from those of more powerful states, but that is a hypothesis that has not yet been explored in research.

If size, type of political system, and level of development do not explain all the variations in diplomatic bargaining styles (and often they explain none of it), what remains? Many authorities on the subject argue at least in hypothetical form that differences derive from national characteristics or, as one author has put it, diplomacy reflects "culturally-conditioned patterns of behavior and thought." This proposition has much to commend it, but it is difficult to establish with much precision. Studies on Japanese diplomacy do reveal some common characteristics or patterns, and, as suggested, a large literature on the subject portrays Soviet diplomats as frequently exhibiting unique forms of behavior.[26] But there are exceptions to any generalizations, so it is difficult to establish precisely what is typical behavior and what is unique. Here are some of the common behavioral traits of Japanese negotiators: They tend to approach discussions with an attitude emphasizing the justice or inherent "goodness" of their position, without examining the proposition that the other side might have valid

---

[25] *Ibid.*, pp. 522–27.

[26] See Michael Blaker, *Japanese International Negotiating Style* (New York: Columbia University Press, 1977); and Hiroshi Kimura, "Soviet and Japanese Negotiating Behavior: The Spring 1977 Fisheries Talks," *Orbis*, 24 (Spring 1980), 43–68.

points as well. With this view of inherent justice, the Japanese then assume that their view will prevail simply by communicating it clearly to the adversaries. Bargaining and tactical ploys, hinting of Machiavellianism, are to be avoided not only because they are repugnant to the Japanese people who admire harmony and order in their social relations, but also because they are often counterproductive. Japanese diplomatic style thus approaches bargaining with the assumption that "right is might" and that fruitful outcomes can be secured through expressions of goodwill and clearly delineating the "goodness" of a position. Japanese style is also unaggressive in the sense that diplomats do not try to shock their opponents by introducing far-fetched maximum positions. Patiently explaining one's own just cause is the way to approach diplomatic discussions. Tactics, to the extent that they might become necessary, are used only in retaliation against the adversaries' gambits. Ad hoc management of negotiations, or bending with the wind, is the typical pattern.

The evidence for this characterization comes from examination of numerous case studies of Japanese diplomacy. Thus, there is some confidence in the findings. But there are also many exceptions—for example, Japanese diplomatic behavior in negotiations with enemy or defeated states during the Pacific War or Japanese commercial diplomacy in Southeast Asia during the past decade. Thus, while the characteristics listed above may be norms, they are *not* in evidence in certain situations and in bargaining with certain types of opponents.

Similar propositions can be related to Soviet bargaining behavior. In contrast to the Japanese who avoid tactical planning, the Russians, as many have noted, are masters at developing preplanned tactics. Strategies are elaborated *before* meetings, and the various ploys and gambits of bargaining are systematically worked out. Use of repetition, accusation, bluffs, warnings, threats, ultimatums, innuendos, "stonewalling," and time limits—whatever tactics are most useful in wearing down opponents—are not responses to the immediate situation but the implementation of carefully orchestrated plans. Also, unlike the Japanese, the Russians have been noted for diplomatic rudeness—for example, by dictating the time and place of negotiations, cancelling sessions at the last moment, and employing intemperate language. But these characteristics also tend to be situationally determined. They are frequently not displayed when the Russians are committed to seeking an agreement or when they are bargaining with equals or superiors. Such demeanor may be more typical in situations where they are bargaining with adversaries whom they consider inferior in rank. We must close, then, with the thought that differences in bargaining style are obvious and sometimes are so pronounced as to constitute norms. But in different situations and at different times, other forms of behavior come to the fore. It should be pointed out as well that as diplomats become enmeshed in a global network of constant contacts, over a long period of time, certain rules or norms of behavior emanating from global diplomatic practice may "wash away" the diplomat's uniquely national characteristics. Moreover, as the nature of problems on the international agenda becomes increasingly complex requiring a high degree of technical competence, individual idiosyncracies, such as intelligence, knowledge, dedication, laziness, alertness, and the like, may be more important in bargaining behavior than culturally conditioned norms.

SELECTED BIBLIOGRAPHY

ACHESON, DEAN, *Meetings at the Summit: A Study in Diplomatic Method.* Durham: University of New Hampshire Press, 1958.

BELL, CORAL, *Negotiating from Strength.* London: Chatto & Windus, 1962.

BLAKER, MICHAEL, *Japanese International Negotiating Style.* New York: Columbia University Press, 1977.

CAMPBELL, JOHN C., "Negotiating with the Soviets: Some Lessons of the War Period," *Foreign Affairs,* 34 (1956), 305–19.

CLARK, ERIC, *Diplomat: The World of International Diplomacy.* New York: Taplinger, 1974.

CLAUDE, INIS L., JR., "Multilateralism: Diplomatic and Otherwise," *International Organization,* 12 (1958), 43–52.

CRAIG, GORDON A., "On the Diplomatic Revolution of Our Times," The Haynes Foundation Lectures, University of California, Riverside, April 1961.

———, "Totalitarian Approaches to Diplomatic Negotiations," in *Studies in Diplomatic History and Historiography in Honour of G.P. Gooch,* ed. A.O. Sarkissian. London: Longmans, Green, 1961.

———, and FELIX GILBERT, eds., *The Diplomats: 1919–1939.* Princeton, N.J.: Princeton University Press, 1953.

HOVET, THOMAS, JR., "United Nations Diplomacy," *Journal of International Affairs,* 17 (1963), 29–41.

IKLE, FRED C., *How Nations Negotiate.* New York: Harper & Row, 1964.

JENSEN, LLOYD, "Soviet-American Bargaining Behavior in the Postwar Disarmament Negotiations," *Journal of Conflict Resolution,* 7 (1963), 522–41.

JERVIS, ROBERT, *The Logic of Images in International Relations.* Princeton, N.J.: Princeton University Press, 1970.

JÖNSSON, CHRISTER, *Soviet Bargaining Behavior: The Nuclear Test Ban Case.* New York: Columbia University Press, 1979.

LALL, ARTHUR S., *How Communist China Negotiates.* New York: Columbia University Press, 1968.

———, *Modern International Negotiation: Principles and Practice.* New York: Columbia University Press, 1966.

LAUREN, PAUL GORDON, ed., *Diplomacy: New Approaches in History, Theory, Policy.* New York: The Free Press, 1979.

LOCKHART, CHARLES, *Bargaining in International Conflict.* New York: Columbia University Press, 1979.

NICOLSON, SIR HAROLD GEORGE, *Diplomacy,* 3d ed. London, New York: Oxford University Press, Inc., 1964.

——, "Diplomacy Then and Now," *Foreign Affairs,* 40 (1961), 39–49.

NOGEE, JOSEPH L., "Propaganda and Negotiation: The Case of the Ten-Nation Disarmament Committee," *Journal of Conflict Resolution,* 7 (1963), 510–21.

REGALA, ROBERTO, *Trends in Modern Diplomatic Practice.* Milan: A. Giuffre, 1959.

RUSK, DEAN, "Parliamentary Diplomacy: Debate versus Negotiation," *World Affairs Interpreter,* 26 (1955), 121–38.

SAMELSON, LOUIS T., *Soviet and Chinese Negotiating Behavior: The Western View* (Beverly Hills, Calif.: Sage Publications, 1976).

SAWYER, JACK, and HAROLD GUETZKOW, "Bargaining and Negotiation in International Relations," in *International Behavior: A Social-Psychological Analysis,* ed. Herbert C. Kelman. New York: Holt, Rinehart & Winston, 1965.

SCHELLING, THOMAS C., *The Strategy of Conflict.* Cambridge, Mass.: Harvard University Press, 1960.

SNYDER, GLENN H., and PAUL DIESING, *Conflict Among Nations: Bargaining, Decision Making, and System Structure in International Crises.* Princeton: Princeton University Press, 1977.

SPANIER, JOHN W., and JOSEPH L. NOGEE, *The Politics of Disarmament: A Study in Soviet-American Gamesmanship.* New York: Praeger, 1962.

STRANG, WILLIAM, *The Diplomatic Career.* London: A. Deutsch, 1962.

TREVELYAN, HUMPHREY, *Diplomatic Channels.* London: Macmillan, 1973.

WINHAM, GILBERT, "International Negotiation in an Age of Transition," *International Journal* (Winter 1979–1980), pp. 1–20.

WOOD, JOHN R., and JEAN SERRS, *Diplomatic Ceremonial and Protocol.* New York: Columbia University Press, 1970.

ZARTMAN, I. WILLIAM, *The Negotiation Process: Theories and Application.* Beverly Hills, Calif.: Sage Publications, 1978.

8

The Instruments of Policy: Propaganda

International political relationships have traditionally been conducted by government officials. Prior to the development of political democracy and modern totalitarianism, the conduct of foreign affairs was the exclusive province of royal emissaries and professional diplomats. Louis XIV's famous phrase, *"l'état, c'est moi,"* may seem strange to those who think of government in impersonal terms; but until the nineteenth century, the interests of any political unit were usually closely related to the personal and dynastic interests of its rulers. The wielding of influence was limited to direct contacts between those who made policy for the state. Diplomats bargained and court officials made policy decisions, but all were relatively indifferent to the public response abroad, if any, to their actions. They had to impress their foreign counterparts, not foreign populations.

Communications across the boundaries of political units were in any case sporadic. Travel was limited and few people had any firsthand knowledge even of their own countrymen. In most societies, nonaristocratic people were illiterate, unknowledgeable about affairs outside their town or valley, and generally apathetic toward any political issue that did not directly concern their everyday life. The instruments of communication were so crude as to permit only a small quantity and languorous flow of information from abroad. Populations were isolated from outside influences; if a diplomat could not achieve his or her government's designs through straightforward bargaining, it would be to no avail to appeal to the foreign population, which had no decisive influence in policy making.

With the development of mass politics—widespread involvement of the average citizen or subject in political affairs—and a widening scope of private contacts between people of different nationalities, the psychological and public opinion dimensions of foreign policy have become increasingly important. Insofar as people, combined into various social classes, movements, and interest groups, play a role in the determining of policy objectives and the means used to achieve or defend them, they themselves become a target of persuasion. Governments no longer make promises of rewards or threats of punishment just to foreign diplomats and foreign office officials; they make them to entire societies. One of the unique aspects of modern international political relationships is the deliberate attempt by governments, through diplomats and propagandists, to influence the attitudes and behavior of foreign populations, or of specific ethnic, class, religious, economic, or language groups within those populations. The officials making propaganda hope that these foreign groups or the entire population will in turn influence the attitudes and actions of their own government. To cite one illustration: During 1974, the military junta in Chile hired an American public relations firm in New York to frame programs for altering Americans' highly unfavorable "image" of that government. This action was by no means untypical; today there are more than 400 active agencies in the United States using propaganda on behalf of a foreign government.[1] Most of the agencies are concerned with promoting tourism and trade, but others have a distinctly political mission: Their task is to influence certain segments of a population in hopes that these will, in turn, affect government programs. The propagandist's model of the influence process appears in the accompanying figure.

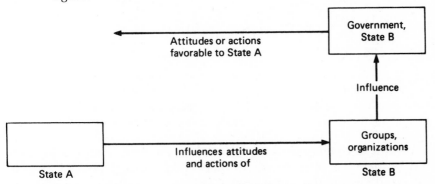

Virtually all governments conduct external information programs. All the major powers have large bureaucracies at home and officials abroad whose task it is to create favorable attitudes abroad for their own government's policies. Even the smallest states have press attachés and public relations men attached

[1] W. Phillips Davison, "Some Trends in International Propaganda," in L. John Martin, ed., *Propaganda in International Affairs* (Philadelphia: Annals of the American Academy of Political and Social Science, Vol. 398, 1971), p. 12.

to their embassies in major countries. Their function is to make contacts with press officials, to send out bulletins and news sheets to all sorts of organizations and individuals that might be interested in events and conditions in the small country, and to answer myriads of questions submitted to them by prospective tourists and school children—in short, their function is to create a favorable "image" of their country abroad.

In view of the extensive networks of nongovernment transactions in the world, propaganda is also conducted at unofficial levels, where a group or movement in one state seeks to alter or reinforce attitudes in another. For example, various spokesmen of black groups in South Africa have toured many countries, telling audiences of the conditions of their people at home and of the South African government's *apartheid* policies. They hope these audiences will somehow influence their own governments to change their policies toward South Africa and thereby promote a change in that government's policies toward the blacks. This is the case where a nonstate actor seeks to improve its condition or achieve its domestic objectives by making linkages with foreign groups or audiences. The model would appear as follows:

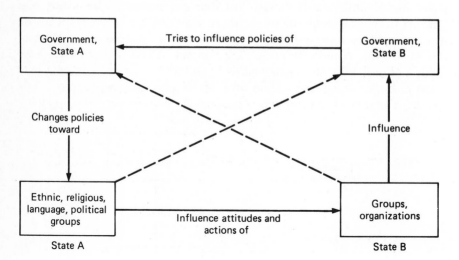

The flow of communication may become even more complex if groups within society attempt to alter directly attitudes and policies of a foreign government. This is indicated by the broken lines. Consumers' boycotts of South African wines are one example. Such "unofficial" lines of persuasion and propaganda are extensive in the world today, particularly as the importance of nonstate actors increases in international politics. Multinational corporations not only disseminate commercial advertising but work on governments and publics, through propaganda campaigns, to try to create a better "climate" for investment and operation. Transnational voluntary associations frequently employ information officers and staff to "tell their story" to audiences around the world. And terrorist groups and individuals have resorted to skyjacking, kidnapping, and seemingly senseless killings as means of publicizing their grievances throughout the world. The sudden, dramatic act can have a much greater political impact than the standard propaganda program disseminated through print or broadcasting. Although the subsequent discussion focuses on government propaganda, we should remember that a variety of nonstate actors and transnational organizations can conduct their tasks successfully only to the extent that they are able to create or sustain favorable public attitudes in many countries. International propaganda is not a monopoly of government information ministries.

WHAT IS PROPAGANDA?

Definitions of propaganda are as plentiful as the books and articles that have been written on the subject. Obviously, not all communication is propaganda, nor are all diplomatic exchanges undertaken to modify foreign attitudes and actions. After a careful review of various definitions, Terence Qualter suggests that propaganda is the

> . . . deliberate attempt by some individual or group to form, control, or alter the attitudes of other groups by the use of the instruments of communication, with the intention that in any given situation the reaction of those so influenced will be that desired by the propagandist. . . . In the phrase "the deliberate attempt" lies the key to the idea of propaganda. This is the one thing that marks propaganda from non-propaganda. . . . It seems clear, therefore, that any act of promotion can be propaganda only if and when it becomes part of a deliberate campaign to induce action through the control of attitudes.[2]

Kimball Young uses a similar definition but places more emphasis on action. He sees propaganda as

> . . . the more or less deliberately planned and systematic use of symbols, chiefly through suggestion and related psychological techniques, with a view to altering and controlling opinions, ideas, and values, and ultimately to changing overt actions along predetermined lines.[3]

Both definitions have four common elements: (1) a communicator with the *intention* of changing attitudes, opinions, and behavior of others; (2) the symbols—written, spoken, or behavioral—used by the communicator; (3) the media of communication; and (4) the audience, or, as it is often called in the terminology of public opinion studies, the "target."

Since propaganda, according to these definitions, involves essentially

[2] Terence H. Qualter, *Propaganda and Psychological Warfare* (New York: Random House, 1962), p. 27.
[3] Quoted in J.A.C. Brown, *Techniques of Persuasion: From Propaganda to Brainwashing* (Middlesex, Eng.: Penguin Books, 1963), p. 19.

a process of persuasion, it cannot be equated with scientific efforts to arrive at some truth. It is not logical discourse or dialectical investigation. It relies more on selection of facts, partial explanations, and predetermined answers. The content of propaganda is therefore seldom completely "true," but neither is it wholly false, as is so often assumed. The propagandist is concerned with maximizing persuasiveness, not with adhering to some standard of scholarship or uncovering some new fact. The common tendency to equate propaganda with falsehood may itself be a result of propaganda. Western newspaper editorials frequently brand Communist speeches or diplomatic maneuvers as "propaganda," while the activities of their own governments abroad are known as "information programs." The implication is usually quite clear: The Soviet version of reality is false, while Western versions are true. In the context of our own values, beliefs, and perceptions of reality, foreign information may indeed seem a deliberate distortion of the truth. Soviet propagandists have in many instances told deliberate lies; but from the point of view of their images of aggressive Western intentions, and from their culture and values, much of their work involves the dissemination of legitimate information. Similarly, to Soviet audiences, who are taught to think in the framework of Marxist-Leninist concepts, information sponsored by Western governments may also be seen as involving distortions of reality.

SELECTING THE TARGET: WHOSE ATTITUDES CAN BE CHANGED?

Soviet and Nazi efforts to institute foreign propaganda programs (they were the first systematic peacetime propaganda programs) were based on intuition, experiment, and revolutionary experience. Some aspects of the programs were self-defeating and, yet, few professional propagandists today could match the skills and insights of Trotsky, Lenin, and Goebbels. During the course of their revolutionary activities, these men developed propaganda techniques based on perceptive analyses of the psychological traits of human beings in their political roles. Soviet propagandists carefully selected targets and attempted to formulate messages that would appeal specifically to particular groups of people.[4]

Despite rapid development of communication media in the past century, only a relatively small number of people in any given society are likely targets of foreign-oriented information. Various studies consistently reveal that even in industrialized societies with high literacy rates and mass consumption of news,

---

[4] The Soviets make an important distinction between propaganda and "agitation." To them, propaganda refers to the intensive instruction and elucidation of the tenets of Marxist-Leninist philosophy to a small audience. Agitation refers to the presentation of one or several ideas, usually slogans, to the masses of people. Thus, their definition of "propaganda" resembles our term *indoctrination,* while "agitation" resembles our definition of *propaganda.*

only a small percentage are interested or involved in international affairs. In many developing countries, the average person's "world" is confined to a small national region or province. Unless a foreign-originated communication has some direct relevance to his or her private everyday life, it is unlikely to reach that person or make any impact.[5] Among those who are potential targets, how effective are communications, and what personal and social characteristics predispose people to react favorably to foreign-sponsored messages?

Some psychologists and sociologists make a distinction between the "nuclear" personality and the "social" personality. The former includes basic attitudes toward objects, ideas, and people, which are usually formed in infancy and reinforced during childhood. These attitudes may or may not relate to political phenomena. In some families, politics are not a matter of general discussion, so the child is left in later years to form his or her own opinions, based on his or her own experiences and social relationships outside the family. Still, any child develops general liberal or authoritarian attitudes, whether they have a political content or not. In other families, fundamental political attitudes—in addition to liberal or authoritarian predispositions—are instilled into the child to the extent that no amount of propaganda, or even experience, is likely to change them. Children born and raised in homes where the parents are vocally prejudiced against specific minorities normally grow up with the same prejudices and do not alter them until they move to a different environment. Some attitudes are so deeply ingrained that even a new environment will not prompt an examination of them. The "nuclear" personality and the attitudes central to that personality, thus, are not amenable to change simply by being subjected to propaganda. This is one reason that people who have been brought up in homes and schools where traditional liberal values were systematically inculcated are seldom converted to any totalitarian organization or faith. For the same reason, Western efforts to convert dedicated Communists who have lived their entire life in a Communist society are not likely to succeed unless these people have already become alienated from the Communist society or have suffered some traumatic experience.

Following the early childhood years, as individuals become a part of larger associations (school, Girl or Boy Scouts), they form attitudes on new ideas, objects, and people; often, these conform to the prevailing attitudes of peer groups. The strength of these group-established attitudes and opinions can be seen in experiments that failed to modify attitudes of individuals contrary to predominating views within the groups to which those individuals belonged. The significance of the "social" personality is that one's political attitudes tend to be functional to the groups to which one belongs. Or, as one of the consistent findings of voting-behavior studies indicates, an individual's political preferences are likely to be similar to those of his or her closest associates.

---

[5] For a review of studies on the limited size of targets, see W. Phillips Davison, *International Political Communication* (New York: Praeger, 1965), Chap. 3.

The implications of these findings are important for the propagandist. They suggest that it is easier to change the attitudes of small associational groups or categorical groups, such as classes, which already share similar attitudes, than of an entire national population, which does not constitute a likely target unless all the members of the national society are united strongly on some value such as the maintenance of national prestige or independence. It is the propagandist's job to find the key groups in society and determine what kinds of appeal will arouse the desired response in the selected targets. To summarize, (1) many people have deep-seated attitudes that have political implications and that become over the years fixed character traits, sometimes liberally disposed and sometimes radically disposed, and seldom amenable to change; (2) other attitudes are also a function of the group and can be changed most easily by altering group attitudes collectively; and (3) a person's attitudes may also be changed by moving into a new milieu or being subjected to a traumatic experience.

The next question is, How do individuals handle information and experience that directly contradict their established attitudes? People are resourceful in resisting information that does not fit their own pictures of reality. Voting-behavior studies in the United States indicate that the more partisan voters are before the election, the less likely they are to subject themselves to the campaign appeals of the party for which they will not vote. Those who do subject themselves to information that contradicts their views may lose confidence in their opinions but will frequently go out of their way to seek any information that substantiates their original position. Others, when exposed to "unfriendly" information, may reject it or perhaps distort its meaning and significance. Or they might question the credibility of the information or its source and pass it off as mere "propaganda." Certainly, one's initial attitude toward the communicator will have an important bearing on one's reception of the information.[6]

We can see these mechanisms operating frequently when we are confronted with information emanating from a hostile country or political party. How often have we failed to read a speech made by a Palestinian leader simply because it came from a hostile source or because we assumed it was mere "propaganda"? Yet we will read carefully a speech by a prime minister of a friendly country or by the candidate of "our" political party because the substance of the speech is not embarrassing to our attitudes.

The presence of these and other mechanisms that insulate us from hostile propaganda would indicate that the propaganda instrument is not equally effective against all types of targets. If there are such resistances, who is susceptible and what kinds of targets are most likely to respond in a desired fashion? The experience of government propagandists and the conclusions of the social sciences seem to point to some answers.

---

[6] Percy H. Tannenbaum, "Initial Attitude toward Source and Content as Factors in Attitude Change through Communications," *Public Opinion Quarterly,* 20 (1956), 414.

Studies reveal that under certain circumstances, communication *can* be effective in shaping attitudes, where no strong predisposition against the communicator and the communicator's ideas already exists. They can form attitudes toward *new* objects; they can change attitudes that are weakly held, or, when several attitudes are fairly evenly balanced, they may be able to strengthen one of them (as is often the case with the "independent voter"). A finding of considerable importance to government information officials is that information of some *personal use* to the target is the most likely to be effective. Information on Soviet economic output, provided by a Russian embassy official to a Canadian student writing an essay on the topic, is more likely to have an impact on the student than is an abstract Leninist tract.[7] Propaganda may also successfully arouse or create desired attitudes and opinions if it is a major or sole source of information for a particular target. The propagandist has an advantage if he or she provides information on a new subject or issue, where public attitudes are not already crystalized and prior information was spotty. This conclusion has been explored in experimental situations, where audiences were subjected to very slanted information on a topic about which they knew very little or possessed few preconceptions. Even when the participants had access to other sources of information, they readily accepted as true the bias of the news media most easily accessible to them.[8]

Propaganda is also apt to be effective when directed toward people who share at least partially the attitudes of the communicator.[9] It is more successful in strengthening *existing* attitudes or crystallizing predispositions than in converting those already hostile. Soviet foreign propaganda does not try to create more Marxist-Leninists all over the world. It seeks, rather, to elicit specific attitudes toward the Soviet Union and its policies—or toward vague symbols such as "peace" or complete disarmament—among people who are neither in a Communist party nor likely to join one as recruits but who, nevertheless, hold some favorable attitudes toward these symbols of Soviet policies.[10] Similarly, the United States International Communications Agency spends more time and money trying to reinforce the pro-American attitudes of selected elites in friendly countries than attempting to convert those whose political leanings go in other directions. The External Service of the B.B.C. takes a slightly different approach. Regardless of the targets' political affiliations, it attempts to maximize its impact by creating a reputation for impartiality. Whereas most governments' foreign information

[7] For a summary of findings on attitude formation and changes in international communication, see Davison, *International Political Communication*, Chap. 3.

[8] For one experiment that establishes this point, see A.D. Annis and Norman C. Meier, "The Induction of Opinion through Suggestion by Means of Planted Content," *Journal of Social Psychology*, 5 (1934), 65–81.

[9] Thus, one of the standard ploys of propagandists sending messages to a hostile audience is not to reveal their own identity. Nazi propagandists frequently used this "black" propaganda, either by failing to mention the source altogether, or by creating some fictitious cover name that would seem legitimate to the audience.

[10] Paul Kecskemeti, "The Soviet Approach to International Political Communication," *Public Opinion Quarterly*, 20 (1956), 304–5.

programs have an identifiable "slant," the B.B.C. presents mostly factual news accounts and critiques of British policies at home and abroad. The purpose is to establish *credibility* for the information source while simultaneously providing a service for those who are regularly subjected to only official government news sources.

Third, propaganda is likely to be effective among youths and apathetic people. Youths are more vulnerable to suggestion and persuasion, because they are the least likely to hold rigid beliefs or attitudes. Results of research projects suggest that children are particularly open to persuasion between the ages of four and eight and that their suggestibility declines steadily with increasing age. Revolutionary parties that create youth groups, religious organizations, and manufacturers of clothing, cigarettes, and cars are all aware of this conclusion and design their propaganda programs accordingly. Apathetic people are also likely targets for the same reason: They do not hold rigid views and tend to be unsure of the political opinions they do adopt. Where such uncertainty persists, persuasion is facilitated, although arousing interest may be difficult.

Finally, propaganda seems to be most effective when directed toward groups whose members share similar attitudes and toward crowds. We have already suggested that attitudes and beliefs are mechanisms that satisfy social adjustment. Individuals are not likely propaganda targets if the content of the propaganda conflicts strongly with the values and opinions that circulate among their closest social connections. We are all wary of adopting and articulating unpopular views—not just because they are unusual, but because we might face social ostracism for expressing them. Crowds, on the other hand, do not necessarily contain an effective network of personal contacts. They are particularly susceptible to propaganda appeals but, as the following statement by J.A.C. Brown suggests, only if there is already some shared attitude between the propagandist and target.

> The study of crowd psychology . . . has shown that, although people do many things whilst in a crowd that they might not otherwise, . . . new attitudes spring . . . from the individual members of the crowd and not, as was formerly thought, from a mysterious entity described as the "crowd" mind. Because of . . . intensification of emotion [in crowds] it is possible to cause disorganized masses of people to behave in other than their everyday manner, to stimulate and lead them more easily than an organized public which is prepared to listen to reason and discuss a problem. But it is not possible to make them do anything. Negro-lynching crowds exist because anti-Negro feelings already exist; the crowd intensifies the feeling to the point of action but does not create it.[11]

It is not clear why people are more suggestible in the crowd, but many observers have noted that individual credulity tends to fall to a low level when emotions are raised in a large gathering. In their domestic propaganda, the Nazis were well aware of this characteristic and put on fantastic parades and party rallies

---

[11] Brown, *Techniques of Persuasion*, p. 68.

to impress the people. There is some evidence that the arousal of any strong emotion may make the individual in the crowd more suggestible, sometimes even when that emotion is directed initially *against* the leader of the crowd.[12]

CREATING IMPACT

After the selection of appropriate targets, the second task of propagandists is to catch the attention of those to whom they will direct their message. Attention-getting may be a difficult endeavor, particularly among people apathetic or hostile to the communicator. Therefore, the devices used by propagandists tend to be spectacular, colorful, or unusual and may not be related to the substance of the message. When attention is elicited, propagandists then attempt to evoke and play on emotions. They cannot do this, obviously, by presenting a calm catalogue of facts (except where the facts "speak for themselves"). Rather, symbols are used to bring about an emotional response, from anxiety and guilt to hatred, which is probably the most potent of all unifying emotions. The common conception that propaganda is synonymous with lying probably arose from efforts of the Allies and Germans during World War I to create hatred toward the enemy by fabricating stories about atrocities and inhumane behavior. Propagandists frequently appeal to hatreds or try to create them, during times of great international tension and in the actual conduct of war, when a maximum number of people and allies have to be mobilized to support a government. In these circumstances, hatred of a national enemy becomes a virtue, while the emotions of love, anxiety, and guilt are seldom included in the various propaganda themes.

These emotions can be raised through almost any communication medium: Orators can inspire a crowd to violent acts simply by giving information; displays of military strength can create fear; and pictures of atrocities can create revulsion and, subsequently, hatred. Probably the most effective technique for foreign propaganda is the coordination of message content with the actual policies and actions of the government.

The adage "actions speak louder than words" undoubtedly applies in international propaganda efforts. The images that foreign populations possess of other countries are usually based on news reports, movies, and cultural events rather than on direct experience. Since most people are uninformed about foreign affairs, their conceptions and attitudes toward foreign countries are seldom detailed. Spectacular, newsmaking foreign-policy actions will be noticed by a relatively broad cross-section of a foreign population, whereas regular government information programs abroad will reach a much smaller audience. In short, people are apt to be more impressed with what governments do than with what propagandists say they do.

Where a great discrepancy between the words and actions of a govern-

[12] *Ibid.*, p. 24.

ment exists, either people abroad become disillusioned or the credibility of the propagandist is compromised, thus making the target populations wary of incoming information. American propaganda toward Eastern Europe, which implied American support of anti-Communist uprisings, had less effect after the United States failed to intervene in Hungary. And the credibility of North Korean propaganda that claimed that the United States had used germ warfare was reduced (except among those who really *wanted* to believe the charges) after the Communists refused to admit an impartial Red Cross investigation. In these instances, all the emotions and expectations that had been raised and attitudes that had been crystallized through verbal and pictorial messages were compromised by the self-defeating actions of the governments that sent the propaganda.

TECHNIQUES
OF PROPAGANDISTS

So far, we have discussed the problem of selecting targets and some aspects of attitude formation and change. Now we can analyze specific propaganda strategies and techniques that have been used in foreign policy during the last several decades. One of the pruposes of external propaganda is to modify the loyalty of particular groups of citizens toward their own government—either to destroy it or to create it, if it did not previously exist. When the Nazis, and often the Soviet government, were attempting through ordinary diplomatic means to achieve their foreign-policy objectives, they simultaneously used propaganda for purposes of subversion. To "soften up" the foreign population, they identified their governments as "cliques," "puppets," and "oppressors," made charges of corruption against them, and, in general, used any means to discredit the established authorities. If various groups' loyalties to their own government could be shaken or destroyed, it became an easier task to substitute another loyalty, such as to a Nazi party, or to create apathy. Those groups or individuals in a society that were already alienated from the government were, of course, a prime target for external propaganda and constituted the material out of which "fifth columns" and subversive elements developed. By playing upon their hatred or revulsion toward the legitimate government, the propagandist could lead them to take political action—riots, mass meetings, or boycotts—that created confusion and embarrassed the regime in power, thus furthering the interests of Nazi Germany or Soviet Russia.

Another strategy exploits potential or actual divisions within a society, often leading to violent action in the form of pogroms, strikes, and riots. This violence damages the international prestige of the government, undermines local confidence in it, and may force it to take unpopular repressive measures. For example, the Nazis directed propaganda toward the Sudeten Germans, urging them to violent action against the majority Czechs. When the Czech government sought to put down Nazi-inspired riots, German propagandists accused it of persecuting a minority. A number of influential Europeans, sympathetic to the position of the Sudeten Germans, consequently made little effort to protest the Munich settlement in 1938 and subsequent Nazi takeover of Czechoslovakia.

A similar strategy attempts to split allies from each other. But instead of provoking class, religious, or ethnic hatreds *within* a society, this type of propaganda tries to *unite* the society by suggesting that a country's allies are unreliable, scheming, or ready to "sell out" the interests of friends. A frequent theme of Nazi propaganda during World War II held that while British soldiers were on the front lines, American troops were in England seducing their wives and girlfriends. Postwar American propaganda has also attempted to arouse Eastern European nationalism by arguing that the Soviet government was exploiting the satellite economies for its own purposes.

Having established a target and appropriate strategy, propagandists then may use a variety of specific techniques in delivering the messages. Among the more prominent are.[13]

1. NAME-CALLING. The propagandist attaches an emotion-laden symbol to a person or country. Targets are expected to respond favorably, from the propagandist's point of view, to the label without examining any evidence. Propagandists relate their appeals to stereotypes that already exist in the audience. Thus, Communists become "reds," labor leaders become "union bosses," and constitutional governments become "capitalist cliques."

2. GLITTERING GENERALITY. This is similar to the preceding technique but is used to describe an idea or policy rather than individuals. The term "free world" is a favorite generality of Western propagandists. "Socialist solidarity" is used in the Communist world to describe the complex relations among Communist states and parties, and "the African soul" is supposed to create a similar image of strength and unity.

3. TRANSFER. The propagandist attempts to identify one idea, person, country, or policy with another to make the target approve or disapprove it. One way to evoke a particularly hostile attitude among religious people against communism is to equate it with atheism. Communists regularly equate capitalism with decadence, and anti-Semites hope to create public support for their bigotry by associating Jews with Communists.

4. "PLAIN FOLKS." Any propagandist is aware that his problems are compounded if he appears to the audience as a "foreigner" or stranger. He

---

[13] These categories are adapted from Alfred McClung Lee and Elizabeth Bryant Lee, *The Fine Art of Propaganda: A Study of Father Coughlin's Speeches* (New York: Harcourt Brace Jovanovich, 1939), pp. 22–25.

seeks, therefore, to identify as closely as possible with the values and style of life of the targets by using local slang, accent, and idiom.

5. TESTIMONIAL. Here, the propagandist uses an esteemed person or institution to endorse or criticize an idea or political entity. A variation of this is the "appeal to authority," where the target is asked to believe something simply because some "authority" says it is true.

6. SELECTION. Almost all propaganda, even when it uses the other techniques discussed above, relies on the selection of facts, although it is seldom very specific in its factual content. When a detailed presentation is given, the propagandist uses only those facts required to "prove" predetermined objectives.

7. BANDWAGON. This technique plays on the audience's desire to "belong"or be in accord with the crowd. It is similar to the testimonial, except that a mass of people, rather than a single esteemed person or institution, serves as the attraction. The messages of Communist propagandists frequently use such phrases as "the whole world knows that . . . ," "all peace-loving people recognize that . . . ," or "all progressive people demand that . . ." This technique implies that the target is in a minority—if he or she opposes the substance of the message—and should join the majority. Or, if the target is sympathetic to the propagandist, this technique will reinforce one's attitudes by demonstrating that one is on the "right" side, along with everyone else.

8. FRUSTRATION SCAPEGOAT. One easy way to create hatred and relieve frustrations is to create a scapegoat. Revolutionary regimes faced with complex internal economic and social disorders and popular frustrations frequently create an internal or external "spook" to account for the people's miseries. The most famous example was the myth created by Hitler that Germany's internal and foreign problems were created by "the Jews"—who were often equated with Communists.

The reader will have noticed that these techniques are used not only in foreign propaganda but in all organized efforts to persuade, including political campaigns, and particularly in commercial advertising. Several of these techniques may be used simultaneously to create the maximum effect.

To this point, the discussion of propaganda as an instrument of foreign policy has been theoretical. To understand better some of the strategies, techniques, and problems that governments face in attempting to influence others, it will be useful to discuss in some detail recent American and Soviet foreign-information programs, even though these are by no means the only governments that use propaganda as an instrument of foreign policy.

The theoretical discussion should not suggest that if the propagandists correctly gauge their audience, carefully select their target, and skillfully combine their techniques, they will always succeed in "winning minds." A review of American and Soviet propaganda policies indicates that, in both governments, there remains considerable uncertainty regarding the kinds of philosophies and techniques that should guide their foreign-information programs.

The American propaganda program is formulated by the International Communication Agency (ICA), an organization created in 1954 by President Eisenhower. The agency organizes the activities of more than 100 libraries and information service offices abroad; a world-wide radio service (the Voice of America); television, film, and news services; and numerous special programs. The State Department handles student and cultural exchanges, which are an important aspect of the American propaganda effort. Until funds were cut off by Congress, the Central Intelligence Agency supplied the resources for Radio Liberty, beamed at the Soviet Union. In a more clandestine fashion, the CIA frequently supports foreign writers or newspaper editors who write favorably of the United States and its policies.[14]

The objectives of American propaganda have shifted over the years. At the beginning of the cold war, anti-Communist themes were prominent and, in a more positive vein, the ICA tried to promote the "truth" about American policies and American society. Exploitation of nationalist sentiments in Eastern Europe has also been a prominent objective, along with efforts to show how American philosophies of economics and government have been instrumental in creating the nation with the highest standard of living in the world.

Perhaps the most serious difficulties have arisen in connection with the choice of targets and types of themes to be used for certain populations in developing countries. There have been instances, for example, where the themes of "democracy" and "private enterprise" were used among landless peasants, whose only experience with private enterprise was one of exploitation and degradation, and where "democracy" meant, at least in their own experience, corrupt rule by closed oligarchies. Similarly, to display visual evidence of the American standard of living—a frequent American propaganda technique—to uneducated and often illiterate peasants often creates either incredulity or outright antagonism.

On the other hand, American propaganda programs have been successful in reinforcing the pro-American attitudes of certain segments of foreign populations, including key economic, cultural, and political elites. People who already have a favorable predisposition toward the United States do visit ICA libraries,

---

[14] Kenneth R. Sparks, "Selling Uncle Sam in the Seventies," in Martin, ed., *Propaganda in International Affairs,* p. 115.

take free English language lessons, or avail themselves of the various recreational and educational programs offered by the agency. It is questionable, however, whether these programs extend to a large majority of the population or whether they make any impact, in the long run, on those who are anti-American or apathetic.

In developing areas of the world, anti-Communist propaganda is less likely to succeed. These areas are usually far removed from the Soviet Union and China, the people have seldom experienced unfavorable Soviet or Chinese policies directly, and communism does not seem a salient problem in their lives. Although some American propaganda in these areas is decidedly anti-Communist, in its main themes—particularly when directed to local elites and property owners—it usually emphasizes that the objectives of American foreign policy are compatible with the interests of the developing country and that the United States can be helpful in assisting in the process of industrialization. Where such themes are coupled with displays of effective foreign-aid programs, the impact may be considerable. American propaganda in developing areas also argues that free enterprise and economic, social, and scientific advancement go together and that the aspirations of less fortunate people can be achieved within a framework of democratic reform rather than totalitarianism.

The ICA has used all the traditional propaganda techniques, but deliberate distortion has been avoided. In addition, instead of relying exclusively on the dissemination of ideas, symbols, information, and messages designed to create some unfavorable image of the Soviet Union or favorable image of the United States and its policies, the ICA has also found it effective to render *services* that have a *direct and immediate benefit to the targets' personal or economic life*. While the Voice of America uses all the traditional techniques of propaganda in its news analyses, it also provides free lessons in the English language and programs for Russian listeners who like, but cannot buy, records of Western jazz or rock music. The ICA *Bulletin* is a news-teletype production that reaches more than 100 countries and is available to local newspapers, political groups, educators, and individuals who request that it be sent to them. Through this service, the ICA disseminates full texts of important speeches by American public officials, so that foreign editors can draw their own conclusions and, in some cases, reprint entire sections of the speech at a very low cost. This service benefits both the propagandist and the target. For the United States, it means wide coverage of the speeches and news items it wants publicized around the world; for the foreign newspapers, it means inexpensive information and news copy. In addition to providing books, periodicals, films, and magazines in ICA libraries around the world, the agency also provides technical and information services to foreign businessmen, labor organizers, educators, and farmers. In other words, the agency seeks to provide information and assistance relevant to the activities of foreign groups and individuals. As one former ICA official has argued, if American propagandists can provide information that is useful to existing foreign organizations or can help new organizations to form, they are much more likely to have a significant political impact than if they focus their attention on influencing isolated individuals.[15]

SOVIET PROPAGANDA

The long-range objectives of the Soviet Union were for many years closely associated with destruction of the contemporary international system and the substitution of a world of socialist states. Whereas the Soviet government has core and middle-range objectives similar to those of many other states, one long-range external purpose, as it often claimed, was that of promoting revolution abroad. Clearly, the Soviet government cannot achieve its long-range objectives simply through diplomatic bargaining or deliberate aggression. Soviet governments from the time of the Bolshevik revolution have thus recognized that both the advocacy of revolution and the promotion of Russian middle-range objectives could be enhanced by formulating systematic propaganda programs that would bypass foreign governments and influence foreign populations instead. These populations, it was hoped, would in turn force their governments to act in a manner consistent with Soviet interests. Propaganda is thus both a technique to assist Soviet diplomats in conferences and bargaining sessions and a means of promoting revolutionary activity abroad.

Soviet propaganda still relies extensively on Marxist–Leninist terminology and traditional Russian demonology, but today it is infused with a pragmatism that was lacking prior to 1953. The flexibility of Soviet propaganda is perhaps nowhere more evident than in the current emphasis on increasing face-to-face contacts. In addition to touring cultural and entertainment troupes, the Soviet government regularly sends abroad scientific, technical, and artistic delegates and willingly invites foreign tourists and delegates to visit some parts of the Soviet Union. Thousands of students from Africa, Asia, and Latin America attend Soviet institutions of higher learning, where the emphasis is on technical training, not the inculcation of Marxism–Leninism. Moscow's Patrice Lumumba University is devoted specifically to students from Africa. In all cases, generous scholarships are provided.

In addition, there are hundreds of "friendship societies" throughout the world. These are voluntary organizations—headed usually by prominent people in a foreign country—that maintain special contacts with counterparts in the Soviet Union. These organizations provide information about Soviet life and promote artistic, literary, and cultural exchanges. From the Soviet point of view, their purpose is to foster generally favorable attitudes abroad toward Russian life in general and Soviet foreign policies in particular. They also provide means of direct communication to key elites in foreign countries.

[15] W. Phillips Davison, "Political Communication as an Instrument of Foreign Policy," *Public Opinion Quarterly*, 27 (1963), 35.

Finally, there are numerous Soviet "front organizations," such as the World Federation of Trade Unions, the World Federation of Democratic Youth, and the International Union of Students. Ostensibly voluntary associations crossing national frontiers, in reality they have been sponsored and are in part funded by Soviet party agencies. The "policies" or resolutions adopted by the organizations often reflect official Soviet foreign policy, and they generally have a strident anti-West tone. If these organizations can mobilize enough popular support within a country on a particular line, they can have some impact on governments. Such was the case when the French section of the World Peace Movement launched a massive campaign in the late 1940s against the formation of NATO and in the 1950s against inclusion of West Germany into the alliance. Using nationalist and anti-American symbols, the movement made a definite impact on domestic French opinion, although it did not achieve its goal of preventing the French government from joining NATO.[16]

Former premier Khrushchev emphasized at the Twentieth Congress of the Soviet Communist Party in 1956 that Russian propaganda must not be concerned too much with inculcating abstract principles of communism but must become increasingly practical. Whereas Stalin conceived of the world as divided into two rigid and unalterably hostile camps—the socialist and capitalist—the present Soviet leadership has recognized the opportunities available for cultivating developing countries through appeals to nationalism and anticolonialism. As Soviet propagandists appeal to broader and more diverse targets abroad, they have replaced the old clichés of Marxism–Leninism with newer slogans. Instead of using such terms as "proletariat" and "working class," which elicited desired attitudes and behavior among only a limited segment of any society, Soviet slogans today include the terms "masses," "all peace-loving people," and, most broadly, simply "the people." Instead of "violent revolution," "class struggle," "imperialist hyenas," and "bloodsuckers of the people," they talk of the "national interest," the "interests of peace-loving peoples," and "aggressive circles."[17]

Aside from propaganda directed at the problems of particular "targets"—that is, information that is relevant to only particular groups of people within a country, in recent years the Soviet government has emphasized three general themes: (1) nationalism (or anti-imperialism), (2) modernization, and (3) peace.[18]

Most of the propaganda that exploits nationalism is not couched in the orthodox phraseology of Marxism–Leninism, for one of the most difficult tasks of Communist theoreticians has been to reconcile Marx's disdain for "bour-

[16] For a discussion of Soviet-sponsored "front organizations" and the World Peace Movement, see Marshall D. Shulman, *Stalin's Foreign Policy Reappraised* (Cambridge, Mass.: Harvard University Press, 1963), pp. 80–103, 199–221.

[17] John H. Kautsky, ed., *Political Change in Underdeveloped Countries: Nationalism and Communism* (New York: John Wiley, 1962), p. 79.

[18] Detailed discussion of these themes is in Frederick C. Barghoorn, *Soviet Foreign Propaganda* (Princeton, N.J.: Princeton University Press, 1964), Chaps. 3–6.

geois nationalism" with the obvious importance of nationalism in the contemporary world. Thus, while in intrabloc propaganda the Soviet government decries manifestations of Eastern European nationalism (although it promotes Russian "patriotism"), propaganda directed to developing areas fully supports policies expressing nationalist attitudes, whether they take the form of territorial claims (such as Soviet support for Indonesia's claim to West Irian in the 1960s), wars of "national liberation," expropriation of Western property, or elimination of Western military bases. Soviet propaganda to Asia, Africa, and the Middle East also emphasizes that any ties with the "imperialists" will jeopardize the independence of the new states and subject them to "neocolonialism."[19] If successful, these appeals based on symbols of nationalism will promote the decline of Western influence and, presumably, simultaneously create good will for the Soviet Union.[20] For European targets, the theme of nationalism is usually put in the form of anti-Americanism, suggesting that America's decadent culture is invading Europe and that the United States supports NATO militarily only to protect itself and maintain domination over weaker NATO members.

Since Soviet leaders have recently argued that other societies, especially the developing countries, will adopt the Communist example if they see the impressive achievements of Soviet science, welfare, and technology, it is natural that Soviet propagandists would use the theme of modernization. This theme is also effective in creating prestige for the Soviet Union. A steady stream of statements, charts, diagrams, and statistics goes via the radio and various publications to the newer countries. These figures emphasize that the Soviet Union has achieved the status of a major power in less than 60 years and that it is winning the "battle of growth rates" over the United States. Soviet space achievements are also acknowledged to be the result of the superiority of communism. Accomplishments of Russian writers and artists and the level of interest in cultural affairs among the Russian people in general are frequently compared with the salacious literature that seems to be so popular in Western countries.[21]

Soviet propaganda in developing countries also places special emphasis on modernization of the Soviet Union's Asiatic areas, particularly Uzbekistan, where natural and economic conditions are in many respects similar to those in other Asian areas. Articles, pictures, and news reports describe the difference between the Central Asian republics during the tsarist period, when indigenous populations lived in ignorance and poverty, and today, when there has been spectacular technological, educational, and cultural progress. The relative religious freedom of Moslems in the area is heavily emphasized in Soviet information directed to the Middle Eastern countries. In propaganda of this sort, the Soviet government is careful to point out that the problems it has faced in building

---

[19] Note that this idea is almost the same as the American propaganda theme that claims that diplomatic, commercial, and foreign-aid ties with the Soviet Union or Communist China will lead to the subversion of nonaligned states.

[20] Barghoorn, *Soviet Foreign Propaganda,* p. 162.

[21] *Ibid.,* Chap. 6.

up the Central Asian republics are similar to the problems faced by the people in developing areas today. It creates an impact by being applicable to the concerns of the target populations.[22]

Another typical technique is to invite foreign Islamic leaders in the arts, literature, history, and religion to a conference sponsored by the "Muslim Spiritual Board of Central Asia and Kazakhstan." Foreign delegates are provided with tours of mosques and one of the few remaining Koranic institutes. But in addition to attending a cultural conference, delegates are asked to pass political—usually anti-Western—resolutions, thus implying a transnational Muslim coalition committed to Soviet foreign-policy objectives.[23]

Peace themes are among the most prominent in Soviet propaganda. These, too, are effective because they play upon rational fears and well-established and widespread attitudes against war. Moreover, these themes appeal to broad groups of people in almost any country, although somewhat different emphasis must be given for each specific target. For Communists and their supporters, classical Leninist strictures about the rapacity and aggressiveness of "imperialists" will be used, while for audiences in nonaligned and pro-Western states, the slogans of peaceful coexistence and "normalization of relations" are more prominent. In either case the objective is to create the assumption that Soviet diplomatic programs are motivated by a sincere desire to create peace. Setbacks and delays are usually attributed to the intransigence of Western governments in general or to Western groups, such as the "military-industrial complex," in particular.

The Soviet government has at its disposal all the modern communication media to disseminate propaganda themes. Face-to-face contacts are emphasized increasingly to supplement the traditional media of books, pamphlets, magazines, and radio. Soviet films, once of such a thoroughly ideological character that no one outside—and few inside—the Soviet Union would pay to watch them, are rated today among the world's artistic achievements. Trade fairs, exhibits, visiting sports teams, circuses, ballets, and technological displays create generally favorable attitudes among a wide variety of people toward the Soviet Union and its economic and cultural achievements.

Emphasis on sports has been particularly notable. Massive programs mobilizing millions of Soviet youth have raised the level of athletic achievement to the world's best in almost all sports. The Russians have even made significant progress in downhill and slalom skiing, once denounced in the Soviet Union as "decadent bourgeois" sports. The growing number of Soviet and East European medals and their total domination of the 1980 Moscow Olympics has one major purpose: to demonstrate to the world the superiority of socialism.

But the largest amount of money is still spent on radio and books. Radio Moscow broadcasts to every area of the world in native languages and

---

[22] Alexander Kaznacheev, *Inside a Soviet Embassy* (Philadelphia: Lippincott, 1962), p. 104.
[23] For elaboration and cases, see Alexandre Bennigsen, "Soviet Muslims and the World of Islam," *Problems of Communism* (March–April 1980), 38–51.

possesses the most powerful transmitting equipment available. Even though the estimated audience of this service is smaller than that of either the Voice of America or the British Broadcasting Corporation's External Service, it can shift attention rapidly to areas suitable for exploitation and can broadcast messages that would not be acceptable for domestic Russian consumption.[24] Soviet propagandists do not have to be concerned with irate legislators or voluntary associations that do not fully agree with the themes or messages being disseminated. The Soviets also publish, at subsidized prices, thousands of foreign-language books and hundreds of magazines and journals. These range from inexpensive editions of Russian literary classics to inflammatory propaganda appeals; every publication is directed toward a particular market. Soviet information officials abroad request local newspapers to reprint or, simply, to sell space in their publications for Soviet articles, news, and photographs.

Among the clandestine means, the best known are the many radio stations broadcasting from unknown headquarters, ostensibly as the "voice" of some liberation movement. Among these are "Radio Peace and Progress," engaged mostly in beaming vitriolic attacks against the United States to Indian audiences. Clandestine radio stations in East Germany have been active in broadcasting to West Germany and, particularly, to Turkey, Iran, and Iraq. China supplies transmitter time to the "Patriotic Youth Front Radio" for Burma and similar facilities for Malaysia and the Philippines. Vast increases in Chinese and Soviet broadcasting to Africa are also notable, particularly since they use each other, as well as the "imperialists," as targets for criticism.

THE EFFECTIVENESS
OF PROPAGANDA
IN INTERNATIONAL POLITICS

It is difficult to generalize about the conditions under which propaganda appeals will succeed and about the extent to which the hundreds of millions of dollars spent each year by the major powers on foreign information programs result in desired attitudes and actions by various "targets." Surveys and studies by propaganda agencies are often unreliable, because administrators have to prove that the resources spent are bringing desired results. And although it is relatively easy to measure the number of listeners to radio programs or attendance at cultural-exchange events, it is virtually impossible to identify the impact these media have on attitudes and actions. Yet, most governments must believe that information programs are an important technique of influence, because they continue to expand their resources in this area.

---

[24] A survey in 1969 found that of regular radio listeners in India, 83% listened occasionally to Radio Ceylon, 66% to the B.B.C., 58% to the Voice of America, and 55% to Radio Moscow. Francis S. Ronalds, Jr., "The Future of International Broadcasting," in Martin, ed., *Propaganda in International Affairs*, p. 79.

As yet, television has not been used extensively for propaganda purposes, although once satellite-beamed television becomes inexpensive and readily available to developing countries, some governments may try to exploit this medium to a greater extent. But an increasing number of governments are beaming radio broadcasts to foreign countries, and a number of them have projects to set up new transmitters or to increase the power of those already in operation. By the early 1980s, various governments were already broadcasting an aggregate of over 17,000 hours weekly, with the Soviet Union leading, at 2,000 hours per week in 88 foreign languages. The Chinese have rapidly expanded their foreign-language broadcasts, and Radio Cairo sends programs to the Arab world on a daily basis. Radio broadcasting is relatively cheap, and the availability and low cost of transistor radios have created an ever-expanding audience, particularly in the developing countries. Thus, relatively small countries such as Saudi Arabia, Zaire, and Albania find it within their means to broadcast abroad extensively.[25] Finally, cultural-exchange programs and propaganda through printed media have grown rapidly as well.

In the long run, most propaganda clearly does not create new attitudes or lead to any particular actions. Indeed, most of it is "facilitative communication," the main purpose of which is simply to keep in contact with foreign audiences and to maintain an awareness of the general foreign-policy goals or social characteristics of a state. Awareness in itself often creates positive attitudes over a period of time, if not political action.[26] In the short run and in highly favorable circumstances of political turmoil, revolution, war, or general fear, however, propaganda can be used very effectively—that is, to the point where "targets" can be motivated to undertake actions desired by the communicator. As the next chapter reveals, propaganda has been used particularly effectively in attempts at subversion where a "revolutionary" situation already prevails in the target state.

SELECTED BIBLIOGRAPHY

ABELSON, H.J., *Persuasion: How Opinions and Attitudes Are Changed.* New York: Springer, 1959.

BARGHOORN, FREDERICK C., *The Soviet Cultural Offensive.* Princeton, N.J.: Princeton University Press, 1960.

——, *Soviet Foreign Propaganda.* Princeton, N.J.: Princeton University Press, 1964.

BETTINGHAUS, ERWIN P., *Persuasive Communication.* New York: Holt, Rinehart & Winston, 1967.

[25] See Ronalds, "The Future of International Broadcasting," pp. 71–80.

[26] L. John Martin, "Effectiveness of International Propaganda," in Martin, ed., *Propaganda in International Affairs,* pp. 62–70.

BIRYUKOV, N., "Broadcasting and Diplomacy," *International Affairs* (Moscow) 10 (1964), 63–68.

BOGART, LEO, *Premises for Propaganda.* New York: Free Press, 1976.

BROWN, J.A.C., *Techniques of Persuasion: From Propaganda to Brainwashing.* Middlesex, Eng.: Penguin Books, 1963.

DAVISON, W. PHILLIPS, *International Political Communication.* New York: Praeger, 1965.

———, "Political Communication as an Instrument of Foreign Policy," *Public Opinion Quarterly,* 27 (1963), 28–36.

DEUTSCH, KARL W., and RICHARD L. MERRITT, "Effects of Events on National and International Images," in *International Behavior: A Social-Psychological Analysis,* ed. Herbert C. Kelman. New York: Holt, Rinehart & Winston, 1965.

DOOB, LEONARD W., *Public Opinion and Propaganda,* 2nd ed. Hamden, Conn.: Archon, 1966.

GORDON, GEORGE N., *War of Ideas: America's International Identity Crisis.* New York: Hastings House, 1973.

JANIS, IRVING L., and M. BREWSTER SMITH, "Effects of Education and Persuasion on National and International Images," in *International Behavior: A Social-Psychological Analysis,* ed. Herbert C. Kelman. New York: Holt, Rinehart & Winston, 1965.

JORDAN, ALEXANDER T., "Political Communication: The Third Dimension of Strategy," *Orbis,* 8 (1964), 670–85.

KECSKEMETI, PAUL, "The Soviet Approach to International Political Communication," *Public Opinion Quarterly,* 20 (1965), 299–308.

LAVES, WALTER H.C., and CHARLES A. THOMSON, *Cultural Relations and U.S. Foreign Policy.* Bloomington: University of Indiana Press, 1963.

LEE, JOHN, ed., *Diplomatic Persuaders.* New York: John Wiley, 1968.

MARTIN, L. JOHN, *International Propaganda: Its Legal and Diplomatic Control.* Gloucester, Mass.: Peter Smith, 1970.

———, ed., *Propaganda in International Affairs.* Philadelphia: Annals of the American Academy of Political and Social Science, Vol. 398, 1971.

MERRITT, RICHARD L., ed., *Communication in International Politics.* Urbana: University of Illinois Press, 1971.

PASSIN, HERBERT, *China's Cultural Diplomacy.* New York: Praeger, 1963.

QUALTER, TERENCE H., *Propaganda and Psychological Warfare.* New York: Random House, 1962.

SORENSON, THOMAS C., *The Word War: The Story of American Propaganda.* New York: Harper & Row, 1968.

ZEMAN, Z.A.B., *Nazi Propaganda,* 2nd ed. New York: Oxford University Press, 1973.

9

Economic Instruments of Policy

Just as modern nations are politically and technologically interdependent, so do they rely upon each other for resources and commodities that enable them to develop and sustain viable economies. Some economic systems are particularly dependent upon external markets and sources of supply and could not function for more than a few weeks if they were cut off from the rest of the world. British farmers, for example, could produce enough food by themselves to support only 12 million of Britain's 56 million people. The British people would starve to death within six months if they could not import food and raw materials; their economy would collapse within several months if they could not sell manufactured products abroad. For almost any national endeavor, whether it is to establish or increase standards of living or to produce capabilities and resources that can be used for domestic or foreign-policy purposes, reliance on others has become one of the paramount conditions of modern international relations.

Needs that cannot be filled within national frontiers help create dependencies on other states. As we have suggested, degree of need is one variable element in the successful exercise of influence in international politics. Because economic resources are often scarce—but necessary to fulfill national values and aspirations—needs in the modern world are frequently of an economic nature. Possession of these resources can be transformed easily into political influence. It is the need for key raw materials by industrial powers that helps explain how "weak" countries, as measured by military or economic capabilities, are able to influence the actions of the "strong." Economic resources are among the major capabilities that can be mobilized for political purposes.

Today, some developing countries use their possession of rare minerals or other commodities to wield effective international influence. But these countries also need capital, machinery, and technical help to develop their economies. They lack a variety of export products and for these reasons are vulnerable to economic pressure from industrialized countries. When a country relies on the export of a few commodities to earn foreign exchange, any drop in the price of these exports can have disastrous effects on the economy. Such forms of dependence are not uncommon between developing and industrialized countries; and they can be exploited for political purposes, provided that alternative markets are not available. If influence is to be created out of economic need, the need must be genuine.

Economic needs and capabilities are not, of course, distributed equally in the international system. Degrees of dependence upon trade as a component of overall economic activity vary considerably among states. Whereas England and Japan rely very heavily on trade (where trade is measured as a proportion of the Gross National Product), other major powers, such as the United States, the Soviet Union, France, and China, are much less vulnerable to fluctuations in trading patterns. Among smaller states, dependence upon trade also varies considerably. Approximately 70 percent of Canada's trade lies with the United States. This trade generates about 18 percent of Canada's GNP. Cyprus, Malta, and Iceland are among the most vulnerable states in the world because a high proportion of their total economic activity is accounted for by exports and imports. Needless to say, if they export most of their commodities to one state or group of states (Iceland sells a large proportion of its fish exports to the Soviet Union), they are potentially vulnerable to threats to break off that trade.

TECHNIQUES OF ECONOMIC REWARD AND PUNISHMENT

When rewards are offered or economic punishments are threatened, at least two conditions must be satisfied to make the exercise of influence effective: (1) the target of the influence act must perceive that there is a genuine need for the reward or for avoidance of the punishment, and (2) no alternative market or source of supply must be easily available to the target. The specific techniques that can be used to reward or punish constitute various controls over the flow of goods between countries: tariffs, quotas, boycotts, and embargoes. Loans, credits, and currency manipulations can be used for rewards as well.

1. Tariffs.   Almost all foreign-made products coming into a country are taxed for the purpose of raising revenue, protecting domestic producers from foreign competition, or other domestic economic reasons. The tariff structure can be used effectively as an inducement or punishment when a country stands to gain or lose important markets for its products by its upward or downward manipulation. The U.S. government, for example, has accorded both Poland and Yugoslavia preferential tariff treatment in an effort to keep these two countries as independent of Moscow as possible. However, the president is authorized by an act of Congress to withdraw this favorable tariff structure any time he deems it to be in the "national interest"—that is, at any time that either Poland or Yugoslavia begins to conduct policies that are too vigorously anti-American.

2. QUOTAS. To control imports of some commodities, governments may establish quotas rather than tariffs (tariffs may, of course, be applied to the items that enter under quotas). Under such arrangements, the supplier usually sends goods into the country at a favorable price but is allowed to sell only a certain amount in a given time period. The U.S. government maintains quotas on the import of sugar from the Philippines, the Dominican Republic, and other sugar-producing nations. Since these countries sell a large portion of sugar (their major export crop) to the United States, any shift in the size of the quotas could either assist or severely damage their economies.

3. BOYCOTT. A trade boycott organized by a government eliminates the import of either a specific commodity or the total range of export products sold by the country against which the boycott is organized. Governments that do not engage in state trading normally enforce boycotts by requiring private importers to secure licenses to purchase any commodities from the boycotted country. If importers do not comply with this requirement, any goods purchased abroad can be confiscated and they can be prosecuted.

4. EMBARGO. A government that seeks to *deprive* another country of goods prohibits its own businesses from concluding any transactions with commercial organizations in the country against which the embargo is organized. An embargo may be enforced either on a specific category of goods, such as strategic materials, or on the total range of goods that private businesses normally send to the country being punished.

5. LOANS, CREDITS, AND CURRENCY MANIPULATIONS. Rewards may include favorable tariff rates and quotas, granting loans (a favorite reward offered by the major powers today to developing countries), or extending credits. The manipulation of currency rates is also used to create more or less favorable terms of trade between countries.

The choice of techniques or combination of techniques to be used will be influenced by the goals being pursued; the type of economic vulnerability or need that exists in the country being rewarded or punished; the estimated effectiveness of alternative techniques; and, since dependence is usually a bilateral proposition, assessment of the possibility of countermeasures. A government will not seriously consider applying an embargo against another country if that country supplies badly needed resources; restrictions on imports through high tariffs or a boycott will not be very effective in damaging the competitor if it sells most of its products in another market; and an embargo will not deprive a competitor if it can easily purchase the commodities elsewhere at comparable prices. Some of the techniques and problems of applying economic rewards and sanctions in attempting to influence the behavior of other nations can best be seen through illustrations from the recent history of international politics.

ECONOMIC REWARDS
AND PUNISHMENTS
IN OPERATION

The postwar history of Soviet-Yugoslav relations provides an excellent example of how economic instruments, along with propaganda, military threats, and diplomacy, played an important role in Soviet attempts to influence developments in Yugoslav foreign and domestic policies. Shortly after World War II, the Soviet Union began to assist the new Communist regime in Yugoslavia by enlarging trade and providing small amounts of economic assistance. In 1948, however, Tito was expelled from the Communist bloc because of his unorthodox domestic policies and unwillingness to submit to Soviet domination in ideological and political matters. The Yugoslav heresy resulted in threats of military action by Hungary, Romania, and Bulgaria; vituperation in Communist propaganda organs; and excommunication of the Yugoslav Communist party from the Cominform. The Soviet Union also organized a Communist bloc embargo and boycott against Yugoslavia. The embargo was potentially an effective technique of punishment because in 1948 Yugoslavia sold over 50 percent of its exports to the bloc and received 95 percent of its imports from the same source.[1] The unfavorable economic impact of the embargo and boycott on Yugoslavia was short-lived, however, because Tito was able to turn to Italy and Great Britain for compensating trade agreements and to the International Bank for Reconstruction and Development for development loans.

After Stalin's death, Soviet-Yugoslav relations intermittently deteriorated and improved. In 1955, the Soviet government signed a barter pact for the exchange of commodities worth over $79 million annually. In the same year, Russia cancelled a $90 million Yugoslav debt and attempted to get other Eastern European countries to expand trade with the former heretic. Between 1955 and 1958, the bloc countries committed themselves to loans of nearly

---

[1] Harold J. Berman, "The Legal Framework of Trade between Planned and Market Economies: The Soviet-American Example," *Law and Contemporary Problems,* 24 (1959), 504.

$500 million in attempting to win back Tito's loyalty and subservience to Moscow on ideological matters. Tito continued to vacillate, however, and each time in 1957 and 1958 that he emphasized his independent Communist line, the Soviet government either threatened to cut off assistance or conveniently "delayed" the granting of new loans. In May 1958, Premier Khrushchev suspended negotiations on loans that amounted to nearly $300 million. By 1963, Tito had mended relations with Soviet Russia—without compromising his independence—and was amply rewarded through new trade agreements and increased Soviet loans.[2]

Considering Yugoslavia's economic dependence on the Soviet bloc, Communist economic punishments and rewards should have succeeded; they failed simply because Yugoslavia turned to the West and found alternative supply and market sources.

A case where alternatives were not available and economic sanctions succeeded occurred in the relations between Finland and the Soviet Union in 1958. After parliamentary elections in 1958, in which Finnish Communists won over one-quarter of the seats, a coalition government headed by a Social Democrat was formed. This government did not include among its ministers any Communists, however. The Soviet government has held a traditional enmity against all Finnish Socialists, and the Soviet premier wasted no time in announcing his displeasure and distrust of the new Finnish prime minister. The Soviet government also objected to inclusion of Conservatives in the new cabinet. Various articles in the Soviet press pointed to the "rightist" government as symptomatic of a general resurgence of "reactionary" forces in Finland and criticized these "rightists" for attempting to destroy friendly Soviet-Finnish relations and planning to increase Finnish trade with the West at the expense of Soviet-Finnish trade. To indicate that it would not tolerate such political leadership in a neighboring country, the Soviet government began to to apply a number of diplomatic and economic pressures:

1. The Soviet ambassador in Helsinki returned to Moscow and was not replaced. The ambassador left without paying the usual courtesy and farewell visit to the Finnish president.
2. The Communist Chinese ambassador left Helsinki for Peking for "consultations."
3. The Soviet government refused on "technical grounds" to sign an agreement with Finland covering fishing rights in the Gulf of Finland.
4. Talks that had proceeded smoothly on the Finnish lease of a Soviet canal (in former Finnish territory) for shipping logs to the Gulf of Finland were suspended.
5. A Finnish trade delegation scheduled to travel to Moscow to negotiate the 1959 trade agreement was left waiting without a Soviet invitation.
6. In November 1958, the Soviet government abruptly halted all trade with Finland, including goods that had already been ordered. This action had the most serious

[2] Figures are provided in Berman, "The Legal Framework of Trade," and in Robert Loring Allen, *Soviet Economic Warfare* (Washington, D.C.: Public Affairs Press, 1960), pp. 16, 41.

effect, since many Finnish metal and machinery products sold in the Soviet Union could not be sold in Western markets because their prices were not competitive. In other words, since no alternative markets existed, the Soviet cancellation of trade threw many Finnish workers out of jobs, adding to an already severe winter unemployment problem.

Recognizing that such economic pressures could seriously damage the Finnish economy and worsen an already serious unemployment problem, several members of the cabinet resigned; and a new government more to the liking of the Kremlin was eventually formed. The Soviet economic pressures in this case worked very efficiently.[3]

That power and influence do not flow only from the major powers or those who possess military might is illustrated in the oil embargo imposed by the Arab countries against Western Europe, Japan, and the United States in 1973. During two previous Arab–Israeli wars, the Arabs had attempted to use oil as a means of reducing Western support for Israel. These efforts did not succeed, however, because the Arab governments were divided among themselves on whether or not to apply an embargo and because the United States, a surplus oil producer until the late 1960s, was willing to share oil purchases from Venezuela with the Europeans. By 1973, in contrast, all the industrial countries were highly dependent upon Arab oil, and the Arab governments presented a united front against all governments that had publicly sympathized with Israel's diplomacy or war-making efforts. The Arab governments, once the October War started, cut back production by 5 percent each month and placed a complete embargo against the United States and the Netherlands. The purpose was clear: to place the industrial countries into a severe energy shortage that could be avoided or overcome only if the targets changed their policies toward Israel. It was hoped, too, that the most vulnerable countries, such as Japan and Great Britain, would urge Washington to reduce its commitment to Israel and take a more sympathetic stand toward the Arabs' claims for land lost to Israel in the 1967 war and for the plight of the Palestine refugees. Japan complied first and publicly disclaimed its policy of diplomatic support for Israel. The European governments, through a series of individual symbolic and policy actions, eventually induced the Arabs to lift the embargo against them. The American position on the Middle East also changed, if very quietly. While military support for Israel did not end, Secretary of State Kissinger began to urge the Israelis to make concessions on key territorial issues. As the American commitment to "peace" through concessions by both sides developed, the oil began to flow again—although at vastly increased prices. Arab solidarity, the extensive dependence of the industrial countries on Arab oil supplies, and lack of stock piles were the conditions that enabled the "weak" successfully to confront the "strong."

[3] K.J. Holsti, "Strategy and Techniques of Influence in Soviet-Finnish Relations," *The Western Political Quarterly,* 17 (1964), 63–84.

Cuban–American relations during the period of the Castro regime provide many examples of American efforts to use economic instruments of policy for foreign-policy objectives. President Eisenhower's decision in March 1960 to organize an emigré force to overthrow Castro gave the Cuban leader, who learned of the decision several months later, justification for arranging what had not been possible earlier—namely, switching his army's dependence from Western to Communist sources and undertaking major programs of expropriation of American assets in Cuba. Cuba was also dependent upon Western sources and facilities for oil until the American secretary of the treasury persuaded the American and British companies to refuse Castro's request for refining Soviet oil. Castro thereupon obtained a commitment from the Communist countries to supply all of Cuba's oil, confiscated American and British refineries, and refused to pay the $50 million owed for earlier deliveries. When Premier Castro began to expropriate other American-owned property in Cuba, the State Department and Congress retaliated by ordering reduction of quotas on the import of Cuban sugar. This hardly subtle measure of punishment failed to deter the Cuban government from adopting an increasingly anti-American foreign policy. Since American officials feared that Premier Castro might also seek to spread revolution beyond the confines of the island, they formulated measures to isolate the regime diplomatically and economically from the rest of the Caribbean and Central American regions. This involved an American embargo on sale of weapons to Cuba; the State Department simultaneously implored other Western governments to control shipments of military goods to the Castro regime. Later, when the Cubans had made explicit their association with the Communist bloc, the American government instituted a complete economic and travel boycott of Cuba. Since the United States had traditionally purchased a majority of Cuba's exports, this punishment seriously crippled the Cuban economy until the Cubans found alternate markets for their products (mainly sugar) in the Soviet Union, Eastern Europe, and Communist China. Although these measures helped to isolate Cuba, they did not bring down the Castro regime, so more pressures were applied. First, the United States imposed almost a complete embargo on exports to Cuba, excluding only food and medicines. Next, American diplomatic officials continued to urge other governments to reduce their exports to the island. To help enforce this policy, the State Department prohibited all foreign vessels carrying goods to Cuba from stopping in American ports to pick up new cargoes on their return voyage. This policy was not received with enthusiasm among foreign shipping companies but did reduce further trade between Europe and Cuba. As a final measure, the American government in 1964 imposed controls even on the export of food and medicine to the island.

How effective was the application of these economic punishments? Cuba briefly became economically isolated from its traditional trading partners, and its economy suffered seriously. Spare parts for automobiles, trucks, boats, and industrial plants became unavailable, and most economic indicators (except unemployment) moved steadily downward. Food rationing was also imposed.

Combined with several poor sugar harvests, the punishments created almost disastrous effects on the Cuban economy.

But, as in the case of Yugoslavia, the Cubans were eventually able to find alternative markets for their exports and some sources of supply to keep the economy running. By granting large loans and providing shipping facilities, the Communist-bloc countries prevented the total collapse of Cuba's economy. At times, Castro might have wondered whether he could keep his regime in power, but the punishments did not modify his aggressively anti-American behavior. The economic isolation of Cuba from the West might have succeeded in one respect, however. Since the Cuban government had to allocate so many resources and so much human energy into keeping the economy from collapsing, it may not have had either the time or resources to undertake major programs of external expansion, revolutionary agitation, or subversion in Latin America.

Another problem with the policy of punishment was that it failed to get total support from European countries. As with many international embargoes and boycotts, unless all the participating countries perceive the target as a threat to their own security or economic interests, they are not likely to sympathize completely with policies that deprive their business community of economic opportunities. In the case of the embargo on Cuba, many NATO allies and nonaligned governments thought that the United States was too sensitive to Castro's presence in Cuba. They did not greet the embargo with much enthusiasm; and when, for example, British and French companies made major sales to Cuba, their governments made no attempts to prevent the fulfillment of the trade contracts. Although the American embargo and boycott continued through the 1970s, American pressures on its allies to conform with the U.S. policy lapsed much earlier.

Does the systematic application of economic pressures to achieve political objectives normally succeed? These four cases would indicate that results are often as unfavorable to the state employing the pressures as to the target of the punishments. In the case of Yugoslavia, Soviet pressures forced it to become more reliant upon the West, a turn of events hardly in keeping with Soviet interests; later offers of rewards were undoubtedly instrumental in obtaining Yugoslav support for selected Soviet foreign-policy proposals. The case of Finland and the Soviet Union illustrates the effective utilization of economic and other pressures to bring about changes in the internal politics of the target country. In the cases of the oil embargo and Cuba, the results were mixed: Although Cuba may have had to concentrate on problems of survival as opposed to revolutionary activity abroad, there is little doubt that American pressures literally forced Cuba to become dependent upon the Soviet bloc. And in the short run, the oil embargo forced some Western governments to change policies toward the Middle East conflict. But in the long run, the dramatic Arab action alerted the major oil-consuming countries to their highly dependent condition. Multibillion-dollar programs to develop alternative sources of supply, as well as emergency oil-sharing schemes, have resulted, so that presumably, in future cases of embargo, the importers of oil will be far less vulnerable. What about other cases?

One study of eighteen cases in which total economic sanctions were employed in international relations between 1918 and 1968 indicates that only two worked effectively.[4] The first occurred in 1933, when the British government threatened and imposed various economic pressures against the Soviet Union to obtain the release of six British subjects who had been arrested by the Russians. Faced with these pressures, the Soviet government released the persons in question. In 1962, the Kennedy administration complied with an international system of sanctions established by the Organization of American States against the Trujillo regime in the Dominican Republic. Even after Trujillo had been assassinated, the American government successfully maintained the embargo and boycott as a means of preventing the takeover of the government by any of Trujillo's heirs.

Aside from these two successes, the Finnish case, and possibly the Arab oil embargo, most other cases of economic sanctions, whether bilateral or multilateral, have had at best mixed results. The study shows, for example, that although the targets of sanctions and pressures may have suffered initially, ultimately they were able to restore their presanction volume of trade within two years after the sanctions were put into effect. Internally, the effects of economic pressures were quite the opposite of those intended. Economic pressures against Cuba and Rhodesia (the former was a bilateral, the latter a multilateral, UN-sponsored sanction program) were based on the assumption that economic hardships would bring about disaffection from the regime and ultimately the collapse of the target government, incapable of meeting the elementary economic needs of its citizens. In fact, most of the eighteen cases in the study, as well as the Cuban, oil, and Rhodesian examples, point out exactly the opposite: Sanctions, even if they create hardships, generally mobilize a population in *support* of their government. The enemy is not the home government, but the state or states that apply the sanctions. With this type of support, the target government can more effectively defy the wishes of the government or states that are applying the economic punishments.

Most of the cases in these examples share two characteristics: (1) The sanctions were imposed by great powers against relatively small states (the Arab oil boycott is the significant exception); and (2) the sanctions were of the most dramatic and publicized types, thus resulting in a surge of patriotism among the population of the target state. What of sanctions where these two conditions do not prevail? Again, recent diplomatic history provides some clues, if not definitive answers. In the case of economic pressures by the major powers against each other, the record indicates a string of failures. NATO strategic embargoes, coordinated by a committee of all NATO members throughout the postwar

[4] See Peter Wallensteen, "Characteristics of Economic Sanctions," *Journal of Peace Research*, No. 2 (1968), 248–67; and Johan Galtung, "On the Effects of Economic Sanctions, with Examples from the Case of Rhodesia," *World Politics*, 19 (1967), 378–416.

period, did not prevent the Soviet Union from developing the most modern and sophisticated military capabilities. (It could be argued, of course, that Soviet military achievements would have been reached earlier had the Russians obtained access to Western military technology.) In the late 1960s the Soviet government attempted to "punish" the West Germans for the latter's attempts to play off one Warsaw Treaty Organization member against the other through lucrative trade arrangements. Russian efforts, primarily through the manipulation of promised gas deliveries, proved useless. The Jackson–Vanik amendment to the United States foreign-trade bill of 1974 made extension of most favored nation treatment to the Soviet Union conditional upon significant liberalization of the Soviet authorities' policies on Jewish emigration. The Soviet response to this tactic was to toughen emigration policies substantially, leading to a significant decline in Jewish emigration. This effort to link trade "carrots" with Soviet domestic policies was also a notable failure. Finally, in 1980, the United States imposed a number of economic sanctions against the Soviet Union for the latter's invasion of Afghanistan in December 1979. These measures included a partial grain embargo, halting the delivery of high technology items such as oil drilling equipment, and, most dramatically, boycotting the Moscow Olympic Games. The costs to the Soviet Union were not negligible. The grain embargo was predicted to reduce meat supplies, as the Russians had to divert more of their wheat to immediate necessities such as bread and away from feeding cattle. Oil-drilling equipment was important to a Soviet industry that was facing declining production rates. And the American Olympic boycott, supported by some key countries such as Germany, Japan, Canada, and Kenya, reduced the significance of all the Soviet gold medals. But in terms of bringing about a change in Soviet policy in Afghanistan, the economic pressures must be judged as a total failure. To the Russians, the costs of pulling out of Afghanistan and seeing the collapse of their client government in that country far outweighed the costs of the American embargoes and boycotts.

What of the second condition, that is, various forms of economic pressures which are more subtle and directed against regimes that are highly dependent? Richard S. Olson had made a study of such techniques, as they have been applied by major powers against developing countries.[5] A prime example would be the "silent blockade" imposed by the United States against Chile after the election of the Marxist president, Salvadore Allende, in 1970. Details of this case are outlined in Chapter 10. Here, it is only important to acknowledge that a variety of "quiet" economic pressures had serious economic consequences in Chile, without engendering a nationalist, anti-American response.

Olson outlines a variety of steps that can be taken that are far less dramatic than embargoes and boycotts but which nevertheless can have significant negative consequences for a developing economy. These include (1) declines

---

[5] For details, see Richard Stuart Olson, "Economic Coercion in World Politics: With a Focus on North–South Relations," *World Politics,* 31 (July 1979), 471–94.

in foreign investment; (2) delays in delivery of spare parts; (3) snags in licensing or other technology transfers; (4) shutting off or reducing bilateral and multilateral loans and credits (as the United States did in Chile); and (5) refusal to refinance existing debts. According to Olson, such measures can create serious economic distress and exacerbate social and political tensions already existing within the society, thus vastly increasing the probabilities of civil turmoil and *coup d'état.* Although not a direct cause, "quiet" economic coercion, according to Olson's studies, can lead to economic decline and such decline, where dependency and social conflicts are already notable, can result in change of regime and ultimate compliance with the major power's economic objectives. Cases where such cause-effect relationships seem impressive include Ghana, 1969–1972; Brazil, 1962–1964; Peru, 1965–1968; and Chile, 1970–1973. In all but the Ghanaian case, the United States was the source of the "invisible blockade." And in each of the Latin American cases, the regime which resulted from internal turmoil was more amenable to American economic policies in the region. While these examples are perhaps not a sufficient sample of the total universe of cases of "quiet" economic coercion, they do indicate a relatively high rate of success— certainly greater than in the case of dramatic trade sanctions.

ECONOMIC WARFARE

Economic warfare refers to those economic policies used as an adjunct to military operations during wartime. The objective is either to hold or conquer strategic resources, so that military forces can operate at maximum strength, or to deprive the enemies of these resources, so that their capacity to fight will be weakened. Economic warfare was used extensively by all the major combatants in both world wars, as none of the belligerents except the United States could raise and sustain a modern army and feed a civilian population by relying solely on its own resources. Mutual dependence thus becomes even more crucial during wartime. Using examples primarily from World War II, one can summarize the techniques that have been used as follows:

1. BLOCKADE. In both wars, the Allies established blockades around Germany in an attempt to "starve" it of materials necessary to prosecute the war. Although rules of international law specifically prescribe the nature and extent of legitimate blockades, the Allies frequently disregarded these rules and blockaded even neutral vessels carrying nonmilitary goods to Germany. In World War II, the Allied blockade was applied at first only to Germany; but as the European neutrals—Sweden, Switzerland, Portugal, Turkey, and Spain—were able to sell and ship valuable raw materials and manufactured goods to the Third Reich, the blockade authorities also threatened to impose strict controls over them. Two American economic-warfare officials have described the function and problems of blockades as follows:

It was theoretically possible for us to cut off all imports from overseas [to the neutrals] in order to force a neutral country to cease its trade with Germany, or to use our blockade controls as a club to compel a neutral citizen to follow a pro-Ally line. In practice, however, the situation was seldom so simple, and open pressure of this sort was rare. Some of the reasons for Allied hesitation . . . involved complex considerations of international law, political and diplomatic expediency, and military strategy, as well as economic warfare pure and simple.

The possibility of such sanctions was always there, however, implicit in all our relations with the neutrals. It was our major source of bargaining power, and in the later stages of the war, as our military and diplomatic position became stronger, it was used more and more effectively to curb neutral aid to our enemies. We prevented Spain from importing essential petroleum products until the Franco government curbed exports of tungsten to the Axis and made other concessions. We employed similar pressure less dramatically against Sweden and Switzerland, to force cuts in their economic aid to Germany.[6]

2. BLACKLIST. Since much of the trade between the neutrals and Germany was conducted by private firms, Allied pressures were exerted directly on them. One device that has been used effectively by governments (sometimes in peacetime as well) against private traders is the blacklist. During World War II, these lists, drafted by British and American economic warfare authorities, included the names of Axis nationals or agents located outside enemy territory, as well as neutral or even Allied citizens who were conducting trade with the Axis states. Persons on the list were considered enemies of the United States or Great Britain; their property was subject to seizure; no American or Briton could deal commercially with them in any way; and they could not travel or ship any of their commodities to occupied Europe through any routes or facilities under Allied control. These people could carry on trade with the Axis only if they were prepared to lose all markets in the Allied countries and face the confiscation of their goods during shipment to Europe.

3. PREEMPTIVE BUYING. Most of the Allied program was concentrated on trying to outbid German agents for materials that the neutrals were willing to export to either side. Where the blacklist was not feasible, the Allies paid greatly inflated prices for commodities in order to keep the Germans from purchasing them. With combined American and British financial resources, the Germans were hard-pressed to match the exorbitant prices the Allies were willing to pay. But preemption did not always take the form of legal market operations. Sometimes it involved smuggling, hijacking, flooding mines, tying up transportation, sabotage, or any other means that would deprive the Axis of needed supplies.

4. REWARDS. Economic warfare during World War II used rewards as well as threats and punishments, although it was normally a combination

---

[6] David L. Gordon and Royden Dangerfield, *The Hidden Weapon: The Story of Economic Warfare* (New York: Harper & Row, 1947), p. 13.

of the two. Sweden, for example, was promised access to Allied oil and other products, which its armed forces desperately needed, when it agreed to reduce the export of bearings to Germany. By selling Spain the materials it needed to maintain its economy, the Allies succeeded at least partially in reducing Spanish economic dependence upon Germany.

The success of economic warfare, according to Gordon and Dangerfield, has been difficult to assess. Certainly the German armies did not collapse as a result of shortages created by Allied preemptive buying and the blockade. But the Germans did have to pay high prices for some needed items, and they had to invest other material and human resources in creating substitutes. Had the materials been readily available, the Germans could have freed thousands of people and millions of dollars for other purposes.

FOREIGN AID AS AN ECONOMIC INSTRUMENT OF POLICY

Foreign aid—the transfer of money, goods, or technical advice from a donor to a recipient—is an instrument of policy that has been used in foreign relations for centuries. In the past it was used primarily for short-run political advantages rather than for humanitarian principles or long-range economic development. In the eighteenth century, statesmen regularly offered their foreign counterparts "pensions" or bribes of cash for the performance of certain services. Governments also used military aid in the form of subsidies and donations of men and equipment. Throughout the eighteenth and nineteenth centuries, the British were often unwilling to sustain the costs of maintaining large standing armies; instead, they provided money, matériel, and naval power while their allies raised troops and fought most of the land battles. Most eighteenth-century alliances included provisions for financial subsidies. In the Treaty of Worms of 1743, for instance, Britain pledged Austria a subsidy of £ 300,000 in addition to 12,000 troops.

Economic needs and expectations today are acute and widespread among more than 65 percent of the world's population. Economic development and industrialization are among the main objectives of public policy in all countries, but many nations cannot hope to achieve these goals without the assistance of those societies that can provide development capital and technological skills. Aid programs benefit simultaneously the donors and the recipients: Recipients receive money, loans, materials, and knowledge, from which they hope to fashion a modern economy, political stability, or military security; the donors, regardless of the types of "strings" they attach to their aid, always hope to receive some political or commercial dividend either immediately or in the long run.

The British were the first to formulate aid policies designed primarily to foster long-range economic development. Through the Colonial Development and Welfare programs beginning in the 1930s, they sought to diversify the economies of their colonies and prepare them for both political and economic independence. After World War II, the United States displaced Britain as the main dispenser of foreign aid, first to help reconstruct war-damaged European economies—for which the Americans spent $12 billion in the European Recovery Program—and later to assist the developing countries in creating modern military forces and begin the long road to economic viability and industrialization. After Stalin's death in 1953, the Soviet Union joined the expanding group of states that was donating funds and technological advice to Asia, Africa, and Latin America. Today, almost all industrialized states of the world contribute at least some of their wealth and skills. Most of the programs are bilateral undertakings negotiated directly between donors and recipients; but, in addition, there are multilateral aid organizations and programs, such as the International Bank for Reconstruction and Development and the United Nations Technical Assistance Program, through which industrialized members of the organization make available personnel with special skills to the developing members. Although these multilateral programs have grown rapidly during the last decade, their value still constitutes less than 25 percent of the aid that flows from industrialized countries to the Third World.

The Donors

All industrial countries, most of the socialist states, and all members of OPEC participate in a variety of bilateral and multilateral aid programs. While the total sums have passed the $30 billion mark annually, this figure, given inflation and the needs of the poorest countries, is judged by most experts to be grossly insufficient. Moreover, since net flows of aid have not kept up with need or demand, use of this economic instrument for political purposes is probably becoming less effective. For one thing, aid donors distribute loans, grants, and technical assistance over a broad range of recipients. Only a few countries receive large sums of aid from a single source today. For example, although the United States in the early 1980s distributed almost $4.5 billion annually (the largest donor), only a few recipients, such as South Korea and Turkey, are significantly dependent upon the United States for aid funds. Most other recipients obtain funds from a variety of bilateral and multilateral donors, making the American contribution relatively insignificant to their total economic activity. Moreover, given inflation, the decline in the value of the dollar, and the virtual cessation of growth in American aid disbursements, the United States is rapidly declining as a major factor in aid-related politics. Table 9–1 indicates that while the United States still allocates the largest total sum annually, its preeminent position in aid flows, so pronounced in the 1950s and 1960s, no longer exists. For example, three relatively minor donors—France, Canada, and Sweden—provided more aid, combined, than the United States. France and West Germany combined provided in 1980 almost $2 billion more than the United States. In 1977, three

Arab countries—Saudi Arabia, Kuwait, and the United Arab Emirates, which, combined, have less than 4 percent of the American population—donated more total funds to foreign aid than the United States did. The point is not only that many states are active in the aid process, but that should one of the actors threaten to stop aid programs, there are many other donors who would be available to step in. In brief, in many cases, aid stoppages as a form of coercion can be effective only if there is a *coalition* of donors who coordinate their policies.

Although not directly related to the wielding of political influence, figures on aid by donors also reveal something about the degrees of commitment to aid programs. Table 9–1 indicates that, after Italy, the United States is the lowest donor among the industrial countries, measured on a per capita basis. Recalling that the official United Nations aid target for industrial countries is 0.7 percent of the GNP, the United States approaches only 26 percent of the target. In fact, only a few countries—none of which has important political or security interests in the Third World—have surpassed the United Nations target. They are Norway, Sweden, Denmark, and the Netherlands. Several OPEC countries have also surpassed the target.

The aid programs of the socialist countries are unimpressive. Soviet aid to a few key client states such as Afghanistan, Ethiopia, and the Peoples' Democratic Republic of Yemen is no doubt crucial. Elsewhere, its impact cannot be translated easily into political influence. Even tiny, isolated Albania, which received considerable largesse from China in the 1960s and early 1970s, was able to break off that relationship with minimal negative economic impact.

Our conclusion must be that, despite a few countries which remain highly dependent on a single donor, the patterns of aid flows throughout the world show considerable dispersion and declining vulnerability of recipients. Taken in combination with other techniques of coercion, such as cutting off credits and loans or trade boycotts, aid cessation may be important. But, in most cases, it has become an insufficient means by itself to alter the domestic and foreign policies of most recipients.

Table 9–1 Official Development Assistance, 1980, in Million U.S. $

DONOR	TOTAL AID	PERCENT DONOR GNP
Sweden	1,125	.95
France	3,836	.59
United Kingdom	2,453	.52
Canada	1,151	.46
West Germany	3,581	.44
Japan	3,071	.27
United States	4,567	.18
Italy	320	.09

Source: Data from International Bank for Reconstruction and Development, *World Development Report, 1980* (Washington, D.C.: World Bank, 1980).

There are four main types of aid programs: (1) military aid, (2) technical assistance, (3) grants and commodity import programs, and (4) development loans. The first is also probably the oldest, for military aid is a traditional technique for buttressing alliances. In the last century, both France and Great Britain spent millions of francs and pounds to strengthen their continental allies. The donors supplied money and matériel, while the recipients provided most of the manpower.[7] Since World War II, the United States and the Soviet Union have spent more resources on military aid than on their foreign economic programs—and the objective has been the traditional one of safeguarding their own security by strengthening the military capabilities of allies. By helping recipients build up modern forces, the donors hope to obtain some immediate political or security objective. For example, since the British withdrawal from the Persian Gulf area in the late 1960s and early 1970s, the United States has donated or sold hundreds of millions of dollars worth of military equipment to Saudi Arabia and Iran, in the hopes that these countries could maintain the status quo in the region and prevent any radical Arab governments from gaining control over oil transportation routes. In short, military aid is used to create local power balances or preponderances, thus reducing the likelihood that the donor will have to station troops abroad or intervene militarily to protect its interests.

Most forms of military aid have the advantages of built-in controls. Not only are the recipients dependent upon the donors for creating a modern military force, but they cannot operate the force effectively unless the donor is willing to provide the necessary training support, replacement parts, and maintenance. Thus, the controls provide a partial guarantee that the recipient will use its military forces in a manner compatible with the interests of the donor—unless the recipient can obtain ammunition, spare parts, and training from alternative sources. In 1954, for example, Syngman Rhee's government in South Korea threatened to break the armistice ending the Korean War and invade North Korea to reunify the country by force. The American government strongly opposed the scheme and threatened to cease all military aid to the Republic of Korea if Rhee carried out his plans. Since the South Koreans were almost totally dependent upon the United States for their military equipment, the Korean government had little choice but to abandon the proposal.

Technical assistance, the least costly of all types of aid programs, is designed to disseminate knowledge and skills rather than goods or funds. Personnel with special skills from industrialized countries go abroad to advise on a wide variety of projects. Some famous American programs and organizations

---

[7] Hans Morgenthau, "A Political Theory of Foreign Aid," *The American Political Science Review*, 56 (1962), 303. Monetary and honorific rewards—or bribes—were also used extensively as a means of achieving diplomatic objectives in the eighteenth century. For a humorous lesson on how to use diplomatic bribes and a description of the various European "customs" for proffering and receiving such bribes, see the essay by François de Callières, *On the Manner of Negotiating with Princes*, trans. A.F. Whyte (South Bend, Ind.: University of Notre Dame Press, 1963), pp. 24–26.

such as "Point Four" and the Peace Corps have been associated with such projects as malaria control, agricultural mechanization, public administration, development of fisheries, teaching programs, land reclamation, road construction, and development of medical and sanitary facilities. The impact of these programs can be very great, particularly in rural areas, while the costs are relatively modest except when they are associated with major development projects.

Until the late 1950s, the preferred method of transferring capital and goods was to donate outright grants or gifts for which no economic repayment was expected. This was the form in which most American funds for the European Recovery Program and the Mutual Security Program were dispensed. But outright gifts of this type always create problems for the donor and recipient, and lately the governments of the major powers have replaced grants with long-term loans. Grants of military equipment are still dispensed regularly, and special economic grants are frequently made available when countries face such emergencies as an immediate military threat, famine, or floods. Under Public Law 480, also known as the "Food for Peace" program, the United States annually distributed abroad several million tons of surplus food for which the recipients paid low prices in their own currencies rather than in dollars. The payments were usually kept in special funds that were lent back to the receiving country for economic development projects. These transactions constitute at once grants, subsidies, and loans.

Foreign aid in the form of loans is not, strictly speaking, aid at all. Loans represent a short-term transfer of funds, but since recipients pay back principal and interest, the transfer is only temporary. Only to the extent that bilateral and multilateral loans are made to recipients with very poor credit ratings, or at interest rates lower than those prevailing in international financial markets, can they be considered aid. And yet, the myth persists that loans somehow constitute an important component of aid programs from the wealthy to the needy.

Considerable disillusionment has spread among recipients of loans. Many are approaching the point where they have to pay more in interest on past loans than they take in on new ones. Loans, in other words, eventually represent a net outflow of funds from the developing countries to the donors. In addition, many loans involve economic "strings" that for a variety of reasons recipients would prefer to avoid. Others are reluctant to borrow abroad because bilateral loans are often "tied." That is, recipients are required to use loan funds to buy products from the donor. Often these are at costs above market rates, or the goods are of inferior quality. Tied loans are, in fact, primarily a subsidy by the donor's government to its own business and shipping interests. Despite these negative features of loans, they can be and have been used to wield political influence over recipients. Regimes that challenge economic orthodoxy in their domestic policies—for example, by nationalizing foreign firms—are frequently turned down in loan requests by Western governments or even by multilateral institutions such as the World Bank.

What proportion each dispensing country devotes to these types of programs will reflect its overall foreign-policy objectives. During and immediately after the Korean War, the United States, fearing military invasions from Communist Russia and China, emphasized military aid and defense support for its main allies. In 1953, for example, the United States allocated $4.2 billion for military grants and only $2.6 billion for economic aid. In the later years of the Eisenhower administration and during the 1960s, the American government reduced military aid and increased lending facilities to support long-range development projects for nonaligned as well as allied countries. In 1961, a typical year of post–Korean War aid programs, the United States spent $5.9 billion on foreign assistance, divided almost equally between grants and loans. But over 75 percent of the sum was made available for economic development loans, technical assistance, emergency relief, and surplus food grants, with the remainder devoted to military grants.[8] In the 1970s, American aid appropriations declined in size. They were broken down almost equally between military aid and defense support on the one hand and economic assistance on the other.

Political Objectives of Foreign Aid

Given the dependence of many developing countries on industrialized nations for capital, advice, and occasionally military assistance, how is foreign aid used as an instrument of policy to influence the behavior of recipients? What criteria do governments use in dispensing aid? Are they purely economic and humanitarian, or do military and political considerations dominate the foreign-aid policy processes?

Most aid programs are obviously not undertaken solely for humanitarian purposes, for a vast portion of the aid goes to a few countries—and sometimes not the countries with the most pressing needs. India, Pakistan, and Egypt, for instance, are large recipients because of their strategic and symbolic importance in world politics. On the other hand, not all aid policies and commitments have an immediate or exclusive political or security objective. Many aid programs are formulated by trained economists, on the basis of economic criteria. Others are designed to relieve immediate suffering or forestall some economic catastrophe. Yet, aside from relieving emergencies, economic development is seldom considered by the donors as an end in itself. Even in the long run, it is designed to help secure certain of the donors' political objectives, which it cannot achieve solely through diplomacy, propaganda, or military policies.

Table 9–2 provides some indirect evidence about the political and security considerations underlying most bilateral aid programs. If most aid funds were committed on the basis of need, then those countries with lowest per capita incomes would receive a substantial amount from donors. The figures

---

[8] Agency for International Development, *U.S. Foreign Assistance and Assistance from International Organizations: Obligations and Loan Authorizations, July 1, 1945–June 30, 1961* (revised) (Washington, D.C.: Agency for International Development, n.d.), p. 1.

Table 9–2 Percent Donor Aid to Low Income Countries, 1978

DONOR	PERCENT AID TO LOW INCOME COUNTRIES
Sweden	39
Canada	37
United Kingdom	29
Japan	26
West Germany	23
United States	22
France	17
Italy	11

Source: Data from International Bank for Reconstruction and Development, *World Development Report, 1980* (Washington, D.C.: World Bank, 1980).

suggest otherwise. Trailing Italy and France, the United States in 1978 distributed only 22 percent of its aid funds to countries designated by the United Nations as "low income." Major recipients of American aid, such as Egypt, South Korea, Brazil, Nigeria, and Turkey, are, in fact, "middle income" countries. In contrast, 39 percent of Sweden's aid in 1978 was directed to low-income countries. It must be recognized, nevertheless, that some low income countries have the capacity to absorb only limited foreign funds, and we must acknowledge as well that important segments of population in the middle income countries suffer equally from want and privation. Yet, these and other figures do suggest that criteria other than need loom important in allocation decisions.

The assumption behind most Western economic development programs is that successful economic development in developing countries will create political stability and reduce the threat of violent revolution and unrest, which can be exploited by Communists. Some also assume, although there is little evidence to support the view, that economic development will help bring liberal democratic regimes into power and prevent the recipients from pursuing adventurous foreign policies. A healthy economy, they argue, brings about a pacific foreign policy.[9]

Another prominent theme governments use to justify their aid programs is that economic development helps buttress the independence of the recipients, enabling them to resist dependence on any one state or group of states. The

[9] As Hans Morgenthau has argued, "The popular mind . . . and much of the practice of foreign aid has proceeded from certain unexamined assumptions, no less doubtful for being deeply embedded in the American folklore of politics. Thus the popular mind has established correlations between the infusion of capital and technology into a primitive society and its domestic development, between economic development and social stability, between social stability and democratic institutions, between democratic institutions and a peaceful foreign policy. However attractive and reassuring these correlations may sound to American ears, they are borne out neither by the experiences we have had with our policies of foreign aid nor by general historic experience." "A Political Theory," pp. 304–5.

stronger they are economically and militarily, the less vulnerable they become to external diplomatic and economic pressures and to subversion. From the American point of view in particular, the presence of a group of genuinely independent states is perceived to have a direct relation to U.S. security interests. It reduces the number of military commitments—including interventions—that the United States must make, and also precludes the necessity for stationing even more troops and bases abroad. From the French and British perspectives, foreign-aid programs are also regarded as a continuing commitment to improvement of former colonial holdings, as a means of expanding commercial opportunities, and as a method of maintaining some diplomatic influence in regions formerly under their exclusive control.

The Soviet Union, even though it often claims the opposite in its propaganda, dispenses aid to help support its political objectives and, like some Western countries, occasionally threatens to cut off aid as a punishment. Not only can the aid be used for short-run political advantages as a reward or punishment and means for increasing Soviet prestige among developing countries, but the Soviet government also conceives of aid as a method by which it can speed up the process of industrialization, create an urban proletariat, and pave the way for eventual liquidation of capitalism and transformation of new countries into socialism.[10]

No matter what the original objective of an aid program, whether economic development or human betterment, *it can be used* for rewarding, threatening, or punishing—that is, for wielding influence over the behavior of recipients in such a manner as to help the donor achieve certain short-run political objectives. When donors manipulate aid programs for immediate political advantages, economic and humanitarian criteria, although still relevant, give way to political desiderata.

It may be difficult, finally, to speculate on all the consequences of an aid program. An economic undertaking, for example, may have considerable effects on the character of local or national politics. American aid to Thailand has had as its main objective the integration of the poverty-stricken and isolated northeastern regions with the rest of the country. Aid programs have helped finance hundreds of miles of all-weather roads in the area. These programs have had an economic impact by making it possible for the peasants, for the first time, to market cash crops in other regions of Thailand. On the other hand, the roads also permit the government in Bangkok to extend both services and control into the region and to police the areas against guerrilla activities.[11]

---

[10] See, for example, Friedrich Ebert Institute, *The Soviet Bloc and the Developing Countries* (Hanover, W. Germany: Verlag für Literatur und Zeitgeschehen, 1962). Both the American and Soviet governments view each other's aid programs as motivated by short-run political considerations—particularly to "enslave" the new nations—whereas they commonly refer to their own humanitarian motivations in undertaking aid programs. For the similarity of their views, see J. David Singer, "Soviet and American Foreign Policy Attitudes: Content Analysis of Elite Articulations," *Journal of Conflict Resolution*, 8 (1964), 446, 450, 461.

[11] Joan M. Nelson, *Aid, Influence, and Foreign Policy* (New York: Macmillan, 1968), p. 22.

Major donor countries have supplied millions of dollars of aid designed to stabilize foreign governments and, through them, their own security interests. Military aid, for example, can have three functions: to help create a modern military force to deter *external* aggression, to establish special military forces trained to put down internal riots and disorders against established authorities, and to raise the prestige of local regimes and military elites. A portion of Soviet, British, French, and American military aid to respective alliance partners and to some developing countries can be understood best in terms of the latter two functions. When the United States sends jet fighters and other modern weapons to a small Latin American country, it is playing on the desire for prestige among the military leaders who, in most cases, wield great influence in Latin American politics. The armaments have little external military utility, but they increase the military's prestige and the recipient government's ability to cope with civil disorders. Similarly, the United States has sent many advisors to Latin America to train local troops in counterinsurgency techniques.

Some economic aid policies are designed primarily to elevate the internal and foreign prestige of a regime, without simultaneously making any significant contribution to the long-range economic development of the country as a whole. Gaudy projects spread around the country illustrate to the indigenous people that their government is pursuing modernization and is capable of possessing the symbols of an industrialized, powerful nation. In Hans Morgenthau's words:

> Prestige aid has in common with modern bribes the fact that its true purpose, too, is concealed by the ostensible purpose of economic development or military aid. The unprofitable or idle steel mill, the highway without traffic and leading nowhere, the airline operating with foreign personnel and at a loss but under the flag of the recipient country—all ostensibly serve the purposes of economic development and under different circumstances might do so. Actually, however, they perform no positive economic function. They owe their existence to the penchant, prevalent in many underdeveloped nations, for what might be called conspicuous industrialization, spectacular symbols of, and monuments to, industrial advancement rather than investments satisfying any objective economic needs of the country. . . . They perform a function similar to that which the cathedral performed for the medieval city and the feudal castle or the monarch's palace for the absolute state.[12]

Finally, some regimes are so weak and the nations they attempt to govern so fractionalized—or even nonexistent—that they must be propped up by the contributions of foreign governments. This subsistence aid, both economic and military, is designed to provide the basic minimal services that keep a political order intact. The Soviet-installed Afghan "revolutionary" government of Babrak Karmal was so weak militarily and administratively that it required the assistance of almost 100,000 Soviet troops and several thousand Soviet administrators to

---

[12] Morgenthau, "A Political Theory," pp. 303, 304.

cope with a poorly equipped and uncoordinated peasant and tribal rebellion in 1980. The military and administrative "assistance" of the Soviet Union will be necessary for years to maintain the client regime in power. Even India, which does not possess many spare resources, distributes economic and military aid to Nepal for the purpose of creating a viable buffer state between itself and China. Although this aid might make only a small contribution to economic development in Nepal, its main effect is to create political and religious strength for the Nepalese government, thereby reducing the possibility of Chinese-inspired disorders.

Aid Designed to Change the Recipient's Domestic or Foreign Policies

Donors can also manipulate economic and military aid programs to change the internal politics of recipients. A regime can be rewarded through increased aid allotments if it promises to institute political reforms, or it can be threatened with a reduction in aid if the reforms are not carried out. In 1963, the American government decided that the war against the Viet Cong could not be prosecuted satisfactorily as long as the Diem regime in Saigon continued to behave as an arbitrary dictatorship. American diplomatic representatives frequently asked Diem and his advisers to observe basic civil liberties in the country and permit other political groups a voice in policy making. When Diem consistently refused to accept the American advice, the United States quietly began to apply pressures by reducing its foreign-assistance program. First, it halted the financing of commercial exports to South Vietnam and later refused to continue payments to Vietnamese Special Forces engaged in persecuting anti-Diem groups rather than fighting against the Viet Cong. It finally "postponed" renewal of the annual agreement on grants of surplus food. By the end of the year, American aid to the Southeast Asian country had been reduced by 75 percent. These steps, which were coordinated with a diplomatic and propaganda campaign against the Diem regime, undoubtedly had an important bearing on the subsequent *coup d'état* by the Vietnamese army that threw out the Diem regime.

Major donors of aid seldom use it in such a crude and open fashion to interfere in the internal politics of the recipients, but virtually all governments have found it necessary on occasion to act this way. Joan Nelson lists some other ways in which aid can be used to affect the internal political processes—in the short run—of recipients:

1. Aid, usually in the form of financial subsidies of commodity import programs, can be used to buy time. Sometimes a new government takes office only to find that it is faced with extreme inflation, a depleted treasury, or an untenable balance-of-payments situation. A financial subsidy from a donor can relieve the government of a crisis situation and give it time to formulate programs to control the economy.

2. A donor can also supply funds to help a government cope with specific economic or political problems, such as unemployment.

3. Occasionally, a grant of aid can be given at a strategic time so as to affect the outcome of an election. In 1964, for example, the United States provided a program for Chile, which was facing a serious problem of inflation. The grant was made several weeks before an election in which the Marxist candidate Allende (subsequently elected president in 1970) had a good chance of defeating the left-of-center candidate supported by the United States.

4. Aid can be suspended following a *coup d'état.* The United States had done this almost routinely in Latin America as a means of promoting constitutional changes of government and discouraging military takeovers.[13]

Examples of aid manipulation designed to change a recipient's foreign policies are equally plentiful. In 1963, the United States decided to cut off almost all economic and military aid to Indonesia after the Indonesian government mobilized resources to achieve its goal of "crushing" Malaysia. Similarly, the Soviet Union quietly withdrew thousands of technicians and millions of rubles worth of aid after the Chinese began to criticize Soviet leadership in the world Communist movement. The Russians claimed that their aid personnel were requested to leave by the Chinese; but it is likely that the Soviet government took the initiative to reduce its economic aid program as an attempted means of inducing the Chinese to change their domestic and foreign policies, as well as their position on certain ideological issues. In 1960, the Soviet Union also seriously curtailed its military aid to China, thus depriving the Chinese of needed modern weapons and spare parts and, in particular, slowing down the Chinese program to build nuclear weapons.

Aid as a Reward for Becoming an Alliance Partner

Promise of large quantities of military and economic aid are also used to obtain or support allies. In return for committing its resources and manpower to the development of a large, modern military capability, targeted toward the main potential enemy of the donor, the alliance partner will receive aid with which to fashion a program for economic development. Since World War II, the largest share of American, British, and Soviet aid has been devoted to obtaining and supporting allies.

Aid to Help the Recipient Achieve Its External Objectives

Donors may grant economic or military aid enabling the recipients to fulfill more easily their foreign-policy goals. This would include military aid to help deter a threat from an external enemy, enhance the recipient's international prestige, or build up its military capabilities to prosecute expansionist policies. Of the last type, a good example was Soviet military aid to Indonesia, which was used by the Indonesians to acquire West Irian under threats of force and to prosecute its policy of confrontation against Malaysia. Although the Soviet

[13] Nelson, *Aid, Influence, and Foreign Policy,* p. 94.

Union made few outright grants of military equipment to Indonesia, it provided extensive credits with which the Indonesian armed forces could secure new equipment. Similar assistance for Syria in recent years has allowed the Syrians to adopt a very tough position regarding the terms of a Middle East peace settlement. No longer can Egypt unilaterally define the conditions under which an agreement with Israel might be possible.

The Problem of "Strings" in Foreign Aid

As the examples cited suggest, almost all aid used primarily to sustain or change internal and foreign policies of recipients has strings attached. Any regime that receives large quantities of economic and military goods to help it remain in power will obviously feel that it must coordinate at least some of its policies to fulfill the expectations—implicit or explicit—of the donor. Even long-range development aid contains a wide variety of economic "strings" or technical standards that the recipient must meet if it wishes to qualify for assistance. Despite what they claim in their propaganda, donors—including multilateral agencies—always insist that their goods and funds be used in a manner consistent with their own purposes. As a minimum, donors maintain rigorous economic and technical requirements. Policy makers thus seldom pose the question of whether their aid should or should not have "strings" attached to it: They are concerned only with defining the *types* of mutual expectations, commitments, and obligations that any aid agreement will impose on both parties.

Since the elites of developing nations place such emphasis on industrialization and modernization, they need the resources and assistance of major industrial countries. In turn, the donors of aid can use these needs for their own purposes and can, in many cases, use aid as an effective instrument for supplementing their diplomacy, propaganda, and military programs. But the recipients are not without influence in their relationships with the donors. Occasionally they are able to obtain external assistance without making explicit commitments to any particular actions or policies. Ruling regimes can also argue that if they do not receive more aid, domestic tranquility will be jeopardized and local Communists will take over. In what has become a frequent bargaining tactic, the potential recipient can always threaten to go to another major power to receive aid if one donor is unwilling to grant it on favorable terms. Any donor, if asked to terminate aid policies, will suffer a blow to its prestige in the recipient country, while the regime, if it succeeds in obtaining goods and services from an alternative source, can demonstrate to both domestic political groups and other nations that the country is independent enough to obtain aid and concessions from a variety of sources. As in any economic transactions where an alternative supply is available, the donor–recipient relationship can be exploited by the recipient for its own purposes. There are, therefore, definite limitations on the use of foreign aid as an instrument of foreign policy to achieve short-run political and military advantages.

Moreover, foreign aid has not accomplished many of the political purposes for which it was originally designed. In the early years of the cold war, many assumed that aid could "buy" allies, or at least keep them from joining the opposite camp. Undoubtedly, military assistance has played a role in local deterrence (it has also allowed some client states to engage in aggressive foreign policies), but there are few examples of a country's changing its major foreign-policy orientations just because of offers of aid or threats to reduce aid.[14] Commercial opportunities and diplomatic influence over the domestic policies of recipients have also been created through aid. But the small sums of money involved and the frequent availability of alternative sources of supply have probably reduced the extent to which aid programs can be manipulated for diplomatic purposes. There is little evidence, besides, that economic assistance has promoted political stability, democratic institutions and practices, or a more "reasonable" foreign policy. Quite the contrary. Many recipients of arms from the major powers have used them to engage in conflicts with neighbors, or to destroy domestic political opposition. And there is some evidence that American military assistance has promoted military coups and the institutionalization of military rule, rather than democratic politics.[15]

Disillusionment with aid programs among recipients arises from the fact that loans have to be repaid and funds have to be used to purchase goods from the donor. Economists and government officials increasingly realize, moreover, that there is no strong relationship between the amount of aid received and the rate of economic growth. Indeed, some studies show that aid correlates negatively with growth: Those countries that have received the most aid also have had subsequently unimpressive growth rates.[16] By creating dependence, by slowing down local initiative, or by the misallocation of scarce resources in ill-conceived aid plans, development may very well be distorted or slowed down. Certainly the Western and Soviet fixation with industrialization rather than agricultural development has led many recipients seriously to distort their economies in favor of heavy industry and to neglect, relatively speaking, the agricultural sector. Massive urban congestion and inadequate food production are among the unfavorable consequences.

Donors, too, show lagging enthusiasm for aid programs. Most of the governments of the major powers have reduced bilateral aid programs or kept them static. Some countries, like Sweden and Canada, have dramatically increased aid allocations, but these have not been adequate to compensate for lower commitments by the major powers. In an era of inflation, high taxes, and the seeming ingratitude of recipients, foreign aid is not a politically popular issue for most donors.

---

[14] One example would be Uganda, which, after having failed to obtain increased support from Israel, turned to Libya. Libya's economic and military assistance to Uganda helps explain the latter's conversion to a strong anti-Israel policy.

[15] Edward T. Rowe, "Aid and Coups d'Etat: Aspects of the Impact of American Military Assistance Programs in the Less Developed Countries." *International Studies Quarterly,* 18 (1974), 239–55.

[16] See, for examples and citation, Tibor Mende, *From Aid to Recolonization: Lessons of a Failure* (New York: Pantheon, 1973), Chap. 7.

If aid as an instrument of diplomatic influence has only a mixed record, it matches that of other economic techniques. Yet, because trade and resource issues are increasingly coming to the fore in the international system, replacing many of the security and military problems of the cold war, we could expect economic means of conducting diplomacy to become increasingly prominent. Talk of trade wars, economic retaliations, cartels of producers, and boycotts fills newspaper headlines. Past experience suggests that little is to be gained from using these instruments, but many governments cannot resist the temptation to coerce by economic means those who are in a dependent position. Compared to other techniques, particularly subversion and warfare (discussed in the following chapters), they might seem particularly inexpensive. That is not to say, they are more effective.

SELECTED BIBLIOGRAPHY

BAILEY, MARTIN, *Oilgate: The Sanctions Scandal.* London: Coronet/Hodder & Stoughton, 1979.

BALDWIN, DAVID A., "Foreign Aid, Intervention and Influence," *World Politics,* 21 (1968), 425–47.

BARBER, JAMES, "Economic Sanctions as a Policy Instrument," *International Affairs* (London), 55 (July 1979), 367–84.

BEIM, DAVID, "The Communist Bloc and the Foreign Aid Game," *The Western Political Quarterly,* 17 (1964), 84–99.

BLACK, LLOYD D., *The Strategy of Foreign Aid.* New York: Van Nostrand Reinhold, 1968.

CLARKSON, STEPHEN. *The Soviet Theory of Development: India and the Third World in Marxist-Leninist Scholarship.* Toronto: University of Toronto Press, 1978.

DOXEY, MARGARET P., *Economic Sanctions and International Enforcement.* New York: Oxford University Press, 1971.

FRANK, LEWIS A., *The Arms Trade in International Relations.* New York: Praeger, 1969.

GALTUNG, JOHAN, "On the Effects of Economic Sanctions, with Examples from the Case of Rhodesia," *World Politics,* 19 (1967), 378–416.

GOLDMAN, MARSHALL L., "The Balance Sheet of Soviet Foreign Aid," *Foreign Affairs,* 43 (1965), 349–61.

GRABER, DORIS A., "Are Foreign Aid Objectives Attainable?" *The Western Political Quarterly,* 19 (1966), 68–84.

HAMMOND, PAUL Y., DAVID J. LOUSCHER, and MICHAEL D. SALOMON, "Controlling U.S. Arms Transfers: The Emerging System," *Orbis,* 23 (Summer 1979), 317–52.

HIRSCHMAN, ALBERT O., *National Power and the Structure of Foreign Trade.* Berkeley, Calif.: University of California Press, 1945. Chap. 2.

HOADLEY, J. STEPHEN, "Small States as Aid Donors," *International Organization,* 34 (Winter 1980), 121–38.

HUNTINGTON, SAMUEL P., "Foreign Aid for What and for Whom?" *Foreign Policy,* 1 (Winter 1970–1971), 161–89.

JASTER, ROBERT S., "Foreign Aid and Economic Development: The Shifting Soviet View," *International Affairs,* 45 (1969), 452–64.

JOSHUA, WYNFRED, and STEPHEN P. GILBERT, *Arms for the Third World: Soviet Military Aid Diplomacy.* Baltimore, Md.: Johns Hopkins University Press, 1969.

KEYFITZ, NATHAN, "Foreign Aid Can Be Rational," *International Journal,* 17 (1962), 247–50.

LYON, PEYTON V., and BRIAN W. TOMLIN, chap. 8 in *Canada as an International Actor.* Toronto: Macmillan of Canada Ltd., 1979.

MENDE, TIBOR, *From Aid to Re-Colonization: Lessons of a Failure.* New York: Pantheon, 1973.

MONTGOMERY, JOHN N., *Foreign Aid in International Politics.* Englewood Cliffs, N.J.: Prentice-Hall, 1967.

MORGENTHAU, HANS, "A Political Theory of Foreign Aid," *The American Political Science Review,* 56 (1962), 301–9.

NELSON, JOAN M., *Aid, Influence and Foreign Policy.* New York: Macmillan, 1968.

OLSON, RICHARD STUART, "Economic Coercion in World Politics: With a Focus on North–South Relations," *World Politics,* 31 (July 1979), 471–94.

PACKENHAM, ROBERT A., *Liberal America and the Third World: Political Development Ideas in Foreign Aid and Social Science.* Princeton, N.J.: Princeton University Press, 1973.

SMITH, HEDRICK, "The Russians Mean Business . . . About Business," *The Atlantic,* 234 (December 1974), 41–48.

TRIANTIS, S.G., "Canada's Interest in Foreign Aid," *World Politics,* 24 (October 1971), 1–18.

WALLENSTEEN, PETER, "Characteristics of Economic Sanctions," *Journal of Peace Research,* No. 2 (1968), 248–67.

WALTERS, ROBERT S., *American and Soviet Aid: A Comparative Analysis.* Pittsburgh, Pa.: Pittsburgh University Press, 1970.

WOLF, THOMAS A., *U.S. East–West Trade Policy: Economic Warfare versus Economic Welfare.* Lexington, Mass.: Heath, 1973.

WRIGGINS, HOWARD, "Political Outcomes of Foreign Assistance: Influence, Involvement or Intervention," *Journal of International Affairs,* 22 (1968), 217–30.

10

Clandestine Actions and Military Intervention

It was a theme of Chapter 3 that social and technological changes in the political units that make up any international system may have important consequences for the processes that occur within that system. Development of sovereign national states and simultaneous decline of other forms of political organization—such as city-states—brought forth new techniques, institutions, and norms of statecraft in the seventeenth and eighteenth centuries. Just as gunpowder helped destroy the foundations of the feudal order, and the growth of dynastic absolutism reduced the international political influence of the Catholic church, mass media of communication, rapid transportation, a complex and interdependent international economy, weapons technology, and mass politics have helped to diminish the "impermeability" of the nation-state. The possibility of obtaining informal or nonofficial access to foreign societies has grown as the size of government missions abroad—once confined to a few diplomats and consular agents—has increased. Short of building walls or iron curtains, most states have relatively few effective means of preventing outside infiltration or the movement of funds, propaganda, or military matériel from abroad. States with lengthy frontiers passing through forests, jungles, deserts, or mountains are often incapable of preventing outside penetration.

As means of achieving objectives, defending interests, or promoting social values abroad, governments may—instead of sending diplomatic notes or making military threats—infiltrate foreign voluntary organizations, sponsor strikes and riots, create political scandals, attempt a *coup d'état*, or, on their own territory, organize, train, and arm a group of foreign dissidents and then send them home to conduct guerrilla warfare or subversion. States that are relatively weak in conventional military capabilities are able to mount campaigns of external subversion and infiltration at little cost, either in funds and matériel or in the risks of military retaliation by the target country. In our era, the capacity to penetrate politically and quasi-militarily into foreign societies may be as important as a capability to make military threats, impose naval blockades, or carry out conventional military assaults. In particular, weak states (militarily speaking) with revolutionary or expansionist objectives may attain objectives by conducting clandestine actions abroad. Certainly a state is no longer powerful *only* if it possesses a vast conventional or nuclear military establishment.[1]

Clandestine activities are not, of course, entirely a product of the modern age. They were organized as well in China during the Chou dynasty, in Greece, and particularly in fifteenth-century Italy. In the dynastic international system of the eighteenth century, intervention for ideological principles seldom occurred, and monarchs were not generally concerned with the domestic policies of their brethren.[2] Louis XIV occasionally conspired to interfere in British constitutional issues, but the main concern over other states' internal political life was with questions of inheritance and royal affairs. Dynasts concluded military alliances, as in the Triple Alliance of 1717, to place certain candidates on foreign thrones, and indulged in all sorts of court intrigues for the same purposes. But there were no attempts to subvert foreign societies in the name of ideological principles, and governments had not yet developed the techniques of mass persuasion or guerrilla warfare commonly observed today in international politics. States were, on the whole, "impermeable" to outside influences.

Intervention became more common in the nineteenth century, particularly as a method of promoting or putting down revolutions inspired by liberal and nationalist movements. The wars of the French Revolution were revolutionary wars, often different in objectives and techniques from the wars in the preceding century. Conservative regimes, following their victories over Napoleon, assigned themselves the obligation to intervene militarily against societies that were experiencing domestic liberal revolutions. Later in the same century, the United States frequently sent contingents of marines to Latin American and Caribbean states to influence the course of local politics and revolutions. In general, however, the principle of nonintervention in other states' internal affairs was observed with considerable regularity.

The record of the twentieth century is a remarkable contrast. In some 200 revolutions that occurred during the first half of the century, some form of foreign intervention took place in almost half; in approximately fifty of these

---

[1] Andrew M. Scott, "Internal Violence as an Instrument of Cold Warfare," in *International Aspects of Civil Strife,* ed. James N. Rosenau (Princeton, N.J.: Princeton University Press, 1964), pp. 154–69.

[2] See Edward V. Gulick, *Europe's Classical Balance of Power* (Ithaca, N.Y.: Cornell University Press, 1955), pp. 62–65.

revolutions, *more than one* outside power intervened. Soviet Russia, Nazi Germany, and Fascist Italy interfered in their neighbors' domestic political life with unprecedented regularity. Since the end of World War II, the record has not improved. Most international crises of the period have started basically as *internal revolutions* or civil disturbances, in which one or more external states eventually became involved. This list would include Greece, China, Algeria, Laos, Lebanon, Jordan, Iraq, Kuwait, Yemen, the Congo, Angola, Vietnam, the Dominican Republic, Czechoslovakia, Cambodia, and Ethiopia. Istvan Kende, in one study of revolution, war, and intervention, records sixty-seven "internal regime" wars between 1945 and 1970.[3] Outside intervention by one or more powers occurred in fifty-two (77 percent) of these civil disruptions. The United States and the Soviet Union, with fourteen interventions each, were the most active foreign powers. But by no means does it follow that only the great powers practice subversive techniques or the use of controlled military means to influence the domestic politics of another country.

True, the clandestine and interventionary actions of the large states are usually the most dramatic because they are the most highly organized or the stakes are bigger, but smaller nations have not failed to use these techniques to achieve objectives or promote political values. Libya and Saudi Arabia have frequently employed propaganda against foreign audiences in efforts to undermine support for certain Middle Eastern regimes; they have financed and organized assassination plots, bribed government officials in neighboring territories, and, as in the Yemen civil war in the 1960s, intervened with their own military troops. Many of the new states in Africa have been no less active. Opposition parties—often driven underground—establish headquarters in neighboring states and even accept foreign nationals in leadership positions. They are given not only sanctuary in foreign territories but, frequently, funds, training, and arms as well. Tunisia and Algeria have provided platforms and headquarters for Morrocan opposition elements, and Morocco has been active in organizing guerrilla activities in Mauritania and neighboring Spanish Sahara. Until President Nkrumah was ousted in a *coup d'état* in 1966, Ghana had both party and government organizations charged with ideological and military training of opposition groups from Nigeria, Togoland, and the Ivory Coast. Ghana was seriously implicated in subversive attempts in both the Ivory Coast and Niger in the early 1960s. Until Premier Ben Bella's demise in 1965, the Algerian government served as perhaps the most well-organized and widespread center in Africa for financing, organizing, and training foreign nationals in the techniques of clandestine political action, subversion, and guerrilla warfare. More recently, the government of Libya has been charged with financing terrorist activities, such as the kidnapping of some OPEC oil ministers from a meeting in Vienna in 1976 and organizing an attempted *coup* against the Sudanese government, also in 1976. And

[3] Istvan Kende, "Twenty-Five Years of Local Wars," *Journal of Peace Research*, 8 (1971), 5–22.

Cuba sent a force of an estimated 10,000 troops in support of the M.P.L.A. faction in the Angolan civil war.

Domestic plots and intrigues in which foreign African and Middle East governments or parties have been involved thus have been and continue to be numerous. What has been distinctive about these efforts is their general ineffectiveness, which can be explained in part by lack of public support among target groups for externally directed operations, political apathy, poor communications, and lack of experience and capabilities on the part of the sponsoring states.[4]

MODERN CONDITIONS THAT ENCOURAGE INTERVENTION

Extensive use of clandestine actions and direct military intervention as techniques of achieving objectives and promoting political values can be accounted for by at least five conditions widespread throughout the contemporary world. First, all the major powers—and some lesser states as well—have added to their traditional diplomatic bargaining techniques vast programs of military and economic assistance. Most of these programs, whether undertaken by a single state or by multilateral organizations such as the United Nations, affect the internal political, economic, and social development of the recipients. Often, economic development cannot be achieved unless important political reforms are also implemented. This may require diplomatic pressures (by threats to withhold economic rewards), which obviously constitute interference in the internal affairs of the recipient. Sometimes foreign efforts to liberalize a regime may result in such political instability that the goal of economic development has to be forfeited. Where such problems confront the donor governments (and they appear in almost all military and economic aid programs), foreign diplomats seek to mold the internal development of a society in ways with no precedent in the eighteenth and nineteenth centuries. In some instances, governments use their large numbers of foreign-aid personnel abroad to conduct propaganda, gather intelligence, and promote revolutionary or counterrevolutionary activities.

Second, there are many inconsistencies between national frontiers, on the one hand, and ethnic, religious, or linguistic frontiers, on the other. Many states today have only conditional viability; that is, they can exist only with the minimal support of all groups within their boundaries. If there are deep social cleavages, and some groups within the society feel oppressed, the likeli-

[4] For details, see I. William Zartman, *International Relations in the New Africa* (Englewood Cliffs, N.J.: Prentice-Hall, 1966), pp. 94–101. Zartman has claimed more recently, however, that because so many of the attempts at subversion in Africa during the 1960s failed, African governments can be expected to rely less in the future on this means of achieving objectives. See his "Intervention among Developing States," *Journal of International Affairs,* 22 (1968), 188–97.

hood of civil disturbances is increased. If these minority groups formulate a strategy that requires highly organized or violent political action, they are apt to need support from the outside. Local Communist parties have obtained funds, propaganda, training, and sometimes weapons from the Soviet Union or Communist China; ethnic minorities, such as the Naga tribes in India, have established contacts with China in order to obtain arms; liberation movements in Rhodesia relied extensively on African governments for sanctuaries, funds, and matériel; and cliques of military leaders have sought foreign support and diplomatic recognition before or during their attempts to seize power. However much these connections may seem to promote purely local interests, there is little doubt that some sort of debt is created between the dissidents and the external patron. The patron can intervene on behalf of the group, faction, or clique, and after it gains power, use its influence with the group to secure its own foreign-policy interests. Any unstable political order—and there are many in the contemporary world—offers opportunities for external intervention. We can suggest the hypothesis that the greater the ethnic, religious, economic, or ideological conflicts within a society, the greater the probability that an external government will intervene to serve its own interests.

The exact processes by which one government becomes involved in the internal affairs of another to the point where it may undertake a major program of intervention have not been studied sufficiently.[5] Recent history would indicate, however, that it is usually a lengthy process in which some particular group in a society establishes contacts with the government of a foreign state. These contacts eventually become translated into commitments. The foreign government may, at first, provide only vague forms of "support"; that is, it announces its support of the group and perhaps disseminates propaganda on its behalf. Ultimately, however, a genuine system of interdependence develops, and vague statements of support become firm commitments involving the training of political leaders and the sending of arms and perhaps manpower. If the political group—whether a revolutionary movement or a regime already in power—is seriously threatened by another force, the outside state may intervene massively with its own troops. The important observation is that at some point, one government perceives that it is in its interest to sustain or change the *internal* structure of another state. All the instruments of statecraft are directed subsequently not so much at influencing the foreign policies of another state, but at determining its internal character. It is at this point that we must recognize the intertwining of domestic and foreign politics.

Third, political loyalties, which have traditionally extended to the predominant political institutions and authorities, whether clan, tribe, nation, or empire, are sometimes directed instead to external political entities or ideologies. In the seventeenth century, religious loyalties frequently superseded national

[5] See C.R. Mitchell, "Civil Strife and the Involvement of External Parties," *International Studies Quarterly*, 14 (1970), 166–94.

or regional sentiments. Similarly, in the late eighteenth century, many European liberals welcomed French "liberation" even if it meant occupation by foreign troops and imposition of alien political institutions. Most people today accept the general proposition of primary loyalty to their own nation ("My country right or wrong"), but there are many exceptions among people who do not accept the legitimacy of the order under which they live. The quip that the postwar French Communist party was neither Right nor Left, but East, illustrates the existence of transnational ideologies and loyalties directed essentially toward foreign states. This characteristic of modern politics naturally creates opportunities for foreign states, symbolizing these transnational ideologies, to become involved in other nations' domestic politics.

Fourth, the current nuclear stalemate has apparently forced the major antagonists of the cold war into the sector of irregular warfare and subversion, where the possibility of uncontrolled military escalation is slight. Blatant military aggression to achieve external objectives may face both universal diplomatic condemnation in the United Nations and instant nuclear retaliation, whereas establishment of client regimes and satellite states through subversion and intervention may be sufficient to achieve some objectives at a minimal cost of national capabilities and resources, with much lower risks.

Fifth, governments with revolutionary external objectives are naturally prone to use for foreign purposes the same kinds of techniques their leaders successfully employed in gaining domestic power. While on one level the French revolutionaries, Soviets, Nazis, and others maintained "correct" diplomatic relations with foreign states, they simultaneously attempted to promote revolutionary activities against the social and political orders of those same states. Using "race" as the basis of political loyalty, Hitler proclaimed that a German's first duty was to the Third Reich, whether he lived in Austria, Czechoslovakia, or the United States. Communist governments have also spoken of "normalization of relations," "peaceful coexistence," and noninterference in other people's affairs; but their ideological pronouncements and domestic-policy statements clearly reveal that when it is in their interest to do so, they will promote, organize, or support foreign revolutions and rebellious uprisings.

This is not to say that Soviet or Chinese support for local rebellions has been indiscriminate. The pronouncements of Communist leaders, of course, support all "wars of national liberation." But in terms of actions, levels of involvement and commitment have varied extensively. In general, the record shows that when it is in the interest of China or the Soviet Union to maintain good relations with another state, it will not become actively involved in a rebellion that may occur in that state. The Russians have generally refrained from open support of Latin American revolutionary movements, and China strongly supported the central government of Pakistan against the secessionist movement in East Pakistan during 1971. Although the Chinese have often promoted and assisted revolutionary movements abroad, their actions are to a certain extent constrained by the Maoist view that revolution should be primarily an indigenous matter. The "bastion of the revolution" role often enunciated in Chinese speeches or editorials is thus inhibited by both ideological principles and considerations of diplomatic expediency.[6]

Many governments with revolutionary external objectives or doctrinal commitments have created a variety of extradiplomatic agencies whose main functions are to dispense propaganda, organize agitation, train foreign revolutionaries, and direct subversion. Among the more prominent of these external revolutionary organizations have been the Comintern, the Cominform, the German Abwehr, and various Soviet and Communist Chinese organizations and institutes that today have the function of providing revolutionary and ideological training for foreign Communist leaders. Although not concerned with doctrines of revolution, the Central Intelligence Agency of the United States has been heavily involved in subversive activities abroad. These organizations sometimes play a major role in defining the objectives and techniques of states' foreign policies and on occasion literally usurp the functions of more traditional diplomatic institutions. During the early 1920s, when the Soviet government was actively engaged in organizing and supporting revolutionary activities throughout Europe, a number of the most important foreign-policy decisions were made within the organization of the Comintern. Soviet diplomats were frequently bypassed as intermediaries between the Soviet government and foreign groups and had to remain content to deal with relatively unimportant aspects of Soviet foreign policy. In any event, the new revolutionary dimensions of foreign relations opened by the Bolsheviks required people with experience and outlook considerably different from those of professional diplomats. The directors of the Comintern and other external revolutionary organizations were primarily revolutionaries and agitators, concerned with the mechanics of organizing violence and political support for doctrinal ends, not men engaged with such mundane matters as trade relations, diplomatic conferences, passports, and territorial treaties.[7]

Throughout the twentieth century, nations have had to face the problem of political change ostensibly inspired by domestic forces but largely engineered by an external power. In addition to reasonably overt actions, where revolutionaries are trained, organized, and armed abroad, intervention may include propaganda, espionage, discriminatory trade policies, or support or denial of support to governments or their opposition in domestic crises where such foreign support might prove to be decisive. Experts do not wholly agree whether one government may give military and political support to another attempting to maintain itself against a possible or actual rebellion or whether some kinds of economic and military assistance constitute intervention.[8] Was the Western democracies' decision not to intervene in the Spanish Civil War really nonintervention? It could

[6] See Peter Van Ness, *Revolution and China's Foreign Policy: Peking's Support for Wars of National Liberation* (Berkeley: University of California Press, 1970).
[7] See Theodore H. Von Laue, "Soviet Diplomacy: G.V. Chicherin, Peoples' Commissar for Foreign Affairs, 1918–1930," in *The Diplomats, 1919–1939*, eds. Gordon A. Craig and Felix Gilbert (Princeton, N.J.: Princeton University Press, 1953), pp. 234–81.
[8] Louis Henkin, "Force, Intervention and Neutrality in Contemporary International Law," *Proceedings of the American Society of International Law* (April 1963), pp. 147–60.

be argued that by deciding *not* to intervene, the democracies paved the way for General Franco's victory.[9] How do we characterize an American program to help train foreign police in riot-control techniques? Since riots and demonstrations are in some countries the most promising or only way to achieve political change, this type of training could be construed in some cases as aid designed to keep unpopular regimes in power. Many other controversial cases could be cited, since they occur almost every day in modern international politics: No aid or trade program, military action, or important diplomatic communication can avoid having some impact on the public internal realm of other sovereign states.

If we classify as intervention all actions that have some impact immediately or in the long run on another state's internal politics, then, today, virtually all forms of persuasion and diplomatic-economic-military programs would qualify. James Rosenau has proposed a more precise definition. In his view, intervention can be distinguished from other forms of state action in that it (1) constitutes a sharp break from conventional forms of interaction in a relationship, and (2) is consciously directed at changing or preserving the structure of political authority in the target state.[10] Thus, foreign-aid programs, even though they might have direct consequences on the authority structure in a society, would not be considered intervention because they would not constitute a radical break from a conventional relationship. In contrast, although the Soviet Union has maintained various forms of control over the internal policies of Czechoslovakia since 1948, the sending of several divisions of troops in a lightning raid on Czechoslovakia in August 1968 would constitute a radical departure from the more conventional means of control. We might add a third characteristic of forms of intervention: Most, but not all, of the unconventional actions are taken *without the consent of the legitimate* (that is, commonly recognized) *government.*

We will discuss five forms of intervention: (1) various types of clandestine political actions, (2) demonstrations of force, (3) subversion, (4) guerrilla warfare (where it is primarily organized and supported from abroad), and (5) military intervention. Governments normally use combinations of these techniques simultaneously, but we shall keep them distinct in examining several cases.

CLANDESTINE POLITICAL ACTION

Probably the oldest technique of interference in other countries' internal affairs is the offering of bribes. In the eighteenth century, granting monetary rewards to foreign diplomats and government officials was a typical means of achieving diplomatic objectives. It was the accepted custom (although not publicized) to pay another dynast's foreign minister or diplomats a "pension"—that is, a bribe—

[9] Manfred Halpern, *The Morality and Politics of Intervention* (New York: Council on Religion and International Affairs, 1962), p. 8.

[10] James N. Rosenau, "The Concept of Intervention," *Journal of International Affairs,* 22 (1968), 165–76.

for performance of certain services or maintenance of certain attitudes on key issues of the day. Documents from the French court of Louis XV reveal that between 1757 and 1769, France subsidized Austrian statesmen by over 82 million livres.[11] American covert political action abroad has included bribery, or at least the subsidy of subversive agents; British and French agents in the nineteenth century frequently gained control of future colonies by bribing native political leaders; and, of course, Nazi and Communist financing of clandestine political action in foreign countries is well documented.

Dissemination of covert propaganda—through unidentified radio transmitters, underground newspapers, or leaflets of unclear origin—can also be classified as clandestine political action that attempts to influence internal political processes in the interests of a foreign government. American propaganda in the crucial Italian provincial elections of 1975, for example, was not always clearly identified, and various other American actions on behalf of the Christian Democratic Party were of a clandestine nature.

Alexandr Kaznacheev, a Soviet diplomat who defected in Rangoon, revealed some of the methods his government used to influence domestic political affairs in Burma. In addition to giving directions and helping finance the underground Burmese Communist Party, the Soviet embassy in Rangoon would "plant" stories in the Burmese press and sometimes blackmail politicians. One of Kaznacheev's jobs in the Soviet embassy was to translate into English copies of articles he received from Soviet intelligence agencies in Moscow. Some of these articles would describe supposed American complicity in various campaigns of subversion in Asian countries (some were reasonably accurate, others pure fabrication); others contained generally anti-American materials. Soviet intelligence officials in Burma would then arrange through local agents to have the articles published in Burmese newspapers, especially pro-Communist publications. The newspaper would translate the article into the native language and sign it as coming from one of its "special correspondents" abroad. Thus a story conceived in Moscow became publicly identified as the testimony of on-the-spot reporters.[12]

Clandestine political action may also include assassination of government officials, diplomats, party leaders, or economic elites. Even though assassination is not a prevalent form of interfering in a country's affairs, foreign governments occasionally finance or encourage local dissident elements who are willing to do the job.[13]

---

[11] Hans Morgenthau, "A Political Theory of Foreign Aid," *The American Political Science Review,* 56 (1962), 302.

[12] Alexandr Kaznacheev, *Inside a Soviet Embassy* (Philadelphia: Lippincott, 1962), p. 172.

[13] It seems to be an unwritten rule of modern international politics—particularly in countries with a Western tradition—that assassination of leaders of hostile states is not an acceptable manner of settling conflicts or achieving objectives. Even Hitler attempted only one assassination (the Austrian chancellor, Dollfuss, in 1934) of a government leader; it is surprising, moreover, that during World War II, Allied leaders never became enthusiastic supporters of the German underground's plots on Hitler's life. Apparently American officials did seriously consider assassinating Fidel Castro, however.

DEMONSTRATIONS OF FORCE

One of the traditionally effective techniques of intervention—with low risks and costs—is to display or threaten to use force either to help or hinder a domestic rebellion in a foreign country. One example of forceful demonstration suggests that this technique may be sufficient in some cases to influence the course of domestic politics in a country.

In 1961, a demonstration of force prevented supporters of the deposed Trujillo dictatorship from overturning the newly established provisional regime in the Dominican Republic. Throughout November, rumors had circulated in Santo Domingo that Trujillo's three sons (one of whom was commander in chief of the Dominican Forces) were ready to launch an assault on the provisional government, whereupon the United States sent twenty-two warships to patrol off the Dominican shore. The provisional government had not asked for this show of force, but it later acknowledged that the American action had prompted the Trujillos to flee the Dominican Republic and had averted a *coup d'état* and possible civil war.

Although the costs and risks of demonstrations of force may be slight, we should not conclude from the case above that they are always an effective means of promoting some change in the internal structure or governing personnel of a state. The events in Czechoslovakia in 1968 would indicate that a government of even a small state may refuse to be intimidated by demonstrations of force on its frontiers. The Dubček government was well aware of Soviet, Polish, and East German antipathy to its reform programs. During the spring of 1968, Warsaw Pact joint maneuvers had taken place in Czechoslovakia, and there were persistent reports that the Soviet contingents were making their withdrawal, after completion of the maneuvers, unduly slow. During the summer, as relations between Prague and Moscow worsened, Soviet troops were mobilized near the Czech frontier and were sent on "maneuvers" for an extended period of time. The meaning of these military steps was of course clear to all the parties concerned: the Soviet Union might intervene militarily if the Dubček government did not abandon some reforms held most distasteful by the Soviet and other European governments. The demonstrations of force did not persuade the Czech authorities to alter their policies, with the result that the Soviet government and four of its East European allies intervened militarily and forced the Czechs to remove Dubček and his associates.

SUBVERSION

The term *subversion* has characterized almost any rebellious activity in a country, but the distinguishing feature of subversion is that it is organized, supported, or directed by a foreign power, using for its own purposes the disaffected elements in a society. Open displays of propaganda by a foreign power would not constitute subversion unless the displays were related to a systematic campaign to help an indigenous rebel group seize power. One of the recent problems of Western policy makers relates to this distinction: is a revolt against an established regime truly serving the interests of the local population or rebels, or is it promoted abroad basically to serve the interests of a foreign power? Where to draw the line is extremely difficult, because almost every revolution today involves some external power. The major Western powers have generally viewed *any* connection between a rebel movement and a Communist state as evidence of Communist subversion. The modern techniques of subversion can be illustrated by describing briefly how Nazi Germany, the Soviet Union, and the United States have enlisted and aided dissident elements in foreign countries to overthrow constituted regimes or pave the way for an outright military assault on the target state.

Nazi Subversion of Czechoslovakia, 1938–1939

The main target of Nazi subversion of Czechoslovakia were the 3.5 million German-speaking Czechs living in the Sudetenland. Shortly after Hitler became the German chancellor, some Sudeten Germans organized a political party (SDP, Sudeten German party) under the leadership of Konrad Henlein. In his early political career, Henlein professed no desire to turn his party into an agency for carrying out Hitler's plans to take over Czechoslovakia. In a 1935 speech, he specifically declared that the German minority in Czechoslovakia would seek to protect its rights and interests only by cooperating with the Czech government and people.[14] Less than seven years later, Henlein boasted publicly of the role that he and his party had played in subverting Czechoslovakia for Nazi Germany. He pointed out that his party, with the support of many Sudetenland Germans, had so completely destroyed internal stability and created so much confusion throughout Czechoslovakia that the entire country became "ripe for liquidation," according to Hitler's plans. He attributed his success to having turned 3.5 million Sudetenlanders into 3.5 million National Socialists.[15]

Henlein's first step in preparing for eventual Nazi "liquidation" of the Czech nation was to mobilize the Sudeten Germans, many of whom were neither Nazis nor pro-German, to his cause. He accomplished the objective by deliberately provoking incidents with Czech authorities, whose reprisals led the Sudeten Germans to believe that they were being persecuted as a minority. The SDP held mass public meetings, circulated manifestos demanding "rights" for the German minority, and issued false or exaggerated propaganda stories about Czech political outrages against the Sudeten Germans. Once a split within the society was achieved through propaganda, it was exacerbated by giving the militant side a feeling of insecurity—in this case by claiming that the Sudeten Ger-

[14] Vincent Urban, *Hitler's Spearhead* (London: Trinity Press, n.d.), p. 16.
[15] *Ibid.*, p. 17.

mans had to remain vigilant lest they be completely destroyed as a distinct nationality by the Czechs. Social perceptions of threat rose to such a high level that political compromise became unacceptable and was, of course, discouraged by the subversive party. Moreover, the Henleinists systematically penetrated Sudeten German social and cultural groups and purged their leadership of anti-Nazi or Czech sympathizers. By 1938, an important part of the German population in Czechoslovakia had become not only anti-Czech, but pro-Nazi as well.

Because some Sudetenlanders, particularly in rural areas, were reluctant to give their support to the SDP, the party also indulged in kidnapping and terrorism. The campaign—which was executed by a corps similar to the German SS, called the Freiwilliger Schutzdienst (FS)—was directed against both uncooperative Germans and innocent Czechs. The terror against the Czechs naturally caused reprisals, which permitted the Henleinists to charge the Czechs with further "atrocities" against the Sudeten Germans. While Henlein's party was active in its work of propaganda, infiltration, and terror, its leaders simultaneously wore a mask of political respectability by entering into formal negotiations with the Czech government to seek "honorable" guarantees for the rights of the Sudetenlanders.

By 1938, it was apparent to the Czech government—if not to foreign diplomats—that Henlein and the Nazis did not wish any real accommodation, but sought only to create a situation that would warrant German diplomatic and military intervention and ultimate cession of the Sudetenland to Germany. On August 6, 1938, Henlein released a fateful order to his followers, inviting them to organize a series of violent acts that would give Nazi Germany an excuse for intervening. His own attempt to seize power one month later failed, and he was forced to flee to the Third Reich. Now without leadership in the SDP, German intervention had to proceed openly. As clashes between Czechs and Sudeten Germans increased in violence and frequency, causing repressive action by the Czech army, Hitler began a series of propaganda broadcasts throughout Europe, which sought through vitriolic language and gross exaggeration to create the impression that the Sudeten Germans were indeed the subject of systematic persecution. Using a combination of military-invasion threats against Czechoslovakia and reasoned appeals for "peace" against the Western governments, Hitler, through the Munich settlement, eventually annexed the Sudetenland to Germany; Czechoslovakia was left a rump state without viable military defenses.

Although the SDP and its paramilitary FS organized and conducted most of the infiltration, propaganda, and terror, the Nazi government of Germany made the policy decisions on the strategy of subversion. Henlein maintained contact with Himmler's SS through a German liaison officer in Czechoslovakia, and his lieutenants frequently traveled to Germany to attend festivals, fairs, and competitions, where they were exhorted and instructed by Nazi officials in the techniques of subversion.[16] Henlein himself agreed, in March 1938, to coordinate and clear all policy with the German Foreign Office and submit all public statements (commands to his followers) to the Germans for approval. The Nazi government also supplied money and weapons to the FS for conducting its campaign of terror and intimidation, and members of the Gestapo occasionally crossed the frontier into Czechoslovakia to kidnap Czech citizens. Throughout the period, the German government also released an avalanche of propaganda directed at three distinct targets: (1) the Sudeten Germans, to rally them behind the SDP and against the Czechs; (2) the Czechs, to undermine their morale; and (3) other European countries, to create the impression that Germany was intervening only to safeguard the rights of a minority. Finally, the German government took advantage of the violence in Czechoslovakia to threaten military intervention. Czechoslovakia did not collapse, then, solely through Henlein's activities. Subversion was used to create conditions that gave the Germans a pretext for threatening and finally carrying out annexation and military invasion.

Communist Subversion of Czechoslovakia

After Czechoslovakia was carved up by the Nazis, most Czech party and government leaders fled either to London or Moscow. As a result of the Nazi–Soviet pact of August 1939, Communist party leaders remaining in Czechoslovakia at first cooperated with German occupation authorities, but after the German invasion of the Soviet Union in June 1941, they went underground and helped lead the anti-Nazi resistance movement. Although the underground Communists displayed bravery and effective activity against the Nazis, their record was not altogether enviable, for they attempted as well to discredit liberal resistance groups—sometimes even by leaking information on their membership to the Gestapo. A number of Communist leaders also went to Moscow to receive training and later returned to Czechoslovakia with orders to dispose of future non-Communist leaders.[17]

Nevertheless, formal diplomatic relations among the exile government of Eduard Beneš in London, the Czech Communist leaders who resided in Moscow during the war, and the Soviet government remained cordial. In December 1943, Stalin signed a Treaty of Friendship, Mutual Aid, and Positive Cooperation with the Beneš government. Klement Gottwald, one of the Czech Communist leaders in Moscow, also agreed with the exile government in London that, pending establishment of a constitutional and freely elected government in Prague after the end of the war, all parties would work together to create "National Committees" to administer Czech territory as it was liberated from the Germans.

The National Committees were established in accordance with the agree-

---

[16] U.S. Department of State, Chief Counsel for the Prosecution of Axis Criminality, *Nazi Conspiracy and Aggression*, 1 (Washington, D.C.: Government Printing Office, 1946), 544, 546.

[17] Josef Korbel, *The Communist Subversion of Czechoslovakia, 1938–1948* (Princeton, N.J.: Princeton University Press, 1959), p. 59.

ment. But since it was the Soviet Red Army that liberated Czechoslovakia, the committees contained mostly trained Communists, who came in to administer the territory after Russian troops had cleared it of Germans. These agents also flooded the zone of military operations with propaganda and agitation and marked non-Communist local leaders (some had collaborated with the Germans) for eventual liquidation. By early 1945, thanks to the Red Army, the Communists had created local strongholds from which they could begin operating as a legitimate political party and simultaneously infiltrate and gain control of social groups. Moreover, the party enjoyed unprecedented popularity, for it was identified among many Czechs with the Soviet Union, which had liberated Czechoslovakia from the Nazis—while the Allies had abandoned the Czechs in 1938—and with a record of bravery as an underground partisan movement during the Nazi occupation.

Thus, when exiled Czech leaders met in Moscow to decide the composition of the provisional government, the Communists possessed a basis of both organization and national prestige for their claims to important cabinet positions. The several portfolios they received were the most important for infiltrating and gaining control over the state's instruments of communication and coercion. The Communists took over the ministries of Interior (which controlled the court system and police), Agriculture, Schools, and Propaganda. A Communist sympathizer was named Minister of Defense.[18]

Communist subversion of Czechoslovakia culminated in the seizure of power in February 1948. To prepare for the *coup d'état,* party leaders and cadres operated on two levels. Using their organizational base in the National Committees, local administration, and important government ministries, they systematically infiltrated and gained control of major economic and social voluntary associations. They simultaneously worked as a traditional political party in parliament, initiating and lending their weight to popular reform measures and conducting party propaganda that emphasized democracy, Czech nationalism, and social reform rather then revolution or dictatorship of the proletariat.

On the more clandestine level, the Communists first gained control over the media of mass communication, through which they could make their promises and sell a program to the people. Even before the war had ended, the Red Army donated captured German printing presses to Czech Communists, and as early as 1945, the Ministry of Information (with the probable assistance of Soviet propaganda experts) started publishing dailies, weeklies, and monthlies disguised as organs of trade unions and other voluntary associations. By 1947, only members of the Czech Journalists' Union (Communist-controlled) were permitted employment as editors of newspapers. Non-Communist editors were either suspended or forced to retire by the Communist-controlled typesetters' union. Communist and pro-Communist ministers were given access to the na-

---

[18] Vratislav Busek and Nicolas Spulber, eds., *Czechoslovakia* (New York: Praeger, 1957), p. 432.

tional radio network as often as they desired, whereas other party leaders were limited to perfunctory appearances. The media of mass communication and the bogus journals were constantly used to extol the Soviet Union and the Czech Communist party and to embarrass non-Communist leaders.[19] Propaganda was also used to heighten social tension and to alter and control the behavior of non-Communists by changing their images of facts and values. In the Czech Communist propaganda, the Soviet Union became the symbol of anti-Fascism and liberation, the Communist party assumed the mantle of progressive democracy and social justice, while all other parties and business classes were pictured as Nazi collaborationists.

A number of techniques were used to gain control of administrative organs. For example, Communist ministers already in the government employed vast numbers of comrades, then recommended economy programs in which they released thousands of non-Communist civil servants. The army, too, was effectively neutralized. "Unreliable" officers were purged and their places filled by Communists or their sympathizers. The General Staff as well as the Directorate of Defense Intelligence passed into Communist hands, and political officers—patterned after the political commissars of the Red Army—systematically indoctrinated Czech troops. The Minister of Interior organized a National Security Corps, an armed body of party adherents, and Provincial Security Departments (ZOB), both of which were staffed with reliable personnel.[20] It was one of the functions of these intelligence networks to identify all potential and actual anti-Communist leaders and subject them to various forms of intimidation. Finally, the party infiltrated the most important agricultural, labor, women's and intellectual groups or copied the prewar pattern of Nazi subversion in Austria and formed various "front" organizations, whose close connections to the Communist party were not revealed. By capturing leadership in the country's most important voluntary associations and by creating "front" organizations, the Communists added an even broader base from which to disseminate propaganda and agitate among the people. Their control or major role in these organizations also helped create additional prestige for the party and afforded them a large amount of favorable publicity.

As a parliamentary organization, the party was no less effective. In the 1946 elections, it won the largest proportion of votes (38 percent), and in alliance with other parties was able to introduce and pass social reform legislation that further increased its popularity throughout the country. Small landholders and tenant farmers, for example, delivered thousands of votes to the Communists after receiving land under agricultural reform legislation. The Communist party, even though it had no parliamentary majority, was able to dominate the legislative branch of the government for almost three years. It enjoyed this position by creating a three-layered parliamentary alliance, which it directed much as a hold-

[19] Rudolf Sturm, "Propaganda," in *Czechoslovakia*, eds. Busek and Spulber, pp. 107–13.
[20] Andrew C. Janos, *The Seizure of Power: A Study of Force and Popular Consent*, Research Monograph No. 16 (Princeton, N.J.: Center for International Studies, 1964), pp. 33–34.

ing company controls several nominally independent corporations. First, it entered into an alliance with the Social Democratic party—the "Marxist Bloc"—in which it made most policy decisions by virtue of its numerical superiority. This alliance was then amalgamated into a "Socialist bloc" of all Marxist and non-Marxist socialist parties. Finally, the Socialist bloc represented a majority in the "National Front," which governed the country without serious opposition.[21]

By the end of 1947, Communist popularity began to wane, as an increasing number of non-Communists were removed from important political and social positions and party leaders resorted increasingly to blackmail, terror, brutality, and intimidation against the opposition.[22] The party feared that in the elections scheduled for March 1948, it would suffer a serious electoral defeat. Even so, the ground had been prepared carefully for the final seizure of power. The state's instruments of coercion were either neutralized or pro-Communist; most media of communication were firmly under the direction of the party; and some of society's most important voluntary organizations could be relied upon to support a *coup d'état*. The crisis came in the winter of 1948. Communist cabinet ministers precipitated a serious government stalemate that forced several non-Communist ministers to resign. Klement Gottwald, the leader of the Communist party in the government, called upon workers to demonstrate, and the Ministry of Interior exhorted other public-spirited groups to send protests to President Beneš. The National Security Corps was ready to lead an insurrection, and in some districts, workers were armed. In others, groups of workers took over factories and transportation facilities. Party and government agents conducted mass arrests of anti-Communists, while special "Action Committees" gained control of the main government administrative offices. Beneš was forced to accept a Communist-dominated cabinet under Gottwald's leadership. It only remained for the Communist-dominated cabinet and ministries to consolidate their power throughout the land. Most political parties were banned, many non-Communist political leaders jailed, and the most important symbols and institutions associated with the democratic regime destroyed. Czechoslovakia's foreign minister, Jan Masaryk, long a popular figure identified with his father's struggle for Czech independence from Austria, committed suicide—although many claim he was murdered by the Communists. With this tragedy, liberal democracy came formally to an end in Czechoslovakia.

We have defined subversion as a series of essentially clandestine actions undertaken by one state, enlisting some citizens abroad through propaganda, infiltration, and terror to overthrow the established regime in their own country. Wasn't the seizure of power in Czechoslovakia really a domestic Communist revolution? It will be years before the role of the Soviet party and government in the Czech subversion is fully revealed, but some facts are already established with reasonable confidence. First, although the operational details of subversion

---

[21] Vlatislav Chalupa, *The Rise and Development of a Totalitarian State* (Leyden, Netherlands: H.E. Stenfert Kroese, 1959), p. 85.

[22] Korbel, *The Communist Subversion of Czechoslovakia*, pp. 185–87.

were locally planned and executed, the main strategy—which had started as early as 1941—was formulated throughout the period in Moscow. Second, during the war, hundreds of Czech Communists were trained in the Soviet Union to prepare the ground for the seizure of power. Third, in 1944, the Red Army played a major role in establishing the National Committees, liquidating Czech anti-Communists, and donating money, arms, and printing presses exclusively to Communist agents—all in violation of the 1943 treaty, in which the Soviet government had sworn not to interfere in the internal affairs of Czechoslovakia. Fourth, every time the Beneš government attempted to resist Communist demands after the war, the Red Army would begin "maneuvers" on the Czech frontiers to intimidate non-Communist political leaders. Much as in the events of 1938, the Czech government faced an organized rebellion at home as well as the threat of external intervention. Finally, it is probably no coincidence that the Soviet deputy foreign minister arrived and remained in Prague during the week of the seizure of power.[23] His exact role in the *coup d'état* has not been revealed through published documentary evidence, but most Western and former Czech authorities claim that he was not in Prague merely to offer a gift of Russian wheat to the Czechs, as the Communists claim. Soviet presence in Czechoslovakia and in the background was an important factor in the collapse of Czechoslovakia's postwar democratic government.

American Subversion in Chile, 1970–1973

American use of force abroad to protect commercial interests, maintain "law and order," and prevent inroads by "international communism" has occurred frequently since the declaration of the Monroe Doctrine in 1823. One study lists more than 100 American military interventions in Latin America between 1806 and 1933.[24] Despite the signature of important articles in both the Rio Treaty (1947) and the Bogotá Charter (1948) prohibiting direct or "indirect" interference in Latin American countries' internal affairs, in practice American governments have never admitted that such principles could invalidate the right and responsibility of the United States to intervene, in case of external armed attack, Communist penetration, or even *anticipated* Communist activity, in Latin America's domestic politics. No Latin American government or revolutionary group is immune from American subversion or intervention if that government or group allows local Communists to play a prominent role in its activities; and any amount of Soviet, Chinese, or Cuban supply of arms, advisors, or technical assistance is usually defined as evidence of Communist subversion, and hence justification for countersubversion or intervention.[25] In short, American govern-

---

[23] See Ivo Duchacek, "The February Coup in Czechoslovakia," *World Politics,* 2 (1950), 511–33.

[24] Cited in C. Neale Ronning, ed., *Intervention in Latin America* (New York: Knopf, 1970), p. 25.

[25] For quotations and the ideological underpinnings of American responses to Latin American social reform, see Melvin Gurtov, *The United States against the Third World: Antinationalism and Intervention* (New York: Praeger, 1974), pp. 82–84.

ments have historically reserved for themselves the right to decide what forms of domestic political change in Latin America are legitimate or illegitimate, tolerable or intolerable. The parallels are striking between American policies and the Brezhnev Doctrine, which allocates to the Soviet government the right to intervene with armed force into Eastern Europe any time a government is threatened by counterrevolution or "imperialism."

Instances of direct American military intervention have declined since 1933, with the launching of Roosevelt's "Good Neighbor" policy. The Bay of Pigs invasion in 1961 (organized and financed by the United States) and the American invasion of the Dominican Republic in 1965 are the only recent cases of direct use of military force. Subversive techniques, however, have been used frequently. In the late 1950s, the United States employed a combination of economic and political pressures to help drive General Trujillo out of the Dominican Republic; and in the early 1950s, the United States, by financing and arming a group of Guatemalan emigrés in Honduras, organized the downfall of the Arbenz regime in Guatemala, which had earned Washington's enmity by expropriating idle lands of the United Fruit Company, importing weapons from East Germany, instituting social reforms, and allowing full civil liberties to reign in the country.

Unlike the case of Guatemala, where Americans subversion was an unqualified success, the case of Chile is difficult to assess, in part because the known facts can lead to different inferences. For example, it is likely, but impossible to prove, that there would have been a military *coup d'état* against the Socialist government of Salvadore Allende even if the United States had maintained a policy of strict nonintervention. Allende's policies were undoubtedly leading to irreconcilable differences in Chile. Numerous radicals, including many who had come to Chile from other countries in Latin America, were pressing Allende to institute a "real" revolution by force of arms. Middle-class groups, facing mounting suppression of civil liberties, were similarly clamoring for fundamental changes in Allende's unsuccessful economic policies. Since Chile was beset with serious economic dislocation and a 350 percent yearly inflation rate (partly caused by American economic steps), the military *coup d'état* was predictable months before it occurred.

The U.S. government's attempts to influence Chilean political life go back as far as 1964, when through covert means it helped finance the electoral victory of Eduardo Frei Montalva, a Christian Democrat with a reformist program, over the Socialist candidate, Salvador Allende. But Frei's victory had been narrow, and Allende's popularity was fully established during the campaign. Since, according to the Chilean constitution, Frei could not run again for the presidency in 1970, Allende was considered by most observers to be the strongest candidate in the elections of that year. The Central Intelligence Agency therefore posted a team in Santiago long before the elections, with instructions to keep the balloting "fair." The CIA operatives interpreted this to mean that they should try to prevent Allende's election. They ultimately spent approximately

$3 million to buy votes and a further $350,000 to bribe Chilean congressmen, who, under the constitution, had to ratify the results of the election. These efforts, of course, failed to prevent Allende's accession to the presidency.

The American government, fearing that Chile would serve as a base for South American revolutionaries (many activists and agents from China, the Soviet Union, Cuba, and Communist parties throughout Latin America flooded into Chile after the election), then set about to create conditions in Chile that would make it difficult for Allende to administer the country effectively. One American corporation with Chilean investments, ITT, put great pressure on Washington to act directly to bring down the Allende government. Indeed, ITT went so far as to approach the CIA with a plan of its own, which would involve a *coup d'état* by the Chilean military forces. After the Chilean government nationalized American-owned copper mines and refused to pay what the companies demanded in compensation, the pressure by private firms on Washington increased, and the response became increasingly positive.

The means used to help create economic and social turmoil in Chile included economic embargoes and classic subversion. Between November 1970 and early 1972, the Export-Import Bank (under the Department of the Treasury, headed by John Connally), the Inter-American Development Bank, and the World Bank cut back credits and new loans to Chile. Private American banks quickly followed the lead of these lending institutions. Although European banks did renegotiate Chilean debts, the United States refused to enter into bilateral discussions with Allende's officials to take similar steps. The Allende government was hardly a good credit risk, but the evidence suggests that shutting off the flow of funds necessary to finance Chile's imports was basically a political decision designed to create further instability in Chile. The credit embargo did not have effects as severe as those of the total American embargo against Cuba, but it did create a shortage of spare parts in important sectors of Chile's economy (most of Chile's trucks, cars, and industrial machinery originally came from the United States). We can infer the political objectives underlying the credit embargo by the fact that it was lifted as soon as the military junta had disposed of Allende.

Direct activities by CIA agents in Chile complemented the muted and "low profile" economic pressures. Personally ordered by President Nixon, a secret attempt by CIA agents to organize a Chilean military *coup d'état* to prevent the installation of Allende as president failed.[26] The CIA then turned its attention not so much toward removing Allende as supporting opposition groups. It channeled funds to the opposition press in an effort to keep it alive—Allende had steered government advertising to only those newspapers that supported him. Additional funds went to opposition politicians, private firms, and trade unions. The CIA also infiltrated Chilean agents into the upper echelons of Allende's

[26] For details, see Thomas Powers, "Inside the Department of Dirty Tricks," *The Atlantic* (August 1979), 45–57.

party; and provocateurs were asked to make deliberate mistakes in their government jobs, thus adding to the economic management problems already facing Allende. Finally, CIA agents organized street demonstrations and funded a truckers' strike that had disastrous consequences on the economy. There is no evidence that the CIA organized or directly supported the ensuing military *coup d'état,* but it was clearly trying to create conditions that would drastically increase the probability of a military intervention into Chilean politics.[27]

GUERRILLA (UNCONVENTIONAL) WARFARE

As the focus of the cold war shifted from Europe to Asia, Africa, and Latin America, guerrilla warfare supplanted some of the conventional techniques of subversion discussed above. This type of revolutionary activity, which combines terror with mobile guerrilla attacks, was used extensively in Yugoslavia and other occupied countries during World War II and has since occurred in more than fifteen countries. Of course, not all guerrilla operations have been organized, supported, or directed by an outside power. Some of the longest and most tragic unconventional military operations have been purely domestic affairs, as in Colombia, where internal strife with characteristics of guerrilla warfare has killed several hundred thousand people over the last thirty years. Successful guerrilla campaigns in Cyprus, China, and Cuba were basically internal rebellions, conducted with a minimum of external interference. In Southeast Asia, however, Noth Vietnam and Communist China played major roles in organizing, training, and supporting "national liberation" movements operating in Malaya, South Vietnam, Laos, Cambodia, Thailand, and Malaysia. This area offers particularly attractive conditions for guerrilla operations, including dense jungles and marshes in which troops can hide, a predominantly rural population often cut off from direct influence from the central government, undeveloped communication facilities between villages and urban centers, and long, unprotected frontiers that permit easy infiltration and supply of matériel from the "active sanctuary" (the country promoting the unconventional warfare). The romantic and ideological inspiration for guerrilla operations originated with Mao Tse-tung and the Chinese Communists and was refined by Che Guevara. Unlike their Western comrades, who were concerned primarily with subversion and infiltration in an urban setting, the Chinese and Cubans engaged in protracted rural guerrilla warfare before achieving power. Because of the different environmental and historical traditions, subversion as practiced in Europe and unconventional warfare as practiced in Asia and Cuba have been basically different means of gaining power.

----

[27] The facts of the Chilean episode come from Elizabeth Farnsworth, "Chile: What Was the U.S. Role? More Than Admitted," and the rebuttal of her arguments by Paul E. Sigmund, "Less Than Charged," in *Foreign Policy,* No. 2 (Spring 1974), 127–56; *Time,* September 30, 1974; and the *New York Times,* September 9, 1974, p. 3.

Guerrilla units, for example, do not wait for a "revolutionary situation" to develop before they begin direct assaults on the state and society. Nor do they necessarily infiltrate voluntary organizations, organize mass demonstrations, run parliamentary candidates, or seek ministerial positions. They usually begin with a small handful of dedicated men who make no pretense of having a popular base or political legitimacy, but nevertheless organize themselves into small military-political units to launch attacks against established authorities at the village level. Although every country poses different strategic and tactical problems arising from varied political, social, economic, and geographic conditions, most of the major postwar guerrilla uprisings have displayed some common characteristics.

The main political strategy of guerrilla warfare is to win positive control over successively larger portions of the civilian population while simultaneously alienating the population from the regime in power. It may require only small groups of highly mobile guerrillas to defeat the state's military forces if the population remains apathetic. As Andrew Janos points out, "Governments fall not because they have too many enemies but because they have too few friends."[28] The military objective of guerrilla warfare is to cause the slow attrition of government forces to the point where they become concentrated in the larger cities, leaving the rebels to consolidate their control to the countryside.

A guerrilla force can be compared to an iceberg. What the observer sees is a small group of full-time guerrilla warriors that continually harasses government troops and drives them from the countryside. Sustaining this "cap" of the iceberg are thousands of civilians—usually peasants—who perform their ordinary routines during the daytime and fight or conduct supporting activities for the "regulars" during the night. They provide food, shelter, transportation, and intelligence about government troop movements and the activities of anti-rebel leaders. Without this civilian base the guerrilla force could not continue to function, for lack of food, supplies, and information. Yet the government, with all its troops and military resources, is little better off than a handful of guerrillas; for it cannot locate and identify the enemy, whose members submerge back into the mass of society after they have performed their services. The government's best hope is to obtain the loyalty of the peasants so that they will identify the rebels and provide information on their activities.

To construct the civilian base and gain control over the civilian population, guerrilla cadres combine positive incentives with terror. The political leaders of guerrilla forces usually offer programs of land and political reform, combined with propaganda campaigns designed to alienate the masses from the government. Themes emphasizing nationalist symbols are also prominent. Rebel agents infiltrate villages and recruit adherents and supporting personnel. Other peasants and civilians are deterred from informing government officials on local guerrilla activities by the knowledge that if their activities are discovered, they will be kidnapped, mutilated, or murdered. Guerrillas and their village agents

[28] Janos, *The Seizure of Power*, p. 20.

also practice selective terror against such government personnel as teachers, local administrators, and village leaders. In each village, a clandestine or "shadow" government is eventually formed, ready to take over control immediately after the area has been purged of protecting government forces.

On the military front, the guerrillas start operating in the most remote areas, where government control and influence are least pervasive. Small units, usually armed with crude weapons, help capture small villages, cut government supply lines, sabotage communication facilities, and ambush government patrols. This type of harassment and attrition ultimately forces government troops to evacuate the rural areas and retreat into larger population centers. Only after several years, in which the guerrillas have gained control of the countryside through military and political operations, are they ready to launch a final military assault on the central political authorities. At this stage, the war of attrition develops into a more conventional war, with the purpose of anihilating the government's military resources. Conventional strategies and tactical principles replace the guerrilla harassing techniques, and the war is fought with more destructive weapons systems, including artillery, tanks, and armored trucks. Mass demonstrations of public support for the revolutionaries are arranged—if at all—only when military defeat of the government appears imminent. The entire process of infiltration and construction of a new order begins only after the revolutionaries have gained power. All the main voluntary organizations still remain to be purged of their leadership, a new mass party to sustain the new regime has to be created, and all of the state administration has to be reconstituted. In short, much of the work that precedes a *coup d'état* in the more traditional forms of subversion still remains to be carried out after the guerrillas have seized power. From the point of view of international politics, once power is gained, the new regime immediately shifts the country's orientation toward the external power that has directed, organized, and supported the guerrillas throughout their struggle.

MILITARY INTERVENTION

A final form of intervention is the sending of large quantities of troops either to stabilize a regime against rebels or to help rebels overthrow an established set of authorities. Massive military intervention may build up over a period of time, as in Vietnam, where the United States started by sending military advisors for training purposes, then had them perform various combat support activities, and finally sent more than a half-million troops to conduct military operations. More often, the intervention is the result of a crisis; troops are then sent in rapidly, often catching the target regime or rebels by surprise.

The classic case of sudden intervention to overthrow a regime is provided by the combined Soviet, East German, Polish, Hungarian, and Bulgarian invasion of Czechoslovakia in August 1968. We have already pointed out how the Soviet government had used demonstrations of force in attempts to alter the Dubček government's policies. In addition, a series of conferences between the Czechs and other Warsaw Treaty governments had failed to convince them that the Dubček regime's policies were not aimed at restoring capitalist and multiparty systems to the country. In particular, Walter Ulbricht of East Germany was afraid that the Czech reforms might lead to civil disturbances in his own country. Indeed, the Soviet and East European governments acted partly on the image of a domino theory: If the reforms in Czechoslovakia were not ended, they might infect the rest of the Communist bloc and seriously threaten the socialist system. The military operations were undertaken with great speed and surprise. After the country was effectively in the hands of the occupation troops, the Soviet government used a combination of kidnappings, threats, and persuasion to have Dubček and his followers deposed from their party and government positions. At the same time, the more orthodox Communists, who had been expelled or demoted from their positions during Dubček's period of reform, reappeared "to restore order." After the Soviet government had achieved its objectives, it negotiated a treaty with the new Czech regime for the withdrawal of all Warsaw Treaty troops.

Intervention may also be ordered as a means of supporting an ally or friendly state against real or supposed rebellion. The American involvement in Vietnam, of course, was justified on the grounds that the legitimate government of South Vietnam was faced with aggression from the north; the situation could not be characterized merely as a civil war pitting the Viet Cong against Saigon authorities. To the American government, the question was always one of North Vietnam's undertaking by military means to reunify the country.

The sudden American intervention against the Dominican Republic in 1965 was also undertaken to prevent a "Communist" revolution in that country. Decisions to intervene were taken rapidly and based on rather scanty information. Indeed, although it is true that civil turmoil had developed in the republic, the notion of a Communist plot has been discredited by subsequent information.

CONCLUSION

In the old European-centered international system (excepting the period 1791–1823, approximately), ideological consensus, impermeability of states, crude media of communication, and the doctrine of noninterference helped to preclude one sovereign's attempts to influence the purely domestic affairs of another.[29]

---

[29] Under the vague understandings comprising the Quadruple (later Quintuple) Alliance of 1815, the major powers of Europe pledged to intervene on behalf of any European monarch who was threatened by liberal revolution. At the Congress of Troppau (1820), devoted to discussion of the liberal revolution in Naples, the assembled Excellencies, Highnesses, and Majesties solemnly declared that "when political changes, brought about by illegal [without royal approval] means, produce dangers to other countries by reason of proximity, and when the Allied Powers can act effectively as regards these conditions, they shall, in order to bring back those countries to their allegiances, employ, first, amicable means, and then coercion." The Allied Powers subsequently intervened in Naples (1821) and Spain (1823) to restore absolute monarchies.

Noninterference is still accepted as one of the foundations of international law and one of the norms that governments should faithfully observe in their foreign relations. The Charter of the United Nations specifically prohibits member states (and presumably the organization itself, in most circumstances) from interfering in each others' domestic problems. The norm does operate, of course, in most international transactions.

But today, complete isolation of internal events from the external environment may be impossible. It can hardly be expected that many governments, as well as international organizations, will be completely indifferent to political, social, and economic developments in foreign countries. Conditions of economic and political instability in many nations create situations that foreign powers will obviously exploit—sometimes for their own gain and, at other times, merely to prevent massacres and social collapse. When major internal conflicts with serious implications for the core security or alliance interests of the major powers occur, intervention and counterintervention will probably take place, even if these conflicts are not originally organized and directed from abroad. At the point where local political problems impinge upon the foreign-policy interests, objectives, and values of external powers, some sort of relationship between the external power and domestic groups will be established. If a dissident faction or revolutionary movement is seeking domestic objectives that coincide with the interests of an external power, the likelihood that it will become dependent on that outside power is dramatically increased. If a regime in power is threatened by revolutionary forces clearly identified as being organized, supported, and perhaps directed from abroad, it will ask its allies and friends to intervene on its behalf, unless it believes it can cope with the problem by employing its own capabilities.

Although actions involving interference in the internal affairs of other states continue to constitute part of the techniques of achieving objectives for many countries, a new set of norms seems to be developing, with less restrictive criteria to indicate when such actions are permissible. Clearly, the old norms of complete noninterference in other states' internal affairs are being violated frequently, but it cannot be claimed that every case is entirely undesirable. Although it is premature to speculate on any long-term trend, many governments take the position that in certain instances, intervention and interference in other states' internal affairs may be legitimate if those actions have the prior approval of some collective body or international organization or if the organization itself assumes such a task. Traditional legal principles prohibiting all forms of external interference are most clearly spelled out in Article 15 of the Charter of Bogotá (1948), in which the Latin American states and the United States solemnly pledged that

> no state or *group* of states has the right to intervene directly or indirectly, for any reason whatever, in the internal or external affairs of any other state. The foregoing principle prohibits not only armed attack but also any other form of interference or attempted threat against the personality of the state or against the political, economic, and cultural elements.

Under Article 16, the signatories further agreed that "no state may use or encourage the use of coercive measures of an economic or political character in order to force the sovereign will of another state or obtain from it advantages of any kind."

In contrast to these strict rules, the recent practice of the Organization of the American States and unilaterally the United States has been quite different. If unilateral intervention has been involved, the acting party has in most cases sought prior approval from the Latin American states, implying that if that approval is forthcoming, the intervention is legitimate. In both the Guatemalan and Cuban episodes, the United States government sought multilateral approval for its actions. In American intervention in the Dominican Republic during 1965, however, the United States took military action *before* it turned to the OAS to seek approval of its policies.

More significant, perhaps, are those occasions when the OAS itself determined to intervene collectively against one or more of its members. In 1960, for instance, the Inter-American Peace Commission of the OAS, in an action hardly compatible with the spirit of the Bogotá charter, condemned the Trujillo regime for "flagrant and widespread" violations of human rights in the Dominican Republic. Later in the same year, the foreign ministers of the Latin American states publicly condemned Trujillo for plotting against the life of Venezuela's president. The foreign ministers' resolution, which called upon members of the OAS to impose partial economic sanctions on the Trujillo regime, was the first time that truly collective action had been applied in the Western Hemisphere. Again, in 1964, the OAS Council voted almost unanimously to impose economic and diplomatic sanctions against the Castro regime in Cuba.

In the United Nations, collective intervention in the internal affairs of member states also seems to have become a legitimate method for coping with widespread domestic chaos that promises to involve external powers extensively. In the Congo (Zaire), United Nations military intervention helped prevent social chaos, secession of Katanga from the central state, and unilateral intervention of the Soviet Union and possibly the United States. In 1964, the organization once again sent troops abroad, this time to Cyprus to establish and police a cease-fire in the civil war on the island, as well as to forestall a Turkish invasion and possible Russian intervention. All these actions were taken in the name of the organization, with the consent of the major governments involved. It is easy to speculate that if the interventions had not been organized, the internal wars and rebellions could have easily become transposed into major international crises.

Diplomatic interference, clandestine political actions, subversion, guerrilla warfare, and military intervention will remain important techniques for influencing or coercing other nations and exploiting or settling periodic domestic crises in unstable political systems. As long as the leaders of some states are committed to supporting and, in some cases, organizing and directing national "wars of liberation," counterintervention can be expected as well. Other states committed to expansive objectives or ideological principles, but lacking the capabilities to achieve them through conventional military means, diplomatic bargaining, or economic pressures, will also be likely to emphasize clandestine techniques. These are often much less expensive, involve lower risks of escalating into a direct military confrontation, and, as the cases of Czechoslovakia and Chile reveal, if the internal conditions in a target state are right, can be brought to a successful conclusion. Where the internal circumstances of a state are less amenable to outside manipulation or two or more states are confronted with incompatible objectives that have little relationship to domestic political processes, then—provided other techniques of inducement fail—the usual decision is to use military threats and violent punishments.

SELECTED BIBLIOGRAPHY

BLECHMAN, BARRY M., and STEPHEN S. KAPLAN, *Force Without War: U.S. Armed Forces as a Political Instrument.* Washington: The Brookings Institution, 1978.

BURCHETT, WILFRED, *Vietnam: Inside Story of the Guerrilla War.* New York: International Publishers, 1965.

COHEN, RAYMOND, "Where Are the Aircraft Carriers?—Nonverbal Communication in International Politics," *Review of International Studies,* 7 (1981), 79–90.

COTTAM, RICHARD W., *Competitive Interference and Twentieth Century Diplomacy.* Pittsburgh, Pa.: University of Pittsburgh Press, 1967.

CROZIER, BRIAN, *The Rebels: A Study of Post-War Insurrections.* Boston: Beacon Press, 1960.

DEBRAY, REGIS, *Revolution in the Revolution.* Middlesex, Eng.: Penguin Books, 1966.

DENNO, BRYCE F., "Sino-Soviet Attitudes toward Revolutionary War," *Orbis,* 11 (1968), 1193–1207.

FALK, RICHARD A., "The United States and the Doctrine of Non-Intervention in the Internal Affairs of Independent States," *Howard Law Journal,* 5 (1959), 163–89.

FELIX, CHRISTOPHER, *A Short Course in the Secret War.* New York: Dutton, 1963.

GIAP, VO NGUYEN, *People's War, People's Army.* New York: Praeger, 1962.

GIBERT, STEPHEN P., "Soviet-American Military Competition in the Third World," *Orbis,* 10 (1970), 1117–38.

GUEVARA, CHE, *Guerrilla Warfare.* New York: Monthly Review Press, 1961.

HENDERSON, WILLIAM, "Diplomacy and Intervention in the Developing Countries," *Virginia Quarterly Review,* 39 (1963), 25–36.

JANOS, ANDREW C., *The Seizure of Power: A Study of Force and Popular Consent,* Research Monograph No. 16. Princeton, N.J.: Center for International Studies, 1964.

KIRKPATRICK, LYMAN B., JR., *Russian Espionage: Communist and Imperialist.* New York: National Strategy Information Center, 1970.

_____, *The United States Intelligence Community: Foreign Policy and Domestic Activities.* New York: Hill & Wang, 1973.

MARCHETTI, VICTOR, and JOHN D. MARKS, *The CIA and the Cult of Intelligence.* New York: Knopf, 1974.

MAO TSE-TUNG, *On Guerrilla Warfare.* New York: Praeger, 1961.

McCONNELL, JAMES M., and BRADFORD DISMUKES, "Soviet Diplomacy of Force in the Third World," *Problems of Communism* (January–February 1979), 14–27.

McGOWAN, PATRICK, and CHARLES W. KEGLEY, JR., *Threat, Weapons, and Foreign Policy.* Beverly Hills, Calif.: Sage Publications, 1980.

MITCHELL, C.R., "Civil Strife and the Involvement of External Parties," *International Studies Quarterly,* 14 (1970), 166–94.

PEARSON, FREDERIC S., "Foreign Military Intervention and Domestic Disputes," *International Studies Quarterly,* 18 (1974), 259–90.

ROSENAU, JAMES N., "Intervention As a Scientific Concept," *Journal of Conflict Resolution,* 13 (1969), 149–71.

_____, ed., *International Aspects of Civil Strife.* Princeton, N.J.: Princeton University Press, 1964.

ROWE, EDWARD THOMAS, "Aid and Coups d'Etat: Aspects of the Impact of American Military Assistance Programs in the Less Developed Countries," *International Studies Quarterly,* 18 (1974), 239–55.

SCOTT, ANDREW, M., *The Revolution in Statecraft: Informal Penetration.* New York: Random House, 1966.

THORNTON, THOMAS, and CYRIL E, BLACK, *Communism and the Strategic Use of Political Violence.* Princeton, N.J.: Princeton University Press, 1965.

WRIGHT, QUINCY, "Subversive Intervention," *American Journal of International Law,* 54 (1960), 520–35.

11

Weapons, War, and Political Influence

The international system is often described as one of anarchy, but such a description overlooks the fact that an overwhelming majority of international transactions are carried on by means of bargaining, persuasion, or reward rather than violence. The routine issues that make up a large proportion of any nation's foreign relations rarely provoke statesmen to use or even threaten to use force. Nevertheless, recourse to violence has been and continues to be an important characteristic of the international system. In his classic study of war, Quincy Wright identified 278 wars occurring between 1480 and 1941.[1] Although the major powers were able to avoid a thermonuclear exchange during the height of the cold war, international violence has erupted at various levels of intensity in nearly every region since World War II. Between 1945 and 1967, there were eighty-two armed conflicts involving the regular forces of a nation, including twenty-six interstate wars. Moreover, many of the remaining fifty-six conflicts—civil wars, insurgencies, and the like—have had significant international implications.[2] There has been no abatement of international conflict during the years since 1967; and many civil wars, including those in Northern Ireland,

---

Note: This chapter was written by Prof. Ole R. Holsti, Department of Political Science, Duke University.

[1] Quincy Wright, *A Study of War,* Vol. 1 (Chicago: University of Chicago Press, 1942), p. 650.

[2] David Wood, *Conflict in the Twentieth Century,* Adelphi Paper No. 48 (London: Institute of Strategic Studies, 1968).

Lebanon, Chad, Angola, Ethiopia, El Salvador, Cambodia, Zimbabwe, Zaire, and elsewhere, have been marked by intervention of external powers.

The legitimacy of force as an instrument of foreign policy, although often denounced by philosophers, historians, and reformers, has rarely been questioned by those responsible for foreign-policy decisions of their nations. Some states have traditionally maintained orientations of nonalignment or isolation; but no nation is "neutral" with respect to its own security, and neutrality does not imply unconditional renunciation of force. Switzerland, for example, maintains active defense forces; India has tested a nuclear device; Sweden has been the scene of an extended debate on the desirability of acquiring nuclear weapons; and some of the staunchest adherents of a posture of nonalignment in the cold war have maintained armed forces proportionately larger than those of the United States, the Soviet Union, or China. Indeed, except in the case of a "puppet regime" established by an outside power, it seems unlikely that any government could long maintain itself in office unless it was committed to the use of all possible means, including force, to preserve the existence of the nation and other interests deemed vital.

Some types of nations may be more prone than others to the use of force as an instrument of foreign policy. In the work cited above, Wright reported that newly established states were more likely to use violence than were older, more mature countries, but that democracies had been involved in war as often as autocracies. Nations with industrial economies were less warlike than those with agricultural economies, and the states with socialist economies have been among the most warlike. On the other hand, some recent studies, based on data since World War II, suggest that democracies are more peaceful than authoritarian nations, and that smaller states tend to engage in more conflictual and high-risk foreign policies.[3]

Beyond the generalization that democratic nations have never gone to war against each other, the relationships in these studies are not always strong, and they should not obscure the fact that even states that have consistently denounced violence in international affairs will use force to achieve objectives or defend their interests *as they define them.* India, whose leaders have been outspoken opponents of violence in international relations, has used its military forces to capture the enclave of Goa from Portugal; to prevent Pakistani control over the disputed area of Kashmir; to defend its northern frontiers against border incursions by Chinese forces; and to dismember Pakistan by forcing it to grant independence to the area that now constitutes the nation of Bangladesh. Many other examples could be cited. The important point is that the decision to use violence reflects the continuing validity of Clausewitz's dictum that war is the continuation of politics by other means. It is the leaders who ultimately

---

[3] Wright, *A Study of War,* pp 828–41; Michael Haas, "Societal Approaches to the Study of War," *Journal of Peace Research,* No. 4 (1965), 307–23; and Maurice A. East, "Size and Foreign Policy Behavior: A Test of Two Models," *World Politics,* 25 (1973), 556–576. Further discussion appears in Chapter 15.

make the choice; indeed, the determination of "core interests" and the decision on appropriate means to defend or attain them have traditionally been considered inherent and legitimate attributes of sovereignty. Serious attempts to modify this aspect of sovereignty are largely a twentieth-century phenomenon. But even the United Nations Charter permits nations to use force individually and collectively for purposes of self-defense, in the event of an armed attack.

In summary, within an international system characterized by an absence of effective institutionalized constraints on the use of force by its member countries, security is a scarce value. Those responsible for national security are rarely willing to rely merely upon the goodwill or professions of peaceful intent of other nations to ensure their own safety; as a consequence, they are likely to perceive few substitutes for procurement, maintenance, and deployment of military forces. A state that makes no provision for defending itself, moreover, is unlikely to find others that will take on the task, because such countries are scarcely desirable allies. Thus, while we may be able to attribute a particular war to an aggressive leader and an expansionist social-political system, a more general reason for the use of violence in international relations is the absence of systemic constraints on its use.[4]

WEAPONS AS INSTRUMENTS OF POLICY

As instruments of national policy, weapons share one important characteristic with all other techniques: Their purpose is to achieve or defend the goals of the nation by influencing the orientations, roles, objectives, and actions of other states. As such, weapons are ethically neutral, and we must distinguish between the goals sought through the use of force and the instruments themselves. The same weapons used by the Soviets to defend their homeland against the invading Nazi armies were also used to suppress the Hungarian revolution in 1956, the liberal Czech regime in 1968, and Afghanistan in 1979–1980. Thus, it is the goals for which the weapons are used rather than the weapons themselves that can properly be judged by ethical standards.

Except for students of tactics (narrowly defined), the role of weapons must be considered in a political rather than in a purely military context. The validity of Clausewitz's strictures against a rigid distinction between politics and military strategy has become more evident as developments in military technology have transformed war from a diversion of monarchs to a potential menace against the continued existence of life on earth. In the nuclear age, it has become more readily apparent than ever that military forces exist not solely for the purpose of inflicting damage upon enemies; they may also be used as a threat

---

[4] Kenneth Waltz, *Man, the State and War: A Theoretical Analysis* (New York: Columbia University Press, 1959).

to buttress bargaining in diplomacy or as means of communicating one's intentions to potential adversaries. In 1938, Hitler invited the chief of the French air force, General Joseph Vuillemin, to inspect the Luftwaffe and to witness a demonstration of precision bombing by high-altitude dive bombers. The ploy was effective, as Vuillemin, terrified by the impressive display of German air power, became a leading exponent of appeasing German demands against Czechoslovakia.[5] Military "maneuvers" near frontiers, putting military units on "alert" status, and the deployment of forces—even small symbolic units—in a conspicuous manner have frequently been used to add credibility to one's diplomacy. Small nations that are prepared to undertake a policy of "punitive resistance" may cause more powerful nations to leave them alone. During the last stages of World War II, Switzerland possessed a well-trained army of fifty divisions, which made the prospects of an invasion too costly for Germany to consider.[6] These examples and the discussion about threats of intervention in the preceding chapter illustrate a few of the ways in which military power may be used as instruments of foreign policy without actually resorting to violence.

Even when violence is employed, the scale of intensity is extremely broad, depending on the amount, duration, and geographical scope within which force is used. At the low end of the scale, we might find actions such as those of infantry troops armed with little more than hand-carried weapons; the brief clashes of Chinese and Soviet troops along the Ussuri River in 1969 and between Ecuador and Peru in 1981 are examples. The high end of the scale is marked by the indiscriminate employment of every available means of destruction, irrespective of costs or consequences. Fortunately, we have had no instance of unlimited violence by the major powers since the advent of nuclear weapons; perhaps actions of this type can best be illustrated by Hitler's desperate efforts to save his Third Reich during its final months, mitigated only by the unwillingness of some German generals to carry out his most demonic orders. Between these extreme examples there are obviously many other possibilities involving the use of force to gain external objectives.

Role of Nuclear Weapons

Force and threats to use force have persistently played a part in international relations, and developments in military technology have often had an important impact on structures and processes of political systems. Thermonuclear weapons and long-range ballistic missile systems are not merely quantitatively different from those that preceded them; they also possess qualitative attributes that have had, and will continue to have, a significant impact on the international system, its member units, and the nature of relations between them. This is not to say, however, that conventional armaments are obsolete; indeed, most nations' military forces are still limited to such weapons, and even the nuclear

---

[5] Leonard Mosely, *On Borrowed Time* (New York: Random House, 1969), pp. 25–27.
[6] Dean Acheson, *Present at the Creation* (New York: Norton, 1969), p. 61.

powers have found it expedient to maintain conventional forces to deal with limited provocations. In most circumstances nuclear power cannot easily be converted into political influence.

The most obvious characteristic of nuclear weapons is their destructive capacity. The bombs that obliterated the Japanese cities of Hiroshima and Nagasaki at the end of World War II had an explosive power of 20 kilotons (20,000 tons of TNT). By recent standards, such weapons are considered almost miniature. In 1961, the Soviet Union tested a bomb rated at 61 megatons (61,000,000 tons of TNT), which exceeded the combined explosive power of all weapons fired during World War II. A single Soviet SS-18 missile is capable of delivering eight to ten multiple independently targetable reentry vehicles (MIRVs) in the megaton range or a single 25-megaton warhead a distance of 7,500 miles, within less than one mile of its target. The United States reportedly possesses over 7,000 strategic nuclear warheads, all with a destructive capacity far greater than those that devastated Hiroshima and Nagasaki in 1945, and the stockpiles of the other nuclear nations add significantly to this total.[7] The U.S. Defense Department has estimated that a general war between the United States and the Soviet Union might kill 149 million Americans and 100 million Russians—and other estimates have been even more pessimistic. Under these circumstances, it is hardly surprising that some traditional views of the function of military forces have been rendered obsolete, and that nuclear war as an instrument of policy has been deemed irrational but, unfortunately, not impossible. Both Soviet and American leaders have expressed the view that there are few, if any, goals that can be served by the actual *use* of nuclear weapons; thus, the threat to use these weapons, rather than their actual use, has become of paramount importance.

It is not only the destructive capacity of thermonuclear weapons that has had an impact on the international system. The development of accurate long-range ballistic missiles has provided the means for their delivery across continents at speeds that have reduced warning time almost to the vanishing point. Space and time, which once provided protection against devastating surprise attack, have all but lost their defensive value in the nuclear-missile age. This development is somewhat analogous to the invention of gunpower in the late Middle Ages, which contributed to the decline of feudalism. With the introduction of the cannon to warfare, the feudal lord was no longer able to ensure the security of his subjects within the walls of his castle or fortified town. Out of the destruction of the feudal system emerged a new unit of security—the nation-state. In a somewhat similar manner, the destructive capacity and range of nuclear missiles lay the territorial state open to total destruction.[8] Before

[7] *The Military Balance, 1980–81* (London: International Institute of Strategic Studies, 1980), pp. 3, 4, 9.

[8] John Herz, "The Rise and Demise of the Territorial State," *World Politics*, 9 (1957), 473–93. However, see also Herz, "The Territorial State Revisited: Reflections on the Future of the Nation-State," *Polity*, 1 (1968), 12–34.

World War I, a nation at war was unable to inflict severe damage on the adversary's territory, industrial capacity, or population without first defeating its armed forces, whereas today it is possible to do so.

The Global Arms Race

Since World War II, the policies of nations armed with nuclear weapons have clearly dominated the international system, but acquisition and deployment of military instruments are by no means limited to the major powers. Nor, despite the huge defense budgets of the five major nuclear powers—the United States, the USSR, Great Britain, France, and China—is the expenditure of vast resources for military means restricted to these nations. As a percentage of their Gross National Products (GNP), the defense expenditures of the "Big Five" are as follows: United States 5.2 percent; Great Britain, 4.9 percent; France, 3.9 percent; USSR, 11–13 percent; and the People's Republic of China, 9 percent. Countries diverting over 10 percent of their GNP to military spending include: Egypt (13.2 percent), Israel (31.1 percent), Saudi Arabia (15.0 percent), Syria (22.1 percent), Iraq (10.9 percent), and North Korea (11.2 percent). At the other end of the spectrum, one major power, Japan, spends less than 1 percent of its GNP on military items, and such nations as Costa Rica, Gambia, Iceland, Lesotho, and Surinam have even smaller defense budgets proportionate to national income. Global military spending was approximately $500 billion in 1980, more than double the 1970 figure. Of that amount, the United States, the USSR, and their NATO and Warsaw Treaty Organization allies accounted for about 75 percent (the comparable figure two decades earlier was 90 percent). But by far the fastest growth in military spending at present is among the developing nations. The huge expenditures for armaments by the newly rich oil-producing nations such as Syria, Libya, and Saudi Arabia—none of which has recently been at war—is impressive evidence of the high priority that even less-developed countries place on acquisition of modern armaments. Using another criterion, percentage of total population in the armed forces, we find that the Republic of China, Israel, Bulgaria, Greece, Albania, Jordan, Libya, Cuba, Vietnam, Laos, Iraq, Turkey, Syria, South Korea, and North Korea have proportionately larger armed forces than any of the major powers.[9]

Thus, although nuclear weapons are of undeniable importance, several important points should be kept in mind: (1) Virtually all nations maintain armed forces; (2) the intensity of violence in military actions may vary across a wide scale, but force is rarely used in an unlimited manner; (3) sources of international instability are by no means confined to the actions and conflicts between nuclear powers; and (4) although nuclear weapons have had a revolutionary impact on some aspects of international relations, many observations about force as

[9] The figures in this paragraph have been calculated from data in *The Military Balance, 1980–81;* and U.S. Arms Control and Disarmament Agency, *World Military Expenditures and Arms Transfers, 1969–1978* (Washington, D.C.: U.S. Government Printing Office, 1980).

an instrument of policy are equally valid for nuclear and for conventional weapons.

THE SPREAD OF NUCLEAR WEAPONS

Military strength has traditionally been one of the attributes distinguishing the so-called great powers from the small powers. Since World War II, this distinction has tended to give way to that between the nuclear powers and those not so armed. The high cost of developing and procuring nuclear capabilities initially prohibited all but a few industrial powers from developing them. The period of Soviet and American nuclear monopoly immediately after World War II coincided with a tendency of nations within the international system to group themselves into opposing alliances led by the two nuclear powers. Paradoxically, however, in the long run, nuclear weapons may have contributed to loosening of a bipolar system. The diffusion of nuclear knowledge, reactors, and materials has dramatically reduced the cost and difficulty of developing nuclear military capabilities. At the same time, as the potential destructiveness of war has risen, junior members of alliances have become more skeptical that other nations will risk devastation to honor treaty commitments. Charles DeGaulle put the question most succinctly: "Will Washington commit suicide to save Paris?" Hence, there is the incentive to develop and rely on one's own nuclear forces. Less than two decades after the first atomic explosion, it was authoritatively estimated that nations economically and technologically capable of supporting a nuclear military program numbered as high as twenty, including Canada, Japan, West Germany, Sweden, Egypt, South Africa, Argentina, Brazil, and Israel. Despite some belated efforts by the United States, Great Britain, and the Soviet Union to delay expansion of the nuclear club—indirectly by the Test Ban Treaty in 1963, and directly by the Nonproliferation Treaty of 1970—the decision of whether or not to acquire nuclear weapons now lies beyond the effective control of leaders in Moscow or Washington; and such decisions are as likely to reflect regional security problems as they are those of the cold war. India's successful nuclear test has increased the motivation for Pakistan to follow suit, and that nation may well be the next to join the nuclear club. Acquisition of nuclear weapons by one of the Middle Eastern nations would almost certainly trigger a local arms race, and that is not the only region in which this might occur.

In a world that faces a growing gap between burgeoning demands for energy and diminishing conventional sources of it, pressures to exploit nuclear power will increase. As India's experience has made dramatically evident, a nation with the capacity to use nuclear technology for "peaceful" purposes also has within its grasp the ability to produce weapons.

At present, nuclear technology has tended to create two classes of international citizenship. In the long run, however, nuclear capabilities may tend to dilute the importance of traditional bases of power—population, territory, industrial capacity, and the like—and therefore reduce rather than expand the differential between large and small nations. To be sure, a nation with a large population, vast territory, and widely dispersed industrial capacity may be in a better position to survive a nuclear attack—and is thus capable of employing threats more effectively—than is a nation with limited population and territory. In the prenuclear era it was unlikely that a minor power could inflict an unacceptable level of damage on one of its large neighbors, much less threaten its existence; it is not inconceivable, however, that in the not too distant future, a small nation armed with nuclear weapons may be in a position to inflict such damage. This is precisely the reasoning that underlies the French nuclear *"force de dissuasion."* The ability to "tear off an arm" is assumed to be sufficient to deter even a much more powerful adversary.

However, for most nations, nuclear power is currently only indirectly relevant to the conduct of their foreign policies. Although possessed of weak and crude military capabilities in comparison to those of the nuclear nations, these countries also enjoy the advantage of being unlikely direct targets of any nuclear exchange. It is thus one of many paradoxes of the nuclear age that the threat of destruction hangs most heavily over those states with the greatest military power; in some respects, then, security is inversely rather than directly related to military capabilities.

DETERRENCE AS A FORM OF INTER-NATION INFLUENCE

The awesome destructive capacity of nuclear weapons has rendered the cost of their use prohibitive except in cases of extreme provocation. Because few, if any, political ends can be gained through nuclear war, the primary function of these weapons is that of posing a threat to potential enemies. Deterrence, by which decision makers in one nation seek to prevent certain actions by potential adversaries by threatening them with military retaliation, can be considered one of the means by which nations attempt to influence others.

Deterrence is not an invention of the nuclear age, as attempts to influence others through threats of sanctions are as old as diplomacy. By posing a threat to the values of a potential attacker, the defender seeks to preclude certain types of behavior—specifically, unacceptable threats to the status quo. Deterrence can also be viewed as a process of communication; decision makers of one nation seek to communicate to their counterparts abroad, "If you undertake activities X, Y, or Z, we shall surely retaliate with actions whose costs to you will outweigh any gains you may achieve." It is generally assumed that the threat of nuclear retaliation is severe enough to deter any nation from attempting an all-out attack on the defender. Some deterrence theorists have also suggested that a powerful nuclear capability will suffice to deter aggression at lower levels of violence, such as conventional attacks, guerrilla incursions, and the like. In the colorful words of Sir John Slessor, former British chief of the air staff, "The dog that we keep to take care of the cat can also take care of the kittens." But, as we shall discuss in more detail later, the assumption that strategic deterrence might deal with a much broader range of challenges is open to serious question.

The premises underlying strategic deterrence are that (1) decisions by both the defender and the challenger will be based on rational calculations of probable costs and gains, accurate evaluations of the situation, and careful assessments of relative capabilities; (2) a high level of threat, such as that posed by nuclear weapons, inhibits rather than provokes aggressive behavior; (3) the value hierarchies of both the defender and the challenger are similar, at least to the point that each places the avoidance of large-scale violence at or near the top; and (4) both sides maintain tight centralized control over decisions that might involve or provoke the use of strategic weapons. Deterrence thus presupposes rational and predictable decision processes. Put somewhat differently, most deterrence theories assume that the nation-state can be thought of as a unitary rational actor. Later we shall consider whether these premises are valid in all circumstances.

Credibility

One obvious requirement for effective deterrence is possession of sufficient capabilities to carry out the threatened retaliation. But influence over the behavior of others is not merely a function of weapon characteristics, as can be illustrated by the case of the bandit who uses a realistic-looking toy pistol to convince a bank teller to hand over some money. Success should be attributed, not to the robber's weapon, but rather to the teller's perception of it. Communicating to potential adversaries about one's strategic capabilities is usually relatively easy. Because weapons and military personnel are tangible objects and their attributes (speed, range, destructive capacity, number, accuracy, and the like) are relatively easy to measure, probabilities of misperceptions are reduced; and any distortions are likely to be on the side of overestimating rather than underestimating the adversary's capabilities—"just to be on the safe side." Also, there are usually ample opportunities for communicating about military capabilities; for example, the annual May Day parade in Moscow provides Soviet leaders an opportunity to impress foreigners with the latest weapons in their arsenal.

Objectively speaking, the destructive capacity of modern weapons and the potentially catastrophic costs of general war should ensure sufficient caution in foreign-policy decisions to make their use unnecessary. Certainly this should be true of nuclear weapons. But success in avoiding general war to date should give rise to only the mildest optimism; the frequency of war indicates that the threat to use force and even the possession of superior military capabilities have often failed to deter.[10] To explain these failures, as well as to understand the conditions for successful deterrence, we must look beyond the attributes of weapons systems. First, as in many diplomatic bargaining situations, the defender must be able to establish the *credibility* of the threat; that is, potential aggressors must be impressed that in case of provocation, the threatened retaliation will in fact be carried out. Mere possession of powerful weapons, even an overwhelming superiority of capabilities, does not ensure credibility, just as in a series of negotiations, threats need more than merely their enunciation to be made believable. Consider again our example of the bank robber, who in this case enters the bank with a genuine weapon. If, for whatever reason, the teller were convinced that the threat was a bluff, she would not meet the bandit's demands. His failure could not be attributed to characteristics of his weapon—in fact, a more powerful weapon might more readily be seen as a bluff—but rather to the low credibility (as perceived by the teller) of his threat to use it. This simple example illustrates the point that credibility is not inherent in the weapon but is rather a function of the challenger's perception of the weapon and of its owner's intentions and motivations. That is:

$$\text{Deterrent effect} = \text{Estimated capability} \times \text{Estimated intent}$$

Although this formula[11] oversimplifies a complex relationship (a point to which we will return later in considering the deterrent effect of "overkill" capacity), it does highlight the key point that if either perceived capability or intent is zero, deterrent effect is also zero.

Because credibility depends upon the challenger's beliefs and perceptions, a crucial problem is that of communicating intent. Compounding the problem is the very real difficulty of gaining hard and verifiable evidence about such elusive and sometimes mercurial attributes as motivations. History is not barren of instances in which disaster arose from faulty assessments of others' capabilities—witness the American estimates of Japanese and Chinese military strength in 1941 and 1950, respectively—but the decidedly more difficult task of adducing intentions has no doubt created far more problems. George Kennan has observed that "in everything that can be statistically expressed—expressed, that is, in such a way as not to imply any judgment on our motivation—I believe the Soviet Government to be excellently informed about us. I am sure that their information on the development of our economies, on the state of our military preparations, on our scientific progress, etc., is absolutely first-rate.

---

[10] Bernard Brodie, "The Anatomy of Deterrence," *World Politics,* 11 (1959), 14–15. Excellent case studies of deterrence failure may be found in Roberta Wohlstetter, *Pearl Harbor: Warning and Decision* (Stanford, Calif.: Stanford University Press, 1962); and Alexander L. George and Richard Smoke, *Deterrence in American Foreign Policy: Theory and Practice* (New York: Columbia University Press, 1974).

[11] Adopted in somewhat modified form from J. David Singer, *Deterrence, Arms Control, and Disarmament* (Columbus: Ohio State University Press, 1962), p. 162.

But when it comes to the analysis of our motives, to the things that make our life tick as it does, I think this whole great system of intelligence-gathering breaks down seriously.''[12] This disability is not, of course, limited to the Soviet Union, or even to totalitarian nations. The Munich Conference, Pearl Harbor, the Korean invasion, the Suez crisis, the American responses to installation of Soviet missiles in Cuba, and the Vietnam War are only a few of the more prominent cases in which leaders of democratic nations seriously misread the motivations and determination of their adversaires. In general, the more ambiguous the information, the greater the likelihood of distortion between the intent behind the sender's message and the meaning assigned to it by the intended audience. Thus, it is much easier to impress opponents about tangible objects such as weapons than about one's motivations to use them in various circumstances.

One method of communicating with potential adversaries is through declaratory policy. Since World War II, American leaders have repeatedly asserted that a Soviet attack on Western Europe would evoke the same response as a direct attack on the United States; Soviet leaders have made similar proclamations with respect to Eastern Europe. But it is difficult to communicate intent by words only; because "actions speak louder than words," visible actions that convey a relatively unambiguous message are usually necessary to buttress policy declarations. During the early 1960s, when Premier Khrushchev was apparently unconvinced of the credibility of certain American defense commitments, President Kennedy is reported to have complained, "That son of a bitch won't pay any attention to words. He has to see you move."[13] Despite repeated American pronouncements concerning the intent to defend West Berlin against Soviet encroachment, the USSR was not deterred from undertaking various efforts to undermine the status of that city. Even such actions as the Berlin airlift of 1948–1949, while adding credibility to the American commitment, did not permanently deter the Soviet Union. On the other hand, repeated failure to carry out a threatened retaliation rapidly erodes credibility. Assertions by British and French leaders that they would support Poland in case of Nazi attack had little deterrent effect, in part owing to their previous failure to act against Italian and German aggression in Ethiopia, Albania, Austria, and Czechoslovakia.

In our discussion of diplomatic bargaining, we pointed out that credibility is enhanced if the threat is roughly commensurate with the importance of the issue in contention. Similarly, in the area of deterrence, it is generally recognized today that the threat to unleash a massive thermonuclear response to aggression, even if supported by the necessary capabilities, is not apt to be credible in cases of limited provocation (such as guerrilla raids). But in the years immediately following World War II, it was widely assumed that the threat of nuclear retaliation would automatically deter aggression at any level. This premise underlay the defense policies of the British Conservative government on its return to

---

[12] George Kennan, *Russia, The Atom, and the West* (New York: Harper & Row, 1957), pp. 21–22.

[13] Arthur M. Schlesinger, Jr., *A Thousand Days* (Boston: Houghton Mifflin, 1965), p. 391.

office in 1951. The invasion of Korea, despite American nuclear superiority and concern for the costs of maintaining large conventional forces, led the Eisenhower administration to adopt a new deterrent posture. In January 1954, Secretary of State John Foster Dulles announced a major change in American defense policy, declaring that henceforth, Soviet-sponsored aggression on the periphery of the free world might be met not in kind (as in the Korean War), but perhaps with "massive retaliatory power" delivered "by means and at places of our own choosing."[14]

In other words, limited aggression might be met with direct retaliation against its presumed sponsor—Moscow. Whatever credibility a policy of massive retaliation might have had during the period of American nuclear monopoly (1945–1949) was drastically reduced after the Soviet Union attained nuclear capabilities. By 1954, both the United States and the Soviet Union could unleash a massive nuclear attack on each other, but neither could escape the frightful costs of a retaliatory attack. Under these circumstances, a threat to respond to any aggressive act with a thermonuclear strike might well be questioned. By 1957, a few months after the successful launching of Sputnik I, even Secretary Dulles accepted the view that Western security would rest in part on local defense, although he stressed the use of tactical nuclear weapons rather than conventional means.[15] By 1961, the doctrine had been abandoned in favor of strategies that could better cope with the full range of warlike acts by an opponent.

Stability

Effective deterrence must be *stable* as well as credible. Adversaries must not only be able to communicate a resolve to carry out a threat if the provocation is severe enough; they must also impress enemy leaders of their intentions without provoking a preventive or preemptive strike out of fear. The possible consequences of the "reciprocal fear of surprise attack" can be illustrated by an analogy:

> If I go downstairs to investigate a noise at night, with a gun in my hand, and find myself face to face with a burglar who has a gun in his hand, there is danger of an outcome that neither of us desires. Even if he prefers just to leave quietly, and I wish him to, there is danger that he may *think* I want to shoot, and shoot first. Worse, there is danger that he may think that I think he wants to shoot. Or he may think that I think he thinks I want to shoot. And so on. "Self-defense" is ambiguous, when one is only trying to preclude being shot in self-defense.[16]

[14] John Foster Dulles, "The Evolution of Foreign Policy," U.S. Department of State, *Bulletin 30* (January 25, 1954), pp. 107–10.

[15] John Foster Dulles, "Challenge and Response in United States Policy," *Foreign Affairs*, 36 (October 1957), 25–43.

[16] Thomas C. Schelling, *The Strategy of Conflict* (Cambridge, Mass.: Harvard University Press, 1960), p. 207.

Leaders of two mutually hostile nations, each possessing powerful military forces that might be capable of destroying the adversary with a surprise attack, may find themselves in a similar situation. Each may prefer to back off but may be unable to convince the other of his preference.

In summary, then, an effective deterrence system requires more than merely possession of powerful military forces—even if they include nuclear weapons. Before 1945, the effectiveness of weapons was measured primarily by their performance against those of enemies and only secondarily for their deterrent effects. The contribution of nuclear weapons to national security is assessed less by their capacity to inflict devastating damage on enemies than according to their ability to influence the behavior of potential adversaries so that the occasion for using them will not arise. The outbreak of war, necessitating actual use of military capabilities, represents a failure of deterrence.[17] Thus, an effective deterrent must be both threatening (sufficiently credible that adversaries are not tempted to undertake prohibited actions) and stable (reassuring enough to reduce any incentives to launch a preemptive strike out of fear).

DETERRENCE IN CRISIS SITUATIONS

Most importantly deterrence must be stable under conditions of great international tensions, when policy makers may be making important decisions while experiencing severe stress. Yet no system of deterrence can be absolutely stable, if only because all weapons are to some degree provocative, because the capacity of individuals and organizations to deal effectively with complex problems is not unlimited and because in any foreseeable international system there will always be nations or subnational groups who are prepared to challenge the status quo with force.

Decision Time

Probably the most pernicious attribute of crisis is time pressure; the aphorism that "haste makes waste" can take on a terrible new meaning in nuclear confrontations. Not only is short decision time likely to constrain full exploration of policy options; it may also materially increase the probabilities of unintended escalation and war. Let's assume that military technology has made nuclear war as an instrument of policy unthinkable because it has become too costly even for the "winner." (A similar argument was, incidentally, also quite popular during the decade before 1914.) We still cannot totally overlook the unintended

---

[17] Glenn H. Snyder and others have pointed out that deterrence may operate *in war* as well as *before war*. This does not negate the point, however, that the outbreak of violence represents a failure of deterrence. Glenn H. Snyder, *Deterrence and Defense: Toward a Theory of National Security* (Princeton. N.J.: Princeton University Press, 1961).

ways in which war might occur: escalation of limited war into a thermonuclear holocaust; catalytic war, in which major powers are drawn into a conflict initiated by other nations; war arising from an accident or a breakdown in discipline among subordinate military personnel; and a war resulting from erroneous intelligence, faulty interpretation of radar images, or other types of communication difficulties.[18]

Most of these occurrences are extremely unlikely, owing to complex devices and procedures designed to circumvent accidents. For example, a number of aircraft armed with nuclear weapons have crashed without a nuclear detonation, owing to safety devices built into the triggering mechanism. The presence of such safeguards does not, however, provide absolute insurance against errors of human perception, judgment, and performance. But in the absence of time pressure, these scenarios can perhaps be dismissed as too improbable for serious concern.

The capacity to respond with weapons of almost incalculable speed of delivery and destructiveness has created one of the crucial paradoxes of the nuclear age: The very decisions that, because of their potentially awesome consequences, should be made with the greatest deliberation may have to be made under the most urgent pressure of time. "He who hesitates is lost" may be a sound rule for card players; we can scarcely afford to have statesmen act on that principle. The ideal deterrence system is thus one that clearly and continually impresses everyone with the fact that striking first is the irrational, not the "safe" choice.

Ample experimental and historical evidence indicates that individual and group decision-making processes tend to become less effective with the compression of decision time. Beyond a moderate level, time pressure has an adverse effect on creativity, memory, productivity, accuracy, and other factors crucial to decision making under conditions of uncertainty. There actually appears to be a two-way relationship between time and stress. On the one hand, the common use during crises of such techniques as ultimata and threats with built-in deadlines—as well as the rapid delivery time of modern weapons—is likely to increase the stress under which the recipient must operate. On the other hand, high stress tends to result in distorted perceptions of time. Finally, when decision time is short, the ability to estimate the probable outcomes— the costs and benefits—of each policy option is likely to be reduced, and concern for short-run consequences of decisions increases. To some extent, then, decisions made under stress may be more apt to violate some of the premises about calculated decision processes that underlie nuclear deterrence: Extreme stress may increase the likelihood of reflexive behavior and concomitantly decrease

---

[18] Singer, *Deterrence, Arms Control, and Disarmament.* A somewhat different set of "scenarios" describing possible causes of war is presented in Herman Kahn, *On Thermonuclear War* (Princeton, N.J.: Princeton University Press, 1960), pp. 524ff. The thesis that the likelihood of nuclear war between the superpowers is disappearing is developed by Werner Levi, *The Coming End of War* (Beverly Hills: Sage, 1981).

the probability of cautious and calculated policies. (For further discussion, see Chapter 15.)

The 1914 Crisis

The events leading up to World War I, a classic example of a minor local crisis that escalated rapidly into a world war, can be used to illustrate how weapons, time, and stress can affect decision making.[19] Archduke Francis Ferdinand, heir apparent to the throne of Austria-Hungary, was assassinated June 28, 1914, in Sarajevo by a young Serbian nationalist. Within a week, Germany had promised "blank-check" support for Austria's policy of punishing and humiliating Serbia and perhaps even provoking a "local war." On July 23, the Austro-Hungarians presented Serbia with an ultimatum of unprecedented severity, the answer to which was regarded as unsatisfactory. Five days later, Vienna declared war against its southern neighbor.

When war between Austria-Hungary and Serbia could no longer be prevented, it also became evident that efforts to localize it might fail As late as August 1, many European statesmen expressed the belief that if time permitted a reconvening of the concert powers, general war might be avoided. But at the same time, attention turned to the risks of being unprepared for the war that might break out.

Here was the dilemma. Time would be required if a general European war was to be averted; above all, a moratorium on military operations was necessary. It was clear that military alerts, mobilizations, and deployment of troops near frontiers would stimulate similar actions by others. But increasingly, these considerations were overshadowed by another: To permit a potential adversary any time advantage in mobilizing the military power of the state was perceived to be disastrous. On July 28, Nicholas II had warned, "I foresee that I will succumb very soon to the pressure put upon me and will be compelled to take extreme measures which will lead to war." Three days later, in the course of his desperate last-minute correspondence with the Kaiser, the Tsar asserted, "It is technically impossible to stop our military preparations which were obligatory owing to Austria's mobilization."

The reaction of German officials to the events leading up to mobilization and war was almost identical. On the one hand, they repeatedly asserted that, owing to the pressure of time, they had no choice but to take vigorous military measures against the threat to the east. On the other hand, they claimed that only Russia was free to act in order to prevent war. "The responsibility for the disaster which is now threatening the whole civilized world will not be laid at my door. In this moment is still lies in your [Nicholas's] power to avert it." And Wilhelm, like the Tsar, finally asserted that he had lost control of his own military and that only the actions of the adversary could stop further escalation.

On July 29, Russia had ordered—and then canceled—a general mobiliza-

[19] The following discussion of the 1914 and Cuban missile crises draws upon Ole R. Holsti, *Crisis, Escalation, War* (Montreal and London: McGill-Queen's University Press, 1972).

tion. Later it was decided in St. Petersburg that the mobilization of the four southern military districts would deter an Austro-Hungarian attack on Serbia without, it was assumed, alarming Germany. But, in part because Russia had no effective plan for a partial mobilization, the Tsar was persuaded to reverse his decision once again on July 30 in favor of general mobilization, German warnings notwithstanding.

In response to what was perceived as a mounting threat against its eastern frontiers, the German government proclaimed a "state of threatening danger of war" on July 31 and dispatched a twelve-hour ultimatum to Russia demanding a cessation of military preparations. The Kaiser then ordered mobilization on August 1. The French government simultaneously ordered general mobilization. Although official British mobilization was delayed until August 2, Winston Churchill, First Lord of the Admiralty, and many others had advocated such action considerably earlier.

Thus, each mobilization was defended as a necessary reaction—made more urgent by the pressure of time—to a previous decision within the other coalition. A gnawing awareness that the probable responses to one's military measures would be counter measures by the opponents failed to deter, and assurances of defensive intent failed to reassure adversaries sufficiently to cause them to abandon their own military steps. Thus, ten days after the small-scale mobilizations by Serbia and Austria-Hungary on July 25, each of the major participants had ordered a general mobilization, a decision commonly regarded in 1914 as an act of war. The armies totaling less than 400,000 troops, called to fight a limited war between two nations, had grown to nearly 12 million men, representing, in addition to Serbia and Austria-Hungary, Montenegro, Russia, France, Germany, Belgium, Turkey, and Great Britain.

One factor contributing to the rapid escalation was the rigidity of the various mobilization plans. Austria-Hungary and Russia had more than one plan for mobilization, but once any one of them was set in motion, it was impossible to change to another. The Russians could order either a general mobilization against both Germany and Austria-Hungary or a partial one directed only at the latter. But, as Russian generals were to argue vehemently during the crucial days at the end of July, a partial mobilization would preclude a general one for months to come, leaving Russia completely at the mercy of Germany. According to General Dobrorolski, "The whole plan of mobilization is worked out ahead to its end in all its detail. When the moment has been chosen, one has only to press the button, and the whole state begins to function automatically with the precision of a clock's mechanism. . . . Once the moment has been fixed, everything is settled; there is no going back; it determines mechanically the beginning of war."[20] Although Austria-Hungary also had a number of different military plans, the condition of her army served as a constraint against diplomatic flexibility.

[20] Sidney B. Fay, *The Origins of the World War,* 2nd ed., 2 (New York: Free Press, 1966), p. 481.

The other two continental powers—France and Germany—each had but a single plan for calling up its armed forces; and, in the case of Germany, political leaders were ill-informed about the rigidity of mobilization and war plans. The Kaiser's last-minute attempt to reverse the Schlieffen plan—to attack only in the east—shattered Moltke, who replied, "That is impossible, Your Majesty. An army of a million cannot be improvised. It would be nothing but a rabble of undisciplined armed men, without a commissariat. . . . It is utterly impossible to advance except according to plan; strong in the west, weak in the east."[21]

Finally, all the mobilization plans existed only on paper; except for the Russo-Japanese War, no major European power had mobilized since 1878. This fact rendered the plans all the more rigid and made military leaders who were responsible for carrying them out less likely to accept any last-minute modifications. It may also have added to the widely believed dictum that one did not mobilize for any purpose other than war.

Does the outbreak of World War I have any relevance for national security policy during an age in which weapons systems have only the slightest resemblance to those existing in 1914? An analysis of European military technology and doctrines would reveal, for example, that objectively, time was of incalculably less importance than in the 1980s. The necessity of harvesting the summer crops was an important consideration in the military calculations of all the continental powers. Russia's ability to mount a rapid offensive against Germany could be discounted; this assumption of Russia's lack of speed in fact underlay the Schlieffen plan.

Yet, any analysis confined to the "objective" situation misses the point that individuals and groups make decisions on the basis of their appraisal of a situation, and that this may or may not correspond to some objective definition of reality. In the high-stress situation in 1914, European statesmen believed that time was of crucial importance, and they acted on that assumption. During the culminating phases of the crisis, foreign-policy officials attributed to potential enemies the ability to deliver a sudden and possibly decisive military blow, even though they knew that their own armed forces lacked such a capability. As a consequence, the costs of delaying immediate military action were perceived as increasingly high. Or, to use the language of modern deterrence theory, decision makers in each alliance perceived those of the other coalition as able and willing to launch a massive first strike and thus hastened their own preparations.

The Missile Crisis of 1962

The events of October 1962, an intense international crisis that escalated to the brink of war and then de-escalated, can be contrasted with the decision making during the weeks immediately preceding the outbreak of World War I. The first nuclear confrontation in history was precipitated by the establishment

---

[21] Quoted in Virginia Cowles, *The Kaiser* (New York: Harper & Row, 1963), p. 343.

of Soviet missile sites in Cuba. For a period of approximately one week, the likelihood of a full-scale nuclear exchange between the United States and the Soviet Union was higher than at any time since World War II.

As in 1914, time pressure was woven inextricably into the entire crisis situation. The pressure created by work on the Soviet missile sites in Cuba has been described by Theodore Sorensen, Special Counsel to the President: "For all of us knew that, once the missile sites under construction became operational, and capable of responding to any apparent threat or command with a nuclear volley, the President's options would be dramatically changed."[22] There was also the countervailing force created by the President and his advisors, who sought to minimize the probability that either side would respond by a "spasm reaction."

One important aspect of American policy making during the crisis was a deep concern for adequate information upon which to make decisions. Despite public pressure, the administration resisted taking action until photographic evidence of the missile sites was available. During the week after discovery of the missiles, a series of alternatives was being considered pending more accurate information; and while the decision to institute a blockade of Cuba was being hammered out, open discussion of the alternatives was encouraged.

Groups that achieve early consensus because dissent on matters of policy is subtly or overtly discouraged often produce decisions of low quality;[23] this was true, for example, of the group in Washington that sanctioned the CIA plan to invade Cuba in 1961. Although many of the same persons were involved in the decisions regarding missiles in Cuba, President Kennedy took various steps to encourage open and sometimes heated debate. As a consequence, at least six significantly different policy options—ranging from doing nothing to launching air strikes and an invasion to dismantle the missiles—were considered and argued in detail. A participant in the decision making at the highest level wrote that President Kennedy, aware that discussions of alternatives in the National Security Council would be franker in his absence, encouraged the group to hold preliminary meetings without him.

It was not until Saturday, October 20, almost a week after the photographic evidence became available, that the consensus developed. The president himself acknowledged that the interim period was crucial to the choice of a policy; he asserted that if the decision had had to be made during the first 24 hours after verification of missile sites, the government would not have chosen as prudently as it did one week later, when it finally settled on the quarantine against introduction of further missiles.

Unlike many decision makers in the 1914 crisis, American leaders also

---

[22] Theodore Sorensen, *Decision-Making in the White House* (New York: Columbia University Press, 1963), p. 31.

[23] Irving Janis, *Victims of Groupthink: A Psychological Study of Foreign Policy Decisions and Fiascos* (Boston: Houghton Mifflin, 1972); and Ole R. Holsti and Alexander L. George, "Effects of Stress on the Performance of Foreign Policy-Makers," in Cornelius P. Cotter, ed., *Political Science Annual: Individual Decision-Making*, Vol. 6 (Indianapolis: Bobbs-Merrill, 1975).

displayed a considerable concern and sensitivity for the manner in which Soviet leaders were apt to interpret American actions. President Kennedy and others were acutely aware of the possibility of misperception by their counterparts in the Kremlin. Only weeks earlier, a serious miscalculation by the president and most of his advisors may have played a major part in the events leading up to the crisis. It was an almost unexamined article of faith in Washington that the Soviets would never place sophisticated weapons in bases so far from Moscow and within reach of a volatile leader such as Fidel Castro. Evidence to the contrary was thus dismissed, all the more easily because it came mostly from Cuban refugee sources that had proved unreliable in the past. The Soviets, for their part, appear to have misperceived how Washington would react to strategic missiles in Cuba, apparently believing that the president was too weak to act resolutely. During the deliberations in Washington, Kennedy even recalled that World War I had developed through a series of misjudgments about each nation's intentions toward the others. This concern for anticipated reactions is evident in all the accounts of discussions regarding an appropriate response to the Soviet missiles.

Sensitivity for the position of the adversary manifested itself throughout the crisis. There were attempts to ensure that Premier Khrushchev and his colleagues not be rushed into an irrevocable decision; it was agreed among members of the decision group that escalation of the crisis should be slowed down to give Soviet leaders time to consider their next move. An interesting example of Kennedy's concern emerges from his management of the naval quarantine. The president ordered the Navy to delay intercepting a Soviet ship until the last possible moment, and he sent his order "in the clear" rather than in code. The Soviets, certain to intercept the message, would thus be assured that they had time in which to consider their decisions. There was, in addition, a conscious effort not to reduce the alternatives of *either* side to two—surrender or total war. An air strike on the missile bases or invasion of the island would have left the Soviets only two alternatives: acquiescence to destruction of the Soviet position in Cuba or counter-attack. A blockade, on the other hand, would give the Soviet government a choice between turning back the weapons-bearing ships or attempting to run the blockade.

Another characteristic of the decision process in October 1962 was the conscious choice of a response at the lowest level of violence or potential violence necessary to achieve withdrawal of the Soviet missiles. Members of the Joint Chiefs of Staff, as well as Senators J. William Fulbright and Richard B. Russell, were among those who urged bombing and an invasion of Cuba in order to ensure removal of the missiles. The decision to impose a naval quarantine was based on the reasoning that it would allow further and more massive actions should the Soviet Union fail to withdraw its missiles. The Kremlin leadership was thus given both the time and the opportunity to reassess its policy. However, although the quarantine succeeded in preventing further shipments of missiles to Cuba, it did not result in removal of those already deployed there. The threat of an air strike was employed in an ultimatum delivered by Attorney General Robert Kennedy to Soviet Ambassador Dobrynin. Just prior to a White House meeting at which the air-strike option would again be discussed, Premier Khrushchev accepted the compromise plan calling for Soviet withdrawal of offensive missiles in exchange for an American pledge not to invade Cuba.

Comparison of the decision processes in 1914 and 1962 underscores the importance, in a crisis, of the ability to lengthen decision time. Although the weapons available to the protagonists of 1962 were of incalculably greater destructive capacity than those available to World War I combatants, those weapons also permitted a more flexible approach to strategic and diplomatic maneuvers. Most important, the policy makers were aware not only of the frightful costs of miscalculation, failures in communication, or panic, but also of the consequences of reducing options to war or total surrender. They appear not to have lost sight of the need to consider the consequences of their decisions for the adversary. Yet, the ability of American and Soviet leaders to avoid a nuclear Armageddon is no assurance that even great skill in crisis management will always yield a peaceful escape from war. As President Kennedy said some months later, referring to the missile crisis, "You can't have too many of those."

DETERRENCE STRATEGIES

It is a truism that no strategy or weapon system can ensure that adversaries will abstain from attack either out of aggressive intent or out of fear. This does not mean, however, that all military doctrines and weapons are equally credible and stable and will therefore contribute equally to national security and to the effectiveness of deterrence. Throughout the remainder of this chapter, we will use these two criteria—credibility and stability—to examine a number of issues relating to strategic doctrines and characteristics or weapons sytems: capability requirements; limited nuclear war; targeting policy; active defense (ABM system); civil defense; and arms control and disarmament. Because the primary purpose of military policy today is to influence the behavior of potential adversaries, our discussion will focus on weapons and strategies as instruments of influence. We will be less concerned with the problems of fighting a war—the ultimate form of punishment—than with the possible consequences of various strategic doctrines on the behavior of others. In short, our focus will be political rather than purely military.

Capability Requirements

Two related "rules" have generally dominated national security policy: the *para bellum* doctrine—"if you want peace, prepare for war"—and the premise that security is a direct function of military superiority vis-à-vis prospective enemies.

Whatever the merits of the *para bellum* doctrine (the frequency of wars prior to 1945 suggests that it may not be a reliable or sufficient guide in all situations), the almost irresistible conventional wisdom that argues that deterrence can be enhanced merely by piling up more and better weapons than the opponent can amass must be qualified in a number of respects.

INVULNERABILITY   An important element of stable deterrence is a mutual second-strike capacity. The speed, range, and destructive capacity of modern weapons may provide a potential attacker with the opportunity and the temptation to destroy the adversary's retaliatory capacity with a surprise attack. If a nation's leaders believe that a surprise attack will permit a quick victory without much likelihood of retaliation because the opponent's weapons can be destroyed before they are used, the latter's deterrent posture is hardly credible. Irrespective of the other attributes, weapons that are a tempting target for a first strike may prove to be no deterrent at all. The concentration of American naval power at Pearl Harbor in 1941 provided Japan with an irresistible temptation to try to gain its objectives with a sudden knockout blow, and the neatly arrayed aircraft on Egyptian airfields gave Israel an opportunity to ensure victory in the Six-Day War of 1967 within the first few hours. Thus, deterrent effect is a function not of *total* destructive capacity, but of reliable *weapons capable of surviving a surprise attack.*

Nor do vulnerable forces satisfy the requirement of stability, because, by failing to provide decision makers with the capacity to delay response, they require a finger to be kept on the trigger at all times. Knowledge that the opponent can launch a crippling surprise attack reduces decision time and increases pressure to launch a preemptive strike at the first signal (which may turn out to be false) that such an attack is imminent. When both nations' deterrent forces are vulnerable, the situation is even less stable, as neither side can afford to delay. Each may prefer to back off, but neither can be certain of not having its "rationality" exploited. A delay of hours, or even minutes, can make the difference between being able to retaliate and having one's military capabilities destroyed. Compressed decision time and the need for a "hair trigger" on retaliatory forces significantly increase the probabilities of accidental war.

Conversely, invulnerable strategic forces—those that cannot be eliminated, even by the most severe attack that the enemy can mount—may mitigate some of the more severe time pressures attending a crisis. Knowledge that one's forces are secure reduces the motive to "shoot first and ask questions later." The temptation to launch a first strike should diminish as the certainty and probable costs of devastating retaliation increase. Equally important, when retaliatory systems are invulnerable, the incentive to undertake a preemptive attack in the absence of complete information (as, for example, in case of a nuclear explosion of unknown origin) declines as the ability to delay response increases decision time.

Survival capability of deterrent forces can be enhanced by a number of methods. An *increase in numbers* can, at least temporarily, make it more difficult for the attacker to succeed in a first strike. This method is relatively crude, and it will be effective only if the adversary does not increase its forces proportionately. The search for numerical superiority may decrease vulnerability in the short run, but its long-term consequences are almost certain to be an arms race that leaves neither side more secure. *Dispersal of forces* at home and in overseas bases may also provide some protection, but this alternative becomes less attractive as delivery systems become more accurate and as the political costs of foreign bases increase. *"Hardening" retaliatory weapons* (such as land-based missiles) by placing them in underground silos, although relatively expensive, can provide adequate protection against all but a direct strike. Assuming a specified probable error in the accuracy of attacking missiles, hardening requires the attacker to expend more weapons on each target, thereby reducing the probability of a crippling first strike. Expectations that missiles in protected silos would prove to be the "ultimate" retaliatory weapons have proved mistaken, however, because reconnaissance satellites can find them and, even more importantly, because missile guidance systems have become increasingly accurate. Multiple independently targetable reentry vehicles (MIRVs) are so accurate that 50 percent of the warheads can be expected to land within a few hundred meters of the target. Research and development work on independently targetable warheads that can be maneuvered in flight (MARVs) may ultimately reduce that figure to 50 meters or less. Thus, although bigger warheads can threaten the invulnerability of retaliatory forces, the far more salient danger arises from the increasing accuracy of missile systems.[24] Placing retaliatory sources at the *maximum possible distance* from a potential enemy ensures their survival only as long as the gap in distance is not closed by longer-range delivery systems. A further measure of protection can be provided by *concealment,* but this method is already somewhat vulnerable to advances in the technology of detection. American U-2 flights over the Soviet Union proved that high-altitude photography can yield considerable intelligence information. Orbiting "spy" satellites have been even more effective than the U-2, without incurring any of the political costs of manned overflights. Finally, a nation may seek to protect its retaliatory forces by adopting a *fire-on-warning* policy. For reasons discussed above, however, doing so would create a highly unstable situation.

At present, the most reliable method of decreasing vulnerability is *mobility.* Missile-launching submarines have become major components of American and Soviet defense forces, and they are an important element in the British and French nuclear deterrent. Important characteristics of this weapon system are these: (1) it combines high mobility with the capabilities for dispersal, distance, and concealment; (2) unlike missile sites or air bases located near cities,

---

[24] According to the "cube root law," the blast effect increases only as the cube root of the increase in yield. Hence, an increase in accuracy will threaten protected targets much more than will an increase in explosive power. For this reason, it is somewhat misleading to assume a linear relationship between "throw weight" (payload capacity of missiles) and ability to threaten retaliatory forces. The "throw weight" controversy was triggered off by the 1974 Vladivostok interim agreement and intensified by the subsequent SALT II Treaty of 1979, both of which permitted the Soviet Union to keep 308 SS-18 multiple-warhead missiles.

it provides the enemy with no incentive to attack major population centers; (3) it does not require foreign bases; and (4) it may remain beyond striking distance of its targets (communicating reassurance), but it can rapidly be brought into firing position without losing its invulnerability.[25]

One point should be emphasized, however. The ability of the invulnerable deterrent forces to delay response may be a necessary, but is not a sufficient, factor to eliminate the incentives to strike first and to ensure crisis-stable deterrence. None of the nations in the 1914 crisis had the ability to unleash a rapid destructive blow, crippling the retaliatory capabilities of the adversary. But in the tense days preceding the outbreak of general war, decision makers in Berlin, St. Petersburg, Paris, and London increasingly attributed to their potential enemies both the *ability* and the *intent* to do so. The penalties for delay were perceived to be too high. The ability to delay response is therefore not likely to contribute to crisis management unless policy makers perceive that the risks of acting in haste are greater than those of using a strategy of delay and, equally important, unless they are willing to attribute the same preferences to the adversary's leadership.

FORCE LEVELS   The theory of a linear relationship between military capability and deterrent effect has been questioned as nuclear arsenals have reached the "overkill" range. Whether the capacity of nuclear weapons to destroy any existing society has tended to make national leaders more cautious in considering decisions that might precipitate a nuclear war has been neither proved nor disproved, but it is at least plausible; the proposition that the capacity to destroy any potential adversary or coalition of opponents five, ten, or 100 times over increases caution proportionately seems untenable. The case for overwhelming strategic superiority was more persuasive when delivery systems were limited to manned bombers, which are vulnerable to surprise attack. Sheer numerical superiority provided some short-run protection against a crippling and decisive first strike. But, as indicated above, greater protection at lower cost (politically and in stability) can be achieved by mobile invulnerable deterrent systems.

FLEXIBILITY   Perhaps the most serious limitation to the theory of a linear relationship between destructive capability and deterrent effect lies in the ability to deter aggression at many levels of intensity. One aspect of the issue has been discussed earlier—the credibility of threatening "massive retaliation" to deter limited aggression.

Before 1945, a single weapons system could generally be counted upon to perform multiple tasks. For example, a strong French army could be deployed

---

[25] Because submarine-launched ballistic missile forces are the most stable element of deterrence, any technological breakthrough in antisubmarine warfare capabilities that threatened their invulnerability would be highly destabilizing. A fuller discussion of this issue may be found in Stockholm International Peace Research Institute, *Tactical and Strategic Antisubmarine Warfare* (Stockholm, Sweden: Almqvist & Wiksell, 1974).

to defend the eastern frontiers against Germany; the same army could, with little modification, also pacify colonial areas. Similarly, the British navy could serve as an instrument for multiple goals—a deterrent against attack on the home island, protection of shipping and commerce, or destruction of an enemy fleet in war.

Whether nuclear arsenals are capable of serving multiple defense requirements is more open to question. For example, can the same weapons to be used to deter an attack against one's home territory, to dissuade adversaries from launching a limited war, and to prevent or cope with various types of limited threats?[26] During the years immediately after World War II, the deterrent function of nuclear weapons was assumed to be self-evident. The invasion of South Korea by Communist forces called this premise of the Truman administration into question. The defense policy of the Eisenhower administration placed considerable emphasis on the deterrent effectiveness of strategic weapons across a broad spectrum of situations. This line of reasoning underlay British defense policies of the 1950s, as well as those of France since the 1960s. Rejecting the "massive retaliation" doctrine of the Eisenhower administration in favor of a policy of "flexible response," Presidents Kennedy and Johnson actively sought to restore a balance between nuclear and conventional forces. With very indifferent success, they also attempted to persuade NATO allies in Europe to focus their resources on forces of the latter type. For fiscal and domestic political reasons, the Nixon and Ford administrations moved toward a reduction of ground forces and back toward greater reliance on the deterrent effects of strategic weapons. According to the "Nixon Doctrine," local forces are to provide the bulk of ground forces. Following the Iran hostage crisis and the Soviet invasion of Afghanistan, the Carter administration announced plans to enhance conventional forces. The Reagan administration is both increasing conventional forces and pressing NATO allies to follow suit.

Defense analysts have generally accepted the need for flexible forces. The credibility of a threatened nuclear response to limited provocation may be quite small and will diminish each time limited aggression goes unchallenged. A commitment to meet *every* provocation automatically with a massive nuclear response denies oneself the possibility for recalculating costs and gains with changed circumstances. Moreover, nuclear retaliation is of questionable validity, either militarily or morally, as a response to limited aggression.

The threat of strategic retaliation may well prove effective against an unambiguous attack against targets of high value. Soviet and American strategic forces have effectively deterred either one from launching a direct attack on the other (assuming that the motivation to do so may in fact have existed). But even in Europe, an area where American alliance commitments are presumably the most credible, the nuclear forces have proved inadequate to deter peri-

---

[26] This distinction between three levels of deterrence and its implications are developed in detail in George and Smoke, *Deterrence in American Foreign Policy.*

odic Soviet attempts to alter the status quo by coercive means—for example, in West Berlin. Nor has a combination of American strategic forces and alliance commitments been sufficient to deter limited probes in other areas or to deal with such issues as the hostages in Iran or the Soviet invasion of Afghanistan. Certainly the threat of nuclear retaliation must be regarded as of very limited utility in areas where frontiers are ambiguous; where the credibility of commitments to allies may be suspect; where regimes are unstable; where the difference between genuine domestic revolutionary movements, private armies of dissident domestic factions, and foreign guerrilla forces is often blurred; and where clandestine aid across frontiers is difficult to identify and even harder to prevent.

Finally, those who intend to challenge the status quo usually have various options for doing so. A defender unable to call upon responses other than strategic threats is unlikely to be successful. For example, even a virtual American monopoly of nuclear weapons in 1950 did not prevent the invasion of South Korea by Communist forces from the north. Once the invasion occurred, had a threat been made to devastate Moscow or Peking unless North Korean forces withdrew beyond the 38th parallel, it might well have been regarded as a bluff. To make the threat without carrying it out would reduce the future credibility of the stategic deterrent; to carry out the threat would have resulted in a major escalation of a limited war to an unlimited one. The American and United Nations response to the Korean invasion, a limited one relying on conventional forces, did not result in a complete victory; but it did restore the frontier between the two Koreas to approximately the pre-1950 position without escalation of the conflict geographically (fighting remained confined to the Korean peninsula as supply bases in Manchuria and Japan remained untouched) and militarily (both sides abstained from the use of nuclear weapons).[27]

One caveat is worth mentioning. A broad range of available capabilities is not an end in itself. Nor does it ensure that, from the wide spectrum of options it makes possible, choices will be made wisely. In 1954, some six months after Secretary of State Dulles's "massive retaliation" speech, the Eisenhower administration decided against intervention in Indochina, partly on the grounds that American conventional forces were insufficient for the task. In response to the logical and political shortcomings of massive retaliation—these had been recognized by Dulles less than four years after the 1954 speech—the Kennedy and Johnson administrations undertook a large buildup of conventional forces to redress existing imbalances. But the availability of multiple military options also made it possible to become committed, step by almost imperceptible step, to a tremendously costly and ultimately unsuccessful war in Vietnam. The value of flexible capabilities is thus no greater than the wisdom with which they are deployed.

[27] However, the unwise decision to pursue North Korean forces back across the 38th parallel did eventually result in expansion of the war, as Chinese armies entered the conflict in November 1950. As a result, the war developed into a bloody stalemate near the 38th parallel for two and a half years.

Another aspect of the relationship between weapons and influence has been identified by Thomas Schelling, who has distinguished between (1) *deterrence,* the ability to prohibit certain policies (negative influence) on the part of enemies; and (2) *compellance* or *coercive diplomacy,* the capacity to persuade the adversary to undertake specified actions (positive influence).[28] American strategic capabilities may have deterred the Soviet Union from overt large-scale aggression in Europe, but attempts to compel North Vietnam to cease supplying its forces in South Vietnam and those of the Viet Cong by bombing transportation routes indicate the difficulty of achieving this type of influence even with conventional weapons. Similarly, Israeli commando raids may deter some types of Arab behavior, but they have not been successful in compelling Arab leaders other than the late Anwar Sadat to negotiate face to face with Tel Aviv. Chinese and Soviet attacks on each other's frontier positions may serve some deterrent functions, but they are not an effective way of compelling the adversary to renounce ideological "heresies" or to acknowledge the other as the leading communist nation. In none of these cases is there reason to believe that threats to use nuclear weapons would enhance the prospects for successful coercion.

Deterrence to Protect Vital Interests at a Distance

Even if the threat of nuclear retaliation is sufficient to forestall an "out of the blue" attack against one's home territory, deterring threats to other vital interests, especially at a substantial distance, poses far greater problems; not the least of these is how to do so credibly without materially increasing the probabilities of escalation into a general war. The contemporary situation in the Middle East illustrates some of the difficulties. The area includes several vital Western interests, notably the security of Israel and access to the oil upon which many Western industrial economies—including France, West Germany, Italy, and Japan—are heavily dependent. The Nixon-Kissinger policy of arming and relying upon Iran to maintain stability in the region proved bankrupt when the Shah's regime in Teheran was replaced in 1978 by a fundamentalist Islamic one that had little interest either in serving Western interests or in preserving stability in the region. Fearing repetition of events in Iran, the Saudi Arabian ruling family is unwilling to take on the role of regional "policeman"; and, furthermore, it has linked its relations with the West to the Arab-Israeli conflict, including the issue of a homeland for the Palestinians. Complicating the problem is the fact that the Soviet Union has provided arms to several of the most radical regimes in the area, including Libya, Iraq, and Syria; moreover, it now has a modern "bluewater" navy able to operate in both the Mediterranean and the Indian Ocean, as well as allies in Ethiopia and North Yemen.

[28] Thomas C. Schelling, *Arms and Influence* (New Haven, Conn.: Yale University Press, 1966). See also Alexander L. George, David K. Hall, and William E. Simons, *The Limits of Coercive Diplomacy: Laos, Cuba, Vietnam* (Boston: Little, Brown, 1971).

In the wake of the Soviet invasion of Afghanistan, the Carter administration announced formation of a "rapid deployment force"; but even those who favor an American military presence in the Persian Gulf region question whether it can ever become effective, either as a credible deterrent or as a fighting force. Efforts to enlist NATO cooperation to secure oil routes have elicited a cool response from most Western European nations, including those most dependent upon oil imports. Moreover, Western allies were increasingly at odds on the Palestinian issue. Military bases may be acquired in the region, but not without some risks of increasing rather than ameliorating existing political instabilities. Finally, an expanded American naval presence in the Persian Gulf area may serve as a deterrent against efforts to disrupt oil-tanker traffic, as well as a "tripwire" against overt Soviet moves toward the oil fields. In the latter case, failure of deterrence might result in an escalation of conflict to the nuclear level, much as would the outbreak of war in central Europe.[29] Moreover, a limited western military presence, whether in the form of bases or an expanded naval task force, could not effectively prevent other threats to oil supplies— for example, an expanded Iran-Iraq war that results in the destruction of both nations' oil industries; sabotage of or guerrilla attacks against vulnerable oil facilities; or revolutionary activity against some of the conservative regimes in the region, notably in Saudi Arabia.

Targeting Policy

Considerable debate has been generated among strategists over the most appropriate target of threat. The debate has generally centered on the probable effects of threatening military targets (counterforce strategy) or population centers (countercity strategy). In assessing the merits of these doctrines, we can again apply our criteria of effectiveness; that is, what do these targeting strategies contribute to the credibility and stability of strategic deterrence?

Counterforce strategy received its first authoritative articulation in an address by Secretary of Defense Robert McNamara to the NATO meeting at Athens in 1962. It has since been given new emphasis by Defense Secretary James Schlesinger's statement of January 10, 1974, and by Presidential Directive 59, issued by the Carter administration in 1980. The stated intent of counterforce is to impress upon potential adversaries that, in the event of war, (1) their strategic striking forces would be destroyed; (2) they would thus suffer a military defeat; but (3) every effort would be made to minimize casualties among noncombatants. Another purpose is to reduce the damage should a nuclear war break out. Hence, a counterforce targeting policy is usually associated with the strategic doctrine of "damage limitation."

Counterforce strategy, according to its advocates, is a more credible deterrent than a countercity doctrine because an authoritarian regime places a

---

[29] NATO and Warsaw Treaty Organization forces have more than 6,000 tactical nuclear weapons—deliverable by aircraft, short-range missiles, and artillery—deployed in Europe.

higher value on its military forces than on the lives of its citizens. Thus, a threat to destroy its ability or will to wage war will prove more effective than a threat against other types of targets, including urban or industrial centers. Counterforce strategists further assert that should deterrence fail and a nuclear war actually break out, striking at the adversary's military targets rather than cities is the least immoral policy, not only because it minimizes the loss of civilian lives in an actual war, but also because it is the only policy short of pacifism that is consistent with the "just war" doctrine that noncombatants must not be held hostage. Such a targeting doctrine also gives the opponent an incentive to avoid cities, thereby potentially reducing loss of life on both sides. And even if enemy leaders are unwilling to spare population centers, their forces, which will have been reduced by a counterforce retaliation, will possess less capacity to strike at cities.

Critics of counterforce doctrines emphasize that the policy cannot be totally divorced from a number of first-strike implications. For example, a strike at the adversary's strategic weapons will clearly prove more effective if undertaken before those weapons have been launched. Although a decision to strike the enemy's cities may be delayed—as targets, their value does not decrease with time—the value of a strike against targets is highest before the enemy has launched any of its forces and is progressively reduced until all bombers or missiles have been launched. Both parties in a crisis will assess the situation in this manner; and each knows that the other is making the same calculations, thereby significantly heightening incentives for a first strike.

Counterforce strategy also serves as an impetus to both quantitative and qualitative arms races. The force level necessary for posing a credible threat to targets other than military ones (assuming that they are unprotected by an effective antiballistic missile system, a point we will examine in more detail later) is finite and relatively easy to calculate. As stationary targets incapable of concealment, cities and industrial sites provide the opponent's leaders with little incentive to increase their arms stockpiles indefinitely; nor do such "soft" targets provide much incentive for continually upgrading strategic forces by replacing older weapons with faster, larger, or more accurate ones. Hence, a countercity strategy, associated with a doctrine of "mutual assured destruction," is compatible with finite deterrent capabilities. On the other hand, a nation committed to a counterforce strategy has considerable reason to build up stockpiles; the greater one's strategic superiority, the greater the likelihood of an effective strike against military targets. The adversary's most predictable response will be to seek safety through (1) sheer numbers, by acquiring sufficient quantities of weapons to "ride out" the worst possible attack; (2) additional steps to protect existing weapons (for example, by deploying land-based missiles on mobile launchers); or—and most likely—(3) both quantitative and qualitative measures. The result of each response to the other side's moves will be an arms race.

An effective counterforce capability against protected strategic systems requires (1) overwhelming strategic superiority, (2) increasingly accurate intelligence and guidance systems to locate and pinpoint strikes against such targets,[30] and (3) command, control, communications, and intelligence (C³I) capabilities that will survive even in the midst of a nuclear war. Efforts toward achievement of this position will succeed only in the unlikely case that the adversary fails to increase his forces. By 1964, Secretary McNamara conceded that the value of striking at Soviet ICBM sites was "questionable" in the light of expected increases in Soviet missile-launching submarine forces. If, however, any country should achieve the ability to destroy the retaliatory capabilities of its potential enemies, the mutual deterrence system will become highly unstable. The latter may be tempted to launch a preventive attack, and the former, aware of the temptation, will have added incentive to unleash a preemptive strike.

If a counterforce strategy is to accomplish its objective of saving the maximum number of lives in case of a failure in deterrence, both sides must move their military targets as far as possible from urban population centers— that is, to take effective steps to deal with the "colocation problem." To assume that, under conditions of a major war, either side would spare military targets in order to save cities is to attribute to leaders of nations at war a degree of magnanimity rarely encountered even in less deadly circumstances. This requirement is virtually impossible to meet in densely populated areas such as Europe; even within the United States, many key military targets are located in or near major urban centers, although, in recent years, public pressures have at times been successful in requiring that military installations be placed away from cities and suburban areas.

Perhaps the most serious problem in counterforce strategy is that neither side believes the other will act with the necessary restraint. Secretary of Defense McNamara had expressed his belief that major population centers would be included as targets in any nuclear attack by the Soviet Union on the United States, and a Soviet spokesman has dismissed as not believable stated intentions to use "humane" methods of warfare that would spare Soviet cities.[31] The deployment of highly accurate missiles with multiple warheads—some 308 SS-18 missiles by the USSR, and the Minuteman II and Titan II missiles, as well as the controversial MX missile system by the United States—appears to be a major step toward acquiring the ability to destroy the other side's retaliatory capabilities. Although the Vladivostok interim agreement of 1974 and the subsequent SALT II Treaty limit each nation to 2,250 bombers and missiles, of which 1,320 can be armed with multiple warheads, it has by no means ensured that neither

---

[30] Submarine-launched ballistic missiles (SLBMs), in many respects the deterrent that comes closest to satisfying our criteria of credibility and stability, can be used only against cities, because the missiles are not at present sufficiently accurate to threaten missiles located in "hardened" underground silos. Missiles ultimately placed in the next generation of strike submarines—the Tridents—will have far greater accuracy.

[31] Kaufmann, *The McNamara Strategy* (New York: Harper & Row, 1964), p. 93; N. Talensky, "Antimissile Systems and Disarmament," *Bulletin of the Atomic Scientists*, 21 (February 1965), 26–29.

one can acquire sufficient "silo-busting" capabilities to threaten land-based missiles and perhaps to make a counterforce first strike a genuine or perceived threat. The failure of the SALT II Treaty to be ratified enhances the prospects for a costly arms race to acquire full counterforce capabilities.

The United States and the Soviet Union each have at most about 200 major population or industrial targets. Thus, even if several missiles are assigned to each such target, there will be a large surplus of deliverable weapons that is certain to be given counterforce missions. Thus, even in the unlikely event that the SALT II Treaty is ratified, it will almost certainly be used in both Moscow and Washington to justify an enormously expensive qualitative arms race.

At present, both the United States and the Soviet Union appear to have acquired the diversified nuclear arsenal for an "all-options" policy that would permit retaliatory strikes against both an adversary's cities and its military targets. It is not unlikely that this state of affairs has been brought about less by a calculated assessment of the arguments for and against the two strategic doctrines than by a process of bureaucratic politics in Washington and Moscow. That is, rather than making a hard choice between the counterforce and countercity viewpoints, both the United States and the USSR have reached a "compromise" by accepting both views—and acquiring the hardware necessary for both.

The debate over targeting doctrines amply illustrates the difficulties of trying to apply ethical criteria to questions of defense policy. Should war break out, any effort to spare lives as envisioned by advocates of counterforce is clearly desirable. But if adherence to such a targeting policy destabilizes deterrence through heightening the reciprocal fear of surprise attack, can claims of greater morality be sustained?[32]

Active Defense (Antiballistic Missile Systems)

A potentially significant component of deterrent capabilities is the ability to protect targets by destroying attacking airplanes or missiles before they reach their destination. Credibility is enhanced if, owing to an effective active defense system, the deterrer can threaten a potential aggressor with the knowledge that the costs of a counterstrike can be reduced if not eliminated.

Up to and during World War II, active defense could prove effective by inflicting only limited damage to the attacker. During the Battle of Britain in 1940, an attrition rate of 10 percent eventually forced the Luftwaffe to abandon its policy of attempting to bomb England into submission. In heavy Allied raids

---

[32] For thoughtful discussions of the relationship of ethics to strategy, see Theodore Roszak, "A Just War Analysis of Deterrence," *Ethics,* 73 (1963), 100–109; David B. Abernethy, "Morality and Armageddon," in *Public Policy,* eds. John D. Montgomery and Arthur Smithies, 13 (Cambridge, Mass.: Harvard University Press, 1964); Arthur Lee Burns, *Ethics and Deterrence: A Nuclear Balance without Hostage Cities,* Adelphi Paper No. 69 (London: Institute for Strategic Studies, 1970); and Michael Walzer, *Just and Unjust War* (New York: Basic Books, 1977).

on Schweinfurt during the summer and autumn of 1943, Germany's ability to down one-sixth and one-quarter of the attacking aircraft was a major victory for the defense.[33]

Intercontinental ballistic missiles armed with thermonuclear weapons have added substantially to the burdens of defense. Identification and destruction of a missile is a considerably more difficult task than that of downing even a supersonic bomber. A second problem is even more serious. The destructive capabilities of thermonuclear weapons and the size of existing stockpiles are such that even an attrition rate of 90 percent (which is currently regarded by virtually all the ablest scientific experts as impossible) cannot prevent utter devastation of most targets.

As a consequence, there is little likelihood that any ABM system can provide protection for cities, industrial sites, airfields, or other "soft" targets. The case for ABMs, then, rests on their ability to provide protection for retaliatory forces such as missiles in underground silos. Whereas the ability to destroy, for example, 50 percent of attacking missiles is totally inadequate to protect cities, such an attrition rate might be sufficient to deter a potential attacker from attempting a counterforce strike against retaliatory forces. But even in this more limited role, the case for ABMs is not unambiguous. The history of military technology suggests that advances in defensive weapons are usually superseded by developments in offensive capabilities. The ABM is not an exception. It is susceptible to penetration by means of decoys, multiple-warhead (MIRV) missiles, evasion by maneuverable (MARV) missiles, or nuclear blasts that render its complex radar systems ineffective.[34]

Finally, as a number of defense analysts have pointed out, ABMs tend to be more useful to the initiator of a nuclear exchange. Thus, their deployment has some first-strike implications that would tend to reinforce the adversary's disbelief about a declaratory second-strike policy.[35]

These difficulties have not, however, been sufficient to prevent deployment of ABM systems. The Soviet Union has installed sixty-four "Galosh" missile

[33] Hans J. Morgenthau, "The Four Paradoxes of Nuclear Strategy," *American Political Science Review,* 5 (1964), 123–35.

[34] Abram Chayes and Jerome B. Weisner, eds., *ABM: An Evaluation of the Decision to Deploy an Antiballistic Missile System* (New York: Harper & Row, 1969), pp. 17–24, 57–60. The case for ABMs is developed in D.G. Brennan and Johan J. Holst, *Ballistic Missile Defence: Two Views,* Adelphi Papers, No. 43 (London: Institute for Strategic Studies, 1967).

[35] There are a number of parallels in this respect between ABMs and civil defense programs. That is, both may save some lives in the case of war, but neither is without first-strike implications.

Except in periods of intense international crisis, such as during the Berlin crisis of 1961, civil defense programs have received relatively little attention in most countries. China appears to have the only large-scale civil defense system currently in existence. Mao Tse-tung's 1973 New Year's message extolled the Chinese people to "dig tunnels deeper, store grain everywhere and accept no hegemony." Harry Gelber, *Nuclear Weapons and Chinese Policy,* Adelphi Papers, No. 99 (London: International Institute of Strategic Studies, 1973), p. 16. Some American defense analysts have recently proposed that a major civil defense effort be undertaken, citing Soviet steps to protect populations and industries. But there is no consensus among western analysts on the magnitude of the Soviet civil defense effort, or even on the practical value of a shelter program.

launchers around Moscow, and a second ABM system has been placed around Leningrad. The American version of the ABM has had a checkered history. When Defense Secretary McNamara announced in 1967 that the Nike-Sentinel system would be deployed in fifteen sites, it was described as protection against the expected threat of Chinese ICBMs. Two years later, the Nixon administration declared that a more limited "Safeguard" system would serve to protect two Minutemen sites; it would also be a bargaining counter in arms-control negotiations with the USSR.

Vocal debates on the ABM issue abated in 1972 with the SALT I Treaty between the United States and the USSR. That agreement limited each nation to two ABM sites, and subsequently the United States chose not even to finish its one site in North Dakota. However, as offensive missiles have become more accurate, possibly threatening land-based retaliatory forces, ABM proponents have advocated new efforts in this direction, even if it means scrapping the SALT I Treaty. The Reagan administration is considering a new ABM program.

DOES DETERRENCE WORK?

If the yardstick is avoidance of a general nuclear war, then we could conclude that since 1945, deterrence has worked effectively. Despite some periods of great international tensions involving nations armed with nuclear weapons, none has attacked or been attacked. Even threats to do so have been avoided—perhaps the sole exception was the Soviet threat during the Suez crisis of 1956 to unleash an attack on France and Britain if they did not withdraw their forces from Egypt.

For several reasons, however, an unqualified positive judgment on deterrence does not seem warranted. First, although none of the major powers has undertaken an attack on another, we can only speculate about the reasons; we cannot prove conclusively that restraint has been the result of successful policies of strategic deterrence. Indeed, evidence that would prove the point is unlikely to be available at any time in the foreseeable future, if ever.

Second, the record since World War II demonstrates rather conclusively that efforts to deter probes, limited attacks, or even outright invasion of allies or client nations have often failed. Moreover, it is as a result of these failures that the international system has been wracked periodically by crises and conflicts—for example, the Korean War, the missile confrontation of 1962, repeated crises over the status of Berlin, battles along the frontier between China and the Soviet Union, and others. In these cases, possession of nuclear weapons probably instilled caution among decision makers and significantly raised the risks of employing highly provocative measures to compel the opponent to retreat or compromise during a crisis. But if a major function of nuclear arms is to prevent those types of moves that *begin* crises, then they can be judged, perhaps, as inadequate.

Finally, it is important to remember that deterrence is not a policy for all seasons. It is but one of many means by which national leaders can attempt to cope with the international environment and to influence other nations. Even during the height of the cold war, when the international system was marked by a tight bipolar configuration, efforts to stretch deterrence into an all-purpose policy were often less than successful. As the relatively simple structure of the cold-war international system undergoes modification—as the result of an increase in the number of nations, a breakdown of alliances, the growing importance of various types of non-national actors, diffusion of effective power, the salience of a broader range of issue areas, and the like—the effectiveness of policies that rely solely on the threat of military retaliation is almost certain to decline. That is not to say that deterrence will cease to be of importance in the relations between nations. Nor is it to argue that the ability to maintain "crisis-stable" deterrence has lost its importance; this is at least a necessary if not a sufficient condition for any meaningful steps toward halting or reversing the global arms race. It is only to state that an effective foreign policy will increasingly need to rely upon a creative mix of negative and positive means of influence. Nations that are able to do so not only will be serving better their national interests, they are also more likely to contribute to a more stable international system.

ARMS CONTROL
AND DISARMAMENT

Arms control and disarmament cannot be divorced from consideration of deterrence. Leaders responsible for national security are unlikely to exhibit much interest in the limitation of weapons if the outcome may reduce their deterrent capabilities. Motives not directly related to national security, such as a desire to reduce the burden on national budgets of military spending, have only rarely proved to be a sufficient incentive to produce lasting and effective disarmament measures. The protracted arms races prior to 1914 and 1939 and since 1945, as well as the example of many developing states that spend a vast proportion of their meager resources on military forces, suggest that purely economic motives will not arrest spiraling arms races. On the other hand, the fear of national, if not global, annihilation provides unprecedented incentives to stabilize deterrence by measures to reduce the fear of surprise attack, arrest the diffusion of nuclear weapons, minimize the probabilities and effects of technological breakthroughs, and diminish the likelihood of unintended war through accident or escalation.

Attempts to control or abolish the use of force are nearly as old as war itself, and they have taken the form of trying to limit both the ends sought through war and the instruments of violence. Included in the former category are the medieval concepts of the "just war," which implied that force could be used only for certain legitimate ends; the 1928 Kellogg-Briand Pact, outlawing the use of war; the Nuremberg war-crimes trials, in which the doctrine of "crimes against humanity" was used to punish top-ranking Nazi leaders; and the United Nations Charter, in which signatories renounced the use of force except in self-defense.

More modest attempts have been made to limit and control the instruments of violence. During the nineteenth century, a movement to "humanize" the conduct of war led to agreements at the Hague Conference of 1899 outlawing certain weapons, including expanding (dumdum) bullets. Delegates at the Washington Conference of 1922 sought to prevent renewal of a naval arms race by limiting capital ships of the five major naval powers—England, the United States, France, Japan, and Italy—according to the ratio of 5–5–3–1.75–1.75, respectively. Subsequent efforts during the interwar years to limit either naval or land forces were unsuccessful, and even the Washington Naval Convention failed to survive the arms race of the 1930s.

Since World War II, considerable activity on questions of arms control and disarmament has produced a number of multilateral agreements—a treaty demilitarizing the Antarctic (entered into force in 1961, ratified by nineteen nations); the Partial Test Ban Treaty (1963, 108 nations); prohibitions on the use of outer space (1967, seventy-four nations) and the sea bed (1972, sixty-two nations) for weapons of mass destruction; the Treaty of Tlatelolco, prohibiting nuclear weapons in Latin America (1967, twenty nations); the Nuclear Non-Proliferation Treaty (1970, 101 nations); and a convention prohibiting the development, production, and stockpiling of biological weapons (signed in 1972, seventy-three ratifications). In addition, since 1963 the United States and the Soviet Union have entered into several bilateral agreements on subjects ranging from the establishment of direct communications links (the "Hot Line" agreement of 1963) to limitations on ABM systems (1972) and ceilings on offensive strategic forces (1972 and 1974). Important as these achievements are, however, they have at best slowed down rather than reversed the global arms race. The 1974 Vladivostok interim agreement and the subsequent SALT II Treaty agreements between the United States and USSR actually permit a large increase in offensive delivery capabilities, and the fate of the latter treaty (as well as the entire SALT process) remains very much in doubt with the deterioration of *détente* in the later 1970s and early 1980s. Effectiveness of the Partial Test Ban Treaty is diminished by the boycott of two nuclear nations, China and France. Paris and Peking have also refused to ratify the Non-Proliferation Treaty, as have a number of important regional powers, including India, Israel, Pakistan, Spain, and South Africa.

The tendency to equate arms control with formal international agreements may, however, lead to overly pessimistic conclusions about the feasibility of placing limits on the procurement or deployment of arms. Self-imposed limits on violence are sometimes more enduring than those found in treaties and have even survived wars. Whether from fear of reprisal, military impracticality, or unwillingness to bear the onus for initiating its use, neither the Allies nor the Axis powers used poison gas during World War II. During the Korean war, both qualitative and geographical limitations were imposed on American and United Nations armed forces; despite considerable domestic pressure to bomb Manchuria, to unleash Chinese forces on Taiwan, and to use tactical nuclear weapons, these plans were firmly rejected by President Truman. Although the USSR provided North Korean forces with vast quantities of military aid, Soviet land forces were withheld from the war and American supply bases in Japan were not attacked.

Other types of self-imposed arms-control measures that have been practiced by the United States and the Soviet Union, in the absence of any formal agreement to do so, include (1) efforts, even prior to the 1970 treaty, to prevent the diffusion of nuclear weapons, although the cost has been high in alienating such important allies as France and China; (2) moratoria on nuclear tests for limited periods of time; (3) occasional reductions in military budgets;[36] and (4) restraint in deployment of certain types of weapons, such as orbiting thermonuclear bombs. Although such limitations pale in comparison to existing stockpiles, they nevertheless illustrate the point that not all efforts to control armaments require formal agreements.

Finally, informal and tacit cooperation on arms-control measures may take place. After an especially harrowing near-accident involving nuclear weapons in early 1961, American scientists developed a sophisticated safety system, the so-called permissive action links, which prevents nuclear weapons from being armed without a release from a responsible command center. The Kennedy administration deliberately alerted the Soviets to the concept and importance of the system at an academic arms-control symposium in late 1962, and the information necessary to build the safety devices was passed to Soviet scientists at the 1963 Pugwash Conference.[37]

Given the unquestionable importance of controlling international violence, why have efforts to control arms not yielded much more substantial results? Not the least of the reasons is the lack of agreement even on the roots of the problem: Are armaments the causes or the symptoms of international tensions? The answer is elusive, and the relationships of arms races to war can be debated. The arms race during the late nineteenth and early twentieth centuries probably contributed to the outbreak of World War I in 1914, but more vigilant French and British defense policies during the 1930s might have enabled them to deter the aggressive ambitions of German and Italian leaders. Moreover, arms have been and are among the most comprehensible instruments for making threats. In situations where objectives are incompatible and where the two sides are

---

[36] For example, in the fall of 1963, American officials announced a 4 percent reduction in defense spending; within weeks, Premier Khrushchev made a similar announcement with respect to the Soviet defense budget. Roswell Gilpatrick, "Our Defense Needs: The Long View," *Foreign Affairs*, 42 (1964), 370.

[37] Edward Klein and Robert Littell, "Shh! Let's Tell the Russians," *Newsweek*, May 5, 1969, pp. 46–47.

strongly committed to their objectives, they may not be able to influence each other's behavior through diplomatic persuasion or by offering rewards. In the absence of some central authority that can legislate peaceful change, states will always have to contemplate those situations in which intolerable demands are made or actions taken against them, and the only possibility of successful resistance lies in deterrence through the threat to retaliate. If arms are viewed not merely as instruments of destruction but as bargaining capabilities, manipulated in various ways to influence other states' behavior, we can better understand why Litvinov's admonition, "The only way to disarm is to disarm," appears deceptively simple. Thus, solution of tension-creating political issues might at least create an atmosphere in which weapons are seen as less necessary. But it is usually assumed that one can negotiate tension-reducing agreements only from a position of strength—that, to use Winston Churchill's words, one must "arm to parley." In this sense, arms can be viewed as symptoms of deeper tensions.

Even though arms can be used for creating bargaining positions, they can also contribute to international tensions, thereby reducing the probabilities of settling outstanding political issues. Decision makers tend to perceive the intent behind their own weapons programs as purely defensive but to infer aggressive intent from those of the adversary. Doubts about the purpose of the enemy's weapons are apt to be resolved on the "safe" side—that is, by assuming the worst ("Why else would they maintain such large arsenals?"). Thus, in high-tension situations, decision makers are unlikely to settle for mere parity in armaments. We cannot, however, assess the probable consequences of arms races merely by examining gross figures for defense spending. Competition to develop weapons of increasingly greater accuracy and capable of destabilizing deterrence is much more likely to raise international tensions, especially in times of crisis. But arms races that add to the invulnerability of one's own deterrent without threatening those of adversaries will be much less likely to do so.[38]

Decisions about levels of armaments are based on estimates of the adversary's current and expected future capabilities. These estimates may or may not be accurate; to the degree that they are incorrect, the error is likely to be in the direction of overestimating the capabilities of potential adversaries. Such misperceptions provide substantial fuel for arms races. One study revealed that military leaders invariably overestimated the military capabilities of potential enemies. In 1914, for example, although the French and Germans accurately calculated the capabilities of third powers, the Germans judged the French army to be larger than their own, whereas the French believed that their army was

---

[38] For this reason, mathematical studies of arms races based solely on gross expenditures (sometimes called "Richardson processes," after the British meteorologist who pioneered such analyses), however valid they may have been for earlier arms races such as that preceding World War I, may not be especially relevant for explaining or predicting the outbreak of war in the contemporary international system.

smaller than that of the Germans.[39] On the other hand, during the 1960s Secretary of Defense McNamara predicted that the USSR had "opted out" of the strategic arms race, settling for a position second to the United States, an assessment not borne out by events of the 1970s.

Further complicating the problem of arms control is the fact that the impetus for acquiring weapons may arise not only from external sources, such as the policies of adversaries or general international tensions. Technological developments may also create pressures for acquiring new weapons—for example, any scientific breakthrough that opens up possibilities for new applications or even for a change of strategic doctrine that is then used to justify acquisition and deployment of the weapons. And if there is no immediately obvious mission for the new weapons, there is always the clinching argument, "If we don't do it, they [the enemy] may." Thus, threats of a technological breakthrough by potential adversaries is a potent inhibitor of agreements that curtail weapons research and development activities. This fear, particularly important as time between generations of weapons has become shorter, was cited more often than any other by those opposing the Nuclear Test Ban Treaty of 1963.

In addition, decisions about defense policies are often as heavily influenced by bureaucratic and other internal political considerations as by the state of international politics. Competition between departments and services for a share of the defense budget may be almost as intense as the international rivalries attending an arms race. This point is illustrated by the removal from office of Soviet Premier Nikita Khrushchev in 1964. His refusal to give the armed forces—or as Khrushchev called them, the "metal-eaters"—all the resources they demanded was, according to many informed observers, the main reason for his ouster. In 1967, President Johnson faced various pressures from pro- and anti-ABM forces, as well as the prospect of being vulnerable to charges of permitting an "ABM gap" if he chose to run for reelection the following year. Johnson's decision to deploy a partial ABM system reflected a compromise that was more sensitive to domestic political realities than to the international strategic situation.[40] Consider also the Anglo-German naval rivalry during the early years of the twentieth century. This was a classic example of an arms race, because each nation was responding directly to the other's naval strength. But specific budget decisions did not reflect merely the increasing military capabilities of the opponent. Winston Churchill, then First Lord of the Admiralty, recalled one instance of bureaucratic disagreement: "In the end a curious and *characteristic solution* was reached. The Admiralty had demanded six ships; the economists offered four; and we finally compromised on eight."[41] No doubt similar episodes

[39] S.F. Huntington, "Arms Races," in *Public Policy, Yearbook of the Graduate School of Public Administration,* 1958, eds. Carl Friedrich and Seymour Harris (Cambridge, Mass.: Harvard University Press, 1958).

[40] Morton Halperin, *Bureaucratic Politics and Foreign Policy* (Washington, D.C.: The Brookings Institution, 1974), Chaps. 1 and 16.

[41] Winston S. Churchill, *The World Crisis: 1911–1914* (New York: Scribner's, 1928), p. 33. Italics added.

occur with regularity in defense ministries everywhere, irrespective of the nation's social, political, or economic system.

Nations may also acquire sophisticated weapons for other reasons, such as "prestige" or to maintain a regime in power. These motives do not, however, preclude the possibility that neighboring countries will then feel the need to follow suit, setting off a regional or local arms race. Nor are leaders of nations that arm themselves for these reasons necessarily more apt to show enthusiasm for arms-control agreements. It is scarcely conceivable that ruling groups in Libya, Ethiopia, Chile, Cuba, East Germany, Paraguay, Albania, and a great many other countries would welcome the prospect of governing without a powerful military.

Earlier we cited fears of surprise attack, technological breakthroughs, and diffusion of nuclear weapons as the primary incentives for stabilizing deterrence through arms control. Paradoxically, these fears are also among the most formidable barriers to arms-control agreements. Unlike the case with trade agreements—which are self-executing and in which violations are immediately apparent and are not likely to endanger national survival—doubts that the other parties are actually carrying out the agreements in good faith are hard to allay. Expecially in a cold-war situation, with a historical background of distrust and tensions, the tendency to expect the worst of others becomes deeply ingrained in the habits and expectations of decision makers. Even gestures that, if taken at face value, would be regarded as conciliatory tend to evoke suspicions of deceit. "Inherent bad-faith models" of the adversary are hard to erode; and although the threats may well be taken at face value, attempts to communicate reassurance, even through unilateral arms reduction, may be discounted. When Secretary of State Dulles was questioned in 1957 about the value for reducing world tensions of a Soviet plan to decrease unilaterally their armed forces by 1,200,000 men, he quickly invoked the theme of the bad faith of the Soviet leadership. He was asked, "Isn't it a fair conclusion from what you have said this morning that you would prefer to have the Soviet Union keep these men in their armed forces?" He replied, "Well, it's a fair conclusion that I would rather have them standing around doing guard duty than making atomic bombs."[42] Similarly, there is little indication that unilateral decisions of the Carter administration to cancel several major weapons programs—for example, the B-1 bomber and the "neutron bomb"—had any influence on Soviet defense policies. Suspicions of bad faith are by no means always unjustified, and each proven violation would not only add to the difficulties of achieving further arms-control agreements; it would also strengthen the hands of those in each nation who resist any limitations on weapons.

If a desire to arrest nuclear proliferation is an incentive for significant arms-control agreements, fear of nonsignatory nations may serve as a counter-

---

[42] John Foster Dulles, "Transcript of News Conference, May 15, 1956," U.S. Department of State, *Bulletin 34* (1956), pp. 884–85.

vailing force. While the United States and the Soviet Union shared a nuclear monopoly, agreements between them would have been influenced and constrained only to a limited extent by the demands and military capabilities of other nations. But the day that the United States and the USSR could impose arms limitations on the rest of the world has long since passed—if, indeed, it ever existed. As China, France, India, and other nations develop increasingly powerful conventional and nuclear capabilities, potential Soviet-American agreements are likely to be inhibited unless other nations can be induced to accept the same limitations. Moreover, as the diffusion of nuclear weapons accelerates, the problems of arms-control negotiations will become more complex. Identifying areas of mutual interest and converting these into acceptable arms-control formulas—difficult even in bilateral negotiations—is not apt to become easier as the number of nations directly involved increases and as the ability of alliance leaders to impose their wishes on junior members declines. China and France have already indicated an unwillingness to follow the lead of the Soviet Union and the United States on many issues involving weapons, and others may choose to follow their example. Indeed, it may be excessively optimistic to believe that the problem of nuclear proliferation is limited to nation-states. Even if security arrangements for every existing nuclear weapon were absolutely foolproof—and there are reports that this is far from the case—the possibility cannot be written off as wholly implausible that criminal gangs, terrorist groups, self-appointed "liberation movements," and other subnational groups could gain access to fissionable materials and the knowledge to assemble a bomb of some kind for purposes of blackmail.

A traditional obstacle to substantial arms-control agreements is the problem of verification. As weapons become more powerful and as the perceived ability of adversaries to alter the existing military balance in a short span of time increases, the need for verification by inspection or other methods also increases. Available evidence indicates that atmospheric and underwater tests can be detected without on-site inspection, but control of production creates more difficult problems, which, despite some ingenious proposals, are still likely to require the presence of inspection teams. Owing to orbiting satellites and other advances in the technology of surveillance, the problem of monitoring has tended to become a less potent obstacle in recent arms-control negotiations. Ironically, should future agreement result in significantly lower levels of armaments, concern over violations could be expected to increase; the smaller the arsenals, the greater the potential premium for cheating, and therefore the greater the fear that adversaries may be doing so.

A further obstacle to arms-control agreements is that of devising formulas that will not work to the disadvantage of any nation. Against a background of different perceived security requirements, *qualitatively* different weapons systems present a problem of comparability. How many bombers are equivalent to a battleship? How many infantry divisions are worth a missile-launching submarine or a squadron of jet aircraft? What is the deterrent value of an intermediate-range ballistic missile (IRBM) compared to that of an ICBM capable of reaching any spot on the globe? A piecemeal approach to disarmament—for example, starting first with nuclear weapons, then moving to conventional land forces—does not wholly resolve the problem. A substantial reduction of foreign bases, in which the Western powers presently enjoy a superiority, would strongly favor the Soviet Union. On the other hand, significant reduction in armored and infantry divisions, in most other conventional forces, or in missiles with the greatest "throw weight" (payload capacity) would favor the West.

Even a purely *quantitative* formula for reduction of a single type of weapon is likely to create controversy. Consider the case of nations A and B, which have stockpiles of 10,000 and 5,000 nuclear weapons respectively. An across-the-board reduction of 50 percent, although requiring nation A to scrap twice as many weapons, might be considered by nation B's leaders a method of perpetuating their inferiority. This may have been a factor in the Soviet rejection of the American "Baruch Plan," introduced in 1946, to create an international monopoly on atomic energy. The Soviets probably viewed the plan as a method to preclude any future Soviet nuclear program, while ensuring an American monopoly of atomic power through its domination of the United Nations and its agencies. To assert that even nation B's smaller stockpiles may be enough to destroy any adversary's society several times over—in short, that when nuclear stockpiles become large enough, "superiority" ceases to have much significance—may not be persuasive to those responsible for national security. These two stockpiles might also be reduced to the same absolute level. Again, whatever its "mathematical equity," such a formula is unlikely to gain enthusiastic support from nation A. A proposal to limit Soviet and American conventional ground forces to the same ceiling might be welcomed by Americans, but the Soviets—unwilling to withdraw their armies from Eastern Europe and faced with perceived requirements for troops deployed along the long frontier with China—would be likely to reject the plan. Although the SALT II Treaty failed to reduce existing arsenals, it did achieve a breakthrough in the problem of defining equivalents between strategic weapons. The formula treats all long-range bombers and ICBMs as equal. Because it avoids complexities, this formula may enhance the prospects for future agreements.

A final factor tending to inhibit arms-control agreements is that arms races and arms control may appear to involve different types of risk. Probably few foreign-policy leaders are unaware that protracted arms races entail a danger of war, but this is at least a familiar risk. On the other hand, dangers associated with disarmament measures are much less familiar and may therefore appear more threatening. Thus, the acquisition of stable deterrent forces is probably a necessary, if not a sufficient, condition for significant reduction of arms. Only when finite deterrent forces are perceived capable of providing adequate security and when arms races and the proliferation of nuclear weapons are perceived to be a greater threat to security than the reduction of arms, are significant steps toward disarmament likely. But even at that point, disarmament efforts must proceed within the context of deterrence. Only arms control or disarmament measures that contribute to heightened confidence in deterrence are likely to gain much support among most nations. Conversely, only under conditions of stable deterrence are there likely to be genuine advances in reversing the global arms race. Unfortunately, recent technological developments that are increasing the accuracy of missile guidance systems, as well as weapon procurement policies of the major powers, do not offer much cause for optimism on this score.

SUMMARY

Weapons have traditionally been used by independent political units to help defend their interests and values when threatened from abroad or to achieve expansionist goals. By their conspicuous deployment or display, they are also used to make diplomatic threats credible in bargaining situations. Unlike conventional military forces, however, nuclear weapons are of no utility in achieving such objectives as defeating a guerrilla movement, controlling strategic waterways, occupying territory, intervening to save a foreign government from internal rebellion, or ensuring supplies of foreign oil. Their main value lies in deterrence, or the capacity to prevent major provocations or massive attack by enemies. Even in this limited area of influence between nations, weapons policies and deployment must be carefully planned, because effective deterrence depends upon credibility. Piling up weapons will not by itself establish credibility if the forces are vulnerable to destruction in a first strike. Various measures such as dispersal, concealment, or protection have been used to lower vulnerability, but none has been totally successful. Defense policy leaders must also consider the consequences of their actions on the policies of their adversaries. Actions that seemingly increase security may, in fact, appear provocative to potential enemies and lead to greater instability or uncontrolled arms races. Arms control, civil defense, and active defense policies also have implications for the complex equations that create both stability and credibility.

SELECTED BIBLIOGRAPHY

ALLISON, GRAHAM T., *Essence of Decision: Explaining the Cuban Missile Crisis.* Boston: Little, Brown, 1971.

ARON, RAYMOND, *The Great Debate: Theories of Nuclear Strategy.* Garden City, N.Y.: Doubleday, 1965.

BARRINGER, RICHARD E., *War: Patterns of Conflict.* Cambridge, Mass.: MIT Press, 1972.

BRODIE, BERNARD, ed., *The Absolute Weapon: Atomic Power and World Order.* New York: Harcourt, Brace and Co., 1946.

BRODIE, BERNARD, *Strategy in the Missile Age.* Princeton, N.J.: Princeton University Press, 1959.

———, *War and Politics.* New York: Macmillian, 1973.

BUCHAN, ALASTAIR F., *War in Modern Society.* London: Watts, 1966.

DIESING, PAUL and GLENN H. SNYDER, *Conflict Among Nations: Bargaining, Decision Making and System Structure in International Crises.* Princeton, N.J.: Princeton University Press, 1977.

GEORGE, ALEXANDER L., DAVID K. HALL, and WILLIAM E. SIMONS, *The Limits of Coercive Diplomacy: Laos, Cuba, Vietnam.* Boston: Little, Brown, 1971.

GEORGE, ALEXANDER L., and RICHARD SMOKE, *Deterrence in American Foreign Policy: Theory and Practice.* New York: Columbia University Press, 1974.

GREEN, PHILIP, *Deadly Logic.* New York: Schocken Books, 1968.

HOFFMANN, STANLEY, *The State of War.* New York: Praeger, 1965.

HOLSTI, OLE R., *Crisis, Escalation, War.* Montreal and London: McGill-Queens' University Press, 1972.

HOWARD, MICHAEL, *War and the Liberal Conscience.* New Brunswick, N.J.: Rutgers University Press, 1978.

HUCK, ARTHUR, *The Security of China: Chinese Approaches to Problems of War.* New York: Columbia University Press, 1970.

HUNTINGTON, SAMUEL, *The Common Defense.* New York: Columbia University Press, 1961.

International Institute for Strategic Studies, *Adelphi Papers.* London: I.I.S.S. Bimonthly.

———, *The Military Balance.* London: I.I.S.S. Annual.

———, *Strategic Survey.* London: I.I.S.S. Annual.

International Security. Quarterly.

KAHAN, JEROME, *Security in the Nuclear Age.* Washington, D.C.: The Brookings Institution, 1975.

KAHN, HERMAN, *On Escalation: Metaphors and Scenarios.* New York: Praeger, 1965.

———, *On Thermonuclear War.* Princeton, N.J.: Princeton University Press, 1960.

KOLKOWICZ, ROMAN, et al., *The Soviet Union and Arms Control: A Superpower Dilemma.* Baltimore: Johns Hopkins Press, 1970.

LEGAULT, ALBERT, and GEORGE LINDSEY, *The Dynamics of the Nuclear Balance,* Ithaca, N.Y.: Cornell University Press, 1974.

LONG, FRANKLIN A., and GEORGE W. RATHJENS, eds., *Arms, Defense Policy, and Arms Control.* New York: Norton, 1976.

MORGAN, PATRICK, *Deterrence: A Conceptual Analysis.* Beverly Hills: Sage, 1977.

MORGENTHAU, HANS J., "The Four Paradoxes of Nuclear Strategy," *American Political Science Review,* 58 (1964), 123–35.

NORTHEDGE, FRED S., *The Use of Force in International Relations.* New York: Free Press, 1974.

OSGOOD, ROBERT E., *Limited War Revisited.* Boulder, Colorado: Westview, 1979.

OSGOOD, ROBERT E. and ROBERT W. TUCKER, *Force, Order and Justice.* Baltimore: Johns Hopkins Press, 1967.

PFALTZGRAFF, ROBERT L., JR., *Contrasting Approaches to Strategic Arms Control.* Lexington, Mass.: Heath, 1975.

QUESTER, GEORGE H., *Deterrence before Hiroshima.* New York: John Wiley, 1966.

———, *Nuclear Diplomacy: The First Twenty-Five Years.* New York: The Dunellen Company, Inc., 1970.

———, *The Politics of Nuclear Proliferation.* Baltimore: Johns Hopkins Press, 1973.

ROPP, THEODORE, *War in the Modern World.* Durham, N.C.: Duke University Press, 1959.

SCHELLING, THOMAS C., *Arms and Influence.* New Haven, Conn.: Yale University Press, 1966.

———, *The Strategy of Conflict.* Cambridge, Mass.: Harvard University Press, 1960.

SINGER, J. DAVID and MELVIN SMALL, *The Wages of War, 1816–1965.* New York: John Wiley, 1972.

SMOKE, RICHARD, *War: Controlling Escalation.* Cambridge, Mass.: Harvard University Press, 1977.

SOKOLOVSKII, V.D., *Soviet Military Strategy,* trans. Herbert S. Dinerstein, Leon Goure, and Thomas W. Wolfe. Englewood Cliffs, N.J.: Prentice-Hall, 1963.

Stockholm International Peace Research Institute, *SIPRI Yearbook of World Armaments and Disarmament.* Stockholm, Sweden: Almqvist & Wiksell, annual.

WALTZ, KENNETH, *Man, the State and War: A Theoretical Analysis.* New York: Columbia University Press, 1959.

WALZER, MICHAEL, *Just and Unjust War.* New York: Basic Books, 1977.

WRIGHT, QUINCY, *A Study of War,* 2 vols. Chicago: University of Chicago Press, 1942.

YOUNG, ORAN, *The Politics of Force.* Princeton, N.J.: Princeton University Press, 1968.

PART IV

Explanations of Foreign-Policy Outputs

12

Explanations of Foreign-Policy Outputs

The previous sections have been primarily descriptive. They have elaborated on the various types of international systems that political units have operated in, on sources of change in those systems, and on the various types of foreign-policy outputs of modern states, ranging from general orientations to specific actions undertaken through diplomacy, propaganda, subversion, and the like. Occasionally we have used a *type* of explanation to show under what conditions certain actions would probably succeed or fail. Part IV of the book attempts more formal explanation; the question is not so much *how* governments and policy makers act, but *why* they act in certain ways. The focus is on foreign policy, particularly on isolating the factors that go into the making of foreign-policy decisions. State actions, such as those discussed in the preceding Part, refer primarily to the execution or implementation of policy. This Part looks at the antecedent condition, the decisions and commands that initiate actions. We will be concerned with the manner in and the conditions under which psychological, bureaucratic, social, systemic, ethical, and legal factors are relevant to policy making.

Efforts to explain foreign policies in all their modes have never been very satisfactory, in part because analyses seldom spell out precisely which aspects of foreign policy need explanation. In the older forms of theoretical determinism—for example, that authoritarian states are militaristic or that democracies are pacific—we are told what the independent variable is (authoritarian or democratic states) but seldom informed about the type of behavior that is to be explained. What does it mean, in terms of the concepts used in this study, that a democratic state is "pacific"? Does the term suggest that such a state avoids forming alliances? Or that its national role conceptions tend toward the passive? Or that in its objectives, it merely seeks security? Or that in its actions, it always avoids threats? In brief, what sorts of foreign-policy outputs should be explained? The meaning of the term "foreign policy" is itself by no means self-evident; hence, we distinguish here orientations from roles, and objectives from decisions and actions.

A second problem in the more traditional studies of foreign policy was their emphasis on single-factor explanations. Thus, for example, it was often claimed that geographic location determined a nation's foreign policy. In recent years, however, scholars have come to appreciate that explanations of foreign policy (no matter how that term is defined) must take into consideration many independent variables. Because there are so many kinds of states, with such diverse socioeconomic characteristics, geographic locations, and types of leadership, it is very difficult to make any firm generalizations about the sources of foreign conduct. Nevertheless, both case studies and explorations using data from many countries over periods of time have appeared with greater frequency, so that today we are in a position to advance at least some tentative generalizations. These, however, refer more to the specific aspects of foreign policy, such as decisions and actions, than to broader types of outputs, such as orientations and roles. Consequently, we will first explore briefly some hypothesized sources or causes of orientations and national roles and then provide a more extensive analysis of the factors that have been used in recent research to explain decisions and actions in foreign policy.

SOURCES OF FOREIGN POLICY: ORIENTATIONS AND ROLES

The structure of the international system is a basic condition affecting the orientations of states. The several historical examples provided in Chapter 2 illustrate the fate of states in various types of systems: In the hierarchical system, submission and dependence are the main orientations; in the polar system, states that seek security through isolation or nonalignment generally fail. They are reduced to vassal states by bloc leaders, or, in some cases, they are simply destroyed and incorporated into the territory of bloc or alliance leaders. For instance, in the polar structure of the Greek system, the smaller allies of Athens and Sparta had few alternatives in their foreign-policy orientations. They had to be faithful allies and pay tributes of taxes and armed forces or face occupation by the bloc leaders. In general we can conclude that the orientations of most states in a bloc, multibloc, or hierarchical system are determined by the interests of the superior powers. Put in the form of a hypothesis, *the more cohesive a polar or hierarchical system, the less latitude of choice or freedom of action remains for the weaker members of the system; likewise, opportunities for changing orientations and roles are limited.* Orientations are determined by the general distribution of power in the system and by the needs and interests of the major actors.

In the diffuse system, where power is distributed widely among the members, orientations may be explained better by the presence or absence of specific threats, geographic location, and internal needs, as well as other factors discussed later in this chapter. Alliances can be explained best by a common perception of threat by two or more states, although common values and ideologies at least help to maintain cohesiveness in the alliance. National needs (apart from security) and geographic location have not been shown to be important conditions underlying decisions to make military alliances. Some have been organized to provide security against *internal* threats; but even in this case, all the parties to the coalition perceive the internal threat in one state to be a threat to their own interests as well.

Explanations of nonalignment are often cast in terms of internal political needs of new regimes, particularly in those states beset by ethnic, religious, and language divisions or by a history of colonial occupation. It has often been asserted that nonalignment is adopted as a means of providing one's independence and giving an outlet for nationalism. However, some of the more traditional nonaligned states, such as Switzerland and Finland, cannot be understood in terms of domestic political needs. Rather, their orientations can be explained better by reference to geographic location (Finland as bordering the Soviet Union), traditional policies (Switzerland's neutrality has been established since 1815), and narrower calculations of the best ways to meet specific problems related to national security. Perception of threat is certainly not a sufficient condition to explain nonalignment or isolation. Some states choose these orientations as a means of coping with external dangers, but there are many nonaligned states today that have no particular security problem.

It should be apparent that these generalizations are not satisfactory from an empirical point of view. Aside from the effect of threats on alliance orientations or the impact of bloc or hierarchical structures on orientations in general, we cannot claim with any degree of accuracy that condition A leads to orientation B. The research that would allow such statements to be made has not yet been undertaken. More important, it is virtually impossible to weigh the *relative impact* of the various systemic or national conditions in explaining any particular orientation. In any given case, all the factors might be relevant, but there is as yet no precise way to measure *how important* each of them is.

High-level policy makers divulge at least some of the sources of national role conceptions. They define their governments' ongoing tasks and functions in the international system or within regions, and, in so doing, they occasionally point out *why* their country should fulfill these roles. In one obvious case, Charles de Gaulle often claimed that France's role of regional leader within Europe was to be understood in terms of the traditional position of that country on the continent. The main source of the role conception was a notion of traditional

Table 12-1 Sources of National Role Conceptions

ROLE CONCEPTION	SOURCES
Bastion of revolution, liberator	Ideological principles; anticolonial attitudes; desire for ethnic unity
Regional leader	Superior capabilities; traditional position in region
Regional protector	Perception of threat; geographic location; traditional position; needs of threatened states
Active independent	Fear that "bloc" conflicts will spread; need to develop trade with all countries; geographic location
Liberator supporter	Anticolonial attitudes; ideological principles
Anti-imperialist agent	Perception of threat; anticolonial attitudes in public opinion; ideological principles
Defender of the faith	Perceptions of threat; ideological principles; traditional national role
Mediator-integrator	Geographic location; traditional role; cultural-ethnic composition of state; traditional noninvolvement in conflicts
Regional collaborator	Economic needs; sense of "belonging" to a region; common political-ideological, cultural traditions with other states; geographic location
Developer	Humanitarian concern; anticipated consequences of development "gap"; superior economic capabilities
Bridge	Geographic location; multiethnic composition of state
Faithful ally	Perception of threat; weak capabilities; traditional policy; ideological compatibility
Example	No sources revealed
Protectee	Perception of threat; weak capabilities

responsibilities of leadership—at least as defined by de Gaulle. In other cases, the presence of certain role conceptions could be explained by such conditions as perceptions of threat, weak or strong capabilities, traditional roles, economic needs, and the like. Table 12–1 lists the sixteen national role conceptions found in recent policy statements of government leaders and some of the factors that were cited in these statements as reasons why the roles were adopted.[1]

If we aggregate these sources, three general types of explanatory variables emerge. National roles can be explained by reference to (1) external conditions, (2) national attributes, and (3) ideological or attitudinal attributes. Table 12–2 displays the individual sources according to these three general categories.

Research that would measure the relative importance of these sources of national role conceptions has not yet been undertaken. In the absence of reasonably precise studies covering many states over a considerable period of time, one cannot make formal casual statements. However, a few impressions can be offered. First, some of the very active roles, such as bastion of the revolution or antiimperialist agent, are strongly linked to ideologies; the governments concerned see themselves as having certain international responsibilities deriving

[1] Table 12–1 is reprinted, with amendments, from K.J. Holsti, "National Role Conceptions in the Study of Foreign Policy," *International Studies Quarterly*, Vol. 14, No. 3, pp. 296–297, copyright © 1970 by Wayne State University Press, with permission of Sage Publications, Inc.

Table 12–2 Types of Variables Linked to National Role Conceptions

GENERAL VARIABLE	INDIVIDUAL SOURCES
1. External conditions	1. Perceptions of threat
	2. Major shifts in conditions abroad
2. National attributes	1. Weak or strong capabilities
	2. Public opinion and attitudes
	3. Economic needs
	4. Ethnic composition of state
3. Ideological and attitudinal attributes	1. Traditional policies or roles
	2. Public opinion and attitudes
	3. Humanitarian concerns
	4. Ideological principles
	5. Identification with region; compatibility of values with other states

from ideological imperatives. An obvious case would be the Soviet Union. The duty to provide moral, propagandist, and physical support for revolutionary movements is clearly spelled out in terms of the internationalist ethic of communism. Roles such as faithful ally and regional protector are strongly linked to common perceptions of threat.

The reader should keep in mind the three general kinds of variable outlined above. Very similar types of variable can be employed in examining explanations for objectives, decisions, and actions.

EXPLANATIONS OF OBJECTIVES, DECISIONS, AND ACTIONS

Moving from the more general types of foreign-policy outputs to the more specific, we must outline the internal and external conditions that can be linked to objectives, decisions, and actions. It can be argued, of course, that these outputs will normally be consistent with orientations and roles. We could predict, for instance, that a government that often refers to its special responsibilities as a regional leader would take various actions to fulfill this role. It could hold conferences, donate aid to regional partners, provide them with military forces, or generally attempt to dominate the weaker states' diplomacy and perhaps their economic life. Similarly, a government that sees itself as an agent of regional integration would probably undertake various actions aimed at increasing regional cooperation. However, roles and orientations by themselves do not necessarily *determine* objectives, decisions, or actions. In Chapter 10, we noted that although the Chinese frequently give assistance to revolutionary movements around the world, they have often refrained from active involvement where such action might create difficulties for their diplomacy. In other words, where there is conflict between immediate "national" interests and the duties deriving from national role conceptions, the former may very well prevail. Also, some governments enunciate inconsistent national roles. In one set of relationships, such a government may portray itself as a faithful ally, while in a broader context it might see itself as a mediator. To the extent that a government has military obligations abroad, normally it would not be a very good candidate for undertaking mediating tasks.

Three other reasons underline the need to explore the kinds of variables that influence objectives, decisions, and actions. First, a significant amount of research has explored the making of decisions in crisis situations. Indeed, we know considerably more about the circumstances surrounding crisis and the typical behavior of decision makers in a crisis than we do about roles or orientations. Where there are rapidly unfolding events in the international environment, furthermore, role conceptions can be notoriously irrelevant to the decisions made and the actions taken. Responding to the diplomatic chaos resulting from Hitler's assault on his neighbors, for example, the Soviet government was quite willing to conclude a nonaggression treaty with Germany, thus completely contradicting its well-established self-portrayal as a prime anti-Nazi agent.

Second, a large part of foreign policy refers to day-to-day problem solving that is essentially unrelated to role conceptions and orientations. A decision to vote a certain way on a resolution at a conference on the law of the sea does not seem related in any way to the role conceptions or orientations outlined previously.

Finally, it can be demonstrated that two states with similar role conceptions will not make the same decisions or take the same action when confronted with similar stimuli. Finland's orientation of nonalignment has been followed by active participation in trade and cultural relations with all European states, whereas Burma's similar orientation has led to avoidance of such involvement with states in Southeast Asia.

The starting point for an analysis of the sources of objectives, decisions, and actions is the view that all these outputs are the result of deliberate choices made by government officials. To explain or understand these outputs, then, we must examine the perceptions, images, attitudes, values, and beliefs of those who are responsible for formulating objectives and ordering actions. We may combine the diverse factors that affect choice of objective, decision, or action under the term "definition of the situation."[2] The definition of the situation would include all external and domestic, historical and contemporary conditions that policy makers consider relevant to any given foreign-policy problem. These might include important events abroad, domestic political needs, social values or ideological imperatives, state of public opinion, availability of capabilities, degree of threat or opportunity perceived in a situation, predicted consequences

---

[2] This concept is introduced and discussed in Richard C. Snyder, H. W. Bruck, and Burton Sapin, eds., *Foreign Policy Decision Making* (New York: Free Press, 1962), pp. 65–68, 80–85. For an application of the concept, see the article by Snyder and Glenn Paige entitled "The United States Decision to Resist Aggression in Korea," in *ibid.*, esp. pp. 239–46.

and costs of proposed courses of action, and the time element or "requiredness" of a situation. It is difficult to generalize about which factors are most important in each situation, since policy makers seldom draw up careful lists assessing the relative weight of each component of the definition of the situation. But for analytical purposes, we can break down the components of any definition of a situation and examine those conditions in the external and domestic environments that are *usually* considered relevant in formulation of objectives and actions.

In this chapter, we will reverse the levels of analysis, starting with individual policy makers, working our way through various societal and national attributes, and ending with events and conditions in the international system. The following discussion will try to demonstrate actual or hypothetical links between objectives and actions (the dependent variables) and (1) the images, values, beliefs, personality characteristics, and political needs of those individuals responsible for establishing goals, priorities among them, and actions needed to achieve them; (2) domestic structures—the influence of bureaucracies, national needs, and attributes; and (3) events and conditions in the external environment. Some other components particularly relevant to policy making, such as perceptions of threat, degree of urgency, and perceptions of alternatives, were already considered in Chapter 11, where policy making in crisis situations was discussed.

IMAGES, ATTITUDES, VALUES, BELIEFS, AND PERSONAL NEEDS AS COMPONENTS OF A DEFINITION OF THE SITUATION

Despite frequent rhetoric to the effect that they have "no choice" but to take certain action, policy makers are confronted with situations abroad and demands by other states that permit many alternative responses, including acquiescence, inaction, threats, or commission of various acts of punishment. When prime ministers say they have been "compelled" to do something, they mean only that they have rejected other alternatives. There is always an element of choice in policy making. In situations perceived as containing only slight threat, will different people in different historical and cultural circumstances behave the same way? Probably not, since so many factors other than immediate stimulus may be considered relevant.

Images

Any delineation of objectives, choice among courses of action, or response to a situation in the environment may be explained partly in terms of policy makers' perceptions of reality. People act and react according to their *images* of the environment. In policy making, the state of the environment does not matter so much as what government officials believe that state to be. By image, we mean individuals' *perceptions* of an object, fact, or condition; their *evaluation* of that object, fact, or condition in terms of its goodness or badness, friendliness or hostility, or value; and the *meaning* ascribed to, or deduced from, that object, fact, or condition. Consider a trained fishing expert and the city-bred novice with no previous experience. The expert can deduce valid conclusions about fishing conditions from a variety of facts, conditions, or "clues," such as water temperature, depth, or color, weather, and time of day. The novice, in spite of seeing the water, feeling its temperature, and knowing it is late afternoon, is unable to draw any paticular conclusions from these indicators because by themselves they have no meaning in terms of past experience. Because they see and interpret the same conditions or facts in different ways (in the case of the novice, hardly interpreted at all), the two will react and behave differently. Experts will go where the fish are and work their tackles in such a way as to catch them. Barring beginner's luck, novices will struggle up and down a stream, flail the water with an assortment of useless lures, scare the fish, and catch nothing. Similarly in foreign policy, different policy makers can read different meanings into a situation; and because they characterize a situation differently and deduce different conclusions from it, they will behave differently. In particular, complex situations involving many interests, historical, economic, or social factors, and value positions are likely to be perceived differently.

Even the most well-informed experts in a policy-making agency cannot know *all* the relevant factors in a situation; their images of reality will always be different from reality. The discrepancy between image and reality is partly a result of physical impediments to the flow of information owing to lack of time, faulty communications, censorship, or lack of competent advisors or intelligence sources. It is also a problem of the distortion of reality caused by attitudes, values, beliefs, or faulty expectations. Individuals are bombarded constantly by messages about the environment; but they select and interpret only a fraction of what they "see," because only a part of it may be relevant to a particular situation. Sometimes people also "see" only information that conforms to their values, beliefs, or expectations. There are both physical and psychological factors that can distort the information upon which policy makers' images of reality are based.

If policy makers rely on faulty information, misinterpret cues, twist the meaning of messages to fit their own preferences, or disregard information that contradicts their values and preferences, their psychological environment— upon which they will act—is quite different from the physical environment—in which their policies have to be executed. The distinction between psychological environment or definition of the situation and physical environment or "reality" must be kept in mind in all analyses of foreign policy. One can readily see the distinction in the case of the attack on Pearl Harbor. In early December 1941, President Roosevelt and American diplomats were attempting to arrange high-level negotiations with the Japanese government to resolve some issues separating the two countries. At this time, American officials had predicted an impending military attack by the Japanese, but they expected it to occur somewhere in Southeast Asia. They could not imagine a direct attack on the American fleet at Pearl Harbor and so took no precautionary measures; they had facts about impending Japanese military actions but could not deduce or predict the correct "meaning" from those facts. The American definition of the situation was thus at odds with reality, and actions designed to cope with the expected Japanese moves were ineffective.

This example illustrates the problem of discrepancies between images and physical environment that arise from faulty or inadequate information and unwarranted expectations.[3] But how do we account for differing interpretations and characterizations of reality when easily verifiable facts are available? Here, the problem of attitudes, values, beliefs, doctrines, and analogies becomes important, for they help determine the meanings ascribed to a set of facts about internal and external conditions. Although distinctions among the concepts of attitude, value, belief, and doctrines are not always clear, they can be defined as follows for the analysis of foreign-policy making.

Attitudes

Attitudes can be conceived as general evaluative propositions about some object, fact, or condition: more or less friendly, desirable, dangerous, or hostile. In any international relationship, policy makers operate—usually implicitly—within some framework of evaluative assumptions of hostility or friendship, trust or distrust, and fear or confidence toward other governments and peoples. These attitudes may have important effects on how policy makers react to the actions, signals, and demands of other states, perceive the intentions of other governments, and define their own objectives toward others. If a Swiss military airplane crosses over the French frontier, we would not expect French officials to behave the same way as if a Soviet military aircraft unexpectedly flew over Paris. Attitudes of hostility and suspicion would probably become operative immediately upon identification of the Soviet aircraft, but not in the Swiss border violation. In the former case, there would probably be serious apprehension about the intention of the Russian action. Similarly, if a high-level policy maker receives a conciliatory message from the government of a state he perceives to be hostile, his attitudes of distrust and hostility may lead him to interpret the message in a different manner than if he had received even a less conciliatory message from the leader of a nonhostile state. Threats that are only potential may be viewed as actual because hostile attitudes predispose policy makers to distort the evidence. Particularly where evidence of intention is ambiguous, policy makers may fall back upon traditional attitudes of distrust and hostility. Intelligence agencies can learn a great deal about the capabilities of states, but policy makers

---

[3] See the careful analysis of this problem by Harold and Margaret Sprout, "Environmental Factors in the Study of International Politics," *Journal of Conflict Resolution,* 1 (1957), 309–28. The most elaborate analysis, with numerous examples, is Robert Jervis, *Perception and Misperception in International Politics* (Princeton: Princeton University Press, 1976).

also have to gauge *intentions*—and these may be badly misinterpreted because of hostile, distrustful, or excessively trustful attitudes.

Values

Our values are the result of upbringing, political socialization in various group contexts, indoctrination, and personal experience. They serve as standards against which our own actions and those of others are judged and are thus the bases of many of our attitudes. Values point out the general direction toward which our actions should be directed (wealth, power, prestige, happiness, isolation), and for policy makers they also serve as reasons and justifications for goals, decisions, and actions. For example, in Western societies, the values of individual freedom, civil liberties, national self-determination, independence, and economic progress are frequently cited as reasons behind certain policy objectives or as the objectives toward which actions are directed. To the policy maker and the public in general, actions that support these values are good; those that do not are to be avoided or resisted if undertaken by other states. In many developing countries, the values of rapid economic development, national unity, freedom from foreign control, and national prestige serve as the main criteria against which to judge one's own policies and those of other states. In socialist societies, the values of working-class solidarity, the struggle against "imperialism," and support for "national liberation movements" would be observed frequently in policy statements. Such values as these do not necessarily prescribe specific responses for particular situations, but they do establish attitudes toward the situation and provide both justifications for, and guides to, the policies designed to cope with them.

Beliefs

Beliefs can be defined as propositions that policy makers hold to be true, even if they cannot be verified. They are the foundation of national "myths" and ideologies, and efforts to question or examine them systematically are often met with hostility or even persecution. Some beliefs that are widespread in societies and expressed in the behavior of policy makers include those claiming that a particular nation, "way of life," or ethnic group is superior to any other, that a particular political system or economic order is superior to others, that human progress and moral improvement are inevitable, that communism is inevitable, or that a particular country will always be a "threat." Some more specific Western beliefs (closely related to liberal values) claim that all conflicts can be resolved through negotiation, that the use or threat of force is unethical except for purposes of self-defense, that foreign aid will produce stability and democracy, and, as a corollary, that hunger and poverty create communism.[4]

In foreign-policy making, such beliefs are important, for they often be-

---

[4] Stanley Hoffmann, "Restraints and Choices in American Foreign Policy," *Daedalus* (Fall 1962), p. 682.

come the unexamined assumptions upon which numerous policy choices are made—for instance, Woodrow Wilson's belief that secret diplomacy, autocracy, and the balance of power caused war; the common Western belief that communism represents basically a military threat; President Eisenhower's beliefs that all political leaders were essentially reasonable and that peace could be secured by frank discussion;[5] and the Chinese Communist belief in the implacable hostility of all "imperialists."

Like most people, policy makers do not like to be told that their beliefs are wrong, or that the images upon which their actions are based are not consonant with reality. Social scientists have repeatedly observed human beings' resistance to "uncomfortable" facts, the stability of our images in the face of rapidly changing events in the environment, and our ability to distort or ignore facts and deny important aspects of reality.[6] When there is some inconsistency between policy makers' attitudes and beliefs on the one hand and incoming information on the other, they can react in one of three ways: (1) ignore the inconsistency by withdrawing from the problem (that is, pretend the problem doesn't exist or isn't important); (2) reject the incoming information and somehow rationalize its lack of worth, thereby maintaining their initial attitudes and values; or (3) yield to the information by a change in values and attitudes. Of course, where the costs of changing attitudes are not very great, or where there are strong social supports or rewards for changing them, the third course may be easy to bring about. But in a highly institutionalized setting such as that in which policy makers work, there may be strong social pressures against changing attitudes and beliefs. Foreign ministers have to contend not only with information that challenges their pet beliefs and attitudes, but also with bureaucratic role and political restraints. They cannot easily change their views of the world if the important people they meet constantly reinforce their initial attitudes and beliefs, and if they find that by adhering to them they achieve more status and political efficacy. One can imagine, for instance, the difficulties faced by career deputy ministers in the Soviet or American defense establishments if they received information indicating that the opposite cold-war nation did not, in fact, constitute some sort of military menace. Even though they might undergo periods of uncertainty about their own attitudes and beliefs, the chances are only slight that they would easily adopt a "new line" and try to influence their colleagues to accept it.[7]

The story of diplomats in the field whose warnings and advice were

[5] Paul C. Davis, "The New Diplomacy: The 1955 Geneva Summit Meeting," in *Foreign Policy in the Sixties,* eds. Roger Hilsman and Robert C. Good (Baltimore, Md.: Johns Hopkins Press, 1965), pp. 166–67.

[6] For a summary of these findings, see Karl W. Deutsch and Richard L. Merritt, "Effects of Events on National and International Images," in *International Behavior: A Social-Psychological Analysis,* ed. Herbert C. Kelman (New York: Holt, Rinehart & Winston, 1965), pp. 132–87.

[7] For a summary of the problem of cognitive dissonance and inconsistency as it applies to international relations, see Milton J. Rosenberg, "Attitude Change and Foreign Policy in the Cold War Era," in *Domestic Sources of Foreign Policy,* ed. James N. Rosenau (New York: Free Press, 1967), pp. 111–59.

shunted aside or ignored by a foreign minister because they contradicted the minister's pet beliefs is a recurring complaint in diplomatic memoirs. To take two examples, a study of President Eisenhower's secretary of state, John Foster Dulles, illustrated how he interpreted facts about, and incoming messages from, the Soviet Union to make them fit his own beliefs about that country, which always emphasized its aggressiveness and great hostility toward the West. In some instances, Dulles interpreted information—often ingeniously—in such a way as to reinforce a previously held belief.[8] Even more clear-cut was Hitler's sensitivity to all information that suggested the imminent defeat of Germany's armed forces. German intelligence sources provided Hitler with accurate statistics of American industrial and military production; but in the last two years of the war, the führer became increasingly annoyed at these figures because they suggested pessimistic conclusions. Finally, Hitler ordered that no more statistics be quoted to him and forbade his officials to believe them or even to discuss them among themselves. Other officials who suggested that the morale of German citizenry was lagging by late 1944 were dismissed from their positions.[9]

Policy makers who do change their views on important foreign-policy programs or who critically examine the assumptions upon which a policy is based, face all the pressures for conformity and loyalty commonly found in small groups or bureaucratic organizations. Sometimes they are welcomed as devil's advocates, but more frequently they are regarded as trouble makers and face considerable personal hostility and sometimes demotion or loss of office. The "Tuesday lunch group" composed of President Johnson and the highest foreign-policy and military officials in his administration regularly made important decisions on the conduct of the war in Vietnam. Those officials who raised critical objections to American military involvement in Vietnam, who provided information that put the American military operations in an unfavorable light, or who asked for fundamental debates on the entire Vietnam policy were subject to sarcastic jibes from the president, appeals for loyalty and unanimity from the others, and eventual rejection from the group. Some were shifted to other government positions; others resigned.

Doctrines and Ideologies

A doctrine can be defined as any explicit set of beliefs that purports to explain reality and usually prescribes goals for political action. Foreign-policy objectives that derive from political doctrines are often put into slogan forms, such as "extending freedom," "trade follows the flag," "he who holds the land will hold the sea," "the throne and the altar," "the white man's burden," "make the world safe for democracy," "the New Order," or "world revolution." In

---

[8] Ole R. Holsti, "The Belief System and National Images: A Case Study," *Journal of Conflict Resolution*, 6 (1962), 244–52.

[9] John K. Galbraith, "Germany Was Badly Run," *Fortune* (December 1945), p. 200.

some political systems, the leadership inculcates into the society a comprehensive framework of doctrines, known also as an ideology. Ideologies not only establish foreign-policy goals, evaluative criteria, and justifications for actions, but have important effects on perceptual processes as well. Marxism-Leninism as an ideology has great consequences in Soviet foreign policy. It can be related to political goals and action in at least five ways.

First, it establishes the intellectual framework through which policy makers observe reality. Messages and cues from the external environment are given meaning, or interpreted, within the categories, predictions, and definitions provided by doctrines comprising the ideology. Soviet policy makers would interpret a foreign civil war as a manifestation of a class struggle (as during the Spanish civil war); they would see conflicts among "capitalist" states as a fight between their ruling classes over markets (as in the official Soviet interpretation of World War I); and they would regard any recession in a free-enterprise economy as evidence of Marx's predictions regarding the laws of economic development.

In its second function, the ideology prescribes for policy makers both national roles and an image of the future state of the world; it establishes the long-range goals of a state's external behavior, to be promoted through diplomacy, propaganda, revolution, or force. Its relevance to day-to-day problem solving and to the development of specific actions in concrete situations, however, may be only very slight. In these realms, a Communist government operates like any other.[10]

Third, the ideology serves as a rationalization and justification for the choice of more specific foreign-policy decisions. As in Western countries, where foreign policies are often justified in terms of such popular values as "preserving freedom," so in the Soviet Union or China, foreign-policy actions can be justified as being consistent with the general values inherent in the communist ideology.

Fourth, the set of doctrines in communism defines for policy makers the main stages in historical development within which specific foreign-policy strategies can be enunciated. For example, when the Soviet Union was weak and the only Socialist state in existence, Soviet theoreticians could define the epoch as one in which the "forces of imperialism" were vastly superior. Defining the world situation as a period of "capitalist encirclement" made certain objectives attractive—namely, building up Russian capabilities rather than concentrating on promoting the "world revolution." But by 1956, Soviet theoreticians could explain that an entirely new epoch, involving a new "balance of forces," had developed, and that Soviet foreign and defense policies would have to change accordingly. Now that the Soviet Union was, they claimed, as strong as the imperialist bloc, it no longer had to fear capitalist encirclement; in the new epoch of "peaceful coexistence," victories could be gained by ideological proselytizing and revolutionary activities, particularly in developing countires. In short,

---

[10] For a discussion of ideological influences in Soviet foreign policy, see Jan F. Triska and David D. Finley, *Soviet Foreign Policy* (New York: Macmillan, 1968), pp. 107–27.

the ideology of Marxism-Leninism provides general outlines for defining the basic characteristics of a given historical era. From these characteristics, Soviet officials can make certain deductions about appropriate foreign-policy goals.

Finally, the communist ideology posits a moral and ethical system that helps prescribe the correct attitudes and evaluative criteria for judging one's own actions and those of others. Communism is distinguished from other ideologies primarily because it claims to be an objective and scientific ideology and moral system, rather than merely the preferred ideology of particular leaders. Communist theoreticians maintain that Marxism-Leninism is all-powerful because it is correct, and, since only Marxist-Leninists are "armed with the truth," only they have a legitimate claim to power in the world. They are on the side of history, they maintain, and all other doctrines or economic systems are retrograde. Good people are those who swim with the current of history, building communism and fighting imperialism and fascism, whereas bad people (or states) are those that are fighting history by clinging to outmoded (capitalist, feudal, and so on) economic systems and their colonies. Capitalism is immoral, according to the evaluative criteria of Marxist doctrines, because it is a barrier to human progress. Any technique used to fight capitalism or imperialism is *ipso facto* moral and justified, because it is in accord with the laws of historical development.[11]

In American foreign policy, liberal values and doctrines play a similar role, although they are much less evident as guides to social and political analysis. Many American foreign-policy actions are organized to promote liberal institutions and private enterprise abroad. When major threats to American economic or security interests are not involved, for instance, policy makers often undertake programs to encourage development of democratic political institutions and discourage authoritarian political practices. In Latin America in particular, American diplomats and propaganda agencies have in recent years attempted to promote free elections and observance of civil liberties.[12] When military regimes have taken command, a frequent American response has been to withhold diplomatic recognition and terminate foreign aid unless the government promised to establish a date for holding free elections in the future. On other occasions, the U.S. government has made a show of force or actually intervened militarily to prevent uprisings against legally constituted governments. However, in in-

[11] The great discrepancies between images of reality in the Soviet Union and the West have led some social scientists to imply that most cold-war conflicts were caused by incongruent images rather than by irreconcilable objectives. See, for example, Urie Bronfenbrenner, "Allowing for Soviet Perceptions," in *International Conflict and Behavioral Science,* ed. Roger Fisher (New York: Basic Books, 1964), pp. 161–78; and the critical discussion by Ralph K. White, "Images in the Context of International Conflict: Soviet Perceptions of the U.S. and the U.S.S.R.," in *International Behavior,* ed. Kelman, pp. 236–76.

[12] See Theodore Wright, "Free Elections in the Latin American Policy of the United States," *Political Science Quarterly,* 74 (1959), 89–112. Active promotion of liberal values abroad was perhaps most pronounced in Woodrow Wilson's foreign policies. During his presidency, he frequently refused to recognize any Latin American regime that came into being through unconstitutional processes. In the case of Mexico, Wilson not only refused to recognize a revolutionary government, he took active steps to overthrow it by getting all major powers to withhold recognition.

stances where democratic political procedures led to corruption, increase in indigenous Communist or radical political strength, economic decay, or threats to American private interests, the United States has been equally prepared to support authoritarian regimes that could more effectively handle these "problems." The promotion of liberal values is thus not an absolute or persistent objective in American foreign policy but is tempered by such other objectives and needs as defending security and economic interests and maintaining the solidarity of alliances. Similarly, when there is inconsistency between promoting purely communist objectives or fulfilling national roles derived from Leninist views of international solidarity on the one hand, and defending or promoting purely national objectives on the other, the latter usually prevail over the former. No Communist state has been willing to commit resources to "world revolution" if by so doing it would seriously endanger its own security or other more specific interests. It is one of the advantages of the flexibility of Marxism-Leninism that when such situations arise—and they do so frequently—some ideological principle can be put forth to justify the choice of national over doctrinal imperatives.[13]

Analogies

We have all experienced attempts to clarify and understand a phenomenon by making analogies. The physiology instructor may make an analogy between the heart and a pump, the eye and a camera, or the brain and a computer. In each case, the object under study is analyzed not in terms of its own properties or characteristics, but with reference to some other object. Similarly, in formulating policy goals and responses to conditions abroad, diplomats and government officials frequently characterize a situation and deduce appropriate actions to cope with it by reference to a different but analogous, set of historical circumstances. The image of reality is based on, or compared to, a past situation, although of course current information must be available in order to suggest the comparison or analogy in the first place. For example, Prime Minister Eden of England found a close analogy between Hitler's foreign-policy objectives and diplomacy in 1938 and President Nasser's behavior in the Middle East in 1956. As a British foreign secretary during the late 1930s, Eden had questioned his government's appeasement policy against the Nazis. Convinced that Nasser presented a threat similar to that posed by Hitler, he deduced that the only way to handle the analogous situation was through a show of force. Even though the decision to invade Egypt in 1956 was formulated in the light of careful intelligence estimates (which were faulty in many ways), Eden did not consult most members of his government to see if they thought his image of the situation and the assumptions of his decision were correct.

During the Vietnam conflict in the 1960s, American policy makers frequently justified their actions and helped characterize the situation by citing

[13] For an argument that ideology plays a subordinate role to interests, see Werner Levi, "Ideology, Interests, and Foreign Policy," *International Studies Quarterly,* 14 (1970), 1–31.

the appeasement analogy of the 1930s: If you let aggressors achieve their objectives, you only whet their appetite for more. Appeasement, they maintained, leads only to general war, usually fought at some disadvantage by the democracies; but a strong display of force and determination can discourage aggressors and save the peace in the long run. In what respects the situation in Southeast Asia in the 1960s was really analogous to Europe in the 1930s can be debated, but the analogy was an important part of the psychological environment in which policy makers formulated their goals and actions.[14]

To this point we have emphasized the role that perceptual and attitudinal characteristics of policy makers may play in the formulation and execution of policy. What about other aspects of personality? Personality, of course, is an elusive concept. For purposes of foreign-policy analysis, we can propose three separate meanings: (1) policy-making *skills;* (2) character traits that predispose individuals to behave in certain ways in given conditions; and (3) pathological traits. Each may have significant influences on types of actions chosen in policy-making situations.

That people have different skills or aptitudes for different kinds of jobs is obvious. In terms of foreign-policy analysis, what may make a difference is traits such as tolerance/intolerance for diverging views, capacity to memorize, ability to weed out the essential information from trivia, capacity to think clearly in conditions of high stress, and the like. It would require a separate book to explore the links between such skills and policy choices. In situations fraught with danger, we are more likely to admire the policy makers who are known to look carefully at alternatives and who remain "cool" rather than those who have a reputation for impulsive behavior, arrogance, and indifference to advice which does not coincide with their hunches. The assumption, of course, is that more successful and safer policy will result from the deliberations of the former than the latter. Yet, some world-historical figures like Adolph Hitler were famous for their impulsive behavior while achieving phenomenal foreign-policy successes—at least in the short run.

Recent research has suggested some intriguing relationships between certain personality traits and propensity to make certain types of decisions in foreign policy. Lloyd Etheredge's study of American government officials and former presidents and secretaries of state establishes reasonably well that *some* types of decisions reflect personality traits.[15] In the case of the top-level policy makers, he found that those with personalities defined as "high dominance"

[14] Taken together, all these components—attitudes, values, beliefs, ideologies, and analogies—can be termed the "operational code." The notion of operational code has been developed by Alexander George. See his "The Operational Code': A Neglected Approach to the Study of Political Leaders and Decision-Making," *International Studies Quarterly,* 13 (1969), 190–222. For an application of the approach, see Ole R. Holsti, "The 'Operational Code' Approach to the Study of Political Leaders: John Foster Dulles' Philosophical and Instrumental Beliefs," *Canadian Journal of Political Science,* 3 (1970), 123–57.

[15] Lloyd Etheredge, *A World of Men: The Private Sources of American Foreign Policy* (Cambridge: MIT Press, 1978).

and "introvert" were significantly more likely to advocate "hard-line policies in international crises than those characterized as "low dominance" and "extrovert."

On a more impressionistic level, some have suggested that at least the *style* of decision making and sometimes the actions ordered reflected Lyndon Johnson's deep-felt insecurities. His inability to adjust policies in Vietnam in light of negative information was due, in part, to his personalization of the war. It was *his* war, with *his* boys getting killed, by *his* personal enemy, Ho Chi Minh.[16] In short, strong ego-involvement tends to reduce consideration of alternatives and condemns the policy maker to stick to a fixed course no matter how ineffective. We might also suggest that certain personality types are more prone to take risks than others.

Finally, writers of psychobiography have suggested that in certain circumstances, policy choices may reflect deep personal needs, which are then rationalized in terms of the national interest. Most experts agree that Stalin was afflicted by paranoia and pathological insecurity. Some of his foreign-policy behavior—his unwillingness to countenance the possibility of a Nazi invasion of Russia despite overwhelming information that it would happen—can perhaps best be understood as a manifestation of personality disorder. (Stalin's responsibility for the mass killings of the 1930s and his propensity to see plots everywhere were obviously related to pathological conditions.) Similarly, certain aspects of Hitler's behavior can be understood best in terms of psychopathological syndromes.[17]

But what of the prime minister of present-day Sweden, or the foreign minister of Japan, or the defense minister of Belgium? Can we best understand and explain the main patterns of those countries' foreign and defense policies today in terms of the personality characteristics of their key decision makers? Clearly the answer is no. The examples cited above are almost invariably taken from persons in unrestricted positions of authority over great powers in crisis situations. Where the policy problem relates to a less threat-laden issue, where it results from considerable bureaucratic discussion, and where it reflects the national needs of a relatively small country, then other types of explanations would be more powerful. We have discussed a variety of personality characteristics (including perceptual variables), because in certain situations, as hypothesized later, they provide a compelling explanation of foreign-policy objectives or actions.

1. Idiosyncratic variables are most likely to provide a significant part of an explanation where (a) policy is made by one or a few key leaders, (b) bureaucracies

---

[16] David Halberstam, *The Best and The Brightest* (New York: Random House, 1972).

[17] Among the prominent attempts at this kind of analysis are Alexander and Juliette George, *Woodrow Wilson and Colonel House: A Personality Study* (New York: John Day, 1956); Arnold Rogow, *James Forrestal: A Study of Personality, Politics, and Policy* (New York: Macmillan, 1963); and Joseph de Rivera, *The Psychological Dimensions of Foreign Policy* (Columbus, Ohio: Charles E. Merrill, 1968).

are uninvolved, (c) public opinion plays traditionally an insignificant role in limiting the executive's options, (d) compelling national needs are not involved, and (e) in a relatively diffuse international system.

2. "Aggressive" foreign-policy decisions and actions are more likely to be taken and ordered by those with the following character traits: (a) introversion/dominance, (b) high propensity to take risks, (c) a tendency to dichotomize foreign-policy actors as good/bad, trustworthy/untrustworthy, and the like, (d) personal insecurity combined with conditions such as sexual frustration, and (e) high need for esteem. Those with opposite characteristics are presumably more likely to be "doves."

The reader may wish to develop further hypotheses. The important point to remember is that no matter how emotionally satisfying it may be to attribute policy to a single person, other factors may be involved as well and may perhaps offer an even more comprehensive explanation. We consider next the *political* needs of key policy makers.

Press analysts and armchair observers often offer explanations of foreign policy which emphasize the domestic political needs of a president, commisar, or prime minister. This is the case where a leader undertakes a particular foreign-policy venture for the sake of augmenting domestic popularity or increasing his or her influence with a legislature. In the United States, at least, studies suggest that *any* foreign-policy move—a new initiative, a foreign tour, a dramatic announcement, or the like—is likely to increase the number of those who say the president is doing a good job.[18] In the spring of 1981, the popularity of Menachem Begin's *Likud* coalition in Israel increased dramatically after the prime minister took a hard line against the emplacement of Syrian SAM missiles in Lebanon, capable of shooting down Israeli reconnaissance flights. (This is not to argue that Begin's only concern was his domestic political problems—that would be another monocausal explanation.) While foreign-policy issues seldom determine the outcome of a country's elections—issues closer to the pocketbook are usually more salient—there is little doubt that some key foreign-policy decisions are timed to create maximum domestic impact and in some cases are taken primarily with a view to improving the leadership's sagging political fortunes.[19]

---

[18] John E. Mueller, *War, Presidents and Public Opinion* (New York: John Wiley, 1973).

[19] This situation raises serious problems for historians. Policy makers may give as reasons for their actions the state of public opinion, conditions abroad, or commitments that have to be fulfilled, whereas privately the most important consideration or component of a definition of the situation is their concern for their own political prestige and reputation. Since such considerations are seldom confessed even in memoirs, it is difficult to establish with certainty the relevance of private motives to public policies. There is also the problem of leaders' giving different reasons for their actions to different audiences at different times. For example, Mussolini emphasized on different occasions at least three reasons—his personal prestige, anticommunism, and strategic advantages—for his decision to intervene in the Spanish civil war. Hugh Thomas, *The Spanish Civil War* (London: Eyre & Spotiswoode, 1961), pp. 226–27. See also Franklin Weinstein, "The Uses of Foreign Policy in Indonesia: An Approach to the Analysis of Foreign Policy in the Less Developed Countries," *World Politics*, 24 (April 1972), 356–81.

DOMESTIC STRUCTURES
AND FOREIGN POLICY

Bureaucratic Needs, Values, and Traditions

Conditions abroad or personality characteristics and ideologies often seem to offer adequate explanations for the decisions and actions of governments. We could assume that the Soviet government would respond to a vast increase in American military spending by some increase in its own armed-forces programs. Deployment of Soviet missiles could be seen as essentially a response to American military initiatives. Yet, *how large* an increase in its defense budget and *what types* of weapons would be emphasized could be better explained or analyzed by investigation of bureaucratic and political processes *within* the Soviet Union.

Thus, in many instances, a full understanding of objectives, decisions, and actions must be based on a model of policy making that is more complicated than one that portrays policy makers as carefully fitting means to ends, gauging other states' intentions, and responding to certain conditions or events abroad. Choices are usually made in a bureaucratic-political context. Graham Allison reminds us that if we think of objectives, decisions, and actions as the result of bargaining between various government agencies, affected by organizational traditions and bureaucratic disputes over jurisdiction, then important facts that may have been ignored in the "rational" model of decision making may emerge.[20] Policy makers, in other words, define the situation not only in terms of conditions abroad, but also in terms of what is feasible bureaucratically. They receive information from various government agencies, and the alternatives they consider are often alternatives that have been drafted and debated by lower officials of various government departments. In part, then, how top-level policy makers see a problem, and the alternatives they contemplate, are an amalgam of how bureaucrats have characterized the situation and what positions they have come up with, taking into consideration organizational rivalries and bureaucratic traditions. Policy outputs, then, can be portrayed as the outcome of the pulling and hauling of bureaucratic politics.

The degree to which the bureaucratic characteristics affect the making of policy will vary from country to country, and in different circumstances. A policy developed over a period of time within the British government bureaucracy may differ significantly from a decision made by a few leaders of a small new state that barely has a foreign ministry. Henry Kissinger has suggested that there are three important styles of foreign policy making today: (1) charismatic-revolutionary, (2) ideological, and (3) bureaucratic-pragmatic.[21]

---

[20] Graham T. Allison, "Conceptual Models and the Cuban Missile Crisis," *American Political Science Review*, 63 (1969), 689–718. See also Allison and Morton H. Halperin, "Bureaucratic Politics: A Paradigm and Some Policy Implications," in Raymond Tanter and Richard H. Ullman, eds., *Theory and Policy in International Relations* (Princeton, N.J.: Princeton University Press, 1972), pp. 40–79.

[21] Kissinger, *American Foreign Policy* (New York: Norton, 1969), pp. 17–43.

In the first, long-range goals emphasizing the reconstruction of the international system or of regional subsystems predominate. Purposes are aimed at construction of a new future, not merely at manipulating the environment. In the early stages of nationhood, these goals can be seen largely as an attempt to put into effect the dreams and aspirations of revolutionary leaders, supported by strong nationalist movements. Bureaucracies in these states are weak and undifferentiated, and lack tradition. Thus, objectives, decisions, and actions largely reflect the ideas and whims of single individuals, often leaders of nationalist revolutionary movements.

In the ideological mode of policy making, as illustrated by most of the socialist states today, policy reflects a constant tension between the bureaucratic elements, with their traditional ways of dealing with problems, and the older revolutionary traditions, which emphasize long-range goals and actions abroad involving high risks.

The bureaucratic-pragmatic style of policy making is characterized by (1) a passive attitude toward the environment, in which policy is made up primarily of responses to situations abroad, rather than initiatives to alter established power relations, (2) a mode of thought that assumes that all events raise "problems" that can be solved by hard work and the give-and-take of diplomatic bargaining, and (3) a strong division of labor, emphasizing specialization. A "problem" is studied extensively by all sorts of bureaucratic experts, extensive data are gathered to illuminate the issue, and formal recommendations are made, reflecting the organizational traditions and biases of various government agencies. By the time objectives are defined and courses of action outlined, it is very difficult to see the imprint of any single individual on the project. According to Kissinger, "Outcomes depend more on the pressure or persuasiveness of the contending [bureaucratic] advocates than on a concept of overall purposes."[22]

It is not difficult to cite cases of policy outcomes that emerged after lengthy bargaining between government agencies. The European Recovery Program (Marshall Plan) was a primary instrument designed to cope with economic reconstruction in Europe and with the possibility of Communist victories there. But not all who engaged in formulating the program saw the objectives in the same way, nor did those who were consulted agree on the appropriate means of coping with the "problem." The final program reflected congressional pressures and bargaining among government agencies; it was a synthesis representing diverse interests, objectives, and attitudes. To understand why this important foreign-policy program emerged as it did, an explanation only in terms of conditions in Europe or the predilections of President Truman or Secretary of State Marshall would be inadequate.

In the state characterized by a highly developed foreign-affairs bureaucracy, there are also unlimited possibilities for foreign offices, military organizations, or intelligence agencies to take actions formulated independently of the

[22] *Ibid.*, p. 40.

top political leadership. This may be a case where bureaucrats deliberately seek to impose their own solutions to problems and attempt to keep the top leadership uninformed of plans and actions. Of the many cases in modern history where policy was vitally affected by bureaucratic actions, perhaps none led to more fatal consequences than the occasion in 1914 when German military and diplomatic officials took steps to goad Austria into war against Serbia and deliberately kept the kaiser uninformed of their own activities, to say nothing of several British diplomatic moves aimed at reducing tensions and preserving peace.

Another variation of policy as the outcome of bureaucratic bargaining or of secrecy is where a top leader formulates an objective or orders the implementation of actions, only to have them sabotaged or forgotten in the bowels of officialdom. This is not to say that all such instances are "bad," because often, as in the case of American-Canadian relations, the bureaucrats of the two countries may have an implicit agreement to "keep down the heat" on a conflict that, were it handled by the top leadership, might lead to an open rupture between the two governments.

The relevant factors in a definition of a situation may become extraordinarily complex and diverse because they involve the interests and attitudes of many competing government agencies. In the United States, for example, many external issues and foreign situations touch upon the interests and jurisdictions of the Departments of Defense, Agriculture, Commerce, and Treasury, in addition to the Department of State. Before decisions can be made, all the people concerned have to be consulted and a policy must be designed to accommodate all those interests. In states deeply involved in the affairs of the system, recurrence of external problems that impinge upon the interests of many government agencies requires establishment of formal interdepartmental machinery, which may very well formulate and administer policies of which the top political leadership has only slight knowledge.[23] Another factor that may complicate the definition of objectives and implementation of policies is the rivalry and suspicion among personalities in different agencies, where some may not accept others' definition of a situation or resent the intrusion of other agencies in problems they feel to be within their exclusive competence.

Even where top policy makers are fully consulted about all major decisions, bureaucratic values will tend to impinge upon individual beliefs, attitudes, and images. Foreign ministers are restrained in their actions and prerogatives partly by constitutional and customary limitations, partly by their own general political position vis-à-vis other policy makers, and also by their expectations of what constitutes proper conduct for a foreign minister. No matter how strong

---

[23] There are more than 160 formal interdepartmental and interagency committees on foreign affairs in the U.S. government. Kenneth Thompson, *Political Realism and the Crisis of World Politics* (Princeton, N.J.: Princeton University Press, 1960), p. 124. For an argument that portrays the president as a virtual captive of the bureaucracy except during crises, see Donald Lampert. "Issues for Global Actors: the U.S.A." in *Issues in Global Politics*, eds. Gavin Boyd and Charles Pentland (New York: The Free Press, 1981), pp. 49–66.

the personality, the foreign minister will always be subjected to influences from the bureaucracy, whether the need to maintain policies consistent with traditional forms of behavior, reliance on organizational sources of information, or more specific resistance by lower-level policy makers against attempted procedural or substantive innovation by the foreign minister. Anyone who has worked in a large organization has learned that whatever one's personal views and beliefs, he or she faces strong pressures to conform with group norms.

Under what circumstances are administrative processes and organizational values, needs, and traditions likely to have an important role in the definition and implementation of objectives? First, where political leadership at the top is weak or unstable, the main administrative organs of the state may have to make policy in the light of their own needs, values, and traditions. Second, most noncritical transactions between states are carried out by the lower echelons of policy-making organizations, often without the explicit direction of a foreign minister or head of government. For routine problems, traditional departmental policies and standard operating procedures, rather than direction from above, serve as the main guidelines for action. The American State Department in any one day receives about 1,300 cables from American diplomatic and consular officials abroad providing information, requesting directions, or seeking permission to make certain decisions in the field. But of that large number of communications, the secretary of state will read only twenty to thirty—about 2 percent of the total. The State Department also sends out approximately 1,000 cables daily, many of which elucidate objectives and provide directions on policies designed to implement them; of these, the secretary of state may see only six, and the president will have only one or two of the most important communications referred to his office.[24] The implication of this type of communications system is clear: On routine and nonvital matters (even if a bad decision made on these may result in a diplomatic crisis), the experts and lower officials of policy-making organizations define specific objectives in the light of their own values, needs, and traditions, often through informal alliances with bureaucrats in other countries. High officials are generally concerned only with suggesting the main outlines of objectives, not with their specifics nor with the detailed means by which to implement them. As Joseph Frankel points out, high-ranking officials within policy-making hierarchies are far removed from information that describes the external environment in detail.[25] They become captives of advisors, oversimplifications, and all the prejudices, established attitudes, and procedures of large bureaucratic organizations. It is little wonder that diplomatic history is replete with cases of top policy makers choosing disastrous courses of action because their images of reality and expectations were at odds with real conditions in the environment.

[24] Testimony of Secretary of State Dean Rusk to a Senate subcommittee, reported in *Time,* 83, No. 4 (January 24, 1964), 19.
[25] Frankel, *The Making of Foreign Policy* (New York: Oxford University Press, 1963), p. 96.

In a crisis, where decisions of great consequence have to be made rapidly, the effect of bureaucratic processes may be reduced considerably. In these circumstances a few key individuals at the highest level of responsibility and authority usually congregate to map strategy and responses to the problem or threat they are confronting. There is no time for detailed consultations, preparation of position papers, or thorough analysis of the situation and its background. Since urgency is the most salient aspect of the definition of the situation, decisions have to be made largely upon the basis of immediately available information, unverified rumors, and the views of upper-level advisers.[26] Under such conditions, individual attitudes, values, beliefs, and images of the highest policy makers become particularly important in defining the situation, choosing responses and goals, and implementing policies.

Social Needs and National Attributes

Some foreign-policy objectives, decisions, and actions are formulated or taken to fulfill general social needs and advance more specific interests of domestic groups, political parties, and economic organizations. In the middle of the nineteenth century, for example, the British government had little interest in establishing new colonies. But by the 1890s, missionary societies, explorers, commercial firms, and military adventurers had prevailed upon the political parties and government to create colonies and protectorates to provide security under which they could conduct activities in Africa with safety. Partly in response to competition from France and Germany, considerations of prestige, and importuning of pressure groups, the British government ultimately made expansion of the empire an official policy objective. The interests of some types of private groups can be secured only by government actions toward other states. If such groups are successful in their agitation, they may obtain official recognition of their interests by policy makers who will raise these private interests into collective objectives, demanding official time and attention, diplomatic representation, spending of public money, and occasional use of armed force. Typical examples occur when a government negotiates a tariff agreement with another state to benefit one of its own business enterprises or industries, or intervenes diplomatically or militarily in another country to protect the property and investments of its own citizens or business enterprises.

More important, the main geographic, demographic, and resource characteristics of a country help create *general* social and economic needs that can be fulfilled only through transactions with other states. The conditions may be so obvious that they are not openly acknowledged as crucial elements in a definition of a situation, but almost every political objective and diplomatic action implicitly gives recognition to their importance. Of the components in

---

[26] Richard C. Snyder and Glenn D. Paige, "The United States Decision to Resist Aggression in Korea," in *Foreign Policy Decision Making,* eds. Richard C. Snyder, H.W. Bruck, and Burton Sapin (New York: The Free Press, 1962).

many definitions of situations, a country's geographic location and topographical features may be the most important, because they are the most permanent. Although modern technology can alter the political and economic significance of geographic characteristics, many of these characteristics still influence policies by providing opportunities or by placing limitations on what is feasible in both domestic and foreign policy programs. A country's size, population, distribution of natural resources, climate, and topography will have an important bearing on its socioeconomic development, needs vis-à-vis other nations, and access to other areas of the world. These conditions also have the greatest relevance to military and defense policies. Topographical features create avenues for invasion and suggest the best lines of defense; economic characteristics and distribution of natural resources determine a nation's self-reliance or dependence on others in wartime as well as during peace; and climate imposes restrictions on the types of warfare that can be conducted in a particular area or the crops that can be grown.

British or Japanese foreign ministers are aware that their country is a small island, heavily populated, unable to grow adequate food supplies, and therefore highly dependent upon foreign trade to maintain an acceptable standard of living. Given the essential goals of maintaining living standards and meeting demands for economic and social security, some foreign-policy objectives, such as trade expansion, naturally proceed from the economic and geographic situation. Lack of raw materials and food within the islands makes it necessary for the British and Japanese to import these commodities; in order to import, they have to manufacture export goods that can compete successfully against the products of other exporting nations. The geographical characteristics of Japan and England thus help create persisting interests and objectives no matter what the circumstances abroad or which political party or foreign minister is in power. This does not mean that all people similarly interpret the significance of geographic and economic conditions or that any two governments will defend or achieve persisting interests in exactly the same way. The British Conservative party, responding to the need to expand trade, may promote this expansion by subsidizing exports; the Labour party may try to accomplish the same goal by lowering the volume of imports. In the 1930s, the Japanese sought to meet their resource needs by creating the "Greater East Asia Co-Prosperity Sphere," a semicolonial region that would provide cheap raw materials, expanding markets, and a region for settling Japan's surplus population. Since World War II, however, the Japanese have sought to satisfy their persisting socioeconomic needs by modernizing industrial capacity, rationalizing agriculture, and conducting vigorous export sales programs in international markets.

Social and economic needs can be linked to policy outputs only in the sense that certain *possibilities* seem logical; in an era when economic welfare is a prime national value, we can predict with reasonable certainty that a resource-poor state will engage in foreign trade, and should that commerce be shut off, policy makers will define the situation as a near crisis and will take action to try to reestablish trade. We cannot say, however, that in all instances the relationship would hold, because needs may be defined in many different ways. What about other national characteristics or attributes as explanations for foreign-policy outputs?

Domestic Instability

One of the oldest propositions has linked domestic instability or turmoil to expansion abroad and hostile diplomatic behavior. The reasoning is that in order to create national unity, governments may undertake foreign adventures. In Quincy Wright's words, a ruler prevents sedition by making external war.[27] In the contemporary context, observers have often asserted that the leaders of developing states display considerable hostility to Western countries or undertake programs of expansion as a means of overcoming or diverting attention from ethnic, religious, and ideological divisions. According to Kissinger, the international arena provides an opportunity for taking dramatic foreign-policy measures that are impossible at home.[28] To what extent can these propositions be supported by historical evidence?

In a study based on European diplomatic history since 1740, Richard Rosecrance concluded that whereas many wars and crises were not related to internal instability or domestic turmoil, many others could be traced to, or explained by, the insecurity of political elites.[29] But the evidence still allows us to state only that internal conflict *may* result in aggressive foreign policy.

Another method of exploring the proposition is to look at a great number of states within a shorter period of time. This way, we can focus attention not only on actors that became involved in wars—as would be the case in diplomatic histories—but on all states. Rudolph J. Rummel has pioneered an extensive body of research that has sought to find links between various national attributes (such as size, number of frontiers, wealth and the like) and national behavior (such as domestic violence) on the one hand and foreign policy conflict on the other. The usual method employed in these studies has been to gather data on the attributes and behavior of a large sample of states (usually more than seventy) for a period of several years and to do the same for external behavior. The national attribute and behavior data are gleaned from standard statistical sources, whereas foreign-policy actions are usually taken from newspaper accounts. The data for the independent and dependent variables are then subjected to statistical treatment.

These studies have not yet uncovered any strong relationships. Rummel's work, for example, has demonstrated that at best, there is only a very weak covariation between foreign and domestic conflict behavior. On the basis of his research, one could not accept the proposition that governments generally display aggressiveness in foreign relations as a means of coping with domestic

[27] Quincy Wright, *A Study of War*, 2nd ed. (Chicago: University of Chicago Press, 1965), p. 140.

[28] Henry Kissinger, *American Foreign Policy: Three Essays* (New York: Norton, 1969), p. 41.

[29] Richard N. Rosecrance, *Action and Reaction in World Politics* (Boston: Little, Brown, 1963), pp. 304–5.

instability.[30] Assuming, however, that there might be a time lag between the incidence of domestic violence and its expression in foreign policy, Raymond Tanter replicated some of Rummel's work and added more extensive data of his own. He found only a weak relationship between the variables. Given a certain level of domestic turmoil at a time x, he could not discover that there was any significant rise in external conflict behavior one or two years later.[31] Using a very broad data base for sixty-nine countries for the period of 1966–1969, Michael Skrein made further investigations relating attributes and behavior to foreign-policy actions. He employed three different statistical manipulations with his data but failed to uncover evidence of any relationships between domestic instability or violence and foreign policy.[32]

Type of Regime

In arriving at this conclusion, however, we have made no distinction between *types* of states. Another popular explanation for national aggressiveness holds that the type of political or economic regime in a state can be crucial. The reasoning is that "closed" systems can maintain secrecy and, by manipulating public opinion, can more easily arouse widespread support. Moreover, it is possible that in a totalitarian or authoritarian political system, where decision making is limited to a few high-ranking individuals often cut off from objective analyses of internal and external conditions, there will be strong imperatives to undertake high-risk policies or to command sudden switches in objectives, roles, orientations, or actions. Since many dictatorships are based on weak foundations, top leaders may also undertake foreign adventures to consolidate their positions. Or, using psychological variables, it could be argued that in regimes headed by charismatic leaders, decision makers can achieve considerable personal gratification from exercising power arbitrarily, seeking international prestige, or glorifying themselves through military displays and expeditions abroad.[33]

Using the Rummel and Tanter data, Jonathan Wilkenfeld has demonstrated that statistical relationships between internal and external conflict behavior do emerge if one takes into account *types* of states, *types* of internal and external conflict, and time lags. Thus, he found that for "centrist" states (mostly

---

[30] Rudolph J. Rummel, "The Relationship between National Attributes and Foreign Conflict Behavior," in *Quantitative International Politics: Insights and Evidence*, ed. J. David Singer (New York: Free Press, 1968), pp. 187–214.

[31] Raymond Tanter, "Dimensions of Conflict Behavior Within and Between Nations, 1958–1960," *Journal of Conflict Resolution*, 10 (1966), 61–62.

[32] Skrein found a tendency for less politically advanced nations to be more generally hostile than the politically mature ones (p. 43), and there were some strong associations between various national attributes and degrees of cooperative behavior. Michael Skrein, "National Attributes and Foreign Policy Output: Tests for a Relationship," Support Study No. 4, World Event/Interaction Survey, Department of International Relations, University of Southern California, Los Angeles, June 1970 (mimeo).

[33] See R. Barry Farrell, "Foreign Policies of Open and Closed Political Societies," in *Approaches to Comparative and International Politics*, ed. R. Barry Farrell (Evanston, Ill.: Northwestern University Press, 1966), pp. 167–206.

one-party, authoritarian states), there is a relationship between (1) revolutions, number killed in domestic conflicts, purges, and general strikes, on the one hand, and (2) *all* types of external conflict behavior after a lag of either one or two years. But in "personalist" states (those ruled by personal dictatorships), *all* types of internal strife (including demonstrations, guerrilla warfare, assassinations, and the like) are related only to certain types of foreign-conflict behavior, including expulsion of ambassadors and officials from other states, and troop movements. For "polyarchic" nations (mostly Western democracies), there is a statistically significant relationship between antigovernment demonstrations, riots, and government crises, on the one hand, and *all* types of external conflict behavior, on the other, for all time periods.[34]

Wilkenfeld's findings support the major propositions linking domestic attributes and foreign-policy actions: There are different patterns of relationship between internal and external behavior when we look at different sorts of regimes. But explanations for these relationships remain to be put forth, and it is significant that, using different data, Skrein did not find meaningful statistical relationships between type of political system, levels of internal conflict, and foreign-policy actions. These contradictory findings are presented to demonstrate the uncertainty that the analyst of foreign policy must face and the necessity to recall that generalizations or explanations are at best *tendency statements.* A reasonable conclusion would be that there is some probability that, given certain manifestations of domestic instability, governments *may* find it necessary to undertake certain hostile actions abroad. President Sukarno's "confrontation" campaign against Malaysia from 1962 to 1966—a policy involving verbal threats, guerrilla warfare, and economic actions—was undertaken in part as a means of creating domestic unity, a heightened sense of nationalism, and a reduction of the divisive political infighting between the Indonesian Communist party (PKI) and the army. The program had an external target, but it was used, partly at least, as a means of bolstering Sukarno's political position in the country.[35]

But we cannot formulate a generalization from a single case. In fact, Wilkenfeld and Zinnes found in a subsequent study that countries experiencing a great degree of internal instability appear to *reduce* levels of externally directed activities.[36] The reasoning must be, as suggested in the case of the United States and Vietnam and many others, that when top bureaucratic and political officials become concerned with the essential foundations of the nation (in coping with a secessionist movement for instance), little time or attention can be paid to foreign policy questions of any kind. A policy of "drift" is not likely to antagonize others.

[34] Jonathan Wilkenfeld, "Domestic and Foreign Conflict Behavior of Nations," *Journal of Peace Research,* 1 (1968), 56–59.

[35] Franklin B. Weinstein, "The Uses of Foreign Policy in Indonesia . . ."

[36] "Analysis of Foreign Conflict Behavior," in *Peace, War, and Numbers,* ed. Bruce Russett (Beverly Hills, Calif.: Sage Publications, 1972). For a review of the literature, see Michael P. Sullivan, *International Relations: Theories and Evidence* (Englewood Cliffs, N.J.: Prentice-Hall, 1976), Ch. 4.

What of the proposition that types of foreign-policy *actions* can best be explained by the sorts of regimes that govern a country? Is there validity to the hypothesis that democratic states are more pacific than "closed" states? A number of research projects have explored this and similar questions. The procedures are like those used in analyzing the relationship between domestic and foreign violence: States are categorized into "open" and "closed" types and compared against data about their foreign-policy actions over a period of time. These studies reveal that closed states do not engage in conflict acts—ranging from verbal threats to the use of force—significantly more than open states do.[37] Nor do states with strong nationalist leaders have more conflict behavior in their foreign policies than do states with other types of leadership.[38] Despite examples such as the late President Sukarno, when nations are aggregated, no important difference exists with respect to type of regime or leadership. Although it is true that *large closed* states give evidence of more conflict acts in their external behavior than do *small open* states, it is the size of the state (measured by population) rather than the type of regime that probably accounts for the difference.

The relationship between type of regime and other forms of policy output such as objectives, roles, and orientations has never been explored. Are closed states more likely to form long-range goals than open states are? Does type of regime dispose a government to have an orientation of isolation, nonalignment, or alliance making? Do closed states have more national role conceptions than open states do? No research has yet uncovered evidence to answer such questions.

Size of Country

If type of regime does not explain differences in types of foreign-policy actions, size, as measured by population, appears very significant. Historically, the major powers have used organized force or have been involved in wars, far out of proportion to their numbers in the international system. To put it another way, the great powers are vastly more prone to war than are small states. The history of war is largely the story of great-power activity.[39] Large states (defined as those with a population over 30 million) are also initiators of more conflict acts, aside from the use of force, than are small states. This is particularly true of the use of economic sanctions.[40] In contrast, small states are more likely to use international organizations as arenas in which to pursue their objectives,

---

[37] Rudolph J. Rummel, *The Dimensions of Nations* (Beverly Hills, Calif.: Sage Publications, 1972), Chap. 14. For different results, cf. James N. Rosenau and Charles F. Hermann, "Final Report to the National Science Foundation on Grant GS-3117" (mimeo, n.d.), p. 20.

[38] Rosenau and Hermann, "Final Report," p. 7.

[39] George Modelski, "War and the Great Powers," *Peace Research Society (International) Papers*, Vol. 18 (1971), 45–60; and Wright, *A Study of War*, pp. 53, 58.

[40] Maurice A. East, "Size and Foreign Policy Behavior: A Test of Two Models," *World Politics*, 25 (July 1973), 571; and Peter Wallensteen, "Characteristics of Economic Sanctions," *Journal of Peace Research*, No. 2 (1968), 248–67.

and, as we might expect, they are more apt to initiate joint foreign-policy ventures.[41]

In the case of national role conceptions, the evidence is also clear. Large states are much more involved in different areas and issues of international politics and see themselves as having a larger number of persisting tasks and functions abroad than do small states.[42]

Although no systematic counts have been made, we can assume that large states, at least those with superior capabilities, also have more objectives to achieve or defend in international politics. Indeed, the scope of objectives, combined with the elements of power, is probably the main characteristic of the great powers. They are able to do more things in international politics because they have superior capabilities; to put it another way, the larger the state, the more power, and the more power, the more ambitious its goals. The more interests it has to extend or protect, the more likely it is to become involved in conflict. States with weak capabilities are less likely to formulate ambitious objectives, although the actions of Indonesia under Sukarno, Egypt under Nasser, and Libya under Qaddafi show that lack of capabilities does not necessarily inhibit a state from pursuing broad revolutionary objectives. There is, nevertheless, a strong relationship between a state's capabilities and the type and number of objectives it pursues.

Level of Development

We might assume that the needs of developing countries are more acute than those of the industrial nations or that the legacies of colonialism might prompt Third World states to embark on aggressive foreign adventures. Although many of the newer states have become involved in other countries' internal problems or have sought to resolve ethnic and language divisions by threats and force, on an aggregate level their actions are not distinct from those of the developed countries. The essential finding of the studies mentioned above is that although *small developed* states tend to be more involved in international political and economic issues than developing states (explained largely in historical terms; Belgium has been an international actor much longer than Chad, for example), they do not initiate more conflict or cooperative acts than small developing states do.[43] On the number and types of national role conceptions, level of development does not explain more than the well-known fact that most developing countries see themselves as nonaligned, whereas most developed countries belong to one of the major military blocs.

In summary, of all the national attributes related to foreign policy, only size—and by implication, capabilities—seems to account for major differences

---

[41] East, "Size and Foreign Policy Behavior," p. 465; and William D. Coplin and Martin J. Rochester, "The PCIJ, the ICJ, the League of Nations, and the United Nations: A Comparative Empirical Survey," *American Political Science Review*, 66 (June 1972), 529–50.

[42] K.J. Holsti, "National Role Conceptions."

[43] Rosenau and Hermann, "Final Report," p. 19.

in foreign actions and national role conceptions. But these studies are based primarily on data from the 1950s and 1960s, when most developing countries faced their positions of dependence with equanimity and often resignation. Those that control scarce raw materials, such as oil, are likely to become more involved and influential in international political and economic issues. It is possible, therefore, that in the 1980s, level of development may be a factor for both more cooperative and more aggressive foreign-policy actions.

Public Opinion

Probably no aspect of the study of foreign policy is more difficult to generalize about than the relationship of public opinion to a government's external objectives and diplomatic behavior. More research on this area, particularly in non-Western countries, needs to be completed before students of international relations can offer generalizations with much confidence. The characteristics of political systems in the world today vary so immensely—from primitive, patriarchal, or religious oligarchies to modern industrial democracies and totalitarian dictatorships—that any proposition would have to be qualified at least in terms of the type of society being considered. Our comments will refer, therefore, primarily to those societies in which the public has relatively free access to information from abroad, where there is a general awareness of the external environment, and where formal political institutions are maintained by widespread political support.

 First, we should eliminate those hypotheses that suggest either that foreign-policy goals and diplomatic behavior are merely a response to domestic opinions or that public attitudes are virtually ignored as important components of a definition of a situation. Some government officials have claimed frankly that their decisions could not be influenced by fickle public attitudes; it is also easy to cite examples where officials yielded to public pressures despite their own preferred policies. Instead of assuming a simple or direct relationship between public opinions on foreign affairs and government policies, we should distinguish (1) *who* is expressing opinions concerning (2) *what* issues in (3) *which* situations. The characteristics of these three qualifiers may have important effects on the ultimate influence of public opinion on the formulation of objectives and actions.

 Studies of public attitudes conclude that the vast majority of people—even in highly literate societies—are unknowledgeable, uninterested, and apathetic with regard to most issues of world affairs.[44] They also reveal that public images and attitudes toward foreign countries are highly resistant to change

---

[44] For example, Gabriel Almond, *The American People and Foreign Policy* (New York: Harcourt Brace Jovanovich, 1950); Gabriel Almond and Sidney Verba, *The Civic Culture* (Princeton, N.J.: Princeton University Press, 1963), esp. Part II regarding knowledge of, and interest in, domestic policies; Warren E. Miller and Donald E. Stokes, "Constituency Influence in Congress," *American Political Science Review*, 57 (1963), 45–56; and Milton J. Rosenberg, "Images in Relation to the Policy Process: American Public Opinion on Cold-War Issues," in *International Behavior*, ed. Kelman, pp. 277–334.

even when dramatic events radically alter the main issues of international politics.[45] Other studies suggest that government, university, and private programs that have sought to create wider public knowledge and appreciation of the complexities of international politics have seldom met with success.[46] An investigation of opinions and actions on the Vietnam conflict, undertaken through a sample survey of American respondents during 1967, revealed that although a large proportion of the people were *concerned* about the war, only 13 percent reported that they had tried to convince someone to change his views on the war, and only 3 percent had done anything such as writing to officials or newspapers. Less than 1 percent of the 1,499 respondents had participated in marches or demonstrations.[47] Considering the very contentious nature of the war and the heated discussion it aroused, the figures are extremely low.

For purposes of analysis, any society has a small top layer of the "attentive" public [48] that is reasonably well informed, articulate, and interested, although not necessarily more prone to change basic attitudes when subjected to new information, propaganda, or dramatic events abroad. In most Western countries, the attentive public is closely correlated with higher education, urban domicile, professional occupation, higher income, middle age, and male sex. Estimates of the size of the attentive public range from 1 to 15 percent, depending on how the category is defined. Next to the attentive public in developed countries exists a layer of the population, normally comprising 30 to 50 percent of the total, that possesses established attitudes toward, and images of, foreign countries and their actions, some knowledge of a limited range of issues, and some capacity to express opinions if asked. Finally, the rest of a society, in some cases constituting 70 percent or more of the population, can be characterized on most issues as apathetic, uninformed, and nonexpressive, although in certain circumstances, these people can display considerable interest in some issue areas and, if properly mobilized, can express great hostility or loyalty to foreign nations or their political leaders.

On what kinds of issues are the opinions found in different layers or groups within society expressed as demands to establish certain foreign-policy goals or to undertake certain actions vis-à-vis other states? The attentive public is likely to be concerned with a wide range of foreign-policy problems and to express opinions on them either directly to policy makers or simply to friends and associates. They constitute probably the only segment of society that *introduces* ideas for the consideration of politicians and foreign-policy officials.[49] They are also likely to have adequate information on a number of foreign countries,

[45] Deutsch and Merritt, "Effects of Events on National and International Images."

[46] Joseph Frankel, *The Making of Foreign Policy* (New York: Oxford University Press, 1963), p. 72.

[47] Sidney Verba and Richard A. Brody, "Participation, Policy Preferences, and the War in Vietnam," *Public Opinion Quarterly*, 34 (1970), 325–32.

[48] The concept is introduced by Almond in *The American People and Foreign Policy.*

[49] For further discussion and some empirical evidence, see Johan Galtung, "Foreign Policy Opinion as a Function of Social Position," in *International Politics and Foreign Policy: A Reader in Research and Theory*, rev. ed., ed. James N. Rosenau (New York: Free Press, 1969), pp. 55–72.

well-defined opinions, and preferred solutions to contemporary problems. Although the bottom layer may be generally apathetic, on certain issues it may become highly involved and express views through diverse channels. Consider one hypothetical example. Wheat farmers in the prairie states may not have much general interest in world affairs, may possess little knowledge about foreign countries and their problems, and may have unrefined attitudes and images based more on family or regional traditions than on a careful examination of contemporary information. But if a problem relating to wheat export programs arises, the farmers will probably become highly involved, express their views in most vigorous terms to friends, associates, and policy makers, and suggest preferred solutions. In other words, apathy and ignorance end when a problem is perceived as having a *direct* impact on the life of the individual. The *scope* of public expression is thus related to the nature of the issue or problem under consideration.

It would still be an oversimplification to argue that those in the bottom layer of a society (in terms of interest and knowledge, not class) become involved only on issues of direct relevance to their private lives, whereas those of the attentive public are interested in a much broader scope of affairs. No matter what the level of interest or knowledge among people, they all hold some notions about appropriate and inappropriate foreign-policy goals and actions. Gabriel Almond has used the term *foreign-policy mood* to suggest those very *general* attitudes or predispositions that prevail in a nation at any given time. In the nineteenth and early twentieth centuries in the United States, the predominant public mood was isolation and indifference to European affairs. In the 1950s and more recently it has been a mood of pronounced fear of, and hostility toward, the Soviet Union. War weariness in Great Britain during the 1930s was an important basis for England's appeasement policy toward Hitler and Mussolini. Such moods, while not suggesting concrete foreign-policy objectives, at least *set limits* around the theoretical policy alternatives of policy makers. The prime minister of neutral Sweden could not, for example, annouce one day that he had concluded a military alliance unless large segments of the population also believed that neutrality was outmoded, ineffective, or incompatible with some value such as national survival. Nor would the president of the United States be likely to proclaim that he would withdraw all American commitments abroad and turn the country into an isolated "Fortress America." On the major questions of a country's general orientation to the rest of the world, war and peace, and general style of diplomacy, everyone has opinions and is likely to express them when challenged. When the *scope* of public opinion is so broad, it is likely to have great influence on the alternatives that policy makers would regard seriously. The mood, in other words, has a constraining effect on policy alternatives, but not much direct impact on specific issues. The American public in the early 1980s seems to support increased defense spending, but their mood does not specify which weapons should be developed. In Galtung's words, the public establishes a vast region of admissible policies surrounded by a belt of inadmissible policies. The vast majority of citizens or subjects thus figure in the definitions of situations by policy makers only in setting bounds to various alternatives. On most specific issues, they must be considered an insignificant element in policy making.

The impact of public attitudes and opinions on the selection of objectives and making decisions can be related, then, to the scope of the public, which in turn is related to the type of issue at stake. A third variable would be the general situation in which opinions are being expressed. Is the role of opinion in times of crisis the same as it is during a period of relative stability and noninvolvement in international affairs? We would expect the scope of the opinion-expressing public to vary directly with the degree of urgency or threat in a situation. More people are probably aroused to take interest in foreign affairs when a conflict develops than when diplomatic conditions are "normal," and there is much historical and experimental evidence suggesting that even societies strongly divided among themselves tend to become united in times of conflict. If a diplomatic-military confrontation creates a public consensus, this opinion is likely to restrict the number of options diplomatic officials would seriously consider.

On the other hand, deep-seated attitudes of distrust toward other countries are not easily changed simply by the development of new circumstances. During the critical period after the outbreak of World War II, President Roosevelt was cautious in making too many commitments in support of England because of the presence of a strong isolationist mood and anti-British sentiments. When the United States joined the war against Germany in December 1941, it took considerable effort at persuasion by the government before a large proportion of the American public would accept the need to create an alliance with the Soviet Union, a nation toward which Americans had directed considerable hostility since the Bolshevik revolution. Similarly, the French government could withdraw from Indochina in 1954 because the French population was weary of supporting a distant military effort that was accomplishing little and involved great sacrifices; but no French government from 1954 to 1958 could have survived in office had it tried to negotiate a withdrawal agreement providing independence for Algeria. In this case, it was not so much that the French population was overwhelmingly in favor of "pacifying" Algeria, but that opinions were split among many different groups, none of which could command a convincing majority. Finally, when the government of Ireland had to decide in 1939 whether to remain neutral or join England against Nazi Germany, the government felt compelled to accept the neutrality opinion because that choice was supported by most of the articulate population—despite some feelings among officials that the other course would have been preferable. Many similar cases could be sited, but they all suggest one conclusion: Public opinion in these critical situations, while it does not prescribe exact policies or responses, establishes limits beyond which few policy makers would normally dare to act.[50]

In a *crisis* situation, however, public opinion probably constitutes only

[50] In examining a noncritical issue, however, one study suggests that policy makers in the United States enjoy considerable freedom from any restraints imposed on their decisions by public groups. See Raymond Bauer, Ithiel Pool, and L.A. Dexter, *American Business and Public Policy: The Politics of Foreign Trade* (New York: Atherton, 1963).

an insignificant factor in definitions of the situation. In contrast to a conflict, which may start slowly and drag on for years, a crisis is characterized by sudden unanticipated actions, high perceptions of threat, and feelings that something has to be done immediately (see Chapter 15 for further discussion). In these circumstances, decisions are almost always made by a few key policy makers; they believe that action of some sort is so necessary that there is little time to consult broadly among legislators or lower administrative officials, to say nothing of the public at large. Developments during a crisis may occur so fast, in any event, that the public seldom has the time to mobilize and express opinions through such institutionalized channels as political parties, legislatures, or interest groups. During the Cuban missile crisis, for instance, those who debated the various policy alternatives deliberately shielded themselves from public scrutiny and did their work mostly in secret. In President Kennedy's opinion, a "good" decision would be more likely if policy makers were immune from considerations of public pressure.

Interaction between Public Pressure and Official Decisions

It would be omitting an important part of the relationship between opinion and foreign policy if we suggested that policy makers only *respond* to public pressures. In fact, the relationship in democratic societies involves complex interaction in which officials and the public or its component groups react to each other's behavior, values, and interests. If in some cases government officials feel constrained to choose policy goals and actions consistent with prevailing public moods, it is no less true that they spend considerable time advocating their own position and characterization of a situation to the population. Because of superior knowledge and access to information, governments occupy a position from which they can interpret reality to the population and actually create attitudes, opinions, and images where none existed before. Although independent communications media may express differing views, a prime minister or president can be very persuasive by virtue of his political prestige and expertise. It has often been observed that information or propaganda emanating from a reliable or prestigious source has more impact on opinions that has information dispersed by less credible sources.[51] Thus, what many people know of, or feel about, a critical situation abroad and their own government's actions and responses to it may originate from the government itself—from press conferences, parliamentary debates, or political speeches. Recent empirical studies demonstrate that changes in public attitudes *follow* government actions, which implies that governments are instrumental in creating the "mood" that also constrains them.[52]

---

[51] See C.I. Hovland, I.L. Janis, and H.H. Kelly, *Communication and Persuasion* (New Haven, Conn.: Yale University Press, 1953), pp. 19–55.

[52] James Rosenau, *National Leadership and Foreign Policy: A Case Study in the Mobilization of Public Support* (Princeton, N.J.: Princeton University Press, 1961); Barry B. Hughes and John E. Schwartz, "Dimensions of Political Integration and the Experience of the European Community,"

In political systems where all information is controlled by the government, public opinion plays predominantly a supporting function. A person whose sources of information about the outside world are restricted to a government-controlled newspaper must have considerable initiative and access to unusual resources in order to develop attitudes and opinions contrary to those prescribed for one by one's government.[53] Since members of such societies normally have no independent sources of information and are not allowed channels of communication through which to express opposition to a government's foreign policies, the government is free to change its objectives, withdraw from untenable positions, or change allies without having to worry about domestic reactions. Domestic attitudes are not, therefore, a salient aspect of the definition of the situation. President Roosevelt, collaborating with members of Congress, executive officers, and many members of the press, labored many months to convince the American public that it should support an alliance with the Soviet Union against Nazi Germany. But Joseph Stalin could easily switch from a policy and propaganda line that emphasized hostility toward Nazi Germany to one of collaboration with Hitler. Clearly, considerations about the state of public opinion in the Soviet Union played little role in Stalin's leadership; Stalin could never quite comprehend that governments in the Western democracies were not similarly free to alter policies with impunity.

THE EXTERNAL ENVIRONMENT

The Objectives and Actions of Others

To this point the discussion has focused on a variety of factors and conditions that give rise to governments' policies toward others. But states do not exist in vacuums; any explanation of foreign policy would be largely incomplete without analyzing the conditions abroad which gave rise to specific foreign-policy actions. Most governments, most of the time do not launch diplomatic-military crusades to change a regional or world order, such as Hitler sought. Rather, they *respond* to a variety of other countries' objectives and actions, or to changing conditions and trends in the international system as a whole or in some of its regions. To illustrate: The Soviet intervention in Afghanistan in 1979–1980 was largely a response to increasingly anarchic conditions in that neighboring country; numerous European and American pressures on Japan to restrict exports were a response to Japan's inroads in their markets, its staggering balance-of-payments surplus, and general technological leadership; and the Israeli

---

International Studies Quarterly, 16 (1972), 263–94; Martin Abravanel and Barry Hughes, "The Relationship between Public Opinion and Governmental Foreign Policy: A Cross-National Study," in *Sage International Yearbook of Foreign Policy Studies,* Vol. I, ed. Patrick J. McGowan (Beverly Hills, Calif.: Sage Publications, 1973), 107–34.

[53] Irving L. Janis and M. Brewster Smith, "Effects of Education and Persuasion on National and International Images," in *International Behavior,* ed. Kelman, p. 193.

bombing of an Iraqi nuclear power plant in June 1981 was a response to the anticipated consequence of having a hostile regime in the Middle East in possible possession of nuclear weapons. More long-range plans, such as the demands for creating a new international trade regime, arduously sponsored by most Third World countries, are a response to the postwar liberal trade regime that was not in their opinion distributing rewards equally, but was rather a factor in hindering development. The objectives and actions of others thus set an *agenda* of foreign-policy problems between two or more governments. The *type* or response (conciliatory, threatening, and the like) will usually be similar to the stimulus; that is, most foreign-policy actions tend to be reciprocal. "Hawkish" behavior tends to beget a similar response, although in a relationship character-ized by deep distrust, a conciliatory signal from one actor may be perceived as more a threat than an opportunity. While diplomacy often takes on a tit-for-tat pattern, the behaviors of foreign offices and leaders are not always unam-biguous. To emphasize a point made previously: It is not the objective conditions that count, but how policy makers interpret them.

There was ample evidence that Hitler's objectives went far beyond the incorporation of certain territories adjacent to the Third Reich. But as long as Allied leaders "saw" Germany as being concerned only with rectifying the injus-tices of the Versailles treaty, their appeasement strategy seemed reasonable. A more appropriate response would have been a multilateral deterrence strategy, but only if one could assume that Hitler's territorial ambitions were virtually unlimited. In retrospect, Hitler's ambitions may seem obvious; but at the time, they were obscure.[54] One reason they were obscure was that the German govern-ment was adept at "mixing its signals." On one occasion, Hitler could proffer the hand of friendship and declare that Germany's capacity for goodwill had no bounds. Later, he could make grandiose demands, hurl threats at neighbors, insult government leaders, and break treaty commitments with impunity. It was not so much that the German government could project a false image, but rather that it deliberately gave indications of incompatible intentions. As Jervis points out, information available to policy makers is seldom unambiguous; even a reasonably clear-cut event such as the North Korean invasion of South Korea may not carry any obvious messages about North Korea's ultimate intentions. Indeed, many American officials believed the invasion was planned and directed by Moscow as part of a general Communist military offensive against the West. In the course of normal diplomatic persuasion, putting forth accurate information does not necessarily mean that it will be either understood or believed by the officials of other governments. Again the interpretation of incoming signals or information on conditions abroad is crucial and can be explained best in terms of the attitudes, beliefs, and values of the policy makers.

[54] Robert Jervis, *The Logic of Images in International Relations* (Princeton, N.J.: Princeton University Press, 1970), pp. 7, 12, 19.

In a world characterized by economic interdependence and dependence, governments continuously have to adapt their domestic and foreign policies to economic and other trends occurring in the system. One hundred years ago, most economies were largely self-contained, so that developments on the other side of the world or region required little adjustment elsewhere. The situation is entirely different now and becoming more complex as governments face an increasing array of problems generated abroad. Unemployment levels in Europe are directly affected by American interest rates; inflation levels throughout the world are partly the consequence of OPEC decisions on oil prices; governments of socialist states, as they become increasingly enmeshed in the world economy also feel the effects of externally generated inflation, once thought to be a disease of only capitalist economies; and the poorest countries, faced with immense bills for import of high-priced machinery and oil, have to spend an astounding share—often 50 percent or more—of their foreign exchange earnings just to pay interest on loans incurred to pay for these imports. The dominant global economic trends of the 1970s and 1980s, including higher fuel costs, depletion of some raw materials, high interest rates, unemployment, and spiralling costs of armaments compel governments to react in some manner. The developing countries have sought loan relief, commodity price stabilization schemes, and producers' cartels, as well as reorganization of the world trade system to gain better access to the markets of industrial countries. Many industrial countries have responded to the same trends by searching for oil alternatives, subsidizing exports, and resorting to protective trade devices such as quotas and "orderly trade mechanisms." Each policy of this kind naturally passes the costs off to other nations.

Other trends require similar attention and have produced problems which so far have escaped reasonable or equitable solution. Population growth rates contribute to immense economic problems in the developing countries. The world supply of food lacks management. The criterion for distribution is ability to pay rather than need. A poor harvest in the Soviet Union—a common phenomenon—drives up the price of wheat as the Russians go on the world market. This brings immediate benefits to North America and Australian farmers but may dramatically increase the cost of wheat imports to very poor countries such as India or Ethiopia. Typically in a world of high economic interconnectedness, those who are most dependent will suffer the most and yet have the least capacity to change or manage the system of which they are a part. Trends in the system appear to be increasingly pervasive in their impact and thus raise an increasing number of foreign-policy problems for all states. These trends create the problem, but how governments will respond will be primarily a function of all the domestic variables already mentioned: national needs, bureaucratic practices, public opinion moods, the political priorities of the leadership, and the like.

The structure of power and influence in the system also provides a set of costs, risks, and opportunities. It was a theme of Chapters 2 and 3 that the structure of the international system limits what the component units can do. Orientations and roles can be linked to configurations of power and influence; similarly, it is not difficult to cite cases where changes in the nature of an international system have brought about changing *objectives* and *actions* among various governments. Particularly for smaller or weaker states, the international power structure establishes conditions over which they have little control; it is a "given" in any definition of the situation. For instance, at the end of World War II, all the Western governments perceived a threat to their security from the Soviet Union. Given their military weakness, compared to that of the United States or the Soviet Union, several means of achieving security, such as constructing bilateral alliances, were out of the question. The choices seemed to be reduced to neutrality or alliance with the United States. Given the experiences of the neutrals, such as Belgium, in World War II, the first option was never considered seriously. However, we can suggest that had the Soviet Union not been perceived as a threat and had the configuration of power not been essentially polar, many more governments would have proposed an orientation of nonalignment as the best method of protecting the core value of national security. In Eastern Europe, the alternatives were even more limited. The Hungarians and Czechoslovakians learned the consequences of attempting to disrupt bloc cohesion; once they were committed to the Communist alliance system, they abandoned their freedom to formulate policies outside those sanctioned by the bloc leader. Only in recent years have Romania and some of the other Eastern states been able to pursue their objectives of internal economic development by creating extensive commercial ties with the rest of Europe.

The influence of systemic structure on foreign-policy objectives and actions is also prominent when the structure is undergoing fundamental changes. New power configurations, the decline of bloc cohesiveness, or the rise of new powerful states creates both new opportunities and new risks; old limitations are cast off, and new possibilities for formulating or stressing national objectives arise. As the Chinese tore themselves away from Soviet leadership and domination in the late 1950s, they began increasingly to concentrate on achieving their own national objectives. For the first decade after the Chinese revolution, the problem of Taiwan was the main preoccupation of authorities in Peking. But after the split with the Soviet Union became increasingly wide, the Chinese began to pay more attention to other border areas, particularly in relation to Burma, India, Pakistan, and the Soviet Union itself. Actions, too, are affected. As the cohesiveness of blocs declines, for example, the lesser members may begin establishing commercial, cultural, and diplomatic relations with states in competing blocs, and relations within loosening blocs may change from threats and domination to genuine bargaining between the small members and the bloc leader.

The external environment can also have a more subtle impact on a state's objectives, for any international system possesses certain values or doctrines that transcend purely local or national values. For example, in the eighteenth century, the doctrine of divine right and the values associated with royal authority were accepted by the European upper classes irrespective of nationality; hence, certain external objectives and actions relating to the preservation or extension of royal authority were highly valued. If dynastic prestige was a goal to which all monarchs aspired, then the various methods of achieving status, such as alliances and marriages, were also considered legitimate. Today, it would appear absurd if Great Britain made an alliance with Sweden in order to enhance the prestige of both countries' royal families. In the late nineteenth century, establishment of empires became a "legitimate" national objective, providing increased international influence, economic rewards, and considerable prestige. In the contemporary setting, one of the great transnational values is self-determination and political independence, while almost no value is placed on colonies. The predominant systemwide value today is economic development. A nation's status is closely related to the level of its technology, military forces, and industrialization, no longer to the personal prestige of dynasts, to colonies, or to royal palaces. Since all the major Western states have placed such high value on industrialization and have achieved so many social goals (including international influence) through industrializing policies, it is little wonder that this objective would have a great impact on the values of newer states as well. Although there are some important indigenous pressures for economic development and modernization—as well as strong resistances—the objective of industrialization is adopted by many governments in part because other states have adopted it as their own goal.

RELATIONSHIPS
AMONG THE COMPONENTS

The analysis of policy makers' attitudes, values, beliefs, and personality needs implied that their relevance to a definition of a situation is related to factors of political role and various administrative procedures. In another section it was suggested that public opinion can impose restrictions on the options available to policy makers in a democratic political system, whereas public opinion in authoritarian political systems, no matter what the situation, plays little or no role in helping to shape foreign-policy objectives and actions. We also argued that organizational needs, values, and traditions are less important in influencing policy making during times of crisis than during consideration of routine problems. All these statements are really *hypotheses* about relationships among the various factors that may influence foreign-policy behavior. It may be useful to know that the state of domestic opinion, the structure of the system, and traditional policies are important aspects, let us say, of the Danish foreign minister's view of a situation to which he must respond. But, ideally, we would also want to know *under what conditions* these are more important than organizational values or personality variables. Too often we assume that only one component of a definition of the situation can explain the behavior of states in their relations with other states.

The problem of assessing the relative importance of different components—and the relationship among them—is well illustrated in analyses of Soviet foreign policy. Some observers of Russian politics claim that ideological imperatives are the paramount consideration in formation of Soviet foreign policy. They argue that the Soviet Union, like any other state, has certain core values and interests, such as national independence and territorial security; but all middle-range and long-range objectives and the diplomatic strategies used to achieve them are deduced from Marxism-Leninism. Others have emphasized the persistence of purely "national" themes in Soviet foreign policy; they claim that by virtue of its geographic position (which creates certain weaknesses and strengths from a military point of view), the Soviet Union is primarily continuing czarist foreign policies, albeit under Communist slogans. This type of analysis suggests that Soviet policy makers define their environment and perceive Russian needs and interests much as their predecessors did, except that they place more emphasis on doctrinaire justifications for actions. A third type of analysis of Soviet foreign policy emphasizes contemporary leadership qualities and role rather than ideology or traditional policies as the most important elements in Russia's external behavior. Diplomatic maneuvers and major policy decisions are thus seen not as tactics designed to implement some grandiose ideological plan, but as a means of establishing or safeguarding the position of the top leadership or a way of fulfilling certain psychological needs. Finally, another generalization explaining Soviet actions abroad claims that the leadership is increasingly concerned with fulfilling domestic needs and responding to consumer demands. Thus, domestic needs and expectations will loom as important components of any definition of a situation. Finally, Soviet foreign policy is often portrayed as changing according to the fortunes of various factions in the Communist party or of certain bureaucratic elements, such as the military.

Which of these interpretations is correct? All would seem at least partially valid, since ideology, traditional policies, personal and political needs, and domestic needs would probably be relevant to many policy-making situations. But this tells us very little about the relative importance of each component in different circumstances. We can use historical data to test our propositions and perhaps even make predictions for the future. For example, an analysis of Soviet foreign policy made in terms of the components listed in this chapter would probably reveal that during the 1930s, the structure of the system (as interpreted in Marxist terms), national needs, traditional policies, and Stalin's personality and political role were the most important aspects of reality considered by Soviet policy makers in selecting goals and diplomatic strategies.

In the absence of systematic, comparative analyses of foreign policies in different countries, it is difficult to make verified statements concerning which phenomena might be considered relevant or significant under different circumstances. Instead, we can suggest some hypotheses about which components are apt to constitute the most salient aspects of a definition of the situation, and under what conditions.

1. The more critical or urgent a situation is perceived to be, the fewer people will become directly involved in defining the situation, choosing responses, and selecting goals.
2. The fewer people making these decisions, the more likely that their actions will reflect personal idiosyncrasies, attitudes, beliefs, and personal political needs.[55]
3. The more people involved in defining a situation, formulating goals, or choosing alternatives, the more the decisions will reflect group and organizational values, needs, and traditions, and the less they will reveal the attitudes, beliefs, or images of any single person.[56]
4. The greater the threat perceived by the policy-making group, the more pressure for conformity and group consensus.[57]
5. The structure of the system is likely to be the most pervasive limitation on the selection of goals or actions when (a) it is polarized, (b) expressions of public opinion or nationalist sentiment are weak, (c) the state has few capabilities and perceives a common threat with the bloc leader, and (d) the situation is generally noncritical.
6. Conversely, a government's foreign policy objectives are *least* likely to be influenced by system structure when (a) the international system has a diffuse structure, (b) the situation is defined essentially by one man who can effectively control his domestic resources, including popular attitudes and opinions, (c) personal values, personality needs, or political needs can be achieved through foreign policies, (d) the state is neither a leader nor a member of an alliance or coalition, and (e) the situation is deemed critical.
7. Domestic needs will be salient aspects of a definition of a situation when (a) the state is dependent upon external sources of food and supply, (b) policy makers are responsive to expressions of domestic opinion, and (c) a territory is perceived to be highly vulnerable to attack from abroad.
8. Capabilities establish limits on objectives for all states, no matter what other internal or external conditions prevail.
9. Capabilities are a less important consideration for governments that subscribe to long-range, revolutionary objectives.

[55] See Snyder and Paige, "The United States Decision to Resist Aggression in Korea."
[56] Verba, "Assumptions of Rationality and Non-Rationality."
[57] See Irving Janis, *Victims of Groupthink: A Psychological Study of Foreign-Policy Decisions and Fiascoes* (Boston: Houghton Mifflin, 1972), Chap. 1.

10. The availability of capabilities may be a less important component of a definition of the situation in crisis situations.[58]

11. Doctrines and ideologies are more important in defining situations in political systems or governments (a) that subscribe to an official set of doctrines, (b) where the top leadership is not responsive to expressions of public opinion or domestic needs, (c) that are new or have undergone recent revolution, and (d) during noncritical situations. In conditions of crisis (such as attack or major threat), responses are seldom deduced from, or closely related to, doctrines or ideologies.

12. Bureaucratic influences will be important components of a definition of the situation (a) in long-established and stable states, (b) in noncritical circumstances, and (c) where the top leadership changes rapidly or is uninvolved in an issue area.

13. Except for size as measured by population, foreign-policy actions do not seem to be linked to other national attributes. No *type* of state is more or less likely to hold a monopoly on diplomatic sin or rectitude.

These hypotheses refer to most governments in a variety of situations. If we were to study many cases of foreign-policy making, we would expect them to be corroborated in most instances by empirical data. However, we can also use the various factors in a definition of the situation to explain the objectives, decisions, or actions of a single government in a particular set of circumstances. Suppose we wished to explain the British government's decision to intervene militarily in the Suez crisis of 1956. The story of that decision is lengthy and complex, but several conclusions emerge. First, the decision was made by very few people. Anthony Eden's position was paramount in policy making, and he let only a few cabinet colleagues into his plans. However, Eden had to act on the basis of information that was supplied to him by intelligence agents. Second, the perception of threat was high. Eden thought the closing of the Suez Canal and its nationalization by Egypt represented an intolerable threat to England's supply lines. Third, Eden's definition of the situation was highly colored by analogies drawn from his past diplomatic experience. He had been a foremost opponent of appeasement of Nazi Germany, and in the 1956 circumstances, he portrayed President Nasser as another Hitler, who had to be stopped early. The consequences of inaction, or further diplomacy, were in his opinion extremely dangerous. Fourth, although Eden was undoubtedly aware that there would be considerable opposition to his scheme for Anglo-French intervention on behalf of the Israelis, he did not anticipate a public furor; more specifically, with a comfortable majority in the House of Commons, he knew he was not staking the fate of his government. Fifth, despite the polar power structure in the world and all the presumed opposition of the project from the United States and the Soviet Union, the perception of threat was so great that independent action (that is, without consulting the United States) had to be taken. Finally,

[58] Dina A. Zinnes, Robert C. North, and Howard E. Koch, Jr., "Capability, Threat, and the Outbreak of War," in *International Politics and Foreign Policy: A Reader in Research and Theory*, ed. James Rosenau (New York: Free Press, 1961), pp. 469–82.

estimations of relative military capabilities revealed that the operation could be conducted easily: The Israeli-French-British forces could gain control of the canal at a relatively low cost. Thus, if we wanted to explain the decisions and actions and list the components in their relative importance, the following order might emerge:

1. Eden's perception of threat (conditions abroad) and his analysis of the consequences of inaction, heavily colored by the use of historical analogies.
2. Domestic needs. (Eden acted on the basis of his estimation of the consequences to Britain's economy and security if Nasser closed the canal to international shipping.)
3. The estimation of relative capabilities, including the participation of Israel and France.
4. Bureaucratic influences, in the sense that top military officers told Eden what was militarily feasible.
5. Structure of the system. This was mostly irrelevant in the decision stage, but in the *execution* of the plan, the vigorous opposition by the United States and the Soviet Union prevented its full realization.
6. Public opinion—in particular, Eden's anticipation of some criticism of the project by members of the Conservative party.

To summarize, making foreign-policy decisions and formulation of goals and objectives involves complex processes in which values, attitudes, and images mediate perceptions of reality provided by various sources of information. The resulting images or definitions of the situation form the reality and expectations upon which decisions are formulated. The components of any definition of a situation will vary with conditions in the system, internal political structure, degree of urgency in a situation, and political roles of policy makers; but most definitions of a situation include estimations of capabilities, domestic reactions, and immediate events or conditions abroad. How important each component may be in a given situation is difficult to predict, although some hypotheses have been presented. In the absence of a verified theory of foreign policy, these statements will have to remain as crude generalizations or untested hypotheses, subject always to qualifications and exceptions provided by new developments in international politics.

SELECTED BIBLIOGRAPHY

ABRAVANEL, MARTIN, and BARRY HUGHES, "The Relationship between Public Opinion and Governmental Foreign Policy: A Cross-National Study," in *Sage International Yearbook of Foreign Policy Studies*, Vol. I, ed. Patrick J. McGowan. Beverly Hills, Calif.: Sage Publications, 1973.

ALLISON, GRAHAM T., and MORTON H. HALPERIN, "Bureaucratic Politics: A Paradigm and Some Policy Implications," in *Theory and Policy in International Rela-*

tions, eds. Raymond Tanter and Richard H. Ullman. Princeton, N.J.: Princeton University Press, 1972.

ALMOND, GABRIEL, *The American People and Foreign Policy.* New York: Harcourt Brace Jovanovich, 1950.

BAUER, RAYMOND E., ITHIEL POOL, and L.A. DEXTER, *American Business and Public Policy: The Politics of Foreign Trade.* New York: Atherton, 1963.

BOARDMAN, ROBERT, and A.J.R. GROOM, eds., *The Management of Britain's External Relations.* London: Macmillan, 1973.

BOULDING, KENNETH E., *The Image.* Ann Arbor: University of Michigan Press, 1956.

BRECHER, MICHAEL, *Decisions in Israel's Foreign Policy.* New Haven, Conn.: Yale University Press, 1975.

BRONFENBRENNER, URIE, "The Mirror Image in Soviet-American Relations: A Social Psychologist's Report," *Journal of Social Issues,* 17 (1961), 45–56.

BUCHANAN, WILLIAM, and HADLEY CANTRIL, *How Nations See Each Other.* Urbana: University of Illinois Press, 1953.

CHRISTIANSEN, BJORN, *Attitudes toward Foreign Affairs as a Function of Personality.* Oslo, Norway: Oslo University Press, 1959.

COHEN, BERNARD C., *The Political Process and Foreign Policy: The Making of the Japanese Peace Settlement.* Princeton, N.J.: Princeton University Press, 1957.

———, *The Press and Foreign Policy.* Princeton, N.J.: Princeton University Press, 1963.

———, *The Public's Impact on Foreign Policy.* Boston: Little, Brown, 1973.

DE RIVERA, JOSEPH, *The Psychological Dimensions of Foreign Policy.* Columbus, O.: Charles E. Merrill, 1968.

DEUTSCH, KARL W., and RICHARD L. MERRITT, "Effects of Events on National and International Images," in *International Behavior: A Social-Psychological Analysis,* ed. Herbert C. Kelman. New York: Holt, Rinehart & Winston, 1965.

EAST, MAURICE A., "Size and Foreign Policy Behavior: A Test of Two Models," *World Politics,* 25 (1973), 560–75.

———, STEPHEN A. SALMORE, and CHARLES F. HERMANN, *Why Nations Act: Theoretical Perspectives for Comparative Foreign Policy Studies.* Beverly Hills, Calif.: Sage Publications, 1978.

ESTERLINE, JOHN H., and ROBERT B. BLACK, *The Department of State Political System and Its Subsystems.* Palo Alto, Calif.: Mayfield Publishing Company, 1975.

ETHEREDGE, LLOYD S., *A World of Men: The Private Sources of American Foreign Policy.* Cambridge: MIT Press, 1978.

FRANKEL, JOSEPH, *The Making of Foreign Policy.* New York: Oxford University Press, 1963.

GALTUNG, JOHAN, "Foreign Policy Opinion as a Function of Social Position," in *International Politics and Foreign Policy: A Reader in Research and Theory,* rev. ed., ed., James N. Rosenau. New York: Free Press, 1969.

GEORGE, ALEXANDER, *Presidential Decisionmaking in Foreign Policy: The Effective Use of Information and Advice.* Boulder, Colo.: Westview Press, 1980.

HALPERIN, MORTON, *Bureaucratic Politics and Foreign Policy.* Washington, D.C.: The Brookings Institution, 1974.

HAYES, CHARLTON J.H., *Essays on Nationalism.* New York: Macmillan, 1926.

HENRICKSON, ALAN K, "The Geographical 'Mental Maps' of American Foreign Policy Makers," *International Political Science Review,* 1 (1980), 495–530.

HERO, ALFRED O., "Americans in World Affairs," Vol. I; "Mass Media and World Affairs," Vol. IV; and "Opinion Leaders in American Communities," 6; in *Studies in Citizen Participation in International Relations.* Boston: World Peace Foundation, 1959.

HOLSTI, K.J., *Why Nations Realign: Foreign Policy Restructuring since World War II.* London: George Allen & Unwin, 1982.

HOLSTI, OLE R., "The Belief System and National Images: A Case Study," *Journal of Conflict Resolution,* 6 (1962), 244–52.

HUGHES, BARRY B., *The Domestic Context of American Foreign Policy.* San Francisco: W.H. Freeman, 1978.

JANIS, IRVING L., *Victims of Groupthink: A Psychological Study of Foreign-Policy Decisions and Fiascoes.* Boston: Houghton Mifflin, 1972.

KISSINGER, HENRY A., "Domestic Structure and Foreign Policy," in *American Foreign Policy: Three Essays by Henry A. Kissinger.* New York: Norton, 1969.

KLINEBERG, OTTO, *The Human Dimension in International Relations.* New York: Holt, Rinehart & Winston, 1964.

KORBONSKI, ANDRZEJ, "Issues for Global Actors: The U.S.S.R.," in *Issues in Global Politics,* eds. Gavin Boyd and Charles Pentland. New York: The Free Press, 1981.

LAMPERT, DONALD E., "Issues for Global Actors: The U.S.A.," in *Issues in Global Politics,* eds. Gavin Boyd and Charles Pentland. New York: The Free Press, 1981.

LEVINSON, DANIEL J., "Authoritarian Personality and Foreign Policy," *Journal of Conflict Resolution,* 1 (1957), 37–47.

LIPPMANN, WALTER, *Public Opinion.* New York: Macmillan, 1922.

OGBURN, CHARLTON, JR., "The Flow of Policy-Making in the Department of State," in *International Politics and Foreign Policy: A Reader in Research and Theory,* ed. James N. Rosenau, pp. 229–33. New York: Free Press, 1961.

PRUITT, DEAN G., "Definition of the Situation as a Determinant of International Action," in *International Behavior: A Social-Psychological Analysis,* ed. Herbert C. Kelman. New York: Holt, Rinehart & Winston, 1965.

ROSENAU, JAMES N., ed., *Comparing Foreign Policies: Theories, Findings, Methods.* Beverly Hills, Calif.: Sage Publications, 1975.

———, *Domestic Sources of Foreign Policy. A Case Study in the Mobilization of Public Support.* Princeton, N.J.: Princeton University Press, 1961.

———, "Pre-Theories and Theories of Foreign Policy," in *Approaches to Comparative and International Politics,* ed. R. Barry Farrell. Evanston, Ill.: Northwestern University Press, 1966.

———, *Public Opinion and Foreign Policy.* New York: Random House, 1961.

RUMMEL, RUDOLF J., "The Relationship between National Attributes and Foreign

Conflict Behavior," in *Quantitative International Politics,* ed. J. David Singer. New York: Free Press, 1968.

SCOTT, WILLIAM A., "Psychological and Social Correlates of International Images," in *International Behavior: A Social-Psychological Analysis,* ed. Herbert C. Kelman. New York: Holt, Rinehart & Winston, 1965.

SNYDER, RICHARD C., H.W. BRUCK, and BURTON SAPIN, "Decision Making as an Approach to the Study of International Politics," in *Foreign Policy Decision Making,* eds. Richard C. Snyder, H.W. Bruck, and Burton Sapin. New York: Free Press, 1962.

SNYDER, RICHARD C., and GLENN D. PAIGE, "The United States Decision to Resist Aggression in Korea," in *Foreign Policy Decision Making,* eds. Richard C. Snyder, H.W. Bruck, and Burton Sapin. New York: Free Press, 1962.

SPROUT, HAROLD and MARGARET SPROUT, "Environmental Factors in the Study of International Politics," *Journal of Conflict Resolution,* 1 (1957), 309–28.

SPYKMAN, NICHOLAS J., "Geography and Foreign Policy," I, *American Political Science Review,* 32 (1938), 28–50.

TRISKA, JAN. F., and DAVID D. FINLEY, *Soviet Foreign Policy.* New York: Macmillan, 1968.

VERBA, SIDNEY, "Assumptions of Rationality and Non-Rationality in Models of the International System," *World Politics,* 14 (1961), 93–117.

WALLACE, WILLIAM, *Foreign Policy and the Political Process.* London: Macmillan, 1971.

WHITE, RALPH K., "Images in the Context of International Conflict: Soviet Perceptions of the U.S. and the U.S.S.R.," in *International Behavior: A Social-Psychological Analysis,* ed. Herbert C. Kelman. New York: Holt, Rinehart & Winston, 1965.

13

Law
and World Opinion
in Explanations
of Foreign Policy

Up to this point, we have related foreign-policy outputs to system structures, national attributes, organizational variables, and personality factors. Orientations, national roles, objectives, and actions have been explained by such diverse concepts or phenomena as the "images" in the heads of policy makers or the degree to which an international system is polarized or diffuse in its power structure. The opinions, beliefs, and values of attentive publics—and, in certain cases, of a national population as a whole—can be linked to some types of policy outputs. In Chapter 2, we pointed out that any international system can be characterized in part by the rules whereby it regulates transactions and actions. The world we know, in terms of its international relationships, would be barely recognizable if governments did not generally adhere to certain fundamental norms of behavior that we often take for granted. If the concepts of sovereignty or freedom of the seas did not exist, for example, contemporary foreign-policy orientations, roles, objectives, and actions, as well as international transactions, would be significantly different. No explanation of foreign policy can therefore be considered adequate unless some effort is made to examine how legal norms and less formal "rules of the game" enter into decision-making processes.

In discussing system structure, capabilities, and public opinion, we implied that orientations, roles, objectives, and actions are often *limited* by these variables. An isolationist orientation can be linked, for example, to weak capabilities; governments choose not to pursue goals that they calculate they cannot achieve, or they refrain from an action they fear might prompt unfavorable public reaction, lack of support, or hostile responses abroad. Similarly, legal norms and traditions create restraints and obligations. Whether explicitly or implicitly, when making decisions, policy makers consider legal obligations and the consequences that their proposed courses of action would have on these obligations.

Any obligation is a limitation on a government's freedom of action. Some parts of international law define what states *may* or *must* do; others point out what states *must not* do; still others attempt to define the *situation* in which positive or negative obligations become operational. If, in their foreign-policy behavior, governments meet these obligations—even at the expense of their interests or efficient conduct of diplomacy or war—we can infer that legal considerations at least in part explain their decisions. If, in other circumstances, governments interpret the rules in an arbitrary fashion or violate their permissive, positive, or negative obligations, we can conclude that other values, interests, or considerations were more important.

The main purpose of this chapter is to illustrate how legal norms enter into the making of foreign policy, particularly in the realm of *decisions* and *actions*. To what extent can we explain any particular decision or action by reference to legal obligations? In decision-making situations, are legal obligations more or less important than policy makers' concern over public opinion, ideological preferences, the situation abroad, or organizational traditions? Are some states more "law-abiding" than others? Considering that there is a vast network of commercial, diplomatic, and military treaties between states, as well as customary rules of law and tradition, how often are actions consistent with the obligations that arise from these sources?

Before exploring the relationship between law and foreign policy—how governments use law—we should establish the extent to which a legal system, or comprehensive network of traditional and treaty law binding all states in the world, really exists. In looking at legal factors in foreign-policy outputs, then, our first problem is to establish the existence, nature, and shortcomings of the legal system, then inquire into the situations in which governments are more or less likely to fashion their objectives and actions to accord with legal obligations.

USE OF LEGAL NORMS IN SOME PREINDUSTRIAL INTERNATIONAL SYSTEMS

A review of preindustrial international systems reveals that legal or ethical norms, backed by religious sanctions, were often considered in organizing actions and transactions between independent political units existing *within a common civilization or culture*. In many civilizations, one can find legal or religious principles that established routines to handle (1) communications between the political

units (various forms of diplomatic immunity, for example), (2) commercial transactions, (3) conduct of warfare, and (4) observance of treaties.[1] There is also
evidence regarding the lack of legal or religious norms in ordering the relations,
between political units of two distinct civilizations or cultures. The laws existing among
the political units of one culture were seldom applied in relations with "barbarians" beyond the geographical and cultural boundaries of the system. Until the
twentieth century, the Europeans, much like the Hindus, Greeks, or Moslems
of earlier ages, did not consider that the legal obligations observed in relations
with each other could be applied equally in transactions with "savages" or "barbarians" of entirely different cultures. Classical European international law and
its historic analogies seem to have been recognized and commonly observed
only within groups of political units that were integrated enough to constitute
a real system.

The second point is that there are many analogies between the rules
found operating effectively in historical systems and those of modern international law. Both the reports of explorers and the more recent studies of anthropologists have noted the rather sophisticated rules and ceremonies that were
associated with economic, diplomatic, and military transactions between tribes,
lineage groups, city-states, and ancient empires. Almost all peoples used various
forms of treaties—as we do—to secure peace, followed by some kind of cere-
mony, ritual, or sacrifice to seal obligations. The sanctions to these treaties
were often religious beliefs that those who broke them would die or receive
some violent punishment. Economic exchanges were normally consummated
according to strict rules, and in many cases, tribes also possessed rules and
customs regulating the outbreak and conduct of warfare. Regular observance
of these religious restraints helps to explain why, despite frequent wars and
violence, many tribes survived for centuries.[2]

In the ancient Hindu international system, the role of law in ordering
transactions between independent units was much less in evidence, and few
analogies with modern international law are to be found. Princes and kings
recognized neither the concept of a family of sovereign states nor a well-defined
body of law.[3] Although some vague understandings pertaining to diplomatic
immunities and commercial transactions seemed to exist, sovereigns did not
faithfully observe them except when they feared serious reprisals. There was
so little faith in treaties that the signatories often exchanged hostages as a guarantee for compliance. Lack of the most basic rules for transactions in the Hindu
system is revealed in a passage of Kautilya's *Arthasastra,* in which he recommends
that a king threatened by a neighboring sovereign invite him to his realm on

---

[1] See, for example, Baron S.A. Korff, "An Introduction to the History of International
Law," *American Journal of International Law,* 18 (1924), 246–59; Bronislaw Malinowski, "An Anthropo-
logical Analysis of War," *American Journal of Sociology,* 46 (1941), 521–50; Rudolf W. Holsti, *The
Relation of War to the Origin of the State* (Helsingfors, 1913), pp. 60–70.

[2] Holsti, *The Relation of War to the Origin of the State,* p. 67.

[3] Adda Bozeman, "Representative Systems of Public Order Today," *American Society of
International Law, Proceedings* (April 1959), p. 18.

the pretext of attending a festival, wedding, or elephant hunt and then take him prisoner and even slay him.[4] War and use of force were accepted as normal activities of the state, whether undertaken for glory, plunder, territory, or creation of vassal states. There grew up later, with the fall of the Mauryan dynasties, a vague principle that certain forms of conquest ("demonaic conquest") involving indiscriminate annihilation and slaughter should be avoided. "Righteous" conquests to create vassal states were the ideal for which Hindu kings were expected to go to war. Other chronicles from the period claim that there were fairly strict rules governing conduct of warfare. These mention that warriors fighting from chariots could not strike those on foot, wounded enemies could not be slain, and, as a form of arms control, poisoned weapons could not be used.[5]

THE GROWTH OF EUROPEAN INTERNATIONAL LAW

Legal, religious, and ethical norms regulating transactions between diverse political units existed in many non-Western, preindustrial international systems and civilizations. However, it was in Greece, the Roman Empire, and particularly seventeenth-century Europe that the first coherent legal system, divorced from religion, developed. Among primitive tribes, and in India, China, and the Islamic empire, the norms observed in interunit transactions were inseparable from general precepts of morality or religion, or from ancient customs. The concepts of legal rights and obligations of sovereign governments, central to modern international law, did not come into existence until the appearance of the European nation-state system in the fifteenth, sixteenth, and seventeenth centuries.[6]

What order existed in late medieval Europe grew out of the authority of the Church to prescribe general rules of conduct and from the customary rules of chivalry. In addition, medieval society incorporated the tradition of natural law and order from Rome, from which other principles relating to the transactions between political units were derived. Generally, however, it was the Church, with its notions of hierarchy, authority, and duty, and its ultimate sanction of excommunication, that had the largest impact in moderating the politics of the period. The Peace of God, declared by the Church in the tenth

[4] George Modelski, "Kautilya: Foreign Policy and International System in the Ancient Hindu World," *American Political Science Review*, 58 (1964), 556. There is other evidence, however, that the ancient Indians did, on the whole, observe treaties and develop some legal norms that were observed for reasons other than immediate gain. See Frank M. Russell, *Theories of International Relations* (New York: Appleton-Century-Crofts, Inc., 1936), pp. 41–46.

[5] A.L. Basham, *The Wonder That Was India* (London: Sidgwick and Jackson, 1954), pp. 122–24, 126.

[6] Quincy Wright, *The Role of International Law in the Elimination of War* (Manchester, Eng.: Manchester University Press, 1961), pp. 18–19.

century, attempted to impose restrictions on war, violence, and plundering, but the results were negligible. The Truce of God (1041), established by the Bishop of Arles and the Abbot of Cluny, was more successful and did effectively limit the scope and degree of violence in certain parts of medieval Europe. There was to be, for example, no fighting between Wednesday evening and Monday morning. Such declaratory laws were never observed with any precision, nor did they gain acceptance as custom except in some localities. Later in the medieval period, the doctrine of "just war" arose and helped to deter some forms of violence. The Church considered war "illegal" and its perpetrators subject to ecclesiastical punishment if it was not properly declared by established authorities, with just causes and legitimate objectives.[7]

The basic premises and rules of modern international law—sovereignty, territorial integrity, equality, and noninterference in other states' internal affairs—developed simultaneously with the growth of centralized dynastic political units that no longer accepted the command of any authorities within or outside of their boundaries. Diplomats and dynasts might have acknowledged certain principles of justice deriving from the "law of nature," but generally their conduct in foreign relations was restrained, if at all, only by obligations undertaken with each other in treaties. Religious principles, the Church, and abstract notions of "natural law" no longer effectively limited what the new sovereigns or principalities could and could not do to their neighbors. Restraints were mostly self-imposed, voluntarily observed, and enforced primarily by the threat of counteraction and retaliation. Customs also played a role in providing criteria for distinguishing legitimate from illegitimate policies, and in some instances, the writings of eminent lawyers and theologians, such as Grotius, Pufendorf, and Vattel, had an impact on restricting the actions of Europe's political units. This is not to suggest that by the eighteenth century there existed either a comprehensive set of legal norms prescribing rights and duties in all kinds of relations or a general practice of observing treaties in conducting diplomatic and commercial relations between dynasts. Claims by dynasts that certain customs were so well established as to be part of international law were seldom met with agreement by other states.[8] Rules observed during the conduct of warfare seemed to arise more from the limitations imposed by a crude military technology than from commonly recognized legal principles or humanitarian sentiments. Nevertheless, jurists and diplomats continued to elaborate on the "law of nations," the number of international treaties proliferated, and dynasts increasingly referred to legal advisers in conducting their politics, even if they did not consistently apply the legal advice they received.

New European needs gave the impetus for rapid development of interna-

---

[7] See for details M.H. Keen, *The Laws of War in the Late Middle Ages* (Toronto: University of Toronto Press, 1965).

[8] See Percy Corbett, *Law in Diplomacy* (Princeton, N.J.: Princeton University Press, 1959), Chap. 1.

tional law in the nineteenth century. In particular, the growing volume of intra-European trade and development of sources of raw materials and markets in non-European areas created similar types of transactions and hence similar outlooks toward the rules needed to place economic relations on a stable and predictable basis. Britain's dominant naval position enabled it to establish almost unilaterally the foundations for the modern law of the sea. The greatest expansion of legal doctrines covered matters pertaining to the obligations of debtor states, sanctity of money, protection of commercial property during civil strife, and expropriation of private property.[9] These aspects of international law expressed the contemporary European doctrines of laissez-faire economics and the mutual interests of European business owners in expanding markets and obtaining security for their foreign investments. Thus, nineteenth-century international law was the law of an expanding commercial civilization. But in regulating the use of force and tempering national and imperial rivalries, the law was much less effective.

The doctrine of "just war," which had placed some limitations on the use of force prior to the eighteenth century, was never carried through to the nineteenth century. On the contrary, governments viewed the threat and use of force as legitimate exercises of a sovereign's will. Some publicists fought for the cause of peace and disarmament, but the law of the period reflected the belief that war was a self-justifying instrument of inducement. The relative military stability of the nineteenth century and the restraints on the use of force flowed from the creation of deterrents and the operation of the Concert of Europe, not from the effectiveness of legal principles.

Nineteenth-century international law did incorporate limitations on the scope and degree of violence.[10] New laws of neutrality established definite rights and obligations for both belligerents and neutrals, helping prevent the extension of bilateral military confrontations into continental or regional holocausts, and certain areas or countries such as Switzerland (1815), Belgium (1831), and the Congo Basin (1885) were premanently neutralized by the great powers, thereby removing them from the arenas of conflict.[11] Series of multilateral conventions and codes were also drafted to prevent undue suffering among troops and civilians alike. In most cases, the laws of neutrality and warfare were observed until developments in military technology in the twentieth century made them more or less obsolete.

[9] See Richard A. Falk, "Historical Tendencies, Modernizing and Revolutionary Nations, and the International Legal Order," in *Legal and Political Problems of World Order,* prelim. ed., ed. Saul H. Mendlovitz (New York: The Fund for Education Concerning World Peace through World Law, 1962), pp. 133–34; Charles De Visscher, *Theory and Reality in Public International Law,* trans. P.E. Corbett (Princeton, N.J.: Princeton University Press, 1957), p. 136; Morton A. Kaplan and Nicholas de B. Katzenbach, *The Political Foundations of International Law* (New York: John Wiley, 1961), p. 28.

[10] Richard A. Falk, "Revolutionary Nations and the Quality of International Legal Order," in *The Revolution in World Politics,* ed. Morton A. Kaplan (New York: John Wiley, 1962), p. 320.

[11] Belgium and the Congo (Zaire) are, of course, no longer neutral.

CONTEMPORARY INTERNATIONAL LAW: THE SOURCE AND EXISTENCE OF LEGAL NORMS AND RESTRAINTS

International law, based on its European origins, has continued to develop in scope and precision during the twentieth century despite the occurrence of two great world wars. An important part of our contemporary law has arisen from the *customary practices of states* over many decades and centuries. In many cases, governments have assembled to translate customary practices into multilateral *treaties* or *codes,* thus setting custom in a more precise framework of written rules. *International and domestic tribunals* have handled thousands of cases involving conflicts between citizens and governments of diverse states, and their decisions, although not strictly binding on subsequent cases, have established many important principles and precedents considered to be part of the modern law of nations. Finally, states have concluded thousands of *bilateral and multilateral treaties* establishing new mutual rights and obligations as well as restrictions on what governments may or may not do in their external relations. Unlike the customary sources of international law, treaties can be drafted, changed, and adapted to particular needs and circumstances and can, therefore, establish immediately new principles, rights, and obligations to regulate the relations between states. For example, since there is no precedent or precise analogy to the problems presented by space exploration, the law covering this area must be *created* by governments through negotiated treaties. Treaties cannot establish new rights or obligations for those states that are not parties to them, whereas customary rules of law can be invoked by all states.

From these sources has grown a modern international law that displays, through custom and precedent, continuity with the past but is infinitely more complex than it was in the past. It seeks to regulate, stabilize, and make predictable types and quantities of commercial and political transactions that are largely unprecedented. In addition, the new law reflects contemporary ethical values that condemn the use of force as an instrument of inducement. The nineteenth-century attitude and doctrine toward war as an instrument of policy to be unleashed by any government solely at its own discretion has been replaced by prohibitions in the United Nations Charter against recourse of force and even the threat to use force, except in cases of self-defense or in conformity to a collective decision. The old laws of neutrality have been superseded by the obligation of *all* states to assist victims of aggression. As an outcome of the Nuremberg trials of Nazi war criminals and the Genocide Convention, personal criminal liability can be imposed against those who launch wars of aggression. In short, as Quincy Wright points out, under the new international law, war is no longer viewed as a duel between legally equal belligerents to be regulated only in its scope, but rather as a crime against all nations that must be prevented.[12]

[12] Wright, *The Role of International Law in the Elimination of War,* pp. 27–28.

It would be difficult to deny the existence of a comprehensive set of rules, rights, obligations, and legal doctrines in numerous treaties, in customs and codes, and in the thousands of decisions of national and international tribunals. These are designed to define rights, limit a state's freedom of action, and prescribe rules of conduct for all types of transactions—technical, commercial, diplomatic, and military. Before we investigate the extent to which these rules and customs effectively restrain action—or in some cases, compel states to take certain actions—it is necessary to point out some of the shortcomings of modern international law, faults found in the body of norms rather than in the actions of governments.

In the first place, no legal norm is so precise as to convey absolutely clear meaning to all people. Although that part of international law based on custom may be more enduring because it reflects common usage and needs,[13] some aspects of it are also vague and imprecise, leaving each state to interpret the custom according to its own interests. Treaties can be formulated more precisely, but these, too, may contain phrases too vague to guide behavior in predictable fashion. Many provisions of the United Nations Charter have been interpreted in different ways by states. Until the day when all conflicts arising out of different interpretations of the law are submitted to impartial tribunals, each government—as do private citizens—will usually construe the meaning of treaties and conventions in such a way as to favor its own political objectives.

Second, legal norms, when they are not legislated by a central political body, tend to change very slowly, with the result that some rules of international law become obsolete before governments acknowledge their obsolescence. Although some governments may feel strong pressures to violate obsolete and unjust norms, their actions are violations nevertheless until a majority of states in the system agree, through practice or conventions, upon new norms. Is it valid, for example, to criticize or make claims against the Allies' persistent violations of the law of neutrality during World War II when the kind of warfare made possible by new industrial technology required vast sources of raw materials, which the neutrals supplied to the Axis powers? The laws of neutrality were drafted in an age of relative economic independence, a condition that no longer prevails. Can the killing of civilians be prevented, as required by the laws of land and naval warfare, when antagonists use nuclear-tipped missiles, long-range artillery, or conventional heavy bombs, or where military and civilian targets are inseparable? The continuing and tortuous debates in the Law of the Sea conferences illustrate the great difficulties involved in trying to fashion a consensus among more than 150 states. Every state agrees there is a problem— the inadequacy of old rules governing maritime matters—but a solution is difficult

---

[13] De Visscher, *Theory and Reality in Public International Law*, p. 155.

to arrange. On the other hand, if changing conditions excuse violations of rules and doctrines, very few norms would be entirely effective, and little predictability would be possible in the relations among states.

Developments in technology require all sorts of new international regimes to regulate the actions and transactions of states and private bodies. Among the problems being grappled with today are those relating to communication. As direct satellite television broadcasting becomes available, what rules should be developed so that two possibly incompatible principles can be observed: free flow of information versus sovereignty? Should the major industrial countries, because they own the technology, be able to broadcast what they wish directly to the citizens of other countries? Or should governments have the right to screen such broadcasts, to black out those programs they judge to be undesirable for their citizens? Such questions are almost impossible to resolve in a manner mutually satisfying to more than 150 governments, yet these are the sorts of issues for which new rules have to be devised. Unlike the nineteenth century when the European countries simply imposed their legal norms on colonial peoples, those who today develop and own technology are finding it increasingly difficult to develop rules which in any way imply inequality between the industrial and developing countries.

We should not place too much emphasis on these inadequacies of the body of legal norms, for it might lead us to conclude that the ineffectiveness of some legal restraints and limitations arises from deficiencies in the law itself. Nor should we assume that the behavior of governments in this respect will change simply because norms are brought up to date or made more precise. Despite the existence of hundreds of arbitration treaties between states, the League of Nations Convenant, the Geneva Protocol of 1924, the Treaty for the Renunciation of War (The Kellogg-Briand Treaty, 1928), the Anti-War Treaty of Rio de Janeiro in 1933, and the United Nations Charter, the use of force has not been effectively regulated yet. Some of these treaties and charters are not entirely clear in their details, but this should not suggest that more and better treaties or international institutions will solve the problem of war. More important is that relatively few disputes and conflicts of objectives arise out of differing interpretations of law. If international politics were defined only as the problems and processes of adjusting conflicts arising from differing conceptions of legal rights and duties, we should be concerned with studying ways to improve the content of the law. But since international politics involve, in addition to collaborative and competitive relationships, the problems and processes of adjusting conflicts arising from more or less incompatible collective objectives, then no matter how clear, precise, and logical the law is, it would not be observed in all instances. The body of the law is far from perfect, but failure to observe legal norms does not necessarily result from imperfections of the law.

THE USE OF LAW IN THE PURSUIT
OF FOREIGN-POLICY OBJECTIVES

In analyzing the role of legal norms in the conduct of foreign policy, it is important to remember that many of the customs, treaties, and doctrines of international law are designed to regulate essentially *private* transactions between citizens of different nations. They are not necessarily concerned with the types of issues arising from conflicts over incompatible *collective* objectives. A substantial portion of existing treaties and legal principles create obligations and provide the ground rules for actions and transactions relating to foreign investment, fishing and conservation, extradition of criminals, maritime traffic, payment of damages of foreign citizens, citizenship, responsibility of minor police officials for actions against noncitizens, and so forth. Such affairs normally do not involve major collective interests, even though violations of established procedures or rules may create nasty incidents. The distinction between a routine and vital matter in foreign policy is not always clear, of course, but great international crises seldom arise out of breaches of law affecting the interests of private citizens.

In dealing with the problems of private citizens and business enterprises, governments tend to rely heavily on established bureaucratic procedures. Since most governments apply approximately similar norms to these transactions, the element of opposition and conflict is reduced and in many cases eliminated. Even where violations of law have occurred against private citizens and their interests, governments are no longer likely to translate these problems into diplomatic conflicts, particularly where relations between the two states are relatively cordial. A great expansion of private and intergovernmental routine transactions has occurred during this century, and even though we are not often reminded of the fact, the vast majority of these transactions and the decisions associated with them are based on principles of international law. In these areas of foreign relations, governments have at least approached the ideal of the "rule of law."

The extreme opposite situation is where governments perceive a threat to vital collective, or core, objectives and interests. What role do legal principles play in the typical crisis situation? In crises, legal obligations and the demands for effective action (in the sense of creating deterrents, making threats, or undertaking policies that essentially seek to punish the opponent) often conflict. In relationships typified by great hostility, incompatibility of objectives, and use of force by the other side, no statesman could be expected to attach absolute value to law observance if by doing so he would sacrifice all his other objectives, including the security of his country. In a crisis, even the most legally minded statesman chooses to use whatever techniques of statecraft or actions are necessary to achieve or defend stated objectives, even when he is fully aware that to do so involves deliberate violation of treaties or legal principles. In 1939, for example, Winston Churchill, as first lord of the Admiralty, recommended that the Royal Navy plant mines in the territorial waters of neutral Norway in order to prevent the shipment of iron ore from Sweden to Nazi Germany. Churchill knew that such action would violate Norway's neutrality and territorial waters, but defended his recommendation on the ground that "the letter of the law must not in supreme emergency obstruct those who are charged with its preservation and enforcement. . . . Humanity, rather than legality, must be our guide."[14] It is not difficult to find instances where even legal scholars have defended the legal violations of governments on the grounds that there were more compelling moral imperatives—particularly the demands of "national security"—than strict adherence to legal norms and treaty obligations. Thus, when advancement of one nation's objectives seriously threatens those of another, military and strategic criteria rather than legal desiderata tend to dominate the making and execution of foreign-policy decisions.

The problem of measuring the influence of legal obligations in decision making is that such influence involves more than the observance or nonobservance of clearly defined rules of law. A government can take action that it *believes* is consistent with legal obligations or the permissive components of international law. Governments normally characterize conflicts in the legal and diplomatic terms *that are most advantageous to their interests and objectives.* This practice is not necessarily a capricious twisting of legal principle to fit facts; it arises out of different perceptions of reality. A government may claim in its attempt to punish or threaten a hostile neighbor that its own aggressive actions are legally justified as "self-defense." Hence, in 1956, when Israel invaded Egypt, it invoked the law of self-defense. A neutral observer may conclude that Israel used aggression, whereas Israeli policy makers may have been quite convinced that their attack on Egypt was a legitimate act of self-defense. In this situation, can it be determined precisely whether or not legal principles and obligations effectively restrained actions? The South African government has consistently characterized its *apartheid* policies as purely a domestic affair, while those on the outside have insisted that these policies are a threat to peace and a violation of the Declaration of Human Rights, hence subject to outside interference. During the uprising in Algeria in the 1950s, the rebels characterized their struggle as a war between two states—France and Algeria—whereas the French maintained that it was a domestic rebellion. One could invoke quite different legal principles as applying to the actions taken in this situation, depending upon which characterization was accepted. When characterizations of one set of events vary so greatly, it becomes extremely difficult to decide which actions are in accord with, or in violation of, the rules of international law. In either case, the policy makers

---

[14] Quoted in Oliver Lissitzyn, "Western and Soviet Perspectives on International Law," *American Society of International Law, Proceedings* (April 1959), p. 25.

may have believed sincerely that their actions were legally justified, given their understanding of the facts.

Governments thus may use the flexibility of the law to their advantage. Moreover, legal norms in crisis situations seem to be used not so much to determine actions as to build justifications for certain actions. Indeed, case studies of recent conflicts between states reveal that governments use law essentially to further their objectives. In this sense, legal norms enter into decision making less as criteria to determine what, substantively, governments should or should not do, than as sets of principles that can be put together into a case to *justify actions that have already been taken.* Legal norms thus become diplomatic capabilities; governments fabricate legal justifications for their decisions and actions in order to mobilize domestic and external support. The American experience in the 1962 Cuban missile crisis reveals, for example, that the legal argument justifying a U.S. "quarantine" against importation of Soviet missiles into Cuba was made *after* the quarantine was already established. There is little evidence showing that the decision, as it was being made, was seriously debated on legal grounds.[15] Similarly, during various crises over Berlin, the confrontation between Malaysia and Indonesia in the mid-1960s, and the Turkish invasion of Cyprus in 1974, law was used primarily to (1) establish the legitimacy of diplomatic positions, and (2) to mobilize diplomatic and public support for each party's own position, while attempting to demonstrate that the opposition's policies or actions were illegitimate.[16]

Thus, we end with three hypotheses about the relevance of legal norms in explaining policy decisions and actions:

1. In (a) issue areas involving primarily private interests, commercial, technological, and cultural actions and transactions, and (b) between states that normally maintain friendly relations, legal norms are at least as important in policy making as are systemic conditions, capabilities, public opinion, organizational values (which probably include a strong commitment to the "legal" way of doing things), or the personal preferences, values, or political needs of individual decision makers. In "routine" matters between two governments, decisions almost always conform to both substantive and procedural norms.
2. In (a) issue areas involving the conflict of collective interests and core values,

---

[15] Lawrence Scheinman and David Wilkinson, eds., *International Law and Political Crisis: An Analytical Casebook* (Boston: Little, Brown, 1968), p. 201. However, one of the participants in the Cuban episode shows that legal considerations were more prominent in decision making than is commonly acknowledged in most memoirs. See Abraham Chayes, *The Cuban Missile Crisis* (New York: Oxford University Press, 1974).

[16] Henkin, in his own case studies, is less pessimistic about the influence of law in crisis decision-making situations. He sees that even where decisions contravene legal norms, policy makers often "soften" their actions, refrain from doing certain things they might otherwise do, because of their awareness of legal prohibitions. Louis Henkin, *How Nations Behave: Law and Foreign Policy,* 2nd ed. (New York: Columbia University Press, 1979), Chaps. 13–16.

and (b) between states that ordinarily maintain friendly relations, governments will attempt to organize their actions to make them consistent with legal obligations. However, perceptions of threat (definition of the situation), the demands of public opinion, and the personal needs of decision makers may require that legal norms be violated, or at least interpreted arbitrarily.[17]

3. In (a) issue areas involving the conflict of important collective interests and core values, and (b) between states that ordinarily do not maintain friendly relations, governments will always choose "effective action" against legal obligations, when the two are incompatible. Perceptions of threat (definitions of the situation), relative capabilities, demands of public opinion, and the political needs of decision makers will be much more important in explaining objectives and actions than will treaty obligations.

Two general conclusions about the place of law in international politics can be offered. First, as a vast proportion of transactions between states are not concerned with crises and conflicts, we can infer that the obligations and procedures established through custom, treaties, and general principles of law predominate in policy making. The fact that most governments respect each other's sovereignty, that they do not seize each other's vessels on the high seas, that they do not arbitrarily incarcerate travelers and tourists, that they do not imprison diplomats, and that they recognize each other's legal equality indicates the pervasiveness of the world's legal system in foreign policy. On the other hand, in crisis situations, law assumes different functions: It is used primarily for mobilizing support at home and abroad rather than for establishing limits on what can or should be done.

[17] The case of shipping routes through the Arctic Ocean illustrates this hypothesis well. In 1969, an American oil tanker successfully navigated the Northwest Passage, opening up a potential oil route between the petroleum fields of northern Alaska and the east coast of the United States. While from a commercial point of view this trip might have proven of great value to the United States, it raised serious problems in Canada. What would happen if, in navigating these ice-filled waters, one of the tankers spilled its oil cargo? The result would be devastation of miles of Canada's Arctic coast. The pollution problem at this latitude is particularly acute, since all living materials maintain a precarious balance; any destruction takes decades to repair through natural processes (unlike the situation in lower latitudes, where natural growth and processes can overcome destruction of the environment in a relatively short time). The Canadian government believed it had to establish some controls over navigation in the north to prevent a potential pollution disaster, even though that control would have to go beyond the traditional 3- to 12-mile territorial limit to be effective. Can a government claim control over high seas in order to protect itself from a perceived threat? Ottawa decided that it should unilaterally declare control for 100 miles beyond the northern coast, and passed legislation establishing restrictions on shipping in the area. From an ecological point of view, the decision was certainly necessary, since it was apparent that the governments of the world would not draft a multilateral treaty governing such problems in time to prevent a possible disaster. The Canadian government, despite strong protests from Washington and London, certainly challenged the well-established principle of freedom of the seas through its action. Moreover, by acting unilaterally, it established a potentially dangerous precedent. Now any government, for whatever reason, could claim similar jurisdiction, arguing, "If Canada can do it, why can't we?" In this case, self-protection was chosen over legal traditions and the views of the government's closest friends.

NONLEGAL OBLIGATIONS
IN FOREIGN POLICY

It would be impossible for governments to regulate all their actions and transactions through legal instruments such as treaties. As Raymond Cohen has pointed out, international politics are too fluid, complicated, and rapidly changing "to permit prior legislation on all possible contingencies and developments."[18] The same is true in personal life: Rules and laws provide guidance for behavior, but it would be impossible to conduct our lives if every conceivable situation calling for action or decision were regulated. In fact, most of us conduct our relationships employing a variety of nonwritten agreements, understandings, and commitments.

Cohen has classified a number of these international "rules of the game" according to the degree of explicitness with which an agreement is communicated. At one end of the continuum are international treaties and covenants, explicit statements outlining behavioral obligations—the do's and don'ts of international politics. Less formal are *nonbinding written understandings.* They do not have the status of treaties but can be just as important in policy making. Cohen provides the example of the 1972 Shanghai Communiqué between the United States and China. After almost twenty-five years of deep hostility between the two governments, the authorities of the two countries were able to hammer out a framework of rules that would guide the establishment of formal diplomatic relations, and a formula that would deal with the tricky problem of Taiwan's status. The communiqué outlined general principles but established no binding obligations; these were to be worked out in detail as the relationship developed. A less happy nonbinding agreement was former President Nixon's famous letter to President Thieu of South Vietnam to the effect that if the North Vietnamese violated the terms of the Paris Agreement (ending the Vietnamese war), the United States would take "swift and severe retaliatory action." In the midst of the Watergate scandal in 1975, the North Vietnamese attacked. Facing a hostile Congress, President Nixon was unable to meet the commitments he had made to Thieu.

Gentlemen's Agreements are also legally nonbinding; they differ from the previous category by not even being written; such agreements are only verbal exchanges of promises. That they are not engraved on paper does not necessarily reduce their effectiveness, however. As in private life, broken promises incur significant costs in a relationship. They are also useful in foreign policy because in some circumstances, particularly in a rapidly changing situation, formal treaties are inappropriate. Where leaders wish to avoid adverse publicity or to bind their successors, they may also rely on gentlemen's agreements.

Tacit Understandings are never written, are certainly not binding, and result from hints, signals, and past behavior rather than from formal communica-

---

[18] "Rules of the Game in International Politics," *International Studies Quarterly,* 24 (March 1980), 129–50.

tion. They develop because they provide some net gain to each of the parties, but for a variety of reasons, they cannot be explicitly stated or put into a document. There are, for example, a variety of conventions and understandings between the intelligence agencies of the major powers. While their agents might indulge in all sorts of skullduggery, deception, and assassination and even turn traitor, some things simply "are not done." Almost all countries expel apprehended spies or hold them until they can obtain the release of their own agents. They do not, however, put them on trial. The few exceptions in the multitude of cases prove the rule. More generally, the Americans and Soviets have tacit understandings that they will not intervene militarily in each other's spheres of influence. This understanding arises more from necessity than choice, yet with the exception of Cuba—which gave rise to the most dangerous crisis in the postwar period—it has been observed. One of the problems of détente is to try to develop new tacit understandings regarding Soviet and American activities in Africa, the Middle East, and South Asia.

These "rules of the game," while not resting on very secure foundations, are nevertheless important considerations in many decision-making situations. They provide flexibility; they can be denounced more easily than treaties; they have no legal status; governments can deny their existence (except the written ones). Despite their informalities, they may have as much importance in policy making as more formal instruments and, in some cases, even more. The important point is that they do guide behavior, and for much the same reasons as treaties: The costs of breaking or repudiating agreements are often very high. We turn, then, to a consideration of those costs, more commonly known as the sanctions of international law and "rules of the game."

LAW IN FOREIGN POLICY: THE SANCTIONS OF INTERNATIONAL NORMS

In most legal systems, rules and customs are normally observed for four distinct, although similar, reasons: (1) self-advantage, (2) habit, (3) prestige, and (4) fear of reprisal. Legal norms are a suitable basis for conducting transactions, particularly where they can help advance the values and interests of one party and where the other party, by observing the rules, can also expect some benefit. Rules simplify procedures between governments and are consequently of advantage to all. The expectation of *reciprocity* is an important factor in the observance of legal norms and obligations. A government accepts the obligations and restrictions imposed by law because it expects, or hopes, that the partners with whom it is in a relationship will base their decisions and responses on similar legal criteria. Self-advantage is mutual. This does not mean that all other considerations are irrelevant to the making of foreign-policy decisions; it means, rather, that governments in most situations recognize and acknowledge the long-run advantages—particularly reciprocity—of conforming their actions to legal norms. This realization tempers considerations of expediency, military "necessity," and short-run political advantages. When the advantages of law observation are clear and persistent, a habit or custom of conducting transactions according to certain principles and routines may also arise.

In addition to reciprocity and habit, another advantage of law observance is that a government may effectively raise its international prestige, and thus its diplomatic influence with other states, if it develops a reputation in the community as a "law-abiding" state. A reputation for meeting treaty obligations and observing well-established legal principles in many types of transactions may be an important asset in the daily dealings of diplomats. Small states, in particular, may be able to obtain a sympathetic hearing from the governments of major powers if their reputation for observing legal obligations is well established.[19] A government that persistently breaks treaties, defies resolutions of international organizations, and capriciously twists the accepted meaning of legal doctrines will lower its credibility in diplomatic negotiations and hence its influence. One need point only to the poor reputation of the Soviet Union until Stalin's death. For many years, Western governments were reluctant to enter into any trade or cultural negotiations with his regime on the ground that the Soviet government had violated the letter or spirit of many important political and commercial treaties to which it had been a signatory.

Negative sanctions, or fear of various forms of reprisal, may also prompt governments to observe their obligations. Development of norms relating to diplomatic immunities is a good example. It was common among new dynastic regimes in Europe not to accord immunities to foreign diplomats, with the result that sometimes foreign diplomats were abused, jailed, and even executed by the government to which they were accredited. But this situation did not prevail, because these governments quickly recognized that if they treated foreign diplomats in this manner, their own representatives abroad could be—and were—treated similarly.

In addition to self-interest, habit, prestige factors, and fear to reprisal, two other considerations must be mentioned as reasons why governments, when faced with alternative courses of action, often choose the one most closely in accord with legal obligations and established practice. First, all governments, whether they explicitly acknowledge it or not, desire at least some convenience, stability, and predictability in their external relations. The ordinary transactions

---

[19] We can cite the case of Finland in the 1930s and 1940s to illustrate this generalization. The American government and people were very sympathetic to Finland's interests during this period, largely because Finland had earned a reputation for honesty as a result of being the only country to repay the United States every dollar it had previously borrowed. This one act of meeting obligations created inestimable public goodwill and official responsiveness toward Finland and, hence, increased Finnish diplomatic influence vis-à-vis the United States. Juhani Paasivirta, *Suomen kuva Yhdysvalloissa* (Helsinki: Werner Söderström, 1962), Chap. 10.

between nations, which are necessary to maintain economic viability, communications, and even security, are based on routines protected by legal doctrines or treaties. If these transactions were made completely unpredictable by lack of law observance, chaos and the impossibility of orderly policy making would ensue. Even revolutionary regimes during their years of external aggressiveness willingly comply with many of the rules of law adhered to by their enemies simply in order to exist. For states with more modest external objectives, law observance for many types of transaction becomes so routine that policy makers would consider other alternatives only in great conflicts or emergencies. The desire for stability and predictability can also be seen when governments convene after great wars or periods of instability to make permanent the changes that had been achieved through political and military actions. The peace treaty— like many other types of treaty—creates a new order out of chaos, stability out of rapid change, and predictability out of uncertainty.

Governments may or may not accept the limitations on actions imposed by legal norms. Certainly, it is not difficult to cite obvious violations of international law. But diplomatic history also reveals abundant evidence that many statesmen do place high value on at least appearing to comply with written and unwritten rules, legal doctrines, and treaties and that in so doing they not only display concern over their prestige or possible retaliation, but demonstrate their belief in the ethical value of law observance. In selecting among alternative courses of action, policy makers do not always adopt a Machiavellian approach, thinking, "This time I will observe the law because I fear retaliation, or a lowering of my prestige, if I do not; but perhaps next time, if I think I can get away with it, I will disregard legal prohibitions and seek to achieve my objectives the quickest way possible and at least material cost." Law is, after all, more than a set of arbitrary rules derived from custom and treaties. Insofar as legal norms and "rules of the game" prevent governments from doing certain things, punish others, or prescribe certain courses of action, they reflect values and moral judgments. The provisions of the United Nations Charter prohibiting the threat or use of force and the principles of the Genocide Convention do not arise from custom, prior treaties, or court decisions. These rules— and many unwritten understandings—emanate directly from a widespread belief that the use of force or the systematic slaying of religious or ethnic groups is inherently immoral and ethically reprehensible.

The observance of these and many other types of rules thus derives from considerations other than convenience. Although policy makers often excuse certain illegal actions as being dictated by the demands of "national security" or "national interest," they do not consistently break rules and norms just because they are acting in the name of the state. Men are usually anxious to do not only what is practical and convenient, but also what they believe is right. Policy makers, like private citizens, will frequently respect a rule or choose that course of action most consistent with legal norms, because they believe that the norms are intrinsically correct and ought to be observed regardless of some particular disadvantage derived from their observance. An eminent international jurist, Charles De Visscher, has written that the observance of international law is ultimately a problem of individual attitudes and morality and not a question of the existence of lack of perfection in legal doctrines.

> The problem of obligation in international law is part of the problem of obligation in general, and this in turn is a moral problem. The distinction between ethical and legal categories, reasonable in itself and in many ways necessary, must not be pushed to the point of completely separating law from the primary moral notions to which all the normative disciplines are attached as to a common stem. Between States as within the State, law belongs to morals insofar as the idea of the just, which forms its specific content, is inseparable from the idea of the good, which is a moral idea. What, then, in the international sphere, is the order of facts, interests, ideas, or sentiments that can provide the moral substratum of obligation? Merely to invoke the idea of an international community . . . is immediately to move into a vicious circle, for it is to postulate in men, shut in their national compartments, something that they will largely lack, namely the community spirit, the deliberate adherence to supranational values. No society has any legal foundation unless men believe in its necessity. The ultimate explanation of society as of law is found beyond society, in individual consciences.[20]

FOREIGN EXPECTATIONS AND "WORLD PUBLIC OPINION" AS FACTORS IN POLICY MAKING

Through treaties, declarations, and traditional methods of dealing with other states, most governments create abroad certain expectations that future actions will conform with past patterns of behavior. American officals expect that the British will conduct their foreign relations according to certain standards, and when these standards are not met or are violated, both governmental and public protests may ensue. Part of the unfavorable American reaction to the British invasion of the Suez Canal and Egypt in 1956 derived from the widespread expectation that the British did not, as a matter of style and tradition, resolve their international conflicts by military aggression. On the other hand, American policy makers for many years held an "image" of the Soviet government as untrustworthy, deceitful, aggressive, and an unreliable partner to treaties and other international commitments.[21] When Soviet behavior did conform to this

---

[20] De Visscher, *Theory and Reality in Public International Law*, p. 98, trans. P.E. Corbett. Copyright © 1957 by Princeton University Press, revised edn. © 1968 by Princeton University Press.

[21] See for example, Harry S. Truman, *Memoirs*, 1 (Garden City, N.Y.: Doubleday, 1955), 320; John R. Beal, *John Foster Dulles*, 1888–1959 (New York: Harper & Row, 1959), pp. 199ff; James Byrnes, *Speaking Frankly* (New York: Harper & Row, 1947); Robert Murphy, *Diplomat among Warriors* (Garden City, N.Y.: Doubleday, 1964), pp. 435ff.

image, indignation was not so strong, because the behavior was expected and predictable.

Opinions expressed by governments and peoples toward the actions of foreign states do not vary only because of different expectations. There is also the problem of different perceptions by peoples with different experiences. Many forms of Soviet or Chinese behavior that Westerners have considered unethical have been similar to types of behavior their own governments have practiced. The predominant American public "image" of Great Britain is that of a loyal ally, courageous and magnanimous in voluntarily adapting its colonial empire into a free commonwealth of nations. To an African nationalist, however, the concept of Britain arising from his personal experience may be that of a rapacious imperial power that exploited his people, practiced the most blatant forms of discrimination, and suppressed legitimate political movements. The same African, who has no experience with Soviet diplomacy and foreign policy, may look upon the Soviet Union as just another great power that has successfully industrialized in a short period of time. In turn, this "image" of the Soviet Union is not likely to be similar to that held by a refugee from the Hungarian revolution of 1956. Different historical experiences greatly affect our perceptions of reality and our expectations concerning the behavior of other governments. It is unlikely, therefore, that when one nation undertakes efforts of rewards or threats of punishment, its actions will be interpreted in a similar way in different areas of the world.

Aside from obvious cases, such as overt aggression or genocide, it is difficult to believe that such a thing as "world public opinion" exists today, if by that we mean a fundamental and popular consensus as to what constitutes legitimate, legal, or ethical behavior in international relationships. Unlike the European international system of the eighteenth century, where a small cosmopolitan aristocracy possessed similar cultural traits and social values, the people who make judgments on international events today do so from the vantage of diverse traditions, ideologies, and ethical standards. With such diverse values, and therefore perceptions, not only may the people in question differ as to what constitutes moral and immoral behavior, but the meanings they ascribe to a set of commonly perceived facts may be so diverse as to preclude development of any common worldwide opinion on a situation.

We must also approach cautiously the concept of "world public opinion" as an important factor explaining foreign-policy decisions because often the demonstrations condemning a foreign government's external policies are not spontaneous expressions of attitudes, but organized incidents led by government officials or professional agitators who wish to embarrass the target government for their own purposes. Freedom of the press is not practiced in most countries, and through government restrictions and censorship, citizens of many countries are able to get only their own government's version of a particular set of events. These governments usually characterize events in the light of their own ideological predilections and foreign-policy interests. Even in those countries where press freedom is observed, reporting of news may be so slanted by stereotypes and omissions, or by under- or overemphasis, that the people who obtain information solely from these news sources may express opinions not congruent with the facts of a situation.

What, then, are we to conclude about the role of "world public opinion" and expectations of other governments in the conduct of a government's foreign relations? Because there are historical examples of both the effectiveness and the impotence of foreign opinion as influences on a government's behavior, it is difficult to generalize. However, some conclusions or hypotheses might be suggested. First, most governments *are* sensitive to the opinions expressed abroad about their policies and how they execute them. Otherwise they would not spend such large sums in trying, through diplomacy and propaganda programs, to create favorable impressions abroad. But they are not equally sensitive to all sources of opinion. Where, for example, perceptions of reality vary greatly, the government being condemned will probably not count hostile opinions as important. If the Soviet Union characterized American intervention in South Vietnam as imperialism and aggression, this was so different from the American government's understanding of the situation that Soviet hostility would probably be discounted. Also, governments are no doubt much more sensitive to opinions expressed by their closest friends and allies than those emanating from noninvolved or hostile countries. Similarly, they are more concerned with conforming their actions to their allies' expectations than to those of states with which they are not so directly involved.

Second, most governments are concerned with their prestige, an important, if intangible, aspect of their diplomatic effectiveness. No government could anticipate with pleasure a resolution in the General Assembly condemning its actions abroad. But in some crises, policy makers place such high value on achieving or defending their objectives that they are willing to break commitments, violate rules to which they normally adhere, and, in short, follow strictly national imperatives. In many other instances, policy makers *anticipate* the reactions of other governments and choose policy alternatives that are least likely to meet with hostile reactions. We can cite cases where resolutions in international organizations both failed and succeeded in persuading governments to observe legal and moral obligations; it is more difficult to know of all those cases where governments did *not* choose a particular course of action because their policy makers anticipated unfavorable responses abroad. If we conceive of "world public opinion" as being both the spontaneous and the organized expressions of attentive publics on particular situations, often communicated through propaganda channels, it can be an effective restraint on policy, provided that there is some agreement among the publics, that the attitudes are also expressed by friendly governments and are not merely the expected hostility of unfriendly states, and that defiance of those attitudes would lower a state's prestige and diplomatic influence.

SELECTED BIBLIOGRAPHY

ANAND, R.P., *New States and International Law*. Delhi, India: Vikas Publishing House, 1972.

BOWIE, ROBERT R., *Suez 1956: International Crises and the Role of Law*. New York and London: Oxford University Press, 1974.

BOZEMAN, ADDA, *The Future of Law in a Multicultural World*. Princeton, N.J.: Princeton University Press, 1971.

———, "Law, Culture and Foreign Policy: East versus West," *Atlantic Community Quarterly*, 12 (1974), 219–32.

COHEN, JEROME, and H. CHIU, *People's China and International Law*. Princeton, N.J.: Princeton University Press, 1974.

COHEN, RAYMOND, *International Politics: The Rules of Game*. (New York and London: Longman, 1981).

CORBETT, PERCY E., *Law in Diplomacy*. Princeton, N.J.: Princeton University Press, 1959.

DE VISSCHER, CHARLES, *Theory and Reality in Public International Law*, trans. Percy E. Corbett. Princeton, N.J.: Princeton University Press, 1957.

FALK, RICHARD A., *Law, Morality and War in the Contemporary World*. New York: Praeger, 1963.

———, *Legal Order in a Violent World*. Princeton, N.J.: Princeton University Press, 1968.

———, "The Reality of International Law," *World Politics*, 14 (1962), 353–63.

FITZMAURICE, GERALD G., "The Foundations of the Authority of International Law and the Problem of Enforcement," *Modern Law Review*, 19 (1956), 1–13.

FRANCK, THOMAS M., "Who Killed Article 2 (4)? or: Changing Norms Governing the Use of Force by States," *American Journal of International Law*, 64 (1970), 809–37.

HENKIN, LOUIS, *How Nations Behave: Law and Foreign Policy*, 2nd ed. New York: Columbia University Press, 1979.

HIGGINS, ROSALYN, *The Development of International Law through the Political Organs of the United Nations*. London: Oxford University Press, 1963.

———, "The Place of International Law in the Settlement of Disputes by the Security Council," *American Journal of International Law*, 64 (1970), 1–18.

———, "Policy Considerations and the International Judicial Process," *International and Comparative Law Quarterly*, 17 (1968), 58–84.

HOFFMANN, STANLEY, "International Systems and International Law," *World Politics*, 14 (1961), 205–37.

KAPLAN, MORTON A., and NICHOLAS DE B. KATZENBACH, *The Political Foundations of International Law*. New York: John Wiley, 1961.

KORFF, BARON S.A., "An Introduction to the History of International Law," *American Journal of International Law*, 18 (1924), 246–59.

LEVI, WERNER, "International Law in a Multicultural World," *International Studies Quarterly,* 18 (1974), 417–49.

———, *Law and Politics in the International Society.* Beverly Hills, Calif.: Sage Publications, 1976.

McDOUGAL, MYRES S., and FLORENTINO P. FELICIANO, *Law and Minimum World Public Order: The Legal Regulation of International Coercion.* New Haven, Conn.: Yale University Press, 1961.

NORTHEDGE, F.S., "Law and Politics Between Nations," *International Relations,* 1 (1957), 291–302.

SCHEINMAN, LAWRENCE, and DAVID WILKINSON, eds., *International Law and Political Crisis: An Analytic Casebook.* Boston: Little, Brown, 1968.

STONE, JULIUS, *Legal Controls of International Conflict: A Treatise on the Dynamics of Disputes and War-Law.* New York: Holt, Rinehart & Winston, 1954.

YOUNG, ORAN, "International Regimes: Problems of Concept Formation," *World Politics,* 33 (April 1980), 331–56.

14

Ethics in Explanations of Foreign Policy

In the past, much of the public and scholarly debate on the place of ethics in a society's foreign relations has assumed that policy makers have a choice between posing as "realists" or "moralists"—that ethical restraints are, in a sense, voluntary or optional. There is, in fact, an intellectual tradition in American diplomatic history reflecting the realists' and moralists' approaches to foreign policy. The moralists often list among their heroes Jefferson, Wilson, Hull, and some lesser figures; Hamilton, Calhoun, and Theodore Roosevelt are often cited as exponents of a realist's approach to foreign relations. Looking at the speeches—although not the actions—of these men, one can see the distinction between the two approaches. In the early 1790s, for instance, Jefferson and Hamilton conducted a debate over the young republic's obligations to revolutionary France. Jefferson claimed that the United States was committed to assist the French in their wars because the Franco-American alliance signed during the War of Independence was still in effect. He asserted that a country had to meet its commitments even if it was not in its direct interest to do so. Hamilton claimed the contrary, arguing that a nation's self-interest can be its only guide to policy. One cannot, he suggested, apply ethical principles to problems of foreign policy.

Regardless of historical context, commitments to self-interest or ethical principles have, to most observers, appeared incompatible. A clear expression of this supposed incompatibility can be found in one of Woodrow Wilson's campaign speeches, when he claimed that:

It is a very perilous thing to determine the foreign policy of a nation in the terms of material interests. . . . We dare not turn from the principle that morality and not expediency is the thing that must guide us, and that we will never condone iniquity because it is most convenient to do so.[1]

The difficulty with this sort of view is that it oversimplifies reality. Both moralists and realists assert that there is a choice between following policies of self-interest and those of principle. The moralists imply that pursuit of self-interest at the expense of principle leads to immoral, or amoral, diplomatic and military behavior. The realists reply that self-interest, when prudently pursued, is ethically justifiable in itself, and that the pursuit of ideals only causes great ideological crusades that end in tragedy. Some would add, quoting Machiavelli, "A man who wishes to make a profession of goodness in everything must necessarily come to grief among so many who are not good."[2] A review of diplomatic history would not support such extreme views of reality. It may be true that in Machiavelli's day, typical forms of diplomatic conduct were notoriously low when judged by today's standards. Diplomats commonly lied, and many took their own cooks abroad for fear that local servants would poison them. The record of assassination, intrigue, and duplicity in Renaissance diplomacy is well documented.

It is undoubtedly true that continued progress in technical and economic development has made it possible for policy decisions to have ever-greater consequences, good and bad, on the lives of ordinary citizens. And as nation-states become more interdependent, the decisions made by one government to protect its interests can have considerable negative impact on the affairs of other societies. Ethical knowledge or moral norms, unlike technical knowledge, are not necessarily additive. It has never been demonstrated that knowledge of past history makes people better or worse. By any standards, Hitler's policies were more evil than those of Prussian monarchs. All we can suggest is that the potential for doing harm to large numbers of people is greater today and that policy decisions may have greater impact on more people than in the past. But explanations of foreign policy that claim that all statesmen are immoral, concerned only with their own power and prestige, and indifferent to the consequences of their actions are surely not warranted by facts. To condemn policy makers as a group overlooks the fact that in their values and moral predispositions, they are probably a fairly representative sample of the educated people in the world. We could not deny that often their calculations are wrong, that they frequently look only to the short run and fail to analyze the long-run impacts of their decisions, or that they often have a propensity to dismiss information that does not fit with their favorite theories or values. Yet are not all people guilty of these shortcomings? This is not to argue that publics should avoid

---

[1] Quoted in Hans Morgenthau and Kenneth W. Thompson, *Principles and Problems of International Politics* (New York: Knopf, 1950), p. 24.

[2] N. Machiavelli, *The Prince*, trans. Luigi Ricci, rev. by E.R.P. Vincent (London: Oxford University Press, 1935), Chap. 15.

criticism of their leaders. Rather, it is to suggest that policy makers are probably no better or worse, from an ethical point of view, than their compatriots. They are in a unique position, however, to make decisions that will have adverse consequences on their own citizens and people all over the world.

Consider, too, that the best of motives may not guarantee that the consequences of policy will do "good." Decisions taken to implement great moral principles may lead to disastrous consequences just as easily as decisions made in the light of selfish interests. As a presidential candidate, Woodrow Wilson could afford to say that morality must precede expediency; but later, in office, he found that the practical application of moral principles could lead to severe injustices. His conduct of relations with Mexico in 1914 and with other governments during the negotiation of the peace settlements following World War I certainly reveals that he was capable of being expedient when it served either American commercial or diplomatic interests or even his personal political fortunes. In fact, the relationship between interests, policy, and ethics is very complicated; we can do well to begin the analysis by rejecting the simple dichotomy between expediency and morality.

ETHICS, MORALITY, AND VALUES AS PSYCHOLOGICAL AND CULTURAL RESTRAINTS

One way of relating ethical considerations to policy making is to conceive of ethics as a combination of cultural, psychological, and ideological "value structures" that inhibit consideration of all possible policy alternatives in a given situation. They establish limits beyond which certain types of behavior become inconceivable. In the framework of Communist ethics and Stalin's personal values, there was nothing unusual in his suggestion to Churchill in 1944 that one way of permanently resolving the German threat would be to capture the German officer corps of 50,000 men and liquidate all of them. To Churchill, the product of an entirely different political culture, the plan seemed totally abhorrent. He rejected it not only because he knew that the British public would not stand for it (anticipated domestic reaction), but also because he found it personally repugnant.[3] Such a scheme had never occurred to Churchill in the first place, and it is in this sense that social values and individual ethical principles limit our perceptions of alternatives. The example also suggests that there is likely to be close correspondence between the ethics, belief systems, and value orientations of policy makers and those held generally in their culture. If a government consistently breaks treaty obligations, practices duplicity in its diplomacy, and uses force and violence without inhibition, it is probable that the society in general and the domestic political system in particular condone such

---

[3] Winston Churchill, *Closing the Ring* (Boston: Houghton Mifflin, 1951), pp. 373–74.

behavior. But how are we to account for decisions and policy actions that *are* beyond the boundaries of normal social or individual value systems?

Churchill could not imagine exterminating 50,000 German officers, but he ordered, apparently with public acquiescence, Allied bombers to kill hundreds of thousands of German civilians in mass incendiary raids that had only indirect consequences on Germany's military strength. An even more dramatic instance of the seeming absence of ethical restraints occurred in the summer of 1945, when the U.S. government decided to drop the newly developed atomic bomb on Japan. Considering that this weapon was known to be unusually destructive of life, what possible justification could be offered as necessitating its use? How could the government consider such an alternative if it meant so much suffering? The decision to use atomic weapons on Japan is instructive because it illustrates the subtle and complex role of ethics in foreign-policy making.

Three groups of people were involved in the decision. First were the scientists who had been working on perfecting the instrument. More than others, they were able to foresee both the frightening and the spectacular implications of the weapon. Many scientists were deeply concerned that such an instrument of destruction should be used at all, while others saw it as the most efficient way of ending the war quickly. The second group was composed of professional military men directly connected with the bomb project. They regarded the bomb project as just another administrative task, which had to be completed in the shortest time possible so that it could be used against the Japanese to force them to surrender. The third group, composed of high-level civilian policy makers, including the secretaries of war, state, and navy, as well as President Truman, also regarded the weapon as a means of forcing the Japanese to surrender, as well as a method of ending the war before the Soviet Union could become deeply involved in military actions against the Japanese. It was commonly anticipated that if the war dragged on and Russian troops participated in an invasion of the Japanese islands, the Soviet government would insist upon being rewarded with a zone of occupation such as it had received in defeated Germany.

How did these three groups react to the situation in which they had to decide between employing or avoiding the use of this weapon of unprecedented destructiveness? Aside from some of the scientists working on the project, no one viewed the choice of using the bomb as essentially a moral or ethical problem. All the policy makers understood that a bomb dropped on a city would cause tens of thousands of deaths and as many injuries, to say nothing of the total devastation of the target cities. The army air force had already been conducting massive fire-bomb (napalm) raids on Japanese cities, causing a loss of life and level of destruction only slightly less than that resulting from some of the most dramatic strategic raids on German cities. In one raid on Tokyo fire bombs destroyed several square miles of the city and caused the death of 83,000 people—considerably more than were to die several months later at Hiroshima. The secretary of war, Henry Stimson, was the only high-level policy maker to question the morality of these raids. They were destroying Japan's capacity to wage the war, to be sure—but at a fantastically high cost in civilian lives.

When it came to making the decision to use atomic weapons, then, ample precedents for slaughter on a massive scale already existed. Both sides had fought World War II with widespread brutality, and there was no expectation that the atomic bomb would introduce any new dimension in suffering. Widespread death would just occur more rapidly. Neither the scientists, the armed-forces officials, nor the civilian policy makers argued against using the bomb on the grounds that it would involve a large loss of life.[4]

In fact, very few of those participating in the bomb project ever questioned that the weapon would be used; this, it seems, was taken pretty much for granted. It was easily rationalized on the ground that the Japanese would never surrender without some dramatic demonstration of force. An invasion of Japan had already been scheduled for the autumn of 1945, and it was anticipated that from one-half to one million American casualties would result from such an operation, plus an even heavier toll of Japanese lives. The perceived alternatives were either to avoid using the bomb and accept an extremely high loss of life on *both* sides, or to use the weapon, at a *relatively* low cost in Japanese lives, hoping that the destruction of one or two cities would induce the Japanese government to surrender. A third alternative—a compromise negotiated peace—was never considered in Washington after the formula of "unconditional surrender" had been agreed upon by the Allied governments in 1943. It was also ignored probably because neither Congress nor the American people would have accepted less than total victory.

The main arguments concerning the bomb thus revolved around two subsidiary questions, and it is here that ethical considerations became more apparent in the making of decisions. Calculation of deaths occurring by atomic bombing as compared to an invasion of Japan was relatively easy to predict; even on hindsight, the decision to use the bomb seems to have been correct, provided that the alternative of a negotiated peace is left out. The first question flowing from the decision to use the weapon was whether or not the Japanese should be warned in some way about the destructiveness of the bomb. Among the civilian policy makers and the scientists, many argued that the United States should first demonstrate the bomb to the Japanese, either in a test in the United States or by exploding it over some unpopulated area in Japan. Those who argued along these lines felt that the United States was morally obligated to give the Japanese a clear warning and visual evidence of what fate should befall them if they did not surrender. In this way, the basic moral choice would pass from the Americans to the leaders of the Japanese government. If they did not surrender, it could not be argued that they had not been given clear warning.

This point of view was not accepted. The counterargument was based

---

[4] Many interesting memoirs regarding Japan's surrender have been published. The facts discussed below are derived from Len Giovannitti and Fred Freed, *The Decision to Drop the Bomb* (New York: Coward-McCann, 1965). This study is based on written memoirs, diaries, and interviews of those who were involved in the decision to use atomic weapons against Japan.

essentially on the American image of the decision-making process in Tokyo, an image that stressed the fanatic zeal of the military leaders in control of the Japanese government. This image was not far off the mark, for subsequent events in Tokyo revealed that even after the two atomic weapons had been dropped, Russia had entered the war, and the United States had instituted an effective blockade of the Japanese islands, Japanese military leaders were willing to surrender only because the emperor ordered them to do so. Most of the Japanese military group had been trained in the view that the only honorable course of action was to fight to the last man. One officer had suggested that Japan might be willing to sacrifice 20 million lives to prevent an Allied occupation and destruction of the emperorship. Indeed, after the decision to surrender had been made, some military officials attempted a *coup d'état* in Tokyo, hoping to take over the government and continue the war. The American government did not know all these details, of course, but it had ample intelligence information indicating that the Japanese would continue to resist no matter how near defeat they were, and that the peace faction within the Japanese government could not overturn or overrule the military. It was argued in Washington, therefore, that in all probability, no demonstration of the bomb in a New Mexico desert or even in some relatively uninhabited area of Japan would adequately indicate to the Japanese the destructiveness of the weapon. This position was supported by the chief scientist on the project in New Mexico, Dr. Robert Oppenheimer.

A further consideration was that the United States possessed only two bombs, and, since it would take several weeks to produce others, the more that were used for purposes of demonstration and warning, the longer the war would continue, with a high American casualty rate in the Pacific islands campaign.

Once the decision to drop one bomb had been made, a second choice remained: Which cities would be destroyed? The American military group selected cities that made important contributions to the Japanese war effort. One of these was Kyoto, from a military point of view the most desirable of targets. But this choice was vetoed by the secretary of war, on the grounds that the city was a former capital of Japan and a great center of culture and historical tradition. Even though Stimson was well aware of the great loss of life involved in dropping the bomb on *any* city, he eliminated the most obvious choice. Clearly, the decision on this target was not made, then, purely on military grounds or reasons of expediency. Other considerations involving moral choices served to restrain action.

What conclusions are we to draw from the decision to use the atomic bomb against Japan, the casual suggestion by Stalin, and the Allied fire raids on Germany and Japan? The first is that as the technical means of destruction in wartime have grown, so has tolerance for destructiveness. When gunpowder was first applied to military uses, many were offended. During World War I, the civilized world was appalled at the loss of life in trench warfare, killing of civilians by long-range artillery, maiming of soldiers with mustard gas, and dropping of puny bombs from airplanes. In World War II, the Germans were characterized as barbarous and inhumane (the real atrocities were not yet even known) for their massive air raids on Coventry, London, Rotterdam, and Warsaw. Within a year or two, those among the Allied powers who were outraged at these German military actions applauded when their own armed forces retaliated in similar, although more thorough, fashion against German and Japanese cities. Were a nuclear war to break out in our own era, policy makers would still make the same kinds of calculations that they did in deciding to drop atomic bombs on Hiroshima and Nagasaki rather than to invade the islands. Military advisers would probably regard their problems from a professional and technical point of view, quite immune from considerations of individual suffering. It remains for civilian policy makers to inject, if they are capable or strong enough, ethical and moral factors in the use of the instruments of violence and to reject certain alternatives offered by their military advisers on the ground that they are ethically reprehensible or politically impracticable.

The second point about these decisions is that they were exceptional rather than typical, taken by policy makers in circumstances of acute tension, of total war. Although, on hindsight, other alternatives might have been possible, the alternatives that *were* considered would probably have involved even greater suffering.

A third aspect of these decisions is that some, like Stalin's suggestion, were made ultimately by individuals with supreme authority, where their perceptions of reality, prejudices, and personal ethical orientations were clearly revealed. Others, like most foreign-policy decisions, were products of lengthy consultation among many government organizations and individual specialists. Stalin's suggestion of liquidating the German officer corps was not in all probability a serious policy alternative that had been worked out in the Soviet bureaucracy. But the decision to drop the bomb or, for instance, to make a loan offer to a developing country is the result of complicated negotiations among various agencies in the government of the donor; it is much less likely to display so dramatically the value orientations of any single policy maker.

Moreover, we must remember that those who make and carry out foreign policies are "role" players. They are officials, which means that they conform more or less to the legal limitations of a particular office, as well as to the expectations of numerous constituents. Role tends to mediate individual attitudes and values to such an extent that policy makers are not always free to use their official position to institute their personal ethics, beliefs, or prejudices. As Louis Halle points out, the position of foreign-policy officials is similar to that of corporate directors, who, however much they may believe in charity, cannot give away the stockholders' assets as if they were their own.[5] Policy makers are responsible for pursuing and protecting collective objectives, and in this capacity cannot always follow the dictates of their conscience. If they honestly disagree with a course of action, they can resign as one means of

---

[5] Louis J. Halle, "Morality and Contemporary Diplomacy," in *Diplomacy in a Changing World,* eds. Stephen Kertesz and M.A. Fitzsimmons (Notre Dame, Ind.: University of Notre Dame Press, 1959), p. 32.

protest—although in totalitarian governments, such a course of action can lead to imprisonment or even liquidation. Despite the effect of role factors on policy making, it should not be assumed that "state" behavior is necessarily less ethical than private behavior. Given the difficult situations with which officials have to deal, their behavior is frequently no less moral than that of private citizens.[6]

ETHICAL COMPONENTS
OF FOREIGN-POLICY OUTPUTS

Ethics and moral principles can be related to all four types of foreign-policy outputs discussed previously. Foreign-policy orientations may reflect not only "hard-headed" responses to conditions in the environment, but also general cultural values or norms that suggest what, in the long run, is ethically good. The orientation of nonalignment, for instance, can be explained only partly by the structure of the system, domestic needs, and the fear of involvement in great power conflicts. It also reflects a widespread contemporary attitude in many developing countries and elsewhere that it is immoral to make military alliances or to become involved with the more unsavory aspects of cold-war politics. Governments whose orientations involve coalition making have similarly justified their policies on moral arguments, or on a combination of practical considerations, historical analogies, and moral judgments. The orientation of collective security through alliances rests in part on analogies drawn from the history of the 1930s (the best way to avoid war is to build overwhelming coalitions against those that are tempted to commit aggression), on common perceptions of threat, *and* on certain ethical views. Some of the last are that powers have a responsibility to protect weaker states faced with external threats; that commitments, if freely entered into, must be kept even if it is to one's disadvantage; and that world peace demands that aggression be punished. Indeed, considerations of expediency or narrow self-interest could easily lead foreign-policy officials to argue the reverse of these views: The best way to avoid war is to mind one's own business; big powers have no responsibilities toward weaker states faced with external threats; commitments should never be kept except when it is clearly in one's own advantage to meet them.

Ethical norms are also revealed in the reasoning behind, and justification of, certain national roles and functions. From the Leninist point of view, fraternal states and parties have a duty to assist each other economically and in defense matters. The regional-defender role conception reflects the view that the Soviet Union, because of its overwhelming military capabilities, has a special responsibility to help "protect" the weaker members of the bloc. The advantage accrues not only to the Soviet Union, but to the bloc as a whole. The role conception of "bastion of the revolution" expresses the moral imperative that the nation

---

[6] Arnold Wolfers, "Statesmanship and Moral Choice," *World Politics*, 1 (1949), 178–80.

should make sacrifices to promote and support revolutionary movements abroad even if doing so is not to its immediate advantage. The role of faithful ally similarly reflects the normative judgment that a government should support the foreign policies of its allies, not just for its own protection, but also for the good of the whole alliance. The developer role is usually spelled out in terms that reflect moral considerations: the developed states have a duty to assist those whose economic needs are greater than their own.

It should be emphasized again that orientations and national roles cannot be explained *only* in ethical terms. We have already seen in Chapter 12 that foreign-policy outputs can be linked to a variety of personal, societal, and systemic attributes and conditions. But ethical norms and moral judgments *are* relevant to any explanation. They enter into the making of policy through the explicit or implicit views of policy makers, the demands and expectations of attentive publics, and occasionally in the expectations of other governments or populations.

Virtually any government's *main* foreign-policy objectives are cast in moral terms and justified with ethical rhetoric. "Détente," "defense of the socialist commonwealth," "Arab unity," "the liberation of Palestine," and like objectives all reflect governments' commitments to a future state of affairs that they perceive as more *just* or desirable than the present. Indeed, on major commercial issues, where it is difficult to clothe greed or self-interest in moral rhetoric, governments often appear uncomfortable; they cannot easily buttress their case on the grounds that it is inherently right, just, or good. Yet, even on such "hard" issues, elements of justice (as distinct from morality, though the two are related) do appear. Justice refers to some "fair" distribution of spoils—whether territory, people, profits, or trade balances. The vast majority of conflicts over these issues are settled according to some formula incorporating an explicit or implicit standard of justice. Seldom is there one party which gains all and the other which loses all. For the same reasons that governments normally observe legal constraints in their foreign-policy actions, they similarly like to appear "fair" in their dealings with others. Yet, there are also problems with justice when one government's objectives—particularly long-range objectives—are portrayed as serving not only national interests, but universal justice and the interests of humanity as well. Lord Wolseley once maintained:

> I have but one great object in this world, and that is to maintain the greatness of the British Empire. But apart from my John Bull sentiment on this point, I firmly believe that in doing so I work in the cause of Christianity, of peace, of civilization, and the happiness of the human race generally.[7]

To the United States, a world of free, independent states, regulating their relations according to law, is eminently just and ethical. A Communist views this

---

[7] Quoted in Kenneth W. Thompson, *Political Realism and the Crisis of World Politics* (Princeton, N.J.: Princeton University Press, 1960), p. 151.

order as representative of American world domination, slavery under capitalism, and an international law that perpetuates inequalities between states and economic exploitation of developing countries by imperialists. Observed in this light, the goals hardly seem just and ethical. Whether or not these goals *are* ethical depends very much from which position they are being viewed.

Rules, which today are contained under such slogans as "free trade," "noninterference in internal affairs," "self-determination," "observance of treaty obligations," or "pacific settlement of disputes" relate not to goals but to the *actions* governments take to influence the behavior of other states. They establish the distinctions between legitimate and illegitimate means of utilizing a state's capabilities. Thus, it is in this realm of *how* states pursue their objectives that ethics might seem most immediately relevant to foreign policy. Since there may still be obvious advantages to following these rules, self-interest and ethics coincide.

However, most problems that confront the policy maker daily do not appear to him as moral problems. They are practical problems that demand practical responses and actions.[8] Some people claim, for example, that it is immoral for a democratic government to maintain an alliance with a regime that practices certain domestic policies not in accordance with democratic principles. But the policy maker is primarily concerned with a security problem or a more general problem of peace, not with the characteristics of foreign political systems. The policy maker would argue that the alliance partner's internal affairs are irrelevant to the alliance relationship, just as he or she does not pass judgment on a grocer's private life before being willing to buy food. The grocer's morals are largely irrelevant to the selling and purchasing relationship.[9]

Is a decision to make an alliance with a dictator really devoid of ethical content? Is this really expediency forsaking principle? It is difficult to predict the costs of *not* making the alliance, but if by not making the alliance, war is the result, who is right in arguing that alliances with dictators are immoral? And, in any case, the policy maker could, instead of forming an alliance, order the invasion and occupation of the dictator's country, thereby creating a more effective deterrent. This would be perhaps a more practical course of action, but the policy maker's values would probably preclude even consideration of such an alternative. *Any* choice of policy alternatives involves selection among ethical standards and values. There is no such thing as a pure realist, if by that term we mean one who sacrifices all values for the quickest gratification of his self-interest. In most diplomatic situations, ethical restraints are not very conspicuous, in the sense that policy is deduced from moral maxims; but they can be observed in the policies that were *not* adopted and in the general manner, whether courteous, respectful, and honest or brusque and deceitful, in which actions were carried out with other involved countries.

[8] Halle, *Diplomacy in a Changing World,* pp. 28–29.
[9] *Ibid.*

In these examples we can see the extent to which both moralists and realists oversimplify. The moralists fail to observe the necessities imposed on the policy maker by conditions abroad over which he or she has no control; they also neglect the possibility that strict observance of rules and commitments might lead to catastrophic consequences. And they fail to realize that policy makers are often cast into a situation where all the alternatives are equally unpleasant. The realists, who say the policy makers' behavior is, or should be, dictated only by "reasons of state," also fail to observe the role of ethical limitations in ruling out what may be more expedient alternatives. Moreover, in focusing on behavior in crisis situations, the realists fail to acknowledge thousands of transactions between states in which diplomatic positions conform rigidly to the principles of international law and the Charter of the United Nations. If in some situations, all possible courses of action are ethically reprehensible, in many others, self-interest and ethical behavior are highly compatible.

In situations where a state's objectives, interests, and values are threatened or frustrated, high-sounding platitudes and general principles do not often serve as realistic guides to action. No foreign policy is conducted exclusively by deducing actions from vague moral principles. Leaders like Jawaharlal Nehru and Woodrow Wilson, who stressed the importance of observing legal and ethical standards of conduct in international relations, did not behave in practical situations very differently from other political leaders who claimed to be "realists." It is, for example, easy for a government to forswear the use and threat of force in its relations with other states. No government admits that it is anything but "peace-loving." But what if that government is subsequently threatened by a neighbor when the international organization is paralyzed because of a veto and little diplomatic support elsewhere can be obtained? Does the general principle of not using threats or force suggest any practical policy in this situation? From the point of view of the observer-moralist, is it ethically more correct to remain faithful to principle and endure certain invasion than to try to create an effective defense with which to deter the perceived enemy? Or suppose that a government had in its policy statements solemnly declared its faith in the principles of international law but found later that a treaty to which it was a partner imposed not only heavy, but clearly unjust, burdens and that the other signatory was unwilling to adjust the treaty through negotiations. When justice and the principle of treaty observation conflict, which is the correct course of action? Is public declaration in support of the "rule of law" a meaningful guide by which to formulate policy in this situation?

Despite their rhetoric, policy makers have to choose constantly among courses of action that represent conflicting values and often feel compelled to accept not the "best" solution, but the one that requires the least sacrifice of direct interests and values. When governments are not deeply involved in a critical situation, they can afford to proclaim fidelity to ultimate purposes and commonly recognized rules; but when they are in the middle of conflict, vague principles such as those in the United Nations Charter may not help very much.

The appeasement strategy of England in the 1930s is a good example of the kinds of conflicting principles and values with which policy makers have to struggle. In this case, British government leaders believed that peace and the principles of conduct in the Covenant of the League of Nations had to be observed. They also believed that reasonable negotiations with the Nazi regime could avert the holocausts experienced during World War I. Prime Minister Chamberlain was a man of great rectitude, and he personally abhorred organized violence. His principles and intentions were above reproach. By surrendering one position after the other through diplomatic negotiations, he was able to keep peace for two years; but, in the process, he and his colleagues sacrificed the independence of Austria, Danzig, and Czechoslovakia. Was two years of "peace" and strict adherence to the League Covenant worth this price? The principles the British observed were commendable, but they did not help to create any effective policies for the Nazi threat.

Policy makers thus confront difficult choices, and absolute fidelity to treaty obligations and other standards of diplomatic behavior may require sacrifices that few people would willingly condone. Fortunately, in most cases, the pursuit of interests and values does not conflict so obviously with the principles a government declares as guides to its external behavior.

ETHICS AS A FUNCTION OF THE PATTERN OF RELATIONS BETWEEN NATIONS

It is still inadequate to argue that in some cases, commitment to ethical or legal principles may cause disaster or unethical consequences. We must also qualify the relationship of ethics to foreign policy by emphasizing that they combine in different ways depending upon the situation abroad or the nature of relations between any two states. We do not hear much criticism about the lack of morality in Swedish-Norwegian, Costa Rican-Panamanian, or British-American relations. In these types of relationships—which comprise a majority of all international relations—governments and their diplomatic representatives commonly observe the accepted forms of diplomatic etiquette, frankness, honesty, good faith, and tolerance. The techniques used to influence each other usually fall within the bounds of international law and the United Nations Charter. Unfortunately, since these relationships seldom make headlines, we are seldom aware of the high standards to which they conform.

But when serious conflicts develop, when the objectives of two or more states are fundamentally incompatible, and where there is no tradition of responsiveness, characteristically any government will be likely to use threats and military force. Observation of treaties, diplomatic niceties, and rules against interference give way to other forms of behavior. But does one instance of the use of violent power, even for unworthy objectives, mean that that state's policy makers are immoral in *all* their relationships? Or does it warrant the cynicism of some observers, who claim that in any case, power is always the final arbiter in international politics and that might makes right?

We should not conclude that violations of some ethical standards in coercive and violent relationships mean that "power politics" have replaced all decency as the basis for a country's foreign policies. Even in violent relationships, as many examples illustrate, ethical norms still limit the vision of policy makers and exclude some policy alternatives that might, in view of the circumstances, be the most expedient. In the most frigid periods of the cold war, the major antagonists refrained from taking certain actions that might have achieved key objectives at a minimum of risk or cost. There are at least tacit agreements, for instance, that neither side would assassinate the leaders of the other, give nuclear weapons to allies, or sabotage each other's economies. These agreements, as well as others, seem to involve modes of conduct where both sides see a common correspondence of self-interest and ethical principles.

During the American-Soviet crisis of 1962 over Cuba, when the Soviet government had secretly shipped missiles to the island to protect Castro's regime from an expected American invasion, several high officials of the American government, including President Kennedy, had to decide among several alternative courses of action in attempting to remove the missiles; two eventually remained for serious consideration. The most practical action would have been to destroy the missiles and bases by a rapid series of bombing raids. Such action would have demonstrated dramatically to the Soviet government that introduction of more missiles would only end in their destruction. Nevertheless, President Kennedy asked his intelligence advisors how many persons would be killed if the United States conducted the bombing raids. The answer was 25,000, including many civilians. The president chose the second alternative—a quarantine of the island by naval forces—partly on the ground that the United States could not be the perpetrator of a Pearl Harbor–type attack on Cuba.[10] He chose a course of action that was less certain of accomplishing the stated objective, but that would cost less lives, even in the territory of a hostile nation. Ethical considerations were operating here, as in many other cases, as criteria upon which to base policies.

SUMMARY

Explanations of various types of foreign-policy outputs are inadequate if they fail to locate the explicit and implicit value judgments and ethical standards that go into choices. They are also deficient if they characterize policy making as a simple choice between good and evil or adherence to mere hard-headed realism where national-interest goals are established and the actions that will achieve them the quickest are outlined. The cases cited above show that the

[10] The president's brother, Robert Kennedy, revealed this aspect of the Cuban missile crises in a speech in New York on October 13, 1964, reported in the *New York Times,* October 14, 1964, p. 1.

policy actions ultimately chosen usually reflect moral considerations; but by no means are the choices made *only* on those considerations. In fact, the ethical content of orientations, roles, objectives, and actions may be imbedded in considerations of other types. President Kennedy's decision on Cuba in 1962 reflected some aspects of "conscience," yet more "realistic" calculations were also involved. For example, he anticipated an unfavorable response around the world to a Pearl harbor–type attack. In other cases, considerations of the responses of a political party, legislative body, pressure group, or the public at large may support what resides in the policy makers' consciences, so that it is difficult to separate the various components in any given decision.

Part of the oversimplification of the relationship between ethics and foreign-policy outputs arises from actions of government officials themselves, for their public pronouncements often refer to foreign policy in terms of ultimate ends or transaction doctrines rather than as practical problems to be resolved. Slogans and principles are useful for mobilizing foreign and domestic opinion, but they are neither substitutes for policy nor necessarily the frames of reference in which actual decisions are made. In their day-to-day positions, policy makers do not approach their problems from the point of view of ethics any more than most business organizations resolve issues by deducing rules of action from ethical or legal principles. Nevertheless, ethics, morals, and values are constantly brought to bear on a government's behavior toward other states. Sometimes the relationship may be explicit: For example, a policy-making body may be aware of, and act to implement, a rule of international law or a prior commitment to an ally despite national disadvantages in so doing. More often, the relationship is more subtle; ethics and values unconsciously block out consideration of policy alternatives.

For reasons of conscience, prestige, and self-interest, governments in most cases conduct their relations with each other in accordance with the commonly accepted "rules of the game." But in many instances, policy makers are confronted with situations in which they have to choose between courses of action that help to secure national values and interests (or minimize sacrifices) and those that are consistent with legal and moral obligations and ethical precepts. When the two courses of action conflict, it is not unusual for governments to choose the path that attains or defends national values and interests. More often, policy represents some sort of compromise between the demands of ethical considerations and rules and the demands of effective action.

SELECTED BIBLIOGRAPHY

ACHESON, DEAN, "Morality, Moralism, and Diplomacy," *Yale Review,* 47 (1958), 481–93.

BUTTERFIELD, HERBERT, *International Conflict in the Twentieth Century: A Christian View.* New York: Harper & Row, 1960.

————, "The Scientific versus the Moralistic Approach in International Affairs," *International Affairs,* 27 (1951), 411–42.

COHEN, MARSHALL, THOMAS NAGEL, and THOMAS SCANLON, eds., *War and Moral Responsibility.* Princeton, N.J.: Princeton University Press, 1974.

EAYRS, JAMES, *Right and Wrong in Foreign Policy.* Toronto: Toronto University Press, 1966.

GEORGE, ALEXANDER L., and RICHARD SMOKE, *Deterrence in American Foreign Policy: Theory and Practice,* Appendix, entitled, "Theory for Policy in International Relations." New York: Columbia University Press, 1974.

HALLE, LOUISE J., "Morality and Contemporary Diplomacy," in *Diplomacy in a Changing World,* eds. Stephen Kertesz and M.A. Fitzsimmons. Notre Dame, Ind.: University of Notre Dame Press, 1959.

KAPLAN, MORTON A., ed., *Strategic Thinking and Its Moral Implications.* Chicago: University of Chicago Press, 1973.

LEFEVER, ERNEST S., *Ethics and World Politics: Four Perspectives.* Baltimore, Md.: Johns Hopkins University Press, 1972.

MORGENTHAU, HANS J., "The Twilight of International Morality," *Ethics,* 58 (1948), 77–99.

NIEBUHR, REINHOLD, *Christian Realism and Political Problems.* New York: Scribner's, 1953.

PETTMANN, RALPH, ed., *Moral Claims in World Affairs.* London: Croom Helm, 1979.

RAMSEY, PAUL, *The Just War: Force and Political Responsibility.* New York: Scribner's, 1968.

THOMPSON, KENNETH W., *Christian Ethics and the Dilemmas of Foreign Policy.* Durham, N.C.: Duke University Press, 1959.

————, *Political Realism and the Crisis of World Politics.* Princeton, N.J.: Princeton University Press, 1960.

————, "New Reflections on Ethics and Foreign Policy: The Problem of Human Rights," *The Journal of Politics,* 40 (1978), 984–1010.

WOLFERS, ARNOLD, "Statesmanship and Moral Choice," *World Politics,* 1 (1949), 175–95.

PART V

Major Forms of Interaction between States

15

The Interaction of States: Conflict and Conflict Resolution

Our attention now draws away from the *actions* of states to the *interactions* of two or more states—to relationships, not foreign policy. Interactions between states in the contemporary system are numerous and diverse. We often classify them according to issue areas, such as trade, international security, tourism, technical cooperation, cultural exchanges, control of nuclear weapons, and the like. Another method of classification focuses on *types* of interaction that predominate in the relations between any given pair of states, no matter what issues are involved. Sociologists similarly classify relationships within, let us say, families. They can be characterized as harmonious, dominant-dependent, or conflictual, regardless of the issues. In this and the next chapter, we will outline the basic conditions and behavioral characteristics of two common types of relationship between states: conflict and collaboration.

This chapter examines conflict relationships in which there is the likelihood of violence or its organized use. The reasons for concentrating on this type of conflict will be outlined later. Here, it should be pointed out that virtually all relationships contain characteristics of conflict. Even in the most collaborative enterprise between governments, some areas of disagreement will arise. In the next chapter, we will examine specifically how conflict is handled in these collaborative relationships. What concerns us here is the type of conflict that can lead to organized violence.

CHARACTERISTICS OF CONFLICT, CRISIS, AND COMPETITION

Conflict leading to organized violence emerges from a particular combination of parties, imcompatible positions over an issue, hostile attitudes, and certain types of diplomatic and military actions. The *parties* to an international conflict are normally, but not necessarily, the governments of nation-states (obvious exceptions would include the various Palestinian guerrilla bands and the Secretary-General of the United Nations). Parties seek to achieve certain objectives, such as additional or more secure territory, security, souls, access to markets, prestige, alliances, world revolution, the overthrow of an unfriendly government, changes in United Nations procedures, and many other things. In efforts to achieve or defend these objectives, their demands, actions, or both will run counter to the interests and objectives of other parties.

An *issue field* is the subject of contention between the parties and includes the positions they are attempting to achieve. Conflict behavior (attitudes and actions) is likely to result when party A occupies a position that is incompatible with the wishes or interests of party B and perhaps others. The critical condition is thus the condition of scarcity, where a move in an issue field by one party is seen to be at the expense of the other party's position. The most traditional issue field is actual territory, but territorial control is hardly the only condition that gives rise to international conflict. There may also be incompatibilities of position on such issue fields as tariff structures, the price of oil, the proliferation of nuclear weapons, the treatment of minorities in a state, or the powers and duties of the Secretary-General of the United Nations. Conflict may arise in these areas because one government wants the problem solved in a manner incompatible with the wishes of another party or parties.

The term *tensions* refers to the set of attitudes and predispositions—such as distrust and suspicion—that populations and policy makers hold toward any other parties. Tensions do not by themselves cause conflict but only predispose parties to employ or manifest conflict behavior should they seek to achieve incompatible objectives. The Israeli and Syrian governments display distrust, fear, and suspicion toward each other, but incompatible positions on an issue, such as control of Jerusalem and the Golan Heights must arise before these predispositions or attitudes lead to diplomatic or military actions. In other words, antagonism, distrust, suspicion, and the like are not sufficient conditions for the occurrence of conflict or crisis.[1]

Finally, conflict includes the *actions*—the diplomatic, propagandist, commercial, or military threats and punishments discussed in Part III—that the con-

[1] See, for example, Raymond W. Mack and Richard C. Snyder, "The Analysis of Social Conflict—Toward an Overview and Synthesis," *Journal of Conflict Resolution*, 1 (1957), 217; Clinton Fink, "Some Conceptual Difficulties in the Theory of Social Conflict," *Journal of Conflict Resolution*, 12 (1968), 434; Lewis A. Coser, *The Functions of Social Conflict* (New York: Free Press, 1956), pp. 37–38.

tending parties take toward each other. We thus distinguish the issues created out of incompatible collective objectives, the attitudes of policy makers that predispose them to make threats and carry out punishments, and the actions taken. Tensions are only a part of conflict, the underlying psychological dimension. What, then, is a crisis?

A crisis is one stage of conflict; its distinguishing features include a sudden eruption of unexpected events caused by previous conflict. A conflict, such as the division of Berlin or sovereignty over Taiwan, may continue for decades, but occasionally, sudden and unexpected hostile actions by one party will raise tensions and perceived threat to such a point that policy makers of the responding state are "forced" to choose between extreme alternatives, including making war or surrendering. From the policy makers' point of view, the hallmarks of crisis are: (1) unanticipated (surprise) actions by the opponent, (2) perception of great threat, (3) perception of limited time to make a decision or response, and (4) perception of disastrous consequences from inaction.[2] None of these events or perceptions is likely to occur unless there has been a preceding conflict.

If we adhere to these definitions of conflict and crisis, we can eliminate some situations that are frequently classified as conflict. First, situations in which private citizens become involved with another government or with citizens of another country over some contentious issue and subsequently call upon their own government to provide them with protection or redress can be called "disputes." We will exclude them from most of the ensuing discussion because, in most cases, they do not involve the collective objectives of governments. To cite some examples: the accidental shooting of farm animals near the frontier by the border police of a neighboring state; the violation of an international frontier by a group of armed bandits; and frontier guards shooting at each other, where such an incident was not organized and commanded by a government. Naturally, such incidents and the ensuing disputes may lead to conflict and even war if there are tensions and other conflicts between the two states. In most cases, however, they are dealt with through legal or administrative procedures and have little bearing on relations between governments.

Second, our definition of conflict and crisis excludes what may be termed international competition. Recall that the perception of scarcity is a central ingredient of conflict, where a move of position by one state in an issue field is considered a loss or threat by the other party. In a conflict, the issue field, like a pie, is usually of a fixed size. If state A obtains a larger piece, state B perceives it will necessarily receive a smaller one. In competition, however,

---

[2] See Charles F. Hermann, "International Crisis as a Situational Variable," in *International Politics and Foreign Policy: A Reader in Research and Theory*, rev. ed., ed. James N. Rosenau (New York: Free Press, 1969), p. 414. For a model of stages in a conflict, see Lincoln P. Bloomfield and Amelia C. Leiss, *Controlling Small Wars: A Strategy for the 1970s* (New York: Knopf, 1969), Chap. 2; and an alternative formulation in Michael Brecher, "A Theoretical Approach to International Crisis Behavior," *The Jerusalem Journal of International Relations*, 3 (Winter–Spring 1978), 5–24.

the size of the pie varies. State A may try to achieve some objective or increase some value, but this effort means neither that state B's share of the value will decrease nor that it will be totally excluded from sharing in that value. An important Soviet feat in space exploration does not mean that the United States has lost the "space race." It can perform its own feats; prestige and scientific knowledge are not limited or constant. In the heyday of European and American imperialism during the latter part of the nineteenth century, the Western states could compete with each other for colonies and markets as long as the territory available for colonization and commercial exploitation kept expanding. However, once all the non-Western areas of the world had been carved up between the imperial nations, none could gain more except at the expense of some other imperial power. Thus, competition changed to conflict.

We can now examine international conflict in the twentieth century according to the four components: parties, issue fields, attitudes, and actions. This will provide us with a basis for assessing the relative effectiveness of means of resolving international conflicts.

THE INCIDENCE
OF INTERNATIONAL CONFLICT

A major study at the International Institute for Comparative Social Research in Berlin has begun to analyze data about the incidence and major characteristics of international conflict in the twentieth century until 1976.[3] Although the work to date has produced few startling findings, it has provided an interesting profile of the participants and escalatory processes of conflict. For the total period of seventy-six years, the investigators found 638 "confrontations," which were defined as any situation between two or more states where force was either threatened (in the verbal form), used without fatalities (e.g., blockades), or employed leading to war. War is defined as a conflict involving at least 1,000 fatalities.

The first finding is that the incidence of international *conflict* has increased significantly since the end of World War II. Of the 638 conflicts, 380 (60 percent) occurred in the twenty-one years, 1945–1976. (However, data from another study suggest that the incidence of *wars*, when we adjust for the increasing number of states in the system, has in fact been declining slightly since the early nineteenth century.[4])

When we break down the figures according to the types of parties involved in conflicts, whether major powers or small powers, other interesting figures appear. The incidence of major power confrontations has declined slightly

---

[3] Wolf-Dieter Eberwein and Thomas Cusack, "International Disputes: A Look at Some New Data" (Berlin: International Institute for Comparative Social Research, March 1980, mimeo). Data provided by J. David Singer, University of Michigan.

[4] J. David Singer and Melvin Small, *The Wages of War, 1816–1965* (New York: John Wiley, 1972).

(2.16 annually 1945–1976 compared to 2.60 prior to World War I), while the incidence of minor power conflicts has grown dramatically—from 2.47 annually, 1900–1914, to 10.10 per year in the postwar period. Most of the minor power conflicts have occurred in the developing world, an area characterized by numerous territorial quarrels and ideological incompatibilities. While the Singer and Small study establishes that the great powers are much more "war-prone" than smaller states, the minor powers are certainly no more virtuous about making threats and becoming involved in confrontations. What particularly distinguishes the major powers is their capacity to intervene militarily in distant countries, something which most minor powers (with the exception of Cuba) have been unable or unwilling to do. A study by Istvan Kende of ninety-seven tribal, ethnic, civil, and interstate wars between 1945 and 1970 indicates that outside intervention occurred in 63 percent of the cases.[5] Most of the interventions were by the major powers, with the Soviet Union and the United States leading the list.

ISSUE FIELDS IN INTERNATIONAL CONFLICT

Still another study has focused on the question of the types of issues which have led to confrontations and wars.[6] In some cases, the conflicts involved so many incompatible objectives that it was impossible to classify any as being of prime importance. The sample of ninety-four conflicts comes from the period 1919 to 1980, of which thirty-eight occurred in the interwar period and fifty-six since 1945. Of these, eighty-seven could be classified as to the major, although not sole, issue field in which incompatible positions led the parties to adopt threats, coercion, and frequently violence. Looking over these conflicts, six major types of state objectives or sources of conflict can be identified.

1. *Limited territorial conflicts,* where there are incompatible positions with reference to possession of a specific piece of territory or to rights enjoyed by one state in or near the territory of another. The attempt to obtain more secure frontiers, such as Israel's conquest of the Golan Heights and the Sinai peninsula in 1967, is fairly common. The issue of sovereignty over ethnic minorities is often related

[5] Istvan Kende, "Twenty-Five Years of Local War," *Journal of Peace Research,* No. 1 (1971), 5–22.

[6] K.J. Holsti, "Resolving International Conflicts: A Taxonomy of Behavior and Some Figures on Procedures," *Journal of Conflict Resolution,* 10 (1966), 272–96; in addition to those cases listed in Appendices A and B of that article, the following conflicts since 1965 have been included: Algeria–Morocco (1958–1970), Morocco–Mauritania (1958–1970), Somalia–Kenya (1960–1969), Arab–Israel (1967), Soviet Union–Czechoslovakia (1968), United States–North Vietnam (1965–1973), India–Pakistan (1971), North Vietnam–South Vietnam (1954–1975), Turkey–Cyprus (1974), Indonesia–East Timor (1975), Vietnam–Cambodia (1977), Uganda–Tanzania (1978), Somalia–Ethiopia (1978), Tanzania–Uganda (1979), China–Vietnam (1979), North Yemen–South Yemen (1979), Iraq–Iran (1980).

to the claim by one state to control territory held by another and, therefore, will also be classified under the limited territorial conflict. Recent examples include a limited Ugandan invasion of Tanzania in 1978 to fulfill a territorial claim; Somalia's 1978 "war of liberation" in the Ogaden region of Ethiopia, claimed on historical grounds and on the fact that the region was populated by ethnic Somalis; and the Iraqi attack on Iran in 1980, with the objective of establishing full Iraqi authority over the commercially and strategically important Shatt-al-Arab waterway dividing the two countries.

2. *Conflicts concerned primarily with the composition of a government.* These types of conflict often contain strong ideological overtones; the purpose is to topple one regime and install in its place a government more favorably disposed to the interests of the intervening party. Examples would include the American efforts to "destabilize" the socialist Allende regime in Chile, 1970–1973 (not included in the list of cases); the Warsaw Pact's invasion of Czechoslovakia in 1968 to restore to authority the orthodox communists who had been replaced by the socialist reformers led by Alexander Dubček; and Tanzania's invasion of Uganda in 1979 to drive out Idi Amin, whose tyrannical regime had been denounced throughout the world as genocidal.

3. *National honor conflicts,* in which governments undertake military threats or actions to vindicate some alleged wrongdoing. States may escalate some relatively minor incident into a full-scale crisis. The Greek invasion of Bulgaria in 1925, arising out of a border incident involving the killing of two Greek frontier guards, is one example. China's "punishment" of Vietnam through limited military operations in 1979 is another.

4. *Regional imperialism,* in which one government seeks to destroy the independence of another state, usually for a combination of ideological, security, and commericial purposes. Nazi Germany's incorporation of Austria in 1938 would be placed in this category.

5. *Liberation conflicts,* or revolutionary wars fought by one state to "liberate" the people of another state, usually for ethnic or ideological reasons.

6. *Conflicts arising from a government's objective of unifying a divided country.* Vietnam is a prominent example.

Table 15–1 shows that incompatible positions in the fields of territorial jurisdiction, rights on territory, and control over ethnic minorities are a major source of international conflict. Ideological confrontations between the great

Table 15–1 Types of Issue Fields as Sources of International Conflict, 1919–1980

ISSUE FIELD	NUMBER OF CONFLICTS, 1919–1939	NUMBER OF CONFLICTS, 1945–1980	TOTAL
Limited territorial	20	25	45
Government composition	3	9	12
National honor	2	2	4
Regional imperialism	9	3	12
Liberation conflicts	—	10	10
National unification	—	5	5
Not classified	4	2	6
Total	38	56	94

powers concerning the composition of governments in small states were a hallmark of the cold war, as were the conflicts over German, Korean, and Vietnamese reunification. On the other hand, the blatant, unlimited imperialism typical of the foreign policies of Nazi Germany, Fascist Italy, and Japan during the 1930s is not to be found in the cold war period, or since.

ATTITUDES

We can say little regarding the unique configuration of attitudes that underlay the action taken in each of these international conflicts. Our comments will refer, therefore, primarily to the general conclusions that can be drawn from the diplomatic-historical literature on crisis behavior, as well as the studies of social scientists who have concerned themselves with foreign-policy decision making in conditions of great stress. These studies show that certain attitudes and psychological predispositions typically surround any serious conflict or crisis. These frames of mind help to explain the propensity to use violence in attempts to achieve or defend collective objectives. The following are some of the most typical attitudes; in each case, we can illustrate how the attitude affects the decisions policy makers ultimately take in a crisis.

1. *Suspicion* is directed toward the opponent, his intentions, and the motives underlying his actions. Intentions and actions of friendly states not in conflict are largely predictable. In a conflict or crisis, however, a sudden change in relationships is likely,[7] as well as a high degree of uncertainty and unpredictability—as indicated by the great lengths hostile governments will go to engage in espionage against each other, and to deduce intentions from capabilities ("Why should he have such large military forces if he doesn't plan to use them against us?"). Suspicion colors (usually pessimistically) speculation as to the other side's intentions. Peace gestures, for example, will probably be rejected as a trick.

2. *Issue escalation*[8] is another attitude common to policy makers operating in a crisis or conflict. They tend to attach symbolic importance to interests that, from a commercial or strategic point of view, are not worth very much. Control of a small and insignificant piece of territory may be defined by policy makers as crucial to national honor or symbolic of a state's willingness to resist the enemy's "aggression." As issues in a conflict or crisis become encrusted with ideological or symbolic importance, compromise may become more difficult, because government officials and publics will regard any withdrawal from a symbolic position as a sacrifice of some great principle.

3. *A feeling of urgency* surrounds the policy makers, at least during the crisis stage of an international conflict. They commonly feel that only a little time is available for making critical decisions and correspondingly believe that unless decisions

---

[7] Dean G. Pruitt, "Stability and Sudden Change in Interpersonal and International Affairs," *Journal of Conflict Resolution*, 13 (1969), 18–38.

[8] E. James Lieberman, "Threat and Assurance in the Conduct of Conflict," in *International Conflict and Behavioral Science*, ed. Roger Fisher (New York: Basic Books, 1964), p. 105.

and actions are taken rapidly, disastrous consequences, ensuing from the enemy's hostile actions, may result.[9]

4. Under the feeling of urgency and the uncertainties surrounding the enemy's motives and actions, policy makers *perceive fewer alternative courses of action* open to themselves than to the enemy. In the typical crisis situation, a government will announce that it has "no choice" but to respond by some military means, yet asserts that it is in the hands of the enemy to decide whether peace or war will result.[10] One's own options appear to be closed, while it is perceived that those of the enemy remain open.

5. Policy makers *perceive the crisis, if not all conflicts, as a turning point* in the relationship between the parties and sometimes in the history of the world.[11] A corollary is the common opinion that a war will somehow "solve" the problems between the conflicting parties.

6. In a crisis, *perceptions of threat are more salient than perceptions of the opponent's relative capabilities.*[12] The practical consequence of this common response is that if a government perceives great threat to a fundamental value, it will be willing to resist with armed force even though the odds of staving off the enemy's military actions are perceived as very slight.

ACTIONS

Various research projects have demonstrated that the presence of these and other attitudes—hostility, lack of trust, and nationalism—are directly linked to the *propensity of people to overreact to provocations.*[13] The studies help to explain why armed force is frequently the action that is ultimately taken in crisis, although other action may precede the use of force. In the early stages of conflict or crisis, protest, rejections, denials, accusations, demands, warnings, threats, and symbolic actions are likely to occur, whereas formal negotiation is more likely

---

[9] Robert F. Kennedy, *Thirteen Days* (New York: Norton, 1969); Charles F. Hermann, *Crises in Foreign Policy Making: A Simulation of International Politics* (China Lake, Calif.: Project Michelson Report, U.S. Naval Ordinance Test Station, April 1965), p. 29; Ole R. Holsti, "The 1914 Case," *American Political Science Review*, 59 (1965), 370.

[10] Karl W. Deutsch, "Mass Communication and the Loss of Freedom in National Decision-Making: A Possible Research Approach to Interstate Conflict," *Journal of Conflict Resolution*, 1 (1957), 200–11; Holsti, "The 1914 Case," pp. 365–78; James A. Robinson, Charles F. Hermann, and Margaret C. Hermann, "Search under Crisis in Political Gaming and Simulation," in *Theory and Research on the Causes of War*, eds. Dean G. Pruitt and Richard C. Snyder (Englewood Cliffs, N.J.: Prentice-Hall, 1969).

[11] Oran R. Young, *The Intermediaries* (Princeton, N.J.: Princeton University Press, 1967), p. 18.

[12] Dina A. Zinnes, Robert C. North, and Howard E. Koch, Jr., "Capability, Threat, and the Outbreak of War," in *International Politics and Foreign Policy: A Reader in Research and Theory*, ed. James N. Rosenau (New York: Free Press, 1961).

[13] Pruitt, "Stability and Sudden Change," p. 32. In a study of thirty-two crises, Michael Haas found that warning signs of impending crises are seldom decoded properly by the future opponents. Inability to interpret "signs" may be related also to overreactions. See Michael Haas, "Communication Factors in Decision-Making," *Peace Research Society (International) Papers*, 12 (1969), 65–86. For a good case study, see Charles Lockhart, *The Efficacy of Threats in International Interaction Strategies*, (Beverly Hills, Calif.: Sage Professional Papers in International Studies, #02–023, 1973).

in the settlement stage of the conflict or crisis.[14] Some common forms of action include:

1. Protest notes
2. Denials and accusations
3. Calling ambassadors home for "consultations"
4. Withdrawal of ambassador assigned to the opponent's capital
5. Threat of "serious consequences" if certain actions by the opponent do not cease
6. Threat of limited or total economic boycott or embargo
7. Extensive official denunciation of the opponent; propaganda at home and abroad
8. Application of limited or total economic boycott or embargo
9. Formal break in diplomatic relations.
10. Exemplary nonviolent military actions—alerts, cancelling leaves, partial or full mobilization
11. Harassment or closing of travel and communication between the antagonists' citizens.
12. Formal blockades
13. Exemplary limited use of force; reprisals
14. War—of which there may be a great variety according to the nature of the objectives, level of force, geographic scope, and so forth

Note that a conflict or crisis may involve any of these actions and that many may be taken simultaneously. Also, it should not be assumed that all conflicts and crises necessarily "escalate" from one step to the next; policy makers may decide to go from denunciation and warnings to use of military force rather than proceed step by step to war. Notice also that many of the actions in the list involve symbolic communication. A decision to call home an ambassador for consultation commonly indicates a government's serious concern with a situation or constitutes a limited form of reprisal. A partial mobilization involves more than just effecting some military plan; its main purpose may be to impress the opponent with one's own resolve to fight.

The propensity to use symbolic actions as means of communication results from another characteristic of crisis behavior: As the level of threat and hostility rises, there is a tendency to reduce formal diplomatic communication.[15] The "mildest" step or action in the crisis, such as withdrawing an ambassador, makes official communication more difficult. One would suppose that explicit communication by authoritative sources is most vital precisely when suspicion, mistrust, and sense of urgency are at their highest.

A review of conflicts and crises reveals a common sequence of actions

[14] Charles A. McClelland, "Access to Berlin: The Quantity and Variety of Events, 1948–1963," in *Quantitative International Politics,* ed. J. David Singer (New York: Free Press, 1968), pp. 159–86.

[15] Holsti, "The 1914 Case"; and Paul Smoker, "Sino-Indian Relations: A Study of Trade, Communication and Defense," *Journal of Peace Research,* 2 (1964), 65–76.

and counteractions that may end in the use of force. One government (the "offensive" party) presents demands or takes actions to change the status quo or its position in an issue field. In almost all cases, it makes its position on some principle of justice. The present situation, in other words, is regarded as violating some standard of justice, whether ethnic unity, "historical rights," rule by a repressive and corrupt government, or the like.[16] The "defensive" party communicates to the initiator that these actions or demands are a violation of a treaty or are a threat to its security or "vital interests." The offensive party responds by claiming that its actions or demands are fully justified according to various historical, legal, moral, or ideological criteria and that it has no intention of withdrawing from them, although it is certainly willing to negotiate. The defensive party thereupon begins to consider various responses to protect its interests, to block (deter) the fulfillment of the offensive state's demands, or to repel the latter's actions if they have already been taken. Moreover, the defensive party usually refuses to negotiate until the initiator has first withdrawn its demands or physical presence from the field or area under contention. The offensive government, however, is publicly committed to its demands or course of action and refuses to withdraw, although it still offers to negotiate. At this point, the defensive party, after indulging in the usual protests and denunciations, begins to take various reprisals and symbolic actions by withdrawing diplomats or ordering mobilizations. If these actions have no effect—and they usually don't—the crisis stage may follow; the decision then has to be made whether to reply with force or to seek some avenue of peaceful settlement.[17]

The Berlin study provides some clues about the incidence of various levels of coercion and violence in international conflict. It classified all 638 conflicts according to the *highest* level of threat, coercion, or force used in each. The possibilities were (1) verbal threat to use force; (2) demonstrations of force (e.g., alerts, mobilizations); (3) use of force with no casualties (e.g., blockades); (4) use of force involving fewer than 1,000 fatalities; and (5) war, involving more than 1,000 fatalities. Only 4 percent of the confrontations ended at the level of *verbal threats;* 22 percent ended with the parties involved in *displays of force;* 27 percent involved forms of *nonviolent coercion* such as blockades and commercial embargoes and boycotts; and 31 percent reached the level of force, but with relatively few fatalities. The remainder, 16 percent, resulted in *war.*

What are the probabilities of conflicts escalating all the way to violence involving large losses of life? Again categorizing by types of states—major powers and minor powers—some interesting differences emerge. Data for the 76-year period indicate that slightly fewer than one in five great power confrontations, including conflicts pitting great powers against minor states, ended in war. How-

[16] See F.S. Northedge and M.D. Donelan, *International Disputes: The Political Aspects* (London: Europa Publications, 1971), Chap. 4.

[17] For full elaboration of bargaining strategies in crisis situations, see Glenn H. Snyder and Paul Diesing, *Conflict Among Nations* (Princeton, N.J.: Princeton University Press, 1977). For theory and case studies, see Michael Brecher, ed., "Studies in Crisis Behavior," special issue of *The Jerusalem Journal of International Relations,* 3 (Winter–Spring 1978).

ever, the probability of war as the outcome of a major power conflict since 1945 has declined to one out of seven. The explanation for the decline is no doubt complicated, but one can speculate that the possession of nuclear weapons has dramatically increased the cost of a crisis getting out of hand; policy makers have become somewhat more prudent as a result. A second argument could be that international norms against the use of force are becoming increasingly secure as effective "rules of the game" restraining brash action. The very high cost of waging warfare—where matériel costing hundreds of millions of dollars can be destroyed in a single battle—could be another factor. In the case of minor powers, the probabilities of a confrontation ending in war are even lower—about one in sixteen during this century. We can conclude, then, that overall the incidence of international conflict is increasing, in large part because of the dramatic increase in the number of states in the system, but that the probability of these conflicts escalating to the point of war appears to be diminishing. This may not be much consolation, but the figures suggest that governments are often reasonably prudent and that various conflict-resolving mechanisms, such as those offered by the United Nations, may have an important role to play in helping to prevent conflicts from breaking out in war. We now turn to the second problem in this chapter: Once a crisis or confrontation has developed and various forms of bargaining involving manipulation of the instruments of coercion and violence come into play, what are the possible outcomes of the situation?

THE POSSIBLE OUTCOMES OF INTERNATIONAL CONFLICT

We will distinguish the *outcomes* or *settlements* from the *procedures* of formal diplomatic bargaining. In our discussion, then, a conflict may be "settled" through conquest—with virtually no "diplomacy" except perhaps in drafting the terms of surrender—or it may be resolved through some official compromise arrived at after extended negotiations and mediation. In other words, we will use the terms "outcome" or "settlement" to mean *any sort of final result of the conflict,* no matter how it was achieved. The term *procedures,* on the other hand, refers only to the formal diplomatic means of arranging some sort of *compromise.* A compromise is only one of at least six possible outcomes or settlements. The other five are avoidance or voluntary withdrawal, violent conquest, forced submission or effective deterrence, award, and passive settlement.[18]

Avoidance

When the incompatibility of goals, values, interests, or positions is perceived by both sides, one possible solution is for one or both parties to withdraw from a physical or bargaining position or to cease the actions that originally

---

[18] Kenneth E. Boulding, *Conflict and Defense* (New York: Harper & Row, 1962).

caused hostile responses. Although this may not seem very likely, it is probably the most common behavior among governments that normally maintain friendly relations.[19] When, for instance, a government initiates a proposal with its neighbor to make certain frontier adjustments in its favor and the neighbor insists that the status quo must be maintained, the initiator may, not wishing to create bad relations, withdraw the request or demand.

Conquest

A second outcome, conquest, requires overwhelming the opponent through the use of force. Even the termination of violent conquest involves some agreement and bargaining between the antagonists, however. One side, as Coser reminds us,[20] must be made to realize that peace, even under terms of unconditional surrender, is more desirable than the continuation of the conflict. One side may achieve this goal by forcing the other to realize that the possibilities of achieving even reduced objectives or successfully defending itself have disappeared. This realization may come only after one side has achieved a symbolic or important military confrontation, such as the defeat of the Spanish Armada, the Battle of Waterloo, the Nazi occupation of Paris, or the fall of Dien Bien Phu. The conflict may also be terminated, however, if the winning side offers lenient peace terms. The policy makers of the losing side may thus be induced to believe that they can still salvage something—their military forces, an intact economy, or the avoidance of foreign occupation—by suing for peace. In 1940, the French surrendered quickly to Germany, expecting that an early capitulation would lead to softer peace terms. This decision, although considered by many a blot on French honor, succeeded in part because it enabled the French to keep their navy—an important bargaining instrument against Nazi Germany later—and to keep the southern portion of the country free of German occupation.[21]

Submission or Deterrence

The criterion used to distinguish submission or deterrence from conquest is whether or not a threat to employ force is implemented. In submission or deterrence, one side withdraws from a previously held value, position, or interest because the opponent makes effective threats to "push" him out by the use of force (in a voluntary withdrawal, of course, no such threats are made). Even though no violence may occur, we will consider any submission resulting from military threats a nonpeaceful mode of conflict resolution. One of the parties accomplishes deterrence or forced submission (deterrence if the initiator of change in the status quo is forced to withdraw the offensive demand, submission

---

[19] *Ibid.*, p. 398.
[20] Lewis A. Coser, "The Termination of Conflict," *Journal of Conflict Resolution*, 5 (1961), 349.
[21] Paul Kecskemeti, *Strategic Surrender* (Stanford, Calif.: Stanford University Press, 1958).

if the initiator of new demands accomplishes them at the expense of the status quo) by demonstrating to another party that the probable risk of pursuing its actions or maintaining its position outweighs the costs of retreating and withdrawing. For instance, most observers believe that the Allied military buildup in Berlin and West Germany in 1961 forced the Soviet government to withdraw its plan to sign a separate peace treaty with East Germany. The Russians apparently concluded that the risks of nuclear war were not worth the possible gain in East German prestige resulting from a peace treaty.

Compromise

The fourth outcome of an international conflict or crisis is some compromise in which both sides agree to a partial withdrawal of their initial objectives, positions, demands, or actions.[22] The withdrawal need not be of the same magnitude to both parties (symmetrical). Any settlement that entails some sacrifice of initial position by both sides can be considered a compromise, even if one side seems to get the better of the bargain.

The main problem in arranging a compromise settlement is to get both sides to realize that the price of continued conflict is higher than the costs and consequences of reducing demands or withdrawing from a diplomatic or military position. An important prerequisite for achieving a compromise thus may be a military stalemate, a condition wherein both parties have neither the resources nor the will to conquer or force submission of the opponent.[23] Unfortunately, many governments do not raise international issues to compromise them and are convinced at the beginning that no goal short of total "victory" is consistent with national honor, some ideological principle, or "sacred trust." Stalemate may thus come only after a protracted and tragic military encounter, as in Korea and Vietnam. In each case, neither side was willing to discuss a settlement seriously until a military stalemate had developed. As long as any party believed it could achieve its objectives, even if slightly altered because of strong resistance, settlement was not likely. The anticipation of possible victory is thus a serious impediment to compromise, as are suspicion and distrust, the constriction of communication, and "issue escalation."

Award

A complicated outcome based on a previous compromise is the award, wherein the opponents agree to a settlement achieved through nonbargaining procedures. An award is any binding decision effected by an independent third party (such as a court) or criterion (such as majority rule), which sets out the substantive terms of settlement. Most conflicts are not, of course, resolved through awards, because procedurally they involve a surrender of bargaining and require a will-

---

[22] Boulding, *Conflict and Defense,* pp. 309–10.
[23] George Modelski, "International Settlement of Internal War," in *International Aspects of Civil Strife,* ed. James N. Rosenau (Princeton, N.J.: Princeton University Press, 1964), pp. 141–43.

ingness to resolve the issue on the basis of some impartial criterion, such as law, under which *there can be only a winner and a loser.* If one side has only a weak chance of gaining a favorable decision, it is not likely to accept such a criterion, especially when it sees a possibility of obtaining more favorable terms through a bargained compromise. On the other hand, if a stalemate develops in a conflict and if both sides trust the third party and expect a fair award, they may be induced to accept the impartial determination of certain issues by means of formal judicial proceedings.

An award settlement need not, however, be made through litigation. As long as some external and impartial criterion for settlement is accepted by both sides, the outcome may be termed an award, even though it is administered by a nonjudicial institution. A plebiscite to determine the allocation of contested territory and population is an impartial device used occasionally to settle both international disputes and conflicts.

Passive Settlement

Often, international conflicts have no formal outcome (deterrence, avoidance, compromise, conquest, or award), but persist for a long period until the parties implicitly accept a new status quo as partially legitimate. Quincy Wright has suggested that most international conflicts are resolved by becoming obsolete.[24] That is, both sides learn to live with a situation over a period of time, even though their formal positions are imcompatible. The involved governments have quietly reduced commitments to their respective objectives to the point where no overt military actions are deemed worth the cost. It is almost impossible, however, to determine when a conflict reaches obsolescence. Some of the postwar territorial conflicts in which the Soviet Union and the United States have had a stake—Korean reunification, German reunification, the Berlin wall, and the like—have been shelved, if not resolved, through the slow acceptance of new positions rather than through formal agreements or settlements. These outcomes may never be very secure, of course, but since many recent conflicts have been handled in this fashion, it suggests that sometimes the least violent method of settlement is the one in which both sides learn to live with their common problem until neither is tempted to impose a solution by force.

Any conflict will culminate in one of these six outcomes. Some, such as compromise and awards, are usually achieved through negotiations, mediation or adjudication, and formal agreements, whereas others, such as avoidance and passive settlement, result from unilateral self-abnegation or bilateral nonaction. The latter do not require formal negotiations or treaties, yet they are just as much a way of settling conflicts and crises as are surrenders or formal agreements. Looking at the 94 conflicts of our study, what has been the incidence of these six types of outcome?

[24] Wright, *A Study of War,* pp. 1256–57.

THE OUTCOMES
OF INTERNATIONAL CONFLICTS,
1919–1980

The figures in Table 15–2 reveal considerable differences in the outcomes of international conflicts in the two periods. The interwar period, culminating in the rush for territorial expansion by Nazi Germany, Italy, the Soviet Union, and Japan, saw a large proportion (42 percent) of all conflicts ultimately settled by violent conquest. The corresponding figure for the postwar period is 27 percent. In the past few years, however, there has been a resurgence of notable conquests, including the Soviet invasion of Czechoslovakia in 1968, Turkey's successful invasion of Cyprus in 1974, North Vietnam's victory over South Vietnam in 1975, and Vietnam's conquest of Cambodia in 1979.

Also of interest is the 21 percent of the conflicts that had award outcomes in the interwar period. This figure reflects the extensive use of plebiscites to settle territorial issues in Eastern Europe. Aside from the lower number of conquests since 1945, the figures to note in the postwar period are the percentages of conflicts solved by passive settlements and voluntary withdrawals, conflicts that have never resulted in formal agreement.

If we group the categories in Table 15–3 into only two types of outcome,

Table 15–2 Outcomes of International Conflict, 1919–1980

OUTCOME	1919–1939 (% OF 38 CONFLICTS)	1945–1980 (% OF 56 CONFLICTS)	% OF 94 CONFLICTS
Conquest	42	27	34
Forced submission, deterrence	21	16	18
Compromise	13	27	21
Award	21	5	12
Passive settlement	—	8	4
Withdrawal–avoidance	3	18	12
Total	100	100	101[a]

[a] Rounding error.

Table 15–3 Forceful and Peaceful Outcomes of International Conflict, 1919–1980

OUTCOME	1919–1939 (% OF 38 CONFLICTS)	1945–1980 (% OF 56 CONFLICTS)	% OF 94 CONFLICTS
Conquest; forced submission, deterrence	63	43	52
Compromise; award; withdrawal—avoidance; passive settlement	37	57	48
Total	100	100	100

"forceful" and "peaceful," the somewhat more peaceful character of the postwar world becomes apparent. In the interwar period, almost two-thirds of all outcomes were forceful. In looking at the total sixty-two-year span, slightly more than one-half of the ninety-four conflicts ended with the defeat—military or otherwise—of one of the parties.

INSTITUTIONS AND PROCEDURES
FOR RESOLVING INTERNATIONAL
CONFLICTS

Conquest, forced submission, and deterrence are outcomes usually achieved by manipulation of the instruments of violence. Diplomats may meet to avert crises or to draft peace treaties at the end of a war, but the ultimate results of these conflicts are usually determined by the threat or actual use of force, not by formal negotiations. Voluntary withdrawals, avoidance, and passive settlements are also usually achieved through unilateral policies and means other than formal negotiations. Consequently, when we discuss conflict resolution in the remainder of the chapter, we will be looking at procedures associated primarily with compromises and awards.

There are three basic procedures for arranging compromises and awards: (1) bilateral or multilateral negotiations among the parties directly involved; (2) mediation, wherein a third party with no direct interest in the issue areas under contention intervenes in the bargaining processes; and (3) adjudication, wherein an independent third party determines a settlement through some type of award.

Negotiations among Parties

Direct negotiations among opponents are as old as conflicts between organized societies. Whereas the character of war and other aspects of international relationships have changed greatly over the centuries, the techniques of diplomatic bargaining have remained essentially the same. Bilateral discussions between special emissaries or professional diplomats have been the historical rule, but since many conflicts involve more than two parties, multilateral conferences have been used extensively as well. The bargaining ploys and gambits used by diplomats or heads of state in direct negotiations are many and varied, so it is not possible to single out any that are particularly effective as means of achieving settlements.

The essence of the bargaining process involves the establishment of commitments to essential positions, determination of areas where concessions can be made, commissioning of credible threats and promises (even if only bluffs), and maintaining patience. The necessary, although not sufficient, condition for the success of any negotiation, however, is a common interest on the part of the opponents to avoid violence, or if that has already occurred, to put an end to it. Without this minimal common interest, there can be no compromise. If negotiations are undertaken when such a common interest does not exist, the purpose can only be to deceive the opponent, to play for time, or to make propaganda. It should not be assumed, therefore, that all negotiations have the purpose of reaching some agreement.[25]

Much has been written on the theory, assumptions, and practices of bilateral or multilateral diplomatic bargaining. Bargaining strategies and tactics are varied and complicated, but case studies and controlled experiments suggest some conditions that are conducive to the arrangement of compromises. These findings suggest, for example, that compromises or successful negotiations are more likely to result if:

1. The issues or objectives under contention are specific and carefully defined rather than vague or symbolic
2. The parties avoid use of threats
3. In their general relationships, the states in conflict have many other common interests
4. The issues are defined in such a way that payoffs can be arranged for both sides, or that the rewards for both parties will increase through cooperation
5. In disarmament negotiations, at least, the parties are equal militarily
6. Similar negotiations have led to compromise outcomes previously[26]

Mediation

One of the potential consequences of international conflict is the "spillover" of violence between two or more parties into the territory or issue fields of third parties. We can imagine that several thousand years ago, the distribution of human population was so sparse that violent conflict between two tribes, rural communities, or city-states had little impact on surrounding areas. Anthropological and historical evidence indicates, however, that even in primitive political systems, mediation by third parties was often practiced as a means of preventing involvement of additional parties in the conflict. In ancient China, India, Greece, and elsewhere, governments commonly recognized that they had an interest in limiting the violent excesses of warring communities. Some societies coped with the problem by formulating rules of neutrality; others, such as the Greeks, developed procedures for mediation and arbitration, whereby an eminent citizen of a noninvolved city-state would bring representatives of the warring communities together and bargain with them until some sort of settlement could be fashioned.[27]

[25] Fred C. Iklé, *How Nations Negotiate* (New York: Harper & Row, 1964).

[26] Many of these findings are summarized in Jack Sawyer and Harold Guetzkow, "Bargaining and Negotiations in International Relations," in *International Behavior: A Social-Psychological Analysis,* ed. Herbert C. Kelman (New York: Holt, Rinehart & Winston, 1965), pp. 464–520.

[27] Coleman Phillipson, *The International Law and Custom of Ancient Greece* (London: Macmillan, 1911).

Efforts to institutionalize mechanisms for interjecting third parties into crises and conflicts have been, in the European historical setting, sporadic. Prior to the development of the nation-state, when Europe was carved into a patchwork of duchies, free cities, city-states, aspiring monarchies, and semi-independent provinces, mediation services were often available and occasionally involved the pope. By the end of the seventeenth century, the states of the European international system had achieved some measure of independence and, through the legal doctrines of sovereignty, recognized no higher authority over their internal affairs or external relations. The international law of the period regarded force as a legitimate instrument for achieving or defending state objectives, and no sovereign would admit that a third party had any right to intervene diplomatically in a crisis or war. The only protection against drawing more parties in was the specific rights and duties ascribed to neutral states.

During the nineteenth century, a number of states concluded treaties that called for arbitration of disputes, and almost 300 unimportant international disputes were resolved through ad hoc arbitral proceedings. In the latter part of the century, owing partly to the influence of the successful arbitration of a dispute verging on conflict between the United States and Great Britain (the Alabama Claims case, 1871), a number of private groups began to agitate for creation of permanent international institutions for handling conflicts and disputes. They argued that establishment of a permanent international tribunal, armed with enforcement powers and supported by limitations on armaments, would give rise to a new era of peace. These sentiments eventually influenced some governments, and in 1899 and 1907, they reluctantly convened international conferences at The Hague to discuss plans for such institutions. The only important result of the first meeting was the "General Act for the Pacific Settlement of International Disputes" (amended in 1907), to which almost fifty states eventually adhered. The delegates also drafted a convention establishing the Permanent Court of Arbitration, which was neither permanent nor a court, but a list of arbitrators (nominated by members of the convention) who could be selected by disputing states to decide a particular case. The convention also delineated common rules of procedure for all arbitral cases. Even though Article 38 of the General Act urged the signatories to use arbitral procedures for "questions of a legal nature, . . . especially in the interpretation or application of international conventions," the same document exempted states from submitting disputes or conflicts involving questions of "national honor." It was left to the states themselves to decide which situations involved "national honor." These arrangements thus gave only a weak basis for the court's jurisdiction and failed to provide it with means for enforcing those few decisions referred to it. As today, submission of cases to arbitral procedures was based on the principle of voluntarism.

The most far-reaching innovation in establishing procedures for peaceful resolution of international conflicts, as well as disputes, came with the creation of the League of Nations in 1919. The major new principle of the League's covenant was that the international community had not only a right but a duty to intervene in international conflicts and, correspondingly, that the parties to a conflict or dispute also had the obligation to submit their differences to some procedure for pacific settlement, ranging from bilateral negotiations to submission of the case to the Permanent Court of International Justice. Primary responsibility for recommending solutions to disputes and conflicts was lodged in the League Council, made up of some of the major powers plus other elected countries, whose number ranged from six in 1922 to eleven in 1936. Under Article 13 of the covenant, which provided for judicial or arbitral procedures, the members accepted the obligation not to resort to force to challenge the decisions or awards of international tribunals. To help prevent noncompliance with such decisions, Article 16 empowered the Council to order economic or military sanctions. Under Article 15, the Council was authorized to consider any matter brought before it, even if one party did not accept the "jurisdiction" of the League. Once the case came before the Council, it could attempt to effect a settlement through any means it wished. In practice, the Council used a variety of procedures, including mediation (often performed by the president of the Council), commissions of inquiry, and conciliation commissions. In one case (the conflict between Poland and Lithuania in 1921 over the city of Vilna), it planned to send an international force to the scene of hostilities to separate the combatants and organize a cease-fire. In other instances, the League supervised plebiscites to determine the outcome of territorial claims. If the Council could not achieve a settlement through these methods, it was authorized to submit a report recommending the terms of settlement. If the report was adopted unanimously by the Council (parties to the conflict or dispute had no vote), no member of the League could use force against the party that complied with the report, upon penalty of having economic or military sanctions imposed upon it. But if the Council could not agree unanimously on the report and its recommendations, the parties to the conflict were free to do as they wished, provided they did not go to war for a period of three months following the vote on the report.

Article 16 of the Covenant provided for automatic sanctions if any member should "resort to war in disregard of its covenants under Articles 12, 13, or 15." All members of the League were to consider the use of force in violation of these articles as an attack on themselves. While the provisions for economic and military sanctions were designed to deter aggression and assure compliance with all decisions or plans of settlement reached through the various settlement procedures, the history of the League in fulfilling these commitments was disappointing. In 1921, three Scandinavian states introduced a resolution proposing that each member of the League, rather than the Council, should decide for itself when a breach of the Convenant had occurred; in 1923, the Canadian government sponsored a resolution that further reserved for each member the decision as to whether or not aggression had occurred and whether or not each should apply sanctions. Although the resolution did not pass, it had only one vote (Persia) against it, indicating clearly that the vast majority of states were not ready to delegate to the Council the authority to order sanctions—or even to determine that an act of aggression had occurred. Thus, the League Council was stripped of whatever authority it had under the Covenant to undertake action on its own authority. From 1923 to 1939, European governments displayed repeatedly that they, rather than the League council, would make all final decisions relating to implementation of the League's efforts in the pacific settlement of disputes and collective security. The League of Nations was notable for introducing flexible procedures to help reach accommodations in disputes and conflicts involving small nations; but when action had to be taken against the aggressions of the major powers, it was powerless.

Under the Charter of the United Nations, provision is again made for use of diverse procedures for handling disputes and conflicts. Chapter VI, entitled "The Pacific Settlement of Disputes" (Articles 33 through 38), obligates the parties to a conflict or dispute "likely to endanger . . . international peace and security" to submit it to some procedure for pacific settlement, whether negotiation, enquiry, mediation, conciliation, arbitration, judicial settlement, resort to some regional agency, or any other method the parties can devise. Under Article 2, the members are prohibited from using force, even if these procedures should fail. There is no assumption in the Charter that the United Nations should, or would, become involved in most threats or breaches of the peace, although Article 37 stipulates that conflicts or disputes *not* resolved outside the United Nations must be referred ultimately to the Security Council. Any party, whether or not a member of the United Nations, can submit an issue to the organization; the General Assembly may notify the Security Council of any dangerous situation; and under Article 99, the Secretary-General may also bring to the attention of the Security Council any matters that in his opinion threaten the maintenance of peace. On its own authority, the Security Council may, if the five permanent members agree, investigate any situation (Article 34) and may recommend at any time "appropriate procedures or methods of adjustment" (Article 36). Any action taken under Chapter VI, including dispatch of mediators or commissions of inquiry, is of a recommending nature only, however, and can be carried out only with the consent of the states directly involved in the conflict or dispute.

In Chapter VII, however, the Security Council is provided with enforcement powers if it has previously determined that there exists a threat to the peace, a breach of the peace, or an act of aggression. If it comes to such a conclusion, as in the Congo crisis of 1960, it can order the parties to a conflict and all member states to accept "provisional measures" (Article 40), such as a cease-fire or an order prohibiting intervention by outside powers. Under Article 41, the Security Council may "decide what measures not involving the use of armed force are to be employed to give effect to its decisions" and may call upon the members of the United Nations to apply such measures. These may include complete or partial interruption of economic relations, that is, boycotts and embargoes. If these measures are considered inadequate as a means of halting aggression or obtaining implementation of provisional measures taken under Article 40, the Security Council can use force. Under Article 43, which has never been implemented, the members of the United Nations are to make available to the Security Council "on its call . . . armed forces, assistance, and facilities, including the right of passage, necessary for the purpose of maintaining international peace and security."

These forces are not to be confused with the international peace groups created for the Suez, Congo, Cyprus, and Middle East conflicts. The latter forces were formed primarily to effect cease-fires, separate combatants, supervise with-drawal of forces, and patrol frontiers. They are not fighting forces in the sense that their function is to halt aggression. The efforts of UNEF, UNOC, UNFICYP, and the Middle East Force have been taken under Chapter VI of the Charter, which deals with pacific settlement of disputes. The forces, made up of contin-gents from many nations, have no directives to engage in hostilities except in self-defense, and have been able to function only because the parties directly involved in the conflicts have accepted their presence. Without this consent, which is the basis of all action and decisions taken under Chapter VI, the peace forces could not operate. It remains, however, for the United Nations to organize an international army that could be used as an instrument of collective security to repel aggression through force of arms.

The Charter gives to the General Assembly only a secondary role in handling international conflicts. Although the Assembly may *discuss* any situation, it can recommend procedures or terms of settlement only if the Security Council is *not* considering the situation. Under the Uniting for Peace resolution of 1950, however, the General Assembly has given itself the authority to determine the existence of a threat to the peace or an act of aggression; and it may recommend appropriate action to its members in case the Security Council, on account of the veto, fails to act. It was under this resolution that the General Assembly organized the United Nations Emergency Force for the Suez crisis to supervise cessation of hostilities and secure a line dividing the combatants. The Hungarian question (1956) was also considered in the General Assembly, although its rec-ommendations were never accepted by the Soviet Union. In 1960, the General Assembly played a key role in the Congo crisis after the agreement of the major powers in the Secirity Council had broken down.

Although the United Nations Charter has covered some of the gaps found in the League Covenant, the procedures for pacific settlement are re-stricted by the necessary agreement among the five permanent members of the Security Council and by the principle that any actions taken under Chapter VI need the consent of the parties to a conflict. In effect, two agreements normally have to be achieved before the Security Council can deal effectively with a danger-ous situation or a breach of the peace: The antagonists, with some exceptions, should agree to submit their conflict to this body, and then the five permanent members of the Council have to agree on the procedures to be used in attempting to effect reconciliation. The Security Council can discuss any situation brought to its attention, but any recommendations or actions, such as establishing commissions of inquiry, are subject to the veto.

We will see below to what extent the United Nations has worked effectively in the fields of conflict prevention, crisis management, and conflict resolution. Before we do so, however, let us review in more detail some of the services and functions that third-party mediators may provide in helping arrange compromise outcomes.

It is generally recognized that in any social conflict, whether between husband and wife, trade union and industrial firm, or two nation-states, the attitudes and patterns of behavior commonly exhibted during the "crisis stage" are precisely those most likely to lead to violence and destruction. We have already noted how, in the international crisis, communications are constricted, symbolic actions replace explicit discussions, and certain attitudes predispose the opponents to overreact to each other's actions. Thus, the most important functions of the third party—a party outside the "emotional field" of the conflict[28]—are to restore communications between the disputants, impose cooling-off periods, investigate conditions in the area of conflict, and provide, if necessary, a variety of services to the parties in conflict. From a bargaining point of view, third-party intervention into a conflict or crisis may provide a feasible avenue of retreat for governments that wish to withdraw gracefully without appearing to back down before threats from the main opponent. As in all conflict relationships, a compromise yielded to a third party may be easier to arrange than withdrawing in the face of the enemy. Finally, a mutually acceptable third party whose sole objective is to achieve a compromise settlement will probably be perceived as a more trustworthy bargaining agent than will a traditional rival.

The role and tasks of the mediator are extremely complex, and the initiatives and bargaining strategies the mediator adopts vary greatly from case to case. Intervention ranges from passing messages between the parties to active engagement in the bargaining and attempts to place pressure on the antagonists to accept peace proposals that the mediator himself has formulated. The activities of the third party may thus vary along several dimensions, such as formality-informality, extensiveness of resources committed, directness of penetration into the bargaining, and identity.[29] The following list, summarizing a fuller exposition by Oran Young, sets out some of the roles and functions that mediators may play in helping to resolve crises and conflicts:

I.   Actions taken to help the opponents begin or continue bilateral discussions, or to help implement any agreements already reached. Here, the third party does not become involved in the essential bargaining.

---

[28] Boulding, *Conflict and Defense,* p. 316.
[29] Young, *The Intermediaries,* p. 31.

A. *"Good Offices."* This refers to the procedures whereby third parties act as channels of communication between the opponents, passing messages between them. In addition, the third parties may propose sites for formal diplomatic sessions and urge the antagonists to begin formal discussions.

B. *Data Source.* This role involves providing opponents with relevant information of an undistorted character. Young cites the activities of the United Nations representative in Jordan during the crisis of 1958, the efforts of Connor Cruise O'Brien in the Congo, and U Thant's messages during the Cuban missile crisis of 1962 as examples of third parties' bringing to the attention of the antagonists information and facts they might otherwise have ignored.

C. *Interposition.* This action, illustrated by the quick dispatch of the United Nations Force to the Middle East after the Arab-Israeli war in 1973, is designed to place military barriers between the forces of the parties that are already employing violence and to supervise the withdrawal of hostile forces from contested areas.

D. *Supervision.* This service comes after the parties to a conflict have already negotiated a preliminary armistice or cease-fire agreement. The third party then delimits truce lines, polices them, handles violations according to established procedures, and occasionally administers contested territory. The long history of the United Truce Supervisory Organization in the Middle East is one example. Others involving supervision and temporary administration of contested territory are the League of Nations Commission, which, during 1933 and 1934, administered the disputed province of Leticia between Peru and Colombia, the international force and plebiscite commission for the Saar in 1934 and 1935, and the United Nations Temporary Executive Authority, which operated in West Irian in 1962 and 1963.

II. Bargaining by a third party during negotiations between two or more disputants. Service functions may also be involved, but in this situation, the main task of the third party is to combine "the elements of a rules keeper and an interested mediator."[30]

A. *Persuasion.* Persuasion involves attempts to keep negotiations going and to persuade the opponents to make progress. For example, the Secretary-General of the United Nations and his staff have often made themselves available during a crisis to point out to the parties the potentially dangerous consequences of rash actions and to emphasize the common and overlapping interests of the opponents.

B. *Enunciation.* This task involves clarification of the issues surrounding a conflict. According to Young, mediators enunciate their understanding of the issues involved and suggest basic principles, procedures, or mechanisms that might be employed in formal bargaining. They may also work on both parties to obtain a common understanding of at least several critical issues.

C. *Elaboration and Initiation.* Here, mediators become actively engaged in the bargaining by helping to formulate common or overlapping interests and making, on their own initiative, substantive proposals for resolving the conflict. If there is no previous single issue area or focus, mediators can create one by their power to make a dramatic suggestion.[31] If they

---

[30] *Ibid.,* p. 51.

[31] Thomas C. Schelling, *The Strategy of Conflict* (Cambridge, Mass.: Harvard University Press, 1969), pp. 143–44.

succeed in initiating a proposal as the basis for discussion, they must then continue to focus the negotiations around these proposals rather than allow the opponents to concentrate on their unilateral demands. Even though League of Nations and United Nations efforts at pacific settlement have usually established only procedures for bilateral bargaining, these organizations have also passed resolutions outlining principles upon which to base a final agreement (e.g., the Security Council resolutions of 1967 outlining the principles for peace between Israel and the Arab states) or initiated peace proposals in private meetings involving a mediator (e.g., Gunnar Jarring's 1971 proposals for a Middle East settlement). In a few cases, such as the handling of the border conflict between Greece and Bulgaria in 1925, the mediator—this time the League Council and a commission of inquiry—is in such a powerful diplomatic and moral position in comparison to the two small states involved in the conflict that it can apply great pressure on the protagonists to accept terms of settlement.

D.   *Participation.*   The last example cited above indicates that on occasion, mediators actually become one of the main parties to the bargaining. Not only will they point out areas of overlapping interest, break down stereotypes and images based on false information and initiate plans or proposals around which the discussions should revolve, but they will make efforts to get the parties to agree to their proposals. At this point there is three-way bargaining and, in a few cases, the mediator virtually dominates the negotiations. United Nations mediation of the Palestine truces of 1948, the solution of the West Irian problem, and the long and confused story of the Congo involved third parties that actively engaged in bargaining and put considerable pressure upon the protagonists to accept United Nations proposals.

These are some of the roles and tasks mediators can fulfill in crisis situations. The extent to which third parties "penetrate" a conflict depends upon many variables, none of which alone could explain success or failure. Since pacific settlement procedures in contemporary international organizations are based on the principle of voluntarism—both parties to a conflict must accept the role and functions of the third party—it is the protagonists themselves, through their responsiveness and willingness to be influenced, who will ultimately determine the third party's success. Power does not seem to be particularly relevant in mediation efforts. Small states as well as large have rejected the initiatives of third parties, a notable example being the unwillingness of Israel and Syria to accept certain formulas proposed by an American mediator during the crisis over Syrian antiaircraft missiles placed in Lebanon in 1981. Also, a weak state may be inclined to continue the conflict rather than agree to mediation if it can generate support for its position among allies and supporters. Impartiality, as perceived by the protagonists, is of course one critical element in creating responsiveness toward mediating efforts. Few parties to a conflict would be likely to accept intervention by an outsider if they perceived that party to hold views on the nature and sources of the conflict greatly at variance with their own or if that party is not disinterested.

Aside from impartiality, diplomatic prestige and the availability of service facilities are other important requirements for mediating efforts.

The final procedure for resolving international conflicts is adjudication and arbitration, whereby the parties, by prior agreement, submit the issues under contention to an independent legal tribunal. The court is supposed to decide the case on the basis of international law, and jurisdiction usually extends only to legal issues.[32] According to the optional clause of the Statute of the International Court of Justice, a legal issue is defined loosely as: (1) the interpretation of a treaty, (2) any question of international law, (3) the existence of any fact that, if established, would constitute a breach of an international obligation, and (4) the nature or extent of the reparation to be made for the breach of an international obligation.

International tribunals can take a case only if both parties agree to its jurisdiction. This means that there must be considerable common interest between the opponents before the procedure can be used. Not only must they both agree that settlement of the conflict is preferable to its continuation, but they must also agree that the settlement should be based on rules of international law and that it should be an award outcome, whereby one party wins and one loses, rather than a compromise. The prerequisites of successful adjudication and arbitration—the existence of legal issues, voluntary submission of the case by both parties, agreement that settlement is preferable to continued conflict, and willingness to accept an award rather than bargain for a compromise outcome—are seldom found simultaneously in conflicts and crises. Hence, as the next section will reveal, this procedure is seldom used except to handle disputes and minor issues between normally friendly states.

THE USE OF SETTLEMENT INSTITUTIONS AND PROCEDURES, 1919–1980

We can now examine the ninety-four conflicts to see which procedures—bilateral negotiations, multilateral conferences, mediation, and adjudication—were used most often to achieve compromise or award outcomes and which were relatively more successful. In most of the conflicts, diplomats and government officials made more than one attempt to resolve the major issues and employed more than one procedure in seeking an outcome. Thus, each attempt was followed through to its conclusion to see whether or not it culminated in some partial or complete agreement. The figures in the second column of Table 15–4 include only formal attempts to use one or more procedures for arranging compromise or award outcomes. They exclude informal attempts at settlement, such as offers of mediation that were immediately rejected, casual communication and bargaining in the form of press conference statements and speeches, or the unpublicized

---

[32] One major difference between adjudication and arbitration is that in the latter, the parties, by previous agreement, may have the issue settled according to other than legal criteria.

discussions that may have occurred in the corridors and salons of international organizations or foreign offices. Informal bilateral discussions that may have led opponents to submit a problem to international organizations or courts, although necessary antecedents to formal settlement, have also been excluded.

Several conclusions can be made from the figures. A large majority (73 percent) of all attempts at resolving conflicts and crises were taken through bilateral negotiations and international organizations. Mediation outside international organizations is relatively rare, as is the submission of conflicts to international tribunals. Multilateral conferences, reflecting the direct involvement of more than two parties in many conflicts, still occur, although not frequently. Perhaps more interesting are the figures on the successes, wherein bargaining within one or more of the settings led to a commonly recognized and legitimate outcome, in the form of a treaty, agreement, or legal decision. In some cases, the "success" was a formal decision to accept some alternative procedure for settlement. For instance, bilateral negotiations were considered successful if they led to an agreement to resolve the conflict formally through a plebiscite (for instance, the negotiations between France and Germany during 1934, when they agreed to use a plebiscite to determine sovereignty over the Saarland).

Based on a percentage of successes to attempts, bilateral and multilateral negotiations appear to provide the best possibility for success if we assume that the trends since 1919 will continue. Cases before international tribunals also had a high ratio of successes to attempts. The number of mediations outside the context of international organization is low (only thirteen attempts), so it is difficult to form conclusions about this procedure. The ratio of successes to attempts is, however, considerably lower than in the other procedures: Only four of thirteen attempts led to compromise. This is not to suggest that third-party intervention into international conflict is as a rule unsuccessful. On the contrary, a large portion of the successes in the "International organizations" row are directly attributable to various conciliating and mediating committees established by interational organizations or the actions, often taken on their own initiative, of the Secretaries-General of the United Nations and its predecessor. It is the context rather than the procedure or technique that is at question: Mediation outside international organizations is seldom attempted, and when it is, it rarely succeeds.

The figures in Table 15–4 also show that international organizations have been used extensively as forums in which conflicts between states have been handled. Of the 156 attempts to resolve the conflicts identified in this study, 58 (37 percent) were undertaken by the League of Nations, the United Nations, or regional organizations. Considering that seventy years ago, internationally organized efforts at conflict resolution or crisis management were rare, it is clear that these bodies have made a significant impact on this endemic problem of international relations. A closer look at the operation of the United Nations in handling conflicts and crises will illustrate the variety of third-party intervention techniques that have been developed and will enable us to make

Table 15–4 Settlement Procedures for 94 Conflicts, 1919–1980

PROCEDURES	ATTEMPTS	AS % OF ALL ATTEMPTS	SUCCESSES	AS % OF ATTEMPTS	AS % OF ALL SUCCESSES
Bilateral negotiations	56	36	27	48	41
Multilateral conferences	18	12	9	50	14
Mediation[a]	13	8	4	31	6
International organizations	58	37	21	36	31
International tribunals	11	7	5	45	8
Total	156	100	66	Average 42%	100

[a] Does not include mediations involving international organizations.

some general assessments about the effectiveness of this organization in meeting its primary task of maintaining international peace and resolving conflicts.

RESOLVING CONFLICTS AND DISPUTES IN THE UNITED NATIONS

To examine pacific settlement procedures and the degrees of success and failure in handling conflicts, this portion of the study will use a sample of thirty-two conflicts and disputes that resulted in some United Nations action aimed at bringing about a compromise. These thirty-two cases, occurring between 1946 and 1965, include bilateral and multilateral conflicts and crises, colonial conflicts, and disputes, as defined at the beginning of the chapter.[33] In all thirty-two situations, at least one of the major consultative organs of the United Nations— the General Assembly, Security Council, and Trusteeship Council—or the Secretary-General took formal *action* aimed at resolving the conflicts and disputes. By action is meant some form of diplomatic initiative, whether fact-finding, reporting, mediation, interposition, or supervision. Any conflict, crisis, or dispute

[33] The cases are: Greece, Indonesia, Indian minorities in South Africa, Southwest Africa, Palestine, Korea, Togoland, India-Pakistan, Libya, Eritrea, Somaliland, Bulgaria-Hungary-Romania, German reunification, Tunisia (Bizerte), apartheid in South Africa, West Irian, UN airmen in China, Suez, Hungary, Oman and Muscat, interventions in Lebanon and Jordan, western Samoa, Cameroons, Cambodia-Thailand, Laos, Ruanda, the Congo crisis, Portugese territories in Africa, Souther Rhodesia, Yemen, incorporation of Sabah and Sarawak into the proposed Federation of Malaysia, and Cyprus. The figures in the tables and most of the following discussion, are based on information found in Carnegie Endowment for International Peace, *Synopses of United Nations Cases in the Field of Peace and Security* (New York: Carnegie Endowment for International Peace, 1966).

in which one of the consultative organs merely discussed a situation or passed a resolution but took no other action was excluded.

What structures and tasks did the United Nations create and undertake in attempting to cope with situations they regarded as serious enough to warrant third-party intervention? The first response to the development of a crisis has usually been for the Security Council or General Assembly to organize an investigatory body, followed by the appointment of some agent (the Secretary-General, one of his representatives, or a conciliating committee) to attempt diplomatic intervention. Table 15–5 shows that of all actions aimed at bringing about a compromise outcome, fact-finding and group or individual mediation have been used most often.

In crises where violence has broken out and where the parties have previously agreed to a cease-fire or truce (usually after extensive United Nations mediation efforts), the United Nations has also been active in separating combatants through interpositionary forces or truce observation teams. Many of the actions of the United Nations in the field of military supervision and interposition are reasonably dramatic, and thus well known. Other supervisory activities are generally less publicized, and yet have been important in helping to implement and police agreements reached by bargaining between the opponents. A few of these are the Korean Repatriation Commission; the Plebiscite Commissioner for Togoland; the United Nations Commissioner for Libya, who drafted a constitution for the country and helped establish a national government; the Temporary Executive Authority for West Irian, which administered contested territory pending transfer of sovereignty from the Netherlands to the Indonesian government; and the Plebiscite Commissioner for Western Samoa. Under the "other" category in Table 15–5 are several agencies that have been used primarily to help civilian victims of violence. These include the Korean Reconstruction

Table 15–5 Agents Used by the United Nations for Intervening in 32 Conflicts, Crises, and Disputes

AGENTS	NUMBER EMPLOYED
Fact-finding or observation committees or commissions, reporting to General Assembly or Security Council	30
Mediation or conciliation committees or commissions created by the General Assembly, Security Council, or Trusteeship Council	28
Mediator appointed by Security Council or General Assembly, other than Secretary-General	3
Secretary-General or his representative as mediator	22
Truce supervisory organizations	4
Other supervisory organizations or commissioners	17
Interpositionary forces	4
Other (mostly civilian relief)	4

[a] Where an agency or person had two or more specific functions listed in its terms of reference, it is counted in all the relevant categories.

Agency and the civilian relief operations undertaken in the Congo and among Palestine refugees. An unusual task was also commissioned by the United Nations, the clearing of the Suez Canal of sunken ships following the 1956 Middle East war.

More important than identifying types of agencies or agents used in attempting to resolve crises, conflicts, and disputes is the task of assessing degrees of success. Judgments here are difficult, because many of the histories of these thirty-two conflicts have not been fully reported. It is difficult, moreover, to speculate whether the cases would have had approximately the same outcomes if the United Nations had not intervened. Did all the fact-finding, mediating, and supervising tasks organized by the United Nations really make any difference? Since we cannot answer this question in many of the cases, we will have to rely instead on a narrow criterion of success: Was each agency or agent able to fulfill the instructions given to it by the consultative organs or the Secretary-General? For example, the major task of a truce supervisory organization is to police cease-fire lines, report violations, and urge the violators to honor the truce agreements. If the agency was able to work as originally planned, even though it could not bring about a formal settlement, we must call it a success. Similarly, if an agency charged with the responsibility of making a report successfully completed that task, it must be deemed a success whether or not that report had any impact on subsequent events. Any effort to inject a third party into the conflict as an active participant was counted as an attempt at mediation.

The figures in Table 15–6 show that of all the activities and tasks that the United Nations undertakes to cope with crises, conflicts, and disputes, mediation is the most difficult, in the sense that only about two out of five attempts succeed. In at least twenty-three of the fifty-three attempts, the parties either refused to enter into serious discussions with the mediator, or if the talks did get under way, neither party changed its actions or positions to accord with the objectives of the mediating agent or agency. This conclusion does not warrant undue pessimism about the effectiveness of the United Nations, however. Many of the failures came in cold-war conflicts, where the United Nations has generally been ineffective, and in a few cases, such as racial policies in South Africa,

Table 15–6 Attempts and Successes in Resolving Conflicts by The United Nations in 32 Cases

TASK	ATTEMPTS	UNDETERMINED CONSEQUENCES	SUCCESSFUL	AS % OF ATTEMPTS
Mediation	53	8	22	42
Fact-finding, reporting	32	1	22	69
Supervisory	23	1	19	83
Interposition	4	—	4	100
Other	4	—	4	100
Total	116	10	71	

where no diplomatic pressures, from whatever source, have had effect. On the other hand, many difficult crises and conflicts were brought to a conclusion essentially in accordance with United Nations objectives because of the mediatory activities of various commissions or individuals. We would include in this category the efforts of mediators in the Indonesian-Dutch war, the Arab-Israeli war in 1948–1949, the violence between India and Pakistan, the release of imprisoned United Nations flyers by Communist China in 1954, and the long and embroiled crises in the Congo.

Information-gathering and service functions of the United Nations have been on the whole more successful than mediation. Fact-finding and reporting, which usually come at the early stages of a conflict, have been hampered only in cases where governments have refused to permit investigating groups to conduct their operations in the territories where the sources of conflict existed. The South African government, for example, has not allowed United Nations fact-finding bodies into its territories to investigate conditions of the black populations.

Various service and supervisory functions normally come at the latter stages of a crisis or conflict, when the parties have already agreed to a cease-fire or to accept more substantive terms of settlement. These prior agreements no doubt account for the high percentage of successful supervisory operations. However, we should not downgrade the importance of these service and supervisory tasks, since the agreements that result from crises seldom by themselves lead to peace, if by that term we mean that neither side would contemplate a renewed use of force. In fact, the high number of cease-fire violations and armistice-line incidents shows that many agreements are built on flimsy foundations. Others are at best truces rather than real settlements. Without truce supervisory organizations, incidents reflecting continued tensions would often lead to resumption of full-scale hostilities.

THE UNITED NATIONS, REGIONAL ORGANIZATIONS, AND PACIFIC SETTLEMENT: SUCCESS OR FAILURE?

How successful have all these efforts by agencies and agents of the United Nations been in helping to manage crises and resolve conflicts and disputes? To what extent, aside from purely tactical successes, has the organization been able to achieve its major purposes as stated in Article 1 of the United Nations Charter?—"To maintain international peace and security . . . and to bring about by peaceful means and in conformity with the principles of justice and international law, adjustment or settlement of international disputes or situations which might lead to a breach of the peace."

In making an assessment, we should distinguish the tactical successes—

such as securing a cease-fire—and the long-range successes of attaining ultimate political objectives. For example, United Nations mediators have arranged cease-fire agreements in many crises, but the organization has failed in those same crises to bring about political settlements that were envisaged in broad resolutions passed by the consultative organs. Although the figures in Table 15–5 on the successes of mediation, fact-finding, interposition, and supervision are reasonably encouraging, they do not reveal much about the general effectiveness of the United Nations in fulfilling its main responsibilities in the field of international peace. A particular agency established by the consultative organs may have completed its task successfully without bringing about the long-range political objectives of the Security Council or General Assembly. All the reporting, bargaining, or supervisory activities of the organization have been aimed *primarily at relieving or managing crises,* not at resolving the underlying conflicts. To make some assessment of the overall effectiveness of the United Nations in maintaining peace and ensuring peaceful change, therefore, let us measure the actual outcomes of the crises, conflicts, and disputes it has handled against the long-range goals or the major outlines of settlement that were enunciated in the resolutions of the General Assembly or Security Council. In all thirty-two cases, these bodies passed resolutions that clearly stated the long-range political objectives to be achieved. In the Korean case, for instance, the stated objective was to bring about the peaceful reunification of the country. The organization played a role in bringing an armistice to the Korean War, but the objective of reunification has not been achieved. In other cases, on the other hand, the stated objective has been to promote the independence of colonial territories. By organizing plebiscites, helping to draft constitutions, and placing diplomatic pressures on metropolitan governments to relinquish control over their overseas territories, the United Nations has successfully assisted in achieving the long-range goals that were originally outlined.

In the thirty-two crises, conflicts, and disputes in our sample, the consultative organs listed in their major resolutions a total of fifty-four ultimate political objectives to be achieved through fact-finding, mediation, interposition, and supervisory activities. Looking at the ultimate outcome of the cases (and remembering that all cases where the consultative organs merely passed resolutions were excluded), we see that thirty-one of the objectives were eventually achieved; the United Nations failed to obtain the desired results, whether acceptance of some particular peace formula and political settlement, "peaceful change," or compromise outcome, in the other twenty-three objectives. In terms of its own goals, the United Nations thus succeeded in 57 percent of the cases where it has taken action beyond mere debate and passage of resolutions. The reader may judge whether this figure represents success or failure.

This figure can be broken down if we wish to judge what issues and conflicts the United Nations has been relatively most successful in resolving. The thirty-two conflicts and disputes in the sample can be reduced, on the basis of the parties involved, to three types: colonial, cold war, and non-cold war.[34] Table 15–7 shows the rates of success and failure of the United Nations in dealing with these three types of conflict. As previously, our measure of success is the number of long-range political objectives, as stated in various resolutions of the consultative organs, that were ultimately achieved.

Even though the sample within each of the categories is small, the differences in achieving stated objectives in the three types of conflicts and disputes are significant. Where the United Nations attempted to achieve compromise outcomes or formal settlements, it was very successful in colonial conflicts and least successful in cold-war conflicts. On the basis of such figures, one would predict that, as in the past, the United Nations will have a higher rate of success in situations where the major powers are not directly involved.[35]

One final point needs to be stated about resolving conflicts through the United Nations, because it is not made apparent in any of the figures presented so far. We have used throughout this chapter the terms "outcome" and

---

[34] The Congo problem could be listed in each of the categories, depending upon the stage of the conflict. For this analysis it is classified as a non-cold-war conflict.

[35] The figures reported in the preceding pages are strongly affected by the definitions of success and the methods used to determine success. Ernst Haas, in his *Collective Security and the Future International System* (Denver: University of Denver Monograph Series in World Affairs, Vol. V, No. 1, 1968), arrives at somewhat different conclusions because he defines the problem differently. The reader may wish to avoid any judgment about the effectiveness of the United Nations mechanisms for conflict resolution until he compares the figures cited above with those listed by Haas. Professor Haas took fifty-five "disputes," which were referred to the United Nations (forty-five cases) or to both the UN and regional organizations (ten cases). The following results emerge from his study:

1. Hostilities occurred in thirty-two of the fifty-five disputes.
2. The hostilities were stopped "largely" as a result of action by international organization in ten of the thirty-two instances, or 31 percent.
3. Eighteen out of the fifty-five cases (33 percent) were resolved partly or wholly on the basis of UN resolutions.
4. Haas included in attempts at conflict resolution only those actions taken by the Security Council or General Assembly, or by organizations established by them. He did not count each attempt at conflict resolution by each organ in each dispute. Thus, if two bodies attempted mediation or conciliation in one case, it was counted only once. The case, rather than the attempt, is the baseline of the Haas study. Keeping these methods in mind, the rates of success are somewhat lower than those reported in Table 15–6.

Procedures	% Successful
Inquiry	43
Collective mediation	57
Single mediator	40
Cease-fire ordered	58
Truce supervisory organizations	56
Enforcement action	50
Police force	75
Secretary-General's "presence"	46
Committee of experts	0

5. Haas also measures the success of the United Nations in terms of the types of parties and issues involved. However, the measure is successful settlements as a proportion of the number of cases, not the number of objectives as a proportion of all the political objectives outlined in UN resolutions. He found that the UN was successful in 42 percent of the colonial conflicts (compared to 71 percent in this study), 26 percent of the cold-war cases (33 percent), and 29 percent of the "other" cases (compared to 56 percent in my non–cold-war category).

Table 15-7 Objectives Achieved by the United Nations in Three Kinds of Conflicts and Disputes

TYPE OF CONFLICT		NUMBER OF STATED OBJECTIVES	NUMBER OF OBJECTIVES ACHIEVED	%
Cold war	7	12	4	33
Non-cold war	13	25	14	56
Colonial	12	17	13	71
Total	32	54	31	

"settlement," as though there were something final about the results achieved through United Nations actions. However, although this organization has been instrumental in bringing about formal settlements to colonial conflicts by helping the territories in question to achieve independence and establish viable governments, in many other cases its efforts have at best merely put a lid on extensive violence, without really resolving the underlying issues. The agenda of the United Nations is still littered with situations, characterized as a threat to the peace, that have been impossible to resolve in terms of substantive settlements based on compromises over conflicting objectives. While the United Nations has undertaken peace supervisory functions in the Kashmir, Suez, Middle East and Cyprus areas, sanctions against Rhodesia, and many queries into apartheid policies in South Africa, it has not been able to achieve in these cases anything that could be called a settlement or compromise outcome, much less peaceful change. Violence in many crises has been reduced, if not completely controlled; the major powers have in some cases been excluded from unilateral interventions; and negotiations between the parties to conflicts have been undertaken occasionally; but no settlements have been achieved. These are "frozen" conflicts, little cold wars that will persist for many years. Some, presumably, will become "passive settlements," rendered obsolete by the passage of time or new diplomatic circumstances. If the United Nations can help to maintain them in a cold state and prevent the intrusions of the major powers, it will, of course, have achieved significant gains, if not formal settlements. One general conclusion about the United Nations must therefore be that, except for easing the transition from colonialism (peaceful change), this organization has been effective primarily as an agent for controlling crises. It has a much less enviable record in actually resolving conflicts; and in cold-war issues, as Hammarskjöld noted, the United Nations has been mostly ineffective.[36]

Another conclusion derives from the record of accomplishments and failures in the United Nations since 1965. In fact, few conflicts have even been submitted to the organization since that time, and on those what have, action has been mostly ineffective. Members debated the Soviet invasion of Czechoslo-

---

[36] General Assembly, 15th Session, Official Records, *Annual Report of the Work of the Organization*, 16 June 1969–15 June 1960, Supplement No. 1 (A/4390 Add. 1), 1960. For further analysis of the UN and international conflict, see Mark W. Zacher, *International Conflict and Collective Security, 1946–1977* (New York: Praeger, 1979).

vakia, the Indian intervention in Bangladesh in 1971, the Arab-Israeli war of 1973, and the Turkish invasion of Cyprus in 1974; but the most they could accomplish was to pass cease-fire resolutions that were ignored or implemented only after a successful military outcome had already been assured. One lengthy mediation attempt in the Middle East on behalf of the United Nations, by Gunnar Jarring, came to no positive conclusion. And some important conflicts, such as the 1978 Ogaden war between Somalia and Ethiopia, were not even referred to the organization. Except for some minor disputes, the perennial issue of apartheid in South Africa, and South Africa's administration of Namibia, it appears that the United Nations has become primarily a forum for discussion of global nonsecurity problems, such as resource development, and a place where the coalition of developing countries will seek to exert influence on the industrial countries to bring about a more equitable world trade system. The United Nations may become, then, more of an arena for conducting a general North-South conflict and dialogue than an institution where more traditional forms of international conflict will be handled.

These comments, however, ignore the records accomplished by regional organizations. In a recent study completed by Ernst Haas and his colleagues, some comparisons are made between the effectiveness of the United Nations and that of regional organizations.[37] Basing their study on all disputes and conflicts—ninety-eight cases in the United Nations and forty-eight cases in regional organizations between 1945 and 1970—the authors show some significant differences. For example, in general, the United Nations has dealt with more significant disputes and conflicts—that is, those representing a greater threat to peace or involving greater loss of life—than those dealt with by regional organizations. Eighty-five percent of the conflicts and disputes handled by regional organizations such as the Organization of American States and the Organization of African Unity were rated as "insignificant" or of low intensity. The corresponding figure for the United Nations is 63 percent. Moreover, the higher the intensity of the conflict, the less the regional organizations seemed to be able to accomplish in terms of helping to stop hostilities, isolating the conflicts, generally abating the levels of tension and hostile activities, or helping to bring about a final settlement. Even though the record of the United Nations is not strong in respect to all these tasks, it has, comparatively speaking, been more successful in bringing some sort of control to bear on high-intensity crises. Haas and his colleagues also found, as we might suspect, that the United Nations has a much better record in dealing with crises involving small and medium states than in the case of conflicts involving great powers. But this pattern does not hold

[37] Haas, Butterworth, and Nye, *Conflict Management by International Organizations.* Haas also presents interesting findings on the success rates of the UN and various regional organizations, identifying types of issues, power of the adversaries, and types of conflict-resolving activities. The number of cases is much larger than that presented in this chapter, since all issues on the international organizations' agendas were included, not only cases involving some form of action. Overall, the chances of an international organization's achieving a significant conflict-management success are about one out of four.

for regional organizations; they have had in many cases somewhat more influence on the major powers' conflict behavior than on that of some of the small states that were involved in the cases.

RESOLVING INTERNATIONAL CONFLICT THROUGH ADJUDICATION

In the history of international politics since 1919, we have identified the procedures used for handling different crises and conflicts, and, in the case of the United Nations, some disputes and colonial conflicts as well. Of those that were controlled or settled by peaceful means, a large majority employed the procedures of formal negotiations and the services of international organizations. During the 1920s, at least eight conflicts were resolved by plebiscites or nonjudicial League awards. But what of judicial procedures? To what extent have governments turned to the International Court of Justice as an avenue for resolving conflicts or disputes? If we maintain our definition of conflict—a situation involving incompatible collective objectives between two or more governments—then the ICJ and its predecessor, the Permanent Court of International Justice, have resolved or helped to resolve only five such situations between 1921 and 1980 (see Table 15–4). Of the 156 attempts to resolve the conflicts and crises, only eleven, or 7 percent, were made through courts. If we look at the record of the ICJ we see that it has considered fifty-two cases (excluding advisory opinions) between 1946 and 1975; of these, only three involved conflicts. The remainder would be classified as disputes, involving relatively minor issues between normally friendly states, cases in which the interests of private citizens, rather than collective national goals, were at stake.

Explanations for this relatively meager record lie in the nature of the Court's jurisdiction, which is based on the principle of voluntarism, on the character of award-type outcomes, on certain attitudes of governments toward contemporary international law, and on the fact that the Court is not expected to deal with issues with a high political content. Before the Court can hear a case— and the case must concern only legal problems—both parties have to agree to the Court's jurisdiction. A government that knows it has only a weak legal position in a contentious situation will probably not agree to this method of conflict resolution, because under it, there can be only a winner and a loser. Compromise, which is the hallmark of diplomatic bargaining and mediation, cannot be the result of judicial proceedings. Moreover, the cases that have been dealt with by international tribunals reveal that the parties have disagreed primarily over the establishment of facts or the meaning of *existing* law or treaties. In most international conflicts, however, one of the parties is deliberately attempting to *change* the other's rights, privileges, or obligations. Thus, most conflicts have important legal aspects, but one or both of the parties do not wish to characterize the situation in legal terms because their political objectives and actions are clearly incompatible with existing legal principles or jurisdictions. In other cases, a justiciable dispute is not handled by legal procedures because it has become too deeply embroiled in, or is symbolic of, greater tensions and conflicts between two states.[38] Finally, there is the problem of the sources of modern international law and governmental attitudes toward that law.

Many existing legal principles were developed to help regulate jurisdictions, forms of interaction, and responsibility of the European states during the eighteenth and nineteenth centuries. Some principles were designed specifically to protect European commercial interests and colonial relationships. Aside from most Communist governments, which have rejected some doctrines of "Western" international law, legal scholars have noted that many of the new states are less than enthusiastic about many of these older principles. They have many economic, political, and commercial needs that cannot be regulated effectively or met by the application of older norms. Hence, the reluctance of many of the new nations to accept the compulsory jurisdiction of the ICJ may be explained in part by their suspicion toward the former colonial powers and the legal principles that they developed to take care of their own needs.

This last point opens another perspective on the problems of conflict resolution: the willingness of *types* of states to employ mechanisms of conflict resolution. If we were to extrapolate from all the figures presented above two types of situation wherein conflict resolution would be most likely to succeed or fail, we would describe them as follows: Conflicts involving (1) two small states, (2) non–cold-war issues, and (3) a combination of bilateral negotiation and Secretary-General mediation would be most likely to result in a successful (such as compromise) outcome. Conflicts involving (1) the major powers, (2) cold-war issues, and (3) mediation outside or within the United Nations structure would be least likely to lead to a successful outcome. But what of the nature of the parties to conflicts? Is it true, as suggested above, that developing states are less likely to make use of judicial procedures when they become involved in conflicts? Do governments with authoritarian characteristics become involved in institutionalized conflict resolution any less than governments that could be characterized as open? William Coplin and Martin Rochester have made a study of 121 cases before the League of Nations, Permanent Court of International Justice, United Nations, and International Court of Justice.[39]

They found that "open" states are more likely than "closed" states to use the major institutional structures for resolving conflicts, although "closed" polities were found to use the United Nations slightly more often than "open"

---

[38] Charles De Visscher, *Theory and Reality in Public International Law,* trans. Percy Corbett (Princeton, N.J.: Princeton University Press, 1957), pp. 322–23. For an argument that international law is too inflexible and conservative as a basis for resolving conflicts, see John W. Burton, *Conflict and Communication* (London: Macmillan, 1969), Chap. 10.

[39] William D. Coplin and J. Martin Rochester, "The Permanent Court of International Justice, the International Court of Justice, the League of Nations, and the United Nations: A Comparative Empirical Survey," *American Political Science Review,* 66 (1972), 529–50.

states. The figures also reveal that "open" societies have taken cases to international courts much more frequently than have either "closed" states or "semi-open" states. This finding would indicate that both developing and Communist states have strong reservations about employing legal procedures, or Western rules of law, as means for resolving conflicts.

In terms of levels of economic development, the figures substantiate the finding: The developed states used the courts three times more often than either developing or "intermediate" states. However, such states used the League and UN more often than the developed states. We can conclude that among the developing states and states with "closed" political systems, judicial procedures have not yet achieved popularity or legitimacy. If they are going to take cases to any institution, the political organs of the League and UN have been favored highly.

In terms of the power of the participants, the study also reveals interesting conclusions. In cases submitted to the courts, the initiator is usually the stronger of the two states involved in the conflict or dispute. In only one out of five submissions is the initiator of legal procedures the weaker of the two states. However, the exact opposite emerges in submissions to the League and UN. In these institutions, the initiators have usually been the weaker of the two parties in a conflict or dispute. According to Coplin and Rochester, these findings suggest that weaker, developing, or Communist states have tended to perceive the courts as the protectors of the status quo, and the League and UN as the most favorable institutions for handling international conflicts and disputes.

CONCLUSION

Most conflicts arise over incompatible positions in various issue areas. If the incompatible values and positions of both parties are perceived as fundamental, the parties' behavior, buttressed by hostile, distrustful, and suspicious attitudes, may well be violent. Unless stalemate, obsolescence, or effective third-party intervention occur, the outcome is likely to be physical conquest or forced withdrawal. The critical point in the conflict occurs when the actions of one state lead the government of another to consider the possibility of using force. Mild threats, pressures, and reprisals can often be controlled, but if tensions are high enough and the actions perceived as extremely threatening, a crisis situation, where a decision to use organized force may be required, results. In a crisis, symbolic communication often increases while overt bargaining and negotiation decrease; and the behavior of policy makers may well be vitally affected by the pressures of time, perceptions of threat, and the need to act quickly. Violence often results. It is in this situation that the fact-finding, mediation, interposition, and supervisory tasks developed in international organizations become important. Both the League of Nations and its successor have in fact dealt primarily with crises rather than conflicts. In this field, they have been reasonably successful. In the most difficult task, mediation, the United Nations has achieved desired results in about 40 percent of the attempts, while in reporting, interposition, and supervision, rates of success have been much higher. In resolving conflicts or promoting peaceful change—that is, arranging some sort of new legal or political situation that is accepted by all the parties directly involved—the record is not nearly so impressive. Indeed, one of the most discouraging facts about international organizations has been their inability or unwillingness to cope with conflicts *before* they reach the crisis stage.[40] Yet it is probably in the crisis stage that formal settlements are least likely to be attained. Only in the area of transition from colonialism has the organization proved truly effective as an instrument of peaceful change.

SELECTED BIBLIOGRAPHY

AUBERT, VILHELM, "Competition and Dissensus: Two Types of Conflict and of Conflict Resolution," *Journal of Conflict Resolution,* 7 (1963), 26–42.

BELL, CORAL, *The Conventions of Crisis.* New York: Oxford University Press, 1971.

BLOOMFIELD, LINCOLN P., ed., *International Military Forces: The Question of Peacekeeping in an Armed and Disarming World.* Boston: Little, Brown, 1964.

———, and AMELIA C. LEISS, *Controlling Small Wars: A Strategy for the 1970s.* New York: Knopf, 1969.

BOULDING, KENNETH E., *Conflict and Defense: A General Theory.* New York: Harper & Row, 1962.

BRECHER, MICHAEL, ed., "Studies in Crisis Behavior," special issue of *The Jerusalem Journal of International Relations,* 3 (Winter–Spring 1978).

BROWNLIE, IAN, *International Law and the Use of Force by States.* London: Oxford University Press, 1963.

BURNS, ARTHUR L., and NINA HEATHCOTE, *Peace-Keeping by U.N. Forces: From Suez to the Congo.* New York: Praeger, 1963.

BURTON, JOHN W., *Conflict and Communication.* London: Macmillan, 1969.

CLAUDE, INIS L., JR., *Swords into Plowshares: The Problems and Prospects of International Organization,* 4th ed. New York: Random House, 1971.

———, "The United Nations and the Use of Force," *International Conciliation,* No. 532 (1961), 325–94.

COSER, LEWIS A., "The Termination of Conflict," *Journal of Conflict Resolution,* 5 (1961), 347–53.

DONELAN, M.D., and M.J. GRIEVE, *International Disputes: Case Histories 1945–1970.* London: Europa Publications, 1973.

FISHER, ROGER, *International Conflict for Beginners.* New York: Harper & Row, 1970.

---

[40] Inis L. Claude, Jr., *Swords into Plowshares,* 4th ed. (New York: Random House, 1971), p. 239.

GOODRICH, LELAND M., *The United Nations in a Changing World.* New York: Columbia University Press, 1974.

HAAS, ERNST B., ROBERT L. BUTTERWORTH, and JOSEPH S. NYE, *Conflict Management by International Organizations.* Morristown, N.J.: General Learning Press, 1972.

HAAS, MICHAEL, *International Conflict.* Indianapolis: Bobbs-Merrill, 1974.

HERMANN, CHARLES F., ed., *International Crises: Insights from Behavioral Research.* New York: Free Press, 1972.

KATZ, MILTON, *The Relevance of International Adjudication.* Cambridge, Mass.: Harvard University Press, 1968.

KECSKEMETI, PAUL, *Strategic Surrender.* Stanford, Calif.: Stanford University Press, 1958.

LARSON, ARTHUR, *When Nations Disagree.* Baton Rouge: Louisiana State University Press, 1961.

LEVI, WERNER, "On the Causes of War and the Conditions of Peace," *Journal of Conflict Resolution,* 4 (1960), 411–20.

LOCKHARD, CHARLES, *Bargaining in International Conflicts.* New York: Columbia University Press, 1979.

LUARD, EVAN, ed., *The International Regulation of Frontier Disputes.* London: Thames & Hudson, 1970.

MODELSKI, GEORGE, "International Settlement of Internal War," in *International Aspects of Civil Strife,* ed. James N. Rosenau. Princeton, N.J.: Princeton University Press, 1964.

NORTHEDGE, FRED S., and MICHAEL DONELAN, *International Disputes: The Political Aspects.* London: Europa Publications, 1971.

PRUITT, DEAN G., and RICHARD C. SNYDER, eds., *Theory and Research on the Causes of War.* Englewood Cliffs, N.J.: Prentice-Hall, 1969.

RIKHYE, INDAR JIT, MICHAEL HARBOTTLE, and BJORN EGGE, *The Thin Blue Line: International Peacekeeping and its Future.* New Haven, Conn.: Yale University Press, 1974.

SCHELLING, THOMAS C., *The Strategy of Conflict.* Cambridge, Mass.: Harvard University Press, 1960.

SINGER, J. DAVID, and MELVIN SMALL, *The Wages of War, 1816–1965: A Statistical Handbook.* New York: John Wiley, 1972.

SNYDER, GLENN H., and PAUL DIESING, *Conflict Among Nations.* Princeton, N.J.: Princeton University Press, 1977.

WRIGHT, QUINCY, "The Escalation of International Conflicts," *Journal of Conflict Resolution,* 9 (1965), 434–49.

YOUNG, ORAN, *The Intermediaries.* Princeton, N.J.: Princeton University Press, 1967.

ZACHER, MARK W., *International Conflict and Collective Security, 1946–1977.* New York: Praeger, 1979.

16

The Interaction of States: Collaboration

A large proportion of the transactions and interactions between the states in our international system are routine and nearly free of conflict. A variety of national, regional, or global problems arise that require the attention of more than one state. In most cases, governments approach each other with proposed solutions, bargain or discuss the problem, adduce technical evidence in favor of one or another solution, and end the negotiations with some treaty or understanding satisfactory to both sides. This process is called collaboration, or cooperation.

The term *collaboration* may create an image of an international organization hard at work resolving common problems, or of technical experts in the field teaching others how to improve agricultural productivity. When we use the term *conflict,* we may mean certain facets of violence or simply a disagreement over some issue. Whatever our common understanding for these terms, we often assume that collaboration and conflict are opposites and that international politics (often defined as the search for power at the expense of others) is primarily a conflictful process. This view is understandable, because our attention is frequently called to the great world crises, whereas we are less often made aware of the tacit or overt collaboration—even in conflict situations—that exists in the world. We should hesitate to identify collaboration as the core of only "good" types of relationships such as those observed in international technical organizations. After all, construction of an aggressive alliance may involve as much collaboration as an international program to raise health and literacy

standards, where governments may disagree seriously about its purposes, organization, and financing. The reason we assume that such programs represent collaboration is that the conflictful content in them seldom leads to violence or
military threats. But the reason they do not lead to violence is not because
there is less conflict; it is largely because the interests involved are not vital
and therefore not worth the risks and costs of military action. Whenever interests
and objectives are inconsistent or incompatible, conflictful relationships will
arise; whenever they are compatible, they are likely to lead to collaborative
transactions. International politics is always a mix of these types of relationships,
as well as of competition. As we will see below, it is virtually impossible to
find examples of collaboration that do not involve some conflict.

CONTEXTS WITHIN WHICH
COLLABORATION TAKES PLACE

Cooperation can take place in different contexts. Most collaborative transactions
and interactions occur directly between two governments facing some problem
or matter of common interest. Brazil and Japan, for example, annually negotiate
a trade agreement; Pakistan and China arrange airline communications between
Rawalpindi and Peking; or two African states agree to survey and demarcate
their common boundary.

     Other collaborative enterprises are undertaken within international orga-
nizations and institutions. Some international organizations, such as the United
Nations, are based on the sovereignty of each member; they cannot act without
the consent of the parties involved in an issue, and agreements to collaborate
are normally made only in accordance with the will of the least cooperative
member. In other organizations, such as the European Community, collaboration
takes on characteristics not often found in the United Nations or its regional
counterparts, and behavior of the member states in fashioning cooperative enterprises is in some ways significantly different. But whatever the differences between international organizations and supranational organizations, collaboration
within them has this in common: The formulation of common policies or coordination of separate national policies is done on a multilateral basis, and often
includes plans and proposals drafted not by national governments but by international civil servants. Moreover, these organizations offer facilities for continual
negotiations and bargaining.

     The number of multinational institutions designed to promote specific
economic, technical, or diplomatic-military objectives or to manage common
problems has grown from fewer than ten in 1870 to more than 270 in 1982.
As the range of problems requiring multilateral management or solution grows
exponentially, the numbers of organizations can be expected to increase at an
ever-faster pace. The most prominent institutions include universal organizations
dealing with problems of peace, security, trade, and development, such as the

United Nations, and a variety of organizations which fulfill the same functions but on a regional basis. These include the highly successful European Community and somewhat less prominent institutions such as the Association of Southeast Asian Nations (ASEAN), the socialist Council of Mutual Economic Assistance (CMEA), the Nordic Council which coordinates the Scandinavian states' economic and social policies, the Arab League which acts both as an anti-Israeli collaborative device and a mechanism to intervene in Arab feuds, and the International Atomic Energy Agency, which inspects national nuclear facilities to see they are not employed to build weapons. NATO promotes defense policy coordination and diplomatic collaboration of fifteen Western countries in their relations with the socialist bloc, while the North Pacific Halibut Commission establishes catch quotas for the member states' fishing fleets. From the mundane, technical institution to the global, high profile organization, these and many others provide some regularity and predictability to international politics.

Expanding technology and commercial activity create a plethora of problems that outpace the capacity of governments to build regional or global institutions. Thus, many issues are addressed by *ad hoc* conferences and meetings designed to create new *regimes,* or rules and regulations that help manage the problems and allocate costs and rewards to all nations. Governments may spend considerable time and effort—the Law of the Sea Conference lasted more than seven years—bargaining and haggling over the rules and regulations, particularly where many private or security interests are involved. While much of the negotiation may be acrimonious, common recognition that even a poor regime is better than no regime compels the delegations to collaborate to the extent of developing a minimally satisfying solution. Transnational organizations, such as international airlines, also become involved in regime creation; without some rules governing routes and fares, chaos involving wars of airlines against each other would ensue. While many regimes are weak and often ineffective, governments have been forced to spend an increasing amount of time negotiating them to avert catastrophic situations caused by unfettered economic and technological activity. The large and lengthy multilateral conference is thus becoming an increasingly visible forum for international collaboration.

In addition to the simple bilateral and intermittent collaboration between pairs of states and multilateral coordination of national policies or regime creation within international or supranational institutions, there is the extensive noninstitutionalized collaboration that occurs within what Karl Deutsch has called "pluralistic security communities." In a pluralistic security community, two or more states have many transactions and almost constant interaction, but not necessarily formal organizations for cooperation. However, the distinguishing feature of the pluralistic security community is that *all* the relationships between the units are predictably peaceful, and when conflicts arise, they are normally resolved by compromise, avoidance, and awards rather than by threats, deterrence, or force.

Deutsch has distinguished pluralistic security communities, where there is no integration of political institutions or authority (Canada and the United States, for example), from amalgamated security communities, where two or more independent political units merge to create a larger entity with a common structure of political authority. Historical examples of the processes leading to amalgamated security communities would include creation of Italy out of a conglomeration of formerly warring city-states, papal holdings, and small kingdoms on the Italian peninsula; establishment of federal authority and nationhood out of thirteen colonies in America; amalgamation of the former nations of Scotland, Wales, Ireland, and England into the United Kingdom by the early eighteenth century; and unification of Germany out of hundreds of principalities, semisovereign towns and cities, and dynastic states during the nineteenth century.

The distinguishing feature of a security community, as compared to ordinary diplomatic dyads, is achievement of "integration," which Deutsch defines as a "sense" of community, and development of diplomatic-political-military practices that ensure "for a long time" the expectation of only peaceful relations among the populations.[1] Deutsch claims that the two main indicators of the existence of a security community are revealed in situations (1) where the policy makers of two or more political units, and their societies in general, cease to contemplate the possibility of mutual warfare; and (2) where the two or more states cease to allocate resources for building military capabilities aimed at each other.[2]

Of course, it may not be easy to state at what particular point in history a security community has emerged. The Rush-Bagot Treaty of 1819 demilitarized the Canadian-American frontier, and there were few official government plans after 1865 indicating any expectation of war between the two countries. Yet there were several instances during the late nineteenth century when some Canadians and Americans expected or planned to use violence against each other. In terms of public attitudes, a true security community between the two countries probably dates only from the early twentieth century. Similarly, there have been no Swedish and Norwegian military forces "targeted" toward each other since the breakup of the Swedish-Norwegian union in 1905, but segments of the population in each country did consider the possibility of warfare against the other until the end of World War I. Another problem of identification arises when two states continue to make routine preparations for defending their borders against each other, even though the societies and governments concerned

---

[1] Karl Deutsch et al., *Political Community and the North Atlantic Area* (Princeton, N.J.: Princeton University Press, 1957), p. 5. Another political scientist, Ernst Haas, argues that true integration and community can develop only where supranational, federal, or confederal institutions exist with powers to direct the policies of the units that are amalgamating. Haas states that while avoidance of force can be achieved outside the context of such institutions, the creation and perpetuation of a new national consciousness cannot be expected to develop unless central political authorities and institutions are established. See Ernst B. Haas, *The Uniting of Europe* (Stanford, Calif.: Stanford University Press, 1968), p. 7.

[2] Deutsch et al., *Political Community*, pp. 31–33.

would not have any expectation of using or threatening force against the neighbor.[3]

A third indicator of the existence of a security community could be mutual acceptance and rigorous observance of certain rules of international law and bilateral treaties when collective objectives of the units are not in harmony. These would include, as well as avoidance of military threats, meeting treaty obligations (except in emergencies, where prior consultation would pave the way for special dispensations), avoidance of interference in the other unit's internal affairs, and observance of normal diplomatic protocol and etiquette in all transactions and negotiations. If behavior conforms to these three indicators—no "targeted" military forces, no public expectations of war, and full observance of treaties—we can say that a security community exists between the two or more independent political units, or within an area where the political units are formally amalgamating.

One might object that in such relationships, the essential collective objectives and values of the political units are so similar that serious conflicts never arise anyway. The indicators of a security community are obvious characteristics of any relationship where goals and values are compatible to begin with. The concept is thus a tautology. But this criticism fails to acknowledge that some very serious differences have arisen among states in security communities, and that some special characteristics of these relationships have prevented the quarreling governments from adopting forms of behavior typical in conflicts involving threat or use of force. For example, relations between France and the United States since World War II have often been strained by diverging collective interests and different long-range goals or concepts regarding the future organization of Europe. Throughout the 1950s, the Algerian rebellion caused considerable mutual recrimination and lack of understanding between the French and American governments; in 1966, President de Gaulle asked the United States and Canada to remove their troops and facilities from French soil and announced his plans to withdraw French commanders from NATO headquarters; ever since the organization of NATO in 1949, there have been unbridgeable differences of view on appropriate military strategies for alliance forces, control over the strategic deterrent held by the United States, and development of independent nuclear capabilities in certain NATO countries. Throughout the 1970s, France and the United States held often incompatible views on trade and economic issues. In each case, the French and American governments sought to change the behavior of each other to conform to their own interests through normal techniques of persuasion, by offering rewards, attempting to persuade by citing common advantages, and in some cases, making nonviolent threats of deprivations or punishments. But in no instance did one party conceive of, or threaten to, employ force against the other; no military capabilities were mobilized to

---

[3] Deutsch et al., *Political Community*, pp. 115–16. For example, the Canadian general staff still had in its files as late as 1931 plans for military expeditions into Washington, Idaho, Montana, Minnesota, and New York, should an American thrust into Ontario occur.

signify total commitment to an objective, and communication between Paris and Washington did not break down. The question arises: Why were characteristics associated with violent conflicts not displayed in conflicts occurring within security communities?[4]

What conditions ameliorate conflict within pluralistic security communities and in international organizations? How are problems typically handled when they arise between states in these two contexts? What are the main forms of collaboration? We will explore these questions by looking at collaboration in two contexts: the Canadian-American relationship (an example of a pluralistic security community with low institutionalization) and diplomacy in the European Community (an example of a security community characterized by joint institutions).

COLLABORATION AND PROBLEM SOLVING BETWEEN OTTAWA AND WASHINGTON

The large volume of transactions across the Canadian-American boundary is bound to offer opportunities for both conflict and collaboration. In many areas, the interests of Americans and Canadians are similar, and cooperative ventures and policies can easily contribute to the advantages of both. In the economic realm, for instance, balanced trade between the two countries contributes mutually to increased national wealth and fulfills critical economic needs. Americans export more products to Canada than to any other country in the world and have found in Canada a lucrative field for investment of private capital. Canadians look south not only for sources of import and export markets (which represent over 70 percent of Canada's foreign trade), but also for capital to help develop Canadian industry, and for investment of their own capital. Through collaboration and coordination of policies, Washington and Ottawa can gain important mutual benefits in flood control, pollution abatement, fisheries management, and tourism. Although of declining importance in the missile age, Canada's geographic location provides the United States with added protection from, and warning against, any attack emanating by air from the north. In the era of the long-distance bomber in particular, the United States would have been highly vulnerable to a Soviet surprise attack unless early warning systems and interceptor fighter bases could be established on Canadian soil. The Canadian government, in defending its continued participation in the North American Air Defense Command (NORAD), argues that a Canadian contribution to the invulnerability of the American retaliatory capacity protects its own interests, since a Soviet-American war could hardly leave Canada unaffected. In general

[4] For a summary of various studies that seek to trace the causes of the development of pluralistic and amalgamated security communities, see Joseph S. Nye, Jr., *Peace in Parts: Integration and Conflict in Regional Organizations* (Boston: Little, Brown, 1971).

diplomacy, Canadian and American objectives have often been similar, so that collaboration, for example through NATO, results naturally. Canada's interest in the Commonwealth, its contributions to the United Nations through peace-keeping efforts, and its initiatives in disarmament negotiations have been either of little interest to the United States or usually consistent with American positions.

Despite the many areas of collaboration, Canadian and American needs and interests are by no means identical in all issue areas. The Canadian approach to Communist nations has been different in many respects from that of the United States. Despite American displeasure, Ottawa has never broken diplomatic relations with Cuba, nor has it stopped trading with that country. Similarly, Canada recognized the government of mainland China and supported its seating in the United Nations long before the United States adopted such positions. While not disagreeing with basic American objectives in Vietnam, the Canadian government occasionally expressed its disapproval of the bombing of North Vietnam and the reluctance of the United States to enter into peace negotiations. But differences of objectives or approaches to problems in the global sphere are not, perhaps, the most significant. Issues relating specifically to Canadian-American relations also raise controversy. The main problem, as seen from Ottawa, is the consequences for Canadian economic interests of policies designed in Washington to relieve specific American problems. Because the two economies are so intricately related, any American decision on matters such as regulation of foreign investment or exchange rates can have profoundly adverse effects on the Canadian economy. It is often not a question of American malevolence, but of decision making in Washington. In seeking to cope with its own economic problems, the American government often fails to consider adequately the consequences of its policies on the needs and interests of closely related states.

Canadian policies have also threatened American interests. The extension of Canadian sovereignty to the 12-mile limit deprived American fishermen of some traditional fishing grounds. Similarly, the U.S. government opposed the unilateral extension of Canadian shipping and antipollution controls to a 100-mile limit in the Arctic. The Canadian government does not allow Canadian advertisers to deduct as a business expense any ads placed on American border stations broadcasting into Canada. American broadcasters lose about $30 million in advertising revenue from this policy and have therefore asked the U.S. government to retaliate.

Perhaps the most contentious issue has centered around Canada's dwindling energy supplies. Americans had for years purchased Canadian oil and natural gas at low prices. As the Canadians began to appreciate the true value of these resources—and recognized that supplies will be exhausted in the foreseeable future—exports to the United States dropped dramatically, or, in the case of natural gas, prices were raised as much as 450 percent within a 12-month period. Canadian decisions on these matters were often taken without previous consultation with American officials. The American government strongly protested these actions, and some officials hinted at American economic retaliation. In these circumstances, protests from Washington could be expected.

Nevertheless, there is little question that Canada and the United States constitute a pluralistic security community. It is difficult to contemplate the two governments using violence against each other, planning military operations to the north or south, or targeting military capabilities toward each other. There is no likelihood of formal unification of the two countries either, but Ottawa and Washington have created some joint institutions to handle the problems that arise between them. Most of the collaboration and coordination, however, occur through normal government channels; bureaucrats at all levels and from all departments communicate and meet to initiate proposals, elicit responses, hammer out details, and draft treaties or establish the frameworks that will guide national policies or coordinated ventures. Finally, transactions occur to fulfill the agreements.

The vast majority of problems that impinge upon the interests of both states are handled in this manner. The negotiations often involve elements of opposition, but there is little likelihood of conflict leading to violence. Looking at the ladder of conflict actions outlined in Chapter 15, we see that Canadian and American diplomats and government officials seldom go beyond the use of warnings, protests, and occasional nonviolent threats.

One of the first conclusions we can make about relations in a security community, then, is that conflict in issue area A does not affect collaboration in issue area B, as would happen when two states' relations were typified by something less than harmony and trust. For example, if some incident or crisis develops between the Soviet Union and the United States, the whole range of relations between the two countries is affected. When the Soviet Union intervened in Afghanistan, all sorts of Soviet-American undertakings were linked together and frozen. The American administration refused to submit the SALT II treaty for approval by the Senate (other reasons were involved as well); technology exports were restricted; sports contacts were terminated; and trade relations were disrupted. Conflict in one domain generated conflict in all others.

When conflicts arise between Ottawa and Washington, how are they typically treated? Certain assumptions and traditions about the appropriate ways of dealing with contentious issues, found in both Ottawa and Washington, help to explain why the two governments seldom carry their behavior beyond the expressions of regret, sending protests, and making mild warnings or threats. First, American and Canadian diplomats and government officials tend to approach problems from a common intellectual starting point: They agree that economic progress is desirable (which makes them sensitive to each other's economic needs), that technology can overcome most problems, and that outcomes must be based on technical criteria and evidence, not emotional responses. Both agree that conflicts of interest and diplomatic irritations are essentially problems to be solved rather than major confrontations to be won at all costs through campaigns and stratagems of diplomacy and threats. Provided that tact, diplomacy, and technical evidence are employed, they assume that few issues are irreconcilable. In addition, they commonly recognize that the benefits of overall cordial relations are not to be sacrificed for the sake of short-run gains in a single policy sector. Hence, both perceive definite limits beyond which they should not press their claims. The great difference in military power between Canada and Washington is largely irrelevant in all negotiations except those involving military matters. The outcome of a series of negotiations will probably reflect the needs of the two parties and their ability to persuade through documentation and evidence, not their military strength.

The results of most disagreements between Washington and Ottawa are typically compromises. In addition, avoidance and passive settlements are frequently observed. Officials in both capitals undoubtedly refuse to take some initiatives for fear of a strong negative response from the neighbor. In other cases, one side will propose a new policy or a particular solution to a problem, only to have the other reject it out of hand. At this point, the proposal is shelved, or the two governments will explain their respective points of view on an issue, acknowledge an unbridgeable difference between these views, and then learn to live with the situation.

What factors can help explain the extensive collaboration between the two countries, the lack of conflict behavior (beyond the occasional warning or protest), and the absence of spillover of conflict from one area into another? In large part, of course, the explanation is the complementary nature of the interests and needs of the two countries. Both sides recognize the advantages to be gained through cooperative efforts, through consultations before major policy decisions are made, and through maintaining a sensitivity toward each other's interests. In addition, certain characteristics of the bureaucracies of the two countries help account for the nature of their mutual relations. Communications are an important factor. The volume of government transactions between Ottawa and Washington is immense. It cannot be handled only between the Department of External Affairs and the State Department. Hence, most bureaucrats in Ottawa correspond directly with their counterparts in Washington, and often simply use the telephone. Common language and slang reduce the possibilities of misunderstandings, and in many cases help significantly to create personal friendships. Bureaucrats represent the interests of their countries, but their close bonds help create alliances against those who might disrupt their special interests and traditions. For instance, if American top-level officials begin discussions on new policies toward Canada, the lower-level officials of the two countries might agree among themselves to resist changes. In particular, when a confrontation is likely to develop, the instinct of the lower-level officials is to handle the problem themselves, quietly, before it becomes "politicized." Finally, both governments exchange a great amount of information. Most of it is done unofficially, but formal consultations and joint institutions are employed widely also.

One consequence of the vast amount of communication is that needs are known and actions are predictable. Many conflicts develop between Washington and Ottawa precisely when the consultative machinery is not used. But overall, mutual knowledge leads to empathy, predictability, and mutual expectations of "responsible" behavior. Each knows generally what policies and actions to expect from the other, and which types of issues are most sensitive. If there are proposed policy changes, they are usually discussed extensively before final decisions are made. Both governments appear reluctant to initiate certain self-serving actions because the shortrun gains do not measure up to the damage of the overall relationships.

But occasionally, policies are changed anyway. Particularly during the past few years, both governments have adopted nationalist economic policies that have had unfavorable consequences on each other's society. As the range of economic incompatibilities has grown, the habits of extensive consultation and policy coordination, at least in the economic realm, have been replaced by more unilateral initiatives, more threats of retaliation, and more extensive use of public accusations. Yet, even in these circumstances, in the long run both governments are inclined to suffer each others' unfavorable policies with equanimity. And of course, in many other issue areas, where collaboration and consultation remain the norm, the occasional conflicts between Washington and Ottawa seem to have little impact.[5]

COLLABORATION AND BARGAINING IN BRUSSELS

The ten states that make up the European Community undoubtedly constitute a pluralistic security community. War between Germany and France—a possibility only a generation ago—seems most unlikely today. The main indicators of such a security community, the lack of targeted military capabilities or military plans, are to be found in these states as well as in North America. But whereas Canada and the United States are in no process of economic or political integration, and possess no institutions with supranational powers, France, Germany, Italy, and the Benelux countries created an organization that does possess such powers. In 1967, the three main institutions of European economic integration—the Common Market, the Coal and Steel Community, and Euratom—were combined into one organization, which we call the European Community. Although the members still conduct most of their foreign and defense policies independently or within the context of NATO, collaboration in economics, trade, tariffs, atomic energy, and transportation goes on primarily within the text of the Community's organizations.

[5] A more detailed account of conflict-resolving procedures in Canadian-American relations is in K.J. Holsti and Thomas Levy, "Bilateral Institutions and Transgovernmental Relations between Canada and the United States," *International Organization*, 28 (1974), 875–902. For evidence of increased conflict in the early 1970s, see Peyton Lyon and Brian Tomlin, *Canada as an International Actor* (Toronto: Macmillan of Canada, 1979), chap. 7.

The main institutions of the Community combine features of both ordinary intergovernmental organizations such as NATO or the United Nations, where the members negotiate and bargain with each other until they can reach some kind of settlement or common policy, and a type of supranational organization, where international civil servants, not responsible to any one government, possess some authority to make binding decisions over member states and their citizens. This is the most important distinction between institutions of an integrated community, diplomatic-type organizations in pluralistic security communities, and intergovernmental organizations. Several other distinctions are also evident. In the European Community, most decisions made by the member governments are reached through majority votes; policies resulting from these votes are binding on all members, including those who oppose them. In the United Nations, on the other hand, no state is compelled to accept or implement decisions reached in the organization relating to pacific settlement of disputes and conflicts. Second, the European Community possesses institutions that themselves administer a common policy; to implement these policies, they are not dependent, in many cases, on national administrative structures, although these necessarily have to cooperate. This feature is seldom observed in intergovernmental organizations. Third, the European Community, through the Commission, has some direct authority over citizens and corporations within the member states and may enforce its policies by bringing suit or levying fines against individuals or corporations that do not conform to the policies established by the organization. Such diversion of law-enforcing authority to a supranational administration is not an ordinary feature of international organizations.

The institutions of the Community that possess these mixed characteristics of intergovernmental and supranational powers include the following:

1. The executive Commission is made up of technical experts appointed by common agreement among the member governments, and responsible only to the organization. They may initiate policy recommendations and administer those policies that have been approved by the member governments. Members of the Commission also sit in on all meetings of the Council of Ministers, and represent the viewpoint of the Community.

2. The Council of Ministers, attended by national representatives, has the final authority to formulate and approve common policies, and to bargain with other member states.

3. The European Council, meeting three times yearly, is attended by the heads of government of members. These are informal meetings, but often important decisions are taken, and it often serves as a useful device for resolving impasses in the Council of Ministers.

4. The Assembly, made up of representatives elected by popular vote, has the authority to discuss and review the policies and actions of the Commission and the Council of Ministers.

5. The Court of Justice of the communities reviews the legality of Commission and Council decisions and disposes of legal cases arising under the founding treaties. It considers conflicts brought by governments against each other, by

governments against the Commission, and by individuals or business enterprises against the Commission. By 1980, the Court had disposed of more than 3,000 cases involving individual, intergovernmental, and organizational matters.

The pattern of decision making and collaboration within the Commission and the Council of Ministers is very complex and involves work by hundreds of bureaucrats, both national and international. Typically, the Commission will begin planning rules, regulations, and directives that would give effect to the goal of economic integration. In making up the multitude of proposals, members of the Commission consult with the Permanent Representatives of the member states, who are all located in Brussels. The Permanent Representatives report to their own governments and naturally consult extensively with their own bureaucrats in the national capital. The Permanent Representatives defend national points of view, but, as they are intimately connected with all the affairs of the Community, they often urge their own governments to support the Commission's point of view as well.[6] When the long process of consultation has been completed and a coherent set of proposals emerges, the Commission presents them to the Council of Ministers, comprising the foreign, economics, finance, or trade ministers of the member states. The Commission sits in the Council as a sort of eleventh member, except that it represents the viewpoint of the Community, not that of any member state. It can argue in favor of its proposals, make new proposals, or act as a mediator should some of the ministers find themselves in a deadlock.

Voting in the Council of Ministers is complicated. Most decisions are based on qualified majorities, based on a system of weighted voting (for example, France has more votes than Luxembourg or Belgium). In other cases, unanimity or a simple majority is required. The important point is that theoretically most decisions of the Council can be taken against the will of one or more of the governments—although, as we will see, the informal "code" of operation in the Council requires the ministers to reach an agreement acceptable to all. De Gaulle's vetoes on Britain's entry to the Common Market in 1963 and 1967, his threat to withdraw from the institutions of the Community in 1966, and Prime Minister Thatcher's showdown over British fees to the Community in 1980 were serious breaches of the normal pattern of decision making. Most policy for the Community is made through the slow and difficult process of fashioning an overall consensus through persuasion, presentation of evidence, and documentation of need. In recent years, however, as the European governments have faced fuel shortages, recession, inflation, and unemployment, the major members of the Community have held a virtual veto power on some decisions. Some programs simply could not be implemented without French, British, and German acquiescence.

As in Canadian-American relations, certain assumptions, traditions, and

[6] Leon N. Lindberg, *The Political Dynamics of European Economic Integration* (Stanford, Calif.: Stanford University Press, 1963), p. 79.

unwritten rules govern the settlement of problems, the pattern of collaboration, or the fashioning of new policies. Most proposals reaching the Council of Ministers involve losses and gains for the member states. Each minister will naturally attempt to see that the final outcome reflects the interests of his government to the maximum extent possible. But unlike negotiations in a violent conflict, where the basic issue is a settlement or the continuation of conflict, the negotiators in the Council of Ministers start with an implicit agreement that a final decision must be the end result; they assume that mutual concessions must be made, since the normal practice, occasional French exceptions notwithstanding, is to exclude the possibility of not reaching an agreement at all.[7] Moreover, in the lengthy discussions, a built-in mediator is always present. The Commission constantly represents the views of the Community, and because it is armed with technical expertise and an aura of legitimacy, it is in a powerful position to influence the bargaining positions of the member states. Ministers are more apt to make concessions and to justify those concessions to their home governments, if they are made in the name of the Community rather than, for example, of another state such as Germany or Luxemburg.[8] The Commission, in sum, is in a strong position to overcome strictly national imperatives.

Moreover, most issues are dealt with as "problems." That is, solutions can be based on data, the elucidation of needs, and the application of technology. Ideological principles seldom color the bargaining that takes place within the European Council, Council of Ministers, or between the Commission and the Permanent Representatives. Thus, decisions and settlements are based less on the power, prestige, capabilities, or reputation of member states than on the objectives of the organization and the most convincing needs of its members. On many issues before the Council, French ministers have reduced their demands to accommodate the Netherlands, and on other issues, the Germans or Italians have retreated from their bargaining positions in order to placate the Belgians. In other words, no government consistently gains or withdraws from its objectives because it is economically or militarily weak or strong.[9]

The bargaining that goes on within the Council of Ministers offers a dramatic contrast to the formality, coldness, and vituperation that goes on in negotiations between hostile states. According to Lindberg, the ministers generally display considerable sensitivity toward the needs of other member states. The atmosphere is informal, in part because the ministers know each other well and are, in some cases, good personal friends. Long, formal speechs are rare; banter and jokes are often in evidence. There seems to be an awareness that the ministers are working on a common problem, one in which compromise is expected from all sides in order to obtain a Community solution.[10] If agreement cannot be fashioned, the proposals or projects are normally returned to the

---

[7] Lindberg, *Political Dynamics of European Economic Integration*, p. 285.
[8] *Ibid.*, p. 286.
[9] Haas, *The Uniting of Europe*, pp. 524–25.
[10] Lindberg, *Political Dynamics of European Economic Integration*, pp. 76–77.

Commission for reworking. The Commission then reestablishes contact with the Permanent Representatives, or with national bureaucrats, and irons out the remaining problems. In these relationships, collaboration rather than conflict is the rule.

Although the Community's practices have altered to some extent because of French threats and vetoes during the 1960s and economic nationalism in the 1970s, the experience since 1952, starting with the Coal and Steel Community, has been the gradual emergence of an unwritten "procedural code" that has come to be called the "Community method." According to Lindberg and Scheingold, the method includes the following expectations and practices:

1. Member governments express strong support for the Community, emphasize the benefits to be gained from participation, and downgrade the possibilities of failure or of withdrawal.
2. The governments recognize the Commission as a legitimate bargaining partner and occasional mediator, as well as a spokesman for the interests of the collectivity.
3. Bargaining is approached in terms of problem solving, not gaining victories for any single member or bloc of members. Negotiations concern how solutions are to be achieved, not whether they should be achieved.
4. All member governments are attentive and responsive to each other's needs and interests. This extends to the Commission as well. Unacceptable demands are avoided, and divisive issues are usually postponed.
5. Governments and the Commission are willing to make compromises and to withdraw from positions in order to uphold the common interest and secure long-range benefits.
6. They agree that unanimity should be achieved on all contentious issues and that bargaining should continue until agreement has been reached and all objections have been overcome. Losses in one area, for a member state, should be compensated for by gains in another. Since bargaining often crosses over from one issue area to another, the governments are able to arrange "package" deals, although often only after lengthy, marathon negotiation sessions.[11]

Repeated exposure to these sorts of bargaining sessions, and the many successful outcomes that have resulted from them, undoubtedly build up personal commitments among the ministers. In conventional diplomatic negotiations, final settlements do not necessarily reflect the technical correctness of a position, but rather degrees of need, dependence, and threat credibility and the bargaining skills of each side. In the negotiations among the ministers and the Commission, however, compromises are often reached on the basis of technical criteria. The ministers' knowledge of each other and of the needs of other member governments (responsiveness) enables them to distinguish between arguments based on bargaining points and arguments based on real needs and

---

[11] Leon N. Lindberg and Stuart A. Scheingold, *Europe's Would-Be Polity* (Englewood Cliffs, N.J.: Prentice-Hall, 1970), pp. 96–97. See also Ernst B. Haas, "The Study of Regional Integration: Reflections on the Joy and Anguish of Pretheorizing," *International Organization*, 24 (1970), 618.

interests. The result is that the discussions focus mainly around technical considerations rather than ideological, sentimental, or national positions.[12]

What conclusions are we to draw from these comparisons of bargaining behavior and conflict resolution in an integrating community and in violent conflicts and disputes? First, we must remember that problems in the European Community are concerned primarily with economic questions, involving issues where technical factors and information can be easily used to influence negotiators. In conflicts arising out of incompatible ideological values, long-range objectives, territorial claims, or more diffuse national aspirations, no such precise criteria for agreement exist. Second, the member governments and their negotiating representatives in the Community are aware of long-run common advantages that can be used to justify short-run economic sacrifices. But when one state makes demands on another country's territory, or in some way threatens its core interests, it is difficult to convince the victim that it will gain some advantage by acceding to those demands or threats. Third, the pattern of collaboration and conflict resolution within economically integrating communities has not yet been completely duplicated in negotiations on military and political questions between the same governments. Within NATO, for example, negotiations on military questions resemble classical bargaining behavior, where agreement is usually based on the lowest common denominator and the military capacity of each member plays an important role in determining its influence in the bargaining process.

On the other hand, within such nonintegrated organizations as NATO, diplomatic bargaining, conflict resolution, and policy making often display the characteristics of responsiveness, adherence to strict rules of negotiating etiquette, and avoidance of military threats to achieve objectives. In short, resolution of conflicts within pluralistic security communities and in many international organizations falls somewhere between the patterns of behavior found in integrating communities and in conflicts involving violence.

COLLABORATION, SECURITY COMMUNITIES, AND PEACE

Collaboration in Western Europe takes place in all three contexts discussed in this chapter. Relations between Spain and Finland, for example, are of the intermittent bilateral type; cooperation on NATO problems takes place within an institution, but one with none of the attributes of supranationality; and collaboration within the European Community occurs primarily in a highly institutionalized context with some supranational features. Western Europe includes, at once, a set of bilateral relationships, a multilateral pluralistic security community as far as most military and diplomatic problems are concerned, and an integrating

---

[12] Haas, *The Uniting of Europe*, pp. 291, 490–91.

community with respect to economic, transportation, agricultural, and atomic-energy problems.

Most students of European integration would not yet predict that successful integration in economic and technical sectors will have much influence on the ways with which diplomatic and military problems are handled between the same governments. As Haas points out, integration forces have an impact on further integration, but not necessarily in integration of other types of political or economic activities such as development of common foreign or defense policies.[13] Another student of the process of amalgamation, Amitai Etzioni, has hypothesized that different types of international or supranational organizations have different potentials for "spilling over" their cooperative patterns of behavior and unique methods of resolving conflicts into other areas.[14] He suggests, for example, that international technical organizations such as postal services or systems of police cooperation between nations have little influence in promoting cooperation between governments on major political or economic issues. International organizations concerned with labor, health, or cultural problems have had somewhat more influence on the political sectors. Etzioni, like others, also points out that the military sector is highly autonomous; even if alliances involve integration of military forces, common military planning, and exchange of defense information, the habits of cooperation and conflict resolution in these organizations do not seem to "spill over" automatically or create any impetus for economic or political integration. It is economic integration, with its pervasive influence on all sectors and groups of society, that seems to have the highest potential for inducing political amalgamation and spilling over its patterns of decision making and bargaining into diplomatic relations between states.[15]

Whether or not Europe will eventually take steps toward political or defense amalgamation remains to be seen. From the point of view of collaboration and conflict, however, amalgamation is not critical. Western Europe today constitutes at least a pluralistic security community; the chances of again seeing a war within Western Europe seem remote at best. Consider what a dramatic change this represents over the past generation. In the 1920s, there were conflicts involving violence between Sweden and Finland, France and Germany, Poland and Lithuania, Poland and Czechoslovakia, Hungary and Austria, and Bulgaria and Greece. In the Locarno Treaties, England was committed militarily to come to the assistance of France, Belgium, or Germany, depending upon which was a victim of aggression. Some people in Norway and Sweden still spoke of the

---

[13] Ernst B. Haas, "International Integration: The European and Universal Process," *International Organization*, 15 (1961), 372–74; see also Leon Lindberg, "Decision-Making and Integration in the European Community," *International Organization*, 19 (1965), 72–77. However, in the last few years the community has developed a common foreign-policy stance on some issues. The ten have formed a cohesive caucus at the meetings of the Conference on Security and Cooperation in Europe.

[14] Amitai Etzioni, "The Dialectics of Supranational Unification," *American Political Science Review*, 56 (1962), 931–32.

[15] However, see Deutsch, *Political Community*, p. 189, for a partly dissenting view.

possibility of war between them. By 1941, every state in Europe, with the exception of Ireland, Sweden, Turkey, Spain, Switzerland, and Portugal, had been the victim of German, Russian, or Italian aggression.

Since 1945, there have been conflicts involving violence in Western Europe only between Yugoslavia and Italy over Trieste, and Greece and Turkey over Cyprus. The military capabilities of Western European states are not aimed toward each other, nor are there expectations or plans for the use of violence. We would not predict that violence in this area could never occur, but only that, compared to the situation forty or fifty years ago, the probabilities have been vastly reduced.

What of the remainder of the world? North America, as we have pointed out, clearly falls in the category of a security community; Scandinavia and New Zealand–Australia would also be included. Other areas of the world are more difficult to classify. Some Latin American states still have military capabilities targeted toward each other, and warfare erupts occasionally in Central America. The United States continues to employ subversive techniques and occasional military intervention to maintain friendly regimes or to oust regimes it considers too radical. In other words, the limits of domestic and foreign policies for all Latin American states are implicitly set in Washington, not in the other national capitals; and if those limits are breached, any state must face the possibility of coercive activity, ranging from economic pressures, through subversion, to outright intervention.

An analogous situation prevails in Eastern Europe. Many of the frontier disputes and minority problems that led to conflict between the Eastern European states in the 1920s and 1930s have been muted by territorial adjustments during and after World War II and by the sense of ideological unity that has permeated this area. Most of the East European states have come to accept Yugoslavia's independent foreign policy and its unique experiments in socialism; among themselves, therefore, the likelihood of violence is low. However, as in Latin America, the region has to be considered also in terms of the intrusion of an extraregional power, in this case the Soviet Union. Its actions in crushing the Hungarian revolt in 1956 and the experiments of the Dubček regime in Czechoslovakia twelve years later as well as unsubtle threats against Poland at the beginning of the 1980s, indicate clearly that developments within the Eastern European states will have to conform more or less to Soviet interests and values. Deviations from the Soviet interpretation of socialism face military extermination, just as "Communist" revolutions in Latin America and the Caribbean will confront American hostility and occasional military intervention.

For the rest of the world, the record is also unfavorable, for there are few other areas that, using the criterion of the possibility of armed violence between independent political units, could be classified as genuine and well-established pluralistic security communities. With the possible exception of the Association for Southeast Asian Nations (ASEAN), none of the non-European regional or federal organizations displays the degree of integration, ideological and cultural homogeneity, or bargaining patterns and procedures for resolving conflicts found in Europe, North America, and Australia–New Zealand. Not only do important territorial and ethnic disputes occasionally mar the unity of these areas, but because of their political and economic instability, they make prime targets for domestic and foreign-inspired intrigues, subversion, and revolution.

In the future, most international crises will probably have as their source the civil wars, *coups d'état,* and revolutions that will occur intermittently in developing countries. These, in turn, will be exploited by the major powers for their own ends, or the domestic factions will appeal to outside powers to intervene on their behalf. Recent agendas of the United Nations indicate that the most serious diplomatic and military crises are related to the problems of building viable nations and establishing within those states regular procedures for transferring political power. The Congo, Lebanon, Laos, Yemen, Cyprus, Dominican, Czechoslovakian, Angolan, and Afghanistan crises were originally domestic quarrels in which one or more external powers intervened, thus turning them into international crises involving the possibility of war. It is these domestic-international conflicts that will probably be most difficult to resolve peacefully, because they involve the interests and values of at least four parties (the United States and China or the Soviet Union, as well as the two major domestic factions), whereas other international conflicts are essentially bilateral confrontations. This is one legacy of the cold war.

Governments will continue, as in the past, to seek their objectives and defend their interests against the demands and actions of others by the traditional means of offering rewards, threatening or implementing punishments, employing diplomatic bargaining, and using force. Within pluralistic and amalgamated security communities, the probabilities are low that conflicts will be resolved through violent threats, deterrence, or conquests. In these types of relationships, the "power" model of international politics—where states seek to increase their power at the expense of others—is a particularly inappropriate tool of analysis. Conflicts arise, but legal and ethical restraints, as well as habits of "getting along," are highly effective in keeping friction to a minimum and helping to provide for settlements by bargaining compromise, and awards.

Elsewhere, the paths to security, peace, and pacific settlement of conflicts will be dangerous and strewn with failures. With the problems most nations in the world face, including building viable states, coping with secessionist movements, and organizing minimally satisfactory economic systems, it may be a wonder that there has not been more international conflict in recent years. Various approaches to the goals of economic well-being and international peace have been, and continue to be, advanced by different observers of international politics. To some, world federalism is the answer; others argue that legal norms must be perfected before they can be expected to restrain effectively the actions of states when their objectives are incompatible. Many believe that international relationships will not improve until the new nations become "developed," a view that overlooks some of the horrendous social problems faced by populations in "developed" states. Still others, perpetuating a long history of simplistic thinking, assume that the only road to international stability is the one that emphasizes perfection of national capacities to threaten and inflict violent punishment. Whatever the panacea, plan, or nostrum, none will work by itself, and none can lead to the goal quickly.

Despite their failures, international organizations have made great contributions to peace in what is, historically, a wisp of time. But this has been possible only because of changing public attitudes toward war and violence. One has only to compare the bellicose views of statesmen, politicians, and publics at the turn of the century with their attitudes today. Then, war was commonly regarded as a positive good, a means of steeling national character and weeding out the poor and weak from the strong and wealthy. It was a game to vindicate honor and prestige, and opportunity to demonstrate the latest toy of destruction. After two world wars, such views seem ludicrous to most people. Today, international violence is mostly seen as a tragedy. Without such views, it is unlikely that security communities could grow, international organizations flourish, or stability develop. Underlying any improvements in the techniques and practices of resolving international conflicts peacefully are the attitudes and ethical principles of those who wield power and those in the general public who support or criticize their leaders. Without the proper values and attitudes, including willingness to experiment in international programs, concede short-run national disadvantages for common long-range advantages, and exercise great caution in the use of military power, mere institutions, laws, plans, and proposals will be inadequate to the task.

What about collaboration in issue contexts other than security? One trend that has become commonly recognized is the multilateralization of nonsecurity issues. Most governments acknowledge today that the fact of interdependence—where the actions of most states have serious consequences on others—requires them to join together to attack problems such as ocean pollution, dwindling natural resources, inadequate food supplies among many developing countries, and possibly regulation of the activities of nonstate actors such as multinational corporations. Individual government action in these realms is simply insufficient and, in many cases, can be harmful. If, for instance, seabed mining corporations begin operating in the open sea, without any international regulation, there may be a mad scramble for the most productive areas, intense pollution of the oceans, and undercutting of the developing countries' incomes from export of raw materials. The consequences of unfettered individual action are not difficult to predict; but this does not always make solutions easier. Governments and nonstate actors are often pressed, unfortunately, to seek maximum gains in a minimum amount of time, so they believe they must protect national advantages even if, in so doing, they diminish the chances of truly collaborative enterprises that could increase everyone's advantage. In other cases, governments are not willing to make short-run sacrifices because they anticipate that the international community will not develop norms or institutions in time to protect everyone's interests.

Reconciling the diverging interests of 150 or more states is by no means easy, even when the necessity of collaboration is commonly recognized. And even if new universal treaties and institutions are created to regulate and attack some of these global problems, it may be a long time before the norms of cooperation and bargaining found, for example, in the European Community will develop in them. One hundred fifty states with conflicting interests, representing different cultural, political, economic, and social systems, will find it much more difficult to develop the procedures of a "security community" than was the case in Europe or North America. This is not to say, however, that the need is any less acute.

CONCLUSIONS

The first chapter of this book made the point that contemporary studies of international politics seek generalizations. That is, they are primarily concerned with looking at state actions, processes, and the settings (systems) within which these actions and processes occur; they are less interested in analyzing events except insofar as those events illustrate general types of actions or processes. In addition, it was pointed out that some phenomena are not unique to international politics; hence, we can learn from the insights of anthropologists, sociologists, and psychologists. Some of the attitudes among policy makers facing an international crisis are certainly comparable to those that people face in some interpersonal situations, for example. Finally, the introduction alerted the reader to the differences among description, explanation, and normative prescription in the study of international politics. Most of this book has been descriptive, but in Chapters 12 through 14 and in the present chapter, where we analyzed *why* violent conflicts are improbable in a security community, the discussion was explanatory. In some cases, the evidence allowed us to generalize with confidence. In other cases, the evidence leads only to educated guesses.

What about prescription? The analysis has generally avoided prescribing what governments *should* do (some parts of Chapter 11 and the last section of this chapter are obvious exceptions). And it has avoided detailed discussion of some contemporary international issues. To some, this omission may appear to indicate indifference toward human suffering; to others, the book evades the real-world excitement of current affairs. Underdevelopment, creation of an equitable world trade system, inadequate food supplies, pollution, seabed mining, the arms race, and direct broadcasting from television satellites—all present immense difficulties. The agenda of international politics is changing—or, perhaps more accurately, new items are being added to it before some of the old items have been resolved. And within five years, still other problems will arise. All will be of important consequence, and broad public understanding of the many issues in each problem may help governments come to satisfactory solutions. But the actions and processes of international politics will remain essentially the same: Governments will continue to develop various types of objectives, roles, and orientations. Alliances and coalitions will not disappear just because some aspects of the cold war are subsiding. Diplomatic bargaining, economic pressures, propaganda, and the many overt and covert uses of organized violence will not change in their fundamental characteristics. Knowledge of the various sources of external actions, ranging from personality characteristics of policy makers to national needs and aspects of the international system, can help us to understand how governments will cope with the new problems. We can hope that ethical norms will play an increasingly important role in policy making. As James Eayrs has put it, policy makers should go beyond asking, "Will it work?" and in each situation, compromise their narrower interests to the question, "Will it help alleviate human suffering?"[16] There is not much evidence that ethical priorities are changing, but before one can begin discussing how governments *should* behave, we should know first how they *do* behave.

Although the amount of international collaboration is impressive, as the role of nonstate actors continues to grow in importance, and as new issues appear on the global agenda, we still face the perennial question of organized violence between nation-states. This remains the most fundamental problem of international politics. My position remains that before one can attack this one overriding problem successfully, or even intelligently, it is necessary to understand the sources and characteristics of foreign policy in general and conflict behavior in particular. To the extent that this book has helped the reader understand this fundamental issue and to distinguish the unique event from recurring actions and processes in international politics, it has achieved its purpose.

SELECTED BIBLIOGRAPHY

ALTING VON GEUSAU, FRANS A.M., *European Organizations and Foreign Relations of States: A Comparative Analysis of Decision-Making.* Leiden, Netherlands: A. W. Sijthoff, 1964.

AXLINE, ANDREW W., "Underdevelopment, Dependence and Integration: The Politics of Regionalism in the Third World," *International Organization,* 31 (1977), 83–105.

DEUTSCH, KARL W., *Political Community at the International Level: Problems of Definition and Measurement.* Garden City, N.Y.: Doubleday, 1954.

———, et al., *Political Community and the North Atlantic Area.* Princeton, N.J.: Princeton University Press, 1957.

ETZIONI, AMITAI, *Political Unification.* New York: Holt, Rinehart & Winston, 1965.

FELD, WERNER J., *The European Community in World Affairs.* Sherman Oaks, Calif.: Alfred Publishers, 1976.

[16] James Eayrs, *Right and Wrong in Foreign Policy* (Toronto: Toronto University Press, 1966), p. 40.

FINLAY, DAVID J., and THOMAS HOVET, JR., *7304: International Relations on the Planet Earth.* New York: Harper & Row, 1975.

GALTUNG, JOHAN, *The European Community: A Superpower in the Making.* London: Allen & Unwin, 1973.

HAAS, ERNST B., *Beyond the Nation State: Functionalism and International Organization.* Stanford, Calif.: Stanford University Press, 1964.

———, "International Integration: The European and Universal Process," *International Organization,* 15 (1961), 366–92.

———, *The Uniting of Europe: Political, Social, and Economic Forces, 1950–1957.* Stanford, Calif.: Stanford University Press, 1968.

———, and PHILIPPE C. SCHMITTER, "Economics and Differential Patterns of Political Integration: Projections about Unity in Latin America," *International Organization,* 18 (1964), 705–37.

HANSEN, ROGER D., "Regional Integration: Reflections on a Decade of Theoretical Efforts," *World Politics,* 21 (1969), 242–71.

JACOB, PHILIP E., and JAMES V. TOSCANO, eds., *The Integration of Political Communities.* Philadelphia: Lippincott, 1964.

LINDBERG, LEON, "Decision-Making and Integration in the European Community," *International Organization,* 19 (1965), 50–80.

———, *The Political Dynamics of European Economic Integration.* Stanford, Calif.: Stanford University Press, 1963.

———, and STUART A. SCHEINGOLD, *Europe's Would-Be Polity: Patterns of Change in the European Community.* Englewood Cliffs, N.J.: Prentice-Hall, 1970.

NYE, JOSEPH S., JR., *Peace in Parts: Integration and Conflict in Regional Organizations.* Boston: Little, Brown, 1971.

PENTLAND, CHARLES, *International Theory and European Integration.* New York: Free Press, 1973.

PINDER, JOHN, "Issues for Global Actors: The European Community," in *Issues in Global Politics,* eds. Gaving Boyd and Charles Pentland. New York: The Free Press, 1981.

SCOTT, ANDREW, *The Dynamics of Interdependence.* Chapel Hill, North Carolina: University of North Carolina Press, 1982.

SPINELLI, ALTIERO, *The Eurocrats: Conflict and Crisis in the European Community.* Baltimore, Md.: Johns Hopkins Press, 1966.

WALLACE, HELEN, WILLIAM WALLACE, and CAROLE WEBB, eds., *Policy-Making in the European Communities.* London: John Wiley, 1977.

Index